INTERIOR TEXTILES

INTERIOR TEXTILES

FABRICS, APPLICATIONS, & HISTORICAL STYLES

KARLA J. NIELSON

John Wiley & Sons, Inc.

For general information about our other products and services, please contact our Customer Care Department within the United States at (800) 762-2974, outside the United States at (317) 572-3993 or fax (317) 572-4002.

Wiley also publishes its books in a variety of electronic formats. Some content that appears in print may not be available in electronic books. For more information about Wiley products, visit our web site at www.wiley.com.

Wiley Bicentennial Logo designed by Richard Pacifico.
Interior text design by Figaro

Library of Congress Cataloging-in-Publication Data:

Nielson, Karla J.
   Interior textiles : fabrics, application, and historical styles / Karla J. Nielson.
       p. cm.
   Includes bibliographical references and index.
   ISBN 978-0-471-60640-6 (cloth)
   1. Textile fabrics in interior decoration. I. Title.
   NK2115.5.F3N53 2007
   747'.5—dc22

Printed in the United States of America

10 9 8 7 6 5 4 3 2 1

Contents

Acknowledgments

Many wonderful people have made contributions to this landmark textbook over the past several years is has been in preparation. My thanks go first to Paul Drougas and Lauren LaFrance, Editors at John Wiley and Sons for their determination, encouragement, suggestions, and patience with the project. I acknowledge industry professionals who have contributed expertise and/or images: Alexis Logan of Lafayette Interior Fashions, Marc J. Geller and Lissette Aliaga of Agency Sacks, New York (representing Stark and Old World Weavers), Kyle Cory of Patterson, Flynn & Martin, Rosecore Carpets, Lori Jurcsak of Comfortex, Sarah P. Fletcher of Lou Hammond & Associates, Inc. (representing Hunter Douglas), Pam Graetzer of Graetzer Communications (Vista Window Films), Virginia Kubler, CP Films, Inc., Linda Baron of Herman Miller, Kathleen Cwirko Spero and Sheryl Boltze of Sure Fit, Inc., Thomas Oder of ADO International, Hillary White of Michael Chaves Advertising, Inc. (representing Giati, Edward Fields), Costikyan, and Madison Leathers, Julia Gillespie of Hi-Tex, Inc. (Crypton Super Fabric), Eileen Meitzner and Donna Hyun of DreamDraper®/ Evan Marsh Designs, Matt Pfingsten of Castec, Fumiaki Odaka of Innovations, Wallcoverings, Vera Vandenboch of Donghia, Elyse Corrado of Carnegie Fabrics, Diane DeZan of AFMA, John Morgan and James Pruden of Cotton, Inc., Vicki Enteen and Janice Langrall of Stroheim, Janan Rabiah of ACT, Association of Contract Textiles, Tammie Hickerson of Arcadia, Trish Hodge of Batik Tambal, David and Jay Nehouray of Caravan Rug Corporation, Elyse Corrado of Carnegie Fabrics, Barbara Skelly of Designtex, Lisa Rivera of Duralee and Highland Court Fabrics, Nick Lomangino of F. Schumacher & Co. Floor Covering Division, Tonja Morrison of Hancock and Moore, Lisa Morrice of On Target Communications (representing Houlès-U.S.A.), Jessica Charles Furniture, David E. Bright of Knoll, Pam Artman of Leggett and Platt, Inc., Amy Behn of Liebco Home, Gordon and Lynn Lonsdale, Catherine DeVestele of CELC-Masters of Linen, Miriam Bajoul of Soroush Custom Rugs & Axminster Carpet, Elise Demboski of Impressions Marketing, Representing Wools of New Zealand, and Maria Cafici of The Woolmark Company, and Merrie Barnett of Bigelow/Mohawk Carpets, Tom Norwood of Royal Carolina Corporation, Gene Banks of Schneider-Banks Inc/SBI Finishing, Gareth Brennan, President, and Elaine Allen-Milne of Eventscape, Inc. Jon Namba, of Certified Floor Covering Installers Association, David Moore and Stephanie Taylor of Uniroyal Corporation (Naugahyde Fabrics).

I am especially indebted to Jim Park of Goose Island Artworks, for his well-developed style and willingness to join forces once again for a quality textbook illustration program.

Special thanks also to Desarae Fowler and Lisset Stevenson for their assistance with photo research. Many interior design students at Brigham Young University over the past decade have contributed to the research and/or artwork behind the scenes under my direction. These include: Jeanine Adams, Neelam Alexander, Kathrin Bates, Gentry Sylvester, Leah Call, Caitlin Carter, Yin Chow, Alex Christensen, Jordan Cushionberry, Becca Cline, Marie Deschamps, Jenny Fosdick, Lacie Gregson, Sarah Hale, Brooke Halverson, Emily Hansen, Heather Harrison, Kate Hickman, Meghan Hollingshaus, Jenni Karpowitz, Maggie Lambourn, Krystle Lowen, Matthew Morrill, Emily Morris, Michelle Morton, Michelle Nixon, Harmony Pearce, Stephanie Rich, Kimber Reeves, Erin Robinson, Nicole Robinson, Heidi Shin, Kim Slobodian, Elise Smith, Sora Smith, Katie Stewart, Christina Snyder, Tayna Sorensen, Rebecca Tuttle, Kathleen Warnick, Erica Williams, Kendyle Willardson, and Steve Wright. And thanks to my son, Philip, for his artwork assistance; to my daughter, Diana for her willingness to help in so many ways; and to my husband, Asa, and the rest of the wonderful Nielson children for their unflagging support during the years of preparation.

KARLA NIELSON
Orem, UT

Introduction

TEXTILES FORM POWERFUL INTERIOR COMPONENTS as they combine three strong design elements: the emotion of color, the impact of pattern, and textural qualities sensed through visual perception and physical touch. Textiles are specified or selected because they are appropriate choices for the aesthetics and practicality of the space and are right for user or occupant needs. Fabric offers physical and psychological advantages to interiors such as sound absorption, privacy, comfort, enhanced safety, and aesthetics.

Textiles absorb sound from within and without, making spaces more humane and comfortable. Carpeting, upholstered walls, and window treatments with lining and interlining are especially good at accomplishing quietude by sponging noise. Properly selected fabric can assure privacy at the window both day and night. This allows the occupant to experience peace of mind. Textiles can be friendly—touchable, enveloping, comforting. They enhance safety as they cushion floors, seating, and beds; they provide visual comfort on walls and at windows. Textiles are powerful emotional tools; they may rest and calm or stimulate and excite. Textiles can be a familiar face in an impersonal world, counted on for warmth and a bit of luxury and loveliness.

Interior textiles are an artist's medium. More aesthetic feats can be accomplished with fabric and soft flooring than any other interior deign component. For example, fabric can be draped, adhered, fastened, attached, grommeted, shirred, stapled, affixed, stiffened, suspended, hung, folded, quilted, appliquéd, upholstered, slipcovered, valanced, pelmeted, sewn, tacked, laminated, glued, stuffed, pleated, ruffled, pleated, piquéd, trimmed, tufted, ruched, layered, banded, contrasted, stretched onto frames, or slid on tracks. There is no limit to the creative ways fabric can be manipulated to create an interior that is unique in design and delightful to the eye, mind, and spirit.

The greatest advantage of interior textiles is the power they possess to set a mood, establish a theme, and secure an ambience. From soft and subtle colors and textures to bold and dynamic materials, the world of interior textiles is an unlimited source in creating great interior design.

Interior Textiles: Fabrics, Applications, and Historical Style is for both new and seasoned students of interior design who value the endless aesthetic wonder and continual technological advancement of contemporary interior design textiles. *Interior Textiles* is a unique and friendly approach to a vast, complex subject. It is divided into three parts.

Part I, "Fabrics," begins with an overview of the textiles industry and explores the spectrum of rewarding textile careers. Chapter 2 explores a relatively new part of textiles — sustainability awareness — now a critical element of interior textiles as it relates to manufacturing, products, and their effects on the world at large, and on the interior environment and its occupants. Chapters 3, 4, and 5 follow the road of textile source and conversion — the study of fibers, yarns, and fabric construction and conversion coloring and finishing.

Part II, "Applications," features chapters that assist the design professional in making the right choice for the right application. Chapter 6 covers the largely nonresidential or contract requirements for textile specifications, including many testing procedures and ratings that assure a fabric will perform as expected. Tests are listed in tables, organized to make a highly technical and complex subject understandable and easily referenced. Chapter 7 discusses the aesthetics of textiles. Chapters 9 through 13 explore the applications of textiles as upholstered furniture, slipcovers, wallcoverings, window treatments, linens and textile accessories, broadloom carpeting, and hand-

and machine-made area rugs. These in-depth chapters cover both contract and residential considerations and are followed by a comprehensive chapter on textile maintenance.

Part III, "Period Styles," addresses the constant elements professionals may rely on throughout their careers, even given the inevitable flux in interior design style and trends. One of these constants is the use of textiles and their colors, patterns, textures, and styles of application in historical periods that continue to influence interior design today. Part III is a richly illustrated section that explores the major uses of interior design textiles through the historical periods. The chapters are divided into major themes: Oriental styles, Formal Traditional styles, Medieval, Colonial, and Country styles, Regional and Thematic styles, and Modern styles. In each period, motifs, upholstered furniture, bed textiles, window treatments, and rugs are described, and many are illustrated. These elements provide endless inspiration for both contract and residential interiors today. For example, in many new contract broadloom carpets, design motifs are taken from periods such as Arts and Crafts or Art Nouveau. This section provides an invaluable and reliable resource for all interiors, as all interior design today is based on designs of the past.

Resources and Website

An outstanding feature of *Interior Textiles* is the highly usable Resources section at the end of each applicable chapter. Associations and organizations are listed whose membership or information may be of direct service to the textile professional. These annotated resources list the Web site, mailing address, phone and fax numbers, and purpose of each organization. They are composited in the Appendix. The Bibliography at the end of the text is also extensive and useful, as well as the Index.

A Companion Web Site, www.wiley.com/go/interior textiles, features a wealth of resources including those found at the end of applicable chapters and manufacturers of the products and styles explored in the textbook. The Web addresses are live so the reader can click through to research educational resources, associations, manufacturers, and specific textile products.

The Companion Web Site also includes supplemental tables referred to specific chapters, an extensive Glossary of Terms, and a Historical Timeline of Manufactured Fibers. An Instructor's Manual is also available for those utilizing this book in a course.

Welcome to the amazing world of interior textiles. Enjoy the journey.

Visit **www.wiley.com/go/interiortextiles** for the expanded supplement and learning resources that accompany this book.

PART I TEXTILES

1

The Textiles Industry: Profession and Careers

Figure 1.1 Fine textiles for interior design offer myriad patterns, colors, and textures. Here, silk protein fibers are used in a luxurious, high-end residential collection, Silk Empire II. *Photo courtesy of Highland Court*. 800-387-3872 www.highlandcourtfabrics.com.

PROFESSIONAL PRACTICES

Professional practices is a business term that indicates the body of generally accepted procedures and conduct in a given industry or profession. It addresses the responsibilities of the professional in two directions: to the employer or suppliers, and to the clients or customers. It also means an individual and collective commitment to fair trade and to ethical conduct. In the interior textiles industry and related professions, a variety of textile producers, manufacturers, distributors, retail businesses, and professionals work cooperatively to nurture a vibrant and financially healthy industry. Economically, the textiles industry and professions are dependent on the same factors as most other U.S. and international manufacturing and consumer-oriented businesses, including the principles of supply and demand and the level of prosperity or intermittent recession.

The textiles profession offers a wide variety of careers in a wide variety of areas and places. Professionals who deal with textiles must work both **upstream** and **downstream.** *Upstream* refers to the business's immediate suppliers, and *downstream* is the outlet for or purchaser of the processed goods. The resulting supply chain is composed of many links, from fiber production at the beginning to the completed end product owned by the consumer.

THE INTERIOR TEXTILES INDUSTRY

The textiles industry is complex, vast, and international. In the United States, the industry employs over 1 million people in fiber production, machinery, textile mills, textile producers, and apparel. It is a $70.8 billion industry, contributing $61.7 billion annually to the gross domestic product (GDP). The textiles complex is third largest among the basic manufacturing industries in the United States. Overall, it is a healthy, vibrant industry, although a rise in imported textiles has caused a decline in the domestic consumption of U.S.-produced textiles. Abroad, particularly in China, Taiwan, Korea, Japan, India, and Vietnam, export of textiles has increased dramatically. The United States imports heavily from these countries, as well as from Mexico.

Production consists of many steps in the processing of raw elements into finished textiles. These steps include:

- Producing and/or procuring natural cellulosic and protein fibers and plant and fossil-fuel components for manufactured polymers.
- Spinning yarn.
- Manufacturing textiles by weaving, needle construction, and nonwoven processes.
- Converting textiles by prefinishing, dyeing, and printing, and by standard and decorative postcoloring finishing.

These steps result in salable textile goods that support and enrich the built environment. The finished goods then move through the distribution network into the hands of wholesalers and then to the trade and the public.

Industry manufacturing is complex because of the varying sizes of facilities, their locations, and their ownership. When a manufacturer is engaged in only one step of the process, the business is termed a **horizontal operation.** Two examples of horizontal operations are the production of fabric to the **greige goods,** or unfinished, state, and the conversion process. *Conversion* refers to the converting or changing of greige into finished fabric.

When a manufacturer is involved in several steps of the process, having financial or operational control over them, the business is termed a **vertical operation.** This type of operation may produce greige goods, convert them, and even distribute them to the trade under a proprietary label or controlled brand name.

Another type of textiles business is seen when mills, or manufacturers, produce goods for a specific product or end-use—for example, commercial fabrics that are tested to meet stringent architectural specifications and codes. A different mill may produce only nonwoven goods such as extruded fabrics or needle-constructed fabrics. A carpet mill specializes entirely in spinning carpet yarn, in producing carpet greige goods, or in tufting or weaving commercial or residential carpeting. Further, one or more corporations may own several such specialized mills, each doing business as (d/b/a) a company or brand name under the umbrella auspices of the larger corporate entity.

The procurement of smaller companies by larger ones is a major trend today. When this happens, the leadership, direction, and even methods of production may change or be updated. Occasionally a corporation elects to close a mill that does not yield a satisfactory return for investors, whose

Figure 1.2 In this step in fabric production, the singer burns the surface fibers from greige or gray goods. *Photo courtesy of Cotton Incorporated.*

sales area is declining, or whose plant is dramatically inefficient. However, the textiles industry is well established and stable, and even with the perceived crisis of a dearth of imported textiles, it remains solid and strong in the United States.

Another feature of the industry is the formation of new corporations by means of shared funding and ownership from successful existing corporations. Companies that join forces may be from more than one country, including the United States and countries in Europe, Central and South America, and the Pacific Rim. These joint ventures may perform research and development (R&D) of existing or new polymer fibers and a variety of useful products, including interior design textiles, and establish and solidify their marketability. Many manufacturing programs exhibit a symbiosis of marketing, research and development, and sensitivity to green design (discussed below). The textiles industry offers many employment opportunities.

Table 1.1 shows the steps in the processing of fiber to finished goods ready for installation. Each line in the table represents a segment of the industry. In the first step, the production of fibers takes place on a continual and concurrent basis, whereas the following steps are largely consecutive, following an order from beginning to end.

TABLE 1.1 TEXTILES MANUFACTURING FLOWCHART

STEP 1—Fiber Production

- Natural cellulosic fiber production: cotton, linen, jute, others

- Natural protein fiber/fabric production: wool, silk, leather

- Manufactured cellulosic fiber production: rayon, acetate

- Manufactured dextrose fiber production: polylactic acid or polylactide (PLA)

- Manufactured synthetic fiber production: acrylic, nylon, olefin, polyester, others

- Manufactured mineral/natural source production: metallic, rubber

Figure 1.3a Staple fibers are blended to enhance yarns and produce varying characteristics. *From Maryrose McGowan*, Specifying Interiors, 2 ed., *John Wiley & Sons, Inc., 2006.*

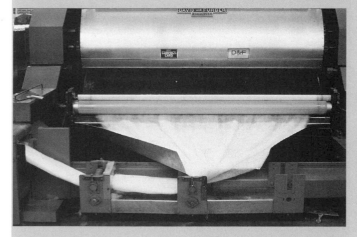

Figure 1.3b Cotton and linen fibers are carded to remove shorter staple, resulting in smooth, long, lustrous fibers. *From Maryrose McGowan*, Specifying Interiors, 2 ed., *John Wiley & Sons, Inc., 2006.*

Figure 1.3c Drafting fibers into slivers increases the length per unit weight. *From Maryrose McGowan*, Specifying Interiors, 2 ed., *John Wiley & Sons, Inc., 2006.*

(continued)

STEP 2—Types of Yarn Manufacturing

- Spinning of natural staple fibers into single- or multi-ply yarn
- Extrusion/spinning of manufactured fibers into continuous monofilaments; texturizing yarn
- Creation of short-length staple from manufactured filaments
- Throwing/compounding filaments or single yarns into plied or complex/novelty yarns

STEP 2 Optional—Types of Yarn or Extruded Fabric Covering

- Dyeing of viscose solution before extrusion of manufactured fibers
- Dyeing or printing of yarn

STEP 3—Greige Goods Manufacturing

- Woven, knitted, needle-constructed, extruded and compound, other fabric construction
- Tufted, needle-constructed, woven carpet greige

STEP 4—Fabric Design and Styling

- Creation of woven and printed design through hand artwork or computer software
- Colorway/dye and pigment engineering selection/specification

STEP 5—Textile Conversion: Coloring and Finishing

- Prefinishing natural fibers: bleaching, mercerizing, stabilizing, precoloring treatments
- Precoloring treaments of manufactured fibers
- Dyeing greige piece goods into solid colors
- Printing pattern on piece goods by screen, roller, transfer, and other printing methods
- Pattern/color applied to carpet roll goods (if not yarn dyed)
- Postcoloring finishes: decorative and/or structural or functional finishes

STEP 6—Distribution of Piece Goods

- **Rolls** or **bolts** of interior textiles are known as **pieces** or **piece goods.** A *full piece* is an average of 60 yards long and a *half-piece* is about 30 yards long, although variations occur. Textiles are sold from the mills or manufacturers in four directions:
  1. To the manufacturers of end-product goods: upholstered furniture and wall coverings; ready-made window treatments; bed, bath, kitchen, and hospitality linens; accessory items; and rugs and carpeting
  2. To distributors, jobbers, or fabric companies or houses, which sell to the trade
  3. Through manufacturers' sales representatives, direct to large corporations or institutions
  4. To piece-goods store retailers

Figure 1.4 Roll or bolt goods, often called **pieces,** are stored in warehouses. Cut orders are taken and shipped to the design professional or fabricator. *Photo by Edward Addeo. Photo courtesy of Donghia, Inc.* www.donghia.com.

1. **Textiles are sold to manufacturers of finished product.** Product manufacturers include upholstered furniture and systems furniture companies; ready-made and alternative window treatment manufacturers; bed, bath, and linen manufacturers; and accessory companies. Manufacturers of product obtain textiles from mills in two ways. The first is to select from fabrics that are already produced. This is done at the mill, at a trade show, or in the manufacturer's showroom, if it is represented in a center of commerce such as New York City. The product manufacturer may also contract for exclusive rights to a fabric so that no other entity may purchase and sell it. This is possible when the manufacturer can guarantee an order large enough to justify selling the entire quantity produced to one company.

The second way is for the product manufacturer to place an order with the textile conversion mill for goods made to custom specifications. In the case of very large companies, such as those that produce alternative window treatments, this may require the services of chemical engineers who design or write specifications for the composition of yarns or textiles—that is, the fibers, construction, coloring methods, and finishes that meet specific criteria for the end product.

2. **Textiles are sold to distributors, jobbers, or fabric companies or houses.** Several dozen distributors stock textiles as merchandise in the United States and abroad. These are discussed later in this chapter.

These industry distributors then sell goods to the trade. The **trade** consists of architects and interior architects, specifiers, facility managers, interior designers, interior consultants and decorators, and specialty retailers. The trade professional specifies an exact amount of cut yardage from distributors, and it is his or her responsibility to specify (or sometimes design) or select and sell textiles for finished applications. The uses or applications of textiles are: upholstery, slipcovers; wall coverings; window treatments; bed, bath, and kitchen linens; accessories; tapestries or wall hangings; and rugs and carpeting.

3. **Textiles are sold through sales representatives direct to large corporations or institutions,** which buy large textile quantities direct from the mills for installation in their privately owned buildings. This is common in commercial carpeting and systems furniture. It may also take place through a vertical operation manufacturer that also acts as a distributor. Examples are large hotels, religious and educational institutions, government agencies, and corporations that purchase substantial quantities on a repeat basis for new construction or as refurbishing needs arise.

4. **Textiles are sold to piece-goods store retailers** that buy overstocked textiles, discontinued pieces, or second-quality (flawed) goods. Piece-goods stores sell textiles that would not otherwise find their way to the general public. Although some stores are independently owned, most are part of a chain or franchise, thus increasing their quantity buying power. For example, if a mill has ten whole or partial pieces or rolls of discontinued fabric for sale, it would be difficult for one store to justify such a large purchase, whereas a chain store company that can distribute one roll or piece to each of ten outlets can. The price these retailers pay to the mill varies and is often negotiated at costs far below wholesale, making below-retail prices available to the public. Piece-goods stores may also purchase overstock or new goods from a few distributors that are a part of a vertical operation for about half the wholesale or cut yardage price per yard. This is another example of quantity discounting. Piece-goods retail stores are discussed later in this chapter as a way for the trade and the public to obtain interior design textiles.

Textile fabrics and carpeting produced for use in interior design is a multibillion-dollar business—one that is always changing to keep up with new directions in style, color and trends, research and development, and ecological and social needs. The industry is also price driven. Salability and profitability are key requirements for the manufacture of textile goods. Although critics feel the quality of textile design is waning in favor of enhancing the bottom line, much good can be said of the many companies that not only try to produce high-quality goods but also consider the effect of their manufacturing processes and products on the environment as well as strive to meet the needs of the end user.

TABLE 1.2 DISTRIBUTION OF FINISHED PIECE-GOODS TEXTILES

I. Fabric sold from mills to manufacturers of product:
- Window treatment manufacturers and distributors
- Furniture manufacturers and distributors
- Wall covering/fabric manufacturers and distributors
- Bed, bath, kitchen, and commercial linens manufacturers
- Accessory items manufacturers

II. Fabric sold from mills to fabric houses, companies, jobbers, or distributors

Fabric house and *company* are more exclusive terms for *jobber* and *distributor*. These companies purchase and warehouse rolls of piece goods, distribute samples, and sell cut orders to the trade.

The Trade
- Architects, interior architects
- Specifiers, facility managers
- Interior designers
- Interior design consultants, interior decorators

The Marketplace
- Residential users: first and second or vacation homes or condominiums, model homes
- Commercial or nonresidential users
- Hospitality, resort, health care, office, institution, retail spaces

III. Fabric or carpeting sold from the mills to large corporations, institutions, government agencies, or religious groups for end-use in their facilities

IV. Specialty retailers, piece-goods and retail stores, carpet mill outlet stores

The Marketplace
- Retail consumers
- Interior design professionals

FIRST- AND SECOND-QUALITY MERCHANDISE

Many nations have fabric manufacturers with a wide range of regional influence and varying degrees of quality merchandise. Not all fabrics and carpeting are perfect, although some fabrics are close. Interestingly, the two countries producing the highest-quality merchandise are among those that sustained heavy destruction of factories during World War II: Japan and Germany. It is said that Japanese textiles are nearly flawless. Excellent goods come from Switzerland as well as Germany, and very fine fabrics are produced in France, England, Italy, and the Scandinavian countries. These countries also rebuilt or upgraded many of their textile mills after World War II. In developing countries, poorer fabrics are produced along with those of finer quality. Millions of yards are imported annually from India, Mexico, and the Pacific Rim, and in interior design, these textiles have achieved a high level of style and fashion acceptance.

In the United States, many newer mills are state-of-the-art and built to the highest European standards. However, some mills date to before the Civil War and utilize antiquated processes in which spun fibers and fine debris can fly through the air and embed in the fabrics, which has a negative impact on their quality. Faults and flaws may also be introduced in the finishing process (see chapter 5), resulting in piece goods that are imperfect even when they are classified as first quality. A catchphrase of the American textile industry, "Firsts are Seconds and Seconds are Firsts," means first-quality (or top-quality) goods may have as many flaws as those classified as seconds (irregular or flawed goods), and occasionally seconds have fewer flaws than some goods certified as firsts. For this reason, all textiles should be examined before being cut and processed into applications.

First-quality goods are sold to manufacturers of product and to the trade. Second-quality merchandise, as well as discontinued fabric that is no longer current or is considered out of style, is sold to piece-goods store retailers.

"TO THE TRADE": THE PROCEDURE FOR OBTAINING TEXTILES

Once a fabric is manufactured, it is sampled and sold to the trade by fabric companies, distributors, or jobbers. The owners or buyers of the hundreds of companies in the United States and abroad often make their selections at international trade shows where manufacturers set up booths with creative, eye-catching displays and samples of the fabrics they are offering for sale downstream. The best known of these interior textiles shows are the international Heim-textil in Frankfurt, Germany, and the Beinalle textile trade show in Paris, France. Heimtextil USA and Interior Lifestyle USA are conveniently located for U.S. companies. New York City is a spring and fall market site for the U.S. mills or converters headquartered nearby. Some distributors and jobbers travel abroad as circumstances dictate.

At all of these locations, piece goods are contracted for purchase by a large number of jobbers and distributors. Thus, the trade professional may see the same fabric in sample books distributed by several companies, each with a different name or stock number and perhaps even priced differently. A fabric that is widely purchased is known as an **open line fabric,** while a fabric that is purchased solely for one fabric company is termed **exclusive fabric.** Such mainstream fabrics have specific markets—some primarily residential, others specifically nonresidential or commercial. That is not to say the two are mutually exclusive. Commercial fabrics may be used in residences, and residential fabrics may be treated to meet fire code specifications, for example, and are potentially useful in nonresidential settings (see chapter 4). Other fabrics are niche-marketed as alternative manufactured window treatment textiles or upholstery for furniture manufacturers.

For some international fabrics, a U.S. company may purchase exclusive rights to distribute a line or a fabric—in the United States only, however, not around the world. Some fabric houses or companies, distributors, or jobbers have a few or many fabrics that are specifically milled and converted with an exclusive pattern. Exclusive or proprietary (solely owned) fabrics have a place in the high-end market as fabrics not widely available to the general public.

There are levels of exclusivity in fabric companies. The more exclusive, unusual, and costly U.S. fabrics are typically sold through **fabric houses** headquartered in New York City and represented in design center showrooms. Their fabrics are distributed to the professional trade only. Such upscale fabric houses advertise in high-end shelter magazines and aim for fabric name brand recognition. Many have warehouses in several major cities.

The terms **distributor** and **jobber** indicate a regional fabric company, headquartered in a city other than New York, whose fabrics are distributed regionally or nationally through sales representatives and at trade shows. Distributors and jobbers offer a wide range of textiles, all priced moderately. They do little, if any, national advertising, which helps keep their costs moderate. The fabrics offered by distributors are considered the bread and butter of thousands of interior design professionals, while the textiles sold by exclusive fabric houses are the cream. Both types of fabric lines are considered essential to a well-rounded design business.

Figure 1.5a Contract textiles and carpet samples are often distributed to the trade in architectural binders that fit neatly on reference shelves.

Figure 1.5b Sample books with cord handles are distributed by fabric companies or jobbers. They vary in size and contain color lines—all the colors available in a fabric or collection of fabrics.

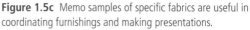

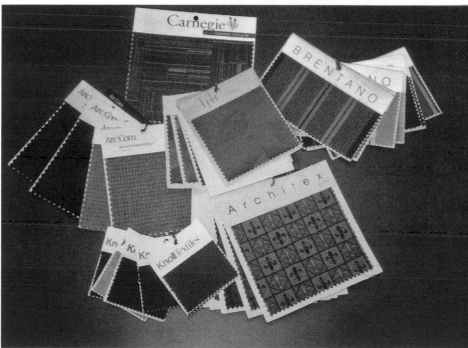

Figure 1.5c Memo samples of specific fabrics are useful in coordinating furnishings and making presentations.

Figure 1.5d Swatch cards of contract textiles are often linked by small chains in groups. These are used in specification books and board presentation layouts.

Commercial or nonresidential fabrics are represented in both fabric houses and regional distributors. It is less critical for commercial fabrics to be in the lay or public fashion spotlight, although advertising in commercial publications and sample distribution through sales representation to designers is essential so such fabrics will be specified.

The term *jobber* (which technically applies to both fabric houses or companies and distributors) comes from the way the distributing company purchases **job lots,** or several pieces of a fabric of the same dye lot at one time, to assure consistency. When a job lot is purchased, some yardage is sent to a sample manufacturer, which cuts the fabric and creates sample books, ringed sample sets, memo samples, showroom hanging samples, swatch/sample cards, and sample one-yard lengths. Each of these sample types has a different purpose:

Architectural binder folders are hardbound books of two–three leaves of small swatches of fabric or carpet.

Sample books are distributed to design firms with a studio, showroom, or retail space. They are a stack of fabric samples cut to the same size and affixed to a cardboard header and cord for hanging. The company name and logo and a name or group title are printed on the header. Sample books may be free or cost about $12 to $60 each as part of a signed purchase agreement between the fabric company and design firm. The firm then owns the samples and can use or cut them to suit its specification or selection needs. The advantage to the designer is that the most recent samples arrive in a timely manner and are on hand even if the studio is nowhere near a design center showroom. Even for urban firms, the time saved not having to search a showroom, the convenience of not having to return samples, and the flexibility of selecting and taking sample books to a job site or customer's interior for selection are all reasons for purchasing sample books. The disadvantages include the investment, the required storage space, the need to change price lists and keep abreast of which samples are discontinued, and the effort to keep the sample books properly marked. Some books are used frequently and some rarely, meaning that some unwanted books must be paid for as part of the set.

Ringed sample sets are flat samples with grommets through which large metal clasped rings are threaded to hold sets. Where the samples are large and heavy, such as upholstery manufacturers' sets, a wooden header handle is often used. The advantage is twofold: When a fabric is discontinued, it can be removed, and new fabrics are easy to add. Samples can also be taken out and viewed in different locations and lighting conditions and used in coordinating with other textiles. Disadvantages include bulk and weight, the lack of a protective book covering, and the effort required to keep track of and replace individual samples.

Memo samples are lengths that range from about 8 × 8 inches to 15 × 36 inches. Sizes vary depending on the company's policy, the fabric type, and the pattern repeat. Memo samples are ordered by computer or by phone, or are checked out in person from a fabric company showroom. Residential memo samples are available free for thirty days and typically must be returned or a fee will be charged to the design firm. **Contract, or nonresidential memo samples** are available at no charge and are not returned to the company. Contract means health care, office, hospitality, etc. and the samples are smaller than residential memo samples. The advantages for residential designers are that the showroom can do the searching for the designer, or that the designer (and perhaps the client) can search for and borrow only the fabric samples that are possibilities for a given installation. The design firm need not purchase or store samples, the size is typically larger than in a sample book, and because they are larger and can be laid flat or hung or held vertically, memo samples are convenient and more flexible than fabric book swatches. Disadvantages include the travel to the showroom or the wait for the mail and the need to return the memo samples in person or through the mail. It takes disciplined efficiency to keep track of memo samples and get them back in the time allotted.

For commercial designers, the fabrics are used most often as upholstery or panels, so memo samples can be placed over a chair or tacked to a wall for aesthetic evaluation.

Showroom hanging samples are similar to memo samples and usually comprise a full set of the fabric lines offered by a given company or jobber. Some hanging samples have a metal hanger attached; others feature small clip-hangers similar to trouser hangers in a clothing store. The company may allow hanging samples to be borrowed, like memo samples, or it may opt to keep them in the showroom only.

Swatch or **sample cards** are free to the design professional and useful in making board presentations (where small swatches are cut and displayed on matte or other art board as a part of a design concept collage). The advantages are economy and the convenience of having a swatch without cutting a sample book or ringed sample set. Cutting for presentations is not an option with memo or showroom samples that must be returned. Swatch cards are most often used for commercial or nonresidential presentations but are also useful to attach to specification paperwork and to coordinate many interior components. Dropping a sample card into a client folder or job book makes a ready reference for large projects in which many textiles and surface finishes must be coordinated.

Sample one-yard lengths are available for commercial projects at no cost when the design firm can assure that the fabric will be ordered. One-yard lengths allow the fabric to be seen *in situ* (at the site) and to be evaluated for aesthetics and tactile acceptability. If the pattern is small in scale, the length may be cut in half vertically to form two half-width one-yard lengths. One-yard lengths may be ordered and paid for by the residential designer for the same purposes.

The remainder of the job lot bolts or pieces are stored in the company's warehouses and used as stock inventory to fill cut orders, as described below.

Textile fabrics may be purchased in one of the following ways:

1. Cut yardage. Most interior design textiles are purchased as cut orders, or yardage of lengths calculated for the application, with 10 yards as an average purchase. Most fabric companies will sell half-yards but will not charge less than the price of one whole yard. If 25 yards are required, a half-bolt may be purchased, and if the yardage is 50 or more, a whole bolt may be obtained at a discount. As discussed in Part II, yardage is a crucial element in the sales and installation of any textile. Too little yardage can halt the project until the missing yardage is ordered and arrives as a perfect dye lot match. Sometimes additional yardage in a dye lot match is unavailable; the balance of the exact dye lot may have been sold from every warehouse. This is a nightmare for the designer. Another problem with undercalculating yardage is that the design firm must pay for the extra yardage needed to complete the job. Once a job price is agreed on, any shortage is usually the responsibility of the design professional, unless the mistake is discovered quickly and renegotiated. When underestimated costs must be absorbed by the design firm, correcting the problem may completely erode the profit margin. Repeats of this kind of mistake will compromise the long-term viability of the business. Thus, yardage must be carefully and accurately calculated and ordered. On the other hand, ordering too much yardage is wasteful, and if a client learns of leftover yardage from his or her installation, then anger and even lawsuits may ensue. Designers must be competent and reliable and exhibit good judgment concerning yardage.

Fabric suppliers and jobbers hold the piece goods in their warehouses on long round tubes. In the apparel industry, the term *bolt* is used to indicate an average of 48-inch-wide goods folded in half and wound around a flat cardboard piece, easily handled by the consumer and sales clerk. However, in interior design, fabrics are an average of 54 inches wide and must be kept flat whenever possible, because many fabrics would permanently crease from folding and thus become unsuitable for most interior design applications. Fabrics for interiors are wound around very strong, round, hollow cardboard tubes about 60 inches long and hung on dowel-like shelves for retail sales, or kept in a deep compartment shelving system in a distributor/jobber warehouse.

When an order is placed for a portion of a roll of piece goods, the fabric is **candled,** or passed over a light table, to inspect it for flaws. In first-quality goods, tiny flaws may be ignored, but when serious flaws are found, the fabric is typically cut to remove the flawed section. This means an order may arrive in more than one length, which could affect the fabrication process.

2. Piece goods or **half-pieces.** A few jobbers or fabric houses sell to the trade in this way. Some give a discount of 50 percent off the wholesale or net price, while other companies that offer piece-goods sales give 5 to 10 percent off the wholesale price. There must be a yardage justification for purchasing piece goods for a final installation. The number of yards required for a job should utilize the entire piece, or the leftover waste must be stored and is very likely unusable.

Purchase Orders

A **purchase order** (PO) is a standard or customized form that instructs a supplier to ship a certain textile to a specific location. Fabric may be sent to a studio, shop, or retail store. It may also be **drop-shipped** to a fabrication workroom (draperies), upholstery shop, warehouse (furniture, carpet), or, infrequently, the site itself. Purchase orders may be standard forms for all items, or they may be specific to the type of textile ordered. For example, cut yardage POs may differ from carpet POs. Do not confuse POs with specification orders or installation orders (see below).

Keeping track of purchase orders is of utmost importance to a well-run professional textile or design business. Copies of purchase orders should be kept in three places:

1. In an electronic file, if ordering online or via computer-linked fax. Two locations on the computer are possible: (a) a folder or file for the customer, and (b) a folder or file for all purchase orders, placed sequentially by number, by date, or by customer.
2. In the customer's manila file folder, known as a *job folder, job notebook,* or *client/customer folder.* These folders are kept in a file cabinet or in the design professional's desk or carrel. The job folder contains sequential loose papers, swatches, notes, and all POs and specification sheets for a job or project. Another option is a three-ring binder; all these papers can be three-hole punched or encased in sheet protectors (helpful for swatch samples and smaller paperwork). Binders are kept in view on a shelf rather than in a drawer. For some designers, visual reminders help keep the project progressing toward completion, whereas in file drawers or in a bin on top of a desk, these same jobs may be temporarily lost or put on hold. "Out of sight, out of mind" is a useful phrase for textile professionals as their work involves many pressing obligations that sometimes erupt in crisis.

PURCHASE ORDER

VENDOR:
NAME AND ADDRESS OF TEXTILE MANUFACTURING OR DISTRIBUTING COMPANY

PURCHASE ORDER NO
00001

SOLD TO _____ NAME AND ADDRESS OF PURCHASER: _____
INTERIOR DESIGN FIRM OR ARCHITECTURAL FIRM
BUSINESS OR SPECIALIST

SHIP TO _____ SAME AS PURCHASER, OR _____
MAY BE "DROP SHIPPED"
TO WORKROOM OR CLIENT

DATE	DATE REQUIRED	HOW SHIP	TERMS

QUANTITY	PLEASE SUPPLY ITEMS LISTED BELOW	PRICE	UNIT
1			
2			
3			
4			
5			
6			
7			
8			
9			
10			
11			
12			
13			
14			
15			
16			
17			
18			
19			
20			
21			
22			

IMPORTANT
OUR ORDER NUMBER MUST APPEAR ON ALL INVOICES, PACKAGES, ETC.
PLEASE NOTIFY US IMMEDIATELY IF YOU ARE UNABLE TO SHIP COMPLETE ORDER BY DATE SPECIFIED.

PLEASE SEND _____ COPIES OF YOUR INVOICE WITH ORIGINAL BILL OF LADING

PURCHASING AGENT

Figure 1.6 Sample purchase order.

3. In a purchase order binder. A wide three-ring variety with a spine label reading "Purchase Orders" is a professional, logical, and organized method of keeping track of all POs placed by the company. Again, if the binder is on a shelf, it is easier to refer to and use properly.

Items entered on a purchase order are as follows:

- The name and address of the design or architectural firm specifier or specialist placing the order.
- The name, address, phone and fax numbers, and email address of the vendor, manufacturer, distributor or jobber, supplier, furniture manufacturer, or carpet wholesale source.
- The date of the purchase order.
- A sequential purchase order number.
- The date the order is expected to be received. This is a precise date and *never* "ASAP," which means nothing to the supplier and may even slow the order because of its presumptuous and unprofessional implication. A real date either can or cannot be met and is the basis for communication concerning the status of the order (see below).
- The name or designation code or number of the person placing the order.
- The name of the person who accepted the phone order and the date of that order. Also, the date and time of day of the phone order and any information given by that person, such as order status or expected delivery date. If appropriate, the words "CONFIRMATION ONLY—DO NOT DUPLICATE" should appear in large, bold letters. A confirming purchase order is important as a part of the paper trail, even when the order is phoned in, serving to avoid duplication and confusion. A paper copy of a purchase order sent electronically may be kept as a backup.
- The name, number, or code of the job, and a shipping address if different from the purchaser's address. This is for cross-reference by the design professional but also is helpful to the supplier.
- The identification, name and/or number, and color name and/or number of the item purchased.
- The quantity in units (furniture pieces, area rugs, wall covering rolls, or accessory items such as pillows), linear feet (carpet), square yards (carpet), or linear yards (fabric).
- Special instructions if the fabric must be cut due to potential flaws. These might read, "30 yards—If necessary to cut, then 10 cut lengths, each 108" or 4 complete pattern repeats of 27" each." This is a safety measure so the yardage is not short with multiple cuts when considering the pattern repeat (adding an extra yard to the purchase order yardage is another way to avert fabrication crises).
- The cost **net** or **wholesale** price per yard or unit (trade purchase price).
- The total cost of the quantity ordered.

Order Status and Delivery

When an order is placed via phone or computer/fax, the condition of the stock should be confirmed. If the merchandise is current, that means it is still available as an item in the merchandise line (not discontinued). If it is in stock, enough is available to fill and ship the order within a few days (according to supplier's customary schedule, unless a rush order is placed at extra cost). If the item or yardage is on backorder, it is still available but out of stock, meaning it will be replaced and shipped at a later date. It is crucial to learn when that date will be, as the information may affect the design work. If the order is for fabric, the supplier may be waiting for mill time (if exclusive) or for the mill to print more of the fabric (this depends on demand). The wait for in-stock status may be from two weeks to several months. Often a two-week wait will not affect the customer or the scheduling of project completion. However, six weeks until in-stock is serious, and the customer must be informed right away to confirm acceptability of the delay. If the replenish time is much longer, which means the fabric may be in danger of being discontinued, the best course is to reselect or choose another item or textile. Discontinued status means reselection must be made immediately. Textiles can be discontinued without notification. This can occur when the stock is depleted and the supplier elects not to replace it. Alternatively, the manufacturer chooses to cease production of that item. A third explanation may be an inherent safety problem or defect in the merchandise.

PIECE-GOODS RETAIL STORES

One way fabrics reach the consumer is through the retail stores that sell piece goods to the public. Interior designers, decorators, and consultants may also shop at these stores for their projects or with their clients. The fabrics stocked in retail stores are either discontinued leftover stock from the mills or second-quality merchandise that has faults or flaws and is not suitable for cut orders. These fabrics are discounted by the mill to the retailer according to the quantities purchased, the quantity that must be moved out of the warehouse, and the age of the goods.

The advantage to piece-goods stores is that textile in-stock merchandise is available for immediate purchase. The disadvantage is that where more yardage is needed to match in-stock goods, it is likely that, unless another store in the chain has the same roll of fabric in stock, it won't be possible to match the dye lot. Thus, the caution "what you see is what you get" pertains to in-stock purchasing.

Piece-goods stores also have samples of current fabrics at low to mid-range prices that can be ordered at retail as specified cut yardage. The wait for cut orders is one to six weeks on average, with backorders always a possibility.

UNDERSTANDING SPECIFICATIONS

Specifications is a critical, twofold word in the textiles profession. It refers to the list of requirements written by the architect so the designer can find acceptable fabrics and carpeting. It also refers to the selected textile as ordered from the manufacturer or supplier, plus documents for fabrication and installation.

Architectural Specifications

First, specifications—specs, for short—are the written requirements prepared by architects or qualified interior designers working with new construction or remodeling buildings. For interior textiles, specs are written for carpeting, upholstery, textiles on walls, and draperies or alternative window treatments. They are listed in order of priority, where cost per yard or financial parameters for the total textile installation or project are given first. Next come the details, such as the fiber to be used, the pleats on the draperies, or the type of carpeting, with minimum acceptable standards for each item. These standards should align with or exceed city or state **codes**, which are enforceable legal requirements that must be met in order to protect the health, safety, and welfare of the public who use the space being designed.

The categories of architectural specifications address the following:

1. **Flammability**—The goal is to select the least flammable textiles.
2. **Physical durability**—How does the fabric stand up to abrasion and traffic? This can be tested and results obtained to match the architectural specifications.
3. **Aesthetic durability**—Based on fiber, yarn, and construction performance, this means the fabric will remain visually appealing for an extended or reasonable period of time from about 6–12 years.

The four types of nonresidential specifications and the stringent tests required for draperies, wallcovering, and upholstery textiles are presented in chapter 6. Flammability tests for carpeting are discussed in chapter 6.

Selection, Fabrication, and Installation Specifications

Once a fabric or carpet is found that meets commercial architectural specifications or residential requirements and is aesthetically the best choice (and approved by the architectural firm, if required), the next steps are to calculate yardage or amounts and place the order via purchase order, as discussed above. The fabric is shipped to the site for installation, to a workroom or manufacturer, to the business location, or to a warehouse.

For textiles that require fabrication, specification sheets or forms are completed with dimensions and all details in writing and possibly drawn to scale. The fabrication workroom or upholstery shop completes the work, and then it can be picked up or shipped to the business or the site of installation. Typically, custom-upholstered furniture and textile applications are not sent to a warehouse but rather planned for completion at the time of the installation or delivery.

Installation sheets or forms may accompany the delivery of applications. This is particularly important in order to ascertain that every item is correctly installed in the right location. Where a residential client owes a balance due on completion of textile goods and finished product, the installer or delivery person customarily collects the funds and submits them to the design professional.

BEING A PROFESSIONAL

A professional is a person who participates for financial gain in a career-oriented job, usually after extensive academic and/or practical training. Professionals conduct themselves in ways that are respected by their peers. They are expected to be honest, ethical, and responsible in their dealings with clients and associates. They are trustworthy with proprietary information. Textile professionals have achieved a command of the processes, terms, materials, and professional business practices related to their field. True professionals are competent and reliable and can be trusted to carry out duties and assignments with integrity.

Professionals are dedicated to their work. They actively participate and are enthusiastic about what they do. They possess a drive for accomplishment. They support or encourage scientific and academic research and product development. They expend energy promoting their profession.

They participate in professional organizations and community affairs. They make real contributions. They are consistent in their efforts to learn, expand their body of knowledge, and then find ways to unselfishly share what they know so others can benefit. They make society better.

Occasionally one finds full-time employees who are not uniformly professional in their conduct, while others who work part-time may be highly regarded professionals. Personal attitude, behavior, and quality of contribution mark the true professional. As a student and throughout your career, your decision to act honorably will invariably yield higher respect from all with whom you associate. The determination to do your best and make the world a better place for your having been a team player will also give you satisfaction and peace of mind, and it will be its own reward. You will also be reimbursed financially, for people who are ethical and professional will always be sought after and paid well for the work they do. Doors of opportunity open to dedicated professionals; promotions and job or project opportunities follow a reputation for excellent performance and ethical behavior.

To clarify the complex and sometimes confusing world of interior textiles, the following table lists many careers in the field. Although in years past a person often stayed with a single job for an entire career of twenty-five or thirty years, today that is not always the case. Three to five years in one area may be a springboard into another career direction. As many people who study textiles are creative by nature, they may find innovative, entrepreneurial avenues to explore beyond those listed below.

CAREERS IN INTERIOR TEXTILES

The textiles industry and marketplace is rich in possible career paths. Some demand a full forty hours or more each week, while others can be part-time careers, flexible in number of hours per week and hours per day.

TABLE 1.3 CAREERS INCLUDING INTERIOR TEXTILES

Architect, interior architect—Architects are trained in structural, mechanical, and electrical systems. Interior architects specialize in systems, finishes, and fixtures. Architectural firms often work closely with interior design firms or have in-house interior design departments that, surprisingly, may earn more revenue than the architecture itself. Architects must be well versed in **building codes,** which are the laws or rules enforced by the local jurisdiction (city, county, etc.) where the building is to be erected. Whether new or remodeled construction, the finishes, fixtures, and furnishings must all be safe for the general public. Thus, the architect prepares the specifications for carpeting, wall materials, office panels, window coverings, and upholstered furniture. It is usually up to the designer to make the actual selections that meet these written criteria.

Carpet and/or rug specialist—This is a full- or part-time, residential or commercial career that can be based in retail, wholesale, or specification. The carpet and rug industry and trade is vast, with multiple opportunities for in-house, travel, and/or sales-oriented work. In the retail market, first-quality cut yardage broadloom carpeting sales have a small profit margin—as little as 10 percent (30 percent is average)—so yardage must be large to yield a good profit or commission. Authentic Oriental rugs typically have a 300 percent markup but often are marked down on sale in what seems a drastic price reduction. Carpet specifiers assist in the selection of a carpet that meets the architect's specifications and may receive a salary or a percent of the purchase price, even when the client purchases direct from a manufacturer. Many design, administrative, manufacturing, and sales jobs are available in the carpet and rug industry.

Corporate design—This field includes the furnishings of corporate offices, banks, and financial institutions. The designer may work directly for a corporation or institution or in a firm that specializes in corporate design.

Government and institutional design—This category of careers covers a wide range of buildings to be furnished, including auditoriums, billets/barracks/clubs, convention centers, day care facilities, embassies, federal buildings, libraries, museums, offices, public facilities, religious facilities, schools or other educational facilities, and universities/colleges/institutes. In all cases, budget, health and safety codes, and durability are key factors in textile specification. Specialists in this field may work directly for the government or bid on furnishing or refurbishing projects.

Healthcare design—This is the planning of spaces and furnishings for assisted living facilities; hospice centers; hospitals; and outpatient, rehabilitation, and wellness centers. The textiles used in these areas must meet stringent codes for fire, abrasion, and microorganism resistance.

Hospitality design—This is the planning of spaces and furnishings for hotels, resorts, restaurants, and cruise ships. Design professionals in hospitality do considerable work with interior textiles.

(continued)

Industry consultant — This is usually a freelance position in which the consultant contracts with manufacturers or distributors to do a specific job such as design work, product evaluation, or textile or color selection for a new or existing line of merchandise. It may entail lecturing or training company personnel. Work may be done on location or in the consultant's office or studio.

Industry personnel — The textile industry offers a wide variety of jobs, from office staff to manufacturing jobs to managerial and administrative positions to sales careers. As in any corporation, pay rates range from low entry-level to moderately high salaries. A commitment to the company and the industry can make working in textiles a long-term career.

Interior decorator, design consultant — This is a professional who, with or without formal design schooling, assists clients in the selection of furnishings, including but not limited to carpeting and flooring, furniture, wallcoverings, draperies and window treatments, bed ensembles, table covers, and accessory items, both decorative and textile. This career path requires good people skills, an understanding of the principles and elements of design, a practical application of business procedures, and the ability to work competently with wholesale sources and to direct installers. Income is usually based on the profit margin. When the decorator or consultant is a sales employee of a retail furnishings or specialty store, he or she is typically paid a commission of 5 to 10 percent of gross sales. Another arrangement is called *draw versus commission*; this situation pays an assured base monthly salary — with the expectation that sales will cover it — and commission in addition to the base salary.

Interior designer is a professional title. Some states license interior designers on the basis of qualifications including, for example, formal education, the passing of the National Council for Interior Design Qualifications (NCIDQ) exam, and a specified minimum years of verified work experience. This career also entails working closely with architects, contractors, and specialty professionals. Interior designers are competent with blueprints, understand building systems and hard materials, and can design fixtures and furnishings from the drawing board stage through fabrication and installation. Thus, they are often qualified to custom design textiles as well. Interior designers work in both residential and commercial areas of specialization. They are often dedicated career professionals who consider sustainability, the needs of special populations, and all aspects of custom design. They focus on programming as well as furnishings in order to design interiors that meet the short- and long-term needs of the occupants.

Figure 1.7 Interior designers study architectural blueprints to determine custom carpeting requirements. *Copyrighted and registered, Soroush Custom Rugs & Axminster Carpet, www.soroush.us.*

Journalist, author — A journalist writes articles for periodicals (magazines) or newspapers. Journalism may be the first career choice, followed by a decision to specialize in writing about interior furnishings. A journalist may be a full-time employee of an interiors magazine or a freelancer who submits articles to or contracts with one or more publications. Other magazine positions are departmental editor and photographer. Freelance fees vary dramatically; freelancing may or may not provide a full-time income for the journalist. An author writes textbooks for college, university, or trade school interior design programs; "reference" books for practicing professionals; or illustrated interior design books for the lay (nonprofessional) market.

Manufacturer's or industry representative — A representative — rep for short, and sometimes called a sales rep — follows a career path that entails travel to architectural and design firms and sometimes to retail stores within a designated region or territory. The rep meets with or calls on the professional who has the authority to purchase samples or to specify products. The rep's responsibilities also include processing special orders, negotiating variable discounts (usually the larger the order, the deeper the discount), and following through when needed to troubleshoot and assure satisfaction of the professionals and their clients. The rep may be salaried but is more often paid as a commission on sales. This means a flexible paycheck, but a secure, lucrative one when the sales rep is enthusiastic, dedicated, skilled, and a good problem solver.

Professional organization personnel — This career is as an administrative or assistant administrative position for a nonprofit organization, such as ASID (American Society of Interior Designers) or IIDA (International Interior Design Association), typically at its national headquarters in a large city. It is a paperwork-heavy, detail-oriented position in which interaction with members and supporting or participating companies (often long distance) may be a large part of the daily routine. Information dissemination to members through e-mail, brochures, and newsletters is a main purpose of these organizations. Another aspect of this career is the organization and execution of trade shows.

Residential — Residential textile careers deal with the sales, specifications, and installation of textile applications in the following types of residences: assisted living, community shelter, multifamily, senior housing, and the most lucrative — single-family homes.

Retail buyer — This position involves making decisions and ordering textile merchandise for a retail store. It is a business-based position rather than an artistic one, although being well versed in styles and trends is critical to success. Buyers travel to trade shows or showrooms and also order from merchandise catalogs. They decide not only which item to buy but also how many and in what color, with an eye toward what will sell in a given marketplace. Buyers for large department or specialty store chains must keep abreast of regional styles and coordinate efforts with each store. The job comes with a lot of pressure and responsibility. It is generally not highly paid, and the hours are often long, especially when visiting multiple stores to assure consistency in stock merchandise, display, and sales.

Recycling industry personnel — The recycling industry is found on every continent and comprises a variety of businesses that deal with the pre-consumer or post-consumer distribution and/or recycling of textiles. Careers include office, sales, supervisory, and distribution positions..

Retail sales associate — yardage, ready-made, or linens — This description may apply to a variety of jobs. In a textile yardage or linens store, for example, this job entails assisting customers in selection and purchase of ready-made goods: window treatments, bed and bath linens, and floor rugs. Pay is hourly wage, usually at or just above minimum. Such jobs are good for getting through college but should not be considered a long-term career in textiles.

Retail sales associate — furniture and carpeting — Being a retail sales associate in a furniture or carpeting store can be a good career choice. Furniture stores often sell window treatments and accessories as well, making this position akin to that of an interior decorator or designer. The job may or may not allow or require the salesperson to go on location to advise, measure, and assist in the selection of merchandise and may entail creativity in putting together a complete interior. The price per sale is substantial enough to pay a commission to the sales associate, which translates to good income potential.

Retail management/ownership — Owning a retail store specializing in textiles may be the dream of some textile professionals. Both owners and managers, however, must deal first with business and second with textiles. A thorough business plan is the first step when considering retail. It requires a host of commitments — from the rental of space, the inventory, the personnel, to the customer — that are not easily broken. Be aware of the cost of setting up a business, the gross revenue required to cover all costs, and when it will be possible to make a profit. Keep in mind that the owner often gets paid last, if at all, in the first three years of business.

Retail and store planning — Store planners often specialize in the design of one or more of the following: boutiques, specialty stores, salons, department stores, home shopping centers, malls, showrooms, and wholesale space. Most of this work is done by a qualified architect interior designer or interior architect, although the furnishings can be accomplished by consultants and decorators.

(continued)

Seamstress, fabricator — These are skilled positions in which textile applications are manufactured on specialized equipment. These professionals produce draperies, bedding ensembles, slipcovers, table covers, and accessory items. Equipment operators for large manufacturers are trained for specific jobs, whereas entrepreneurs may run a business from the home or another modest location and do custom work. As a business of this type grows, the owner may become a manager as employees are hired and trained.

Seminar leader — This is a freelance full-time or part-time career that consists of developing and presenting training and design seminars. The classes may be as short as one hour or up to eight hours or even several days. When seminars are offered at large or national conventions, it is to the advantage of the seminar leader to have organized and submitted the course for approval as a CEU (continuing education unit) course (see also "Continuing Education and Professional Development" at the end of this chapter). Presenters often have standard prepared seminars they adapt to meet the needs of varying audiences. However, some seminars presented for corporations are custom organized, which requires research and preparation time. Seminar leaders must first be recognized as qualified experts in the field. This entails years of preparation and a track record of success. As a general rule, the greater the credentials and years of accomplishment or the more famous the presenter, the higher the seminar fees. Presenters are paid on a per-course basis they negotiate with the sponsoring organization or corporation.

Shop-at-home decorator or sales professional — Shop-at-home is a custom service in which a professional brings samples to the home (or other location to be furnished) for the client's consideration. The sale is often concluded in the first sales call and may comprise the selection and order of carpeting, upholstery, window treatments, bed ensembles, table covers, and accessory items. Shop-at-home professionals specialize in one area, such as window treatments, or may offer a limited number of the items listed below. The decorator makes appointments based on telephone or walk-in customer inquiries. The sales appointments are fitted to the customer's schedule, during the day or in the evening or on weekends. The future for this career looks strong as more private customers are seeking the convenience of having the professional come to them with all the necessary tools to furnish their interiors. When the studio is located in the decorator or designer's home, the overhead is low, and the designer's vehicle is the main "studio," with the home office serving as the place where orders are processed. When a laptop or notebook computer is used with electronic design programs and specification forms and for faxing or electronically placing and tracking orders, the process can be efficient, with little need for office space. When the professional works for a company, commission as percentage of the sale is the standard means of income. Independent decorators (some call themselves interior designers or design consultants, where no law prevents it) make their money from the gross profit margin, or the difference between the cost of sales and the retail price charged to the customer, less overhead costs.

Sustainability expert/consultant — This professional may be employed by a large manufacturing facility where he or she holds advanced knowledge and responsibility for green production. A consultant can advise several kinds of companies on how to improve their environmental practices. Employees are paid in line with the individual company's budget, whereas consultants charge a fee, often based on their credentials and industry respect. See also industry consultant.

Teacher — Teaching is a career for those with terminal degrees — a PhD (Doctor of Philosophy), an MFA (Master of Fine Arts), or, in some cases, an MA (Master of Arts). These final higher education degrees qualify one for teaching at the university, college, institute, or trade school level. Often, a variety of skills and knowledge areas is required, from hands-on studio skills to computer knowledge to specialties such as sustainability, historical design, and commercial and residential design in addition to the textile courses offered in a balanced curriculum. Depending on the degree completed upon hiring, teaching ranks are as follows:

- **Adjunct instructor** — A part-time contract teaching appointment in which the teacher has lesser credentials than required for higher rank.

- **Instructor** — A full-time appointment in which the teacher has not completed at least a master's degree and has insufficient credentials for a higher rank.

- **Adjunct assistant, associate, or full professor** — A part-time contract appointment in which the teacher has notable professional experience and/or a terminal degree.

- **Assistant professor** — The entry-level rank for a new teacher with a terminal degree.

- **Associate professor** — The next level for an experienced teacher who has prepared and submitted a dossier in application for rank advancement and who meets all criteria in teaching excellence, campus community contributions, and professional development (publications or achievements). A salary raise ensues.

- **Professor or full professor** — The highest teaching rank at colleges and universities. It denotes accomplishments, a high level of teaching or research skills, and publications, plus a considerable number of years of participation and teaching that shows commitment to the career.

Teaching may be a year-round occupation, or the contract may be for nine months or for six or seven months (the school year less the summer terms). Because teaching pay begins modestly

Figure 1.8a Archives of historic textile design inspire updated and recolored versions of traditional motifs created by textile designers. *Photo by Karla J. Nielson.*

Figure 1.8b Textile and carpeting designers utilize state-of-the-art software programs. *Copyrighted and registered, Soroush Custom Rugs & Axminster Carpet, www.soroush.us.*

and takes many years to advance to a comfortable living, many teachers do freelance design work, write texts or manuals, give lectures or seminars, or consult in the industry.

Textile designer — Textile designers are artists; they may or may not use a sketchpad and paints. Today, most textile design for fabrics and carpeting is accomplished through computer software. This is especially true for woven goods. Software expertise can be obtained in a textiles school or independently. Textile designers may have a degree in textiles or training as an artist or interior or graphic designer. This is an excellent career for artistic individuals who enjoy seeing their designs come to life and like to work with processes and with precision and detail.

Textile designers may be in-house, meaning they are hourly or salaried employees who work in the offices of a textile manufacturer, or they may own their own studio and sell their designs as piecework (paid by the piece or design). Another option is to be paid royalties, which is a percentage of sales. If a design does not sell well, then the investment return is minimal, but if the design is highly successful, then the monetary rewards are handsome.

Trainer — Trainers are typically found in corporations where employee turnover is such that new training and professional development are continually offered. They may work under different titles, as determined by the organization, and may work in instruction or administration. They may teach or organize single classes or a full curriculum. They may hire other trainers or instructors. They may also shoulder other corpo-

rate responsibilities such as the organization of conferences, conventions, or trade shows.

Upholsterer — These laborers work applying textile to furniture, often learning to do so on the job. The upholstery shop owner often has design training and leads the sales force, while the manager oversees the sales and the upholstery process and furniture delivery. Upholstery shops can be one-person operations or much larger businesses with several employees. Income for a hired upholsterer is modest, but the income from wise management of an owned business can be moderate to substantial. Some upholstery shops also fabricate and install draperies. Greater diversity can yield higher sales volume.

Visual merchandiser — The job of a visual merchandiser involves both design and the physical labor of assembling retail store displays. The position may be paid by the hour, by the job, or possibly as a full-time salary. Where retail stores do not have enough work for full-time positions, the visual specialist may freelance, doing display work for several stores.

Window treatment specialist — These specialists can conduct their career from a retail space, a studio, a home office, or a vehicle. However, they necessarily spend much time on the site, taking measurements and, sometimes making selections. The job requires samples of alternative (hard and soft) manufactured treatments and fabric samples. Designing soft custom window treatments—draperies, top treatments, and shades—allows for artistic creativity and can be profitable. Wallcoverings, custom bedding, and accessories may be part of this career.

POST-OCCUPANCY EVALUATION

Much of the valuable information a design professional acquires about textile performance is from the evaluation after the installation. This is obtained at two stages. The first is a thorough walk-through about ten days following complete installation. This reveals the aesthetic suitability of the choices and the level of success of the actual coordination of color, pattern, and texture. The quality of the fabrication, shop manufacturing, and installation is also evident. The completeness of the project give confidence to the designer or team concerning their abilities. When an interior is particularly beautiful and its unique problems have been solved, it may be photographed for publication in periodicals or marketing brochures. These photographs show potential clients the quality of work, a selection of styles, and the overall competence of the firm to create workable solutions and handsome, livable interiors.

The second type of evaluation comes after the installation has been in use for some time. The test of time is often the best way to gauge whether a selection was "right." To classify a textile as a right selection means that it is fully satisfactory given the effects of wear and tear and subsequent changes in style and trends. If the design professional used green design philosophy as a guide, then the long-term post-occupancy evaluation, conducted five to seven years after installation, should reveal that the specified materials have withstood the effects of time. It is expected that upholstery has resisted abrasion and that rugs and carpets have proven crush resistant; neither should have pilled, stained, or otherwise shown undue wear. Drapery fabrics and wall upholstery or panels should still perform well, without fading, sagging, or other problems.

Often designers do not follow through with the long-term post-occupancy evaluation (POE); they more often perform the short-term POE, and, as the design firm's longevity proves its competence, the installations speak for its work. Word of mouth is the best form of advertising for any design, architectural, or interior furnishings firm. Personal recommendations follow excellence in design style, quality, and serviceability.

CONTINUING EDUCATION AND PROFESSIONAL DEVELOPMENT

Once textile professionals embark on a career, whether on the fast track and full-time or paced and part-time to balance personal lifestyle or family demands, they must maintain and enhance their level of professionalism. Continuing education and professional development are expected in the research-driven, competitive textile world. Successful professionals look for ways to integrate their continuing education while on the job, during downtime (waiting for a client or sitting in traffic, for example), or during off-hours in the evenings and on the weekends. Dedicated textiles professionals take seriously opportunities to enhance their knowledge and understanding. They want to know more about the industry, the marketplace, sustainability, textile science, applications, and historical style. They can learn by means of personal study of textbooks and professional books, brochures, newsletters, online searching and communication, and their own experience. Such independent study requires an extra measure of motivation and self-discipline.

Seminars, conferences, and trade shows are excellent ways to increase professionalism. These are sponsored by professional associations, fabric companies or distributors, or product manufacturers, including window treatment, furniture, and carpeting manufacturers. Seminar lectures are typically offered at conferences and trade shows, often for **continuing education unit (CEU)** credits. Many professional organizations require a minimum number of CEUs in order to maintain membership. This is motivation to enhance professionalism and to be informed of new technologies, trends, and product developments.

Certification programs are offered by many professional organizations and within an industry. Some large companies have designed their own certification programs. The goal of certification is to reward participants who advance their knowledge and skills to a higher plane of expertise and to recognize their leadership and authority on a given subject. Certification is typically based on study of a text or written materials, seminars or courses attended in person or online, a minimum number of hours of professional experience, and usually an examination.

Certified professionals possess greater credentials and are better qualified or respected as leaders in their field than those who are not certified. They may also add the certification acronym after their name as they would for an advanced college degree or as a member of a professional organization.

PROFESSIONAL AND TRADE ASSOCIATIONS

Professional and trade associations are nonprofit organizations whose members, whether individuals or companies, are in similar types of business. They are joined through a national or international organization, often with an executive director (paid), a board of directors (volunteer, expenses paid), and other paid administrative positions. Design professionals, businesses, and corporations recognize the benefits of belonging to organizations that strengthen their positions in the marketplace or industry, promote and protect their interests, and provide financial or insurance benefits. Associations often have committees or branches that support research or product development and liaisons who work with governmental agencies. Associations inform members about conferences and trade shows via brochure and e-mail, and may themselves sponsor such conventions in conjunction with training or educational seminars. They may list job openings and provide information about opportunities for professional development. Many companies pay for corporate membership and send one or more designated representatives to the meetings or training sessions. These individuals are responsible for implementing changes or updates in the products or organization of the company.

An important trend in the interior design and architectural market is one of specialization, as listed in Table 1.3. Once they select a specialty career path, it behooves interior professionals to seek affiliation in a related professional association. Small design firms and independent design or textile professionals may join professional associations for different reasons, and include these:

1. To stay abreast of new developments, laws, status of licensing requirements, codes, technologies, and trends within the profession.
2. To enjoy a network of professionals who work in the same field of expertise. Design can be a lonely profession, and associations can help fill a void in connecting people to their peers. This in turn provides encouragement, enthusiasm, and the discovery of solutions to similar problems.
3. To learn of new work opportunities and projects, and to obtain career direction.
4. To continue education and enhance professional skills and expertise through trade shows, conventions, and seminars.

For large and small design firms and textile professionals, associations may offer access to exclusive industry resources (for example, furnishings suppliers to the trade only); discounts for services such as insurance; professional publications; and travel, business, and entertainment opportunities, including conferences and conventions.

Following is an annotated list of professional architectural and interior design associations. Specialized product trade associations are listed as Resources at the end of applicable chapters. Most maintain websites where their purpose, goals, scope of services, and contact information is listed.

RESOURCES

American Institute of Architects (AIA)
www.aia.org
1735 New York Avenue NW
Washington, DC 20006
Tel 800-AIA-3837
Fax 202-626-7547

The AIA comprises 300 component organizations across the country and around the world to serve the needs of U.S. architects in any location. These components also assist individuals seeking information about architecture in specific areas.

The American Society of Interior Designers (ASID)
www.asid.org
608 Massachusetts Avenue NE
Washington, DC 20002
Tel 202-546-3480
Fax 202-546-3240

ASID is the world's largest association of professional interior designers. Members have access to an array of marketing tools, research information, and exclusive products and services through the ASID Advantage program. Some of these products are available to nonmembers also. A list of ASID student chapters can be obtained from the national headquarters.

Council for Higher Education Accreditation (CHEA)
www.chea.org
One Dupont Circle NW, Suite 510
Washington, DC 20036
Tel 202-955-6126
Fax 202-955-6129

The organization that accredits the Council for Interior Design Education, a voice for self-regulation of academic quality through accreditations, CHEA is an association of 3,000 degree-granting colleges and universities that recognizes 60 institutional and programmatic accrediting organizations.

Council for Interior Design Education (formerly FIDER)
www.accredit-id.org
146 Monroe Center NW, Suite 1318
Grand Rapids, MI 49503-2822
Tel 616-458-0400
Fax 616-458-0460

The Council for Interior Design Education provides a foundation for excellence in the interior design profession by setting standards for education, accrediting academic programs that meet those standards, and publishing a list of accredited programs. It is recognized as a reliable authority on interior design education by CHEA and is a member of the Association of Specialized and Professional Accreditors (ASPA).

Interior Design Educators Council (IDEC)
www.idec.org
9202 North Meridian Street, Suite 200
Indianapolis, IN 46260
Tel 317-817-6261
Fax 317-571-5603

IDEC is dedicated to strengthening lines of communication among educators, institutions, and other organizations concerned with interior design. Available from IDEC are the following: a career guide brochure, a listing of graduate programs, newsletters and membership information.

Interior Designers of Canada (IDC)
www.interiordesigncanada.org
260 King Street East, Suite 414
Toronto, ONT MSA 1K3
Canada
Tel 416-594-9310
Fax 416-594-9313

IDC is the national interior design association of Canada, with member associations in eight provinces.

International Interior Design Association (IIDA)
www.iida.org
341 Merchandise Mart
Chicago, IL 60654
Tel 312-467-1950
Fax 312-467-0779

IIDA is an internationally recognized organization representing design educators and professional interior designers practicing commercial, education and research, facility planning, government, healthcare, hospitality, residential, and retail design.

National Council for Interior Design Qualifications (NCIDQ)
www.ncidq.org
1200 Eighteenth Street NW, Suite 1001
Washington, DC 20036
Tel 202-721-0220
Fax 202-721-0221

NCIDQ identifies to the public those interior designers who have met the minimum standards for professional practice by passing the NCIDQ exam. It endeavors to maintain the most advanced examining procedures and to update continually the examination to reflect expanding professional knowledge and design development techniques. It seeks the acceptance of the NCIDQ examination as a universal standard by which to measure the competency of interior designers to practice as professionals.

Figure A-1 Visa window film protects the vibrant color of the drapery, upholstery, and accessory textiles against sunlight UV and heat damage. *Jamie Drake/Drake Design Associates. Photo courtesy of Vista® Window Film.*

Figure A-2 Contemporary patterns from the Tatoo Upholstery and Upholstered Wall collection, left to right: "Wired," "Ink," "Soleil," "Full Sleeve," and "Co-Exist." *Photo courtesy of Carnegie Fabrics www.carnegiefabrics.com.*

Figure A-3 "In the Fold" upholstery fabric is a successful blend of natural and manufactured fibers: 41% cotton, 22% linen, 15% polyacrylic, 12% rayon, and 10% polyester. *Photo courtesy of Carnegie Fabrics www.carnegiefabrics.com.*

Figure A-4 Fresh colors are seen in the carpeting, upholstery and drapery fabric of this room. Drapery fabric "Palermo" unites the bold color scheme. *Photo courtesy of Stroheim & Romann, Inc., www.stroheim.com.*

Figure A-5 A new range of colorways for the popluar line of eco-friendly wallcovering, "Grasscloth," this natural-hewn texture is woven from the honeysuckle vine. *Photo by Fumiaki Odaka. Courtesy of Innovations in Wall-coverings, www.innovationsusa.com.*

Figure A-6 The Country Woods® Collection alternative window treatment blinds control light and glare while side draperies from Carole Fabrics (800-439-8260) set a stunning background in this richly colored interior. *Photo courtesy of Hunter Douglas.*

Figure A-7 This richly furnished den features a Bessarabian rug #242954A from the Doris Leslie Blau Collection. Fabric and furniture: Devon armchair with Florence Café, Sally custom sofa with Clermont gold/green/beige, Dubois brown pillow, and Directoire coffee table. Interior design by Penny Drue Baird, Dessing, LLC. Photo Courtesy of Stark Carpets.

Figure A-8 "Faux What" from the Remix Collection of luxurious multi tasking textiles designed by Susan Lyons for Innovations. This collection is for commercial, hospitality, and healthcare environments, addressing a multitude of installations: seating, drapery, cubical curtain, wallcovering, wrapped panels, all with style and substance. *Photo by Fumiaki Odaka, courtesy of Innovations in Wallcoverings, Inc., www.innovationsusa.com.*

Figure A-9 Castec's inverted pleat valance on a headboard with French pleat draw draperies and Roman shade from Castec's Natural Woven Shades product line. *Photography courtesy of Castec, Inc., North Hollywood, CA.*

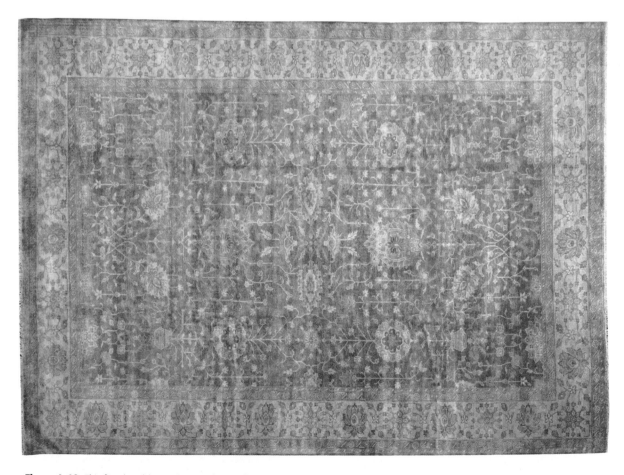

Figure A-10 This fine, hand-knotted Oriental rug is from Caravan Rug's Ushak Collection and shows the antique streaked quality known as abrash. *Courtesy of David and Jay Nehouray, Caravan oriental Rugs, www.caravanrugs.com.*

Figure A-11 Donghia's "Sherwood Green" updated cut velvet is a botanical motif inspired by knightly crests. A soft matte ground contrasts beautifully with the raised, slightly siny velvet design. For use as drapery and meets heavy-duty abrasion rating for upholstery. 80% cotton, 20% modal. *Photography by Edward Addeo. Photo courtesy of Donghia, Inc., www.donghia.com.*

Figure A-12 Multihued braid, fringe, rope, and tassels from the Arthur Trimmings collection add luxurious elegance and refinement to fine textiles. *Photo courtesy of Houlè's-USA.*

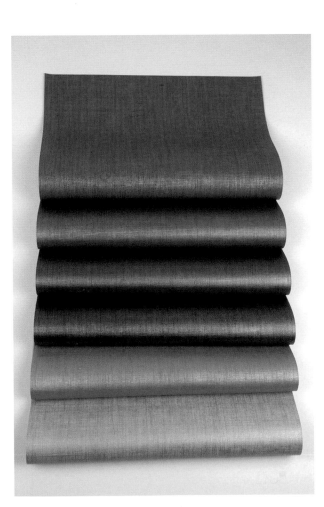

Figure A-13 A sophisticated addition to Innovation's Vinyl Series wallcoverings, "Murano Thai Silk" is a versatile wallcovering that captures the elusive beauty of shimmering hand-woven silks from Thailand. Thai Silk recreates the irregular weave of its namesake in an embossed vinyl pattern that would fool even the most discerning eye. This 50" wide, Type II wallcovering is both elegant and durable. *Photo by Fumiaki Odaka; courtesy of Innovations in Wallcoverings, Inc., www.innovationsusa.com.*

Figure A-14 The warmth and beauty of wool in the "Tartan & Jacquard collection" features, clockwise from left to right, a classic Scottish Lomond Clan Tartan (180475H) in a soft pallet of persimmon, copper, yellow, and green. Next, a subtle Jacquard in variant shades of the same color scheme (180480H) adds fluidity to the linear plaid. Ascending from the bottom of the photo, a delicate plaid with a herringbone weave (180476H-Clay). *Photo courtesy of Highland Court Fabrics, www.highlandcourtfabrics.com.*

Figure A-15 "Abracadabra" is silk shantung with a glowing warp that shines through the weft. Flipping the fabric over can create an instant border, as the reverse side is equally beautiful. *Photography by Edward Addeo. Photo courtesy of Donghia, Inc., www.donghia.com.*

Figure A-16 Fabrics from "The Avalon Collection." From left to right from the Marigold and Green-Apple color books is a sunny floral paisley (13761-346) bordered by a small green and white gingham check with an overlay of woven gold threads in a diamond pattern (#13797-212). The predominant pattern is a French Jacobean floral lampas in shades of coral and green on a neutral ground (13765-430). A soft plaid (13839-3043) of coordinating colors borders on the right. *Photo courtesy of Duralee, www.duralee.com.*

Sustainable Interior Textiles

Figure 2.1 This contract panel fabric "Insight," by Carnegie Fabrics is composed of the highly sustainable polylactic acid (PLA), made from plant starch, predominantly corn. The resulting fiber shares many characteristics with petroleum-based polymers, including low flammability, high resistance to fading, excellent color characteristics, and light weight. *Photo courtesy of Carnegie Fabrics, www.carnegiefabrics.com.*

SUSTAINABILITY: SPECIFYING GREEN DESIGN

A knowledge of textile manufacture, procurement, and professional practices forms a basis for ethical decision making. It is assumed that all textiles professionals will consciously decide to conduct business in an honest and ethical manner as generally stipulated by professional organizations.

In addition, there are issues in which individual and firm policies are based on a guiding belief. One such area is **sustainability** and **green design**. These are a part of the complex, high-profile issue of how the manufacture and use of textiles affects the built environment and the natural environment. A commitment to sustainability often guides the specification and selection of interior textiles where professionals have gained an interest in and knowledge of the benefits of green design. Now it is considered by many a collective and individual responsibility; for an increasing number of professionals, green design is not pursued only when convenient but rather with a zeal to change the attitudes and opinions of people who do not understand the seriousness of the damage that textile production has done to the earth, the atmosphere, and the air quality of interior environments. Today's students are likely to be aware of the problem of contemporary societies whose consumption has controlled the economy. This is not to condemn older generations but to charge younger or beginning designers to learn from cutting-edge professionals who deem green design a critical issue and to educate their clients and other designers.

Sustainability, or green design, is a multiphased term that applies to every stage of a fabric's lifespan, from beginning to end. It means managing waste and avoiding pollution, conserving resources, and utilizing materials and furnishings whose components are renewable. A sustainable environment utilizes furnishings from **renewable resources** with a long lifespan requiring minimal upkeep. Green design also means the creation of healthy, clean environments for users. Further, a sustainable environment incorporates reuse and recycling to avoid waste and buildup of landfills, which takes us, full circle, back to the goal of avoiding pollution.

According to the U.S. Green Building Council, the built environment is growing globally at a rate three times faster than the population growth rate. Buildings have a huge impact on the resources of a finite earth, consuming 30 to 40 percent of all energy used and gobbling up as much as 30 percent of all raw materials produced annually. These statistics represent a crisis in depletion. Natural resources are being consumed at an alarming rate, and the energy used in modern society in the production and manufacturing of goods is also a major contributor to the crisis. Fortunately, many individual and collective voices have made the public aware of the real state of the world with a charge to preserve natural resources for future generations. Thus, we have entered a new era in which sustainability is more than a buzzword. It is a beacon illuminating all facets of procuring materials, manufacturing, and living in the built environment with an eye to conservation of existing resources, both material and energy. It also means the environment is safe and healthy for its occupants, thus increasing good health and workforce productivity.

Sustainability is a comprehensive approach to respecting the environment. Creating sustainable interiors includes specifying sustainable or "green" materials and products; improving indoor air quality, which enhances productivity and enhances general health and well-being; extending textile lifespans; and enhancing resource efficiency through efforts to reduce, reuse, recycle, and repair. The result is not only the improvement of life in the built environment but, surprisingly often, substantial cost savings from conservation of energy and resources. Everyone can participate in creating sustainability by committing to recycle or to use less electricity, to reuse or repair rather than replace textiles,

or to specify green or recycled products. The immediate or short-term benefits of sustainability in an office or business include improved employee health and productivity, cost savings, and improved life cycle for furnishings.

It helps to think of green design as a circular or closed system, much like the water cycle. The water we drink, bathe in, and swim in, that we use to water plants and wash our vehicles today is the same water that has been in circulation since the dinosaurs roamed the earth. With this in mind, we must ask ourselves a searching question: Are we assuring that future generations will receive their entitled legacy to a whole, clean, and cared-for earth? What is taken from the earth, whether alive or inert, eventually returns to begin its life cycle again. Are we allowing this process to take place, even encouraging it, or are we a part of the now-recognized problem of living in a world that is no longer sustainable, where resources are being depleted without being replenished, and where landfills contain products that cannot disintegrate? We must consider that our part in the procurement, use, and discard of textiles has a real and significant impact on the environment. With this realization, we should commit to participate in the major movement toward green design. Specific ways to make a difference include avoiding pollution and managing waste, utilizing renewable resources, understanding and specifying green materials, paying attention to indoor air quality (IAQ), selecting long-lived products, expanding lifespans, understanding ways to expand lifespans, and encouraging people to reduce, reuse, recycle, and repair.

AVOIDING POLLUTION AND MANAGING WASTE

Compared to many other industries, the textile industry, particularly in the United States and Europe, is succeeding today in waste and pollution management. This reflects the commitment of fiber producers, yarn spinners, textile mills, and converters or fabric finishers to use less energy and resources in any way possible during the manufacturing process and to avoid polluting the ground, streams, or atmosphere during production. Certain chemicals used in the past that are known to be environmentally or physically harmful have been eliminated by many large manufacturers or are off the market. Water used in processing and dyeing is being conserved, recycled, and purified. Air pollution constraints are firmly in place. Manufacturers in developed countries are committed to **green manufacturing** in the production of textile products.

Internationally recognized certification programs support and motivate green manufacturing. Two available certifications sought by textile industry manufacturers are the

ISO 14000 and ATMI E3 status. The International Organization for Standardization (ISO) is a private Swiss organization dedicated to promoting standardization and marketing activities among nations to enhance free trade. With input from industry, research groups, governments, and consumer and international organizations, the ISO 14000 series requirements establish stringent criteria industries must meet to manage the impact of their activities on the environment.

The American Textile Manufacturers Institute (ATMI) offers textile factories a rating system known as Encouraging Environmental Excellence, or E3, created in 1992 to improve the U.S. textile industry's environmental record. The program's main purpose is to challenge U.S. textile companies to strengthen their commitment to the environment by going beyond simply complying with existing environmental laws. E3 encourages U.S. textile companies to get out in front of regulations and set standards for other industries to follow. Once compliance is met for all federal, state, and local laws, companies must set and then exceed their own standards for environmental excellence. To qualify for E3 certification, an ATMI member company must comply with all federal, state, and local environmental laws. In addition, it must adopt a ten-point plan. Guidelines require that a company develop a corporate environmental policy and set annual goals for reducing waste and conserving water and energy. The company must also develop an outreach program for customers and suppliers to encourage pollution prevention and waste minimization, develop employee education and community awareness programs, and audit its facilities. Once a company is eligible to participate in the E3 program, annual certification is required. The Environmental Protection Agency (EPA) rates ATMI among the most proactive trade associations on pollution prevention, waste reduction, and environment improvement.

RENEWABLE RESOURCES

Renewable resources are raw or natural resources that are not depleted when used but that can be replanted or recreated on a continual basis — for example, harvesting wood pulp from sustainably managed forests to use in fabric production.

A new sustainable renewable resource polymer fiber is known as polylactide, or **PLA,** which is now a generic description for synthetic fibers made from annually renewable resources. PLA was developed by Cargill Dow LLC. This independent company, founded in 1997 after fourteen years and a $750 million investment in research and development by its parent companies and funding sources, is located in Minnetonka, Minnesota.

One PLA company name is NatureWorks, and its resulting fiber has a trademark name of Ingeo™. It is made from lactic acid, the product of fermented dextrose. While PLA can be made from the sugars of many plants, the selection was cornstarch, which is made of carbon dioxide and water.

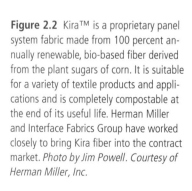

Figure 2.2 Kira™ is a proprietary panel system fabric made from 100 percent annually renewable, bio-based fiber derived from the plant sugars of corn. It is suitable for a variety of textile products and applications and is completely compostable at the end of its useful life. Herman Miller and Interface Fabrics Group have worked closely to bring Kira fiber into the contract market. *Photo by Jim Powell. Courtesy of Herman Miller, Inc.*

The production facility is in Blair, Nebraska. At full capacity, the total corn needed for PLA will be 0.15 percent, or less than one fifth of 1 percent of annual U.S. grain production. PLA represents an optimal combination of agricultural processes and biological and chemical technologies, while using up to 50 percent less energy in its manufacturing. PLA fabrics are suited for use in a wide range of interior textiles and industrial applications at a cost and performance level that competes with the petrochemical synthetic fibers nylon and polyester. This example shows where we may be headed in the future as new fibers are developed.

GREEN SPECIFICATION

Green specification is the selection of products made from renewable resources that will not harm the earth's environment if they are removed. Green products are also manufactured with fewer adverse effects on the environment than comparable traditional products. Green specification also means the selection of textiles that can be recycled or reused. The EPA has established a certification system whereby manufactured items can be designated "Environmentally Preferable Products". These have a reduced effect on human health and the environment than do other products that serve the same purpose. To earn this certification, the product undergoes evaluation according to the following criteria: product performance; total environmental impact of product manufacturing; use of green energy manufacturing; and safety, health, environment, and end-of-life responsibility.

Leadership in Energy and Environmental Design (LEED®)

The many design professionals who need assistance in green specification can turn to excellent resources such as the LEED-CI Leadership in Energy and Environmental Design Contract Interiors section of the LEED Green Building Rating System. The Green Building Rating System, developed by the U.S. Green Building Council (USGBC), is a voluntary, consensus-based certification system for developing high-performance, sustainable buildings, created to define *green building* by establishing a common standard of measurement. The USGBC also aims to raise awareness of green building benefits and thus help transform the building market. LEED provides a complete framework for assessing building performance and meeting sustainability goals. Based on well-founded scientific standards, LEED emphasizes strategies for sustainable site development, water savings, energy efficiency, materials selection, and indoor environmental quality. LEED recognizes achievements and promotes expertise in green building through a comprehensive system of project certification, professional accreditation, training, and practical resources.

In the United States, buildings use one-third of the total energy, two-thirds of the electricity, and one-eighth of the water consumed. Introduced in 1999, the LEED-NC Green Building Rating Systems for New Construction has helped improve the quality of buildings and their impact on the environment, helping produce a sustainable community. Project teams interested in the LEED certification must register online during the early phases of a project to ensure maximum potential for certification success. Credits are assigned in construction and furnishing areas and to remodel and tenant improvements.

LEED-CI—Contract Interiors

The portion of LEED that applies to textiles is found within the LEED-CI (Contract Interiors). This certification applies to tenant improvements to new or existing office space. Those who choose to participate in the LEED Rating Systems may be recognized for their commitment to environmental issues, receive recognition for their achievements, qualify for funding initiatives, and receive marketing exposure for their project. These sections include Credit 3.3 Resource Reuse; Credit 4.3 Low-Emitting Materials: Carpet Systems; and Credit 4.5 Low-Emitting Materials: Systems Furniture and Seating. Another section is Credit 8.2–8.3 Daylight and Views. Although this section is based on quantity and placement of windows, it may be said that window treatments can either enhance daylight and views or detract from natural daylighting.

Credit 3.3 Resource Reuse encompasses three areas:

1. **Resource Reuse, 30 Percent Furniture and Furnishings:** Requirements are to use salvaged, refurbished, or used furniture and furnishings for 30 percent of the total furniture and furnishing budget.
2. **Recycled Content, 20 Percent** (post-consumer, half pre-consumer): Requirements are to use materials, including Division R Furniture and Furnishings, with recycled content such that the sum of post-consumer recycled content plus one-half of the pre-consumer (post-industrial) content constitutes at least 20 percent of the total value of the materials in the project.
3. **Rapidly Renewable Materials:** Requirements are to use rapidly renewable construction and Division 12 (Furniture and Furnishings) materials and products made from plants that are typically within a ten-year cycle or shorter for 5 percent of the total value of all materials used in the project.

Credit 4.3 Low-Emitting Materials, Carpet Systems: Carpets must meet or exceed the Carpet and Rug Institute's Green Label, plus testing and product requirements.

Credit 4.5 Low-Emitting Materials, Systems Furniture and Seating: Systems furniture is defined as either a panel-based workstation comprising modular interconnecting panels, hang-on components, and drawer-filing components, or a grouping of furniture items and their components that have been designed to work in concert. Occasional furniture is not included.

Requirements are that all systems furniture and seating introduced into the project space that has been manufactured, refurbished, or refinished within one year prior to occupancy must meet one of these specified requirements:

Option A: Greenguard Indoor Air Quality Certified

Option B: Calculated indoor air concentrations less than or equal to those established for furniture systems and seating determined by a procedure based on the U.S. Environmental Technology Verification (ETV) Large Chamber Test Protocol for measuring emissions of **volatile air compounds (VOCs)** and aldehydes testing protocol for commercial furniture.

INDOOR AIR QUALITY (IAQ)

The USGBC has estimated that one-third of all buildings have serious IAQ problems. In fact, the EPA ranks indoor environmental pollution as one of the top five environmental risks to public health, with a number of federal reports confirming this ranking. The indoor air we breathe can be 10 to 50 times more toxic than outdoor air (EPA, 1998). The term **sick building syndrome (SBS)** describes those buildings with poor air quality that affects the health and productivity of people who work, obtain services, or live there. Buildings are saddled with poor indoor air quality for a variety of reasons. Today, chemicals are infused into every type of building and furnishing product, whether in laminated subflooring or the carpeting installed over it. Many combine with heat, light, and interior environmental air quality to emit toxins or poisons that are difficult to measure.

The EPA states that we live, work, and play in a chemical soup, with over 60,000 chemicals now in use, with less than a 10 percent understanding of their effects and combinations of effects. As buildings are constructed much tighter than at any point in the past in order to prevent escape of energy, chemicals are typically trapped inside the buildings. Once installed, building products and furnishings **off-gas**, or emit VOCs, volatile organic compounds. VOCs are vapor or gaseous indoor air pollutants or chemical compounds. Besides VOC sources such as inks (from photocopy machines, for example), dyes (from textiles), paint, and housekeeping products, many preservatives and product enhancers are integrated into textiles and building products. These include formaldehyde (a suspected carcinogen used in fabrics and carpeting), benzene (a known carcinogen), acetone, toluene, and xylene, to name some of the better-known chemicals. VOCs potentially pose a greater health risk than hazardous waste sites, and we allow ourselves to be exposed to them daily. With low outside air infiltration

Figure 2.3 Indoor air quality (IAQ) can be enhanced by selecting textiles and carpeting low in volatile organic compounds (VOCs). *Freestanding system furniture, Steelcase Context show. Steelcase.*

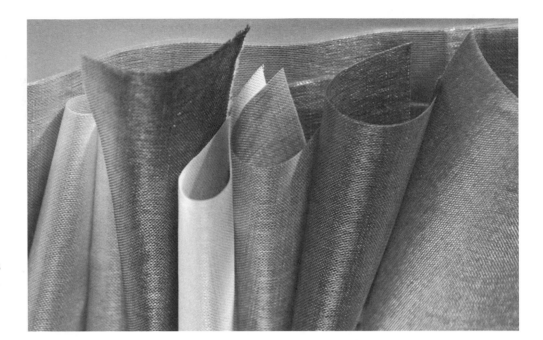

Figure 2.4 Xorel® combines beauty and performance in a high-tech yarn woven from environmentally sound polyethylene without the use of chlorine, plasticizers, or PVC. Xorel® offers extremely low toxicity and off-gassing, which makes it a sustainable choice. *Photo courtesy of Carnegie Fabrics, www.carnegiefabrics.com.*

in most buildings today, it is little wonder that many people experience headaches, nausea, lack of concentration, overall malaise, and a host of other symptoms as they work indoor jobs. A large percentage of sick days can be blamed on the effects, slight or profound, of sick building syndrome.

Controlling Indoor Air Pollution

Indoor air pollution is best reduced by controlling the sources. Although there are few federal, state, or local law controls, voluntary standards are worthwhile. The Greenguard Certification Program can help find low-emitting interior products and building materials. Other ways to voluntarily reduce indoor air pollution include the following:

- Wherever possible, new textiles, carpeting, and wallcoverings should be allowed to off-gas for a minimum of 24 hours before occupancy. Open-window cross-ventilation, augmented with fans to push the escaping fumes outside, will help detoxify the indoor air.
- Apply paints and wallcovering or flooring adhesives before carpeting.
- Allow new products to off-gas or air out before the space is occupied.
- Use exhaust fans in areas that tend to trap or hold odors and in cooking areas.
- Store construction materials or unused lengths of carpeting outside the building.
- Do not allow smoking indoors.
- Do not use indoor fragrance, deodorizers, burning candles, or aerosol sprays.

- Regularly have ductwork cleaned. Dust, dirt, and microbial contamination can build up, spewing toxins into the air from heating and cooling ductwork. Be certain no construction debris is left in the ductwork of new construction.
- Regularly clean textiles that may trap toxins such as tobacco smoke, and equipment that may retain toxins such as photocopy toner.
- Use an ionizing air purifier to enhance air quality.
- Introduce the many indoor plants that can absorb toxins and produce clean air. Specifically, **benzene** can be allayed with English ivy, *Dracaena marginata,* Janet Craig, *warneckei,* chrysanthemum, gerbera daisy, and peace lily; **formaldehyde** can be treated with azalea, philodendron, spider plant, golden pothos, bamboo palm, corn plant, chrysanthemum, and mother-in-law's tongue; **trichloroethylene** can be mitigated with gerbera daisy, chrysanthemum, peace lily, *warneckei,* and *Dracaena marginata.*

Greenguard Certification Program™

The Greenguard Certification Program is an independent third-party testing program for low-emitting products and materials. The Greenguard Product Guide, an IAQ resource available at no charge, features products that are regularly tested to ensure their chemical and particle emissions meet acceptable IAQ pollutant guidelines and standards. Greenguard certification is a tool design professionals, specifiers, and purchasing organizations can use to locate, specify, and purchase off-the-shelf low-emitting products for indoor environments. Greenguard certification is a voluntary program available to all manufacturers and their suppliers.

Today, people spend over 90 percent of their time indoors and are exposed to thousands of airborne pollutants. Products and materials indoors release volatile chemicals and particles into the air; these may negatively affect human health or result in unacceptable odors. Inadequate ventilation, high temperatures, and high humidity increase concentrations of some pollutants, leading to indoor air pollution levels up to 100 times higher than those outdoors. The EPA, the American Lung Association, the World Health Organization, and other public health and environmental organizations view indoor air pollution as one of the greatest risks to human health. Poor IAQ can lead to allergies, asthma, reproductive and developmental problems, and cancer.

The economic impact of indoor air pollution is equally alarming. Poor IAQ can adversely affect employee health and productivity. The EPA has estimated these costs to U.S. businesses in the "tens of billions of dollars per year" (USEPA Report to Congress on Indoor Air Quality, 1989). Improvements in the indoor air environment may substantially increase employee morale and productivity and reduce healthcare costs.

Indoor Air Quality Health Issues

People can experience health effects from indoor air pollutants soon after exposure or years later. Immediate effects include irritation of the eyes, nose, and throat, headaches, dizziness, and fatigue. Such immediate effects are usually short-term and treatable. Indoor air pollution may also trigger symptoms of some diseases, including asthma, dermatitis, allergic rhinitis, and hypersensitivity pneumonitis soon after exposure. More serious health effects may show up either years after exposure or only after long or repeated periods of exposure. These effects include some respiratory diseases, heart disease, reproductive and developmental problems, and cancer, and they can be severely debilitating or fatal.

Many complaints about the indoor environment are triggered by odors. Odors, which result from the presence of volatile chemicals in the air, can severely impair people's quality of life and their work performance. These chemicals may or may not be hazardous at the levels present. However, they do signal the presence of unacceptable air quality and may result in considerable concern and anxiety among building occupants.

Carpet and Rug Institute Green Label

The Carpet and Rug Institute (CRI) developed and administers the **Green Label IAQ** testing and labeling program for carpet, adhesives, cushion materials, and vacuum cleaners. **Green Label Plus,** an enhancement to the CRI Green Label, incorporates additional requirements to meet the criteria for low-emitting materials issued by California's Collaborative for High-Performance Schools (CHPS). Products listed as CHPS-compliant materials have been chamber tested to meet the IAQ guidelines outlined in California's specification section 01350. Green Label Plus, in addition, incorporates ongoing product testing, making it an exceptionally stringent program for new carpet.

LONG-LIVED SELECTIONS: EXTENDING TEXTILE LIFESPAN

The cycle of fashion is a driving force in interior design. To their credit, interior textiles play a major role in the updating, refurbishing, and renewal of interiors, even when the interior architecture stays the same. This is problematic in the matter of sustainability. For each yard of replacement textile that is purchased and installed, one yard of used fabric or carpeting becomes an encumbrance. Because throwing something away is a fallacy — where is "away"? — we need to look at all the alternatives for sustainability, including extending the lifespan.

One approach is to keep textiles for a longer period in their present installation. Because selling new textiles is the lifeblood of the industry and marketplace, this suggestion sounds heretical. However, sometimes carpeting, upholstery, draperies, wall panels, bedding, or linens are slightly dated as to color, pattern, or texture, but the condition of the textile is still good. To keep the installation intact, try changing paint color, enhancing lighting, rearranging furnishings, or replacing some but not all of the fabric.

This attitude is born of a commitment to green design rather than sales. In the long run, however, a conservative, don't-replace-it-yet approach may win friends and influence people. The design firm that espouses conservation may earn not only respect but also a commitment from clients to continue use of textiles that are not yet worn out.

Reduce, reuse, recycle, and *repair* are buzzwords of **resource efficiency.**

To **reduce** means to use less energy and to produce less waste in the manufacture of a product. It also means to delay replacement by reusing or repairing that item. Preventive maintenance reduces the drive to replace a textile prematurely by keeping it clean so that soiling does not do

Figure 2.5 Good design with long-lasting appeal in contract or nonresidential settings is often seen in fabrics that are simple and neutral in design. Ingeo™ fabric, made of polylactic acid (PLA), offers great durability and is derived from the highly sustainable resource of plant sugars. *Photo courtesy of NatureWorks®.*

irreparable damage. In addition, the placement of textiles may be rotated to distribute use where possible—for example, upholstery cushions and rugs may be reversed. All textiles are subject to wear and tear and the effects of aging.

Reuse is a type of recycling in which the interior design textile is removed from its original location and placed in another space with little or no alteration. This can be done within the original building or home—by reinstalling a carpet in a different room, for example, or by moving window treatments, upholstered furniture, or linens. Textile items can be sold by the user or consumer directly to another user at a yard sale or on the Internet. Textiles can be donated to a charitable organization for resale in a secondhand store.

The EPA's definition of **recycle/reclaim** is "the collection, separation, and processing by which products or other materials are recovered from or otherwise diverted from the solid waste stream." The *cradle-to-cradle protocol* means a product is developed using green practices and at the end of its life can be recycled as a new textile or another product or can return to the earth as compostable or biodegradable. The phrase was coined by architect William McDonough and chemist Michael Braungart, who jointly established the McDonough Braungart Design Chemistry protocol, which sets strict criteria for evaluating environmental impact at every stage of a product's development (see Resources at the end of this chapter and the Bibliography).

Recycling occurs at two levels: pre-consumer/post-industrial waste and post-consumer waste. Pre-consumer/post-industrial textile waste is byproduct material from the fiber, cotton, wool, and other textile industries. Annually,

750,000 tons of pre-consumer/post-industrial waste are recycled into new raw materials for mattresses, furniture, coarse yarn, home furnishings, and other industrial products. Post-industrial recycled yarns are called *seconds*. In manufacturing polyester products, post-industrial seconds that do not meet bottle or film specifications are still acceptable for fiber end-uses. Polyester can be broken down, remelted, and extruded into continuous monofilament yarns.

One type of post-consumer recycled yarn comes from used soda bottles that have been sorted, cleaned, chopped into pellets, melted, and extruded into staple yarns. Recycled polyester is used in commercial upholstery. One company leading the way in green manufacturing and recycled polyester is The Designtex Group, which offers a broad range of sustainable materials, including recycled upholstery and panel textiles. Examples include the Designtex/Sustainable Initiatives brand, which is a green alternative to vinyl. The Duraprene family of sustainable wallcoverings is produced with water-based inks and has a recycled fiber content of 50 percent wood pulp from sustainably managed forests, 40 percent post-industrial waste, and 10 percent post-consumer waste.

A large portion of post-consumer textile waste is apparel, much of which is sold to Third World countries. According to the Council for Textile Recycling, the textile recycling industry removes 2.5 billion pounds of post-consumer textile product waste annually from the solid waste stream, which represents 10 pounds for every person in the United States. Of this amount, approximately 500 million pounds are used by the collecting agency, with the balance sold to textile recyclers, including used clothing dealers and exporters, wiping rag graders, and fiber recyclers. In addition, textile recycling firms purchase a large percentage of their raw materials from charitable institutions, which in turn use these funds to house, feed, and train people in need of such assistance. Industry members are able to recycle 93 percent of the waste they process without producing new hazardous waste or harmful byproducts. Interior design textiles can be recycled in the same way. Carpeting companies are increasing their ability to reclaim carpet fiber and produce new carpet fiber from recycled sources, including recycled plastic soda bottles. Unfortunately, much of the carpeting that is removed is taken to landfills. Carpet recycling, or value recovery, is also known as *carpet take-back* when carpet manufacturers receive carpets for recycling at the end of their original life cycle. The CRI and its member companies are working to develop value recovery pyramids for all of the carpet systems in use today, including vinyl-backed carpet.

To **repair** is to extend a textile's lifespan by bringing it back to a state of acceptability in order to continue its usefulness. Sometimes a thorough cleaning brings fabric and carpet back to life. Other times, evident wear makes the

Figure 2.6a Designtex Group "Box Lunch" © 2003 William McDonogh & Michael Braungart is part of the McDonough & Braungart collection of sustainable initiatives, as defined by MBDC criteria. The biological nutrients are 91 percent wool, 9 percent ramie. The fabric is produced using the Climatex® Lifecycle™ manufacturing process. This fabric is 100 percent biodegradable. *Photo courtesy of Designtex.*

optimized by

△MBDC

● ● ● ● ○

Figure 2.6b McDonough Braungart Design Chemistry label.

owner feel it's time to throw it out and replace it. However, many items can be repaired, continuing to be useful. Examples include the restoration of worn areas of oriental rugs and the repair of small tears in fabric applications. Keeping useful products by repairing them rather than discarding them is an old-fashioned notion. The familiar aphorism "a stitch in time saves nine" is still valid, especially if we are conscious of green design philosophy.

The Resources section below lists associations, companies, and educational organizations closely associated with green design in interior textiles. Many of the websites contain a wealth of information and links to other organizations.

THE FUTURE OF GREEN

Environmental issues and solutions that relate to interior textiles are constantly changing. Students and professionals must stay up-to-date and informed. The resources listed below and on www.wiley.com/go/interiortextiles should lead to a basis for understanding the latest problems and explorations toward solving them. There is no consensus about how to specify green nor how to evaluate the greenness of a material. Manufacturers should develop properly researched data that ensure their products are, in fact, green. Unsubstantiated claims by manufacturers are known as *greenwashing;* all design professionals should be wary of this problem. However, a number of green-related organizations and programs are credible and have achieved a level of respect from government agencies and the public. Several of the organizations listed below offer certification programs and comprehensive databases and listings of products that can be consulted, although they can make no absolute guarantee of claim reliability for individual companies or products. Those

companies that claim to sell green products are required by law to back their claims as specified under Life Cycle Assessment (LCA) (see Resources). This makes it more difficult for companies to falsely claim a product is green. Certification programs that are consensus-based, meaning many professionals approve of and accept the standards they set forth, are gaining momentum and, ideally, promote companies and products whose commitment to sustainability and healthy environments is real. As more materials are tested and claims are made public, the subject of environmental responsibility will only get more complicated. Yet from the mass of information have come some conclusions:

- The quality of the natural and built environment matters to many people; more each day are concerned about environmental ethics and protecting future environmental resources and human health.
- All design professionals can and should be informed about and be advocates of sustainability.
- More can be and is being done to ensure sustainability and enhanced quality of the built environment on a continuing basis.
- Each person's and each company's efforts count. The future will be shaped by those who are aware of the impact of their efforts.

Although this chapter considers textile sustainability at an undergraduate level, there is much room for topic research for upper-division undergraduate, classroom, or team projects; graduate work; and professional grant or product development in this relatively new arena and in IAQ. Suggestions can be gleaned from the following organizations listed under the following Resources and by researching these and related groups on www.wiley.com/go/interiortextiles.

RESOURCES

The American Textile Manufacturers Institute (ATMI)
1130 Connecticut Avenue NW, Suite 1200
Washington, DC 20036-3954
Tel 202-862-0500
Fax 202-862-0570

The U.S. national trade association for the domestic textile industry. ATMI's organizational objective is to help member companies deal with programs and problems on an industrywide national basis. ATMI works with legislative and administrative branches of the federal government and news media. It also sponsors a certification program entitled Encouraging Environmental Excellence (E3).

The U.S. Green Building Council (USGBC)
www.usgbc.org

The USGBC is a coalition of leaders from across the building industry working to promote buildings that are environmentally responsible, profitable, and healthy places to live and work. It is leading a national consensus for producing a new generation of buildings that deliver high performance inside and out. Council members work together to develop LEED products and resources, the Greenbuild Annual International Conference and Expo, policy guidance, and educational and marketing tools that support the adoption of sustainable building. Members also forge strategic alliances with key industry and research organizations and federal, state, and local government agencies to transform the built environment. Application for membership is on the website.

Greenbuild Conference
www.greenbuildexpo.org
USGBC Greenbuild Expo
PO Box 714502
Columbus, OH 43271-4502
Fax 330-963-0319

This conference for professionals in the public and private sectors comprises educational sessions; LEED workshops, including LEED Professional Accreditation workshops; exhibits showcasing green technologies, materials, and services; workshop tours of schools, homes and offices, where attendees learn about a broad spectrum of projects from the integrated design teams who created the projects; and USGBC Day, when new USGBC programs and initiatives are presented.

MSDS Solutions, Inc.
www.msds.com
Two Mid-America Plaza, Suite 800
Oakbrook Terrace, IL 60181
Tel 630-928-1002
Fax 630-928-1003
Offices also in Montreal, Canada, and the Netherlands

MSDS Solutions™ offers health and safety managers a database of Material Safety Data Sheets (MSDSs) containing over 1.5 million original documents from over 15,000 manufacturers worldwide in an indexed, searchable electronic format. MSDS offers management and distribution tools and compliance services.

Greenguard Environmental Institute
www.greenguard.org
1341 Capital Circle, Suite A
Atlanta, GA 30067
Tel 800-427-9681
Fax 770-980-0072

Greenguard is an independent third-party testing program for low-emitting products and materials. The GREENGUARD Product Guide, an IAQ resource available at no charge, features products that are regularly tested to ensure their chemical and particle emissions meet acceptable IAQ pollutant guidelines and standards. Greenguard Certification is a tool design professionals, specifiers, and purchasing organizations can use to locate, specify, and purchase off-the-shelf low-emitting products for indoor environments. Greenguard Certification is a voluntary program available to all manufacturers and their suppliers.

The Institute for Market Transformation to Sustainability
mts.sustainableproducts.com

The Institute for Market Transformation to Sustainability has developed a standard textile rating system called the **SMART® Sustainable Textile Standard®**. This promotes sustainable textile achievement for public health and environment in order to increase the economic value of sustainable textiles through the supply chain, provides information that enables specifiers to sort out complex sustainable attribute information, identifies other consensus-based standards, educates and instructs, and encourages competition to increase sustainability at all levels. Certification in this Sustainable Textile Standard is intended to allow inclusive participation and encourage the progressive movement of the textile industry toward sustainability. The standard is voluntary yet emphasizes disclosure of information on both negative impacts and benefits of a textile or textile product from an environmental and sustainability perspective.

The results should provide the following benefits: cost savings, design innovation, product differentiation, long-term customer relationships, liability reduction, and ecological restoration. The standard is inclusive, is based on life cycle assessment (LCA) principles, and provides benchmarks for continuous improvement and innovation.

This program is partnered with the International Interior Design Association (IIDA) Launched Sustainable Textile Online Training Module with MTS, Gensler, DMJM, Milliken Carpet, Fabric and Apparel, Shaw, Catalyst Partners, the Carpet and Rug Institute, and 80 other training partners.

Life Cycle Assessment (LCA)

www.sustainbleproducts.com

As required by international law, any product communication about sustainable, green, or environmentally preferable products, or about more than one environmental benefit — for example, "ozone-friendly and nontoxic," must be backed by LCA. LCA evaluates and discloses the environmental benefits of products over their full commercial cycle, from raw materials extraction to final disposition.

Green Seal Product Standards

www.greenseal.org

Green Seal is an independent nonprofit organization dedicated to protecting the environment by promoting the manufacture and sale of environmentally responsible consumer products. It sets life-cycle–based environmental standards and awards a Green Seal of Approval to products that cause less harm to the environment than other similar products. By setting standards for environmentally responsible products, Green Seal seeks to reduce air and water pollution; cut the waste of energy and natural resources; slow ozone depletion and the risk of global warming; prevent toxic contamination; and protect fish and wildlife and their habitats.

Aerias AQS IAQ Resource Center

info@aerias.org
1337 Capital Circle
Marietta, GA 30067
Tel 770-933-0638 ext. 251

Aerias AQS IAQ Resource Center offers some of the most comprehensive, in-depth, and up-to-date information on indoor air quality available online. The reports, articles, and statistics featured exclusively on Aerias have been compiled based on studies conducted in Air Quality Sciences (AQS) laboratories, knowledge gathered from AQS experience in the field, research and scientific literature surveys, and AQS's extensive database of pollutants and sources.

The Cleaner and Greener® Program of the Leonardo Academy, Inc.

www.cleanerandgreener.org
1526 Chandler Street
Madison, WI 53711
Tel 608-280-0256; 877-977-9277
Fax 608-255-7202

The Leonardo Academy is a nonprofit organization dedicated to reducing pollution. The Cleaner and Greener Environment Program helps individuals, organizations, and businesses have a direct impact on reducing pollution. Companies can earn the Certified Cleaner and Greener Seal so consumers can easily identify environmentally responsible businesses. This certification helps businesses, organizations, and participants who reduce environmental emissions create market rewards for their reductions, including recognition, preferential purchasing by consumers of products from certified companies, and adding rewards for emissions reductions from energy efficiency

regulations. All certified entities are required to reduce their emissions. This is important because 65 to 85 percent of all energy use in the United States comes from product production, delivery, and use.

American Lung Association

www.lungusa.org

The nonprofit American Lung Association fights lung diseases in all forms with educational programs and strategies to increase air quality and promote lung health.

Clean Air Council

www.cleanair.org
135 S. Nineteenth Street 300
Philadelphia, PA 19103
Tel 215-567-4004
Fax 215-567-5791

A member-supported nonprofit environmental organization dedicated to protecting everyone's right to breathe clean air. The Clean Air Council works through community advocacy, public education, and government oversight to ensure enforcement of environmental laws.

Buy Recycled Business Alliance

www.nrc-recycle.org/brba
Tel 202-347-0450

This professional organization, established in 1992, is now a broad-based group of over 3,000 organizations committed to enhancing the purchase of recycled products and materials. The alliance provides strategic support to U.S. businesses through national workshops and support materials, including the *Growing a Buy Recycled Program: A Manager's Guide.*

Council for Textile Recycling

www.textilerecycle.org
7910 Woodmont Avenue, Suite 1130
Bethesda, MD 20814
Tel 310-656-1077
Fax 301-656-1079

The Council for Textile Recycling works in partnership with the Secondary Materials and Recycled Textile Association (SMART). The goals of the Council for Textile Recycling are to increase the amount of textile waste that can be recovered and at the same time develop new uses, products, and markets for products derived from pre-consumer and post-consumer textile waste. The council encourages trends toward the increased use of recycled materials in products and the increased recovery of material for recycling.

Green@worktoday.com

www.greenatworktoday.com

green@worktoday is a website portal for tracking environmental news for those who would like to stay informed but lack the time to peruse the ever-growing number of resources. Articles are gathered about positive progress that deals with the environment and sustainability.

The Carpet and Rug Institute (CRI)

www.carpet-rug.org
Mailing Address: PO Box 2048, Dalton, GA 30722-2048
Street Address: 730 College Drive, Dalton, GA 30720
Tel 706-278-3176
Fax 706-278-8835

CRI developed and administers the Green Label IAQ testing and labeling program for carpet, adhesives, cushion materials, and vacuum cleaners. Green Label Plus, an enhancement to the CRI Green Label, incorporates additional requirements to meet the criteria for low-emitting materials issued by California's Collaborative for High-Performance Schools (CHPS).

InformeDesign: Where Research Informs Design

www.informedesign.com

Informdesign is an extensive website of information available free on registration. It is sponsored by the American Society of Interior Designers (ASID) and created by University of Minnesota. For green design information, go to Specializations and click on Green/Eco-Design Recycling.

International Organization for Standardization (ISO)

www.iso.ch
1, rue de Varembé
Case postale 56
CH-1211 Geneva 20
Switzerland
Tel 41-22-749-01-11
Fax 41-22-733-34-30

ISO is the source of the ISO 9000 and 14000 series Family of International Standards certifications programs for business, government, and society. It also comprises a network of national standards institutes from 147 countries working in partnership with international organizations, governments, industry, business, and consumer representatives. It is a bridge between public and private sectors.

McDonough Braungart Design Chemistry LLC

www.mbdc.com
401 E. Market Street, Suite 201
Charlottesville, VA 22901
Tel 434-295-1111
Fax 434-295-1500

McDonough Braungart provides presentations and business/industry consulting, including on-demand materials research and tools for management based on the Cradle-to-Cradle Design Protocol and the Hannover Principles. Also see the bibliography. The concepts of founders architect William McDonough and chemist Michael Braungart have shifted paradigms all over the world toward prosperous and safe sustainability based on natural processes.

The Secondary Materials and Recycled Textile Association (SMART)

www.smartasn.org
7910 Woodmont Avenue, Suite 1130
Bethesda, MD 20814

Tel 310-656-1077
Fax 301-656-1079

SMART is an international trade association dedicated to serving and promoting the textiles industry. Member companies work in many areas of the industry, including the grading and sorting of mixed post-consumer textiles for the wiping materials and used clothing markets; manufacturing and converting of nonwoven and paper products; sorting and distributing new textile products and byproducts; manufacturing textiles; and distributing remnants, fibers, and related materials.

Sustainable Design Leadership Awards

sustainabledesign@att.net

The Sustainable Design Leadership Awards were created to honor sustainable design contributions as recognized by a jury of prominent designers and business leaders as well as the national media. Three notable organizations have joined forces to honor leaders who have integrated design excellence, sustainable design, and best business practices for the interior built and workplace environment. They are the International Interior Design Association (IIDA), www.iida.org; the American Institute of Architects/Interiors Committee, www.air.org/interiors; and CoreNet Global, www.cornet.com. For more information or to receive an entry form, call 888-548-5800. Details are available on the website.

Textile Fiberspace

www.textilefiberspace.com

This website lists fibers resources and associations, including those related to recycling.

Scorecard

www.scorecard.org

Scorecard is a website that ranks communities on environmental pollution issues. Information is accessible through ZIP code input.

The U.S. General Services Administration (GSA)

www.gsa.gov

The GSA helps federal agencies serve the public by offering at best value superior workplaces, expert solutions, acquisition services, and management policies. The GSA aims for a better environment by buying green, building green, saving green, driving green, and managing green. It has six goals: (1) Provide best value for customer agencies and taxpayers; (2) Achieve responsible asset management; (3) Operate efficiently and effectively; (4) Ensure financial accountability; (5) Maintain a world-class workforce and a world-class workplace; and (6) Carry out social, environmental, and other responsibilities as a federal agency. The GSA produces the Internet-accessible "Environmental Products and Services Guide."

CARE Carpet America Recovery Effort

www.carpetrecovery.org

A voluntary initiative of the carpet industry and government focusing on methods of carpet reclamation and recycling methods.

chapter

Natural and Manufactured Fibers

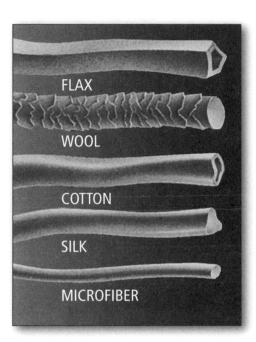

Figure 3.1a Fiber shapes from top to bottom: flax (linen), wool, cotton, silk, and microfiber. Microfibers are extremely fine filaments extruded to less than 1.0 denier while maintaining strength and uniformity; they have been referred to as supernatural—luxurious and high-performing manufactured fibers. *Courtesy of FiberSource/ American Fiber Manufacturers Association*.

Figure 3.1b "Great Lash" fabric from Donghia consists of 92 percent tow linen flax, 8 percent wool. The inconsistent character of the linen yarns is enhanced by clipping half the weft yarns out of the weave and leaving their ends exposed on the fabric face to create a rustic, feathery effect. *Photo by Edward Addeo. Product by Donghia, Inc.*

FIBER QUALIFICATIONS

Throughout history and until the mid-nineteenth century, the only fibers available for interior furnishing fabrics were natural fibers. Of the dozens of tested and usable natural fibers, only a few have proven suitable for decorative fabrics. These are the natural cellulosic fibers, especially cotton and linen, with some fibers as less-used textiles, and the natural proteins, silk, wool, and leather. These natural fibers and fabrics have been in use for thousands of years. In the past

150 years, since the beginning of the industrial revolution, new frontiers of research and development have resulted in an amazing array of engineered or manufactured textiles. Today, fiber manufacturers invest millions of dollars annually on research and development of existing and new fibers. The term *generation* is often used to distinguish a manufactured fiber with a new feature. Chemically and mechanically engineered improvements take place continually. The quality of natural fibers production is also deliberately improved.

TEXTILE SCIENCE

Textile science is the chemistry, composition, and manufacture of textiles. Although most interior design professionals, given a choice, prefer not to deal with the chemistry and composition of fibers, some understanding is essential. The extent to which readers will utilize textile science depends entirely on the direction of their career track.

Textile science is expressed in the language of chemical engineers or in a "lay" nomenclature that is more understandable to professionals whose expertise is in business and artistic endeavors. Because interior design professionals lean toward the latter category, this chapter employs the more popular format. This allows selective study according to the textile course directives.

The chapter includes tables and a Resources section useful to the professional who, with deadlines and the pressures of a demanding career, needs a ready reference for fiber selection. The book's accompanying website (www.wiley.com/go/interior textiles) provides quick online access to further information that may be needed to meet code specifications.

Natural and Manufactured Fiber Composition

Fibers vary in their composition, structure, and inherent characteristics. This is important because the inherent fiber composition determines its overall physical structure, which in turn affects the yarn and the resulting fabric. Six qualities must be present in any fiber, natural or manufactured, for it to be a viable yarn. These qualities are among the inherent characteristics of the fiber.

Length-to-width ratio—The fiber must be at least 100 times longer than its width. This ratio is written 100:1. Fibers must be longer than ½ inch (1.5 cm) to be usable.

Uniformity—Fibers must be relatively uniform along their length and from yarn to yarn in order to accept dyes evenly and to be spinnable and flexible.

Strength or tenacity—A fiber's strength is its ability to withstand the pressure of spinning and textile construction. As manufactured fibers are tested, they are assigned a **denier** unit, which is a yarn measurement equal to the grams weight of 9,000 meters of yarn. The minimum fiber tenacity is 2.5 grams per denier (gpd), although other characteristics, such as resilience or elasticity, may make up for a low gpd so the fiber still makes a viable textile yarn. *Note:* Separate count systems are used for natural fibers. Efforts are under way to simplify this situation.

Pliability or flexibility—Pliability is the ability of fibers to bend without breaking, resist crushing, and drape well.

Cohesiveness or spinnability—Cohesiveness is a fiber's capacity to be spun into a yarn and hold together, interlocking or fitting together snugly as the fibers are twisted. Fiber with slightly irregular shapes holds together in shorter staple form, whereas long, smooth filaments are spinnable due to their length.

Absorption—A fiber's ability to take up water or oil is called absorption. This quality makes fibers better or less suited to a given circumstance. Terms that describe absorption include the following:

- **Hydrophilic**—Literally, "water loving," or a fiber that holds water easily. Hydrophilic fibers respond well to wet cleaning.
- **Hygroscopic**—A fiber that absorbs significant amounts of moisture without feeling wet.
- **Hydrophobic**—A "water-rejecting" fiber, or one that repels or avoids water.
- **Oleophilic**—Literally, "oil loving," or a fiber that readily absorbs oil. Oleophilic fibers respond well to solution or dry cleaning, and sometimes to wet cleaning. Heat applied before an oil-borne stain is removed may permanently set the stain, making its removal impossible.

The suitability of a fiber as an interior textile is a matter both simple and complex. In some residential applications, the fabric simply must possess the right aesthetics, color, pattern, texture, and price point. These are fairly simple and straightforward characteristics. In nonresidential or commercial design, however, many more characteristics must be weighed to determine if a fabric is acceptable in a given application. These criteria require that the fiber and finished textile meet stringent code requirements for user safety and product durability. For example, a carpet in a commercial, heavy-use area must meet flammability codes, resist pilling and crushing, and be aesthetically durable for several years. At the same time, it must be affordable. If sustainability is a criterion, then the carpet must also be recyclable or biodegradable, or a component carpet whose tiles or squares can be replaced when worn without replacing the entire carpet. Relatively few fibers meet these specific performance standards.

An important and demanding task of the design professional is to find fabrics or carpets that meet performance requirements, cost limitations, and aesthetic coordination for a given interior application. As each natural and manufactured fiber has both unique positive characteristics and inherent limitations, the professional who has this working knowledge can competently make appropriate selections.

Inherent Fiber Characteristic Terms

The categories listed below are compared to major interior fibers in a chart titled "Major Interior Fibers Composition: Natural and Manufactured Fibers" on www.wiley.com/go/interiortextiles.

Abrasion resistance — The ability of a fiber to resist deterioration or thinning of yarns through rubbing or foot traffic.

Absorbency — The ability of a fiber to absorb water without damage to the fabric. A fabric with good absorbency is more likely to release soil in wet cleaning, although it may be less dimensionally stable in humid environments.

Acid reactivity — The level of resistance to damage caused to the fiber or fabric from acids.

Alkali reactivity — The level of resistance to damage caused to a fiber or fabric from alkalis.

Colorfastness — The resistance to fading of a dyed or printed fiber or textile due to prolonged sunlight exposure or artificial light. Colorfastness is measured by a device called a *fadometer*, which simulates an accelerated exposure to sunlight. Results are measurable and are used to meet architectural specifications. **Gas fading** is the changing of a dyestuff color due to impurities in the air. Generally, brighter and darker colors fade faster than light colors or neutrals. Colors may also fade inconsistently, meaning that a color changes identity as one component of the dye solution fades at a different rate than other components. In a blue-green dye, the blue may fade faster so that the green becomes dominant, for example. **Crocking** is the wet or dry transfer of color from a textile, which makes a difference in seating fabrics.

Dimensional stability — The ability of a fiber to remain stable; the resistance of draped fabric to sagging or hiking as humidity fluxes; the resistance to stretching in upholstery.

Drapability — The ability of a fiber to hang in a manipulable gentle and fluid fashion.

Flame resistance — The inherent resistance to combustion and sustained burning, and the ability to self-extinguish.

Grease/oil reactivity — The fiber's ability to resist staining or damage from exposure to grease or oil substances.

Heat sensitivity — The level of damage a fiber sustains from prolonged exposure to heat, as in a heavily sunlit environment, or to heat from clothes dryers or irons.

Figure 3.2a Silhouette® polyester window shadings, with soft fabric vanes suspended between sheer fabric facings, resists sunlight fading or yellowing. UV light rays are diffused through the sheers, also helping prevent sunlight fading of valuable textile furnishings. *Photo courtesy of Hunter Douglas, Inc.*

Figure 3.2b Giati solution-dyed textiles feature a high degree of colorfastness against fading. *Images courtesy of Giati Designs, Inc.*

Microorganism and insect reactivity—The degree to which a fiber supports or resists microorganism or bacteria growth, which can destroy the fabric and is also a health and safety issue. Also, the susceptibility or resistance to insects that eat the fiber.

Moisture reactivity—The level of damage incurred to a fiber when it is subjected to humidity or water exposure, such as floods or spills.

Solvent reactivity—The level of potential damage done to a fiber when exposed to solvents or cleaning agents.

Strength/tenacity—The ability of a fiber to withstand the force of spinning into yarn and to withstand the rigors of use.

Sunlight reactivity—Damage to the fiber itself from deterioration that results from ultraviolet rays and heat combined.

TABLE 3.1 FIBER/FABRIC SOURCES

Natural Fiber Sources

Cellulosic: Seed/Fruit	Cellulosic Bast/Leaf
Cotton (fruit/boll)	Banana (leaf)
Coir (coconut; hull fibers)	Pina (pineapple; bast/leaf)
	Henequen (leaf)

Cellulosic: Bast/Stem	Protein
Linen (bast/stalk)	Wool (sheep; wool)
Jute (bast/stalk)	Hair (goat; llama; rabbit; hair)
Maize (corn; bast/stalk)	Silk (silkworm cocoons; filament)
	Leather fabric (cattle/swine; tanned hide)
	Sisal, hemp (leaf)

Manufactured (Man-made) Fibers

Cellulose	Fossil Fuel
Acetate (wood/linters)	Acrylic (natural gas, water, air, petroleum)
Rayon (wood/linters)	Aramid
Lyocell (wood pulp)	Anadex
Dextrose (noncellulose)	Modacrylic (Acrylonitrile, vinyl bromide)
	Nylon (petroleum, or natural gas, air, and water)
Polylactide (cornstarch)	Novoloid
	Olefin
Plant Extract	Polyester
Rubber (rubber tree)	Spandex
	Vinyon
Mineral	
Glass (silica sand)	
Gold, silver, bronze (mineral)	

INTERIORS FIBERS

Many fibers are used in interior design textiles, each with its own strengths and weaknesses. As no single fiber contains every positive characteristic for each installation, the interior design professional often must make choices where there is no perfect solution.

In this chapter, the major interior design textile fibers are presented in this format: Name of fiber, brief history, source (including genus, species, or chemistry), types, processes and finishes (natural fibers), positive characteristics, limitations, and textile price range.

Because the study of fibers is complex, this chapter includes tables that categorize information in grouped comparisons in tables found on www.wiley.com/go/interiortextiles.

NATURAL CELLULOSIC FIBERS

Cotton

Brief History

Cotton fiber and boll fragments over 7,000 years old have been discovered in the Tuacan Valley of Mexico (from 3500 B.C.), and cotton has been cultivated in India for over 5,000 years. Fragments of cotton fabrics have been found in India dating to 3000 B.C., in Peru dating to 2500 B.C., and in the southwestern United States dating to 500 B.C. Arab merchants introduced cotton cloth to Europe about A.D. 800, and Columbus found cotton growing in the Bahama Islands when he arrived. Cotton was used by ancient North and South Americans, Chinese, and Egyptians. It is believed that cotton was first planted in Florida in 1556 and that it was one of the first crops planted in the Jamestown colony in 1607. By 1616, colonists were growing cotton along the James River in Virginia.

Modern cotton manufacturing began in England, where it was first machine spun in 1730. In the United States, Eli Whitney invented the cotton gin (*gin* is short for "engine"), which separated fiber from seed 50 times faster than hand labor. Patented in 1793, the cotton gin facilitated the delivery of large quantities of fiber to the fast-growing textile industry.

Source and Types of Cotton

Cotton is a genus the mallow family, a small shrub cultivated in several parts of the world. The cotton flower bud, or *square*, blossoms to produce the oval-shaped boll that at maturity splits open, exposing long, fluffy seed hairs. These consist of spiral-twisted, flattened, tubular cells attached to seeds. These hairs range in length from 1.3 to 6 cm, or 0.5 to 2.5 inches. Shorter fibers grow from the seeds and are

Figure 3.3a Cotton blossom

Figure 3.3b Cotton boll or seed pods

Figure 3.3c Cotton seed hairs, removed and processed into cotton yarn

Figure 3.3d Cotton Incorporated® logo

Figure 3.3e Cotton has long been termed *the decorator fiber* because it accepts dyes readily and is made into a variety of pleasing and functional designer fabrics. Here, a large-scale cotton toile fabric is used as sofa upholstery, pillows, upholstered screen, and dust ruffle or bedskirt. At the window, Silhouette® window shades protect these furnishings by blocking up to 66 percent of UV light when open and up to 99 percent when closed. *Photo courtesy of Hunter Douglas.*

Figure 3.3f "Wisteria" cotton floral chintz is a classic floral design in four new colorways. Inspired by document artwork to emulate the English and French styles of the 1920s and 1930s, this fabric is from the Ellington Print Collection, the Cyrus Clark Archives. *Photo courtesy of Duralee® Fabrics, 800-275-3872 www.duralee.com.*

called *lint*. The three major species of cotton grown commercially are as follows (*Note: G.* means *genus*).

G. hirsutum, commonly known as American Upland cotton, or simply Upland cotton, is grown worldwide, accounting for about 90 percent of planted acreage. It is a medium-length cotton. Many countries produce Upland cotton. China is one of the world's largest producers of raw cotton.

G. barbadense is an extra-long staple cotton, originally from Egypt. It is engineered into three kinds of cotton: Egyptian, Pima, and Sea Island. Egyptian and Pima (originally called American-Egyptian) are produced in Egypt, the United States, Israel, Peru, and the Central Asian countries. Sea Island cotton is cultivated in the islands of the West Indies, to which climate it is particularly suited. Long-fiber

cottons can be spun into extremely fine yarns, resulting in smooth and lustrous fabrics.

G. arboreum and *G. herbacum* are varieties of Asiatic short-staple, coarse cotton. Russia and the Central Asian states produce large quantities of this cotton.

Bt cotton is a genetically engineered cotton carrying the *Bacillus thuringiensis* (Bt) gene, which produces protein crystals in every cotton plant cell that are toxic to some insects.

Organic cotton is raised using crop rotation, beneficial insects, compost, and other nonchemical farming methods rather than chemical fertilizers and pest controls.

Engineered cotton produces cotton that is already colored in shades of pale and beige hues. This cotton is useful where allergies to dyes are a concern.

Processes or Finishes

Cotton must be harvested. It can be *picked,* which leaves the hull and removes only the boll (selectively repeated by hand or machine), or *stripped* (a mechanical operation that pulls all the bolls and hulls off the plant at once. The harvested pulp is then processed through a cotton gin, which separates the fibers from impurities. The fibers are then graded according to length—very short (½ inch), short, medium, long, and extra-long (2½ inches). Grading is determined by color, brightness, and purity of fiber.

Cotton is also given a character rating according to the fibers' degree of sameness, strength, elasticity, cohesiveness, and fineness or coarseness. Once graded, cotton is opened, cleaned or blended, carded, combed, spun into *slivers* and then yarns, woven into *gray goods* or *greige,* treated with prefinishes, and then dyed, printed, and finished.

Mercerization is the exposure of the yarn or greige fabric to sodium hydroxide (a strong alkali) or to liquid ammonia. This process realigns the cotton polymers (molecular structure), imparting greater strength and absorption. The fiber swells and untwists, evening the diameter and allowing it to better absorb dye. This results in a smoother and more evenly colored textile with a larger surface for better light reflection.

Cotton may also be given flame-retardant finishes and soil- or water-repellent finishes.

Positive Characteristics

- Versatile in application
- Excellent drapability
- Easily dyed and printed
- Dimensionally stable
- Hydrophilic/absorbent
- Low luster
- Good hand; comfortable
- Releases soil readily through wet cleaning
- Long lived with proper care and maintenance
- Releases oil-borne stains through dry cleaning solvents
- Colorfast if the appropriate dye is used to bond to the structure of the fiber

Fiber Limitations/Weaknesses

- Wrinkles unless blended or treated
- Low abrasion resistance
- Disintegrates from lengthy sunlight and air pollution
- Mildews if kept moist
- Low resilience and abrasion resistance
- Dries slowly
- Acids, air pollution cause eventual degradation

Flammability

Cotton is flammable and burns readily. The smell of burning cotton resembles burnt paper. The residue is a fluffy gray ash. Cotton can be chemically finished for flame resistance in order to meet nonresidential code.

Care and Maintenance

Cotton is a washable fiber because it is hydrophilic; absorbing water allows it to release most soiling. Bed, bath, and table linens may be primarily cotton and can be machine washed and dried according to manufacturers' instructions.

Many interior decorative and fabrics are cotton or cotton blends with an average of six finishes, many of which can be removed by wet cleaning. Therefore, it is recommended that cotton products other than linens be dry or solvent cleaned to maintain their appearance and body. The exception to this is cotton upholstery, which is cleaned on the furniture piece and where wet cleaning can work well. Ask for credentials and check references before hiring an upholstery cleaning service.

Spots should be cleaned quickly with mild soap and water or with a solvent, depending on the type of stain. Then the item may require only infrequent major professional cleaning. Go to www.wiley.com/go/interiortextiles for more information on textile maintenance.

Textile Price Range

Depending on grade, blend, and fabric construction, cotton is priced from very low to moderately high in a moderate or mid-range cost structure.

Linen

Brief History

Linen is the oldest of all domestically produced fibers (wild plants are not used). Remnants of all stages of linen manufacture, including straw, seeds, fibers, yarns, ropes, and fabric fragments that date back to over 8000 B.C., have been found in Swiss lake dwellings. Linen was used extensively at the height of great civilizations, including the eras of the Egyptian pharoahs, the Golden Age of Greece, and the Imperial Age of Rome. In the early medieval centuries, linen use declined, but it began to rise again in the eleventh century A.D., when it was discovered that linen helped cure skin diseases, including leprosy.

Source and Types

Linen is produced from the fibers within the stalks of the flax plant, *Linum usitatssimum,* widely produced in the Far East, Europe, Russia, and the British Isles. Irish and Belgian fine table linens, for example, are world famous. During much of the twentieth century, 80 percent of European flax was grown in Russia. Flax is also produced in New Zealand.

Figure 3.4a Linen fibers are obtained from the long stems of the flax plant.

Figure 3.4b Logo of MASTERS OF LINEN: European Linen of Quality.

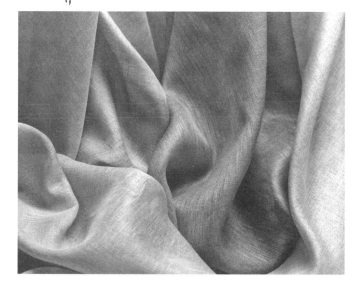

Figure 3.4c Linen is used for many applications, including bedding and accessory items such as pillows. *Photo courtesy of MASTERS OF LINEN: European Linen of Quality.*

Figure 3.4d "Summer Squall," a highly refined 100 percent linen sheer, is an elegant casement with a subtle sheen. *Photo by Edward Addeo. Product by Donghia, Inc.*

Linen has long been termed the fiber of luxury. It is a crisp, long-lived fiber, the best known of the bast family of fibers, or those made from the stems and leaves of plants. **Ramie** or **China grass** is a cousin to the linen plant; the fabric is also a bast plant, derived from the stems. It is used as a minor blended fiber in a variety of fabrics to give crispness and texture.

Processes or Finishes

Flax is planted in March or April and harvested in around 100 days.

Linen is obtained by gathering and bundling the rippled flax stalks. First they are threshed to remove any remaining seed pods, then *retted,* or rotted, a process taking several days or weeks, to soften and loosen the outer bark of the stalk. Dew retting is the laying of the flax stalks on the ground, which can take up to six weeks. Stream or pool retting is placing the bundles in stagnant or slow-moving water, which also takes up to six weeks. Tank retting is placing the stalks in warm water tanks, which yields decomposed bark in less than a week. Chemical retting is the addition of chemicals to tank retting to hasten the process.

The retted stalks are broken open by passing them through corrugated rollers. A scutching machine pulls out the linen fibers, which are then hackled or carded and combed. Hackling separates the long **line linen** fibers from the shorter **tow linen** fibers. The bundle is known as a *sliver* and in its creamy white state resembles a blonde-haired child's ponytail (thus the expression *towhead*).

Positive Characteristics

- Moderately strong to very strong fiber
- Crisp appearance
- Strong when wet; good for table linens
- Hydrophilic; absorbent
- Low luster; increases with use/cleaning
- Natural hand
- Coarse tow linen textures are appealing
- Smooth, lustrous line linen are prestigious

Fiber Limitations/Weaknesses

- Inflexible; may break when creased
- Wrinkles hard to remove
- Decomposes with prolonged sunlight
- Creases, wrinkles
- Rough hand not always appealing
- Prone to mildew
- Stretches in damp climates; poor recovery
- Loses body when damp

Flammability

Linen is flammable. However, when applied as a wallcovering, linen typically meets fire code requirements. Burnt linen smells like burnt paper, and, like cotton, leaves a residue of fluffy gray ash.

Care and Maintenance

Linen is a hydrophilic and hydroscopic fiber, making it suitable for table linens. Its slightly abrasive quality is useful for polishing stemware, dinnerware, and silverware. Table and kitchen linens may be laundered with care. Tow linens wrinkle easily. Ironing is needed at high temperatures and requires moisture. If tablecloths are laid over dowels rather than hung on wire hangers or folded for storage, there will be considerably less creasing.

Drapery and upholstery blends containing linen should be professionally dry-cleaned.

As linen will decompose with prolonged heat and sunlight as well as dampness, long-lived linens are protected and kept in a dry and light-controlled environment. Lining linen draperies increases the lifespan of the fiber.

Textile Price Range

Linen is moderately priced, although some exclusive fabrics are moderately high in price.

Other Bast or Seed/Fruit Fibers

Abaca comes from a banana family plant grown mainly in the Philippines. Its fibers are extracted from the leaf and may be as long as 15 feet (4.5 m). A strong, lightweight, and delicate-appearing fiber, it is used for rope or cordage and for table coverings or place mats for use indoors and outdoors.

Coir is the seed hair or fibrous mass from the inner coconut shell. It is obtained by soaking the husk in saltwater for several months. It is a brown color. Resists abrasion, water, and most weather conditions, and thus it is used for outdoor doormats.

Hemp, from the *Cannabis sativa* plant, has been used primarily for cording or ropes. Today it is used as a minority specialty fiber for wallcoverings and casement draperies. It is a coarse fiber, similar to but rougher than tow linen.

Jute comes from the jute plant, grown in India and Southeast Asia. Jute is used for **burlap** cloth, which has a variety of industrial uses. It is used for webbing (about 3-inch-wide woven goods left in its natural state) or base cloth to cover springs in furniture upholstery. Jute may also be a blend fiber in natural wallcoverings. Until recent years, it was used as primary or secondary carpet backing; it was fairly economical and did not slip, although it did stretch and was subject to rotting if the carpet was subjected to flooding or prolonged moisture. Jute has been replaced by olefin or polyproplene as a carpet backing. Jute has fewer applications today in interior design products, as its weaknesses include difficulty in spinning and weave due to its stiffness, its relative inability to hold dyestuffs without fading, and its flammability.

Kapok is grown in Java and extracted from seed hairs that are light and bouyant. It is used in life preservers, where it can support 30 times its weight. Historically kapok has been used as upholstery padding and pillow stuffing. Polyester and other synthetics are now used for these applications.

Maize is a fiber from the stalks of the corn plant. It is made into floor mats for indoor or outdoor use.

Piña is the fiber from the leaves of the pineapple plant, produced primarily in the Philippines. It is mainly used for lightweight sheer, stiff fabrics. It is frequently seen as mats and table linens, sometimes embroidered.

Sisal comes from the leaves of the sisalana cactus or yucca plant, which is grown in warm climates, particularly in Mexico and Brazil, with fibers extracted from the large leaves. Used in heavily textured, rough wallcoverings and floor mats, sisal is used in a natural or bleached state and is not spun, as the fibers are very stiff. Its texture is rough and abrasive. Sisal rugs are discussed in chapter 10.

NATURAL PROTEIN FIBERS

Silk

Brief History

According to legend, silk was discovered about 2690 B.C. by Princess Si Ling Chi of China, who discovered the filament of a particular moth cocoon could be unwound into

Figure 3.5a The silk moth

Figure 3.5b Moth eggs grow into a chrysalis.

Figure 3.5d The silk caterpillar spins a cocoon of silk filament.

Figure 3.5c The silk caterpillar emerges from the chrysalis, eating voraciously and growing rapidly.

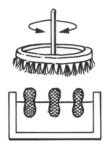

Figure 3.5e Silk cocoons are abraded to brush loose the silk filament.

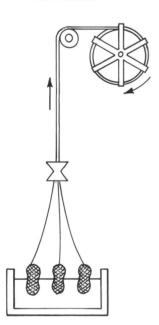

Figure 3.5g Fine filaments are reeled in groups onto spools.

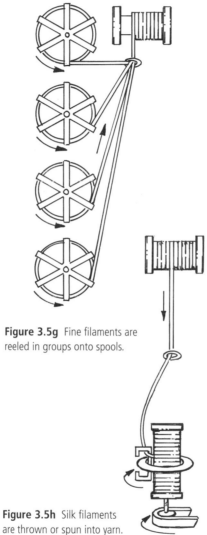

Figure 3.5f Drawing or extrusion process

Figure 3.5h Silk filaments are thrown or spun into yarn.

Figure 3.5i 100 percent cultivated silk "Spectrum" glows brilliantly; wide bands are formed with three rich tonal hues. *Photo by Edward Addeo. Product by Donghia, Inc.*

a lustrous, continuous length. It has been said she made this discovery when a cocoon fell into her hot tea on the veranda and she fished it out. The secret of silk was jealously guarded until two Nestorian monks sent to China by the Byzantine emperor Justinian managed to smuggle silkworm eggs and seeds of the mulberry tree, for its leaves on which the silkworm feeds, in hollowed-out walking canes and brought them to Europe in the sixth century A.D. along what became known as the Silk Road. Italy, France, and England have been particularly successful in producing silk fabric.

Although for several centuries silk was mainly produced in Asia and Europe, it is now produced profitably in many countries around the world, including developing nations. Production is a laborious process that calls for patience, diligence, and hand labor. Silk fabrics for interior design were in high demand by aristocracy during the formal traditional eras, until rayon and acetate became viable competitors in the late 1800s.

Source and Types

Cultivated silk comes from the *Bombyx mori* silkworm (caterpillars) and feeds on mulberry tree leaves.

Wild silk is produced by the *Antheraea myllita* and *Antheraea pernyi* and feeds on oak leaves.

Processes or Finishes

Degumming is the process of removing sericin from the raw silk by wet heat.

Weighting is the addition of metallic salts to give weight to the silk. This causes deterioration, and the amount of weighting is governed by legislative act. Some is allowed, but not enough to affect silk fabric performance.

Positive Characteristics

- Cool, dry hand
- Exceptional drapability
- High luster (cultivated silk)
- Medium to low luster (wild silk)
- Versatile applications
- Resists solvents and organic acids
- Dimensionally stable
- Lightweight
- Accepts dyes well
- Ages gracefully when protected

Fiber Limitations/Weaknesses

- Ultraviolet light sensitive
- Susceptible to beetle damage
- Moderate tenacity
- May scorch, stretch, or deteriorate (see "Care and Maintenance" below)
- Susceptible to abrasion
- May yellow with age
- Subject to mildew and rot in hot climates
- Wrinkles easily (although this may add to its natural beauty)

Flammability

Silk has good resistance to flame. Once combusted, it smells like burning hair. It will self-extinguish and leave a brittle ash.

Care and Maintenance

Silk is susceptible to sunlight deterioration, so it must be protected from direct sunlight. In draperies, this means lin-ing the fabric right to the edge (called *pillowcase lining*). Move silk applications out of the path of direct sunlight and provide screening such as sheer window treatments or window film that screens ultraviolet (UV) light. Artificial light sources that contain UV light can also cause deterioration, so silk should be kept at a distance from direct light sources.

Silk is also readily degraded by mineral acids found in perspiration; hence, many silk applications are placed in a restrained or relaxed environment where people are calm and cool. It is attacked by carpet beetles and other insects. If it is clean when stored, it is less likely to attract insects. For long-term storage, such as the museum display of vintage silk, oxygen must be controlled, as silk degrades by atmospheric oxygen.

Generally, silk applications such as draperies, bed linens, carpets, and accessory items should be dry-cleaned by professionals with expertise in silk. Silk should always be handled gently.

Silk is both hydrophilic and hygroscopic, absorbing up to 33 percent of its weight without feeling wet. Some silk items are hand washable, depending on the finishes and dyes used. Water-soluble dyes and sizings require solvent cleaning, and solvent-soluble dyes and sizings require hand washing. When hand-laundering silk items, only non-chlorine bleach may be used. Water should be gently squeezed and never wrung through the fabric. Silk loses strength and elongates when wet. High dryer heat or hot iron temperatures will scorch and discolor the fabric.

Textile Price Range

Silk is available in the medium to high price range. Some silk textiles are priced very high.

Wool and Specialty Wool (Hair)

Brief History

High-quality wool is the major reason historical pieces are treasures. Good-quality antique carpets are ever rarer, as prices have soared. Wool has been a major part of many civilizations, providing essentials for clothing and domestic items and for capital and luxury goods. In ancient Mesopotamia, wool production was second only to food production, leading to both trade and wealth. Sumerian economic texts found in Ur III dating from about 1900 B.C. detail an annual production of about 2,000 tons of new wool for processing. Wool is noted throughout ancient Near East literature. The Bible lists information about flocks and garments, such as Joseph's coat and Jesus' robe. The Assyrian Annals indicate wool was seized as tribute along with gold and silver. The Mediterranean world, including the

Figure 3.6a Wool and hair are taken from the fleece of domesticated sheep, goats, and camels.

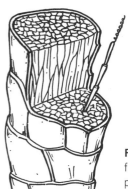

Figure 3.6b Cross section of the wool fiber showing core, cuticle, and overlapping scales.

Greek and Roman empires, traded in wool. Wool was a key factor in Italian Renaissance prosperity and, later, in England, where it set off the industrial revolution—but then fell victim as manufactured fibers were discovered in chemistry laboratories.

Today, mass wool production and mass marketing have lowered prices to increase sales. This means less demand for select wools of higher prices, so luxury wools are less familiar than in the glory days.

Source and Types

Wool is from sheep; specialty wool, or hair, is from goats or horses. A *skin* is the pelt of a dead animal, soft and tanned, and with wool or hair still attached. Most wool and hair is obtained by shearing the animal in the spring, and is called *clipped* or *fleece wool*. If the animal has been slaughtered for its meat, it is *pulled wool*. The cleanest and coarsest wool comes from the back and shoulders of the animal, while that from the underbelly contains more debris but is softer.

Sheep for wool are raised in temperate climates. The British Isles, Australia, New Zealand, and Spain are noted for their production of fine wools, although wool is produced in nearly every country in the world for export or domestic use.

Long-staple wool, taken from Cotswold, Lincoln, and Romney sheep, is used for sheer interior textiles and refined apparel. The longer, straighter, stronger, and sometimes coarser yarns are spun on the **worsted system.**

In the United States, much of the wool comes from Suffolk sheep, whose wool is average in quality and characteristics. The original Navajo churro sheep, with their strong luster wools, are being redeveloped. Merino breed sheep wool is the standard for quality U.S. grading. Called *short merino,* it is characterized by short, fine wool with a good crimp. Wools are graded according to characteristics but divided into rather large categories. In the United States, wool is often processed to homogenize its characteristics so that it can be machine-spun into an even yarn. In this way, wool breeds matter less today than in the past. This presents a major challenge to the modern wool industry as well as to carpet buyers as higher quality American wool is less readily available. To this end, Wools of New Zealand® markets a high-quality proprietary wool for carpeting.

Short-staple wool is sheared from the legs of all types of sheep. It is used for rugs and carpeting.

Medium- to short-staple yarns are soft and highly crimped or springy. They are spun on the **woolen system.**

Virgin wool has not been spun or woven previously; it comes directly from the fleece of a live sheep.

Pulled wool is removed from a dead sheep.

Lamb's wool is the first shearing from a sheep younger than seven months old.

Figure 3.6c The Woolmark logo. *The Woolmark logo is owned by the Australian wool services group of companies, including the Woolmark Company. Permission has been granted for its use in this publication.*

Figure 3.6d The Woolmark Blend logo. *The Woolmark Blend logo is owned by the Australian wool services group of companies, including the Woolmark Company. Permission has been granted for its use in this publication.*

Natural Protein Fibers **45**

WOOLS OF NEW ZEALAND®

Figure 3.6f The Wools of New Zealand logo is owned by Wool Interiors, an international provider of innovation, technologies, and research to the global wool carpet value chain, from woolgrowers to retailers. The company owns and manages the Wools of New Zealand brand program and works in partnership with the world's leading carpet and rug manufacturers, spinners, importers, and retailers to make them more profitable. Wools of New Zealand offers its partners value-added services in the areas of brand management, commercialization of new technologies, product development and testing, technical support, wool education, marketing, merchandising, and public relations. The Wools of New Zealand brand is a symbol of excellence applied only to products that have passed numerous quality and performance tests. *Wools of New Zealand, 1-800-367-0462, www.woolcarpet.com.*

The **Woolmark** indicates 100 percent new wool that has been approved and endorsed by the Australian wool services.

The **Woolmark Blend** denotes a fiber blend containing new wool in fabrics that must comply with strict quality control standards established by the Woolmark company. Wool may be reprocessed or rewoven into new products from scrap or leftover virgin textiles, and it may be reused or recycled from previously processed wool. **Noil wool** indicates waste or impure wool that can be used for carpet felt padding.

The terms *fine, medium,* and *coarse* describe the diameter or thickness of the fiber. These are terms of measurement, not quality.

Wool is not inherently a strong fiber. It does possess a considerable amount of resiliency, a combination of elasticity and recovery that makes durable textiles. This resiliency is the result of the natural crimp or waviness of the wool fiber. Wool also is highly absorbent, takes dyes well, and resists abrasion.

WOOLMARK

Figure 3.6e The Woolmark Gold Label logo. *The Woolmark Gold Label logo is owned by the Australian wool services group of companies, including the Woolmark Company. Permission has been granted for its use in this publication.*

Wool and hair vary in color from off-white and cream to brown, gray, and black. **Berber** is a fabric or carpet (looped or cut pile) where these natural colors are blended and left undyed, producing a creamy color with flecks of browns, grays, and blacks.

Specialty wool, or **hair,** is generally less resilient and durable than sheep wool, with the exception of mohair from the Angora goat. Specialty wool comes from these animals:

Alpaca is a South American member of the camel family whose fine, strong hairs are used in drapery and accessory items and in luxury upholstery in a manner similar to mohair—in plush pile weaves. Alpaca are sheared every two years. Often the fibers are used in their natural color state of white, brown, or black.

Angora rabbit hair is technically fur and is clipped four times annually. The fur or hair is used as a blend or accent fiber in luxury throws or accessory items to add softness and luster. It is known to shed and must be handled with care.

Camel hair is taken from the shedding or molting of the two-humped Bactrian camel, raised in China, Mongolia, Iran, Afghanistan, Russia, New Zealand, and Australia. The outer, coarse guard hairs are used in brushes, and the fine, short underhair is a luxury fiber similar to fine wool; it is used for throw blankets or accessory items.

Cashmere is the fine hair of the Cashmere/Kashmir or down goat, originally named for the Indian province. Little hair is now exported from Kashmir province; the goats are raised on the high plateaus of Asia and in China, Mongolia, and Tibet. The hair is combed or sheared. Dehairing separates the coarse from the down hair, which is a soft, expensive, and luxurious fiber used in throw blankets and accessory items.

Flokati (floccati, flocati) goats are raised in Greece and produce long, fluffy hair that is sheared and cleaned, then lightly twisted and tufted as a long pile into a woven backing for deep shag area rugs. Flokati rugs are especially popular in Scandinavian countries, as their warmth and natural appearance blend well with the Scandinavian modern or folk interior. These wool rugs are widely available at retail outlets and online.

Goat hair from the common goat has been used as a component in folk rugs and mats by peasants for centuries. It is not a commercially viable hair, however, as the hair length is very short and difficult to spin into an acceptable yarn.

Horsehair, taken from the manes and tails of horses, is a strong, coarse monofilament thread from 1 to 3 feet long. It is a historic fiber primarily used for padding or decorative upholstery fabric.

Llama, like alpaca, is a South American camel relative that is sheared annually. Fibers are often blended with wool, as llama is not as strong as alpaca. It is used as a blend in a variety of specialty applications.

Mohair comes from the Angora goat. It is more resilient, lustrous, and absorbent than wool and is often used in plush upholstery velvet suitable for high-end residential and commercial use, such as theater seats. It is also used alone and in blends for draperies, upholstery, rugs, and carpeting.

Vicuña, another camel relative, is a small wild animal that lives in the Andes mountains of South America. It must be killed to obtain the fiber, and Peru limits the number harvested annually. The fiber is stiff, strong, and lustrous. It is a costly luxury fiber.

Processes or Finishes

After shearing, wool must be sorted and graded, scoured to remove grease, dirt, and impurities, carded, spun, and woven. Prefinishes and treatments also include:

Perching—Visual inspection over a lighted frame.

Burling—Pulling out loose fibers and knots with burling irons (special tweezers).

Specking—Pulling out specks, burrs, and other vegetable matter.

Mending or **sewing**—May be required when finished textiles have holes from the processes above.

Carbonizing—Applying sulfuric acid and then burning it out to remove vegetable matter.

Fulling—Softening and shrinking in warm, sudsy water, then rinsing with cold water.

Crabbing—Immersing in hot or cold water, then pressing to set the weave.

Positive Characteristics
- Versatile applications
- Accepts dyes well
- Resists abrasion
- Resists soil, water, and grease stains
- Flame resistant
- Excellent insulator
- Dimensionally stable
- Wrinkle resistant
- Exceptional resilience
- Blends well with other fibers
- Available in a wide range of textures, from fine and soft to coarse and wiry

Fiber Limitations/Weaknesses
- Susceptible to moth damage
- Triggers allergic reaction in some people
- Upholstery may irritate skin
- May shrink
- Expense limits use

- Emits a distinctive animal smell when wet
- May shed, fuzz, and pill
- Darker fibers cannot be successfully dyed

Flammability

Wool resists combustion, burns slowly when in direct contact with flames, and self-extinguishes when the source of the flame is removed. It smells of burning hair and leaves a black, brittle bead residue. As such, it meets stringent flammability codes for most commercial specifications for upholstery, wall panels, draperies, and carpeting.

Care and Maintenance

Wool may be wet-cleaned gently by hand in cold water, as it shrinks when exposed to hot, wet cleaning methods, particularly if agitated. Wet heat weakens and stiffens fibers; dry heat over 270°F (132°C) causes decomposition and yellows the fiber. As is true of many interior design fibers, it is best to dry-clean wool textiles. Choose a professional dry cleaner who has a specialized knowledge of wool textiles.

Cleaning and maintenance of wool carpets include vacuuming regularly, removing spills immediately, and professionally cleaning as needed. Residential wool carpets should be cleaned once every year or two.

Textile Price Range

Moderate to high price range.

Leather

Brief History

In prehistoric times, animal pelts were preserved with grease and smoke and used mainly for garments, tents, containers, coverings, and shoes. Throughout the written history of the world's great civilizations, leather is recorded as a valued and long-lived material with a great number of uses. By the 1700s, leather tanning had become a well-respected albeit tedious trade. It took nearly a year before the prepared hides could be delivered to a craftsman who might make of them saddles, harnesses, and other items. In the eighteenth century, a machine was invented that split tanned leather into a flesh layer and a grain or hair-side layer. This opened the way for more applications for leather, as the material became available in lighter weights as a supple and manipulable material.

During the formal traditional periods in Europe, leather was a preferred writing desk inlay; it is still available in upscale period desks today. Its use as a bookbinding has long been a cherished application. Leather upholstery was especially valued in countries and periods where durability took precedence over fashion. In U.S. and European history and

Figure 3.7a Leather for interior design comes primarily from the tanned hides of cattle and swine.

Figure 3.7b "Tower Sofa" is an example of high-quality leather upholstery. *Photo by Jim Koch, courtesy of Hancock & Moore.*

in contemporary upscale applications, leather has been used as floor tiles and even in strips as a type of shag rug. Leather may be used as a pelmet-type window treatment, as side panels at the window, or as panel door coverings. On beds, leather is used to upholster head and footboards and as bed hangings or even coverlets. Leather tiles used as wallcoverings has a rich effect. All these are occasional uses of leather. By far the most extensive and common use of leather today is for upholstery for seating pieces, footstools and ottomans, for pillows, and bookbindings, and small accessory items such as leather boxes.

Source and Types

Leather is the skin or hide of any animal, with the greatest quantity coming from cattle or swine that has been converted by tanning into a stable, nondecaying material. Skins or hides are cured by tanning to prevent decay and to impart flexibility and durability. Tanned leather is split into two or more thicknesses to produce a flexible material. The upper side is called *top grain,* and the under part, called the *split,* is used for suede products. Horsehide is tanned with the hair on. *Note:* Chapter 13 discusses skin rugs, also known as *processed pelts.* The leather is tanned and the hair intact. These rugs come from bear, zebra, and many other animals.

Leather Terms

Bend—The center or top of a hide from which the shoulder, belly, and butt have been cut off. The bend is the best part of the hide.

Buffalo or **water buffalo**—Leather with a distinctive rough grain from the hide of domesticated water and land buffalo of the Far East.

Calf or **calfskin**—The skin of a young bovine; it has considerable strength compared to its lighter weight. It is soft, fine grained, and supple, and contains about 32 square feet of leather.

Cattle hide—The skin of a fully grown bovine animal (cow). European steer hides average 52 square feet.

Full-grain leather or **full top-grain leather**—Leather treated to retain its natural grain or texture, including imperfections. However, *full top-grain leather* usually refers to premium leathers that are without noticeable flaws.

Grain—The unique and unaltered surface of the hide with distinctive pore patterns. The best grain comes from the bend because it has the fewest markings. Neck and shoulder grain is deep and furrowed.

Hide—The whole skin covering of large animals, usually cattle. The sources of hides are worldwide, and the quality of hides varies according to where they are raised. The best hides come from small farms enclosed with wooden fences where the animal is protected against injury from barbed wire, rocks, animals of prey, and other kinds of injury that could result in scars and markings on the hide. Both horsehide and cowhide can be screen-printed and/or embossed to imitate exotic or endangered animal hide.

Horsehide leather—This leather is tanned with the hair on. Horsehide is strong and soft and can be silkscreened to imitate the color patterns of endangered species such as leopards, jaguars, and tigers. It might be noted that the horse is used for food throughout Europe and Asia, so, like cattle, nothing is wasted in horse products.

Figure 3.8a Leather floor tiles offer high aesthetics and luxury underfoot. *Photo courtesy of Patterson, Flynn & Martin/Rosecore.*

Figure 3.8b Exotic animal prints on cowhides create a look of authenticity for area rugs. *Photo courtesy of Patterson, Flynn & Martin/Rosecore.*

Markings—The natural grain pattern of the hide, neck, and shoulder wrinkles that appear as elongated furrows, scars such as tears or scratches from barbed wire or fences, cattle ranch brands, scraping from rocks, wounds, and bug bites. Markings can be a character mark, or they can be buffed out.

Rawhide—This brittle untanned leather is similar to parchment and unusable except for wall hangings in rustic settings.

Spanish leather or **cordovan leather**—A soft colored leather originally made in Cordoba, Spain, in the Middle Ages. Today it is real or imitation leather that is tooled or embossed, sometimes gilded, and used for wallcoverings, screens or panels, and accessory items.

Split leather or **suede split**—Portions of hides or skins split into two or more thickness other than the grain side. This product is used most often for shoes and garments.

Suede and **nubuck**—Leathers buffed to achieve a soft, velvety nap. Nubuck, made from top-grain leather and buffed on the upper or outside, is a product of excellent durability. Suede is typically made from the bottom split by buffing the flesh side of the hide to make a soft nap. Special care is required in the maintenance of suede.

Top-grain leather or **corrected top-grain leather**—The outer layer of the hide, buffed or sanded to smooth the grain.

Vegetable-tanned calfskin or **Russian leather**—Leather dressed with birk oil and dyed red with brazilwood extract. This term now covers a variety of rich-appearing leathers.

Processes or Finishes

The process of converting hides to supple and stable leather has changed little throughout history, although modern equipment and processes have streamlined the procedures. There are about nineteen steps in tanning and finishing, with variables to allow processing for a particular end-use.

Hides are prepared for tanning by de-hairing, which is usually done in a lime-based chemical solution bath, followed by fleshing and cleaning. At this point, the hides are inspected and graded. Then they are split, and, for upholstery, the top $\frac{3}{64}$" of the hide is separated into a top-grain leather, no thicker than the edge of a coin, the typical thickness of leather upholstery material.

Tanning is a chemical process of converting raw hides into a stable product that is no longer susceptible to decay. High-quality tanning takes place in large wooden drums, where hides are tumbled for up to a half a day with chemically mixed tanning solutions, or *tannins*, which are obtained from bark, wood, or other parts of plants and trees, notably oak and sumac. Chromium salts and natural and synthetic vegetable agents are also used. Leather exposed to tannins becomes claylike and pliable when wet; when dried, it retains its shape indefinitely.

Finishing is the application of coloring substances that provide resistance to stain and abrasion as well as enhancing color.

Buffing is mechanical sanding used to even or smooth a grain and to remove markings.

Conditioning and lubricating replace natural oils displaced by tanning. This step also calls for tumbling in large drums. Aniline dyes may be added at this point, when the hides are absorbent.

Vegetable tanning solution is extracted from trees such as the mimosa, chestnut, and quebracho. The advantages of vegetable tannin are the resulting leather's resilient and springy hand and its mellow charm as it ages. The disadvantage is that it tends to fade in sunlight.

Dyeing is the application of color. **Full aniline dyeing** is the leather's immersion in an aniline dye bath without pigment or other opaque materials in the top finish so the grain pattern is fully exposed, including any scars. Aniline dyes are translucent. **Protected aniline dyes**, or **semianiline dyes**, include some pigment in the top finish. Pigment gives color and hides flaws. Additional dyes may be hand-rubbed or sprayed on.

Finishing means giving the leather a unique or specialty finish, typically by hand. Leather adapts to a wide variety of finishes, from dull or matte to shiny and glazed. Grain irregularities may be enhanced or emphasized, or they may be minimized to yield a uniform material. Finishes include:

Hand-finishing or **hand-antiquing** is the hand application of an accent color—typically a darker color padded over a lighter base to emphasize the grain.

Embossing is the imprinting of a pattern with a raised bas-relief embossing plate under heat and pressure. Embossing may enhance a grain for greater emphasis. It may imprint a design, such as the hand-tooled effect of Spanish or cordovan leather. Another contemporary favorite is to emboss a cattle or swine leather to imitate lizard, alligator, or other specialty leather material.

Enameling or **lacquering** is the application of chemical treatments that produce a high sheen. A familiar term is *patent leather,* well known in shoes.

Glazing is achieved by rolling the leather with a glass cylinder to produce a high-gloss, transparent coat.

Grain enhancement may be brought out by rubbing or imitated by embossing.

Printing is the application of color to imitate the hide of another animal, such as zebra. When combined with embossing, many specialty effects can be achieved.

Sueding is raising a nap by buffing with emery or carborundum wheels, usually on the flesh side. Suede leather products require greater care or upkeep and can be stained and damaged more easily than fully finished leather.

Massaging is a final finish that ensures the leather remains soft and pliable.

Hides are dried under controlled temperature and humidity and slightly stretched in the process so they remain supple.

Grading is based on suppleness, uniformity of color and thickness, and the extent of markings. For leather upholstery, the thickness must be 1.0 to 1.2 mm and/or a weight of 2½ to 2¾ ounces per square foot.

Positive Characteristics

- Tough, strong, durable material
- Resists fading
- Repels liquids and oils
- Resists fire; no toxic fumes
- Resists tearing and cracking
- Maintains shape, won't stretch
- Sensuous, tactile feel and look
- Easy maintenance
- Excellent value; long life is economical
- Visually richer with age
- "Breathes" or absorbs and transmits moisture, which yields comfort
- Leather softens a little after years of use. Softness is also achieved by tumbling at the tannery. Leather never gets so soft it rips or tears easily. Generally, the softness of the leather you purchase will stay the same as long as you have it. This, of course, also depends on the quality of the leather.
- Leather adjusts itself constantly to its environment. It is cool to the initial touch and then adjusts to body heat in a matter of seconds. Leather is neither cold in winter nor hot in summer.

Fiber Limitations/Weaknesses

- As a natural textile, it cannot be blended with fibers.
- It is stiff and has applications only as upholstery and other uses as listed above.
- Leather's high cost restricts its use.
- Some people object to the killing of animals to obtain this material.

Flammability

Leather is inherently flame resistant and will meet most nonresidential and commercial flammability codes.

Care and Maintenance

Dust furniture that is not frequently used. Spills bead and can be wiped away easily with a cloth. If the leather appears dirty, use mild soap such as castile soap in warm water and wipe with a damp, not wet, cloth. Saddle soap may be used on pure aniline leathers or natural vegetable leathers, but as a second choice. Many high-quality furniture stores sell leather restoration kits available specifically for leather upholstery.

Tearing or ripping and scratching of high-quality leather is not common. If it does occur, however, leather can be repaired, and specialty repair shops can be found in most large cities.

Suede must be treated gently. The nap can crush and, over time, even deface. Use a suede brush to lift and restore the nap. Suede is more absorbent of stains than smooth leather, so anything oily, even fingers, can soil it. Blot spills immediately. To clean spots, gently rub in a small amount of powered detergent with a damp cloth or brush, then blot with a clean damp cloth. Use a dry, clean cloth to remove moisture and brush gently.

Textile Price Range

Leather is a costly material. However, it can outlast nearly all other materials, so its life-cycle costing is economical. A chair covered in leather typically has four times the lifespan of other high-quality upholstery materials, so the cost per year is considerably less.

MANUFACTURED FIBERS

Since the mid-1800s, manufactured fibers have been discovered and developed by chemists and chemical engineers who continue to research and reengineer them to meet the evolving needs of a complex world. Some fibers have been developed and marketed for a short time, only to be re-placed by another fiber that does a better job. Some fibers are not useful in interior design but have extensive application in apparel, packaging, disposable products, science, and industry. The focus of this section is on fibers that are used in interior design.

Figure 3.9 Extruded fibers are seen in these textiles of Xorel®, registered trademark of Carnegie Fabrics, *www.carnegiefabrics.com.*

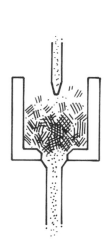

Figure 3.10a Pulverizing raw material for manufactured fiber production

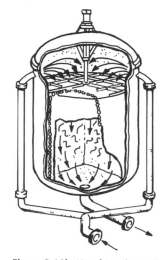

Figure 3.10b Liquefying chemically compounded viscose or dope solution

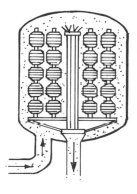

Figure 3.10c Mixing and extruding viscose solution into monofilamrents

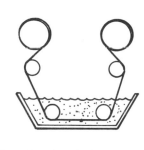

Figure 3.10d Prefinishing treatments

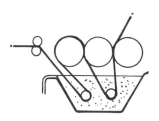

Figure 3.10e Calendaring process; straightening or smoothing

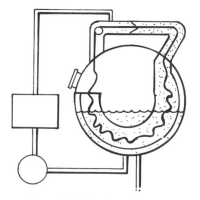

Figure 3.10f Dyeing yarns

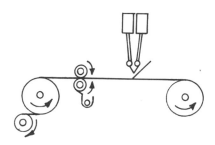

Figure 3.10g Drying and straightening yarns

Manufactured fibers, which are sometimes referred to as *man-made fibers*, are extracted from elements or ingredients found in nature and divided into categories according to their source. These are cellulose, petrochemicals, dextrose, minerals, and liquid extractor proteins. The raw sources are chemically engineered and compounded through many complex steps (which are beyond the scope of this book) to become polymers, which are then liquefied by the addition of either heat or solvents to become a thick syrup known as *viscose solution* or *dope*.

The viscose or dope solution is forced or *extruded* through the tiny showerhead-like orifice openings of a **spinneret** to become a liquid strand called a **filament** or **monofilament** that cools or solidifies in warm or cool air or in a liquid bath. This process of **extrusion** is sometimes referred to as **spinning**, a term with two meanings; it also describes the process of twisting threads together to make yarns.

Filament or monofilament is typically drawn or stretched to align the polymers, then may be twisted or spun into smooth yarns, texturized or crimped before yarn production, or chopped into shorter lengths, called *staple*, which is then twisted into yarns. All manufactured fibers have these similar steps in common. The terms that apply to the body of manufactured fibers are listed alphabetically in Table 3.2.

TABLE 3.2 MANUFACTURED FIBER TERMS

Cellulosic polymers — Manufactured fibers derived from cellulosic sources—specifically wood chips, and, to a lesser degree, cotton linters—pulverized and treated to become a liquid that is extruded into continuous monofilaments. Manufactured cellulosic fibers are rayon and acetate. (Lyocell is a cellulosic fiber from wood pulp).

Dope or viscose solution — The liquid state of manufactured fibers prior to extrusion. The term *viscose* originally meant rayon only, but now it is a more general term for the liquid step in the manufacturing process.

Dry spinning — Polymer solutions dissolved by solvent are extruded into filaments that solidify in a warm air chamber. Acetate (and triacetate for apparel), acrylic (and modacrylic), spandex, and vinyon are dry-spun fibers.

Extrusion — The process of forcing the liquid viscose or dope solution through the spinneret, similar to the way water is forced by pressure through a showerhead. The liquid solidifies by immediate exposure to chambers containing warm air (dry spinning), cool air (melt spinning), or liquid bath (wet spinning).

Filament — The extruded length of fiber before it is twisted into a thread or yarn.

Manufactured cellulose fiber — Rayon and lyocell.

Modified cellulose fibers — Acetate and triacetate.

Manufactured fibers — The general term for chemically engineered and produced fibers, also known as man-made fibers.

Melt spinning — The solidification of extruded filaments in cool air. Nylon, olefin, and polyester are melt spun.

Monofilament — A filament extruded without interruption to be a continuous length. Monofilaments are twisted into yarns or thread and can be texturized or cut into staple before twisting.

Multifilament or floss — Bundles or grouped filaments that can be texturized in bulk or spun or twisted into yarn.

Staple — Short lengths of filaments that are twisted or spun into yarns that have bulk and loft and greater variety of texture than monofilaments. Staple of one fiber may be combined with other fiber staple to create a blended yarn.

Solution dyeing — The addition of dyestuff to the liquid polymer before extrusion so the color is fast or resists fading.

Spinning — The process of extrusion, or forcing a liquid solution through a showerhead-like orifice to form long strands that are cooled in warm air, cool air, or a chemical liquid bath. (*Note:* The twisting of filaments to create yarn or thread is also called *spinning*, and is a separate process.)

Spinneret, spinnerette — The showerhead-like orifice through which the liquid manufactured solution is forced to become continuous monofilament. It is made of heavy, noncorrosive material. The openings can be a variety of sizes and shapes to meet specifications.

Synthetic or non-cellulosic — A term, now used infrequently, distinguishing manufactured fibers from a source other than cellulose.

Texturizing — False twisting, crimping, or air texturizing of multifilament yarn to produce loft and variety in the spun yarn.

Wet spinning — Filaments are extruded directly into a liquid chemical bath, where they solidify. Acrylic, rayon, and lyocell are wet-spun fibers.

The history of manufactured fibers began in 1664 and continues to develop today. A timeline of this fascinating history is on www.wiley.com/go/interiortextiles.

Most manufactured fibers are spun or extruded as a single fiber. A textile identification or hang tag may list two or more fibers that have been blended to create the textile. Blends may include both a natural and a manufactured fiber in one fabric. Commonly, one fiber is the warp and the other the weft. Alternatively, the fibers may be blended as they are made into yarn. Manufactured fibers may also be combined before extrusion by mixing viscose solutions. This is known as *fiber modification*. There are four ways to modify manufactured fibers:

1. In the viscose state, chemicals can be added to give special effects—for example, solution dyeing or soil-repellent finish. See also chapter 4.
2. The holes through which the solution is extruded can be modified into various shapes, each with an end-use property—for example, enhanced light reflection (greater shine or luster), light absorption (less luster or more matte appearance), increased bulk, enhanced dye acceptance, greater tenacity (strength), or enhanced shape retention. Shapes include kidney, octagonal, trilobal, triangular, mushroom, bone, and surface striation and pitting, among others.
3. A *bicomponent fiber* filament is made when two or more generic fiber solutions are mixed and extruded as a homogenous blended fiber.
4. A *biconstituent fiber* filament is formed where two or more generic fiber solutions are extruded side by side or one inside the other in a hollow pipe-inside-pipe or sheath-around-core configuration.

MANUFACTURED CELLULOSIC FIBERS

Rayon

Types

Ninety-five percent of all rayon is viscose, with a subcategory of high wet modulus (HWM), which is a higher performance type of viscose rayon. When this type of rayon is crimped or texturized, it is known as *crimped high-performance HWM*. Another type sometimes used in interiors is cuprammonium rayon.

Positive Characteristics

- Highly absorbent
- Flexible; may imitate wool, silk, or cotton
- Excellent drapability
- Blends well with other fibers; acetate is most common
- Silk-like luster
- HWM rayon is a strong fiber
- Filament or staple yarns
- Good insect resistance
- Long-lived
- Can be delustered and enhanced with optical brighteners

Fiber Limitations/Weaknesses

- Weak when wet
- Sensitive to acids, alkalis, and bleaches
- Low abrasion resistence
- Susceptible to sunlight deterioration
- Mildews if kept damp

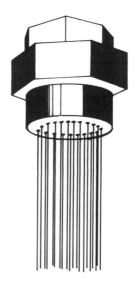

Figure 3.11a Yarns being extruded through spinneret

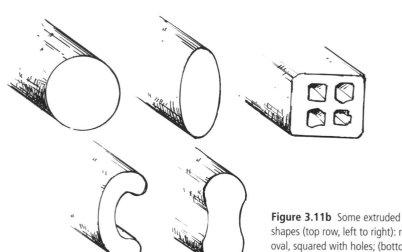

Figure 3.11b Some extruded shapes (top row, left to right): round, oval, squared with holes; (bottom row): crescent or kidney, dog bone. Each shape imparts specific fiber characteristics.

Flammability

Rayon burns readily, smells like burning paper, and leaves a fluffy gray ash. It must be treated with flame-retardant finishes to meet nonresidential codes.

Care and Maintenance

Although some rayons are considered machine washable, it is recommended that all interior design textiles with rayon or rayon blend be professionally dry cleaned. Rayon has good solvent resistance and dry cleans well. Rayon can be ironed at high temperatures. Rayon fabrics should be protected against sunlight, as the fabric fades and deteriorates with continuous exposure.

Textile Price Range

Rayon is moderate in price. It is sometimes blended with silk or wool to decrease the price of the natural fibers.

Lyocell

Lyocell is a wood-pulp cellulosic fiber. Developed by Courtaulds Fibers (now Acordis Cellulosic Fibers) as a rayon consumer (apparel) fiber in 1991, the Federal Trade Commission (FTC) designated lyocell a separate fiber group because its properties and production processes differed from those of rayon. Lyocell's properties are somewhat closer to cotton than rayon. It is breathable, absorbent, and generally comfortable, can take high ironing temperatures, and scorches rather than melts. It is susceptible to mildew and damage by silverfish. It may wrinkle—though less than rayon, cotton, or linen, and wrinkles may be steamed out. Lyocell is moderately resilient and shrinks slightly. Its stability is similar to that of silk. Lyocell has begun to enter the interior design marketplace in bath towels, sheets, pillowcases, and window treatments. It also has numerous industrial applications. It may be wet- or dry-cleaned. Trade names are Tencel® and Lenzing®.

Lyocell is environmentally friendly, as the chemicals used in production are reclaimed. It is recyclable and biodegradable, and can be blended with cotton and polyester.

Modal® is a registered trademark of Lenzing AG, an Austrian company specializing in textiles and fibers, particularly natural fibers made from cellulose. Modal is a variety of rayon derived from beech. It is about 50 percent more hygroscopic per unit volume than cotton, although it dyes like cotton and is colorfast when washed in warm water. In the United States, pure Modal has begun being used in household linens such as towels and bedsheets. For example, Bed, Bath, and Beyond sells Modal sheets under the name Pure Beech™. Indian fabric companies in particular have taken to Modal and produced about 4,000 tons of Modal in 2005. Textiles made from Modal do not fibrillate, or pill, as cotton does, and are resistant to shrinkage and fading. They are smooth and soft, more so than even mercerized cotton, to the point where mineral deposits from hard water do not adhere to the fabric surface. Modal must be ironed after washing.

Acetate

Types

Acetate and triacetate are modified manufactured cellulosic fibers. Triacetate is primarily an apparel fiber.

Positive Characteristics
- Silk-like sheen and hand
- Low absorbency
- Solvent resistant; dry-cleans well
- Excellent dimensional stability

Fiber Limitations/Weaknesses
- Low abrasion resistance
- Deteriorates in prolonged sunlight
- Mildews if kept damp
- Discolors, weakens with age, prolonged sunlight

Flammability

Acetate, a cellulosic fiber, ignites readily and melts. It must be surface treated with topical flame retardants to meet codes for nonresidential application.

Care and Maintenance

Dry cleaning is recommended. Some acetates are now washable.

Textile Price Range

Low to moderate.

MANUFACTURED DEXTROSE FIBERS

Polylactide (Polylactic Acid, or PLA)

Manufactured dextrose fiber, Polylactide (Polylactic acid, or PLA), Ingeo™ fibers (manufactured by Cargill Dow LLC)

Positive Characteristics
- Excellent hand, drape, and luster
- Outstanding resistance to ultraviolet (UV) degradation

- High tenacity
- Inherent wicking (of moisture away from the body)
- Low moisture regain
- Superior evaporative properties
- Inherently stain resistant
- Low specific gravity
- Excellent loft
- Does not support bacterial growth
- Low odor retention
- Hypoallergenic
- Optical composition allows control of crystalline melting point
- Low refractive index produces intense dyed colors
- Lower energy costs due to lower wet processing temperature requirements
- Solution dyeable for applications with high colorfastness requirements

Fiber Limitations/Weaknesses:

- Low melt temperature leads to low ironing temperature and limits end use applications.
- Hydrolytic weakening potential due to its sensitivity to aqueous alkaline conditions limits the number of corrective additions during dyeing.
- Lower yarn manufacturing speeds. Thirty percent speed reduction during carding and ring spinning for spun yarns as compared to cotton and PET fibers. Forty percent speed reduction during false twist texturing as compared to PET filament yarns.

Figure 3.12a The PLA fiber production cycle for Kira™. *Photo courtesy of NatureWorks®.*

Figure 3.12b The process of Ingeo® Kira™ high-performance extruded polymer PLA. *Jim Powell. Photo courtesy of Herman Miller.*

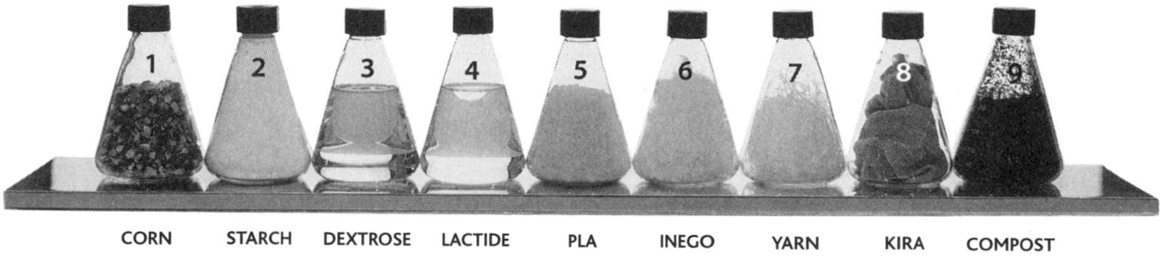

Flammability

Inherent flame resistance. Releases significantly less smoke than other synthetic or cotton fibers. High limited oxygen index (LOI), which makes it harder to support combustion. Lower heat generation during combustion as compared to PET and polyamide fibers.

Care and Maintenance

Dry- or wet-clean.

Textile Price Range

Moderately priced.

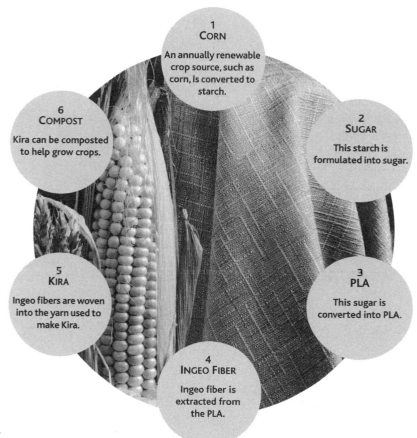

1 **CORN** An annually renewable crop source, such as corn, is converted to starch.

2 **SUGAR** This starch is formulated into sugar.

3 **PLA** This sugar is converted into PLA.

4 **INGEO FIBER** Ingeo fiber is extracted from the PLA.

5 **KIRA** Ingeo fibers are woven into the yarn used to make Kira.

6 **COMPOST** Kira can be composted to help grow crops.

CORN STARCH DEXTROSE LACTIDE PLA INEGO YARN KIRA COMPOST

Figure 3.13a "Bridge and Tunnel" ©2003 Designtex contract upholstery fabric is 40 percent nylon, 30 percent wool, and 24 percent polyester. From the New York Collection, this grid pattern brings to mind New York City's bustling commuter population en route. Abrasion rating of 100,000 Wyzenbeek. *Photo courtesy of Designtex.*

Figure 3.13b Nylon is the carpeting fiber of choice in many contract settings, as it ranks high in durability and cleanability. *Photo courtesy of Mohawk Carpets.*

MANUFACTURED SYNTHENTIC FIBERS

Nylon

Types
Nylon 6 and Nylon 6,6 are the two types of nylon used in interior design products. They are named for the chemical alignment of the monomers. Nylon 6 consists of six carbon atoms that repeat as a unit, and Nylon 6,6 has two sets that likewise repeat.

Positive Characteristics
- Exceptionally strong
- Lustrous; inherent sheen
- Elastic with good recovery
- Wet cleanable (rugs and carpeting)
- Abrasion resistant
- Solution dyeable to eliminate color fading
- Resilient; good shape retention
- Dyed in a wide range of colors
- Low moisture absorbency
- Resists damage from oil and chemicals
- Filament yarns yield smooth, soft, long-lasting fabrics
- Spun yarns lend fabric light weight and warmth

Fiber Limitations/Weaknesses
- Harsh hand unless modified
- Susceptible to sunlight deterioration
- Sheen can appear artificial
- Conducts static electricity (carpeting)

Flammability
Flame resistant. Nylon melts before burning and self-extinguishes when the flame is removed.

Care and Maintenance
Dry-clean or wet-clean.

Textile Price Range
Low to moderate.

Acrylic

Types
Acrylic and modacrylic (modified acrylic).

Positive Characteristics
- Good resilience
- Wool-like texture, loft (springiness), hand, appearance

- Accepts dyes well
- Resists chemicals, insects, aging, mildew

Fiber Limitations/Weaknesses
- May fuzz and pill
- Oleophilic
- May crush in high traffic
- Variable strength and stability

Flammability
Flammable; melts, and then burns slowly.

Care and Maintenance
Treat oil-borne spots quickly. Dry cleaning recommended. Acrylic may be wet-cleaned in some products such as carpeting; be aware of blends before wet-cleaning.

Textile Price Range
Low to moderate.

Modacrylic (Modified Acrylic)

Note: The use of modacrylic in interior design is limited. Polyester has become the fiber of choice in most former modacrylic applications. Modacrylic is still used as a blend percentage in upholstery and drapery textiles.

Positive Characteristics
- Soft yet buoyant or lofty fiber
- Often a texturized fiber or complex yarn
- Good drapability
- Resists chemicals, aging
- Not affected by water

Fiber Limitations/Weaknesses
- Heat sensitive
- Low abrasion resistance
- Moderate strength
- Uses in interiors are restricted

Flammability
Flame resistant; burns only in flame source, self-extinguishes when flame is removed.

Care and Maintenance
Dry cleaning recommended. May be wet-cleaned in some modacrylic-only products. Used as a blend with other fibers that may be harmed by wet cleaning.

Textile Price Range
Moderate.

Olefin

Positive Characteristics
- Dyes easily
- Second usage to nylon in manufactured fiber carpeting
- Good resilience; durable
- Resists both acid and alkali damage

Fiber Limitations/Weaknesses
- Rough texture
- Low melting point
- Oily hand or feel
- Susceptible to sunlight and heat deterioration

Flammability
Flammable, but burns slowly. When flame is removed, burns and melts slowly.

Care and Maintenance
Dry- or wet-clean. Oily stains easily removed with water and detergent.

Textile Price Range
Economical; low to moderate.

Polyester

Positive Characteristics
- Soft hand
- Resembles wool in carpet appearance
- Dimensionally stable
- Resists sunlight fading and deterioration
- May be heat set
- Resists damage from mildew or insects
- Durable, multiuse fiber
- Accepts dyes well; may be solution dyed
- Excellent drapability
- Not affected by water, heat, or aging

Fiber Limitations/Weaknesses
- May have oily texture
- Crushes; weak carpet fiber
- Low abrasion resistance
- Oleophilic

Flammability
Polyester burns with a heat source and self-extinguishes when the flame is removed. It may be treated in solution or topically to become flame retardant.

Figure 3.14a Manufactured waterfall Roman shades in 100 percent polyester are an ideal selection for this residential bathroom. © *Lafayette Venetian Blind, Inc.*

Figure 3.14b Polyester draperies perform well in sunny settings, such as this European residence. *Photo courtesy of ADO Corporation www.ado-usa.com.*

Care and Maintenance

Dry- or wet-clean. Can be spot treated. Not affected by water; unless finishes will be removed, some products clean better with mild detergent and water.

Textile Price Range

Economical fiber; low to moderate price range. Some polyester fabrics are priced higher due to costly special finishes or blends.

Vinyl (Vinyon)

Types

Vinyon polymer blended into a substrate (extruded as a film) and bonded to a jersey knit or nonwoven backing creates vinyl. The best-known brand is Naugahyde®. Vinyl upholstery, or artificial leather, has been made since about 1950 and was originally a strong fabric coated with a rubber composition or a synthetic substance like pyroxylin. Since World War II, most materials made from vinyl polymers have far outstripped the earlier artificial leathers in commercial importance. Vinyl upholstery is used in hospitality, health care, office, and residential interiors. Vinyl wallcoverings are specified for both contract and residential applications and offer ease of care and durability. Vinyl wallcoverings are extruded in a wide variety of styles, colors, and textures.

Positive Characteristics
- Imitates leather upholstery
- Highly resistant to chemicals
- Produced in many colors and lusters
- Durable, abrasion resistant
- Can be embossed for pattern or texture
- Stain resistant; easily cleaned
- Useful in all upholstery suitable for leather
- Long-lived wallcoverings, residential and nonresidential

Fiber Limitations/Weaknesses
- Softens at low temperatures
- May crack and split over time
- May be damaged by punctures
- Repair is difficult or impossible
- Nonabsorbent, does not breathe
- Becomes brittle, inflexible with age

Flammability
Melts, then burns slowly.

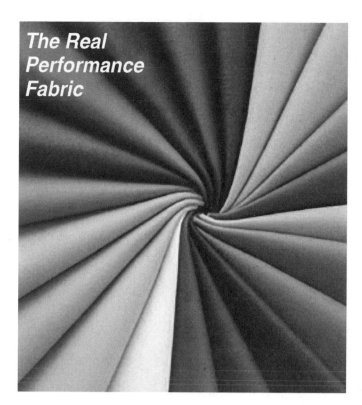

The Real Performance Fabric

Figure 3.15a Naugahyde vinyl upholstery is often specified for healthcare and hospitality contract settings. *Photo courtesy of Uniroyal Engineered Products, LLC.*

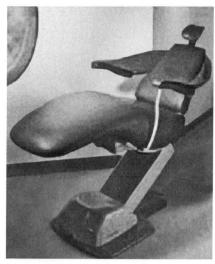

Figure 3.15b High-performance Naugahyde vinyl is considered an economical alternative to leather. It is sometimes referred to as *pleather* or *faux leather*. *Photo courtesy of Uniroyal Engineered Products, LLC.*

Figure 3.15c "Sonic" is a Type II vinyl wallcovering that meets or exceeds the ASTME84 tunnel test with a Class "A" fire rating. *Photo by Fumiaki Odaka, courtesy of Innovations® in Wallcoverings, Inc.*

Care and Maintenance

For light soiling: Warm water with 10 percent household liquid dish soap applied with a soft damp cloth or, if necessary, a soft bristle brush. Wipe away the residue with a water-dampened cloth. To clean stained or soiled areas, a soft white cloth is recommended. Avoid use of paper towels.

For heavy stains, apply lighter fluid or hairspray with a soft cloth. Wipe with a water-dampened cloth. Use with caution in a well-ventilated area and away from any open flame. Try on an inconspicuous spot before using it on a large, obvious area.

For difficult stains not removed by the above methods: Dampen a soft white cloth with a 10 percent solution of household bleach (sodium hypochlorite). Rub gently. Rinse with a water-dampened cloth to remove bleach concentration. If necessary, allow a 1:10 diluted bleach solution to puddle on the affected area or apply with a soaked cloth for approximately 30 minutes. Rinse with a water-dampened cloth to remove any remaining bleach concentration. Try this method on an inconspicuous spot before using it on a large, obvious area. Avoid harsh solvents or cleaners intended for industrial applications.

A light coat of spray furniture wax can be used to restore luster. Apply for 30 seconds and then buff lightly with a clean white cloth.

Textile Price Range

Moderate.

Note: Chapter 6 discusses textile flammability testing, which is a nonresidential or commercial specification concern.

Other Manufactured Fibers

Aramid is an aromatic compound polyamide with properties similar to nylon and with additional heat and flame resistance and strength. The two recognized tradenames are Kevlar® and Nomex®. Aramid fibers are used in aircraft components, spacesuits, and firefighting clothing. It is rarely used in interior design.

Azlons are a category of fibers made of proteins sometimes referred to as *not-natural proteins, prolon,* or *protan.* The Textile Fiber Products Identification Act assigned azlon as the generic name for regenerated (manufactured) fibers of peanuts, milk, corn (zein), and soybeans.

TABLE 3.3 APPLICATIONS/USES INTERIORS FIBERS

Fiber	Accessories	Awnings	Bath Items	Bed Linens	Bedspreads Comforters	Blankets Throws	Broadloom Carpet	Carpet Backing	Curtains	Draperies	Fiberfill Padding	Kitchen Linens	Lamp-shades
Cotton	•	•	•		•	•			•	•	•	•	•
Linen	•			•	•				•	•		•	•
Silk	•			•	•				•	•		•	
Sisal/Grass													
Wool	•				•	•	•			•			
Leather	•												
Acetate	•	•			•			•	•	•	•		•
Acrylic	•		•	•	•	•	•			•			
Lyocell						•							
Modacrylic	•					•							
Nylon							•						•
Olefin		•					•	•	•				•
Polyester	•	•	•	•	•	•	•	•	•	•	•	•	•
Polylactide		•	•	•	•	•	•	•	•	•	•	•	
Rayon	•		•	•		•		•		•			
Saran		•								•			
Spandex													
Syn Metallic	•												
Vinyl	•												

Fiber	Linings	Mattress Pads	Mattress Ticking	Oriental Folk, Designer Rugs	Outdoor Carpeting and/or Upholst.	Passementerie (Fringe)	Scatter, Accent Rugs	Slipcovers	Table-cloths, Linens	Upholstery	Wall-coverings	Wall Tapestries	Woven Floor Mats, Squares
Cotton	•	•	•	•			•	•	•	•	•	•	
Linen								•	•	•	•	•	
Silk				•	•		•		•	•	•	•	
Sisal/Grass											•		•
Wool				•	•		•			•	•	•	
Leather				•			•		•	•	•	•	
Acetate	•		•		•					•			
Acrylic					•		•	•		•	•	•	•
Lyocell													
Modacrylic										•			
Nylon				•	•		•	•		•		•	•
Olefin		•			•		•			•	•		•
Polyester	•	•	•		•		•	•	•	•	•	•	
Polylactide		•	•				•						
Rayon	•							•		•			
Saran					•								
Spandex											•		
Syn Metallic						•				•	•	•	
Vinyl					•					•	•		

Figure 3.16a Fiber blends create unique designer fabrics such as "Intaglio" damask, named for the process by which a metal plate is carved with grooves and filled with ink to create an image. This fabric mimics the look with an overall design reminiscent of Victorian tin ceilings. It is made of 38 percent cotton, 29 percent linen, 21 percent silk, and 12 percent viscose rayon. *Photo by Edward Addeo. Product by Donghia, Inc.*

Figure 3.16b "Palazzo" creation Baumann for Carnegie, is a shantung-like fabric of 34 percent ramie, 30 percent rayon, 13 percent linen, 12 percent silk, and 11 percent polyester. It is used for window treatments, upholstered walls, and, if paperbacked, wallcoverings. *Photo courtesy of Carnegie Fabrics, www.carnegiefabrics.com.*

Casein (milk) protein fibers are considered animal protein. Trade names for the early casein fibers, no longer in production, included Lanital, Aralac, R-53, and Caslen. Fabrics of these fibers are referred to as *vintage fabrics* and include quilts and garments from the 1930s to the 1960s.

Corn (zein) protein comes from corn seeds (39 percent kernel protein, or about 4 percent kernel weight). Vicara was a brand name for one corn (zein) protein, marketed from 1948 to 1958. *Note:* Corn fiber research today is discussed above under "Manufactured Dextrose Fibers: Polylactide (Polylactic Acid, or PLA)."

Soybean protein fiber (SPF) was produced as early as 1937. Today, China claims to have taken the lead in SPF, calling it a healthy and comfortable apparel fiber for the twenty-first century. Its qualities are absorbing and releasing moisture for both ventilation and warmth and a soft luster that rivals silk and cashmere. SPF yarns can be mixed with wool, flax, silk, cashmere, and spandex. Its use in interior design applications remains to be developed.

FIBER BLENDS

Fiber blending is the bringing together of two or more fibers for one of the following reasons:

1. To create a textile with positive qualities of two or more different fibers.
2. To compensate for a limitation or disadvantage of one fiber with the positive qualities of another. An example is the combination of cotton and polyester. Cotton is absorbent (hydrophilic) and comfortable to the touch, but it wrinkles and shrinks. Polyester is stable and does not wrinkle or shrink, but it is nonabsorbent (hydrophobic) and has a harsh or oily feel.
3. To produce variety in yarn, sheen, or appearance.
4. To decrease the cost of an expensive fiber by adding a percentage content of an economical fiber.

Fiber blending can be done in one of two ways:

1. By blending fibers in the extruded state
2. By blending filaments or yarns

RESOURCES

American Fiber Manufacturers Association (AFMA)
www.afma.org
1530 Wilson Boulevard, Suite 690
Arlington, VA 22209

Tel 703-875-0432
Fax 703-875-0907

The AFMA (formerly the Man-Made Fiber Producers Association) is the trade association for U.S. companies that manufacture synthetic and cellulosic fibers. Membership is limited to U.S. producers that sell manufactured fiber in the open market.

American Textile Manufacturers Institute (ATMI)

1130 Connecticut Avenue NW, Suite 1200
Washington, DC 20036-3954
Tel 202-862-0500
Fax 202-862-0570

ATMI is the national trade association for the textile mill products industry. Its members manufacture yarns, fabrics, home furnishings, and other textile products. Through its Safety and Health Committee, ATMI addresses workplace safety and health issues, including cotton dust, personal protective equipment, and ergonomics.

Cashmere and Camel Hair Manufacturers Institute (CCMI)

www.cashmere.org
6 Beacon Street, Suite 1125
Boston MA 02108-3812
Tel 617-542-7481
Fax 617-542-2199

The CCMI was established in 1984 to promote the use of genuine cashmere and camel hair products and to protect the interests of manufacturers, retailers, and consumers of these products. Its objective is to maintain the integrity of cashmere and camel hair products through education, information, and industry cooperation.

Cotton Incorporated

www.cottoninc.com
6399 Weston Parkway
Cary, NC 27513
Tel 919-678-2200
Fax 919-678-2230

Cotton Incorporated is an independent, nonpolitical company, funded by cotton growers and cotton textile importers, that is dedicated to building markets for its commodity. Cotton Incorporated works to stimulate and meet demand along the entire chain of production and distribution, from planting cotton to its final sale in the form of retail consumer goods.

National Cotton Council of America

www.cotton.org
Street Address: 1918 N Parkway, Memphis, TN 38112-5000

Mailing Address: PO Box 820285, Memphis TN 38182-0285
Tel 901-274-9030
Fax 901-725-0510

Washington Office: 521 New Hampshire Avenue N, Washington DC 20036-1205
Tel 202-745-7805
Fax 202-483-4040

The National Cotton Council of America's mission is to ensure the ability of all U.S. cotton industry segments to compete effectively and profitably in the raw cotton, oilseed, and U.S.–manufactured product markets at home and abroad. The council serves as the central forum for consensus building among producers, ginners, warehousers, merchants, cottonseed crushers, cooperatives, and textile manufacturers. It is the unifying force in working with the government to ensure that cotton's interests are considered.

The Woolmark Company

www.woolmark.com
Australian Wool Services Ltd.
Level 9 Wool House
369 Royal Parade
Parkville, VIC 3052 Australia
Tel+61-39341-9111
Fax+61-39341-9273

1230 Avenue of the Americas, 7th Floor
New York, NY 10020
Tel 646-756-2535
Fax 646-756-2538

The Woolmark Company specializes in the commercialization of wool technologies and innovations, technical consulting, business information, and commercial testing of wool fabrics. It owns and licenses the Woolmark, Woolmark Blend, and Wool Blend brands and symbols, providing unique worldwide quality endorsement protected by rigorous and extensive control checks that are recognized globally as signs of quality and performance.

CELC—MASTERS OF LINEN

www.mastersoflinen.com
15, rue du Louvre
75001 Paris, France
Tel +33 (0) 1 42 21 06 83
Fax +33 (0) 1 42 21 48 22

MASTERS OF LINEN is a subsidiary of the CELC (European Flax and Hemp Confederation), the only European agro-industrial body to bring together players working in all stages of the flax/linen supply chain. MASTERS OF LINEN acts as the interface between the European linen industry and other sectors, providing information and promoting high-quality European linen throughout the world.

Wools of New Zealand USA

www.woolsnz.com
PO Box 172
Marble Hill, GA 30148
Tel 706-579-1484
Fax 706-579-1495

Working in partnership with the world's leading carpet and rug manufacturers, spinners, importers, and retailers, the Wools of New Zealand brand program is focused on creating, developing, and promoting carpets and rugs of exceptional quality and beauty.

chapter

Yarns and Fabric Construction

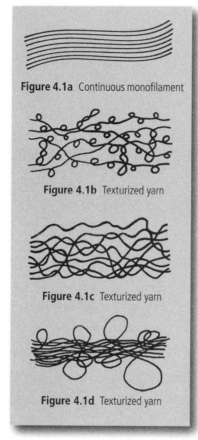

Figure 4.1a Continuous monofilament

Figure 4.1b Texturized yarn

Figure 4.1c Texturized yarn

Figure 4.1d Texturized yarn

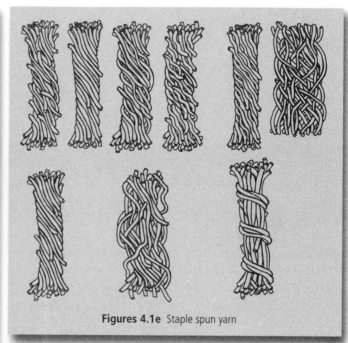

Figures 4.1e Staple spun yarn

Figure 4.1f "Sedona." Like the desert striations of the American Southwest, chunky chenille yarns have variegated horizontal stripes without uniformity or repeat, resulting in a random ripple effect. *Photo by Edward Addeo. Product by Donghia, Inc.*

HOW TEXTILES ARE MADE: FROM FIBER TO FABRIC

Textiles travel a fascinating journey from their raw goods state to the finished, salable, and aesthetically pleasing condition in which they can be specified, purchased, fabricated, and installed in an interior. As discussed in chapter 3, there are two sources from which fibers are derived: natural sources (cellulosic and protein) and manufactured (cellulosic, dextrose, and synthetic). The raw goods state of natural cellulosic fibers is the plant itself: cotton bolls, linen tow, or other fibers. The most raw goods condition of protein fibers is the wool of animals, the cocoon of the silkworm, or the hide of cattle or swine.

Manufactured cellulosic fibers begin with a plant source, including pulverized wood chips, to which chemicals are added through many steps of chemical engineering to yield a liquid viscose or chemical dope solution. Dextrose sources typically begin as cornstarch and are further engineered to the same liquid state as cellulosic viscose. Synthetic fibers begin as raw materials such as petroleum, coal, natural gas, air, and water, which may be formed into hard pellets or other materials that can be melted or converted into the liquid solution. At this point the process of making manufactured yarns begins.

YARN

Yarn can be defined as continuous strands of filaments, fibers, or other materials that are suitable for weaving, needle constructing, or otherwise intertwining to produce a textile. Yarn has much to do with the texture and hand of fabric. The majority of textiles produced for interior use today are made of yarn that is later woven, needle constructed, or fused. Some textiles are made of structures that resemble yarns, and other fabrics are made of extruded solution. Yarn is important to interior textiles because of its versatility. It can establish the formality or informality of a fabric—from smooth to coarse, compact to lofty, simple to complex. When combined with a construction technique and with coloring and finishes, yarn often defines the appearance, durability, and usefulness of interior textiles. There are two basic divisions of yarn types: spun and filament. These come both from natural sources and by extruding filaments.

Spun yarns are derived from all natural fibers, except cultured silk, and from manufactured fibers cut into staple lengths that are thrown—that is, twisted or revolved into a continuous strand. Spun yarns are bulky, lofty, and coarse, with protruding fibers; hence they are lightweight. They are generally matte or dull, somewhat inconsistent, soft, and warm because the loft traps tiny pockets of air that insulate. They tend to be flexible, with more give due to their short lengths, unless they are very bulky or heavy. Spun yarns are not structurally as strong as filament yarns, being vulnerable to breakage, again due to short lengths and weaker internal structure.

Filament yarns are made from cultured silk and manufactured fibers. They are first drawn or extruded into continuous lengths of filament (or monofilament). As filament, they may be used for clear monofilament sewing thread (discussed below). Filaments may be twisted into smooth, lustrous, uniform, strong, stable yarns. They have less flexibility and are cool to the touch.

Throwsters is the term commonly used for yarn manufacturers. It covers the entire facility and all the staff who operate the machinery. Several spinning or throwing methods accomplish a wide variety of types and textures of yarns.

Natural Yarn

Natural fibers are obtained in two forms: as filaments or lengths (silk and horsehair) and as various lengths of staple or relatively short fibers (wool, cotton, linen, etc.). Filament

Figure 4.2a Cotton, Inc. logo. *Courtesy of Cotton Incorporated.*

Figure 4.2b Cotton ring-spin Zinser machine. *Photo courtesy of Cotton Incorporated.*

and the longer staple fibers produce smooth, tight, and perhaps lustrous yarns. Shorter staple fibers produce bulkier, more textural, and matte or dull yarns. Specific systems are used in the processing of natural fiber yarns.

Cotton Spinning System

1. Samples are cut from 500-pound bales of opened, cleaned, and blended fibers and graded according to length. Short staple yields a coarser or bulkier yarn, and the longer cottons—indicated by the words *combed cotton* or designated by types such as Pima, Egyptian, or Sea Island cotton—are smooth and lustrous.
2. The fibers are fluffed, or picked, into a compacted mass known as a **picker lap.**
3. The picker lap is fed into a carding machine, cleaned and straightened into a thin web, and then formed into a long, loose strand, about 1 inch in diameter, called a **card sliver** or **sliver.**
4. Slivers may be further straightened, or **combed** (optional for fine yarn).
5. Drawn or condensed slivers are twisted slightly and readied for spinning into the finished yarn.

Linen Spinning System

1. Flax stalks are retted, or slightly decomposed.
2. The retted stalks are fed through a scutching machine to open and remove the bast fibers.
3. The fibers are hackled to card and comb them.
4. The combed fibers are divided into three categories: short or **tow** fibers (about 12 inches), medium-length or **demiline** fibers (13–23 inches), and long or **line** linen fibers (approximately 24 inches).
5. Two spinning techniques are used in linen. Linens that are **wet-spun,** typically line or demiline linens, are tight and smooth. Linens that are **dry-spun** make loftier and bulkier yarns.

Silk System

Silk is both a staple and a filament fiber.

1. Wild silk cocoons harvested after moths have broken open and left the cocoons are short staple lengths.
2. Cultivated silk cocoon moths are killed with dry or wet heat to keep the cocoon intact.
3. Cocoons are placed in very hot vats of water to degum. Seven or eight filaments are typically drawn out together to form one filament substantial enough for spinning.
4. Silk may be spun into single or ply yarns.

Figure 4.3 "Abracadabra," a 100 percent silk shantung yarn, is woven with different colors in the warp and weft, creating a glowing warp shining through the weft yarns. *Photo by Edward Addeo. Product by Donghia, Inc. Note:* Shantung is defined in the textile glossary (www.wiley.com/go/interiortextiles).

Wool Spinning Systems

1. Wool is sheared, cleaned, and blended, sometimes from different breeds and from different parts of the body, making the distinction less clear between long and short staple.
2a. The **woolen** method produces a shorter-staple, bulky loft, and fuzzy yarn.
2b. The **worsted** method tightly twists longer staple to produce a smoother, stronger, typically finer yarn.

Other Natural Yarnlike Structures

Natural rush, used for seating materials in place of covered fabric, is made of two to three cattail leaves twisted tightly into a type of yarn. **Fiber rush** or **kraftcord** comes from twisting paper to imitate natural rush. **Sea grass, China grass,** and **Hong Kong grass** are used as unspun weft (and sometimes warp) in grass cloth wallcoverings.

Manufactured Filament Film and Yarns

Manufactured fibers must be melted and/or chemically compounded into the viscose state before they can be made into yarn. They are extruded through a **spinneret** as film or as **continuous monofilament,** also called **filament** or **monofilament.** Continuous filaments can be used in their filament state or thrown or spun into yarn useful for fabrics with a smooth, lustrous, or hard finish, including many smooth sheer and semisheer fabrics, plain weave fabrics, smooth satin or sateen weaves, and refined Jacquard weaves. Some heavy textiles, such as frieze and some tapestries, also require a smooth filament yarn to accomplish the regular surface effect. Monofilament may also be texturized and/or cut into staple lengths, discussed below.

Yarn Texture and Texturizing

Natural fibers often produce yarns that are highly textural, meaning that many natural yarns are inconsistent or uneven due to their inherent nature or the way the short fibers are spun, with slubs or nubs evident. Wool and hair, wild silk, and tow linen are examples of natural texturized yarns. **Slub** yarns are an example of texturized yarns. Another example in natural yarns is the uneven quality of tow linen in the fabric crash. These yarns are calendared somewhat flat but are still uneven, creating a "linen look" that has great appeal and popularity in both home textiles and apparel.

Yet another example of natural yarn texturization is seen in cotton fabrics that have **nubs,** almost like tiny knots that feel as if they could be picked off the face of the fabric but that are actually spun into the yarn to create a rough texture. Wool yarns also are often nubby and uneven where the look of natural, coarse, or unrefined textiles is desirable.

Jack Lenor Larsen, a master weaver and renowned fabric purveyor who has sought unusual textures and construction techniques from all parts of the world, once said, "The great loss of hand-loomed textiles is not the loss of the hand-weaving, but in the loss of hand-spinning." This is because modern machinery, which can indeed create slubs and nubs and irregular yarns, must accomplish it with precision and regularity, whereas hand-spun yarns have an irregularity that is beguiling and intriguing.

Monofilaments can become part of textured yarn in a variety of ways:

1. By engineering slubs, nubs, or other irregularities in the yarn spinning process.

2. By texturizing or adding crimp or curl that makes the fibers less parallel and even. The American Society of Testing and Materials (ASTM) defined textured yarns as "that group of filament or spun yarns that have been given notably greater apparent volume than conventional yarn of similar fiber (filament) count and linear density." For thermoplastic fibers (which soften with heat and harden when cooled), including polyester, texturizing produces crimp, curl, or configures an extruded filament into another forced shape. This is achieved by heating the fiber to the point where the molecules begin to flow—the melting point—and then immediately cooling the filament. All texturizing methods, except the air jet method, utilize heat.

Advantages of texturizing yarn include the increased bulk or apparent volume of grouped monofilaments in order to produce greater coverage. There is also an increase in fiber cohesiveness, elasticity, warmth, and softness due to greater bulk. Bundles of filaments to be texturized are called **tow.** Texturized tow is known as **bulked continuous filament (BCF).** BCF may also be cut into staple length and spun for extra bulk and loft. These yarns are light and springy and thus imitate wool and other natural fibers.

3. By cutting texturized yarns into staple lengths, generally 1 to 6 inches, and then spinning them into yarns that are light, bulky, and lofty. These can imitate natural textiles in interesting and effective ways; for example, rayon can be made to appear as cotton, and acrylic can look and feel as wool. When cut into staple, manufactured fibers are used in fabrics where the textile must elicit interest or exhibit character, depth, bulk or loft, special effects, and perhaps even enhanced sturdiness and resilience. Texturizing methods include the following:

Air jet texturizing—Straight yarns are fed through a stream of controlled, turbulent air that partially explodes the filament, causing the outermost fibers to curl into loops on the surface. The loops may resemble bouclé or other complex yarns. This process does not produce a stretch yarn.

False twisting or false-twist coiling—Tow filament is twisted around a spindle, heated, untwisted, and cooled in a continuous operation. The yarn itself is not twisted, hence the name *false twist.* These yarns may have considerable stretch and recovery. After cooling, false-set yarns may be heat-set again to become a **set** or **stabilized yarn,** which has no stretch.

Gear crimping—Filament bundles are passed between intermeshing gears to produce a crimp. The size of the gears and hence the crimp varies.

Knife-edge—Filaments are curled by drawing them tightly over the edge of a knife as one would curl gift-wrap ribbon. The curl reverses occasionally to balance the yarn.

Knit-deknit—This procedure begins by creating a knitted fabric, typically a jersey-knit tube. The fabric is heat-set and then unraveled or deknit. The effect is yarn that is crinkled or wavy. The size of the wave is determined by the knitting guage, or number of loops per inch. Knit-deknit pile yarns that are space-dyed often become carpet yarns with variegated effects.

Stuffer-box crimping—Filaments are stuffed quickly into a heated box-shaped chamber, then slowly removed, causing a buckle and backlash crimp.

Thread

Thread is a very fine yarn used to hold fabrics together. It may be twisted and fed onto spools and used in the fabrication process of sewing lengths of fabric together to make upholstery, window treatments, linens, or accessories. Threads can be made of 100 percent polyester, 100 percent cotton, cotton-wrapped polyester, or other combinations.

Clear polypropylene monofilament (extruded and not twisted or spun) looks like a thin fishing line and is used in the fabrication of many interior design textile products where strength in the sewing thread is essential, including fabrication of upholstery or other heavy or sturdy fabrication processes where no color should show. Clear monofilament takes on the color of the textile. Other clear monofilament uses include the computerized quilting of bedspreads and heavy drapery construction.

Small spools of thread for home sewing are available in a wide array of colors at fabric stores, whereas cones of thread are used with serging machines for many items where edges or seams are joined and finished with an overlapping stitch in one operation.

Spinning Fiber into Yarn

Spinning is the twisting of filaments or staple into a designed yarn for a specific end-use. Yarns must be twisted for all spun yarns and many multifilament yarns in order to create a stable yarn. The two ways of spinning:

1. Groups of long filaments are spun, or twisted together.
2. Short-length staple is joined and twisted into yarns.

S- and Z-Twist
Filaments or staple are twisted in one of two directions, the right-hand or *S*-twist, typically used for the warp threads or yarns. A left-hand or *Z*-twist is often used for weft or filler yarn. The resulting tension of yarns twisted in different di-

Figure 4.4a Slack-twisted yarn   **Figure 4.4b** Tight-twisted yarn

rections makes the fabric more sturdy. The term *thrown* may be used to indicate the action of feeding fibers or filaments into the spinning wheel or spinning mechanism. Throwing may be automated or accomplished by hand.

Turns per Inch
Much of the variety and control in yarn production comes from the number of **turns per inch**, or **turns/inch**, or **tpi.** Tightly spun or twisted yarns may have as many as 30 to 40 tpi, making them strong, durable, or very fine and hard. Loosely spun yarns that have more textural effects may have as few as 2 or 3 tpi. The result is specified in interior textiles according to specifications for use, durability, hand, and textural interest.

Yarns that are very loosely twisted are called **slack-twisted yarns.** These enhance the coarse or natural appearance of a textile. On the other extreme are **crepe-twisted yarns,** which are so tightly twisted they may curl back on themselves. Crepe yarns create a slightly bumpy surface texture. However, they are typically so fine that the fabric is thin or perhaps fine, and the crepe creates only a slight texture with sturdiness and even a hard or smooth quality.

Yarns progress from simple to complex in their construction methods. *Single-ply* yarns are made of one spun filament or of staple; *ply* yarns are made of two or more single yarns; and *cable* yarns are made of two or more ply yarns.

Simple Yarns

Simple yarns may be spun or extruded as filament. They have in common a regular diameter and are relatively smooth. They include single-ply, cord, cable/rope, and hawser yarns. These simple thrown yarns progress by combining like members.

Yarns that are produced in one operation, such as fiber to thrown yarn or simple twisted multifilament or multiple filament yarn, are termed **simple single yarns.** Where two or more simple single yarns are twisted together, a **ply yarn** is the result. Throwing or twisting two or more ply yarns produces a **cord yarn,** and two or more cord yarns twisted together result in a **cable** or **rope yarn.** Two or more cable or rope yarns combined become a **hawser** yarn.

Complex Single Yarns

Complex yarns include complex single yarns, plies, and cords. To form single yarns from these sources, these processes are employed:

Single complex yarns are those with texture spun into a yarn that is extruded or spun. These include nub, slub, speck, and thick-and-thin yarns. Small knotlike **nubs** are tiny tufts randomly spun into the yarn in the same color as the yarn. They may appear as pills that can be picked off the fabric face. Nubs give surface texture to an otherwise plain and simple yarn. The addition of an enlarged area that imitates the way wild silk is joined with a knot slightly enlarged in diameter and profile is a **slub yarn.** Slubs differ from nubs in that they are gradual enlargements and do not lie on the surface of the yarn but are spun into the body of the yarn. In manufactured fibers, slubs are formed by coarser yarns and fewer tpi (twists per inch) in that spot, making the slub a weaker component in the yarn while adding an antique or **dupioni** silk-like texture where two cocoons grown together create an irregular yarn.

Speck yarns are produced by incorporating a nub in a contrasting color to produce a gnarled or tweedlike effect. The specks may be in one contrasting color or several to create a lively visual effect.

Thick-and-thin yarns are spun with areas that are twisted more tightly and areas looser, with fewer tpi. In extruded yarns, the thick-and-thin effect is controlled at the spinneret, where pressure can regulate the amount of viscose solution that flows; spurts create the thicker areas, and streams produce thin filaments.

Eiderdown yarn is made by abrading a staple ply yarn (originally wool) so it becomes fluffy or fuzzy.

Figure 4.5a Slub-textured yarn   **Figure 4.5b** Nub-textured yarn

Figure 4.5c "Summer Squall Stripe" features contrasting bands of transparent linen. Slubs and nubs lend interest and character to this casement textile. *Photo by Edward Addeo. Product by Donghia, Inc.*

Complex Novelty Yarns

Complex novelty yarns, also called **plies** and sometimes **cords,** are constructed of three components: a core or base yarn around which an **effect** or **fancy yarn** is plied or twisted—this is a nub, slub, crepe, or texturized yarn, wound or laid in a regular or irregular zigzag pattern—and a fine, clear monofilament that holds these two yarns together. Novelty yarns are used in casement drapery fabric and upholstery goods.

Twisting together two slub yarns results in a **plied slub yarn. Flock** or **flake yarns** employ an effect thread—a spun flock yarn—where bits of fiber are inserted during the single-spinning, enlarging and making a lofty, fibrous yarn. A complex **corkscrew yarn** resembles a tight candy cane with spiral stripes. A **spiral yarn** is similar. but with a looser, bulkier appearance. Plied yarns that produce special effects from simple yarns include **spot, knap,** or **complex**

Figure 4.6 Complex bouclé yarn composition

nub yarns, which expose projected spots or nubs along the yarn face. Tiny nubs are called **seed yarns,** and exposed, elongated slubs are termed **splash yarns.**

Loop or **curl yarns** have a fuzzy or loose effect, and **bouclé** yarns have uneven loops as the effect yarn; this is the yarn used in poodle cloth. In **ratiné,** the yarns are tightly curled or texturized and plied in a regular zigzag or rick-rack pattern across the core yarn. **Spike** or **snarl yarns** are composed of two or more effect yarns combined with a **bouclé yarn,** where very tightly twisted yarns create a kinky-curly effect; this is sometimes used in heavy upholstery as **poodle cloth** or **bouclé cloth.**

When one yarn is spirally warped tightly around another yarn or braided three or more around one yarn, the base yarn is entirely covered. These are called **gimp yarns.** One of the special effects achieved with gimp yarns is lamé (metallic-appearing) yarns, used for decorative trimmings similar to passementerie. Gimp may have a stretch base yarn. When the effect yarn is a staple spun yarn, the result is a **core-spun yarn;** when the elastic yarn is wrapped with a filament thread, it is a **covered core yarn.**

Yarnlike structures are created by several methods. Some of the best-known or most commonly used are **chenille, felted wool yarns, split film tapes,** and **metallic yarns.**

Chenille yarns are made by leno-weaving a thick fabric with thick spaced warp yarns and fine weft threads. The fabric is cut into lengthwise strips and the fine weft threads abraded to create a pipe cleaner or fuzzy caterpillar look.

Film extruded into a polymer sheet, cooled, then cut with heat into thin strips and rolled becomes **flat** or **crimped (fibrillated) polymer tape yarn** or **slit/split film yarn.** Slit/split tape yarns are hard and smooth and not pleasant to the touch, although they are dimensionally stable and abrasion resistant and can produce interesting decorative effects. Flat olefin/polypropelene tape yarns are used for secondary carpet backing, artificial turf carpeting, furniture webbing, sack or bag materials, awnings, and exterior upholstery or covers. They may also be used as a component in a complex yarn for casement-type draperies and accessory fabrics.

FABRIC CONSTRUCTION

It is important for interior design professionals to be knowledgeable about textile construction for these reasons:

1. The suitability for a specific end-use is often established in the construction process.
2. The durability of a textile, its ability to withstand use and cleaning, is usually a direct result of fabric construction.
3. Identification of a textile is based on the construction first, then on specialty factors such as yarn type, coloring, or finish.
4. Special effects are possible through textile construction; a basic knowledge is imperative in communicating with a client or other professional about any given textile.

Figure 4.7 "Bouclé Stripe" upholstery, a 100% recycled polyester, re: Solutions™, shows complex bouclé yarns woven tightly as a horizontal textured yarn. *Photo by Fumiaki Odaka, courtesy of Innovations® in Wallcoverings, Inc.*

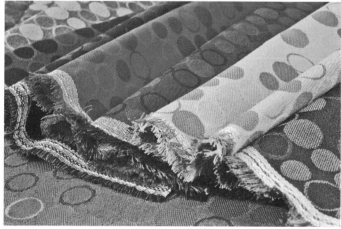

Figure 4.8 Earth friendly 100% recycled Polyester re: Solutions™ upholstery, is "Circle, Circle," a Jacquard weave. Here is shown the selvage of this geometric patterned fabric. *Photo by Fumiaki Odaka, courtesy of Innovations® in Wallcoverings, Inc.*

Fabric is constructed in one of four ways:

1. Nonwoven and extruded methods
2. Weaving
3. Needle construction
4. Combination methods, called compound cloth or textiles

Each of these is discussed below.

Nonwoven and Extruded Fabrics

Nonwoven fabrics can be achieved in several ways. Fabrics may be constructed entirely of fibers where no yarns are used.

Tapa cloth is a natural nonwoven traditional material made in the South Sea Islands of the Pacific. It comes from mulberry tree bark, which is pounded until it is very thin, and then painted. Tapa cloth is used for flooring, wallcoverings, and traditional apparel.

Fiber web construction includes webs or scrims made by a wet, dry, or melt method.

The **wet method** suspends the fibers in a water solution, where they are tangled. A screen is brought up from underneath; this strains the water and leaves a mesh of fibers. When the fibers dry, they are tangled and hold together as a fabric mass.

The **punch-bonding method** uses barbed needles to punch or work up and down through a mass of fibers, pulling and interlocking them. Punch-bonded polyster fiber batts are used for the interlining of quilts and referred to as *batting*. This subject is discussed below under "Quilting."

Spin bonding produces nonwoven textiles by heating a thermoplastic fiber mass until the fiber begin to melt or flow. Then it is quickly cooled and welded together. Spin bonding can create nonwoven carpet square in flat or ribbed textures.

These nonwoven textiles are useful as scrim applied to the underneath or bottom of upholstered pieces, for nonwoven buckram or crinoline used to reinforce the top of draperies to be stiff-pleated, or for some types of mass-produced or manufactured pleated fabric shades. Heavier mesh is used for indoor-outdoor carpet squares. Typically, synthetic manufactured fibers and used to make these products.

Another form of nonwoven textile is **foam,** which is made of synthetic or rubber-synthetic blend sources that is engineered into a thick liquid. This viscose is poured into large, flat pans on conveyor belts and baked into forms of varying weight, height, and density. Foam is used as upholstery padding and cushions, carpet underlay or padding (more on padding is found in chapter 12), and other interior design uses.

Nonwoven textiles also include extruded fabrics that are produced from a liquid into a **flat sheet** form. Thin extruded films slit or cut into tape "yarns" are one example. Vinyl upholstery is an extruded textile, discussed later in this chapter.

Nonwoven textile examples: Tapa cloth/bark cloth, buckram/crinoline, batting (interlining and upholstery padding), craft felt, cushion and carpet underlay or padding, extruded fabric, foam materials, interfacing or interlining, upholstery scrim. See www.wiley.com/go/interiortextiles for glossary definitions.

Weaving

Weaving is the process by which nearly all historic or period textiles were made, and it is still today the method by which the vast majority of fabrics are constructed. Weaving can be simple or complex. In **biaxal weaving,** one set of long or lengthwise **warp yarns** is interlaced at right angles with the crosswise **weft** or **filling yarns** in one of several over-and-under sequences (discussed below). One single weft or filling yarn is called a **pick** or **filling pick.** When warp and weft are at perfect 90-degree angles, the fabric is **on-grain** or **grain-straight.** This means the 45-degree angle or **bias** of the goods is also perfect, or has a **true bias.** When the interlacing is skewed or twisted, the quality of the fabric may be unacceptable, although the grain may be straightened during the conversion or coloring and finishing stage.

Selvages, the reinforced sides of woven textiles, prevent fabric fraying. They are created in four standard ways:

1. **Conventional selvage**—A smooth, rounded return of the continuous weft yarn
2. **Tucked-in selvage**—The partial return-interlacing of a single pick, useful where a yarn is inserted as a single row of color, for example
3. **Compacted selvage**—Where the warp yarns are threaded closer together on the edges
4. **Leno selvage**—An hourglass twist in the insertion of the weft threads secures the sides.

Thread count or **fabric count** is the number of warp and weft yarns in a square inch of fabric. It is most often referred to in bed linens. When the warp and weft are equal numbers, the fabric is said to be a **balanced construction.** The higher the count, the finer and denser the weave, translating into more durable goods. The more dense or **compact** the weave, the more serviceable the fabric; upholstery textiles are typically more compact than drapery fabric, for example.

The Loom

The loom is the machinery for weaving textiles. Looms vary in width, complexity, and efficiency—from simple hand-operated units, where hand labor creates unique and artistic pieces, to computerized, sensitive machines that produce goods at lightning speeds. All have a place in interior design textiles. Primitive looms produce a wide variety of unique goods, often filled with character and sometimes exquisitely executed. Simple hand-operated looms include the **box loom,** made of a simple box with nails for attaching the warp and weft, and the **backstrap loom,** a narrow set of weft threads that require only a top and a bottom stick that can be secured to nearly any object, such as a tree or table, on one side, and to the weaver's waist or a stationary object on the other, then woven in a suspended state. These simple looms are used for craft purposes and for items such as belts and straps.

The quality of woven goods is an indicator of the level of a society's cultural achievements. The more complex and finely woven the textiles, the more advanced the culture. Beautiful and complex textiles were and are possible where peace and prosperity reign, where a high premium is placed on refinement and aesthetics, and where pride of craftsmanship, tradition, and weaving skill are developed.

Weaving has been an integral part of many cultures, and not just of fabrics for interiors or apparel. Traditional hand-tied rugmaking is a weaving process, but the loom is an upright loom where the colored yarns that create the pattern are looped around or tied to the vertical warp threads, and then a weft thread is inserted every few rows and tamped in place to secure the construction. Two types of looms are used to create the majority of fabrics today: hand looms and power looms.

Hand looms include **floor looms** and **table looms.** The term **jack loom** refers to how the harnesses move—one type is counterbalanced; another is countermarche. Weaving is accomplished by securing lengthwise or vertical simple (stronger than complex) yarns laid perfectly straight

Figure 4.9 A simple loom. The warp (long yarns) is threaded onto the loom, and the shuttle is used to insert weft (filling yarns).

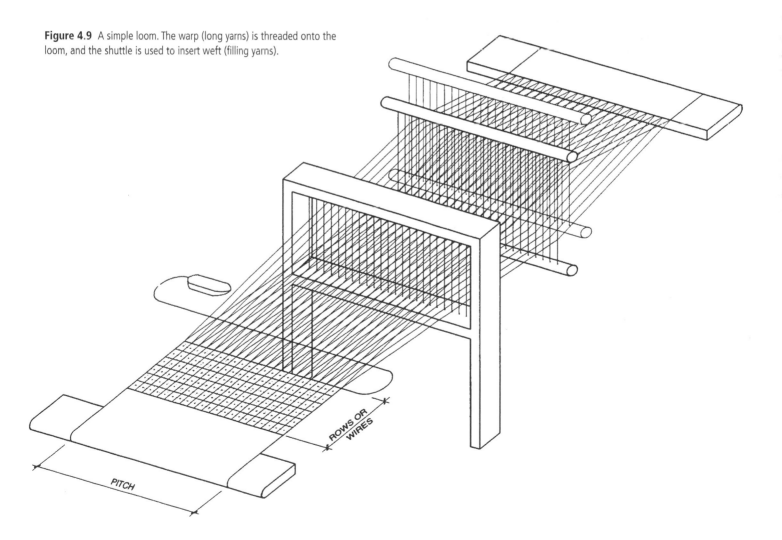

ROWS OR WIRES

PITCH

from large packages, known as **cheeses**, onto a **creel frame**, a unit that lays the yarns straight in preparation for winding onto the **warp** or **loom beam**. The beam may hold up to 150 yards of warp yarn that, when woven, becomes the **piece** or **bolt** of finished textile. The warp or loom beam yarns may be **slashed**—sized or starched—then dried for greater strength and more consistent roundness to the warp yarn. The sized yarns on the warp or loom beam are then mounted onto the loom.

Yarns are individually threaded through a *heddle,* a metal, nylon, or string strip with a small hole in the center. There may be as few as two heddles for simple weaves and up to sixteen heddles for complex patterns. The threading or drawing-in of heddles follows a **pattern draft.** For a plain weave, even-numbered yarns are threaded on heddle A and odd-numbered yarns on heddle B, for example. One or more heddle units are lifted to form a **shed**—a sideways V—that allows the weft thread to be inserted.

The horizontal weft yarns are inserted with a **shuttle,** which is a boat-shaped unit with yarns wrapped around a **quill.** The weaving is done by operating or opening the warp shed with a foot pedal and inserting by hand a shuttle encasing a bobbin that unwinds and deposits the weft yarn. The shed is closed, and the **beater bar** or **lay,** a frame that holds a **reed** or **comb** through which each yarn is held separately to keep it in perfect alignment, is pulled forward to tamp down or **batten** the weft yarn, holding it snugly in place. This step assures uniform spacing and keeps the weft on-grain. The shed is then reopened in a different configuration. The shed configurations are determined by the lacing of the heddles, which are raised and lowered by the pedal operation. Plain, twill, satin, and combination weaves and their variations can be executed on the hand loom. Plain weave requires only two heddles; the other weaves require more. Finished textiles are wound around a **cloth beam** or **breast beam.** The finished fabric may be one continuous length of up to about 150 yards, or it may accommodate several lengths of fabric with one set of warp yarns, including possible changes in the interlacing configuration by rethreading the heddles.

Hand looms were used to create all textiles until the seventeenth century, when the first automated or power looms were invented. Today, hand looms are utilized for textiles that are created one at a time as unique and personalized or artistically individual creations. The ability hand looms give to change designs or yarn colors and to be inventive yields textiles that are sought after for their distinctiveness or custom qualities. Fabrics hand-loomed include rag rugs, rug or wall tapestries, blankets, table linens, and decorative textiles. Some people enjoy the craft of hand-loomed weaving and its artistic and therapeutic effect to the extent that

weaving is a hobby of first choice, and some even have looms in a studio portion of their homes. Hand-loomed textiles created by artisans or craftspersons are often sought by interior designers and artistically sensitive people who want a one-of-a-kind piece or textile with unique or coordinating coloration or special effects.

Power looms were first deployed in the seventeenth century in Europe, revolutionizing the textile industry. Today, the vast majority of textiles, excluding authentic Oriental, folk, and rag rugs, are constructed on power looms in mills around the world. For both the power loom and the hand loom, the steps of weaving are essentially the same: (1) shedding, (2) picking, (3) battening, and (4) taking up and letting off.

1. Shedding is the opening of the shed. In power looms, this process is automated; in hand looms, it is hand- or foot-operated.
2. Picking is the insertion of a pick or single warp yarn. In hand looms, the shuttle is hand thrown. In conventional power looms, the shuttle is sent flying through the shed by a hammerlike device. These are called **flying shuttle looms.** Other power looms do not use shuttles. One type of **shuttleless loom** is a **rapier loom** (*rapier* is French for "sword"); the rapier is a projectile device that carries the pick halfway across the shed, where it is grasped by another rapier that carries it the rest of the way. Then the process reverses. In the **air jet** method, a burst of air shoots the picks through the shed. In the **projectile** method, a pick attached to a projectile is shot through the shed; both ends are cut and tucked into the next shed to form a tucked-in selvage.
3. Battening is the tamping down of the heddle or lay to secure the weft yarn in place and keep the fabric construction consistent.
4. Taking up and letting off comprise a two-part, simultaneous process. Taking up is the cutting of the warp yarns to remove a finished length of fabric from the loom, and letting off is the beginning of a new piece of fabric where the warp yarns are attached to the cloth beam.

The power loom is far faster and more efficient than the hand loom. Today they are primarily computer-controlled. Fabrics are cut from the last of the warp threads with a laser instead of with scissors, another technique that speeds production.

Attachments to the power loom create variations such as embroidered detail (lappet, swivel embellishment) or dobby patterns.

Types of Weaves

Weaving can be distinguished or categorized by the order of interlacing. There are five basic weaves: the *plain* weave, the *twill* weave, the *satin* weave, the *jacquard* weave, and the *pile* weave. These weaves are described and illustrated below, together with a list of some of the fabrics constructed with each weave. Decorative and support fabrics, marked with an ending asterisk*, may also be constructed in a different weave as well. For example, many casement textiles are plain weave, but they are also often needle constructions: rachel knits, malimo, and arnache.

The Plain Weave

The plain weave may be accomplished on box and backstrap looms, the floor/jack/hand-operated loom, or the power loom. It is the simplest type of interlacing: one weft or filling yarn over and one under one weft yarn—or, in other words, an interlacing of one over and one under in a regular order. It is also called the **taffeta** weave and the **tabby**

Figure 4.10a
Plain, regular, or tabby weave

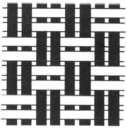

Figure 4.10b
Basketweave, plain weave variation

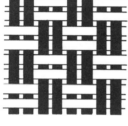

Figure 4.10c
Leno weave, plain weave variation

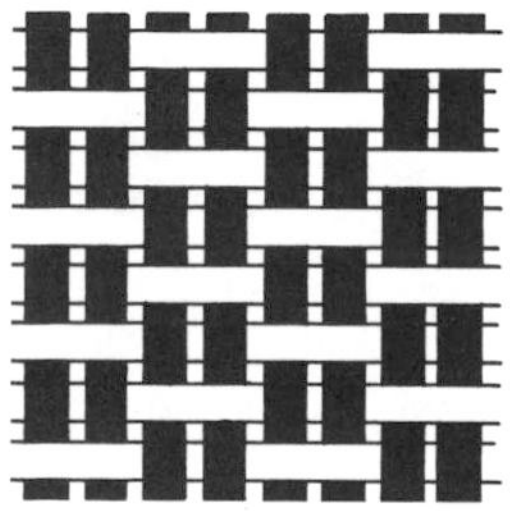

Figure 4.10d
Oxford weave, plain weave variation

Figure 4.10e The Power Loom makes textile construction efficient. *Audrey M. Pecott.*

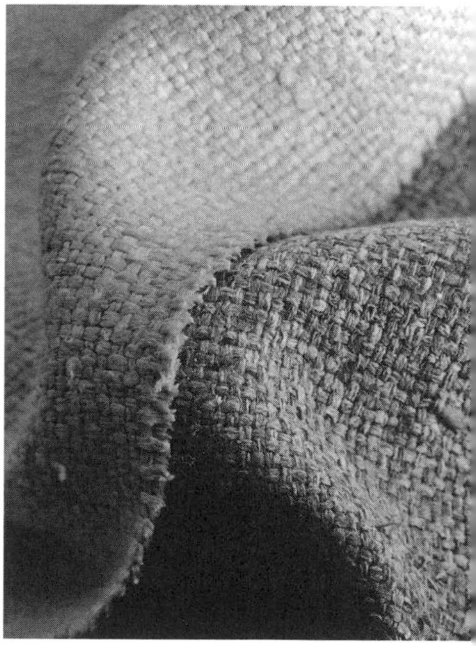

Figure 4.10f The plain weave is evident in "Sauvage," French for "savage." This 100 percent tussah organic raw silk is spun from wild silk cocoons after the moths have escaped, giving the silk a thicker, less delicate nature. The nondyed fibers become natural colors. *Photo by Edward Addeo. Product by Donghia, Inc.*

Figure 4.10g A plain weave, "Gatsby" is a multipurpose classic American seersucker with contrasting smooth and puckered surfaces achieved by slack tension weaving. *Photo by Edward Addeo. Product by Donghia, Inc.*

weave, and because the technique is used in hand tapestry weaving, it is also called the **tapestry** weave, not to be confused with tapestry fabric, which is usually woven on Jacquard looms.

Plain weaves may be woven into thin, sheer, lightweight, medium-weight, or heavyweight textiles, and even into floor coverings such as tapestry-weave rugs. The plain weave is very versatile. Through variations in the interlacing order or through the addition of more warp or weft yarns or with an attachment to the loom, dozens of plain-weave fabrics are used in today's interiors.

Balanced Plain Weave

A balanced plain weave has an even, orderly interlacing of yarns where each warp yarn is interlaced with a single weft or filling yarn, or pick. The count of balanced plain weaves is the number of warp yarns over the number of weft yarns; it is a unit of measurement for sheeting and fine cloths, as discussed in chapter 11. Higher thread counts are due to the fineness of the yarns, as fine yarns can be woven more tightly.

Balanced plain weaves may be woven of yarns of varying sizes or denier, yarns inconsistent in diameter and profile, or complex or novelty yarns, giving textural interest to the face of the cloth.

Balanced plain weave examples: go to www.wiley.com/go /interiortextiles for fabric glossary definitions.

Sheers and semisheer fabrics —angeline, batiste, casement*, cheesecloth/gauze, cheviot*, chiffon, China silk, crepe, crepe chiffon, cretonne, dimity, eolienne, georgette, lawn, net, ninon, organdy, organza, semi-organdy, sheer, Swiss, tarlatan, tergal, tissue, voile, French voile

Lightweight opaque fabrics —batik, broadcloth, buckram/crinoline*, calico, cambric, challis, chambray*, crepe de chine, dimity, eponge, eyelet, gingham, lining*, madras, muslin, nainsook, nun's veiling, percale, percaline, plissé, printed paisley* , seersucker, sheeting, taffeta*

Medium-weight fabrics —bark cloth, butcher linen, chintz, crepe, cretonne, flannel*, flannelette, granite cloth, homespun, hopsacking, interfacing*, interlining*, jaspé/strié/ombre*, khaki*, lamé*, lampas*, lining, osnaburg, plaid*, rajah*, tabby cloth, tartan*, toile*, union cloth*

Heavyweight fabrics —art linen, bouclé/poodle cloth, canvas*, felt (woven, abraded)*, chenille, grass cloth, Holland cloth, interlining*, oatmeal cloth, ratiné, repp, suedecloth*, tapestry*, tartan*, tattersall, tweed, union cloth*

Plain Weave Variations

Many fabrics in interior design are variations of the plain weave. Some of these are balanced, but many are unbalanced, meaning that two or more yarns may be carried as one, either warp or weft direction, or that the yarns are of differing sizes or woven in such a way that the one-over-one-under sequence is inconsistent.

Plain weave variation examples: basket weave, crammed or rib weave, dobby weave, hand-loomed tapestry, lapped or swivel weave, leno or doup weave, oxford weave, piqué weave

These are described, with examples, below.

Basket weave The basket weave is a plain weave variation where groups of two or more yarns are carried as one. In balanced basket weaves, the number of grouped yarns is the same in both the warp and weft directions, producing an even pattern. Typically seen are yarns grouped to interlace two-over-two, three-over-three, and four-over-four. Unbalanced basket weaves have groups of yarns that are not even. Warp or weft threads, or both, may be grouped in a sequence of two, then four, then three, for example. Oxford cloth and duck are unbalanced basketweaves that carry two fine warp threads as one interlaced with one slightly heavier weft thread.

Balanced basket weave examples: basketweave cloth, casement,* tweed*

Unbalanced basket weave examples: duck/sailcloth, khaki,* oxford cloth, tweed,* union cloth*

Note: Go to www.wiley.com/go/interiortextiles for fabric glossary definitions.

Crammed or Ribbed Weave This variation of the plain weave produces raised, rounded ribs accomplished either by pushing more yarns tightly together in one direction (warp or weft) or by weaving larger yarns in one direction. Ribbed fabrics are usually accomplished by weaving heavier weft yarns, yielding a horizontal or crosswise rib. The fabrics listed here all have crosswise ribs except piqué, which has lengthwise ribs (see also "Piqué Weave" below)

Crammed weave examples: bengaline, corded fabric, faille, grosgrain ribbon, moiré, ottoman, piqué, poplin, taffeta*

Note: Go to www.wiley.com/go/interiortextiles for fabric glossary definitions.

Hand-Loomed Tapestry This category of plain weave goods refers to fabric produced by hand by either native or ethnic artisans or modern or contemporary craftspersons. The pattern may be constructed as the artisan proceeds, and the motifs are often simple, abstract, and primitive or ethnic. Looms may be upright looms or similar to jack looms. The artisan may or may not follow a pattern or cartoon.

Hand-loomed tapestry examples: hand-loomed tapestry, Aubusson rugs and tapestries, Bessarabian rugs, dhurrie rugs, kilim rugs, Navajo rugs, rya rugs, flokatti rugs, other flat ethnic rugs, wall tapestries (artistic, one of a kind).

Note: See chapter 13 and www.wiley.com/go/interiortextiles for rug glossary definitions.

Leno or Doup Weave This plain weave variation constructs the cloth so a twisted hourglass design is seen in the vertical or warp yarns spaced across the face of the goods. The repeat of the leno or doup crisscross pattern can be very fine and fairly closely woven (although not tight), as in the semisheer fabrics listed below. In coarser fabric, such as casement, the repeat is usually 1 to 4 inches with, typically, an open weave, although the yarns can vary from fine to ply or novelty.

Note: A faux leno or doup is seen where yarns are woven to come together in hourglass fashion but do not twist or overlap.

Leno or doup weave examples: bouclé marquisette, casement,* gauze,* grenadine, leno, marquisette

Note: Go to www.wiley.com/go/interiortextiles for fabric glossary definitions.

Piqué Weave A piqué weave is a plain weave variation accomplished with a dobby loom attachment. It yields raised lengthwise cords or geometric designs in the fabric, creating a three-dimensional effect. Piqué fabrics vary from semisheer dimity to heavyweight waffle cloth. The third dimension may appear to be embossed or stamped patterns.

Piqué weave examples: dimity, Bedford cord, bengaline, bird's eye, gooseye, huckaback or diaper cloth, waffle weave/cloth

Note: Go to www.wiley.com/go/interiortextiles for fabric glossary definitions.

Oxford Weave This is a simple variation of the plain weave where two finer warp yarns interlace around a larger or heavier weft yarn. The relative weights and consistencies of the yarns are determiners of the decorative fabric. Men's shirting oxford cloth (not an interiors textile but familiar to many people) is very fine and smooth, whereas canvas is heavy, stiff, and sturdy.

Oxford weave examples: awning cloth, duck/sailcloth, canvas,* chambray,* poplin, oxford cloth, sailcloth, toile*

Note: Go to www.wiley.com/go/interiortextiles for fabric glossary definitions.

Dobby Weave

The dobby weave is typically a plain weave background cloth, although it may be twill or satin weave. Its defining characteristic is a small geometric pattern woven into the cloth. Typical patterns are diamonds, squares, dots, shells, diagonal slashes, and short lines. The pattern repeat is under 4 inches and is often a drop repeat, where vertical lines of dobby patterns are staggered to fall horizontally between flanking lines. In other words, every other line matches, and the alternate lines are placed halfway between them. Dobby fabrics are plain weave variations.

Dobby weave examples: armure, bird's eye, dobby cloth, gooseye, huckaback or diaper cloth, waffle weave/cloth

Note: Go to www.wiley.com/go/interiortextiles for fabric glossary definitions.

Lappet or Swivel Weave

Typically woven into a plain weave background, this is a woven ornamentation technique where a pattern is embroidered in discontinuous spots, dots, or motifs, or creates a small isolated fringe or novelty effect. The term *swivel* indicates that an embroidery arm can swivel across the face of the cloth to accomplish the surface ornamentation.

Lappet or swivel weave examples: dotted Swiss (embroidered), eyelash, eyelet (embroidered), lappet embroidery

Note: Go to www.wiley.com/go/interiortextiles for fabric glossary definitions.

The Twill Weave

The twill weave is accomplished by weaving one weft yarn over a warp, then skipping two, three, or four, and then interlacing under one, called the *tie-down*. The twill weave produces sturdy textiles with a raised diagonal cord or *wale*. The direction of the wale can be a left-hand twill—proceeding upward to the left on the face of the fabric—or a right-hand twill—from lower left to upper right. The pitch of the wale varies from low to steep. Because twill weaves typically yield stout textiles, the yarns most commonly used are cotton, nylon, and wool, which also accounts for their sturdiness. Twill weaves are categorized into regular or balanced twill weaves and novelty or unbalanced twill weaves.

Figure 4.11a Balanced twill weave with floating weft

Figure 4.11b Twill weave with floating warp

Figure 4.11c The Raffia Textures collection features (clockwise from left to right): a luxurious chevron twill pattern reminiscent of Japanese ikebana baskets; a plain weave variation that achieves the look of woven leather; a fabric with a hemp-style basket texture; and a wickerlike plain weave. *Photo courtesy of Highland Court, 800-387-2533 www.highlandcourtfabrics.com.*

Regular or Balanced Twill Weave A regular or balanced twill weave interlaces yarns in the same manner throughout the fabric, so the wale never changes direction. This method is used in textiles that are somewhat smooth, even, and necessarily predictable. Regular or balanced twill weave textiles are frequently multipurpose, medium weight fabrics.

> *Regular twill weave examples:* broadcloth*, cheviot, chinchilla cloth, chino, denim, drill, duvetyn, flannel*, jean, khaki*, gabardine, granada, rajah*, serge, surrah, tartan* ticking, tricotine, tweed, twill

Note: Go to www.wiley.com/go/interiortextiles for fabric glossary definitions.

Novelty or Unbalanced Twill Weave This variation of the twill weave yields fabrics with different face designs achieved by reversing or changing the direction of the twill from a right-hand to a left-hand interlacing sequence. For example, the herringbone or chevron design reverses on a regular basis, creating an even zigzag design. The woven flame-stitch pattern reverses irregularly, creating the uneven leaping flames. The houndstooth pattern is a check with a dog/canine-tooth appendage near the corner on the flat side of the check square. Novelty tweed may change the direction in seemingly unpredictable ways; this develops a random effect in the unbalanced twill, which enhances the rugged or casual texture of the tweed.

> *Novelty, compound, or unbalanced twill examples:* barathea, charvet, herringbone, flame stitch (woven pattern), houndstooth, chevron, novelty tweed, tartan

Note: Go to www.wiley.com/go/interiortextiles for fabric glossary definitions.

The Satin Weave

The satin weave is accomplished by floating a fine warp yarn over several (up to eight) weft yarns, then tying down that one yarn. A tie-down is where the yarn interlaces perpendicularly. The order of interlacing may be less even. The face texture is smooth and without a determined pattern (no rib, wale, or woven pattern is discernible). The fact that yarns selected for satin weaves are typically fine, smooth, and lustrous also accounts for the smooth sheen of the face. Historically and before the invention of manufactured fibers, all satins were silk; the word *satin* is derived from the port city of Zaytoun, China. Hence, silk and satin have been near synonyms for hundreds of years. Today, however, satin is also woven of very fine yarns of rayon, acetate, and polyester that imitate silk.

Antique satin is a cloth construction that imitates shantung silk. The satin weave is woven with heavier, slub weft or filler yarns, creating a slightly ribbed surface.

> *Satin weave examples:* amazon cloth, antique satin, charmeuse, ombré/strié, peau de peche, satin, shantung,* upholstery satin

Note: Go to www.wiley.com/go/interiortextiles for fabric glossary definitions.

Sateen or Satine Weave The sateen or satine weave, a variation of the satin weave, appears in two ways: (1) a cotton textile woven in a satin weave, called a *warp sateen,* which

Figure 4.12a Satin weave floats a fine warp yarn over as many as eight weft yarns.

Figure 4.12b "Byzance," a trimming collection by Houlès, is laid over smooth, lustrous satin weave fabric. *Image courtesy of Houlès-USA.*

is the base cloth for nearly all cotton prints that are slightly heavier than chintz, broadcloth, or muslin, or (2) the interlacing of yarns so the weft yarns float and are tied down by warp yarns. This is also called a *horizontal satin*.

Sateen or satine weave examples: drapery lining,* polished cotton, sateen/satine, warp sateen

Note: Go to www.wiley.com/go/interiortextiles for fabric glossary definitions.

Satin-Jacquard Combination Weave The satin weave is often used as the background weave in jacquard fabrics that are more smooth or formal, where the goal is a lustrous background. This is nearly always seen as coverings (ticking) of new mattresses, where the fabric must appear luxurious, and in many drapery and upholstery Jacquards. The manufactured fibers (rayon, acetate, and polyester) usually appear shiny and slick, and cotton textiles are usually matte in texture.

Satin-jacquard combination weave examples: brocade, brocatelle, cotton damask, damask (any fiber), lampas, and single damask

Note: Go to www.wiley.com/go/interiortextiles for fabric glossary definitions.

The Jacquard Weave

The Jacquard weave is named for the inventor of the loom attachment that makes it possible. In 1901, Joseph Marie Jacquard developed a remarkable way of creating large, complex designs. The warp yarns were threaded through special heddles, each attached to a vertical cord with a weighted needle at the top. In Jacquard's day, as the shed opened, some warp yarns were lifted by allowing the heddle at the top of the heddle cord to pass through a punched hole in a card—similar to the original computer cards of the 1960s. Heddles that struck the card did not raise that particular warp end (single warp yarn). The design had to be hand-calculated, one interlacing at a time, and the Jacquard loom had to be threaded and sequenced by hand. These were both lengthy processes. However, once the design was determined and the loom threaded, the ability to quickly manufacture woven designs of nearly any size and complexity was realized. This was a vast improvement in time and efficiency over hand-weaving methods, and it made Jacquard fabrics available and affordable to a much wider range of potential purchasers.

The Jacquard loom today is completely computerized. Not only are computers used to design the textile but also the patterns are stored on hard disks, which control the loom. The patterns can be changed not by rethreading the loom but by a computer command, even when the loom is in production. The background or ground cloth of a Jacquard weave can be plain weave, satin weave, twill weave, or a combination of weaves.

Jacquard weave examples: Aubusson, brocade, brocatelle, damask, flame stitch,* Jacquard, lampas, matelasse, needlepoint (patterned, combined with pile), paisley (woven pattern), single damask, tapestry, velvet* (cut and moquette, combined with pile weave)

Note: Go to www.wiley.com/go/interiortextiles for fabric glossary definitions.

Figure 4.13a The Jacquard weave interlaces yarns to achieve a woven pattern.

Figure 4.13b "Labyrinth" is a Jacquard damask of 78 percent cotton and 22 percent silk, inspired by an antique Chinese textile. *Photo by Edward Addeo. Product by Donghia, Inc.*

Figure 4.13c "Flora Noblis," from the Highland Court Tapestry collection, is a jacquard-weave bouquet design of stylized peonies, leaves, and buds on a sharply contrasting black ground. *Photo courtesy of Highland Court, 800-387-2533, www.highlandcourtfabrics.com.*

The Pile Weave

The pile weave creates a third dimension, depth, or face pile in textiles. It is accomplished in one of two ways. In warp piles, an extra set of warp threads is woven around wires. Then the wires are removed and the loops cut into a cut pile, or they are left round and looped, called an *uncut pile*.

Another method of creating a cut pile is to weave two textiles face-to-face, then cut the pile yarns that connect them to produce two cut pile textiles. This method is often employed in constructing velvet. It can produce varying depths, from short-pile velveteen to deep-pile upholstery velvet.

Pile fabrics can be embossed or panné finished, as discussed in chapter 4. Pile fabrics and carpeting can also be combined with the Jacquard weave, as in the case of cut, jacquard, and moquette velvets. Axminster and Wilton carpets are pile weave textiles, discussed in chapter 12. Another approach is to shear or cut the pile to different heights. The result is called *sculptured pile* or *pile on pile*.

Pile weave examples: Axminster carpet, corduroy, frieze, needlepoint (all types), terry cloth, velvet (all types), velvet carpet, Wilton carpet

Note: See chapter 12 and www.wiley.com/go/interiortextiles for fabric glossary definitions.

Figure 4.14 This pile weave, "Roy," is a 100 percent cotton striped chenille corduroy, both functional and attractive. *Photo by Edward Addeo. Product by Donghia, Inc.*

Combination Weaves

It is common to combine two or more weaves in a textile to achieve a result such as woven stripes (crammed weave and satin weave) or many jacquard damasks (satin background, jacquard figures). Twill weave and plain weave may also form the background for jacquard-woven textiles. Novelty tweed textiles often include plain and twill weaves in interesting combinations or patterns. A host of other fabrics are made of two or more weaves, and they are identified by the decorative names or the duplicity of weaves.

NEEDLE CONSTRUCTIONS

Needle-constructed textiles constitute a broad category of textiles that achieve various effects, including knits and lacy or open-constructed textiles. Handmade needle-constructed fabrics in interior design have played a key role in furnishings as accessories or small upholstery fabrics. Examples include knitted or crocheted afghans, throws, pillows, and accessory items. These can contribute a personal stamp of creativity to a home. Handmade laces such as doilies, dresser scarves, or runners protected (and perhaps still do) fine furniture from being scratched by objects of art. Lace has many uses, including curtains, bed canopies and hangings, bed skirts, pillow tops, and even altar covers in churches.

Mass-produced needle-constructed fabrics are a significant part of textile manufacturing today. They include machine knitting, malimo and arnache, tufting, and passementerie.

Note: Go to www.wiley.com/go/interiortextiles for fabric glossary definitions.

KNITTING

Knitting is the process of interlacing a single yarn into fabric. Hand-knitted textiles are constructed with a pair of knitting needles. Such needles come in many sizes; the size is chosen according to the size of the yarn. Machine knitting utilizes hundreds of needles on complex machines. Knitting has limited usage in interiors, although it is extensively used in the apparel market.

Hand-Knitted Textiles

Hand-knitted textiles in interior design are limited to afghans or throws, hot pads, and craft accessory items. They are a somewhat contemporary application compared to the history of handmade lace (below). The design integrity of knitted textiles for the home varies: Some knitted afghans are lofty, soft, and beautiful, and, if relatively neutral in color, have long-lasting appeal. Hand-crocheted baby blankets can be treasured items. On the other hand, some craft items are incidental and of questionable design quality— brightly colored knitted toilet paper roll holders, for example. Color and yarn selection have a great deal to do with the beauty and long-term appropriateness of the finished items.

Hand-knitted examples: afghans or knitted blankets, hot pads, craft accessory items

Machine Knitting

Circular knitting machines yield jersey-knit or single-knit textiles, double knits, and stretch knits. Single- or jersey-knit textiles, particularly of nylon, including tricot, are used for some bedding and limp draped applications. The heavier double knit may be used for upholstery, but stretch knit is more likely used for modern sculptural upholstered pieces that require fabric that hugs the form.

Knitted textile examples: jersey or single knit, tricot, double knit, milanese, suede cloth, stretch-knit upholstery fabric

Note: Go to www.wiley.com/go/interiortextiles for fabric glossary definitions.

Rachel or Raschel Knits

The rachel or raschel knit is a needle-construction method of producing casement drapery fabrics. It is also called a *warp knit.* Here, the horizontal yarns—often unusual novelty yarns—are held together by knitting very fine thread, sometimes fine, clear monofilament, spaced vertically, or in the lengthwise warp direction. The fabric is semisheer with novelty effects. Rachel knits can construct fabrics up to 118 inches wide for seamless draperies (see chapter 10).

Rachel or raschel knit examples: Rachel or raschel knit, casement*

Note: Go to www.wiley.com/go/interiortextiles for fabric glossary definitions.

Malimo and Arnache

These needle-construction methods produce drapery casement fabrics quickly and economically. Malimo or maliwatt fabrics, named after the respective machines on which they are produced, which were invented in Germany, are constructed by laying down banks of weft yarns and then interlocking them with a lace-like interlocking stitch in a clear, fine monofilament. These banks or swatches of yarns may not lie perfectly straight but may overlap each other in a random horizontal manner. Arnache textiles are similar, but just one yarn at a time is inserted, creating a more precisely even or horizontal appearance. In both the malimo and arnache constructions, a nonwoven substrate layer can be laminated or stitched to the surface so the fabric becomes translucent rather than semisheer, useful for installation where privacy is important.

Malimo and arnache examples: Malimo, maliwatt, arnache, casement*

Note: Go to www.wiley.com/go/interiortextiles for fabric glossary definitions.

NEEDLE CONSTRUCTION: LACE

Handmade Lace

Handmade lace is a centuries-old art form that afficionados believe constitutes the way "real lace" is created. There are five handmade lace techniques: bobbin or pillow lace, needlepoint or point lace, tatting, tape lace, and crocheted lace.

Note: Go to www.wiley.com/go/interiortextiles for fabric glossary definitions.

Bobbin or Pillow Lace
Bobbin or pillow lace takes its name from the bobbins used to pull the threads tight during the process; pins hold the work in progress to a pillow form. A design is first created by pricking holes in paper; the pins go into the holes to act as guides for the threads. Complex designs may require hundreds of bobbins. Bobbin lace is traditionally used for window treatments, tablecloths, and accessory items such as pillows.

Bobbin lace examples: Antwerp, Binche, Brabant, Bruges, Chantilly, Cluny, duchess, genoese, milanese, rosaline

Needlepoint or Point Lace
This lacemaking technique spread throughout Europe during the Renaissance. It is a type of embroidery using a needle in a buttonhole stitch. Needlepoint or point lace is also used for window treatments, table covers, and accessory items.

Needlepoint lace examples: Alençon, argentan, gros point, rose point, point de France, reseau

Tatted Lace
Tatted lace is the most recent handmade lace, being invented in the mid-nineteenth century. Tatting is made by knotting thread in a lark's-head knot or stitch with a very small shuttle. The stitches are tied together in circles or along a foundation thread, with decorative loops protruding from the circles. Tatted lace is used for edges and trimmings.

Tape Lace
This technique involves weaving thin strips of plain weave to form leaves or flowers by folding corners to make curves and points, then filling in the spaces with a looped stitch. The leaves are held together with slack-twisted thread. Tape lace is usually made of linen or cotton and is the form most often used in Battenberg lace, imported from China or Europe. In interiors, Battenberg consists of cotton tape lace sewn onto cotton muslin or percale in white, off-white, or pale colors. It is used for bed linens, window treatments, and accessory items.

Crocheted Lace
Crocheting is the interlooping of a single yarn to form a pattern. To form lace, the yarn is typically the size of a sturdy, thick thread. A single instrument, the crochet hook, about the size of a pencil, is thin, with a small hook used to catch and loop yarns together. Crocheted lace can form the edging of textiles, such as pillowcase or blanket edging, or it may be used for an allover lace piece suitable for coverlets or altar covers, for example.

Machine-Made Lace or Leaver Lace

Machines that produce lace were first invented by Englishmen John Heathcoat and John Leavers in the early nineteenth century. Today, lacemaking machines work on many of the same principles as the original mechanisms. Machine-made lace is even and nearly flawless, compared to the potential inconsistencies in handmade lace. However, lace purists sometimes refer to machine lace as "imitation lace" because it does not possess the character and labor of love of handmade lace. Machine-made lace is typically seen as floral or geometric patterns on a background of hexagonal or geometric mesh or net. The weight of this lace varies from fine and thin to heavy, with heavier yarns imitating cotton lace. Machine-made lace mainly is imported from Europe, with a few sources in the United States.

For window treatments, lace yardage is available in America in a wide variety of styles in widths of 24, 36, 48, 54, 72, 104, and 118 inches. Curtain lace often has finished edges such as scallops. Valance and café curtain lace yardage may also have a finished heading, some with large loops through which a curtain rod may be inserted as self-curtain rings. Other laces have slit openings so ribbon can be threaded vertically to create a poufed shade or decorative effect. Some lace that is 24 to 30 inches wide is scalloped on both selvages to become finished French door panels.

Most machine lace is polyester and can be safely washed or dry-cleaned. Because of this, machine-made lace can be made into nearly any type of window treatment, decorative bedding, table linens, accessory items, and trimmings. Polyester laces are dimensionally stable and, when layered with a lining fabric, can be fabricated into items that typically require light- to medium-weight opaque textiles. The same names are used for machine-made and handmade laces, but of course the machine-made laces are imitations of a particular style. More often, the manufacturer or jobber who has purchased piece yardage from a lace manufacturer will give each lace a pattern name to identify it within the line of goods.

Lace construction without pattern is called net and comes in different sizes and weights. *Mesh* is large, *net* is a medium scale, and *tulle* is very fine net. Net is used for underling to give fullness and stiffness, such as for bed skirts. Net may also be used for window and bed drapery for decorative purposes. *Mosquito netting* is gauze, a plain, loosely woven semisheer textile with a netlike appearance. It is draped over beds to keep the sleeping occupant safe from mosquitoes. Such netting also may be used decoratively.

> *Machine-made lace examples:* lace named by manufacturer or jobber, Nottingham lace, imitations of handmade laces, mesh, net, tulle

Figure 4.15a This Victorian-style machine-made or leavers lace softens the practical hard edge of 2-inch metal blinds. *Photo compliments of Comfortex Window Fashions.*

Figure 4.15b Swagged machine-made lace in this Empire-style room is featured at windows.

Figure 4.16a Tassels, fringe, braid, and gimp are all part of this "Arthur" passementerie collection. *Image courtesy of Houlès-USA.*

Figure 4.16b Tassels on rope tie-backs and drapery edge strings are part of this exclusive "Paloma" passementerie collection. *Image courtesy of Houlès-USA.*

TUFTED TEXTILES

Tufting is the insertion of yarns into a nonwoven or plain weave base fabric in order to create a pile. The yarns can be cut or uncut. In carpeting, there must be an application of latex or another compound to hold the back of the tufted yarns in place. Most tufted textiles are broadloom carpeting (see chapter 12), although some velour and chenille textiles are tufted. Tufted bedspreads have Colonial or Victorian patterns. Bath mats or rugs are also tufted: cotton without a backing and nylon or polyester with a rubber backing that eventually peels or flakes off with age and exposure to heat from washing and drying. Cold-water washing and line drying extend the life of the rubber backing.

Tufting examples: broadloom tufted carpeting, upholstery velour,* tufted bedspreads, bath mats, throw rugs

Note: See chapter 13 and for fabric glossary definitions go to www.wiley.com/go/interiortextiles.

PASSEMENTERIE

Passementerie is manufactured trimmings: fringe, gimp, tassels, cord, and braid. The processes for creating passementerie are hand methods related to lacemaking, often automated. Trimmings are made by twisting, knotting, and weaving in various configurations with fine silk, rayon, polyester, or cotton threads or yarns. Some trimmings are made with coarser cord or of less refined or natural linen or cotton fibers. Fringe and tassels are used for trimming draperies, upholstery, pillows, and bedding. Large tassels held with cord are used as tie-backs. Smaller key tassels, named because they were historically attached to a house key as a sort of key chain, are often used as accents hung on a drawer handle or arranged as part of a grouping of small accessory items. Gimp and deep boullé fringe is used to cover upholstery tacks or in place of an upholstery skirt on chairs, sofas, or ottomans respectively. Boullé fringe was originally fashionable in the Victorian era.

Passementerie examples: braid or galloon, flat braid or galloon, raised openwork braid or galloon, border, cord and rope cord, barrier rope, cord tie-backs, rail rope or stair cord, fringe, base fringe, boullé or bullion fringe, cut moss or moss-edge fringe, fine-cut fringe, glass bead fringe, loop fringe, netted tassel fringe, rat-tail fringe, tassel fringe, multitasseled fringe, wood mold fringe, gimp or guimpe, flat gimp, raised-surface gimp, corded gimp, grosgrain, ribbon, rosettes, bows, tufts, frogs, tie-backs, tassels, chair tassels, chair ties, chandelier tassels, key tassels, tassel tie-backs

Note: See www.wiley.com/go/interiortextiles for passamenterie definitions.

COMPOUND TEXTILE CONSTRUCTION

Textiles that consist of more than one layer are termed compound (cloth) textiles. They are produced via hand or hand-guided machine constructions, so many compound textiles have a one-of-a-kind flavor or character. Types include embroidery, quilting and appliqué, and laminated or bonded and coated fabrics. These categories vary from handmade to mass-produced, from residential-only applications to a broad range of nonresidential specified product installations.

Note: Go to www.wiley.com/go/interiortextiles for fabric glossary definitions.

Embroidery

Embroidery is a form of compound cloth construction where a fabric, complete in itself before being embellished, or printed or unprinted scrim or art cloth, is ornamented with designs from a threaded needle. There are several well-respected forms of embroidery: needlepoint, crewel, candlewicking, cross-stitch, fancywork, and categories of machine embroidery.

Needlepoint

Needlepoint is a hand-embroidery form where rounded stitches fill the base scrim or needlepoint cloth completely. The resulting piece is heavy and stiff. Needlepoint is used for upholstery, pillow tops, hand-made rugs/carpeting, and framed wall art. Very small stitches are termed *petit point,* and very large stitches are called *gros point.* Needlepoint is an artistic pastime and hobby for many people. Commercially produced needlepoint rugs originated in Portugal and are now produced for lower cost in China. Manufactured fabrics that imitate handmade needlepoint include uncut frieze (single-color pile weave or combined with patterned jacquard weave) and velvet moquette (pile and Jacquard combination weaves). Jacquard weave tapestry fabric may also imitate common needlepoint designs (dark and floral) and thus be a type of trompe l'oeil or fool-the-eye-trickery. Tapestry can be comparable in sturdiness to needlepoint. Jobbers or manufacturers may give names as needlepoint, petit point, and gros point fabrics, even though they are technically imitations of authentic hand-embroidered needlepoint.

Crewel Embroidery

Crewel embroidery is hand- or machine-embroidered designs on a coarse, medium-weight plain weave cotton, linen, or wool cloth—cretonne, monk's cloth, or basket weave—

Figure 4.17a "Tudor Garden," 100 percent worsted wool crewel embroidery hand-stitched on a hand-loomed cotton, is a nineteenth-century English Jacobean–inspired tree-of-life design. *Photo courtesy of Highland Court. 800-387-2533, www.highlandcourtfabrics.com.*

Figure 4.17b Subtle and sophisticated "Linen Brode'" is an example of schiffli embroidery. *Photo courtesy of MASTERS OF LINEN: European Linen of Quality.*

in a neutral or natural beige. The crewel stitch is a looped chain stitch in a coarse, woolen yarn, off-white, a variety of single colors, or multicolored. The crewel stitches form designs of rambling tree branches or vines with a variety of leaves, flowers, and exotic fruit.

Originating in India in tree-of-life patterns, crewel became a popular domestic embroidery form during the Elizabethan age and the spin-off Colonial years in America. Crewel embroidery can be accomplished by hand as a needlework project. However, jobber yardage for interior applications is hand-guided machine-embroidery and imported for the Western market primarily from India today. Crewel embroidery is used as bed coverlets, bed skirts, drapery and top treatments (particularly pelmets), upholstery, pillow and cushion covers, and decorative table covers and accessories. It can be used lavishly as the only furnishing fabric or as a single accessory. Crewel has authentic acceptance as the front, back, or allover upholstery of early Georgian Queen Anne wing chairs. Its use historically dates to the Medieval English and to the Colonial periods in America (seventeenth-century American Colonial and American Early and Late Georgian periods).

Candlewicking

Candlewicking is an embroidery form similar to crewel, and an imitation of it developed during American Colonial years. Lacking woolen crewel yarns, embroiderers used the cotton cord made for candle wicks as embroidery yarn. These cords were all natural and uncolored. Patterns are similar to crewel, but smaller and lighter in scale and less complicated. Candlewick is also a less sturdy fabric, based on muslin or osnaburg fabric, and so is used mostly for bedding, window treatments, and accessory items.

Cross-Stitch and Fancywork

Cross-stitch and **fancywork** are other forms of hand embroidery that find many decorative uses in historic and contemporary interiors. Cross-stitch and fancywork embroidery projects are sold in packages at craft and needlework stores, where the fabric is typically a white cotton broadcloth with a stamped design; the kit may even include the embroidery floss to do the work. Counted cross-stitch is executed on a cross-stitch art cloth or canvas where the embroiderer follows a pattern printed on a piece of paper, counting the number of squares in the fabric, then embroidering stitches that are categorized as fancywork.

During the Colonial era, it was common for adolescent girls to learn a variety of cross- and fancywork stitches by creating a sampler. Authentic samplers that date to the Colonial period are collectors' items and seen as framed art in museums and in Colonial-style homes. Today, samplers can be purchased and accomplished as a piece of wall art.

As late as the mid-twentieth century in the United States, a bride's dowry was not considered complete without hand-embroidered pillowcases and kitchen linens. In many developing countries today, hand embroidery is still alive as a revered domestic embellishment.

The fabric to be embroidered in cross-stitch and fancywork must be held taut. Two types of frames are used: embroidery hoops, which are pairs of circular hoops, held in the hand, that clamp the fabric tight in a radius of 5 to 20 inches, and freestanding frames, which are used for larger projects.

Cross-stitch and fancywork examples: pillow and quilt tops, open edges of pillowcases, kitchen and dining linens, samplers, framed and pictorial calligraphy designs such as family trees or embroidered inspirational phrases

Machine and Schiffli Embroidery

Machine embroidery can be accomplished on a small scale with domestic sewing machines. For commercial monogramming and embroidery, the machines are run by computers. Monogram work is useful in interiors for initials on bath towels for homes or hospitality design, bath mats, and pillow shams, for example.

Schiffli embroidery is the process whereby mass-produced textiles are embroidered after the fabric is constructed. Schiffli is utilized where the patterns are complex and the amount of thread or yarn used in the embroidery is generous. Like other machine processes, schiffli is computerized, giving substantial freedom of design, from large scale to small areas, from floral patterns to monogrammed designs or isolated motifs.

Machine embroidery is also seen as lappet and swivel weaves that create simple patterns such as eyelet and dotted Swiss. These were discussed above under plain weave variations.

Machine and schiffli embroidery examples: embroidered sheers, motif-embroidered upholstery, bath and table linen embroidered work, including commercial applications

Quilting and Appliqué

Quilting is the process of stitching together two or more layers of fabric with thread or by a fusion process. Here we discuss hand quilting and appliqué; we cover forms of machine

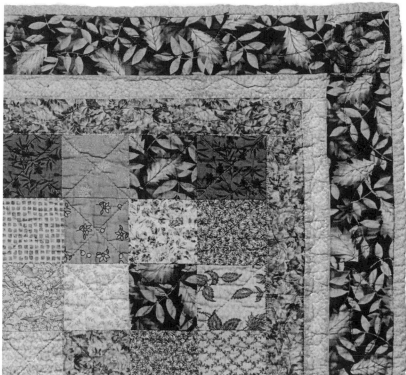

Figure 4.18 "Angelina," a paisley in the tradition of Indian couture embroidery, is a contemporary tone-on-tone in 100 percent cotton ground and 100 percent rayon embroidery. *Photo by Edward Addeo. Product by Donghia, Inc.*

Figure 4.19 This simple two-block pieced quilt by Lynn Lonsdale illustrates the enduring charm of the pattern. Each handmade quilt is unique, with individual fabric selections and placement. The curved lines indicate hand quilting. Needle artisan skills are receiving renewed interest and popularity. *Photo by Gordon Lonsdale.*

quilting next.) Many people today have once again become involved in the art of hand and machine quilting, making quilting both a traditional and a contemporary skill. It is a pleasurable pastime and a meaningful expression of fabric artistry. It is also a way of producing income for fabric artisans both in America and abroad.

Hand Quilting

Hand quilting is the method of layering fabrics and then stitching them together to form one unit. Quilting is a folk art and handicraft form as well as a fabric construction method utilized in many countries, including the United States. Even though today the vast majority of blankets and bedding is mass-produced, quilt-making as a hobby is alive and well, and handmade quilts and pillows are available for purchase through specialty sources and catalogs or direct from quiltmakers.

Quilting is accomplished by marking a pattern with a marking pencil on a fabric, usually a cotton or cotton-polyester broadcloth, nylon tricot, or other lightweight opaque textile. The markings wash out after the quilt is completed. Fabrics are deliberately shrunk prior to marking, but they typically pucker a little with subsequent washing. This adds to the charm of a handmade piece. A layer of polyester quilt batting is sandwiched between the marked quilt top and the plain or printed backing, and the layers are pinned together. This fabric sandwich is secured to a quilting frame. Traditional quilt frames allowed several quilters to be seated on the four sides and to work simultaneously to sew the layers together. This arrangement makes for a social activity known as a *quilting bee,* where industrious quilters visit as they work, creating a pleasant buzz as they laugh and exchange stories.

Contemporary quilt frames may be compact and roll the fabric like a scroll from each end so the quilt can be managed by one or two quilters. Wood is the traditional quilting frame material, although frames of other materials, such as lightweight PVC pipe, can be disassembled when not in use and easily handled and stored. Quilt frames come in various sizes; some can accommodate any size quilt, from baby blankets to king-size bedspreads. Parallel sides are wound or rolled to make the exposed quilt smaller, so the center of the quilt can be reached. When the quilting is completed, the quilt is taken off the frame. Then a binding is sewn onto the edge, typically one side by machine, then folded around to the other side and hand-stitched in place. Quilts are sometimes self-bound with the face or backing fabric.

An expert quilter takes four or five stitches each time she pulls the needle through the fabric sandwich. Tiny stitches are considered highest quality. Quilts may also be tied with yarn, fine or coarse, in a matching or contrasting color. Large needles are used to make a tied double knot in a selected style; knots are spaced 4 to 6 inches apart in a random or planned pattern. The yarn is cut midway between stitches to form fringe. Uncut stitches, such as the turkey track, are a tied-quilt alternative. Refer to chapter 16 for Colonial quilting patterns.

Pieced Quilts

Another quilt-top form is the **pieced** or **patchwork quilt**, made of small squares or triangles of contrasting, often patterned calico fabrics. The pieces may be stitched together by hand, or, more commonly today, sewn on a sewing machine to form the patterned top. Quilting may contrast or follow next to the seams. Extra-wide broadloom fabrics printed to look like patchwork quilts come in twin, full, queen-, or king-size widths and lengths. This saves time, although it is not authentic piecework. In this case, quilt stitches or tying can be done right on the "seam" lines, because the design is printed.

Appliqué

In many cultures, appliqué is integral to the history of quilt-making. Appliqué is an art form where the quilt top is made by stitching small pieces of fabric directly onto the quilt top in a pattern. The pattern may be geometric or floral, or may consist of blocks that are hand-painted, signed, or embroidered. Representations of geography, architecture, people, or commemorative events can be accomplished with appliqué. The size of the appliqué and the texture and pattern of the carefully selected and coordinated design fabrics, allow for complexity and charm in this type of quilt. Fancywork embroidery may also embellish the patterns, including embroidered writing to document people, places, events, or dates. These works may become wall hangings in both homes and public places.

Many people today seek handmade appliqué quilts, either new or antique, as interior textile treasures to be hung on a mounting board for display on a large wall, used as a coverlet for a bed, or displayed as a throw quilt for snuggling under on a chair, sofa, chaise, or window seat. Appliqué quilts may be employed as an artistic textile accessory laid across beds or seating pieces or displayed on quilt stands. Small piecework makes charming country-style pillows and accessory items.

Although the complete story of quilt-making is beyond the scope of this book, here we can at least give respect to those (primarily) women who, throughout history, worked diligently to keep their families warm. At the same time, they lovingly created with the passion of their hearts and the labor of their own hands beautiful and durable textiles that have become an integral and artistic part of our domestic heritage.

Patterns such as the wedding ring, the lover's knot, the chimney sweep, and the friendship quilt are well known. Historically, appliqué quilts were often made of clothing that was worn out, outgrown, or no longer fashionable. This was a practical as well as sentimental way to preserve family memories. During the Victorian era, the seemingly nonsensical **crazy quilts,** made of uncoordinated fabrics in random shapes and sizes and joined together and quilted with decorative stitches, added humor and nostalgia. They were often made of recycled apparel textiles. Amish quilts today, particularly antiques, command dear prices due to the excitement of their design and their superb craftsmanship. Appliqué is also seen as a key ingredient in smaller handcrafted items generated for country-style interiors, including handmade appliqué dolls, doll crib quilts, and stuffed animals, for example.

In many countries where folk crafts still thrive, one can find examples of appliqué, each with its own native terminology. From the islands of the Caribbean to the islands of the South Pacific, from South America to Asia to Africa to the Nordic countries, appliqué textiles for domestic and decorative use are an important art and craft form. These items can also make a fine addition to contemporary, modern, or eclectic interiors.

Trapunto or Trapunta

This is a quilting form where one area is quilted, and then only that area is stuffed with batting. This makes the quilted area stand in relief from the flatter fabric. One example is the puff quilt, in which individual squares are stuffed and then sewn together to form a bed quilt or craft item. Technically, trapunta is created by hand, whereas trapunto is machine-quilted. In machine trapunto, the area is first layered with batting and backing, then quilted; next, the excess batting around the quilting is trimmed away. This method is somewhat uncommon today.

Quilting and appliqué examples: bed quilts, pillows, wall hangings, craft items, table covers, throw covers, art or craft display items, accent work on any of these applications (especially trapunto or trapunta)

Machine Quilting

There are three forms of machine quilting: hand-guided, automated, and fuse-bonded.

Hand-Guided Machine Quilting

The free-arm quilting machine allows the quilter to quilt any pattern by tracing an outline or following a patterned fabric or by creating a pattern, including standard allover designs and isolated quilting. As with hand quilting, the layers—the top decorative fabric, the batting, and the lining—are pinned together. The quilt is then rolled so a narrow strip is exposed. The quilter typically works in these long strip areas, moving lengthwise or crosswise along the piece.

Hand-guided quilted goods examples: custom bedspreads and pillow shams, pillow tops, upholstery (cushion seats and backs), window treatment valances, long insulating drapery panels

Automated Quilting

Automated quilting machines can quilt wide widths of fabric with multiple quilting needles very quickly. Such machines are usually computerized and include a variety of patterns from which to choose. The advantage is a lower cost and perhaps a quicker turnaround because automated quilting requires less human labor. Quantities of bedspreads for hospitality interiors (hotels, resorts) are either automated-quilted or fuse-bond quilted because this method is efficient for mass production.

Automated quilted goods examples: mass-produced or ready-made bedspreads, comforters, and economical custom bedspread ensembles

Fuse Bonding

Fuse bonding is sometimes called *pinsonic quilting* because tiny sonic waves heat up a spot in order to melt and fuse the layers together. This technique is efficient and leaves no holes in the fabric nor threads that can fray or come loose. It is also a rapid method of mass-producing goods, so it is used in mattress pads and commercially produced (ready-made) bedspreads and window treatment products that are energy efficient (sewn holes decrease the R-value; see chapter 10). Commonly used patterns include the straight lattice pattern and the ogive or ogee shape (bulbous, with a pointed top and bottom). Fuse-bonding or pinsonic quilting is moderate in aesthetic appeal.

Fuse-bonded or pinsonic quilted goods examples: ready-made bedspreads and comforters or ensembles, mattress pads, energy-efficient window shade textiles

Laminated or Bonded Fabrics

Lamination or bonding is a compound cloth process of joining two fabric layers together in a permanent, fused construction. Typically, one layer is in a liquid form; the liquid is extruded in a wide layer on top of the companion fabric. This is seen in vinyl upholstery, where the liquid solution is extruded onto a base, backing, or substrate layer, which might be a jersey knit or a nonwoven web.

Lamination is also achieved by adhering a clear vinyl fabric to the surface of a decorative fabric. Lamination turns nearly any fabric, including popular decorative cotton fabrics such as chintz and warp sateen, into textiles that can be used in restaurants, hospice care settings, and for homes where spills are likely and water protection is needful, such as upholstered furniture and seat cushions for indoor or outdoor applications.

Note that lamination can be applied to the decorative surface or to the reverse, wrong, or back side of fabrics. The advantage of a surface application is the user's ability to wipe clean any spill, wetting, or soiling; thus the decorative fabric is not subject to spots or stains. The disadvantage is the unpleasantness of sitting on a plastic surface; the lamination tends to diminish the fabric aesthetics and the human dignity of the user.

Another viable choice, often used in care and hospitality centers, is to laminate the fabric's reverse, wrong, or back side. This results in a fabric with greater tactile and aesthetic appeal that will not allow spills or accidental wetting to penetrate to the batting. Because spills, soiling, and wetting do not sink into the fabric, the odors of food, urine, and feces are minimized.

Laminated or bonded fabric examples: vinyl upholstery, clear vinyl laminated fabrics

Coated Fabrics

Textiles are coated for dimensional stability, to add privacy, or to conserve energy. In one type of coated fabric, the backing or substrate layer is liquid that is flowed onto the back of a decorative fabric; this is sometimes called a *foam-backed textile*. A very light application may be flowed or sprayed onto the back of fabric to provide dimensional stability and sturdiness to a fabric for upholstery. This light coat is sometimes called a *kiss coat*. Some fabrics are coated as they are manufactured, and others are sent to fabric finishing companies to be treated with a stabilizing coating (refer to chapter 5). Coated textiles are also used for linings where heat or noise insulation or darkening qualities are specified, as in hotel rooms and residential bedrooms where occupants must sleep during the day.

Coated textiles examples: insulative fabrics for draperies, stabilized fabrics for upholstery, insulative and blackout drapery linings, wallcovering textiles.

RESOURCES

American Textile Manufacturers Institute (ATMI)
1130 Connecticut Avenue NW, Suite 1200
Washington, DC 20036-3954
Tel 202-862-0500
Fax 202-862-0570

ATMI is the national trade association for the textile mill products industry. Its members manufacture yarns, fabrics, home furnishings, and other textile products.

Fibersource
www.fibersource.com

Fibersource features its member organizations, which manufacture fibers, yarns, and constructed fabrics, online, accessible as live website links.

The Embroiders' Guild of America, Inc. (EGA)
www.egausa.org
335 West Broadway, Suite 100
Louisville, KY 40202
Tel 502-589-6956
Fax 502-584-7900

The Embroiders' Guild of America is an organization supporting more than 20,000 talented needle artists in developing and growing to their full potential.

International Machine Quilters Association (IMQA)
www.imqa.org
PO Box 6647
Monona, WI 53716

IMQA membership is open to any corporation, partnership, sole proprietorship, or individual engaged in the machine quilting industry or in selling machines, materials, supplies, or services directly related to the industry.

Quilters News
www.quiltersnews.com

Quilters News is a fully scheduled affinity market broadcast network addressing the quilting industry needs for project-based media.

QuiltersBee
www.quiltersbee.com

QuiltersBee is a website for an Internet quilting guild. It contains instructions and lists of quilt guilds.

chapter

5

Fabric Conversion: Coloring and Finishing

Figure 5.1 The fabric conversion process yields marketable fabrics, such as this grouping from the "Black and Camel" color book, with its Art Nouveau quality. Counterclockwise: taupe and gold calla lilies in a chenille and rayon fabric with decorative stylized leaves on a black background; a vertical stripe with a hint of metallic opalescence; and a multi-yarn with a grass cloth texture. An Art Deco–style striated leopard print in black and bone completes the group. *Photo courtesy of Duralee® Fabrics, 800-275-3872, www.duralee.com.*

FABRIC CONVERSION

Fabric conversion means the series of treatments a textile must undergo in order to be finished or complete and to become salable or marketable. From the raw goods state, commonly referred to as **greige** or **gray goods** because of its dingy off-white color, a textile undergoes an average of six coloring and finishing processes.

While some processes are customary or assumed for a given fiber, most of the conversion processes are planned by a fabric stylist, specifier, or design professional to meet the expectations of the contemporary consumer or the requirements of a specific end-use. For example, the residential market is one where trends are paramount. Pattern, texture, and color work hand in hand to create textiles that have current appeal. This is evident in the introduction of spring and fall lines of textiles, discussed in chapter 1. While the nonresidential or contract market is less influenced by the latest style, criteria for conversion are equally compelling. These include dimensional stability, serviceability, resistance to wear and crushing, flame resistance, and resistance to microbial bacteria.

Conversion steps or processes can occur at varying stages. These are:

1. As prefinishes or coloring in the natural fiber stage or man-made fiber solution stage
2. As a prefinish in the greige textile stage, performed to help the fabric accept or absorb color better and to produce greater uniformity in the textile
3. As a coloring process — dyeing, printing, or a combination of the two
4. As post-finishes, applied after the fabric is colored, to enhance durability or performance or to give a specific aesthetic finish.

Durable and Nondurable Finishes

Finishes that are topically applied to the surface of a yarn or textile fall into two categories:

1. **Durable finishes** are those that can withstand repeated wet (washing) or dry cleaning. These are applied for the life of the fabric. Permanent press is one example of a durable finish.
2. **Nondurable finishes** are those that are removed, weakened, or damaged when wet- or dry-cleaned. One example is chintz, a glaze that can be removed with wet cleaning.

Prefinishes

To prepare a textile for coloring, one or more prefinish processes must be employed, although they can take place in the fiber or yarn stage, or after the textile is constructed. Prefinishes performed on greige or gray goods are either dry or wet processes. **Dry processes** include brushing, heat setting, singeing, stabilizing, and tenter drying. **Wet processes** include bleaching, boiling or scouring, carbonizing, crabbing, decatizing, fulling, mercerizing, and preshrinking. These are listed here along with the fibers that utilize each finish.

Dry Prefinish Processes

Brushing is done to fabrics to pull out tiny fibers from natural or manufactured fibers in order to produce a smoother surface. **Wool** textiles were originally brushed with thistles. The thistle motif is still used today to symbolize some Scottish woolen textiles.

Heat setting is a method of permanently pressing a **polyester** or **polyester blend** textile into a pleat, wrinkle, or other configuration. It is done by folding or compress-configuring the fabric, heating the textile until the fabric polymers begin to flow or melt, and then cooling the fabric

very quickly. This permanently alters the polymer chain into the new direction or pattern so the wrinkle or pleat will not wash out or wear off over the life of the fabric.

Singeing is a process where cotton, wool, or linen fabrics are passed over the top of a gas-fired jet in order to burn out vegetable matter.

Stabilizing is a process for setting the weave or knit in wool textiles by heating the greige to hot temperatures or by treating it with resins (in which case it may be classified as a wet treatment). The heat process and resins may be combined.

Sun bleaching is a historical treatment for lightening linen or cotton textiles by laying the gray goods or the finished cloth, if it is white, "on the green" for ten to fourteen days, allowing the sun to naturally brighten and bleach the textiles. This is sometimes called *grassing*. It is used rarely today, but it has the advantage of keeping linen fibers strong for fine table linens by not subjecting them to the wet process of bleaching.

Tenter drying involves pulling fabrics tightly and clamping them onto a tenter frame, where they dry in the stretched-tight position. This helps correct the grain, straightening the warp and weft threads to more perfect right angles to each other and more nearly parallel to the selvages. This is done before the fabric is colored and finished.

Wet Processes

Bleaching to remove inherent color (gray or off-white) is the submerging of any greige fiber in a solution containing bleach, which removes the gray, allows further coloring to be clearer and brighter, and helps unprinted areas remain white in a given colorway. The type of bleach — typically hydrogen peroxide (H_2O_2) and sodium hypochlorite (NaCLO) — and amount of exposure must be carefully selected, as some fibers quickly deteriorate with exposure to certain kinds of bleaches or whiteners.

Boiling is a process for cotton, linen, wool, and silk where the fabric or yarn is boiled in water to encourage the release of natural substances such as pectin, wax, gum, and grease.

Carbonizing is a wool process for removing fibers and organic foreign matter. The greige is treated with sulfuric acid and then burned out via singeing.

Crabbing is a wool process whereby the greige is submerged in very hot water, then immediately in cold water, and then ironed to set the weave. This procedure makes wool fabric stable.

Decatizing is a process for cotton, wool, and rayon. Cold water is used to preshrink the textile.

Desizing is the application to manufactured fibers of an enzyme that breaks down sizing or starch during boiling or scouring. The result is a more supple, softer fabric.

Fulling is the process of immersing a wool textile in hot, agitating detergent water and then rinsing it in cold water. This shrinks or felts the fibers and softens the textiles.

Mercerizing cotton or linen is the process of exposing the yarn or fabric to caustic soda while it is stretched taut on a tenter frame. The yarns become more even, full, rounded, and lustrous, and as a result absorb and hold dyes better.

Preshrinking is a process common in cotton, rayon, and wool fabrics. Typically, preshrinking involves exposing the textile to hot water and then drying it with hot air. Methods vary and include decatizing. Preshrunk fabrics stay dimensionally stable during subsequent cleanings.

Scouring is a process of boiling cotton, linen, wool, and silk in water to which detergents are added or in a solvent solution to remove natural pectins, waxes, gums, or grease. It is also used to remove sizing and other additives from manufactured fibers.

Sizing is a wet finish applied to fibers to enhance their dyeability. Sizing is a light starch.

Figure 5.2 Singeing is the process whereby greige is passed over a gas jet to burn off any vegetable matter. *Photo courtesy of Cotton Incorporated.*

Coloring

Adding color to a textile can be a simple or a complex process. Dyeing is the complete submersion of a yarn or fabric in a dye bath or liquid; it can be accomplished in manufactured fibers before the viscose solution is extruded into monofilament. Printing is the application of dyes dispersed in liquid that penetrates the textile or of a pigment held onto the surface of the textile with resin binders. Fabrics may be first dyed and then printed, or may be woven of dyed yarns that also may be printed on top, though this is less common. Dyeing methods can alter the cost of the fabric; more elaborate methods yield higher prices.

Dyeing

Throughout the ages, before the discovery of chemical dyes, all colorants came from natural sources. For example, yellows and browns were obtained from leaves and bark, red from sources such as the root of the madder plant, blue from the indigo plant and inorganic compounds such as cobalt, and purple from *Murex,* a mollusk from the ocean's depths. Most textile dyes were acquired from plants—leaves, stalks, bark, flowers, berries, or seeds. Today, natural dyes are being rediscovered as environmental consciousness makes its impact in the textile field. Natural dyes are used not only by the single textile artisan but also by companies whose products are 100 percent natural as an expression of a green design philosophy. This serves a segment of the public that prefers natural materials, including people allergic to synthetic dyestuffs.

Dyestuffs and Pigments

The chemical makeup of both natural and manufactured fibers must be carefully aligned with the chemical composition of the dyestuff and the method of applying the dye or pigment. If not compatible, the fabric may not accept or hold the color. This is referred to as **dye affinity.**

The vast majority of dyes and pigments in use today are synthetic, derived from sources such as coal tar derivatives and inorganic compounds that are chemically engineered as a dry powder or concentrated liquid known as **dyestuff** or **synthetic dye.**

A **pigment** is a nonsoluble coloring agent that, ordinarily, cannot be dissolved in water, and therefore is usually held to the surface of the textile with resin (adhesive) binders. However, pigments can undergo a chemical process whereby they become soluble **pigment dyes** with an affinity for the fiber. Pigments can be used to dye or to print textiles in the fabric stage, whereas dyestuffs can also be used to color viscose solution, natural fibers, and yarns. White is the most common pigment color, and metallic colors—gold, silver, copper—are typically pigments. Pigments held to the surface with resin binders appear more as paint lying on the surface than do dyestuffs, which are absorbed into the textile.

The four general classifications of dyestuffs are based on the way they bind to the textile. These are **surface absorption, ionic bonding, covalent bonding,** and **pigmentation.** The categories of dyestuffs are listed below, with the fibers that chemically align with or have an affinity for that dye. Also listed are the benefits and drawbacks to each type of dyestuff.

Surface Absorption Dyes Surface absorption dyes are physically absorbed into the surface of the textile. The two dye classifications that adhere to textiles in this manner are direct and disperse dyes.

Direct dyes are used on cotton, linen, rayon, and acetate (cellulosic fibers). Direct dyes, also called *salt dyes,* are bright, economical, water soluble, and colorfast during wet cleaning when resin finishes are applied, although they tend to bleed and lose their color without the resin application. They usually need no pretreatment, and the salt helps the dye be absorbed into the fiber. **Developed direct dyes** are post-treated with compounds that help the dye develop the final shade and become more colorfast.

Disperse dyes are used on hydrophobic fibers that do not absorb water: acetate, nylon, and polyester. The fine organic dye compounds are suspended or dispersed in a very hot water solution. They possess good colorfastness in cleaning and in sunlight, although they will gas fade unless protective finishes are applied.

Ionic Bonding Ionic bonding is the adhering of dyestuffs to the fiber structure itself. Three classes of dyes that work in this manner are acid dyes, basic dyes, and mordant dyes.

Acid dyes are used on silk, wool (protein fibers), and some rayons and synthetic (noncellulosic) fibers. These dyestuffs require an acidic solution to charge the positive ions onto the fiber. They exhibit good colorfastness, although appropriateness of use is variable, meaning the dye must be used selectively according to the textile end-use.

Basic dyes are used on acrylic, some nylons, and polyester. This class of dyestuffs bonds to negatively charged ions. Colors may be brilliant but not fast, except on acrylic. If combined with other dyes, basic dyes can increase the brilliance of those dyes.

Mordant dyes are used on acrylic, some olefins, rayons, polyester, silk, and wool. This dye type ionically charges or adheres to metallic substances rather than to the fiber, so the fabric may be pretreated with a mordant, which is a metal compound—chrome (used most frequently), tin, copper, aluminum, or iron—to which the dye bonds. A variety of mordant dyes is known as *premetalized dye* when the dyestuff is mixed with the metallic substance, eliminating the need to pretreat with metalized solution. Colorfastness increases during cleaning. Mordant dyes are good for lightfastness as well. Colors are dull rather than brilliant.

Covalent Bonding Covalent bonding is a process used for cellulosic fibers where the dye and the fiber form a strong molecular or covalent bond. These include reactive dyes.

Reactive dyes are used on cotton, linen, rayon, and silk. These dyestuffs work in two steps. First, salt is added to the solution containing the reactive dye to reduce its solubility and to spread it evenly. Second, alkali is added to cause the covalent or molecular bond. Excess dyes are washed out. Reactive dyes can achieve bright colors without crocking or rubbing off onto other textiles, and they are colorfast during cleaning and in sunlight.

Pigmentation or Mechanical Adhesion In this last classification of dyestuffs, the fiber or textile is subjected to a solution where pigments or water-insoluble dyes are made to adhere through resin binders or by undergoing a process whereby they become water soluble and are thus absorbed into or have an affinity for the fiber.

Azoic or **naphthol dyes** are used primarily on cotton but also on other fibers. These dyes are economical, have good colorfastness, and can achieve brilliant colors, although they may rub off when wet or dry. The textile is first immersed in a colorless alkaline solution of naphthol. A diazoic acid is added to react and produce the color within the fiber structure itself.

Vat dyes are used on cotton, rayon, and silk. These dyes are among the oldest (indigo blue and Tyrian purple) and get their name from the vats where they were fermented to remove oxygen. The dyes are today reduced in an alkaline solution, which produces a strong affinity for cellulosic fibers. After dyeing, exposure to air (oxidation) develops the color. These are fairly colorfast dyes.

Sulfur dyes are used on cotton and rayon. They must be reduced in order to become soluble. They possess relatively good colorfastness, although they can be hard on the fiber and must be carefully aligned and applied.

Dyeing Methods

Dyeing is the means by which fibers, yarns, or piece goods are saturated with color. This can take place in any of these four stages: the stock/fiber stage, the solution stage, the yarn stage, or the finished textile stage. Various methods pertain to each stage, and these are discussed below. Dyeing may be the first step in the coloring process. A textile may be dyed, then printed, then finished.

Dyeing textiles is a wet coloring process. When a color is determined according to the design marketing plan or jobber's specifications, a small amount of solution is mixed. A swatch of fiber, yarn, viscose solution, or prepared piece goods is dyed for examination and approval. This sample dye formula and solution then becomes the **master** or **standard formula.** A larger amount of dye is mixed to color a specific amount of stock or fiber, yarn, solution, or piece goods, after which the dye bath is used up, and any remaining or leftover solution is typically discarded. Converters with green manufacturing procedures (discussed in chapter 2) do not dump the dye solution but clean the water and recycle or reclaim it in each part of the process.

One batch of dye solution is referred to as a **job lot** or **dye lot,** and the dyed or printed textiles within that dye lot are exactly the same. When subsequent batches are mixed according to the master or standard formula, they may be slightly different. Blue dyes seem to be the most variable. This means that a set piece-goods bolt may be just off from the standard, and a precise **match** may be impossible. Textiles for interior design are particularly vulnerable to the problems that arise through dye lot variation because one application may be draperies, another bedspreads, another upholstery. When these items are made from bolts of different dye lots, the colors can appear entirely different. For this reason, when ordering more for a particular fabric or when matching to an existing item, it is wise to request cuttings from the warehouse in order to select the right dye lot color. Although dye lots are assigned numbers in wallcoverings within a given time frame, no dye lot numbers are indicated in fabric. This means there is no way to trace which dye lot a textile came from. The problem is compounded because the finished goods may be sold to any number of jobbers. If the textile is exclusive to one fabric company, it may be distributed to more than one warehouse.

This dye lot mismatch problem also affects finished piece goods, wallcoverings, and, to a lesser degree, carpeting. Because the problem can dramatically affect the ordering of cut goods and processing of custom textile products, the design professional must be keenly aware of ordering procedures and cautions.

Fiber/Stock Dyeing Dyeing fibers before they are spun into yarn can be accomplished in cotton, linen, wool, silk, and extruded filaments of man-made fibers. The advantage of dyeing in this stage is the saturation of the dye to the core of the fiber. The disadvantage is the limitation of end-use of the colored fiber because the color is committed.

Solution Dyeing Adding dye to manufactured fiber viscose or liquid solution is known as **solution dyeing** or *melt-coloring*. Because the dyestuff becomes a part of the fiber itself as it is extruded, it is truly colorfast. It is a relatively costly method of dyeing, and the downside is the commitment to a color; careful planning is necessary to utilize all the fiber in a textile, get it to the marketplace, and sell it before the color is out of fashion. In some instances, solution dyeing may be specified for a particular end-use where a great deal of yardage is custom-colored for a specific installation and where the risk of color fading is high.

Yarn Dyeing Dyeing yarns is crucial for textiles whose color is accomplished through weaving colored yarns into the pattern. Examples include tweed and Jacquard weaves such as tapestry, brocade and moquette, and Wilton and Axminster carpets. Yarn is dyed first in a beaker or cup to determine the exact color desired, which then becomes the standard or master. Large quantities are then dyed in one of four methods: skein or hank dyeing, package dyeing, beam dyeing, and space dyeing.

Skein or **hank dyeing** is done by immersing skeins or hanks—a measure of yarn loosely wound—in a dye vat. The advantage is that the quantities of yarn may vary and the color distribution and penetration are good.

Package dyeing dyes yarns that are wound around perforated tubes or packages that weigh 1 pound each. The stacked packages are loaded into a dye vat or kettle that holds up to 3,000 pounds. Dye solution is forced through the perforated tubes. The advantage is shorter lengths of dyed yarn.

Figure 5.3 The "Pebble Beach" group, a 100 percent solution-dyed acrylic for both interior and exterior use, is guaranteed for three years against fading, splitting, peeling, and cracking. Abrasion tests classify the collection suitable for both residential and contract settings. Seen here are "Suman Azul," "Vitale Azul," "Pace Coco," "Riven Rock Cocoa," "Jacinthe Slate," "Rilassanto," "Crema," "Neroli Chocolate," and "Mirquet Cocoa." *Images courtesy of Giati Designs, Inc.*

Beam dyeing is accomplished by winding longer lengths of yarn around a perforated warp beam. The yarns are dyed in a large vat, where the dye solution is forced from the inside of the beam outward through the yarns and then from the outside into the center so the dye is evenly distributed. When the yarn on the warp beam is dry, it can be loaded directly onto the loom, thus saving time and labor. This method is generally used for finer yarns.

Space dyeing is the method used to achieve a variegated or heathered color in yarn. This includes light-to-dark single hues, tone-on-tone hue variations, and a transition from one color to another in a predetermined progressive order. It is achieved by winding the yarns around a dye package or beam and controlling the color and amount of dye that pours through certain holes.

Piece Dyeing Dyeing textiles once they are in fabric form as piece goods is referred to as **piece dyeing**. Even though piece dyeing is a particular method, it is also sometimes used as a generic term. A **piece** is a length of textile that typically varies from 30 to 120 linear yards (27.5 to 110 meters), with 60 yards (approximately 55 meters) the most common length of piece goods or fabric. It might be noted that some piece dyeing is done in lengths of up to 250 yards (approximately 191 meters).

The methods of dyeing woven or needle-constructed fabrics include **bale dyeing**, **chain** or **continuous dyeing**, **jig dyeing**, **piece dyeing**, **polychrome dyeing**, **pressure dyeing**, and **pressure jet dyeing**.

Bale dyeing is a method where the warp yarns are pretreated with sizing so they will accept the dye more readily. The fabric is then dyed in a cold-water dye bath so the sizing will not disperse or dissolve. Thus the warp yarns are darker, creating a slight two-tone effect as in chambray, for example.

Chain or **continuous dyeing** is used for more delicate fabrics in order to prevent stretching. A textile piece is connected into a link similar to a continuous loop of a chain, placed on a reel, and run through the dye bath in a continuous motion.

In **jig dyeing**, the fabric is stretched to its fullest width and then run back and forth through the dye bath until the desired result is obtained.

Piece dyeing is achieved by twisting the fabric in a rope-like configuration and passing it back and forth through the dye bath. This process requires less horizontal space than jig dyeing.

Polychrome or **polychromatic dyeing** produces random, indistinct patterns by one of two methods:

1. **Flow-form dyeing**, where dye is sent through a perforated roller in a timed manner to give the effect of inconsistency. This achieves a marbled effect.
2. **Dye-weave dyeing**, where dye is spurted through a spray jet onto metal plates set at a 45-degree angle to the fabric. The dye runs down and onto fabric that moves beneath it. The dye bleeds and creates a fuzzy, irregular pattern.

In **pressure dyeing**, the fabric is enclosed so temperatures can be escalated above boiling.

Pressure jet dyeing sprays a very hot dye bath on manufactured fibers that are less receptive to dyes in order to set the color.

Printing Methods

Printing, also a wet coloring method, is the creation of a pattern in one or more colors by the application of a liquid dye, ink, or paste onto the surface of textiles by hand or machine. Historically, all methods were accomplished by hand until the industrial revolution of the mid-nineteenth century, when some hand methods were motorized and other methods invented.

Hand Printing Hand methods are diverse. Interestingly, regions seemingly unrelated have, throughout history, utilized similar methods to create printed textiles for their interiors. Some of the best-known hand-printing methods include resist methods (**batik** and **tie-dye printing**), and surface ornamentation techniques (**block printing**, **hand-painting**, and **stencil and screen printing**). These are briefly described here.

Batik is a resist-dye technique of applying pattern to cloth. In Africa, Indonesia, India, and Japan, this hand-printing method, known in English as **batik** or **tjanting** or **tjap**, has been a primary means of printing for several hundred years. Beeswax (or, these days, paraffin wax) is applied by hand with a small hand-held dispensing container. The fabric is then immerse-dyed. The pattern created by the wax resists the dye. The wax is removed by heating it and absorbing it with paper. Typically, the resulting fabric has a pattern and background in high contrast colors such as dark blue or pinkish red against white. Multiple colors can be achieved by rewaxing the surface in another design and then dyeing it in a different dye bath. When the wax is applied and has dried, the textile can be crushed to crack the wax surface so the dye will seep into an interesting striated textural pattern.

Tie-dye is similar to batik in that it is an ancient resist method developed in the same countries. It is particularly associated with Japan, where it is considered a historic art form. Fabric is folded, gathered, knotted, and tied with

Figure 5.4 "Pulco," a 100 percent linen striped table linen, is woven with yarn-dyed warp. *Photo courtesy of Libeco Home, www.libecohomestores.com.*

Figure 5.5 Hand-created and -dyed batik fabric, "Birds." *By Thoms© of Batik Tambal 2004, www.batiktambal.com.*

waxed strings or rubber bands and then dipped into a dye bath. Where the string is tied, and where the fabric is thick from being bundled, the dye is resisted. The fabric may be rebundled and retied and immersed in the same or a different color and the process repeated until all the desired colors and effect are complete. Tie-dye may also be monochromatic. The pattern is often concentric circles with an uncertain or bleeding effect.

Tie-dye textiles have had two recent surges of popularity. The first was in the 1960s and 1970s, when Asian cultures were examined and their influence felt in association with the hippie era. Again, tie-dye became popular in the late 1990s with a reminiscent revival of the 1970s. Tie-dye can be an enjoyable and creative craft.

Ikat printing results when warp yarns are tie-dyed using the method described above and then threaded onto a loom, shifted to an irregular placement, and woven with contrasting colors—plain or in horizontal stripes—the fabric is known as an **ikat.** Ikat fabrics are produced in many developing countries, particularly Indonesia and Southeast Asia.

Block printing or **hand block printing** is another hand technique used in both ancient and modern times. The Chinese perfected block printing. The fabrics they made were imported to Europe, where the method was copied, and England in particular became famous for block-printed fabrics for interior design use in large floral patterns. Originally, the blocks were made of wood and, later, of linoleum. The background design is cut away so the highest area will produce the pattern when inked and stamped onto the textile. Hard block materials produce crisper, more accurate

designs (as compared to, say, rubber stamps), although other materials can be formed or built up rather than carved out by hand.

Hand painting dates to the dynasties of ancient Egypt, where it is suspected to be the method of decorating textiles found in the tombs. Ancient Chinese and Japanese cultures also painted silk textiles for many centuries. Today, hand-painted scrolls and byobu screens (folding Japanese paper screens) of silk or mulberry paper are still produced and esteemed. Hand painting is also available via custom order or stock patterns, typically on silk textiles or wallcoverings.

Stencil and flat-bed (silk) screen printing is another method used for several hundred years in countries around the world. A stencil is a cut-out area of a thin material where a colored medium is applied. In screen printing, the process is more sophisticated. The screen consists of a frame or sides of a box the width of the fabric, 45 to 60 inches, and up to 80 inches long. It is covered on one open side with a fine, sheer silk (originally), nylon, or polyester (common today) fabric with a cut-out stencil film adhered to the surface. Several methods may be employed to create the stencil, including computer-generated designs on film. Dye, ink, or paste is forced through the open cut-out area by means of a squeegee, which is a rubber blade set in a wood or metal handle. The fineness of the fabric determines the amount of dye paste that can be applied to the textile. (On paper, screen printing is also known as *serigraphy,* meaning graphics made possible through silk screens.)

Interior textiles printed by hand screening require that the box screen be placed in perfect alignment. One person holds the screen in place while the other squeegees toward his or her body. Then they trade duties to reverse the ink flow and ensure an even distribution of color. This technique is used to produce one-of-a-kind crafts rather than large quantities of printed textiles. One screen is used for each color, with the film stencil opening configured for that portion of the design. One set of screens can produce several colorways of the same design.

Semi-automated Printing There are two methods of semi-automated printing: semi-automated silk screen printing and air brush painting. In **semi-automated silk screen printing,** a machine lowers the screen and holds it in place. There may be one screen or up to twenty screens, one for each color in the pattern. If the process is semi-automated, hand labor is used to squeegee the paste through the screen, and the workers move along a stationary piece of greige. This method is used for smaller yardage in custom designs rather than for quantity yardage.

Air brush painting is an automated hand technique where the artist follows a pattern freehand or fills in a stencil area with an air-powered gun that produces a light and even layer of color.

Mechanical Printing Mechanical printing methods include **automated roller silk screen printing, discharge printing, roller printing,** and **transfer printing.**

Automated flat-bed screen printing is similar to the descriptions above, except all portions of the screen printing process are automated. The screens are mechanically raised and lowered; the dye paste is dispensed automatically, and the squeegee is automated; the textile piece moves along a conveyor belt. This method, when used for carpeting, is known as **Zimmer flat-bed screen printing.** To penetrate the pile, a magnet is placed beneath the carpet, creating a field that draws the dye paste downward. A vacuum system can achieve the same effect.

Automated rotary (silk) screen printing is the automated version of silk screen printing using nickel-plated screens that allow up to 215 holes per linear inch, compared to 120 holes in earlier screens. The stenciled areas are created by blocking some holes with water-soluble lacquer, meaning the screens can be used again for other patterns. The screens are fastened in cylinders and the ink or dye paste automatically forced through the stencil. The circumference of the screen depends on the size of the pattern repeat. The mechanism involves a dyestuff pipe that feeds the paste onto the inside of the screen, forced through the holes with a squeegee blade and a durable synthetic tip. Rotary-screened fabric may be monotone — one screen, one color — or multicolored, with up to twenty rotary screens placed next to one another, rotating with perfect precision simultaneously onto a fabric that moves along on a conveyor belt. Colors can be laid down quickly and economically in succession, which is a key factor to the success of this method.

Rotary screen printing is the most widely used method of textile printing. It is useful on flat as well as nap fabrics, such as velvet, and on warp yarns. It can produce detailed, realistic patterns as well as subtly shaded and imprecise patterns. *Note:* Automated warp printing includes roller printing, flat-bed screen printing, and rotary screen printing.

Discharge printing, also known as **extract printing,** is used primarily on cotton. In this method, dye is removed from a pre-dyed textile by printing a design on the fabric with a bleaching agent. The pattern becomes the lightened or white area, which may be solid or mottled or streaked.

Roller printing invention is credited to Christophe Philippe Oberkampf, a Bavarian who, in the early eighteenth century, developed the roller printing device in Jouy, France. His *toiles de Jouy* are famous as one-color roller-printed designs on natural linen or cotton. The designs were popular because they depicted contemporary political and fashionable scenes and motifs. Since then, roller printing has been a highly successful process.

The roller, made of heavy engraved metal, is continuously inked and prints the fabric as it travels around the roller. A separate roller is required for each color. The greige or dyed fabric is fed around a large support cylinder coupled with a support blanket, and each etched roller is continually inked with a paste transfer roller that rotates through a trough of dye paste. The etched roller is equipped with a doctor blade that squeegees off the excess paste. The etched rollers transfer the design to the piece goods. Each roller must be perfectly aligned in order to build up each subsequent color and design component.

Roller printing is capable of producing precise detail and high-quality printed goods. It is not the method of choice for printing large blotch or background areas. That may be better accomplished with transfer printing. However, roller printing is more costly than screen printing because of the copper used for the rollers and the labor involved in preparation. It is therefore declining in use.

Broadloom carpeting may be roller-printed using a method known as **Stalwart roller printing.** In order to penetrate the pile, the rollers are fitted with three-dimensional sponge forms that rotate into dye pans. This method has become less common with the introduction and success of jet printing.

Another form of roller printing was developed by a German carpet firm, Textile Austustungs, and Kusters, a machinery supplier. Known by the resulting acronym, **TAK printing,** the roller is a sheet of dye liquid that is interrupted with oscillating chains that cause the dye liquid to be dropped randomly, or sprinkled, onto the surface of the carpet, creating a random pattern. Another machine, the Mult-

Figure 5.6 Nine screens are used to lay down sequential color in this rotary screenprinting process. The finished print is seen in the background, drawn vertically to dry the dye and pigment. *Image courtesy of Royal Carolina Corp., Greensboro, NC.*

TAK®, also developed by Kusters, can produce simplified geometric or wavelike patterns and variations.

Jet printing is used to continuously color or print carpet surface by means of nozzle jets through which dye liquid is sprayed in solid colors or patterns. A wide variety of effects is possible with carpet jet printing. Some of these systems include Kuster's Foamcolor® unit, where computer-controlled jets shoot air into dye foam streams, deflecting their descent; the Jet Foam Printer® and the Colorburst® units utilize solenoid and photoelectric cells to regulate the value spray to the nozzles.

Where the jets are positioned as close as 0.1 inch apart, jet spraying produces accurate patterns that may even imitate fine oriental rugs. One such system, used by Milliken Carpets, is the Millitron®, a computer-controlled jet printing system with great accuracy. In order to make the designs precise, the greige is sheared and vacuumed in preparation for printing.

Heat transfer printing or **sublistatic printing** is a method utilizing a colored design on a specially prepared paper that can be stored for a long time at a minimal cost and in little space. Three methods are used for printing the design onto the paper: **gravure** (engraved copper rollers print the paper); **flexo** (engraved rubber covered rollers, a more flexible material); and **rotary screen** (described above). When the order is placed for the textile, the prefinished greige is purchased, and only the ordered quantity is printed by heat and pressure transfer. The dyestuffs have a greater affinity for the greige than the paper, so when heat and pressure are applied, the dyestuffs sublime, or transfer, from solid to gas and then back into a solid on the fabric. This is the same system used to make decals for small craft projects, only on a larger scale.

The advantages of transfer printing include the relative quickness of the process, its efficiency, and the absence of environmental pollutants from the disposal of dye liquor. Transfer-printed goods are subject to little relaxation shrinkage resulting in pattern distortion. The weight of fabric can also be changed; the same design can be transfer-printed onto warp sateen as onto polished cotton or cretonne, for example, giving greater flexibility and less waste.

Disadvantages include shallow dye penetration, making the process less suitable for napped or pile textiles. Pile fabrics are also distorted during this pressure-printing process.

Pigment, as discussed above, is water-insoluble coloring matter that will not diffuse into a dye liquor or paste. In **pigment printing**, pigments are used to add white or metallic color as a form of **overprinting** on the top layer of a dyed or printed fabric. White in a printed pattern cannot be created as a soluble dye paste and applied in screen or roller printing, for example. In many textiles, white is seen as a bleached yarn or as the bleached background of the unprinted greige, with all other colors dyed or printed around it. White pigment creates a different effect than bleached greige. White pigments yield sharp accents or precise definition in motifs.

Metallic pigments include gold, silver, and bronze coloration and may be used as tiny accents or in an allover design. They may be mixed or layered for special or complex effects. Metallic pigments can simulate metallic-colored threads used in lamé. White can also be mixed with metallic pigments to form a white, off-white, or tinted mother-of-pearl effect.

As pigments do not penetrate the surface but rather lie on top of the fabric, they result in a slight bas-relief effect. This can be detected both visually and by running a hand over the surface and feeling the raised pigment. Pigments are usually durable.

Acid printing, **etch printing**, and **burn-out printing** refer to sheer patterns inside a more opaque fabric that result from printing sulfuric acid on a textile composed of an acid-resistant fiber such as polyester or nylon (synthetic) and an acid-degradable fiber such as cotton or rayon (cellulose fibers). Where the acid eats or dissolves one fiber, the fiber remaining is thinner, often becoming sheer. This technique is used for drapery fabric and may be combined with unusual printed designs in abstract or contemporary themes.

Mechanical resist printing combines dyeing with printing. The fabric is first printed with an agent that will not absorb water, then dyed. The result is a reverse design—greige pattern surrounded by dyed color. Batik, tie-dye, and ikat (described above) are the hand-technique forms of resist printing.

Gum printing is resist printing used on pile fabrics and carpeting to achieve a frosted effect. A gum compound is applied to the tips of the yarns, the fabric is dyed, and the gum is removed. The dye is darker or deeper at the base of the yarn pile than at the surface. This effect is sometimes called **frostiness.**

Pile restoration is necessary in fabrics subject to pressure during a dyeing, printing, finishing, lamination, or adhesion process. Methods used to return pile to its upright position include vacuum techniques and a reverse panné, where a metal blade pushes the pile up.

COLORING STANDARD TERMS AND SPECIAL EFFECTS

Beaker dyeing—Where dye is mixed in a small beaker or cup and samples colored in order to determine the exact dye composition and result.

Blotch—A solid-colored background area.

Conversion—The process of coloring and finishing fabrics to bring them to a completed, salable state.

Coverage—The amount of the surface that is dyed or printed. For example, 100 percent coverage is when the decorative surface is completely dyed or printed, with no exposed or uncolored areas.

Cross-dyeing—The creation of a heathered or two-tone effect by subjecting a fabric of two different fibers with different dye affinities to the same dye bath. One fiber will readily accept the dye, and the other will only partially accept it.

Design or **motif**—A pattern unit, such as a single flower. *Design* also refers to the entire composition of the textile pattern.

Dye or **dyestuff**—The colorant compound suspended in a liquid to become the dye bath.

Dye bath—The hot or cold liquid, a water and chemical mixture, to which the dye or colorant is added and into which the fibers, yarns, or piece goods are immersed to become colored.

Dye lot or **job lot**—The bath of dye liquor or liquid mixed according to the standard or master, used to color a specific amount of yarn or textile. Dye lots may vary slightly in color.

Fall-ons or **overlays**—Printing designs so they purposefully overlap or fall on each other. An area may be double-printed to achieve a darker effect or a different color. Often used in plaid and floral design configurations.

First-quality goods or **firsts**—Textile goods that meet all the manufacturer's criteria for quality construction and coloring and so can be sold at retail pricing.

Job lot—See Dye lot.

Figure 5.7 Tenter (fabric pulled taut) drying and color finishing in process
Image courtesy of Royal Carolina Corp., Greensboro, NC.

Master—See Standard.

Metamerism—The appearance of one color in one light and another color in another light. Dye lots may appear different under varying lighting conditions.

Motif—A single unit within a larger design.

Overdyeing—A method of achieving a marbled or heathered effect by dyeing the piece twice, once in a darker hue, then in a lighter hue.

Overlays—See Fall-ons.

Pattern repeat—A complete pattern unit measured from one point to the same point in the next repeated pattern or design. A pattern may be measured from the beginning of the pattern to the beginning of the next pattern, from the middle to the middle, or from the bottom to the bottom. Small pattern repeats are 2 to 4 inches, large pattern repeats from 27 to 40 inches.

Penetration—The depth of dye absorption into the textile. A deep penetration will show the printed dye on the back, while a shallow penetration will reveal the white or off-white prefinished color on the reverse or back side of the fabric.

Pigments—Insoluble coloring agents, typically held to the surface of the fabric with resin binders.

Selvage legend—This is a strip of information printed along the uncolored selvage of a printed textile. It contains the written name of the designer or design studio, the trademark, and/or the manufacturer/jobber or fabric house. It also includes a square or circle of each color used in the printed design.

Shade—The hue or color specified in a textile. When a color is **off-shade,** it is not an exact match to the standard or master.

Standard or **master**—The chemical formula for the dye or colorant that becomes the dye bath. It is the result of the beaker dyeing or sample printing approved for the dye lot or job lot.

Strike-off—A short length of a few yards that is dyed or printed in the master or standard formula to determine the color in quantity and to obtain approval of the color, coverage, registration, penetration, finishes, and other criteria. The strike-off is essential to **custom-colored orders** and must be approved by the designers or clients, after which they must purchase the goods even if they change their minds or the order changes.

Union dyeing—The uniform dyeing of a fabric with two fibers with different dye affinities in a single dye process, achieved by mixing the dyes. When the dyes are not mixable, two separate dye baths are used for a smooth, even color.

FAULTS AND FLAWS

Textiles are available as **firsts** and **seconds.** A first is a fabric or broadloom carpet that is, ideally, without faults or flaws, while seconds have some mechanical or aesthetic problems that render them less suitable. However, there is an expression that refers to textiles, particularly those manufactured in U.S. facilities that date to the 1800s: "Firsts are seconds and seconds are firsts," meaning that both first-quality and second quality merchandise may be equally flawed and pass for one another. Whereas new manufacturing facilities have considerable quality control, many goods from older plants have a series of problems that justify the warning "designer or consumer beware!"

It is of paramount importance that fabrics be **candled.** This means the fabric is passed over an inspection frame lighted from behind, typically a backlit glass table. Candling allows the inspector to identify flaws in first-quality goods, stop the machinery when one is sighted, and cut that section out of the length. The danger is that a designer, decorator, or workroom fabricator may receive the cut order in shorter lengths, causing inadequate pattern repeats. For this reason, the workroom fabricators or upholsterers should also candle the fabric and check the yardage, including pattern repeats. If a problem is found, the fabric should be shipped back and replaced immediately. If no time is lost in dealing with fabric problems, the same dye lot is more likely to still be available in the warehouse. If proper candling does not take place and the textile is fabricated into, for example, a drapery, and installed at the window before the fault or flaw becomes apparent, this is a much bigger problem. The fabric jobber will replace flawed fabrics within a given time frame but will not reimburse costs to remake or reinstall the product. Thus, all the profit is used for the labor.

Fabricators typically are held blameless for flawed goods unless a written contract exists between the design professional and fabricator holding the latter responsible for careful inspection of the fabric. Likewise, flaws in carpeting are rarely discovered until it is either rolled out and ready for installation or after the installation takes place. Again, it behooves the professional to have a written agreement with the installer to carefully inspect goods before installing them.

The replacement of textiles can be a somewhat lengthy process. In some cases, the textile must be inspected by a regional sales representative who travels a territory and may not be available immediately. It may be necessary for this sales rep to write or phone in an authorized replacement order. Where installations must meet a time deadline, the professional may face tough decisions and unhappy clients. The expression "design is the process of solving problems" then has new meaning.

Figure 5.8 Fabrics are candled, or inspected for flaws under bright overhead light and over a backlit glass table, to reveal any imperfections. A perfect sample of the fabric is hung to the left for color and pattern comparison. *Image courtesy of Royal Carolina Corp., Greensboro, NC.*

Typically, one of three scenarios will result.

1. The fabric or carpet is rejected and not fabricated or installed, and new goods are reordered.
2. The fault or flaw is not discovered until installation, and one of two choices is made.
3a. The installation stays until a replacement is secured, and then the flawed product is returned to the manufacturer or jobber.
3b. The product remains in place, and the design professional negotiates a reduced price for the client to keep it. In some cases, the jobber may not want the flawed merchandise returned to the warehouse, in which case the product may be kept by the designer for personal use; a warehouse, tent, or yard sale; or for donation to a charitable cause, such as Habitat for Humanity, Salvation Army, or another used-item store. In no case should a design professional consider throwing away new merchandise that is flawed. Such action would be environmentally irresponsible and ethically unacceptable.

A **fault** is a coloring error that takes place in manufacturing or after installation. A **flaw** is an irregularity in the surface construction of textiles. However, *flaw* may be substituted for *fault*, as it is a more familiar term in the industry. Seconds are often lumped into one category, "flawed goods." Following is an alphabetized list of faults and flaws.

Bar marks, bars, or **barres**—A flaw where weft/filler yarns produce horizontal bands of color due to color variations in the filling picks or irregularities in the filling yarn tension.

Dye migration—A concentration of dye puddled on the yarn tips in pile fabrics and carpeting. The tips are darker than the rest of the yarn and often uneven across the face of the pile.

Gas fading—A fault where a gradual shifting, lightening, or changing of color emerges after the textile is installed due to atmospheric gases or impurities. This is rare, and when it occurs, it may be past the textile performance guarantee period allotted by the jobber.

Grins or **grinning**—This fault is the exposure of thin slices of background color (colored or greige) where the pattern was off-register or misaligned. Because many textile designs are floral, the off-registration produces the shape of a smile or grin. This flaw usually makes the textile aesthetically unacceptable.

Off-grain—A flaw where warp and weft yarns in a biaxial weave are not perpendicular. Two problems can occur: **bowed yarn alignment,** where weft yarns sag in the center of the piece, causing a scalloped or sagged effect when the piece is fabricated into seamed widths; and **skewed yarn alignment,** where weft yarns are higher on one side than the other, creating a lopsided effect that, if joined and matched, makes the top and bottom of the product appear crooked. These flaws are remedied through tentering, described below.

Off-registration—A printing fault where the alignment of patterns in subsequent screens or rollers does not line up or register perfectly. This off-registration or misalignment causes the colors to appear incorrect and grins to appear.

Off-shade—A coloring fault in which the color varies from the standard or master in dyed or printed textiles. A dramatically off-shade piece will usually become a second, whereas slightly off-shade textiles are considered firsts.

Second-quality goods—Textiles whose flaws or faults make them unacceptable as first-quality goods. Many kinds of faults do not necessarily diminish the performance quality of the textile because they can often be cut out. In the case of off-shade, it may not need to match the standard or master in order for the color to be acceptable to the end user. Seconds are discounted and typically sold at outlets that carry bolts or pieces at retail to-the-public prices that approximate the wholesale or net price of cut orders placed by a designer. These stores often give interior design professionals an additional discount of 10 to 15 percent when they make purchases for their clientele.

Shading—A fault where there is a color gradation from selvage to selvage or from one end of the piece to the other. The problem is that in sewing lengths together, a striped effect results, and this is usually unacceptable to the end user. One technique that may allay the problem, if the shading is very slight and the fabric is plain or piece-dyed, is to turn every other length upside down so the vertical shades match. This is no guarantee of success, and often the fabric must be replaced.

FINISHES

Finishes are surface or submersion treatments that complete a textile. Some finishes are applied wet, some dry, some cold, and some hot. Often, a combination of methods is used to complete the finish. Finishes on textiles vary with the end-use. Fewer procedures are required for fabrics to be used in residential settings than in nonresidential settings. Specification requirements are discussed in chapter 6.

Finish longevity varies and is categorized as durable or nondurable. A **durable finish** is one that will endure through successive wet or dry cleanings. A **nondurable** or **solution** finish will be removed through successive washing or dry cleaning. Whether a finish is durable or nondurable is not likely apparent. If the quality of yardage or the nonresidential specification dictates, the design professional should research the finishes to document durability. This is particularly important with flame-retardant finishes. Another consideration is whether or not the finish will meet the required codes. This is also discussed in chapter 6.

Standard Finishes and Decorative Finishes

Textile finishes applied after the coloring process generally fall into one of two general categories according to purpose or end result. These are **standard, wet,** or **chemical finishes,** and **decorative** or **mechanical finishes.**

Standard Finishes
Standard, chemical, or wet finishes augment the textile's durability or ability to perform in a given way. These include antibacterial or antiseptic finishes, antistatic finishes, carefree finishes, flame-retardant finishes, insulative finishes, mothproofing, soil-repellent finishes, and water-repellent finishes.

Antibacterial or **antiseptic finishes** are typically applied in the form of bacteriostats—chemicals that suppress mold and mildew and that slow or prevent rotting. These finishes are especially important in healthcare settings.

Antistatic finish is primarily a finish for carpeting and wall or furniture upholstery. Antistatic properties can be applied by adding chemical inhibitors to the manufactured fiber viscose solution or as a topical application after the carpet or fabric is complete. If added to the viscose, the antistatic finish will be durable; if applied topically, it is a soluble or nondurable finish. The antistatic finish is meant to reduce shocks received after walking across a carpet and then touching a light switch. It is also important in office settings, where computers or other delicate equipment can be protected against damage by a reduction in potential static electricity.

Carefree finishes are those that make a textile easier to care for. Bedding and other fabrics that are washed and upholstery fabrics that receive much use can benefit from a wrinkle-resistant finish. **Smoothness-retention finishes** include **heat setting,** or subjecting a thermoplastic fiber to heat in a smooth, flat state; and **wrinkle-resistant** or **durable press finishing,** which is the addition of resins or a formaldehyde-based or other reactant compound before smooth heat setting. (*Note:* The terms *durable press finishing* and *permanent press* are used interchangeably. Here, *durable press* refers to smoothness retention. Below, *permanent press* refers to setting a crease or crinkle into the fabric permanently.) The permanently creased, pleated, crushed, or wrinkled appearance desired in some wall and drapery fabrics and upholstery textiles may be accomplished by means of a **permanent press** finish, which may include the addition of resins or a formaldehyde-based reactant compound before configuring and heat-setting the fabric. These are topical finishes that are heat-set or calendared into the fabric. Hence, they are also calendared finishes.

Note: Research is under way to find a substitute for formaldehyde, which is potentially harmful to humans through long-term release. It may well be a contributing factor to increased interior allergies. *Also note:* Resins decrease absorption and increase soil retention, have a somewhat distasteful odor when new, weaken fibers, decrease abrasion resistance, and shorten lifespans. Fabric subjected to abrasion may be thus weakened, resulting in a wearing down of fiber and hence color. This is known as *frosting.*

Flame-retardant finishes inhibit the ignition rate and flame spread, and encourage a fabric to self-extinguish. These topical or submerged applications are heat-set into the textile and are required for many nonresidential settings to meet flammability code. Because of flame-retardant finishes, a wide variety of beautiful textiles may be used in nonresidential settings. The durability of flame-retardant finishes may vary, as there are several levels of resistance effectiveness. *A word of caution:* Flame-retardant finishes can alter the color of textiles and weaken the fiber or construction. This means a flame-retardant fabric may become unacceptable in color or durability. A sample length of fabric should be treated and tested before treating multiple yards.

Insulative finishes are typically a foam product sprayed or flowed onto the back of fabrics to insulate against temperature and noise. These durable finishes are most often used for drapery fabric. An insulative finish tends to make the fabric heavier and more opaque.

Lamination or **bonding** is the process of joining two textiles through the application of heat, pressure, and, sometimes, adhesives. Vinyl upholstery and clear vinyl-laminated fabrics are the most common. Because the unfriendly nature of plastic is unacceptable in some settings, lamination may be applied to the back or wrong side of a fabric. This allows spills or urine (as in the case of care centers or hospices, for example) to stay on the surface and make cleanup much easier.

Mothproof finish is a topical finish applied to wool or cellulosic fabrics that are vulnerable to insect damage. Moth and carpet beetle larvae eat the yarns, breaking down the disulfide cross-links in the cystine monomer. The finish renders the disulfide linkage indigestible, and when the process is combined with dyeing or finishing, the finish is integral and thus durable.

Nonresidential or commercial wools produced in the United States are given a mothproof finish, although imported wool labels must be inspected to determine finishes. For products not treated, mothballs, blocks, crystals, or sprays may be used in the areas of greatest vulnerability—the dark, cool areas where larvae thrive. These naphthalene-based compounds release a distasteful odor to the insects, and they are potentially harmful to companion pets and humans. To avoid accidental ingestion, place mothballs, blocks, or crystals in a sheer fabric that allows for fume release.

Soil-release finish is a fluorocarbon-based finish that enhances a fiber's hydrophilic quality, increasing water absorbency to augment detergent's power to lift and release soil.

Soil-repellent finish is available as both durable and nondurable. The treatment to the fabric when it is manufactured or when sent to a fabric finishing company is durable; topical application from a spray can or in the back room of the furniture warehouse is nondurable. Fluorocarbon-based soil-repellent finishes hold dirt and oily stains on the surface of the textile for a time so they can be readily removed. They do so by enhancing the high surface tension of spills and oil-based particles, causing them to bead like water does on an oily surface. It is important to blot and remove the spill or soil quickly. If spills are left on the surface and the upholstery continues to be used, the surface tension relaxes, the spill or soil spreads, and it is finally absorbed through tiny cracks in the finish that occur with time and use. The soil eventually works its way under the finish, locking in the stain.

Water-repellent finish is sometimes added to soil-repellent finish; it can also be durable or nondurable. It makes the textile less hydrophilic or water-absorbing in order to protect it against moisture damage and waterborne soil and stains. Textiles used outdoors, some drapery fabrics, and some nonresidential installation textiles benefit from water-repellent finishes.

Water absorbency finish enhances the textile's ability to absorb water, making it more easily washable and more able to release soil and stains that are absorbed into the surface.

Decorative Finishes

Decorative finishes achieve a decorative result or enhanced aesthetic hand or appearance. A decorative finish may give a fabric its name; examples include moiré, plissé, and chintz. Some decorative effects are not apparent because they enhance the surface texture or finish by brightening or dulling it. Some finishes increase the durability of the decorative effect.

Beetling finish is a pre- or postcoloring finish for linen where the piece is hammered with heavy wooden planks to flatten the yarns and increase the luster. It is effective in damask-woven textiles to augment the visibility of the woven design.

Brightening finish is a durable or nondurable finish that augments the clarity or brightness of the colors in a textile, making it look crisp and new for a length of time.

Calendaring finishes are applied and pressed in with a calendaring machine—a heavy cylinder roller that applies heat and pressure. Starches, glazes, or resins can be forced deeper into the textile surface by calendaring, and when the roller is engraved or has raised designs, specialty textural effects such as Palmer or moiré finishes are achieved. Calendared finishes can be durable or nondurable.

Ciré (chintz) finish is a calendared finish where a glaze, usually in the form of a resin, is applied and then pressed in. It may be durable if dry-cleaned but is nondurable through washing or wet cleaning. It is a glossy finish.

Delustering finish, a treatment for either yarns or finished fabric, diminishes the shininess of a textile. A high luster in textiles is sometimes considered a cheap look; by the same token, a low-luster finish enhances the richness of a particular fabric or carpeting.

Durable press calendaring is the application of resins to a textile that is stretched tight and then cured at very high temperatures in order to make it more wrinkle resistant and to retain shape. Durable press is also used in the calendaring process to create or add a greater degree of permanence to the embossing. Durable press is a flat curing procedure.

Etch printing or **burn-out finish** prints a design on a fabric, such as a polyester-cotton blend, with an acid compound that burns or etches (dissolves) the cellulosic fiber to reveal a sheer pattern.

Flocked finish is the adherence of tiny fibers or fine particles to create a pile effect on a fabric or wallcovering through one of these methods:

1. Adhesive applied to the surface of the fabric, possibly in a design or pattern. Excess flocked fibers are vacuumed, the adhesive cured, and the fabric brushed and cleaned.
2. Electrostatic flocking, which also utilizes adhesive on the ground cloth and then passes the fabric through a high-voltage chamber that charges the fibers, causing them to be attracted to the adhesive and aligning them.

Flocked fabrics can be embossed and printed. The finish is generally durable.

French wax finish is a ciré finish where resins are applied and then calendared. A French wax is the shiniest or highest-gloss finish. It is durable when dry-cleaned.

Moiré finish is an embossed method where the calendaring roller is engraved or raised into a watermark design pressed into faille fabric (fine crosswise or weft ribs). Moiré fabrics also include embossed velvets in a pattern. The moiré look can also be achieved by pigment printing and jacquard weaves.

Napped finish is the brushing-up of fibers to loosen them and create a fuzzy finish or depth similar to a short pile.

Panné finish is achieved by an embossing method where a velvet, ribbed velvet, or other pile textile is pressed down in one direction, resulting in enhanced luster.

Plissé finish is achieved by applying a caustic acid that causes the yarns to pucker. The plissé pattern is typically a stripe, plaid, or allover pucker. Ironing may remove plissé.

Resin finishes involve the application of a resin, a natural or synthetic clear, translucent substance, to the fabric. When applied and calendared, the resin becomes a lustrous glaze or the basis for waterproofing or soil repellency.

Schreiner calendaring is attained by means of tiny engraved lines on the calendar, which produce an increased luster in a textile without the application of resins or starches. Also called Schreiner finishing.

Post-Finishing

Finishes may be applied to finished fabrics to meet specified requirements. A fabric finishing company is one that specializes in treating fabrics prior to their fabrication into draperies, bedspreads, upholstered furniture, wallcoverings, or accessory items. The key advantage to post-finishing is that a fabric that has the right color, texture, and pattern but does not meet a certain nonresidential or fabrication requirement such as weight, stability, durability, or stain or flame resistance can still be fabricated and installed after finishing. This allows the interiors professional as well as the client far greater latitude in fabric selection. Finishing companies work closely with interior design professionals to help customize and expand their interior design options. Fabric finishing companies are listed at www.wiley.com /go/interiortextiles. Look for speedy, high-quality service and personnel with a knowledge of fabrics. Also note that finishing companies have proprietary names for their finishes, so when comparing one fabric finisher's products and services to another the name of the finish may not fully reveal its parameters.

The process for having fabric finished is as follows:

1. Contact the fabric finishing company of your choice and obtain specifications about the finishes it is equipped to apply, its policies and procedures, minimum yardage requirements, time frame turnaround, guarantees, quantity of return after shrinkage, risks to the fabric, charges per yard, and so on.

2. Select the fabric and add the finishing price before presenting the client with the cost, including fabrication. *Note:* Finishing prices are wholesale. You may opt to pass on this price, but more typically design professionals add a fee to cover their time and handling of the fabric specification and transport. Include shipping costs, and be aware of shrinkage, which means extra fabric will be required.

3. Send a short length to the fabric finisher for a finishing sample.

4. Compare this to the yardage and inspect for color or texture change. Test for strength. Unless guarantees exist, it may be wise to send the post-finished sample to an independent testing laboratory to ascertain that the fabric will still perform to other standards. For example, if a flame-retardant finish has weakened the textile, it may not meet nonresidential upholstery durability standards (discussed in chapter 6).

5. Once the sample is deemed acceptable, the entire length may be shipped for post-finishing.

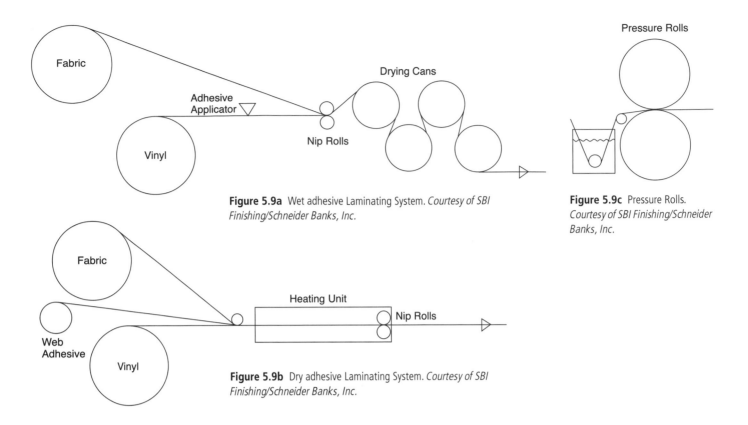

Figure 5.9a Wet adhesive Laminating System. *Courtesy of SBI Finishing/Schneider Banks, Inc.*

Figure 5.9c Pressure Rolls. *Courtesy of SBI Finishing/Schneider Banks, Inc.*

Figure 5.9b Dry adhesive Laminating System. *Courtesy of SBI Finishing/Schneider Banks, Inc.*

There are two general categories of post-finishing piece-goods fabric:

1. The lamination to a fabric of another material, such as a vinyl, knit, or paper
2. The adhesion of a liquid that solidifies on the back of the fabric, including foam flame-retardant finishes, acrylic latex, and silicone

Lamination

Lamination is the converting of fabric to suit it for an application other than one for which it would normally be used. For example, a delicate fabric cannot be used as upholstery unless it is laminated to a knit backing to increase strength and durability and to help prevent fraying and tearing. Other processes can be used for fabric protection, fire protection, water protection, and saving time and money in sewing or upholstering. Lamination is the combining of a fabric with a fabric or other material. The types of lamination are listed below. A few rules to remember when considering a lamination follow. Many of these rules apply to all types of lamination, but some only to vinyl and others only to flame-retardant finish lamination.

Points to consider about **clear lamination:**

- Colors are subject to minor variations when fabric is laminated due to the idiosyncrasies of color, pigments, dyes, fabric construction, and the heat processes of lamination. Fabric finishers do not assume responsi-

bility for variations that make the fabric unsuitable for a finished installation. Obtaining a trial sample is always recommended to avoid potential unsuitability.
- Laminated fabrics are generally not machine-washable, and the end-use of the product should not involve exterior exposure, which can cause fabric to delaminate, crack, bleed through, bubble, or shrink. Fabric finishers assume no responsibility for problems that occur when the fabric is mistreated in use or cleaning or by exposure to extremes in temperature unless specified and guaranteed as a finish feature or benefit.
- Inherently flame-retardant fabrics, including 100 percent polyester, will not pass fire code requirements after lamination unless flameproofed prior to lamination.
- Fabrics sent to a laminating company should be rolled, not folded, with different cuts on separate rolls and correct yardage indicated.
- Generally, goods can be laminated at widths from 45 to 58 inches. Nothing smaller or larger can be laminated.
- If the selected fabric may not be suitable for lamination, most laminating companies will provide up to a full-width, ½-yard sample at no charge.
- Laminating film is typically a 0.006-gauge translucent film with a cold-crack factor of −10° Fahrenheit. Laminated outdoor furniture cushions thus should be brought indoors in cold weather. Fabric finishers may offer lamination suitable for outdoor installations.

Mildew inhibitor may be added, but it will not prevent microbial growth under continual exposure. Clear laminated fabrics are not machine-washable.

- When ordering, specify matte or shiny finish.
- The return, or amount of yardage that comes back from the fabric finisher, is less than the yardage sent. For example: from 11 to 100 yards, approximately 86 percent will be returned. From 101 to 200 yards, 95 percent will be returned; from 201 to 1,000 yards, 96 percent will be returned; and over 1,000 yards, 97 percent will be returned. Lengths of less than 10 yards have no guarantee of minimum return.
- Approximate shipping time is 3 to 4 weeks after receipt of fabric. This can vary according to workload.

Types of Lamination Vinyl lamination film is a clear matte or shiny film, typically 0.006 gauge, that will often withstand temperatures of −10° Fahrenheit. Mildew inhibitor may be added to the clear film. Vinyl lamination is commonly used for seat cushions, headboards, table covers, shower curtains, and upholstery, and it has a dull finish. Shiny or polish vinyl lamination has a glossy finish. High-quality vinyl lamination will meet most upholstery flammability standards and should contain an ultraviolet (UV) inhibitor to deter fabric fading and deterioration from sunlight and other light sources. Indoor use only.

Moisture-barrier (interlining) backing is a vinyl barrier laminated to the back of upholstery fabrics used in institutional and healthcare applications to protect from fluids (spills and urine). It helps in maintaining a clean, sanitary environment and often has antibacterial and antifungal properties as well.

Water-repellent finish or **waterproofing** enhances the performance of outdoor fabrics. The degree of repellency is determined by the fabric's fiber content and construction. This finish is durable to laundering and dry cleaning.

Stain protection or **siliconizing** is fabric protection without lamination. It is used to protect fabric from both oil- and waterborne stains and helps repel dust and dry soil. Stain protection may extend the life of the fabric by increasing rub resistance. It has no visible effect on hand or appearance. Stain-protected fabric is durable to commercial cleanings. Branded fluorocarbon products include Scotchgard™ (3M) and Teflon® and Zepel (DuPont). Fabric finishing companies have their own house brand. Compare claim guarantees.

Moth and mildew resistance provides extended protection against mold, mildew, and fungus growth. This can be applied in conjunction with other finishes.

Antimicrobial finish is a broad-spectrum growth inhibitor that retards the growth of most gram-negative and gram-positive bacteria as well as many viruses. It is code-specified for institutions and healthcare facilities.

Urethane film is clear, stretchable film for lamination. It allows stretchable fabrics meant for stretch upholstery or accessory items to maintain stretchability after lamination.

Acrylic latex backcoat lamination stabilizes and reinforces fabrics for upholstery use, improves handling characteristics, and helps prevent fraying and seam slippage. It is recommended for directional fabrics but not for silks. Additional stain protection may be required. This type of lamination is an alternative to paper backing in wallcovering applications.

Paper backing lamination is used to back fabric for wallcovering applications.

Canvas backing laminated to a lightweight fabric gives it more body. It is used for bags, patio furniture, and so on.

Blackout backing in the form of blackout vinyl is laminated to window coverings and window shade materials to block out the sun.

Knit backing is bonded to the back of fabric to increase the strength and durability of upholstery fabric. It is often specified by major furniture manufacturers. Cotton knit backing helps prevent seam slippage and provides a luxurious hand to lightweight fabrics.

Foam backing is the lamination of ⅛-, 3/16-, or ¼-inch foam to fabric to make it suitable for acoustic control and quilted items, for example.

Wall upholstery backing is a multilayer-barrier backcoating designed to improve fabric handling and help prevent *adhesive strikethrough,* the bleeding of adhesive to the surface of wall upholstery. Additional stain protection is required.

Flame-retardant (FR) finish is perhaps the most important fabric finish, as nonresidential fabrics must meet architect specifications that include it. Nonresidential fabrics from contract distributors are already FR fabrics, yet many fabrics selected for nonresidential settings are not treated and must be flame-retarded. Because the United States does not have a national code, architects specify the tests or standards to be met for each given installation. These tests are discussed in chapter 6. When placing an order for FR finishes, you must give this information to the fabric finishing company, which then applies the product that will meet those specs. The company also provides written certification, which must be kept on file and copied to the architect. When in doubt, contact the local fire marshal where the fabric is to be installed.

Drapery codes require more chemical application than upholstery codes. The most stringent code for drapery fabrics is the NFPA 701, 1989 small-scale test, and for upholstery fabrics the NFPA 260/UFAC class 1. These codes, explained in chapter 6, are widely accepted by municipalities and fire departments in the United States. Be aware that California, Massachusetts, Boston, and New York have their own testing requirements. Their codes are often specified because they are the most stringent.

The two kinds of FR finishes used are polymer finishes and saline finishes.

Polymer flame-resistant or **-retardant finishes** are applied by submerging the fabric in a chemical bath and then heat-setting the treatment. Shrinkage is at least 5 percent. The process may produce stiffness or change the appearance, as discussed below, but it is the more durable of the treatments. **Saline flame-resistant** or **-retardant finishes** are salt-based and can corrode metal drapery pins, tacks, staples, and sewing and fabrication machinery. They increase the fabric's moisture absorption and may cause loss of dimensional stability. Saline solutions may cause fading, as they tend to leach out dye.

Several factors affect the results of FR finishes. These are listed below. A high-quality fabric finisher will work closely with the design professional to ascertain the fabric is the right choice and the aesthetic result satisfactory. Do compare companies to check state-of-the-art chemical formulations and application techniques. Look for environmentally nontoxic processes and products. FR finishes are solvent dry-cleanable. *Note:* Vinyl-laminated textiles are flame resistant if bonded to fabrics that have been flameproofed.

The content of a fabric is the most important factor in determining its suitability for a flame-retardant fabric finish.

1. Natural fiber fabrics are the best choice to be flame-retarded. Natural fibers best absorb the flame retardant and can be treated to meet the most stringent flammability standards.
2. Polyester and rayon respond well to FR treatments, and polyester can be treated with a washable finish. The other manufactured fibers are more difficult to treat for flame retardance. Acrylic, acetate, nylon, and polypropylene are not recommended for drapery use; they are hydrophobic (nonabsorbent), so the chemical remains on the surface of the fabric. All manufactured fabrics can be treated with FR backing (discussed below) for upholstery use.
3. Blends are commonly flame-retarded. A higher percentage of natural fiber yields better results. Higher concentrations of synthetic fibers make it necessary to add more chemical to meet the flammability standard. Some blends cannot be treated to meet a vertical test. Keep in mind that acrylic backings and stain protection are rarely, if ever, listed as part of a fabric's content; their presence increases fabric flammability and can substantially affect test results. Refer to the resources at the end of chapter 6 for fabric testing companies.

Flameproofing is a wet finish process; the fabric is moistened with a water-based flame-retardant solution and then heat-dried to cure the finish. Shrinkage may be uneven in some fabrics, rendering them unsuitable for use after finishing. Fabrics respond to the treatment much as they would to being moistened with pure water. These weaves require special attention:

1. Fabrics with varying thicknesses or densities, woven stripes, or embroidery may shrink at different rates. This can cause puckers or wrinkles to develop in the fabric.
2. Fabrics with a nap, such as chenille, velvet, and velour, may pose problems. Silk and cotton velvets tend to flatten, although polyester and mohair velvets respond well to treatment.
3. Moiré and optically sensitive fabrics can develop markings or patterns because of their hypersensitivity. Delicate moiré marks may diminish or disappear when flame-retarded.

All fabrics considered for FR finishes should be provided so the finisher can evaluate and conduct screening tests. There will likely be a charge for this service.

FR treatments often do not adversely affect the hand and appearance of the goods, with the exception of acrylic, nylon, and certain blends that require higher levels of chemical to pass tests. A tightly woven fabric may become stiff. Also, the finish applied to a nonabsorbent fabric may be visible in some form on the fabric.

As FR chemicals are water soluble, treated fabrics must be dry-cleaned only in an uncharged system containing no water. Fabric should be evaluated for flammability after each cleaning. The flame retardant will be partially or completely removed by washing. Other rules include avoiding applications where contact with moisture or dampness may exist, installing in climate-controlled indoor environments, and, for hung installations, using drapery pins and fasteners designed for use with FR. Also, the fabric should not come in contact with metal surfaces and should be sewn on very clean sewing machines.

Flame-retardant backing treats only the back of the fabric to prevent flame spread. Obtain verification of standards met. The advantages are the absence of visible effect on the decorative surface of the fabric and the potential to meet the most stringent flammability codes. This also reduces the need for a second moisture-barrier fabric in institutional settings. FR backings may be durable to both laundering and dry cleaning. Obtain verification from the fabric finisher. FR backings are recommended for all applications where fabrics may come in contact with moisture.

Flame and stain protection is a recommended nonresidential finish that combines flame-retardant and stain protection. It is especially useful for dark and solid-colored fabrics for commercial upholstery applications.

Fabric inspection is a service that may be offered by a fabric finisher where each yard of material is visually inspected for flaws and general condition before finishing. This procedure is recommended when the quality of goods sent for finishing is questionable.

Preshrinking is a wet, natural shrinkage and drying process designed to increase stability in natural fiber fabrics. The degree of shrinkage is determined by the content and construction of the fabric.

Measure/cut includes surcharge processes where fabrics are measured prior to finishing, cut, and rerolled onto separate bolts. High-quality fabric finishing companies also offer customer services that include administrative services, research, testing, and fabric storage.

ENHANCING TEXTILE PERFORMANCE

Textiles perform by being durable and serviceable; by resisting fading, crocking, and abrasion; and by remaining dimensionally stable and aesthetically pleasing. Enhanced performance is accomplished as follows:

Stabilizing Yarn Placement

Two problems may occur in yarn placement: sliding and unraveling. Yarns that slip, slide, or travel out of their placement distort patterns, are unsightly, and may pull away at the seams, leaving potential gaps. A test for seam yarn slippage is discussed in chapter 6. Yarns can be stabilized with a backcoating of latex, polyurethane, or polyacrylonitrile. A light spray or coat, called a *kiss coat,* is used on the back of drapery and upholstery fabrics to stabilize the yarn placement. Heavier coating flowed onto the back of fabric is for temperature or noise insulation and for light-darkening qualities.

Unraveling may take place where yarns are loose along cut edges. If a seam is trimmed close to the stitching and then subjected to pressure or stress, it can pop open. This problem is difficult to remedy. As a precaution, all seams should be serged with an overlocking double-stitch to prevent fraying and to reinforce the seam stitching. Where serging is not used, the fabric should be cut a minimum of ⅝ inch from the seam line. Another technique used for small handmade projects is to paint a ravel-stopping liquid onto the edges of the textile.

TABLE 5.1 FINISHES BY CATEGORY

Removing Color

Bleaching	Grassing

Increasing or Decreasing Luster

Beetling finish (linen)	Brightening finish
Calendaring finishes	Ciré (chintz) finish
Delustering finish	French wax finish
Resin finishes	Schreiner calendaring finish

Adding Designs, Motifs, or Apparent Texture

Embossed finish	Etch printing or burn-out finish
Moiré finish	Plissé finish

Adding, Changing, or Restoring Pile

Flocked finish	Napped finish	Panné finish

Enhancing Performance or Serviceability

Antibacterial or antiseptic finishes (microbial resistance)
Antistatic finish

Carefree finishes: smoothness-retention or wrinkle-resistant finish, permanent press finish.

Durable press finish	Lamination or bonding
Mothproof finish	Soil-release finish
Soil-repellent finish	Smoothness-retention finishes:
Water-repellent finish	heat setting and durable press

Increasing Flame Resistance

Flame-retardant finishes

Enhancing Insulative Value

Insulative finishes: foam, blackout

Correcting Off-Grain

The flaw of **off-grain—bowed** (weft yarns sag in center of width) and **skewed** (lopsided) yarns—is listed earlier in this chapter under "Faults and Flaws." To rectify offgrain fabrics, a **tenter frame** is used. The fabric is mounted with metal clips or pins (leaving tiny holes in the selvages), and then tension is applied to straighten the grain. The fabric is then subjected to steam and heat and dried to set the corrected grain. If the fabric is to be printed, **tentering** is done as a pretreatment.

Enhancing Dimensional Stability

A dimensionally stable textile retains its size and shape. Several factors can render a fabric less dimensionally stable. One is when warp and weft yarns are stressed or pulled tight as they are extruded or spun. As yarns gradually relax over time, they shrink slightly. This is **residual shrinkage.** Another factor is found in the weaving process, which also stretches yarns in the completed textile. This stretching or stressing results in the slow, gradual relaxation of the fabric known as **relaxation shrinkage.** To allay these problems, manufacturers may use one of the following techniques.

Fulling, used on wool fabrics, involves subjecting the fabric to moisture, heat, and pressure, causing the yarns to shrink and relax so the fabric is stable and compacted. Fulled wool fabrics may still shrink and compact further through successive cleanings after fabrication. This undesirable progression is called **felting.**

Compression or **compressive shrinkage** is conducted for cotton. The fabric is subjected to moisture and heat during the tentering process, resulting in what is known as a *preshrunk cotton textile.*

Heat setting is used to stabilize thermoplastic manufactured fibers such as polyester. When the tentering process is combined with high heat and a controlled cooling procedure, the yarns stay permanently in alignment. If, however, heat setting is done on slightly skewed or bowed yardage, those flaws become permanent.

Crypton®

Crypton is a patented technology whereby distributor or jobber fabrics are treated for upholstery and cubicle wallcoverings. Once treated, the fabric becomes a **Crypton Super Fabric.** Not a coating, topical treatment, or laminate, Crypton is a patented chemical process engineered to en-

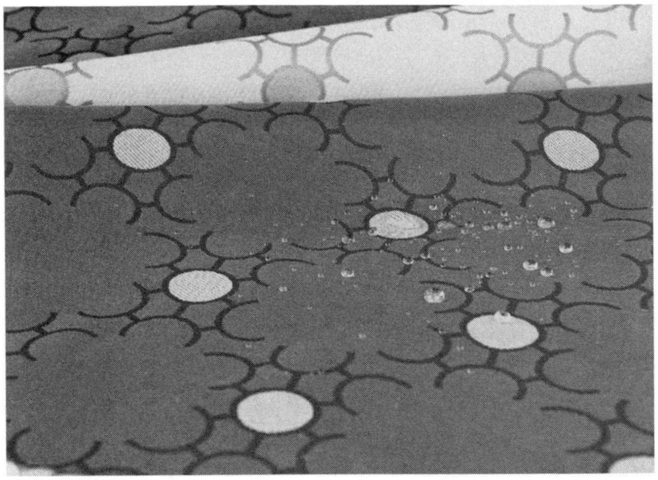

Figure 5.10 "Oh, Suouzani" a Crypton performance fabric from the Remix collection designed by Susan Lyons is a multitask textile for commercial and healthcare environments. *Photo by Fumiaki Odaka, courtesy of Innovations® in Wallcoverings, Inc.*

capsulate the fiber within the fabric, preventing moisture, bacteria, and stains from entering. Foreign substances can be easily removed from between the fiber's pores, and most stains can be wiped away. Crypton's five-year warranty guarantees that spills, stains, fluid, or bacteria will never penetrate the fabric or enter into a cushion where microbial organisms and bacteria could grow and odor develop. This antimicrobial chemistry and engineered moisture barrier results in clean, safe upholstery fabrics. Crypton has been a lead supplier in the hospitality, contract, and healthcare industries since 1993, with a 90 percent awareness in the hospitality market. Today, Crypton is the most specified fabric in the healthcare market and the only performance fabric specified by the U.S. government. The company is expanding its reach to include residential, automotive, and aviation markets. Fabric is available to the trade through the distributor list. A limited open line is available through the website at www.cryptonfabric.com.

RESOURCES

Go to www.wiley.com/go/interiortextiles for a list of fabric finishing companies.

Textile Directory
http://textile.us/directory
Extensive listing of fabric manufacturing and fabric finishing companies.

The American Textile Manufacturers Institute (ATMI)
1130 Connecticut Avenue NW, Suite 1200
Washington, DC 20036-3954
Tel 202-862-0500
Fax 202-862-0570

ATMI is the national trade association for the textile mill products industry. Its members manufacture yarns, fabrics, home furnishings, and other textile products.

PART II TEXTILE APPLICATIONS

6

Textile Specifications, Testing, and Labeling

Figure 6.1 Specifications are parameters for selecting a fabric and the fabrication sheets and forms that comprise instructions for fabrication into textile applications. Here, Crypton® Super Fabric piece goods await fabrication. *Photo courtesy of Crypton.*

TEXTILE SPECIFICATIONS, testing, and labeling are closely related topics in contemporary textiles. The process of selecting textiles must begin with a clear understanding of the parameters and requirements of a project. In contract interior design, those parameters do not originate with the interior designer but rather with the architectural firm, which is legally bound to meet the building codes and minimum or specified requirements for cost, fiber, life, safety, and durability. The architectural firm writes specifications listing general or specific types of products or parameters of acceptable construction and installation. This is done to protect the health, safety, and well-being of the public and to ensure both cost efficiency and the long-term durability of the textile products.

In order to specify requirements that a textile must meet, or pass, for the above criteria, testing is accomplished with rated results. These results appear on labels or are otherwise accessible to the design professionals, who then choose textiles that meet the specification criteria. These interdependent actions make possible the selection of acceptable contract interior textiles that are safe, practical, and within budget limitations—and that also contribute to the project's aesthetic success as handsome products and installations that will withstand time, use, and fashion trends.

While the majority of the information in this chapter is geared toward the technical rigors of contract interior design, much is also applicable to residential spaces. Design professionals often link contract requirements to the selection of durable and aesthetically pleasing textiles for residential spaces. The processes of selection specifications and installations are also residential topics.

CONTRACT CODES AND SPECIFICATIONS

As discussed in chapter 1, the word *specifications,* or "specs," has two meanings. The first meaning includes the parameters, written by the architectural firm, for selecting a textile for a commercial or residential project. Each contract textile carries a description or documentation of its fiber, construction, finishes, and tests it has passed. This description is known as a *product specification* or *specs.* These are the parameters specified by the architectural firm. See figure 6.2.

The second meaning of *specifications* covers the forms and action of ordering of textile yardage, the fabrication sheets or forms whereby that yardage is made into product, and the installation forms and instructions.

The design professional selects textiles with specifications or descriptions that meet the criteria or specifications written by the architect. These criteria are presented in this chapter. The details pertaining to the second interpretation of *specifications* are presented in the application chapters on upholstered furniture, slipcovers, textile wallcoverings, window treatments, linens and accessories, broadloom carpeting, and rugs.

Specifications are written by an architectural firm for nonresidential or contract application. They exist because public spaces experience heavy textile use. Multiple users may cause damage to textiles through abuse and soiling. Cleaning must be frequent, and health and safety factors are mandatory. The parameters of textiles and carpeting used in contract settings include environmental requirements, user or occupant requirements, aesthetic requirements, performance or functional specifications, descriptive specifications, proprietary specifications, and reference standard specifications.

Environmental requirements include the ethical use of renewable resources, the protection of the earth's environment, and the specification of materials that will enhance rather than diminish the quality of life and air indoors. These may or may not be a part of the written specifications. Refer to chapter 2.

User or occupant requirements are those that demand effort or resources on the part of the purchaser or user. They include the cost of materials, fabrication, and installation, as well as efforts in decision making, the longevity as well as physical and psychological comfort of the textiles, and upkeep or maintenance. Cost is customarily a priority in nonresidential specifications.

Aesthetic requirements concern the coordination of textiles as critical components of a whole interior or exterior private or public space. The long-term livability or aesthetic durability depends on several factors, including the performance of the fiber and textile construction, finishes, upkeep, the cycle of color trends, the timeless versus trendy choice of pattern, and the appeal of texture. All these components are balanced against the purpose of the interior and the real-life reactions of the people who will use the space. Aesthetics and beauty are transient. If well chosen, however, textiles can last as long as they are functional and durable. Poor aesthetic choices result in interiors that become trite, tiresome, dated, or nonfunctional. Likewise, where a fabric or carpet is not durable, its aesthetic is short-lived, as it physically wears out before it goes out of style. It should be the determined goal of every design professional to ensure the best quality and highest level of aesthetic design the budget will allow, thus increasing the longevity and enjoyment of the textiles. Aspects of textile aesthetics and coordination comprise chapter 7.

Performance or functional specifications are always present for textiles used in the public sector. They include flammability requirements, wet and dry crocking, colorfastness to light, physical properties, abrasion or crush resistance, and resistance to microbes or bacterial growth and moisture barrier. Architectural firms specify minimum acceptable performance or functional standards according to the type of installation and the specific parameters and use of the space. Flammability standards are imperative for all public spaces, while other criteria are more use-specific. For example, resistance to microbes or bacterial growth and moisture is necessary for healthcare facilities. Abrasion resistance standards are required for high-use seating and crush resistance for high-traffic carpeting. Colorfastness against fading is critical for applications where natural or intense artificial lighting is a key design element.

Performance or functional requirements are established locally as codes or enforceable regulations assured by testing results. Architects include in the specification documents lists of functional requirements. Standardization is achieved by the Association for Contract Textiles (ACT), listed in the Resources section at the end of this chapter.

A **descriptive specification,** in which the product is described in detail—including fiber content, construction

Figure 6.2 Xorel® specifications.

SINCE ITS INTRODUCTION IN 1981, Xorel fabrics have a proven track record in thousands of installations around the world. Woven from a single high performance fiber, Xorel's extraordinary utility and beauty belies the simplicity of its design process.

Contents 100% Xorel or 100% IFR (Inherently Flame Retardant) Xorel Polyethylene

Backing/Width   Paperbacked 52 inches
Acrylic backed 54 inches
Unbacked 56 inches

Uses Wallcovering, Upholstery, Upholstered Walls, Panels

Dyeing All Xorel yarns are solution dyed and virtually fade proof.

Flame Retardancy All Xorel fabrics, both IFR and non-IFR, qualify for use in Class A and Class 1 areas under the ASTM E-84 Tunnel Test. They also pass NFPA 265 Room Corner Test.

IFR Xorel passes NFPA 701. IFR Xorel fabrics also pass other major vertical tests in the U.S., Canada, and Europe, as well as the IMO standards for shipboard use.

Durability Wyzenbeek Abrasion Method. No wear after one million (1,000,000) double rubs.

Stain Resistance In tests conducted at intervals of one hour, one day, and seven days, 27 common stains were completely removed by cleaning procedures specified by Carnegie.

Colorfastness Under the Fadeometer Test, Xorel fabrics achieved highest rating Class 5 (no fading) after 80 to 200 hours, two to five times the normal testing time required for upholstery and wallcovering fabrics

Indoor Air Quality Xorel meets the requirements of Section 01350, California State Building Guideline for Indoor Environmental and Air Quality

Toxicity in Fire IFR Xorel easily passes the International Maritime Organization's (IMO) test for toxicity in a fire, which measures the 7 deadliest gasses produced in a fire. Xorel is accepted by the New York City Department of Buildings under the Pittsburgh Protocol Test Method.

Hospital Use Xorel fabrics will not support the growth of fungi, bacteria, or staphylococcus aureus and when paper backed will not permit the passage of bacteria.

Acoustics In NCR (noise reduction coefficient) testing. Xorel fabrics are acoustically neutral in key frequencies. In tests on multiple patterns, the NRC of the tested fiberglass core covered with Xorel fabric changed only minimally from a decrease of .20 to an increase of .05.

Dimensional Stability In a high humidity test Xorel fabrics were completely stable, neither expanding nor shrinking.

Maintenance Since Xorel yarns are inherently nonabsorbent, Xorel fabrics are uniquely stain resistant and do not require any topical finishes. Most stains can be removed with hot water. For information on specific stains, ask for our Suggested Maintenance Procedures brochure, or view it on our web site.

Installation Instructions Contact us for a copy of our wallcovering and upholstery installation instructions or view them on our web site.

Carnegie

110 North Centre Avenue
Rockville Center, NY 11570
T 800 727 6770
www.carnegiefabrics.com

method, weight, and so on, but without mention of manufacturer or jobber—is often used for textiles and carpeting. For example, a drapery specification may list an inherently flame-resistant (FR) fiber; the type of fabric, including weight or weave; the kind of construction and type of pleat; and drapery hardware. Carpeting specs list fiber, construction, and weight and cost parameters, among other details, as selected by the architect. Performance and descriptive specifications are typically combined in draperies, wallcoverings, and carpeting, and often used in upholstered seating.

A **proprietary specification** is a specific product identified by its brand name or number from a specific manufacturer. Use of a proprietary spec means the finished interior will match the approved interior design program plan. Proprietary specifications are often named in upholstered furniture and paneled workstations, particularly where the fixtures are planned by proprietary CAD (computer-aided design) software; only the specified manufactured fixtures will work in the space as designed, for example. If specific products are not obtainable, comparable substitutions may be acceptable.

A **reference standard** is where the specs follow guidelines from an acknowledged authoritative source or organization that has established a minimum standard of quality acceptable for nonresidential interior design. In this case,

the architect has only to quote or refer to the reference standard, and design professionals will access that information through online or library sources to determine the specifications.

Fabrication specifications are forms and written instructions, often accompanied by drawings, that are given to a fabricator whose job it is to custom upholster or sew textiles into the applications. These applications include upholstery, draperies, slipcovers, bedding, linens, and accessory items.

Custom and installation specifications may include drawings that show the style or shape or placement of the textile product. These may be floor plans, wall elevations, or product drawings. Written directions for installation, and sometimes installation drawings, are included as well. These assist the design professional in carrying out the master plan with little room for error or change that could compromise the integrity of the master architectural or interior design plan.

Specifications may stand alone if the textile application is a subcontracted refurbishing or replacement element not attached to new construction. In this case, requirements may be altered to fit the parameters of the installation and the preferences or needs of the tenant's workspace.

RESIDENTIAL SPECIFICATIONS

Standards for flammability, abrasion resistance, colorfastness, and resistance to bacterial growth do not apply to residential interior design unless assurance is sought by the homeowner or the design professional. Keeping the interior safe for occupancy should always be a high priority, and nonresidential textiles are occasionally used in private design because of their durability and timeless design qualities with the added advantage of higher performance standards. Likewise, wise selection with respect to environmental responsibility relates to both residential and nonresidential projects, even though codes or requirements do not exist for private residences.

Specifications for residential textiles are rarely written by an architect. Rather, the selection of textiles is a decision made by the client and the interior design professional, or sometimes by one without assistance of the other. Often, several design professionals assist the residential customer —one or more for each area of textile application. It is

Figure 6.3 When specifying correct yardage for multiple applications, such as draperies and bedspreads, calculate carefully to avoid reordering fabric; the later order may be from a different dye lot. *Photo courtesy of ADO Corporation, www.ado-usa.com*

more likely that the term *specifications* will relate to the actual ordering of textile, the forms of instruction for upholstery or fabrication into product, and the installation instruction forms. In the ordering process, some scenarios should be avoided. The following residential examples illustrate the need to be precise and thorough in specifying textiles.

A designer orders from the jobber or fabric house yardage for custom draperies and bedspreads. A decision is later made to also create matching pillows and table skirts. When the fabric is reordered, the dye lot is off, or unmatched. The jobber or fabric house will accept the cut order back into the warehouse only with a restocking fee of as much as 30 percent.

Another example: A customer places a cut order based on the sample book swatch. The fabric shipped does not match the swatch and consequently does not look right in the interior. In both instances, a small swatch of the fabric at hand was mailed to the jobber or fabric house order desk, which then searched each warehouse in the United States. Fabric was found to match the draperies and bedspread ensemble, but the sample swatch could not be matched in any of the warehouses, requiring the customer to reselect another fabric.

These situations recur often. The design professional should be careful in three ways when specifying or placing orders:

1. Ascertain the extent of the customer's desire or the complete parameters of the items that require matching or exact fabric. Be thorough.
2. Calculated yardage may contain errors. Before placing an order, recheck the calculations.
3. Never be in a hurry. Mistakes often occur when fabric is ordered quickly. These mistakes often consume the profit in a custom job. When goods must be reordered, ordering and delivery time, shipping expense, and time handling the fabric must be considered. If the dye lots do not match, this process may be repeated, sometimes two or more times.

An ironic aspect of the recurring dye lot problem is that for each new set of piece-goods bolts reordered and placed in stock in the warehouse, there are usually a few remnant bolts with so few yards as to be largely unusable for custom order. When the fabric is eventually discontinued and orders cease to be placed for the in-stock goods, there is a need to dispose of the goods to a retail outlet specializing in fabrics that are flawed or of varying dye lots. Alternatively, the jobber may elect to hold a parking lot or tent sale, or to donate the goods to charity.

CONTRACT AND RESIDENTIAL FABRICATION

Both contract and residential fabrication specifications must be accurate to avoid scenarios such as these:

- The wrong textile is upholstered onto a piece or into a specified product. This may happen when the fabric is not checked for accuracy on arrival or when the specification instructions are vague.
- A textile is upholstered in the wrong direction—railroaded (horizontal) instead of vertical, for example.
- Styling is incorrect in fabricated products such as window treatments, bedding, linens, or accessories.
- Installation is incorrect in style, placement, or location. The wrong product—possibly one belonging to a different client—may be installed.
- Dimensions for fabrication are inaccurate, causing the finished product to be the wrong size. This problem sometimes cannot be corrected, and the textile may have to be reordered and refabricated.

OVERSEEING INSTALLATION

Professionals who specialize in interior textiles are responsible for providing accurate installation instructions. However, they are often not present in person during installation. The steps in ensuring a well-executed installation are as follows:

1. High-quality installers are the key to high-quality installations. Finding and keeping skilled and reliable installers should be a high priority for interior design professionals. Experienced installers can make all the difference in the quality of a textile installation, whether for floor coverings, wallcoverings, window treatments, bed appointments, or furniture. Although no installer has a magic wand to correct mistakes made by the textile professional, there are times when the installer can make a product look even better than was envisioned.

2. Decide on the hiring arrangements for installers. There are two ways to engage the services of textile application installers. One is to work with independent contractors. This means the installer owns his or her own tools and works independently for other professionals as well. If all the installer's time is spent in serving one design firm, and if the installer is considered full-time and depends on that firm for all his or her work, then the firm is obligated to pay a full-time salary, including taxes and benefits. A full-time employee gives dedicated service

Figure 6.4 Expert installation is evident in the carpeting, window treatment, furniture placement, and perfection of the VISTA® Window Film.

but is also a financial burden to the firm, whereas an independent contractor keeps a schedule the firm must accommodate.

3. Specification sheets or work orders are given to installers with the product to be installed. For example, a floor plan with carpet layout plotted indicates to the installer which direction carpet is to be installed and where the seams and cuts are to be placed. For window treatments, a copy of the workroom specification sheet indicates the rod width placement or exact dimensions. A drapery spec sheet is often accompanied by sketches or photocopied illustrations indicating how the finished product will appear. Installers of upholstered furniture need a furniture placement plan. They should also remove all packaging materials from the site once the furniture is in place.

4. The interior design professional may or may not accompany the installer to a job site. If the installer is competent and understands the parameters of the job, there is usually no need. Some design professionals visit the site at the completion of the work, or within some period, such as a week, to inspect. If problems arise during the installation, the design professional should be accessible to seek a solution or remedy.

Installers often collect the balance due upon completion of an installation, per the sales contract. It may be the custom of an installer to bring the check to the textile professional and be paid quickly, sometimes even the same day, as the installation takes place.

Professionals and Process

The types of design professionals whose job it is to fulfill the parameters of the specifications include interior designers or interior design or interior architectural firms—possibly a department within an architectural firm—facilities managers, specifiers, manufacturer's representatives, and specialty design professionals whose business is in one or more segments such as upholstery, wallcoverings, window treatments, or carpeting.

The awarding of a project may result from a comprehensive *bid procedure* wherein each bidding party supplies samples and product specifications that meet the architectural specifications, including cost, product quality, time frame, and capability to deliver. Bidding parties typically propose different products except in cases of proprietary specifications. This may result in changes to the aesthetics or color scheme. The bids are compared and the project is awarded based on the lowest price, the reputation of the bidding party, or other parameters. There is inherent risk for the design professional, as bids are typically undisclosed. Sometimes no minimum or maximum budget is given. Further, the bidding party is usually not told why it lost the bid. Much time may be dedicated to preparing a bid, with disappointment a real possibility. The professional who wins the bid is bound by that bid to provide product at that price.

If unexpected circumstances arise, the professional may seek to modify the contract with a **change directive,** which allows the parties to approve a specific change. This may be a textile or product that was discontinued after the bid was submitted (discontinuation takes place without prior notification) or a product that is otherwise unavailable or unsuitable.

When the contract price must be modified, a **change order** is required, which, like the change directive, is signed by all authorized parties. The change order is necessary to make changes in product, installation, time frame, or cost. When a clarification or interpretation is required but does not change the sum or cost, then a **supplemental instruction** is used. These items become amended parts of the contract documents.

If furnishings are part of a major remodel or new project, the specifications may be a subsection of larger contract documents that form an agreement between the contractor and the owner. These may include construction, systems, fixtures, finishes, and furnishings documents.

TEXTILE AND PRODUCT TESTING

Textile fabric and product testing consists of experiments conducted under controlled conditions where a fabric, mock-up of furniture, mattress, drapery or wallcovering, or carpeting sample is tested such that results can be measured, evaluated, and reported. Testing categories include flammability, wet and dry crocking, colorfastness to light, physical properties, and abrasion or crush resistance. Test results enable the professional to meet Flammable Fabric Act flammability standards as well as local or regional codes or regulations. Testing is conducted by independent testing laboratories, governmental laboratories, and fabric finishing companies. Test results are individualized as a rating based on minimum standards or as a pass/fail. Where a textile passes a test, a certificate is issued or documentation made available upon request. In this chapter, tests concerning textiles are presented first. Later in the chapter, carpeting testing is presented.

Testing is a difficult issue for many design professionals to understand and comply with because codes or standards are state or municipal ordinances rather than national standards. In new construction, the architectural firm traditionally selects the codes based on local ordinance but often looks to more stringent codes. For example, the California Technical Bulletins, the New York Port Authority, and the Boston city fire codes are particularly stringent because of human life tragedies in those places spurred lawmakers to regulate flammable materials in public spaces. The gamut of tests can be bewildering and has long cried out for an organization to standardize both tests and results. As no national laws exist, the process must be voluntary by fabric manufacturers so contract design professionals can more easily recognize and select textiles that meet the most frequently written functional specifications for contract installations.

The Association for Contract Textiles (ACT) has developed five symbols that assure, with respect to contract fabrics that bear them, that those fabrics meet industry standards and pass all applicable testing. These icons are included on most contract/nonresidential textile samples and are easily recognizable. At a glance, the symbols displayed on labels indicate a level of acceptance for stringent specification guidelines in these five categories: **flame resistance, colorfastness to wet and dry crocking, colorfastness to light, physical properties,** and **abrasion.** These are listed in Table 6.1, and descriptions are listed in the tables that follow. *Note:* For American Society for Testing and Materials (ASTM) tests listed in the following tables, the last two digits indicate the year the test was updated. For example, "-02" indicates the test was updated in 2002.

TABLE 6.1 ASSOCIATION FOR CONTRACT TEXTILES (ACT) PERFORMANCE GUIDELINES

 Flammability

The measurement of a fabric's performance when it is exposed to specific sources of ignition.

NOTE: ACT guidelines specify different flammability tests dictated by the intended end-use for the fabric.

ACT GUIDELINES

Upholstery
California Technical Bulletin #117 Section E –
Class 1 (Pass)

Direct Glue Wallcoverings
ASTM E 84-03 (Adhered Mounting Method) –
Class A or Class 1

Wrapped Panels and Upholstered Walls
ASTM E 84-03 (Unadhered Mounting Method) –
Class A or Class 1

Drapery
NFPA 701-89 (Small Scale)*—Pass
*NFPA 701-99 Test #1 is being phased in at this time, but is not yet cited in all relevant codes. Therefore, the small-scale test remains the ACT standard until further notice.

(continued)

TABLE 6.1 ACT PERFORMANCE GUIDELINES *continued*

 Wet & Dry Crocking

Transfer of dye from the surface of a dyed or printed fabric onto another surface by rubbing.

ACT GUIDELINES

Upholstery
AATCC 8-2001
Dry Crocking, Grade 4 minimum.
Wet Crocking, Grade 3 minimum.

Direct Glue Wallcovering
AATCC 8-2001
Dry Crocking, Grade 3 minimum.
Wet Crocking, Grade 3 minimum.

Wrapped Panels & Upholstered Walls
AATCC 8-2001
Dry Crocking, Grade 3 minimum.
Wet Crocking, Grade 3 minimum.

Drapery
AATCC 8-2001 (Solids)
Dry Crocking, Grade 3 minimum.
Wet Crocking, Grade 3 minimum.

AATCC 16-2001 (Prints)
Dry Crocking, Grade 3 minimum.
Wet Crocking, Grade 3 minimum.

 Colorfastness to Light

A material's degree of resistance to the fading effect of light.

Upholstery
AATCC 16 Option 1 or 3-2003
Grade 4 minimum at 40 hours

Direct Glue Wallcoverings
AATCC 16 Option 1 or 3-2003
Grade 4 minimum at 40 hours

Wrapped Panels and Upholstered Walls
AATCC 16 Option 1 or 3-2003
Grade 4 minimum at 40 hours

Drapery
AATCC 16 Option 1 or 3-2003
Grade 4 minimum at 60 hours

 Physical Properties

Physical property tests include: Brush Pill, Breaking Strength and Seam Slippage. *Pilling* is the formation of fuzzy balls of fiber on the surface of a fabric that remain attached to the fabric. *Breaking strength* is the measurement of stress exerted to pull a fabric apart under tension. *Seam slippage* is the movement of yarns in a fabric that occurs when it is pulled apart at a seam.

ACT GUIDELINES

Upholstery
Brush pill
ASTM D3511-02, Class 3 minimum

Breaking strength
ASTM D5034-95 (2001) (Grab Test)
50 lbs. minimum in warp and weft

Seam slippage
ASTM D4034
25 lbs. minimum in warp and weft

Wrapped Panels and Upholstered Walls
Breaking strength
ASTM D5034-95 (2001) (Grab Test)
35 lbs. minimum in warp and weft

Drapery
Seam slippage
ASTM D3597-02-D434-95
for fabrics over 6 oz./sq. yard
25 lbs. minimum in warp and weft

 **Abrasion**

The surface wear of a fabric caused by rubbing and contact with another fabric.

ACT GUIDELINES

General Contract Upholstery
ASTM D4157-02 (ACT approved #10 Cotton Duck)
15,000 double rubs Wyzenbeek method

ASTM D4966-98 (12 kPa pressure)
20,000 cycles Martindale method

Heavy Duty
ASTM D4157-02 (ACT approved #10 Cotton Duck)
30,000 double rubs Wyzenbeek method

ASTM D4966-98 (12 kPa pressure)
40,000 cycles Martindale method

End-use examples of heavy-duty installations where upholstery fabrics rated at 30,000 double rubs should be appropriate are single shift corporate, hotel rooms/suites, conference rooms and dining area usage.

ACT acknowledges that there are extreme wear situations that may require higher levels of abrasion resistance. End-use examples that may require higher than 30,000 double rubs include: 24 hour transportation terminals, 24 hour telemarketing, 24 hour healthcare emergency rooms, 24 hour casino gambling areas, and such public gathering places as theatres, stadiums, lecture halls, and fast food restaurants.

It is strongly suggested that double rubs exceeding 100,000 are not meaningful in providing additional value in use. Higher abrasion resistance does not necessarily indicate a significant extension of the service life of the fabric.

FLAMMABILITY: CONUMER SAFETY

Flammability, or the ability to inflame or catch on fire, is of crucial importance in all public spaces because of the potential loss of life that can occur when a textile propagates a fire. The loss of life in well-known fires has resulted in strict standards and codes or regulations. Tragedies that resulted in investigation and eventual standards and regulations include the 1913 fire at the Triangle Shirtwaist Company of New York City, where 145 female workers died, and the 1942 fire at the Coconut Grove nightclub in Boston, where 492 people lost their lives. Today, New York and Boston fire codes, as well as the California Technical Bulletins, are among the most stringent in the United States.

Flammability standards include the material specifications and also the practices or test methods used to render a textile safe for public use. Standards are established by both public and private organizations. The National Fire Protection Association (NFPA) publishes the NFPA 101 Life Safety Code (LSC), a primary source for fire protection information. As a voluntary, private nonprofit organization, NFPA standards and information cover all aspects of fire prevention. The NFPA 5000, the International Building Code (IBC), and the Uniform Building Code (UBC) publications have chapters on interior wall and ceiling finishes, floor finishes, decorations and trim, and special finishes. The NFPA LSC also includes furnishings requirements. The ASTM also establishes standards for products and materials used in construction and manufacturing. And, although the American National Standards Institute (ANSI) does not develop standards, it does coordinate the efforts of the public and governmental organizations by forming a consensus and enhancing credibility. ANSI then becomes a joint sponsor with other organizations, and the resulting standards are often referred to as ANSI standards.

Requirements for office workstation or systems furniture, upholstered walls, and divider panels listed with Underwriters Laboratories (UL) clarify that they apply only to electrified panel systems. In general, panel products are expected to meet Class A requirements. Only the Boston firecode and the federal General Services Administration (GSA) require that the systems be Class A, though some occupancies have more relaxed standards. There is a test for the NFPA 101 Life Safety. Office systems do not have to be Class A, even though the fabrics themselves do. However, the test procedure itself describes neither a classification system nor pass/fail criteria.

The Flammable Fabrics Act (FFA) was passed in 1954, largely to restrict the use of flammable apparel fabric. In 1967, the act was amended to include interior furnishings and to permit the establishment of flammability standards for interior textiles. A federal agency known as the Consumer Product Safety Commission (CPSC) was established in 1972 and operative in 1973. This agency administers the FFA by compiling and analyzing statistics and data concerning fire-related injuries. If a textile or furnishing product is deemed an unreasonable risk to consumer safety, the CPSC may work toward the establishment of revised FFA safety standards. The CPSC is authorized to research textiles and product flammability, conduct feasibility studies on ways to reduce flammability, and develop and offer training on testing methods and devices.

Much of the investigative work is carried out by the federally funded National Institute of Standards and Technology (NIST), which provides statistical injury data and laboratory test results to the CPSC and other federal agencies. These results may eventually lead to the development of new standards. If that should take place, the CPSC must follow strict procedures that allow the textile industry to fully cooperate with the new standard. The CPSC must first publish a notice in the *Federal Register* of the proposed new standard, invite and consider response from affected and interested parties, publish the final version of the new standard in the *Federal Register,* allow approximately one year for the manufacture of textiles or products to meet the standard, and prohibit noncomplying products to be distributed after the imposed date. Exceptions are possible.

As the standards are made known, they are labeled so that reference may be made to their origin. The Department of Commerce (DOC) acronym appears on some standards. The indicators Flammable Fabric (FF) or Proposed Flammable Fabric (PFF) and numbers are used to notate these standards. The first number, as seen below, indicates the sequence of proposed standards; the second number is the year the action was taken (not necessarily the effective date or year). The DOC notation has largely been replaced by the Code of Federal Regulations (CFR) acronym and identifying numbers. See the Resources section at the end of this chapter for procuring information.

Four standards have been established that pertain to interiors; others are being considered. These four are of special interest to design professionals:

FF 1-70 Large Carpets and Rugs (16 CFR 1630)

FF 2-70 Small Carpets and Rugs (16 CFR 1631)

FF 4-74 Mattresses and Mattress Pads (16 CFR 1632)

PFF 6-81 Upholstered Furniture (16 CFR 1633)

This last standard, for upholstered furniture, did not reach the mandatory stage because, when the draft was posted, members of the upholstered furniture industry worked to prevent the standard from becoming too restrictive. The Upholstered Furniture Action Council (UFAC) was launched in 1979 to facilitate a voluntary program to ensure safer products. The focus was flammability from lighted cigarette ignition, the primary source of upholstered furniture fire. All parts of furniture have been made flame resistant, including construction components, padding, and especially the covering fabric. To participate in the UFAC Voluntary Action Program, upholstered furniture manufacturers must agree to produce their furniture in accordance with the basic UFAC construction criteria. Manufacturers participating in this program label the furniture with UFAC hangtags. In order to identify component materials that meet the UFAC requirements, a test method is needed to define acceptable performance in each criterion.

Tests are briefly described in Table 6.3, with website references for further information.

As listed above, performance specifications, written into project contracts by architects, are the result of codes or standards established on a local, state, or national level to ensure the health, safety, and welfare of the public who use the spaces. Regulatory standards and codes, which often reference the standards, are the result of the combined efforts of people who have worked long and hard for protection for the public—government agency personnel, architecture and design industry professionals, and consumers or users of the spaces. In particular, flammability has been a focus of

safety studies, as textiles have the potential to ignite, spread a fire, and produce toxicants and smoke that are potentially lethal to occupants.

Codes are enforceable by the office of the local fire marshal within the jurisdiction where the building is located. Even if no flammability specifications are written, or if the refurnishing items are not under the direction of an architectural firm, the supplier or design professional is still obligated to meet local requirements. Therefore, to become knowledgeable about local code is imperative.

Flammability, Smoke, and Toxicity

Both the terms *flammable* and *inflammable* indicate a textile or component that can combust, or catch on fire. This occurs where oxygen combines with other elements or compounds and produces heat energy and, eventually, fire.

Table 6.2 lists the combustion process, the three stages of interior fire, and the terms and definitions associated with flammability commonly used in the interior design textile industry.

Byproducts of combustion include smoke, toxicants or toxic gases, and molten polymer compounds. A key danger in the combustion process is the production of smoke and toxic gases. Carbon monoxide (CO), the most toxic or poisonous gas, is present in all fires. It prevents the absorption of oxygen by red blood cells. Other toxic gases include carbon dioxide (CO_2), hydrogen cyanide (HCN), hydrogen sulfide (HS), nitrogen oxide plus nitrogen dioxide (NO + NO_2), and vinyl cyanide ($CH_2 CHCN$). Research is underway to devise a test method for inhaled toxicants.

The combination of toxic gases and smoke, which prevents air from reaching the lungs and prevents clear vision of exits, usually causes death by suffocation and inhaled poisons before a person can die from the heat of a fire. While some tests measure smoke spread and density, others do not consider smoke or toxicants.

Molten polymer compounds are synthetic thermoplastic fibers such as polyester and vinyl products that melt and form droplets. If the melting fabric hardens into pellet-like droplets and does not contribute to the fuel load, this is a positive; however, if the melting droplets drip onto a rug or carpet that may smolder or ignite, the fabric may increase the fire danger.

Flammability Testing

Flammability testing is one of the most important testing procedures within the textile industry because of crucial safety implications. A major cause of fatalities in fire is the accidental ignition of upholstery and textiles.

TABLE 6.2 FLAMMABILITY TERMS

Stage 1 fire — The fire is contained within the item that is burning. Related terms are *time of ignition* and *initial growth* of a fire. Smoke produced in a Stage 1 fire may travel many feet and pose a risk to humans. Ideally, a fire alarm alerts occupants, and handheld fire extinguishers can be used to stop the fire from spreading. If the textiles selected do not support or sustain a fire for the first five to ten minutes, the chances of the fire progressing to Stage 2 are reduced, giving occupants time to evacuate the building safely.

Stage 2 fire — The fire is in the growth stage, spreading from its point of origin and igniting other items nearby. Operative smoke detectors that activate ceiling sprinkler system fire extinguishers may stop the flame propagation. If not, the combined heat builds up and the flames flash over, simultaneously igniting all the combustible material in a room or area. This explosion takes place when the fire reaches the 1200°F range, dramatically increasing the flame spread and rate of toxic smoke generation.

Stage 3 fire — The fire is fully developed and spreads or spills out from the origination space to adjoining spaces — other rooms, corridors, or open spaces. The entire building is now dangerous to those within range from significant heat, smoke, toxicants, and potential structural collapse.

Smoldering — Combustion without a flame that generates heat, smoke, and toxicants and results in black, charred damage.

Flammability — In testing, the amount of flame spread under test conditions.

Flame spread — The rate at which flame travels along the surface of a finish.

Inherently flame-resistant — Describes fibers that resist burning or are slow to ignite and melt before burning. These include aramid, asbestos, glass fiber, novoloid and modacrylic, Kevlar®, Nomex®, Trivera CS (comfort and safety — a European brand) polyester, and Avora® FR polyester.

Flame resistant — Describes inherently flame-resistant fabrics and fabrics given a flame-resistant finish that resist flame or terminate the flame following ignition. To be flame-resistant, the textile should not propagate or spread the fire and should self-extinguish. Wool is slow to ignite and self-extinguishes when the flame source is removed.

Flame retardant (FR) — Describes finishes added to the fiber's liquid state before extrusion, or applied as a post-finishing treatment. Depending on the chemicals and method of application, a flame-retardant treatment may secure a textile's ability to meet stringent flammability codes.

Fire block — A separate material underneath or behind a finish or building material that creates a fire barrier. A fire block may make the installation compliant (meet the standards or codes).

Heat barrier — A liner between an upholstery and padding to prevent flame spread or smoldering heat.

FR backcoating — A finish applied to the reverse of a fabric or finish that serves as a heat barrier stability factor, improves durability, or both. FR fabrics often are backcoated, which is also an option for post-finishing a textile to meet flame-resistance requirements.

There are currently no national rules that regulate the requirements of either contract fabrics or the furniture they cover. Instead, regulation is left to local fire officers or building code officials, who most often follow one of a number of possible models. For this reason, this text lists the tests required by ACT. The three general types of tests for flammability are small scale, large scale, and full scale.

Small-scale tests utilize small specimens, typically less than 1 foot square or in diameter, actual product, or easily managed mock-ups of a single item.

Large-scale tests incorporate large samples or fabric specimens to be used for carpeting and rugs, window treatments, and mattresses.

Full-scale tests replicate an entire furnished room or a corridor to underscore safe egress in case of stage 3 fire.

Although high-quality fabric finishers test the samples they finish and provide certification, independent testing sometimes is required by the architect. This is an extra charge beyond the fabric finishing. See Resources at the end of this chapter for a noninclusive list of testing labs.

The **flame spread index (FSI)** indicates the rate of speed at which a fire may spread across the surface of a material. A low number indicates a slow fire spread that allows more time for occupants to evacuate. This index is determined by comparing test results to glass-reinforced cement board and red oak flooring. The cement board is given an index of 0 (lowest index number) and red oak 100 (highest, most flammable number).

The **smoke development index (SDI)** measures visibility to egress. Underwriters Laboratories determined a maximum of 450 based on the level of visibility. Over 450 means an occupant could not see enough to find the way out of a burning space or building.

The numerical classification method of reporting indicates that Class A is the most restrictive and Class C is the least.

Notes:

- Tests required by the Association for Contract Textiles (ACT) are listed in this table.

- The results of the various flammability tests are recorded differently. The flame spread index, the smoke development index, classifications, and pass/fail designations are the most frequently used approaches.

- These are brief descriptions for overview purposes only. Refer to the website listing for each test for complete technical information.

California Technical Bulletins (TB)

California is one of the few states to regulate seating products through both mandatory and voluntary requirements. For complete technical details about the California bulletins, refer to http://www.bhfti.ca.gov/techbulletin/117.pdf (the 117 indicates the bulletin number, as indicated below).

Small-Scale Upholstery Fabric: California Technical Bulletin #117 Section E — Class 1 (Pass)

The California TB #117 Section E is a test method of the California Bureau of Home Furnishings and Thermal Insulation. It is a mandatory requirement for components of upholstered furniture. Section E looks at a fabric's resistance to a small flame.

Procedure: Fabric mounted at a 45-degree angle is exposed to a ⅝-inch (1.6 cm) butane flame for 1 second. A pass is achieved if:

1. A 5-inch section of the fabric is consumed in 3.5 seconds (less than 3.5 seconds is a failure). For raised surface fabric, the minimum burn time is increased to 4 seconds.

2. The fabric does not ignite.

Note: As local codes become more stringent and reference more standards, some consider that the California TB 117 Section E, in its current form, is a minimal commercial test for upholstery tests.

Rating: Pass/Fail

For complete technical details about California Bulletin #117 Section E, see http://www.bhfti.ca.gov/techbulletin/117.pdf.

Small-Scale Upholstered Furniture: State of California Technical Bulletin # 116

This is a voluntary cigarette ignition test for mock-ups of or completed upholstered furniture.

Procedure: Lighted cigarettes are placed on all horizontal surfaces that could conceivably support a dropped cigarette — cushions, arms, base, etc. Three cigarettes are placed in each area, no closer than 6 inches apart, and a 6-inch square of white cotton or cotton/polyester sheeting fabric is used to cover each cigarette. A fail is recorded if obvious flaming occurs or if a char develops more than 2 inches long in any direction from the cigarette.

Rating: Pass/Fail

Note: The NFPA 260 UFAC Cigarette Test is similar to TB 116 and is not described here.

Full-Scale Upholstery: State of California Technical Bulletin #133

This is another test for completed furniture pieces intended for use in high-risk occupancies, including hospitals, nursing homes, prisons, and public areas of hotels. In California, it is a mandatory standard in these kinds of occupancy, although the requirements are relaxed in areas with sprinklers. The city of Boston has also adopted TB 133, but here it is specified for all nondomestic properties, and sprinkler systems are not taken into account. The test is stringent, with rigorous pass/fail criteria.

Procedure: The test consists of exposing a piece of upholstered furniture to an open flame in a standard room. The ignition source is a square gas burner placed in the furniture seat, 2 inches from the back and 1 inch above the base. The flame exposure time is 80 seconds.

The pass/fail criteria are given below. Criteria A were the original parameters and are still acceptable, although Criteria B are currently preferred.

Note: The test's stringent pass/fail criteria make all upholstered furniture that passes this test the most resistant to fire. As more jurisdictions increase the strictness of their own codes or laws and standards, it behooves design professionals to ensure that specified upholstered furniture in high-risk occupancies pass TB 133. Not all furniture is required to pass this test if it is placed under sprinkler systems, yet if the sprinklers fail, any upholstered furniture not tested to meet this criteria could be questioned, with design professional liability a possibility. If a fabric is tested, the cost is absorbed by the design professional, who should be certain to pass it on the client with contract approval. If a mock-up is tested, the fabric will be ruined. In some instances, a fire block liner can be added to a fabric during upholstery to make the piece TB 133 compliant. However, certain chairs or furniture pieces, depending on their component parts, can never be compliant — for example, if the chair or component has plastic parts or where there is airflow on an upholstered piece or through certain fabrics, the piece becomes flammable and cannot become compliant.

Criteria A: A failure is recorded if any of the following occur: (1) The temperature measured at the ceiling thermocouple increases by 200°F or more above ambient; (2) The temperature, measured at the 4-foot thermocouple, increases by 50°F or more; (3) Opacity is greater than 75 percent at the 4-foot smoke opacity monitor; (4) CO concentration is at 1,000 ppm or more for 5 minutes; (5) Chair weight loss is 3 pounds or more during the first 5 minutes.

Rating: Pass/Fail

Criteria B: (1) Maximum heat release is 80 kW or greater; (2) Total heat release is 25 mJ or greater in the first 10 minutes; (3) Opacity is greater than 75 percent; (4) CO concentration is 1,000 ppm or greater.

Rating: Pass/Fail

For complete technical details about California TB #133, see http://www.bhfti.ca.gov/techbulletin/133.pdf.

ASTM E 84-03 Tunnel Test

The ASTM E 84, a test method of the American Society for Testing and Materials (ASTM), is commonly called the *tunnel test* and sometimes the *Steiner tunnel test*, after Albert J. Steiner, who developed the first tunnel test chamber in 1922 (and other tests). It has been in use since 1968. This test can be performed under two methods, adhered or non-adhered; the only difference is in specimen preparation. This test may also be used for carpeting.

Adhered: The fabric is bonded to either a CA board substitute or gypsum board. This is the prescribed method for wall coverings whose actual use will be altered.

Non-adhered: If the fabric is a panel fabric or for upholstered walls, it is tested in a frame without being bonded to any other material.

In both cases, the fabric is placed on the ceiling of the test tunnel and subjected at one end to a high-intensity flame that spreads over the first 4.5 feet of the 24-foot test specimen. The distance of flame front progression and total burning time are used to calculate a flame spread index. Smoke monitors are used to calculate a smoke developed value. The flame spread index and smoke developed value are calculated from the results of the test fabric compared to the characteristics of cement board and red oak materials resulting in the indexes.

Tunnel Test Results/Rating: Class A, B, or C

Class A: Flame spread index of 25 or less and smoke developed value of 450 or less

Class B: Flame spread index of 25 to 75 and smoke developed value of 450 or less

Class C: Flame spread index of 76 to 200 and smoke developed value of 450 or less

Caution: The ASTM E 84 test is valid only if the textile or vinyl wallcovering is used in a sprinklered occupancy. If not, the Room Corner Test (NFPA 265 for textiles; NFPA 286 for vinyl) is mandated in many jurisdictions.

For complete technical details about ASTM E 84-03, see http://www.astm.org.

NFPA 701-89 Small-Scale Test

The NFPA 701-89 Small-Scale Test is a method of the National Fire Protection Association (NFPA). It measures the ignition resistance of a fabric after it is exposed to a flame for 12 seconds. The flame, char length, and flaming residue are recorded. The fabric passes the test if all samples meet the following criteria. (If one sample fails, the fabric fails.)

1. An after-flame of less than 2.0 seconds
2. A char length of less than 6.5 inches
3. The specimen does not continue to flame after reaching the floor of the test chamber.

Note: NFPA 701-99 Test #1 is being phased in at this time, but it is not yet cited in all relevant codes. Therefore, the small-scale test remains the ACT standard until further notice.

For complete technical details about NFPA 701, see http://www.nfpa.org.

NFPA 701 Large-Scale Test

This test is useful where small-scale test results show shrinkage or melting and for large-scale window treatment fabric tests.

Procedure: Specimens may be tested in folded or flat application. Flat specimens measure 7 feet × 5 inches; folded specimens are 7 feet × 25 inches, folded. Both are suspended in the apparatus with the lower edge 4 inches above a burner tip with an 11-inch flame ignited for 2 minutes.

Rating: Pass/Fail

Pass is based on four criteria: (1) Fabric does not burn longer than 2 seconds after flame is removed; (2) Vertical flame spread is no more than 10 inches above the test flame tip; (3) Folded specimen flame spread is no more than 35 inches above test flame; (4) No continued burning of portions that break off or dripping.

For complete technical details about NFPA 701 Large Scale, see http://www.nfpa.org.

16 CFR (FF 4-72) Standard for the Flammability of Mattresses and Mattress Pads

This test is against the most common cause of mattress fire: burning cigarettes.

(continued)

Procedure: The mattress is exposed to 9 ignited unfiltered cigarettes, 85 mm long, placed between cotton bedsheets. The mattress pad test procedure is similar. The pad is tested before and after dry cleaning.

ASTM D 1230 Standard Test Method for Flammability of Apparel Textiles is used also for toweling to determine the direction of the most rapid rate of flame spread.

Rating: Class 1, 2, and 3

UFAC (Upholstered Furniture Action Council) Voluntary Action Program Test Definitions

- **Ignition**—Continuous, self-sustaining smoldering combustion of upholstered furniture substrates after exposure to burning cigarettes.

- **Obvious ignition**—Pronounced continuous and self-sustaining combustion of the test system. Determination is a matter of operator judgment based on experience in this type of testing.

- **Sample**—Slab or garneted filling/padding material being tested.

- **Specimen**—Individual piece of sample used in one test assembly.

- **Char**—Area of fabric destroyed or degraded from face to back, not including the area that is discolored by smoke.

UFAC Voluntary Action Program Tests: UFAC Fabric Classification Test Method—1990

Procedure: Fabrics that meet the requirements of this test method are approved and may be labeled as UFAC Class I and used directly over conventional polyurethane in the horizontal seating surfaces of upholstered furniture bearing the UFAC hangtag. All other fabrics are UFAC Class II and require an approved barrier between the cover fabric and conventional polyurethane foam in the horizontal seating surfaces. Vertical and horizontal panels of 2-inch UFAC Standard Polyurethane Foam substrate are covered, using the fabric to be tested. The panels are placed in three specimen holders, and a lighted cigarette is placed in each crevice formed by the abutment of vertical and horizontal panels of each assembly. Each cigarette is covered with a piece of sheeting fabric. The cigarettes are allowed to burn their entire length, unless an obvious ignition occurs. Test measurements and observations are recorded. A minimum of three test specimens is required for each cover fabric sample to be classified.

Results

Class I—vertical char length of less than 1¾ inches

Class II—vertical char length of 1¾ inches or more and/or the fabric ignites

Other criteria apply. For complete technical details about UFAC Fabric Classification Test Method—1990, see http://www.homefurnish.com.

UFAC Voluntary Action Program Tests: UFAC Interior Fabrics Test Method—1990

Cigarette ignition resistance for interior fabrics in intimate contact with outer fabrics in upholstered furniture bearing the UFAC hangtag. Vertical and horizontal panels are assembled on three specimen holders, using UFAC standard polyurethane foam as the substrate. The vertical foam substrate is covered with the standard mattress ticking only. The interior fabric is placed over the polyurethane foam on the horizontal panel and covered with UFAC Standard Type I mattress ticking. A lighted cigarette is placed in the crevice formed by the abutment of vertical and horizontal panels and covered by a piece of sheeting fabric. The cigarette is allowed to burn its full length unless an obvious ignition occurs. A minimum of three test specimens is required for each interior fabric sample tested.

Rating: Pass/Fail

If all test specimens have no ignition, or if the vertical char of each is less than 1½ inches (38 mm) upward from the crevice, the test material passes. Other criteria apply.

UFAC Voluntary Action Program Test: Filling/Padding Component Test Method

Procedure: Part A—For Slab or Garneted Materials

The materials covered by this test method include but are not limited to natural and manufactured battings, foam/cellular filling or cushioning materials, and resilient pads of natural or manufactured fibers. Vertical and horizontal panels are assembled on three specimen holders, using the UFAC Standard Type I mattress ticking as the cover fabric. A lighted cigarette is placed in the crevice formed by the abutment of the vertical and horizontal panels in each test assembly and covered by sheeting fabric. The cigarettes are allowed to burn their full length unless an obvious ignition occurs. A minimum of three test specimens is required for each sample tested.

Rating: Pass/Fail

If all test specimens have no ignition, or if the vertical char of each is less than 1½ inches (38 mm) upward from the crevice, the test material passes. Other criteria apply. For complete technical details about UFAC Filling/Padding Component Test Method Procedure: Part A—For Slab or Garneted Materials, see http://www.homefurnish.com.

UFAC Voluntary Action Program Test: Filling/Padding Component Test Method

Procedure: Part B — For Fibrous or Particulate Materials

Commonly used for loose or semiattached backs, arms, or throw pillows. The materials covered by this test method include but are not limited to staple of natural and manufactured fibers, shredded foam or cellular filling materials, and composites of any of these, together with any protective interliners that may be necessary to meet the requirements of the test method. Vertical and horizontal panels are assembled on three specimen holders, using the UFAC Standard Type I mattress ticking as the cover fabric. A lighted cigarette is placed in the crevice formed by the abutment of the vertical and horizontal panels in each test assembly and covered by sheeting fabric. The cigarettes are allowed to burn their full length unless an obvious ignition occurs. A minimum of three test specimens is required for each sample tested.

Rating: Pass/Fail

If all test specimens have no ignition, or if the vertical char of each is less than 1½ inches (38 mm) upward from the crevice, the test material passes. For complete technical details about UFAC Filling/Padding Component Test Part B, see http://www.homefurnish.com.

UFAC Voluntary Action Program Test: UFAC Decking Materials Test Method — 1990

Decking is the upholstered furniture covering, and includes padding material such as foam, fiber, or cotton pads beneath loose cushions. Three burning cigarettes are placed on a decking assembly and allowed to burn completely.

Rating: Pass/Fail

The material passes if ignition or vertical char length is less than 1½ inches and fails if vertical char length is more than 1½ inches. Other criteria apply. For complete technical details

about UFAC Decking Materials Test Method — 1990, see http://www.homefurnish.com.

UFAC Voluntary Action Program Test: Welt Cord Test Method — 1990

Procedure: A lit cigarette is laid on a UFAC Standard Type II fabric laid around a welt cord placed in the joint of a back and seat cushion upholstered assembly and covered with cotton bedsheet fabric. The test is repeated three times.

Rating: Pass/Fail

The material passes if ignition or vertical char length is less than 1½ inches and fails if vertical char length is more than 1½ inches.

For further information on UFAC Welt Cord Test Method — 1990, see http://www.homefurnish.com.

UFAC Voluntary Action Program Test: Standard Test Methods for Decorative Trims, Edging, and Brush Fringes — 1990

Testing is where lighted cigarettes could become lodged or entrapped if dropped onto the sofa. Round or elliptical cord is tested using the Standard UFAC Welt Cord test method.

Trim, edging, or brush fringe is placed at the abutment of the horizontal and vertical panels of the small-scale test assembly, just barely in contact with the vertical panel. A lighted cigarette, covered by a piece of sheeting material, is placed on the specimen and against the vertical panel of the test assembly and allowed to burn its entire length unless an obvious ignition occurs. Char is measured on the vertical panel upward from the crevice. Three to six specimens are tested.

Results: If all test specimens have no ignition, or if the vertical char of each is less than 1½ inches (38 mm) upward from the crevice, the test material passes. Other criteria apply.

For complete technical information about UFAC Standard Test Methods for Decorative Trims, Edging, and Brush Fringes — 1990, see http://www.homefurnish.com.

European Flammability Tests

Many standards in force internationally reflect different ways of approaching flammability issues. One test widely accepted throughout the European Union is Test EN 1021-102: 2003/2004. Many other tests are also being standardized as European Nation (EN) tests that will serve the European Union.

Specific testing standards are also established in countries such as Germany, Italy, France, and England. However, EN standards are being encouraged to develop greater uniformity throughout Europe. When researching these standards, note that *watersoak* is a European term. This procedure, defined in Great Britain under Standard BS 5651:1990 Clause 3, requires that a fabric be soaked in water and dried prior to testing. This is done because chemically treated material may be adversely affected by watersoaking, and its additional flame-retardant characteristics may be greatly reduced or completely eliminated, thus qualifying as a nondurable finish.

Figure 6.5a Knoll Currents® office system furniture features covered panels of flame-retardant panel fabric. *Photo courtesy of Knoll.*

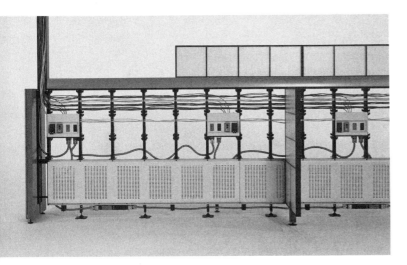

Figure 6.5b Knoll Currents® service wall accommodates unlimited lay-in cable distribution behind removable covers, supporting technology while facilitating change. *Photo courtesy of Knoll.*

UL Component Recognition Program for Office Systems Furniture

The Underwriters Laboratories (UL) Component Recognition Program for Office Systems Furniture was developed to clarify and expedite the FR approval process for customers' own materials (COM) fabric on office systems furniture. Fabric suppliers and furniture manufacturers individually work with UL to meet qualifications that allow their specific products to be added to the UL Recognized Components directory. Once a fabric or office system is approved and listed as a UL Recognized Component, it can be used in combination with any other approved fabric or office systems furniture. This allows more design freedom without significant burn testing fees and extended lead times due to additional UL testing.

SOFT FLOOR COVERINGS TESTING

A large number of tests are performed on rugs and carpet. Flammability testing is mandatory and described in Table 6.8. In addition, performance tests evaluate the absorption of sound; level of noise transmission; insulative value (carpet and cushion); light reflectance; static generation; wear resistance; textural changes; abrasion resistance; colorfastness to crocking, gases, and light; and colorfastness to shampoo and water (wet-cleaning method color removal). Some of these tests are listed in Table 6.9. *Note:* Carpet evaluation factors and a sample of carpeting specification labeling are presented in chapter 12.

TABLE 6.4 WET AND DRY CROCKING TESTS FOR UPHOLSTERY, DIRECT GLUE WALLCOVERINGS, WRAPPED PANELS, AND UPHOLSTERED WALLS AND DRAPERY

Crocking is the transfer of dye from the surface of a dyed or printed fabric onto another surface by rubbing.

Upholstery, Direct Glue, Wrapped Panels, and Upholstered Walls and Drapery: AATCC 8-2001

The AATCC 8-2001 is a test method of the American Association of Textile Chemists and Colorists (AATCC). This method involves rubbing a standard white cotton fabric against the surface of the test fabric. To test for wet crocking, the standard fabric is wet before rubbing against the test fabric. After rubbing under controlled pressure for a specific number of times, the amount of color transferred to the white test square is compared to an AATCC color chart and a rating established.

  Grade 5 = no color transfer

  Grade 1 = high degree of color transfer

For complete technical details about AATCC 8, see http://www.aatcc.org.

Drapery (Prints): AATCC 116-2001

The AATCC 116-2001 is a test method of the AATCC. This test is specifically used for printed fabrics that do not lend themselves to the AATCC 8-2001 method. The test fabric is held at the base of a Rotary Vertical Crockmeter and rubbed with a standard cotton white fabric, either dry or wet. After rubbing under controlled pressure for a specific number of times, the amount of color transferred to the white test square is compared to a chart and a rating established.

  Grade 5 = no color transfer

  Grade 1 = high degree of color transfer

For complete technical details about AATCC 16, see http://www.aatcc.org.

TABLE 6.5 LIGHT COLORFASTNESS TESTS FOR UPHOLSTERY, DIRECT GLUE WALLCOVERINGS, WRAPPED PANELS, AND UPHOLSTERED WALLS AND DRAPERY

Colorfastness Tests

Colorfastness is a measure of the permanence of a color on fabric. Color can be adversely affected by a number of factors including exposure to light, water, and normal wear and tear. Various tests assess how color is affected by these factors. A numerical value is then established to indicate the degree of color change.

Test Methods

Upholstery, Direct Glue, Wrapped Panels, Upholstered Walls, Drapery, and Toweling: AATCC 16 Options 1 and 3 — 2003

The AATCC 16 Options 1 and 3 are test methods of the American Association of Textile Chemists and Colorists (AATCC). The Association for Contract Textiles (ACT) recognizes both methods; the only difference is the light source used. In AATCC 16 Option 1, a carbon-arc lamp is used as the light source, and in AATCC 16 Option 3, a zenon-arc lamp is used. Under both methods, a strip of fabric (part of which is protected by a special paper card) is placed in a fadometer and exposed to 40 hours of accelerated fading units (AFU). After the exposure, the difference in color between the exposed and protected parts of the fabric is compared to the AATCC gray scale and the degree of fading rated.

Grade 5 = no fading

Grade 4 = slight fading

Grade 1 = high degree of fading

For complete technical details about AATCC 16 Options 1 and 3 — 2003, see http://www.aatcc.org.

TABLE 6.6 PHYSICAL PROPERTIES TESTS FOR UPHOLSTERY, WRAPPED PANELS, AND UPHOLSTERED WALLS AND DRAPERY

Physical property tests include brush pill, breaking strength, and seam slippage.

- **Pilling** is the formation of fuzzy balls of fiber on the surface of a fabric that remain attached to it.
- **Breaking strength** is the measurement of stress exerted to pull a fabric apart under tension.
- **Seam slippage** is the movement of yarns in a fabric that occurs when it is pulled apart at a seam.

Upholstery: ASTM D3511-02 Brush Pill Test

The ASTM D3511-02 is a test method of the American Society for Testing and Materials (ASTM). This test utilizes nylon bristles to rub the surface of the test fabric for a specific amount of time. The number of pill balls is counted and given a rating of 1 to 5.

Class 5 = no pilling

Class 1 = severe pilling

For complete technical details about ASTM D3511-02, see http://www.astm.org.

Upholstery: ASTM D5034-95 Grab Test

The ASTM D5034-95 (2001) (Grab Test) is a test method of ASTM. The fabric being tested is put into a machine that grips it with two clamps. One clamp is stationary and the other moves away, applying tension until the fabric breaks or ruptures. This test is performed in both the warp and weft directions. The number of pounds required to cause a fabric to break or rupture determines the rating.

Breaking Strength Test

This test is performed in both the warp and weft directions. Fabric is clamped at one end and weight applied from the other end to form tension. The rating is determined by the number of pounds required to cause the fabric to tear or break. At least 50 pounds is required for upholstery and at least 35 pounds for panel and vertical surface fabrics.

For complete technical details about ASTM D5034-95, see http://www.astm.org.

Upholstery, Wrapped Panels, Upholstered Walls, Drapery: ASTM D3597-02-D434-05

The ASTM D3597-02-D434-05 is a test method of the ASTM. To measure a fabric's ability to resist seam slippage, a seam is sewn in the test fabric using a standard thread, specific seam allowance, and specific number of stitches per inch. The sewn fabric is then clamped at opposing sides of the seam. One clamp is moved away from the other, applying tension at the sewn seam. This test is performed in both the warp and weft directions. The tension is increased until the seam separates to a specific distance. The number of pounds required to cause separation due to yarn slippage determines the rating. For both upholstery and panel/vertical surface fabrics, 25 pounds is the minimum requirement.

For complete technical details about ASTM D3597-02-D434-05, see http://www.astm.org.

Other Specifications Tests for Carpeting

ASTM has designed several tests for fibers, pile, yarn, density, carpet backing, and criteria for terminology. These include the following:

ASTM D-418 Standard Test Methods for Testing Pile Yarn Floor Covering Construction

ASTM D-629 Standard Test Methods for Quantitative Analysis of Textiles

ASTM D-861 Standard Practice for Use of the Tex System to Designate Linear Density of Fibers, Yarn Intermediates, and Yarns

ASTM D-1244 Standard Practice for Designation of Yarn Construction

ASTM D-2646 Standard Test Methods for Backing Fabric Characteristics of Pile Yarn Floor Coverings

ASTM D-5684 Standard Terminology Relating to Pile Floor Coverings

ASTM D-5793 Standard Test Method for Binding Sites per Unit Length or Width of Pile Yarn Floor Coverings

ASTM D-5823 Standard Test Method for Tuft Height of Pile Floor Coverings

For technical details, see http://www.astm.org.

TABLE 6.7 UPHOLSTERY ABRASION TESTS

Abrasion is the surface wear of a fabric caused by rubbing and contact with another fabric.

The Wyzenbeek and Martindale tests are the two methods commonly used to predict wearability. Actual performance is determined by many factors, such as fiber content, weaves, finishes, furniture design, maintenance, cleaning, and usage. The durability rating of an upholstery fabric is a complex interaction of a number of performance tests that, in addition to abrasion, includes seam slippage, pilling, tensile strength, and usage.

There is no correlation between the Wyzenbeek and Martindale test methods, so it is not possible to estimate the number of cycles that would be achieved on one test if the results from the other test are known. In Table 6.1, ACT Performance Guidelines, the following results are the minimum requirements.

For general contract upholstery, 15,000 double rubs Wyzenbeek and 20,000 cycles Martindale. For heavy-duty contract upholstery, 30,000 double rubs Wyzenbeek and 40,000 cycles Martindale. Examples of heavy-duty installations include conference rooms, dining areas, hotel rooms/suites, and single-shift corporate offices. Extreme wear situations that may require higher levels of abrasion resistance, up to 100,000 double rubs, include theaters, stadiums, lecture halls, fast food restaurants, and other places of public gathering, and twenty-four-hour facilities such as telemarketing, emergency health-care, and casino gambling areas.

ASTM 4157-02 Oscillatory Cylinder Method (Wyzenbeek)

The ASTM 4157-02 is a test method of the American Society for Testing and Materials (ASTM). A Wyzenbeek machine, which allows samples to be pulled taut, held stationary, and rubbed both in the warp and weft directions, is used for this test. Individual test specimens cut from the warp and weft directions are rubbed back and forth, using a #10 cotton duck fabric as the abradant. The number of cycles, or double rubs, endured before the fabric shows "noticeable wear" (two yarn breaks) indicates the level of abrasion resistance.

For complete technical details about ASTM D4157-02, see http://www.astm.org.

Note: A wire screen abradant is recommended by ACT for use with vinyl and polyurethane coated upholstery and may also be used for testing 100 percent olefin fabrics.

ASTM D 4966-98 Martindale

The ASTM D4966-98 is a test method of the ASTM. In this test, undertaken on a Martindale machine, the fabric is rubbed against a worsted fabric to simulate wear and tear. The apparatus records the number of cycles or rubs to which the fabric is exposed until a physically significant end point is reached. The end point is when three threads on the fabric have worn to the extent of actually breaking. The abrasion value is the number of cycles completed at the time of breaking. The fabric is abraded at a pressure of 800 g/12 kilopascals, and abradants are changed every 50,000 cycles. Within BS 2543, five classifications and associated fabric performance levels are specified for various types of end-usage.

For complete technical details about ASTM D4966-98, see http://www.astm.org.

TABLE 6.8 CARPETING FLAMMABILITY AND SMOKE GENERATION TESTS

Flammability resistance of carpeting and rugs is under the jurisdiction of federal, state, or local municipalities, often following the NFPA 101® Life Safety Code®. Carpet can be installed on floors or walls; testing takes this into account. All carpet flammability tests are based on a **critical radiant flux (CRF)**, calculated from the distance of flame spread converted into watts per square centimeter (watts/sq. cm, or watts/cm²), indicating the critical or threshold level to sustain burning. The shorter the distance of burning, the higher the safety level, measured as a decimal percentage watt. For example, 0.40 is a higher and therefore safer rating than 0.15.

Radiant Panel Test: NFPA 253 Standard Method of Test for Critical Radiant Flux of Floor Covering Systems Using a Radiant Heat Source, and ASTM E 648 Standard Test Method for Critical Radiant Flux of Floor Covering Systems Using a Radiant Heat Energy Source

Small-Scale Carpeting (and Resilient and Hardwood Flooring) or NBSIR 79-950

The radiant panel test simulates a Stage 3 fire. This test measures the fire spread of floor coverings (although they are not regarded as a primary cause of flame spread), corridors, and egress areas. This test may be used with or without cushion.

Notes: If carpeting is to be installed over a flammable subflooring, other test criteria apply. Also, this test is increasingly selected for carpeting in lieu of the ASTM E 84-03 Tunnel Test, described in Table 6.3.

Procedure: A specimen measuring 42 × 10 inches is placed on the floor of the test chamber. It is preheated by a 30-degree inclined radiant panel, and then a gas burner flame contacts the sample for 10 minutes with the added heat from the inclined radiant panel. To further simulate a hallway exposed to fire, air flows through the chamber bottom and exits at the top in a type of chimney. Testing is complete when the floor ceases burning. The distance the flooring burns before self-extinguishing is converted to watts/cm² from a calibration graph and becomes a critical radiant flux (CRF). The higher the CRF value, the more resistant the carpet to flame propagation.

For complete technical details about ASTM E 648, see http://www.astm.org.

For complete technical details about NFPA 253, see http://www.nfpa.org.

Rating: CRF (critical radiant flux) measured in watts/sq. cm.

ASTM D 2859 Methenamine Pill Test

This test simulates a carpet exposed to a limited source of ignition—a glowing ember, burning match, or cigarette. If the carpet does not support or propagate the flame, the fire would likely be a Stage 1 fire (see Table 6.2). The Methenamine Pill Test has been adopted as a method within the scope of 16 CFR (Code of Federal Regulations) 1630 (modular carpeting; carpets and rugs over 24 square feet with one side more than 6 feet) and 16 CFR 1631 (small accent or throw rugs).

Procedure: Eight samples of 9-inch square carpet are oven-dried to make them moisture-free. Each sample is placed in a draft-protected burn chamber anchored with a steel frame exposing a round opening 8 inches in diameter. A **methenamine pill** or **tablet** formulated to burn for two minutes is placed in the center of the specimen and ignited. When the pill or carpet, whichever is last, ceases to burn, the testing is complete and analysis begins. A measurement from the ignition source to the end of the burn scar is termed a **char length.** If the char lengths of at least seven of the eight specimens do not come to within 1 inch of the diameter opening, the carpet passes. If the char length does come within 1 inch of the diameter opening, the product must be labeled with a warning that it fails U.S. Consumer Product Safety Commission Standard 16 CRF 1631 and should not be used near sources of fire.

For complete technical details about ASTM D 2859, see http://www.astm.org.

Rating: Pass/Fail

ASTM E 662 and NFPA 258 Smoke Chamber Test

This test measures the quantity of smoke generation of solid materials exposed to flame and nonflame conditions. Dense smoke prevents efficient egress through visual obstruction and can overcome occupants, who can choke or die from inhalation. Thus, smoke generation testing is becoming more generally required by governing agencies.

Procedure: A 3-inch square specimen up to 1 inch thick is suspended vertically in a fully enclosed chamber.

Flaming method: The specimen is exposed to 6 small flames augmented with radiant heat to achieve 2.5 watts per square centimeter or CRF.

Nonflaming method: This test utilizes radiant heat to simulate smoldering conditions. A light beam shown through the smoke is measured in terms of light transmittance value. Testing is complete after 20 minutes or when a minimum light transmittance value is reached.

Results: Optical density values are measured from a low of 50 to a high of 450. The flaming and nonflaming tests may be averaged.

> **Class A:** CRF 0.50 watt/cm² (flame spread of 0–25); maximum specific optical density 450 flaming or less.
>
> **Class B:** CRF 0.25 watt/cm² or greater (flame spread of 26–75); maximum optical density 450 flaming or less.
>
> **Class C:** face, back, and cushion each pass 16 CFR 1630; flame spread of 76–200; smoke development of 0–450

Note: These are not the same classifications as the Tunnel Test results.

TABLE 6.9 CARPET PERFORMANCE TESTS

ASTM D 3936 Standard Test Method for Delamination Strength of Secondary Backing of Pile Floor Coverings

Lamination is the gluing together of primary and secondary carpet backings. Delamination is the separation of these layers due to excessive traffic flow or equipment abuse, resulting in shearing or movement of the layers against each other until the face of the carpet ripples, bubbles, or works loose at the seams. In this test, stress is applied by attaching one clamp to the pile and primary backing layer and another clamp to the secondary backing, and then pulling them apart.

Results: Force required for layer separation is measured for each of three specimens and recorded as pounds per linear inch—generally from 2.5 to 8.33 per inch.

See http://www.astm.org.

ASTM D 1335 Standard Test Method for Tuft Bind or Pile Floor Coverings

A tuft bind is a measurement of the force necessary to pull a single loop of carpet pile from the primary backing. The sample is clamped, a hook is inserted into a loop, and adjoining loops on each side of the test loop are cut.

Rating: Reported in pounds of force to pull the test loop from the primary backing, generally 4½ to 20 pounds.

See http://www.astm.org.

AATCC 134 Electrostatic Propensity of Carpets

This test utilizes a person walking across carpet wearing clean, neolite-soled shoes that are connected to an electrometer. Given an ambient temperature of 70°F temperature and 20 percent relative humidity, the measurement of voltage buildup on the body is recorded in static volts. For complete technical information, see www.aatcc.org or www.techstreet.com.

AATCC 8 Colorfastness to Crocking; AATCC 23 Colorfastness to Gas Fading; AATCC 109 and 129 Colorfastness to Ozone Fading

These results are given numerical ratings. Overall lightfastness, **AATCC 16E**, is given a class rating. For complete technical information, see www.aatcc.org or www.techstreet.com.

AATCC 107 Colorfastness to Water and AATCC 138 Shampooing: Washing of Textile Floor Coverings

These tests analyze dye bleeding, staining, and change of yarn (dye) color as compared to a gray scale. Results are rated numerically. For complete technical information, see http://www.astm.org.

ASTM D 6119 Standard Practice for Creating Surface Appearance Changes in Pile Yarn Floor Coverings from Foot Traffic

This test measures foot traffic units as recorded from the effect of persons walking on the carpet sample. A comparison of samples results in evaluation data.

For complete technical information, see http://www.astm.org

ASTM D 5251 Standard Practice for the Operation of the Tetrapod Walker Drum Tester

A cylinder chamber is lined with carpet, pile side up. As the drum cylinder revolves, plastic-covered tetrapod feet hit against the pile to imitate foot traffic. This test measures the change in pile thickness and loss of pile weight, indicating a level of abrasion resistance. For complete technical information, see http://www.astm.org.

ASTM D-6119 Standard Practice for Creating Surface Appearance Changes in Pile Yarn Floor Covering from Foot Traffic

This test grades appearance change observed in all types of carpet intended for residential or commercial use due to matting, flattening, and change in pile fiber configuration and *not* by soiling. It is not a test for pile reversal or watermarking. Scales are used as an aid in assessing appearance change in carpets. The test utilizes a hexapod or Vettermann drum tester and six sets of digitally imaged increments of change, representing a 5-point scale with intermediate half steps. Up to three grades may be recommended.

Rating: Rated to the half step as grades on a 5-point scale. Carpet with a higher appearance retention rating (ARR), such as 4.5 or 4.0, will retain its original appearance longer under various traffic conditions than carpet with a lower ARR.

ASTM D 3884 Standard Test Method for Abrasion Resistance of Textile Fabric—Rotary, Platform, Double Head Method

In this test, two carpet samples are mounted onto rotating disks under the pressure of an abrading wheel on each sample. The samples are rotated in opposite directions until the primary backing of the carpet is fully exposed. The results are measured in number of cycles, pile weight loss, or breaking load percent loss. Five tests are conducted to achieve an average. *Note:* This test is also known as the **Taber Abrasion Test.** For complete technical information, see http://www.astm.org.

Acoustical and Impact Noise Ratings

Carpeting reduces airborne and surface sounds to a degree that can be translated into a **noise reduction coefficient (NRC)**, given as a decimal number. For example, 0.20 is a low rating and 0.70 a high rating. The **ISO R 140 Tapping Machine** tests the ability of the carpet or cushion to reduce impact noise transmission. An **impact noise rating (INR)** of +25 is good. Another rating is by **impact insulation class (IIC)**, where 76 to 80 is considered high insulation against noise. Generally, carpet plus cushion as an assembly is more effective. See www.carpet-rug.org for information from the Carpet and Rug Institute.

Light Reflectance

Light reflectance can be tested and given a **light reflectance factor (LRF)**; this rating is the percentage of incident light reflected. Out of 100 percent, a carpet may absorb 85 percent and reflect 15 percent, or 15 LRF, which is the maximum recommended for areas with heavy traffic, such as nonresidential installations. However, lighter carpets with lower LRF numbers are appropriate in low-traffic areas and in residential installations.

R-Values or R-Factors

The R-value is the resistance to heat flow, or insulation against heat exchange. R-values for carpeting range from approximately 0.55 to 2.46, where thickness, pile density, and cushioning are factors in increasing the effectiveness. Higher numbers mean greater effectiveness. For further information, see the Carpet and Rug Institute, at www.carpet-rug.org.

CARPETING AND ENVIRONMENTAL SPECIFICATIONS

As discussed in chapter 2, today's design professionals have a serious responsibility to specify environmentally friendly or green design textiles. The issues are conserving natural resources by specifying materials that are from renewable resources or from recycled or recyclable sources and reducing the level of **volatile organic compounds (VOCs)** in order to preserve **indoor air quality (IAQ)**.

One test that measures VOC level is the Green Label of the Carpet and Rug Institute. The test is the ASTM D-5116 Guide for Small-Scale Environmental Chamber Determinations of Organic Emissions from Indoor Materials/Products. The current criteria for the program are based on a maximum emission factor measured in $mg/m^2/hr$, as follows:

Total volatile organic compounds (TVOC)	0.5
4-PC (4-phenylcyclohexene)	0.05
Formaldehyde (to prove that none is used)	0.05
Styrene	0.4

Since the inception of the program in 1992, the industry has made substantial reductions in the levels of TVOCs, as well as reductions in 4-phenylcyclohexene (4-PC), the compound most associated with new carpet odor.

For complete technical details about ASTM D-5116-95, see http://www.astm.org.

ASTM protocol testing is also conducted for carpeting soil removal performance by measuring soil removal via X-ray fluorescence (XRF) technology. Testing is also for residual water following carpet cleaning. Excess water creates the potential for the growth of mold spores and may harm carpet fibers. Tests measure a carpet sample before and after to determine how much water remains. Surface appearance change in the carpet pile, a result of extraction cleaning, is measured using the **Carpet and Rug Institute's Appearance Retention Reference Scales,** which assist in assessing appearance change in carpets. In order to qualify for the Seal of Approval, an extractor must not affect the appearance of the carpet pile surface more than a one-step change based on one year of normal extractor use. This test criterion is included because experience has shown that some machines can cause excessive wear on the carpet.

The *CRI Seal of Approval* program began in 2004 with the setting of test methods and performance criteria for two categories of cleaning products: spot removers and prespray/in-tank cleaning solutions. In 2005, the program expanded to include a significant new element in the testing protocol, X-ray fluorescence (XRF), a sophisticated testing method that measures the precise amount of soil removed from carpet. Soon, vacuum cleaners—currently tested under the Green Label Vacuum program—will be added to the Seal of Approval testing program. Interim extractors and cleaning systems (i.e., the testing of equipment and cleaning chemicals combined) will be added to the testing and certification program at a later date. The Seal of Approval is awarded only to those cleaning products with high performance in all of the testing categories. The green and blue Seal of Approval helps customers differentiate between high- and low-quality products. Because CRI's Seal of Approval extractor program takes advantage of space technology, companies certified under the Seal of Approval XRF testing program are eligible to display the Space Foundation Seal.

LABELING

Labels are written information printed on paper as packaging, glued, affixed, sewn, or stapled onto a fabric or product, or attached with a plastic extruded loop as a **hangtag** on furniture. By law (see TFPIA below), labels appear on the following: fibers, yarns, fabrics, carpeting (pile or face fibers), bedding and bath linens, curtains, casements, draperies, furniture slipcovers, and throws (afghans). Interior design items exempt from labeling include upholstery padding and stuffing, outer coverings of upholstered furniture (even though upholstery yardage must be labeled, the finished product does not require labeling), and mattresses and box springs and their coverings.

Labels and hangtags are a means of informing the professional and the consumer about a textile or product's fiber content, specifications, and test rating, which assists in making appropriate selections for a given installation. Labels are also a means of product and trade association recognition and are a form of both advertising and public relations. Where a logo or icon symbol and/or company or trade association name is a part of a label, these may assure quality based on the performance of the same or similar products and a level of dependability on the part of the manufacturer or endorser.

Many items on labels are voluntary, such as the icons authorized by the Association of Contract Textiles and language assuring that no child labor was used in the construction of a Tibetan-made carpet. Some labels are recognized by the industry and have met guidelines assuring truthfulness in labeling.

The following laws require specific labels:

1. The **Wool Products Labeling Act (WPL)** of 1939 and its amendments include:
   a. The definition of wool (fiber from the fleece of sheep or lamb or hair from the angora, mohair, or cashmere goat and specialty fiber hair from camel, alpaca, llama, and vicuña)
   b. The definition of recycled wool (prior processed or reused wool where fibers are shredded or reduced from previously manufactured product, whether used or unused)
   c. The definition for virgin wool, new wool, and wool (now synonymous terms for unreclaimed wool)
   d. The registered FTC number or name of the product manufacturer
   e. The country of origin or "Made in the USA." When manufactured in the United States from foreign product, the label is to read, approximately, "Sewn in the USA of Imported Components."

2. **The Textile Fiber Products Identification Act (TFPIA)** of 1960 and its amendments require that interior design fabrics bear a conspicuous label or hangtag. Exceptions are:
   1. upholstery stuffing, except labels indicating the stuffing is reused
   2. outer coverings of furniture, mattresses, and box springs;
   3. linings or interlinings incorporated primarily for structural purposes and not for warmth;
   4. filling or padding incorporated primarily for structural purposes and not for warmth;
   5. stiffenings, trimmings, facings, or interfacings;
   6. backings of, and paddings or cushions to be used under, floor coverings.

As labels are often voluntary, deceptive practices are possible. Therefore, the U.S. Congress created the Federal Trade Commission (FTC) in 1914 (and further empowered it by the Wheeler-Lea Act of 1938) to prevent unfair methods of competition and unfair or deceptive acts or practices, to investigate commercial trade practices, to encourage voluntary corrective action and compliance, to instigate necessary legal action, and to issue rules and guidelines for textile labeling and marketing. The **Magnuson-Moss Warranty Act,** enforced under the FTC's Product Reliability Division, establishes written warranties procedures. The FTC maintains regional offices that enforce mandatory fiber product labeling. The FTC does not handle consumer complaints but does investigate evidence that may result in a hearing or further ruling.

The TFPIA mandates these items of information on applicable textiles or products:

1. Standard terminology for specifications
2. Type of fiber, including the generic and common names
3. The percentage of each fiber that composes the item
4. The manufacturer's name
5. The country of origin, meaning one of the following:
   a. Made in [name of offshore country]
   b. Made in the USA
   c. Made in the USA of Imported Components
   d. Partially Manufactured in the USA and Partially Offshore

Note: For apparel, the laws specify care instructions that include standard terminology, dry-cleaning instructions, and washing instructions. These rules generally do not apply to interior textiles or products. However, some labels do read "dry cleaning recommended." This is largely because of finishes that are easily removed during the laundering process.

In addition, the **FTC Guides for the Household Furniture Industry** became effective in March 1974. These specify that vinyl or other nonleather or man-made upholstery coverings disclose textile content and not use terms such as *skin, hide,* or *leather,* although homophones such as *hyde* (as in Naugahyde) are acceptable.

Design professionals and consumers who are aware of trademarks or trade names will be able to identify the generic fiber. In interior design, care labels are not required, although some products do list the icons listed on www.wiley.com/go/interiortextiles.

Flammability ratings are often listed on labels for protection of the consumer along with the information required for contract interiors. In some cases, flammability is affected by the care given the product. For example, the labels for mattress pads treated with flame retardant must list precautionary maintenance information to prevent the finish from being removed by cleaning.

Maintenance Labeling

Although labeling for textile product care is not written into law, ASTM composed ASTM D-5253 Standard Terminology of Writing Care Instructions and General Refurbishing Procedures for Textile Floor Coverings and Textile Upholstered Furniture, which document provides standardized instruction for the proper maintenance of carpets, rugs, and upholstered furniture (except leather), as well as ASTM D-3136 Standard Terminology Relating to Care Labels for Textile and Leather Products Other Than Textile Floor Coverings as Upholstery. As international trade has increased worldwide, symbols that represent care procedures are represented. These symbols, now widely used throughout the textile industry, are found on www.wiley.com/go/interiortextiles. Use of the symbols and care instructions is voluntary.

For more information about these standardized instructions and glossary logos in ASTM D-5253 and ASTM D-3136, see http://www.astm.org.

RESOURCES

Association for Contract Textiles (ACT)
www.contracttexiles.org
PO Box 101981
Fort Worth, TX 76185
Tel 817-924-8048
Fax 817-924-8050

The Association for Contract Textiles is a trade group founded in 1985 to address diverse issues related to contract fabrics. are Registered Certification Marks of the U.S. Patent and Trademark Office and are owned by the Association for Contract Textiles, Inc.

The Upholstered Furniture Action Council (UFAC)
www.homefurnish.com
PO Box 2436
High Point, NC 27261
Tel 336-885-5065
Fax 336-884-5072

UFAC was founded in 1978 to make upholstered furniture more resistant to ignition from smoldering cigarettes, which are the leading cause of upholstery fires in the home. Household fires from smoldering ignition have been reduced substantially since its inception—a decline of 79.3 percent, according to the latest figures. UFAC provides technical assistance, promotes compliance, and encourages all segments of the industry to participate through independent testing.

The Carpet and Rug Institute (CRI)
www.carpet-rug.org
Street Address: 730 College Drive, Dalton, GA 30720
Mailing Address: PO Box 2048, Dalton, GA 30722-2048
Tel 706-278-3176
Fax 706-278-8835

CRI is the national trade association representing the carpet and rug industry. Its membership consists of manufacturers (representing over 90 percent of all carpet produced in the United States) and suppliers of raw materials and services to the industry. There is continued coordination with other industry segments, such as distributors, retailers, and installers. CRI is a source of extensive carpet information.

ASTM International
www.astm.org
100 Barr Harbor Drive
West Conshohocken, PA 19428
Tel 610-832-9585
Fax 610-832-9555

ASTM International, originally known as the American Society for Testing and Materials (ASTM), provides consensus standards and is one of the largest voluntary standards development organizations in the world. It is a trusted source of technical standards for materials, products, systems, and services. Technical experts represent producers, users, consumers, government, and academia from over 100 countries. The *Annual Book of ASTM Standards* is available through the website and by mail.

National Fire Protection Association (NFPA)

www.nfpa.org
1 Batterymarch Park
Quincy, MA 02169-7471
Tel 617-770-3000
Tel 800-344-3555
Fax 617-770-0700

NFPA is an international nonprofit organization that is an authority on fire, electrical, and building safety. It provides and advocates consensus codes and standards, research, training, and education. NFPA focuses on fire prevention and is an authoritative source on public safety. NFPA's 300 codes and standards influence every building, process, service, design, and installation in the United States as well as many of those used in other countries. NFPA is accredited by the American National Standards Institute (ANSI).

American Association of Textile Chemists and Colorists (AATCC)

www.aatcc.org
777 E. Eisenhower Parkway
Ann Arbor, MI 48108
Tel 800-699-9277 (U.S. and Canada); 734-913-3930 (International)
Fax 734-913-3946

AATCC provides the textile wet processing industry with a communication center and a clearinghouse for new ideas and innovation in textile chemistry and color science. AATCC works for all professionals associated with the application of chemistry to textiles and has published more than 175 test methods addressing such topics as colorfastness, staining, laundering, and electrostatics.

Code of Federal Regulations (CFR) Resources

Legal Books Depot
www.legalbooksdepot.com
Tel: 323-463-3999

Textile Guide

www.thetextileguide.com

Sponsored by Interface Fabrics Group, the *Textile Guide* assists the professional fabric specifier, covering topics from flammability to the environment.

Underwriters Laboratories (UL)

www.ul.com
333 Pfingsten Road
Northbrook, IL 60062-2096
Tel 877-854-3577

UL offers an online directory where searches can be conducted for approved fabrics using the Office Panel Fabrics category Code QAXN2. Office systems furniture can be found using Category Code QAWZ.

Testing: The Govmark Organization, Inc.

www.govmark.com
96D Allen Boulevard
Farmingdale, NY 11735-5626
Tel 631-293-8944
Fax 631-293-8956

Testing: Northwest Labs

www.nwlabs1896.com
241 S. Holden Street
Seattle, WA 98108
Tel 206-763-6252
Fax 206-763-3949

Testing: Vartest

www.vartest.com
19 W. Thirty-sixth Street
New York, NY 10018
Tel 212-947-8391
Fax 212-947-8719

Commercial Testing Co.

www.commercialtesting.com
PO Box 985
1215 S. Hamilton Street
Dalton, GA 30720
Tel 706-278-3935
Fax 706-278-3936

Figure B-1 "Serafina" lounge series designed by David Dahl for Arcadia is a functional and flexible modular group of lounge chair, love seat, and three-cushion sofa that boast tapered angles and sophisticated design. This modular series is ideal for a variety of options and quick and easy reconfiguring made possible with a series of distinctive and stylish bridges. *Photo courtesy of Arcadia, www.arcadia.com.*

Figure B-2 These sunscreens give daytime privacy and cut heat, glare, and intense light. *Photo compliments of Comfortex Window Fashions.*

Figure B-3 From the G P & J Baker "Perandor Collection," brilliant colors in large scale linen textiles give this chair a fresh, updated historic appeal. Chair fabric is "Giant Peony." G P & J Baker, www.gpjbaker.com. *Photo courtesy of MASTERS OF LINEN, www.mastersoflinen.com.*

Figure B-4 The classic "linen look" in vivid color line from Elitis, an innovative French textiles company known for combining advanced technologies to produce commercial fabrics and wallcoverings, www.elitis.fr. *Photo courtesy of MASTERS OF LINEN, www.mastersoflinen.com.*

Figure B-5 From Desio, Paris, France a custom made "Maxi Diablo," sofa/canapé with 3 ½-seats in linen fabric "Johana" color plum. Quality is assured through a 3 year warranty beech frame, a 5 year seating warranty, and back cushions made of duck down (80%) and synthetic down (20%), a very soft mixture is especially meant for backrest. Cushions are all double sided for reversible convenience, www.desio.com. *Photo courtesy of MASTERS OF LINEN, www.mastersoflinen.com.*

Figure B-6 The "London Valance" by Castec is perfectly suited to this bow window grouping, creating a softly scalloped top treatment that provides rhythm and interest to this white interior. Matching blue lumbar pillows are a high contrast element placed on the white custom slip-covered wing chairs. *Photo courtesy of Castec, Inc., North Hollywood, CA.*

Figure B-7 This richly colored bedroom with deep chocolate walls and red Oriental rug benefits from the sun-screening fabric of these roller shades that diminish heat gain and glare and provide daytime privacy. The scalloped hem, echoed by the coverlet-scalloped hem, give gentility and softness to the commanding architectural detail. *Photo © Lafayette Venetian Blind, Inc. Used by permission.*

Figure B-8 Comfortex Roman shades are a custom manufactured alternative fabric treatment in the waterfall Roman style. These practical, easily operated and easily maintained shades achieve privacy, enhance sound insulation, and create a handsome background for this comfortable contemporary leather furniture set on a striking red Caucasian Oriental rug. *Photo courtesy of Comrtex Window Fashions.*

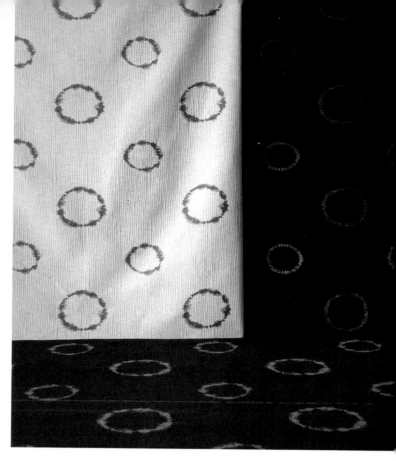

Figure B-9 Dramatic red, black, and plum coloration in 100% linen fabric from Dominque Picquier www.dominiquepicquier.com. *Photo courtesy of MASTERS OF LINEN, www.mastersoflinen.com.*

Figure B-10 "Eclipse" Jacquard reproduces the look of traditional Japanese resist dye technique called "shibori," creating a tie-dyed circle motif with small stitch-like silver highlights. Both residential and nonresidential, Eclipse meets 45,00 double rubs 30% cotton, 39% rayon, 28% acetate, 3% polyester. *Photography by Edward Addeo. Photo courtesy of Donghia, Inc., www.donghia.com.*

Figure B-11 Dynamic Art Deco styling in this sleek and sophisiticated "Main Street Club Sofa" here is seen in brilliant solid red. *Photography by Edward Addeo. Photo courtesy of Donghia, Inc. www.donghia.com.*

Figure B-12 Natural Hair hides are a dramatic and luxurious wall and floor covering application. High quality European hides are used, preferred for the length and softness of the hair, with attractive and colorful markings. Selections are then hand sewn into custom sizes in limitless custom color options. *Natural Hair Hide Carpet courtesy of Madison Leathers.*

Figure B-13 A sophisticated blend of fine textiles is seen in this interior design by Randall A. Ridless. Rug: New Oriental Egyptian #248134A from the Doris Leslie Blau Collection. Sofa: Chambord color beige Sofa throw: Bear color polar bear. Sofa pillows: Bonita color cream. Chairs: Vermenton color neige. Lumbar pillows on chairs: Narcia Damask color rosso/tabaco. Tufted ottoman: Katherine color bear. Oval stool: Tiger color brown gold. *Photo courtesy of Stark Carpets.*

Figure B-14 A stunning window treatment consisting of a wide box pleated valance and broadly striped silk drapery trimmed with tassel fringe and tied with rope/large tassel passementerie are protected against sunlight damage by "Alouette ™ Light Louvers." These elliptical soft fabric louvers in a cellular shape soften and diffuse light. Interior design by Melissa Brown for the 2003 International Designer Showhouse in New York City. *Photo courtesy of Hunter Douglas, Inc.*

Figure B-15 "Timepiece"™ is a yarn-dyed, durable upholstery contract textile in a variety of colorways. *Photo Courtesy of Herman Miller, Inc.*

Figure B-16 Xorel® Registered trademark of Carnegie Fabrics is an inherently flame retardant (IFR) fabric with high performance contract capabilities. *Photo courtesy of Carnegie Fabrics www.carnegiefabrics.com.*

Textile Aesthetics

Figure 7.1 The custom-designed Axminster carpeting in this University of Maryland dining facility is as practical as it is beautiful. *Copyrighted and registered, Soroush Custom Rugs & Axminster Carpet, www.soroushcustomrugs.com.*

BOTH NATURAL AND MANUFACTURED FIBERS have inherent visual or optical properties that determine the visual effect and aesthetic appeal of finished textiles. The level of luster is affected by the shape and relative smoothness of the fiber, and the resulting yarn is a monofilament or staple fiber. Smooth filament yarns are inherently lustrous, an appropriate texture in more formal settings, for example. Smooth, lustrous, or shiny textiles may magnify soiling, making them suitable in areas where low use or controlled cleaning is expected. Staple yarn and fibers such as wool, with its overlapping scales, are inherently dull or matte, making fabrics

from these yarns more aesthetically suitable for hiding soil and wear in installations where durability is paramount. Chemical treatments may deluster fabrics for a softer or less shiny appearance, as discussed in chapter 5.

Color is an inherent quality in all natural fibers and includes shades of off-white, cream, tan, brown, and black. These fibers may change or migrate with age and exposure to sunlight. Off-whites may yellow and browns may fade, for example. Many natural colors are bleached and then dyed to a preferred color to eliminate undertones that may migrate. Manufactured fibers are inherently dingy gray and

...ly lightened before conversion to a finished textile. ...s that do not fade or crock stay aesthetically pleasing ...ime.

Aesthetics are also affected by the tactile characteristics of the fabric—its feel. A fabric that is pleasant to the touch, whether it is smooth or heavily textured, will be perceived as a more acceptable fabric visually. Mechanical properties also contribute to aesthetic success. Fabrics that resist abrasion, that do not pull, sag, stretch, snag, or soil easily, hold their good looks for much longer. Fabrics with low specific gravity—that is, that are heavy or dense—have greater covering power, making them more able to fill space. This gives the aesthetic impression of a more substantial fabric, a quality important for all upholstered or opaque installations.

Aesthetics are more likely to be pleasing when fabrics are correctly specified for products that are appropriate selections considering the weight, texture, drapability, or suitability for their installation. To this end, the *Interior Textiles* website, www.wiley.com/go/interiortextiles, features a lengthy chapter, entitled "Decorative and Supportive Fabrics," that contains a wealth of information about the appropriate use for hundreds of defined decorative fabrics.

AESTHETIC COORDINATION

Aesthetic coordination of textiles is the aspect of interior design many professionals enjoy the most. In fact, many enter the field because of an innate talent and passion for artistic textile combinations and creative design placement. For many of these professionals, rules of coordination are unnecessary. The abilities of others may lean toward the business or scientific side of textiles, so guidelines for selecting and coordinating fabrics into an aesthetically pleasing whole are needed and appreciated.

Selection of textile combinations for both residential and nonresidential design is best established by a design program plan—the sum of the parameters and data gathered in the design process. In the exploratory part of the design process, needs and wants are examined, both physical and emotional. This is a personal statement in residential design, sometimes called the power of self-expression. In nonresidential design, the use requirements for many people must be considered, so the textiles will necessarily be far less expressive and more subtle, neutral, or universally appealing. Contract upholstery fabrics tend to feature darker or small or complex patterns that mask soiling and wear.

In all well-designed interiors, a recognizable theme in the master plan guides the selection of textiles. The term **thematic design** indicates a master plan that adheres to a specific look, mood, theme, or historic or contemporary period.

Approaches to thematic design include these guidelines:

1. Accurate or adapted—Where an interior is an authentic or adapted historic theme, such as neoclassic, the types of textiles are established, as indicated in Part III, Period Style, including chapters 14–18. However, experienced design professionals sometimes opt for interesting and unusual fabrics on period furniture pieces to freshen or update a historic look.

2. Grouped or unified—A broader approach involves general themes such as Oriental, Renaissance, formal traditional, medieval, Colonial, country or provincial, regional, ethnic, or modern.

3. Place-specific—A theme may focus on a place or region associated with feelings or moods meant to influence the mind-set of the user. Examples include tropical island or beach (natural, relaxing), mountain cabin or ski lodge (solid, earthy), cosmopolitan or urban (sleek, sophisticated), contemporary European (high-style, unique).

4. Activity themes—Examples include sports (active, stimulating), recreational activities (idyllic, sturdy), high-tech (no-nonsense, powerful), air flight (imaginative, soaring).

5. Stages of life—Examples include nursery (innocent, pure), juvenile (lighthearted, whimsical), teen girl (fashion-forward, perky), adolescent to teen boy (action, techno), professional adult (serious, discriminating), family (organized, interactive), retirement (leisure, hobby-oriented).

6. Entertainment themes—Examples include action movies (dramatic, action-filled), romantic (ethereal, gentle), comedy or animation (humorous, delightful).

When a theme is considered, each textile is evaluated according to its textural and aesthetic compliance with the governing design theme. If unity is sought, the textiles should all be compatible and contribute to a sense of oneness. However, for harmony to be effective, the unity must be balanced with variety in texture. As a general rule, an interior should have several types of textiles that all work within a theme.

Color, Pattern, and Texture

The three aspects of textile coordination, which encompasses all materials and finishes in interiors, are color, pattern, and texture. So important are these three attributes that the period chapters contain descriptive sections of color, pattern/motif, and texture for each historical style.

Color is the most emotionally charged element of design. Color evokes psychologically positive or negative occu-

Figure 7.2a "Young at Heart" is a collection of patterns designed to lift the spirits of the truly young and eternally young. Clockwise from top right: "Zoology," "Jester," "Petal Pusher." *Photo courtesy of Duralee® Fabrics, www.duralee.com.*

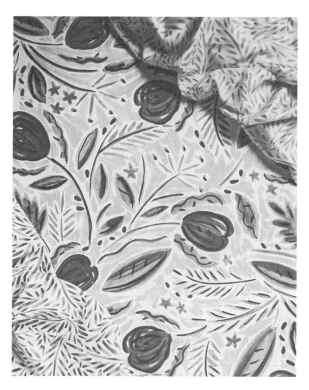

Figure 7.2b The Caribbean Exclusive Print Collection features tropical designs, here in "Palm Beach" and "Palm Frond." *Photo courtesy of Duralee® Fabrics, www.duralee.com.*

Figure 7.2c Featured in the "Aquamarine" book of the Transitions Vol. II collection, from left to right: "Swirl," a striking contemporary motif of large flowing gold swirls on a sea of jeweled aqua; a smaller pattern of abstract leaf shapes reminiscent of Moorish tiles. *Photo courtesy of Duralee® Fabrics, www.duralee.com.*

Figure 7.2d From the Silk Empire Collection, Vol. I, for the high-end residential designer. Featured at the top right is a beautiful silk Jacquard with stylized flowers and leaves and dragonflies dotting a neutral ground of gold. Next is a warm vertical stripe. The lower left is a small plaid. *Photo courtesy of Duralee® Fabrics, www.duralee.com.*

pant responses. A knowledge of color theory and application is a basic requirement for every design professional.

Color is visible to the human eye because of the physics of energy and color in light and in dyestuffs or pigments in textiles. Colored light is, essentially, electromagnetic wave bands of energy. All wavelengths of the electromagnetic spectrum are measured in nanometers (nm); 1 nm = 0.000000039 inch. White light is made up of all the **spectral colors,** familiar as the seven colors of the rainbow. Energy bands that can be seen by the human eye are called the **visible energy spectrum,** where violet or purple, the shortest wave of visible light, borders the invisible ultraviolet rays (400 nm). Next to violet or purple, in sequential order, are the visible energy bands of blue, green, yellow, orange, and red. After red, the next is the invisible infrared energy wave band (700 nm). Colored pigments and dyestuffs in yarn and finished textile absorb all the light source wavelengths except for the hue(s)—that is, the tangible color. That color is reflected, so it is evident to the human eye. Thus we see color through the process of color subtraction.

A **hue** is the identifying name of a color. Thousands of hues are created in textiles by mixing colors, resulting in slight variations. There are also thousands of off-whites, off-blacks, and true and tinted browns and grays, making the colors available in textiles nearly limitless. Textiles and surface colors that are blended and related rather than precise matches will yield a more pleasing scheme or grouping of colors. If effort is made to match the hues, disappointment is nearly always the result, as the surface texture reflects color differently; a smooth fabric and a rough-textured textile dyed the same will make a single color appear slightly different, creating a visual dissonance. The variables are the type of yarn, the fiber, and the placement of the textile in relation to the angle at which the light strikes it, as well as the spectral energy distribution of the light (warm or cool light). For these reasons, textiles that blend rather than match may be more successful. The exception is a set of designs printed or woven on identical base cloths, where matching of dye lots can be more closely assured.

General rules for color include the **law of chromatic distribution,** which states that the largest areas in an interior are filled with the most neutralized colors of the scheme. The smaller the area, the more intense the color proportionately becomes. The **law of value distribution** states that the lightest colors are placed on the ceiling, medium values around, and the darkest colors underfoot, creating a sense of stability. **Color value** means the lightness or darkness of a fabric. A clear, clean, lightened hue is a **tint,** a neutralized or dulled lighter value is a **pastel,** a darker value obtained by adding black is a **shade,** and a deeper value obtained by neutralizing (adding the complementary color or more than one darker value, including black or brown, to create a dull or dirty shade) is called a **tone.** Any color that is not pure but rather contains another color in increments has an **undertone.** Colors can be categorized as **warm colors** (yellow, orange, red), considered friendly, advancing, and less formal, or **cool colors** (green, blue, violet), which are more aloof, distant, and formal. An undertone can render a color warmer or cooler, or it may prove to be a warm-undertoned cool color or a cool-undertoned warm color. As a general rule, aesthetics are enhanced if undertones are similar.

Figure 7.3 Custom rug designs may be selected from an extensive archive of designs ranging from ancient Persian to ultracontemporary motifs or custom-created to specifications. Here, colors are selected from carpet tuft samples. *Copyrighted and registered, Soroush Custom Rugs & Axminster Carpet, www.soroushcustomrugs.com.*

Color schemes specified for an interior may be based on standard color wheel theory (the prismatic or rainbow colors—red, yellow, green, blue, violet—arranged in a circle). These include:

1. Monochromatic scheme—One color in several varieties, ample white, and accents of black.
2. Analogous schemes—Two to six colors adjacent on the color wheel. Generally, one dominates.
3. Complementary schemes—Direct complement, or two colors directly across on the color wheel: red/green, blue/orange, yellow/violet; split complement, or three colors: one hue and the colors on either side of its complement, such as blue, red-orange, and red-violet; triadic complement, or three colors equidistant on the color wheel; alternate complement, or four colors, a triad with one hue's direct complement; tetrad complement, or four colors equidistant on the color wheel; and double complement, or four colors, adjacent double complements.

More often, a textile-based color scheme will be drawn from the colors in a fabric, not because they conform to one of the standard schemes above. A textile that meets all the necessary specifications listed and also is an excellent choice aesthetically will usually form the basis for the color scheme. Coupled with a design theme, textiles carry much influence in the interior.

In specifying colored textiles, it is best to lay the samples together to carefully evaluate how the applications will affect one another. It has been said there is no such thing as an ugly color, only colors used in the wrong amounts, intensities, or combinations.

Lighting effects can cause fabrics to appear different. Large quantities of light appear to wash out or lighten color, whereas low lighting may cause color to be darker or more dead or lifeless. **Metamerism,** or the **metameric effect,** is the ability of a textile to appear as one color under one light and another color in another light. Artificial light is not always balanced or pure, depending on the season and weather conditions and surrounding landscape or buildingscape. Most artificial light has unbalanced spectrums, leaning toward warmer yellowish light or cooler bluish light. Colors or hues will be manifested according to the lighting spectrum. Also, because textiles are often three-dimensional, they may catch or reflect light in unexpected ways. Colors appear to vary from one room to another and may even appear different when viewed on opposite sides of the same room. Therefore, it is best to try combinations of textile samples in the space where they will be installed together, including evaluation at different times of the day and under different lighting conditions—daylight, incandescent

light, and fluorescent light, day and night. For example, warm or yellow light is missing part or all of the blue components of light, and cool or blue light is missing the yellow components. This means that under warm light, fabrics will appear more yellowish or orange-tinged. Under cool light, fabrics will appear more bluish or violet-tinged.

Color matching requires the use of a standard light box with several illuminants, including D65 (daylight), A (tungsten), CWF (Cool White Fluorescent), WWF (Warm White Fluorescent), and a variety of incandescent lamps. Color perception may vary according to visual acuity (individual ability to see color, which varies). Light boxes are therefore employed so that whenever samples are viewed, the conditions are exactly the same.

Pattern or Motif

Pattern or **motif** is the application of a design to or on the surface of a textile. The pattern or motif establishes a fabric's theme, historical style, or overall mood or aesthetic. People have a tremendous psychological response to pattern, second in intensity only to their response to color. Pattern can evoke positive or negative reactions from users according to their background, life experience, or exposure to design elements.

Because pattern can be very personal, in residential design the clients who most frequently occupy the space should be given an opportunity to make guided selections for their individual taste satisfaction. Rooms with fewer patterns may seem larger but less interesting; pattern utilizes color and form to give style and interest to an interior. In nonresidential spaces, dramatic or well-defined patterns are kept at a minimum in favor of less defined or more universally appealing patterns, which may appear from a distance as texture. In this way, several nonassertive patterns can be used together when colors are carefully coordinated. However, fabrics with definite patterns must be used judiciously.

If a pattern on a major fabric has a large scale, then smaller applications may be more successful in small scale. Generally, two similarly scaled fabrics are competitive and awkward together unless they are coordinates and planned for use as companions. Note that this is not necessarily the case just because a fabric book offers a grouping of patterns in the same colorway. There must be a lead fabric and a support fabric, not two equally competing fabrics used together. As a general rule, a room can often support a large pattern (or a medium-sized pattern), a small pattern, a tiny pattern (often a geometric, a stripe, or possibly a plaid), plus textures. Although all rules can be broken with skill and artistic license belonging to one who has achieved good taste and judgment through a careful study of design, this rule is

Figure 7.4a "Sparta" area rug, by designer Marion Dorn, is inspired by an ancient Greek mosaic tile floor. *Photo courtesy of Edward Fields, Incorporated.*

Figure 7.4b "Botanica" is an asymmetrical burst of tropical flowers on a ground of rectangular shapes, with a sense of the Japanese shibui aesthetic. *Photo courtesy of Edward Fields, Incorporated.*

Figure 7.4c The "Carrington" designer rug features symmetrically placed botanical motifs resting on vivid rectangles of color and contrasted with circles and crosshatched design elements. *Photo courtesy of Edward Fields, Incorporated.*

Figure 7.4d "Saguaro III" is a Frank Lloyd Wright design of geometric patterns expressed in a luxurious wool pile from the Tibetan Silk and Wool Collection. *Saguaro III area rug from the Schumacher Frank Lloyd Wright Collection, F. Schumacher & Co.*

a safe and consistent one that will help assure proper use of coordinated fabric patterns. Patterns should be thematic to achieve harmony, which can be lost if the interior becomes visually busy or confusing.

Texture

Texture is the visual or tactile surface achieved by the form of construction and by special finishes. Texture may be judged as **relief,** the difference between high and low areas. Textures that are calendared to increase luster and those that are smooth, shiny, or low relief (flat) are considered sleek, sophisticated, and more formal and require higher upkeep, making them more suitable for light to moderately used spaces. Textures that are rough, matte, or inconsistent are less formal, hide dirt, and are perhaps more livable. If the textile is readily cleanable (less, not more, surface depth), then the relative hand may render it suitable for highly used applications. The surprising contrast of texture is a hallmark of late postmodern design. The contrast of a rough textile with a smooth often is a delight to the eye, but it must be accomplished with experience and great care.

Texture is also a variable when it is subject to crushing. A carpet pile that compresses with repeated traffic will appear lighter or darker than at installation.

Soiling is a color perception factor related to texture; soil will darken colors and cause inconsistencies in coloration where repeated abrasion or traffic is evident. Hence, the Crypton treatment can ensure a truer color for a longer period. (Refer to chapter 5.)

Fading is a factor in how colors appear over time; colors do not fade only to a lighter hue but often change hues as mixed colors fade at different rates. Window film or low-e glass can help deter fading in fabrics. *Note:* Solution-dyed textiles generally do not fade.

GUIDELINES TO FURNISHING WITH TEXTILES

There are several approaches to furnishings, examined here as philosophies that can guide the selection and coordination of textiles. One furnishing ideology involves structural and practical interior furnishing products, sensibly put together into a serviceable whole. The look is pragmatic and functional. Upkeep is minimal, colors are typically neutral, and the decorating scheme could change with little concern for the window treatments. There is staying power, or endurance over time.

Another direction is more personalized, with consideration given to the lifestyle or work style preferences of the

Figure 7.5 A stunning carpet is the focal point in this custom interior. Interior design by Randall A. Ridless. Rug: New Oriental Egyptian #248134 from the Doris Leslie Blau collection. Sofa: Chambord color beige. Sofa throw: Bear color polar bear. Sofa pillows: Bonia color cream. Chairs: Vermenton color beige. Lumbar pillows on chairs: Narcia Damask color rosso/tabaco. Tufted ottoman: Katherine color bear. Oval stool: Tiger color brown gold. *Photo courtesy of Stark Carpets.*

client; custom interior design is inevitable. Thought is devoted to the goals of the interior, the users who will live or work there, and how furnishings should function to support the activities that will take place there. A plan should be in place for completing a fully executed design theme, even if it is accomplished in increments. Carefully coordinated colors, patterns, and textures work together to create a harmonious whole, where all elements are interdependent for an effectively furnished and complete look. More selections are offered to the customer with price and quality as factors, but appropriateness, beauty, and significance are the key deciding factors—what is really the right look, the right fabric, the right style.

A third approach is seen in high-quality furnishings that include lavish textile applications. This philosophy assumes that the interior has already achieved function and a fully executed design theme, as described above. This type of interior may become fine design, meaning the pinnacle of good taste. The ability to focus on details is inherent to this approach. Then creativity is put into action through add-ons, which make an ordinary interior into a special, unique space tailored to the desires or even the justifiable whims of the client. The details are the icing on the cake, so to speak. Examples include dressmaker details such as buttons or welting, passementerie, and appliqué.

The approach also includes coordinating two or more fabrics in delightful ways that result in great visual satisfaction through the skillful coordination of color, pattern, and texture. The best interior design is never trite or obvious or boring or tedious. No trimming or banding or contrast jumps out to grab the eye's attention. Rather, the eye must do a bit of searching. Subtlety is a critical element of excellent design. This is especially true in fabric. For example, if a fabric has three or more colors, do not pick out the smallest quantity color for a major-use fabric or even as trimming, as the eye has difficulty in making the connect. It is better to select a color that is most clearly the key player in the fabric for trimming or accents. This will assure that the scheme will appear cohesive and harmonized.

Referring to the rules of pattern coordination to vary the scale or size of the pattern in coordinated applications is a key to fine design. Discrimination is also required for the sophisticated and appropriate use of passementerie—fringe, cording, tassels, and other trimmings. Very elegant passementerie should be reserved for formal, traditional rooms. The heavier the scale, the larger the room, and the more exquisite the furnishings, the greater the use of trimmings. Appropriate trimmings, such as braid and banding, are often effective in both formal and less formal settings. Similar to the rule above about contrasting colors, the best-designed interiors use trimmings in an understated contrast—not harsh or high contrast, but soft and subtle. This rule assures that the eye will not be offended nor tire of the passementerie. The result is details that will stand the test of time and hence be beautiful for years.

At times, simplicity and structural, unadorned design is the best direction, while at others, many trimmings will be appropriate. That is part of the enormous responsibility of the interior design professional—to gather the facts that yield excellence in aesthetic specifications.

COST VERSUS AESTHETICS

Budget is a first priority in nonresidential interiors and often in residential interiors as well. The price tag for interior textiles can be the restricting factor. The challenge is to find a single textile or a group of textiles that meet the functional,

environmental, user, and aesthetic requirements. Often, a fabric meets the nonresidential specifications but is unfriendly in terms of texture and aesthetics. Many residential fabrics are post-finished to be applied in public spaces. Contract fabrics may also have a residential design flavor as micro-fibers increase in use.

There is a tremendous range in the cost of textiles—from $2.00 per yard for discontinued or flawed textiles to several hundred dollars per yard for custom or exclusive fabric. Average textile prices range from about $12.00 to $60.00 per yard. When comparing two textiles that are similar in construction or style, the one with the lower price simply may be not a brand name, or the quality of construction or finishing may be poorer. Discrimination is requisite in determining the best quality for the money, and the time involved in making this determination is often substantial. However, a fabric that performs better is worth the effort to find.

One approach used by design professionals is termed the *lion's share* policy. Fabrics are selected that are economical but durable and perhaps more serviceable and practical, and then a larger portion of the budget per yard is spent on accent pieces or limited applications that are dramatic, lavish, and stunning. Thus, by not utilizing complete equity in the budget, surprisingly effective results can be achieved.

SELLING FABRIC: THE POWER OF VERBAL PERSUASION

It has been said that the larger one's vocabulary, the more money one makes. Certainly persuasion is one skill a design professional must possess in order to sell. Although most clients have difficulty picturing a product or complete interior in their mind's eye, to designers who love working with textiles and design elements, the finished product or space is a clear vision—they simply see it. The problem is that such designers often have difficulty communicating their vision to others. Here is where a running list of adjectives will not only aid communication but also help paint a picture of what the product is or can be.

On www.wiley.com/go/interiortextiles, "Textiles Aesthetics Adjectives" is a list of words for describing fabrics according to general styles. The comparison of these terms to those in chapters 14–18 will be valuable in building a vocabulary for describing textile selection and application as well as the finished product. These are suggestions—they can act as a springboard for a larger, more commanding vocabulary of aesthetic coordination. As a theme is developed, the words that describe each fabric should be similar or compatible, and readily applied to the samples scrutinized by the client.

Upholstered Furniture and Slipcovers

Figure 8.1 "Serafina Modular" armless upholstered chairs are fitted with connecting computer support tables to create an informal yet handsome open conference room. *Photo courtesy of Arcadia, www.arcadiacontract.com.*

SPECIFYING CONTRACT UPHOLSTERY

Project Analysis

The first step in specifying contract upholstery is to analyze the project. In contract applications, upholstery is used in offices, hospitality venues (hotels and restaurants), healthcare institutions, and commercial settings (stores and businesses). Depending on the type of project and client, specific needs must be addressed. This may seem obvious, but identifying the type of project is important and will immediately narrow the upholstery options to be considered.

In a restaurant, for example, fabrics for seating must be easily cleaned and durable. As a contrast, seating pieces in a law firm executive conference room involve other factors— a reflection of professionalism, status, comfort, and long-term appeal—so more aesthetically pleasing fabrics may be considered. These two examples point out that needs and considerations vary greatly from project to project.

Product/Application Analysis

After determining the scope of the project, the products to be upholstered are analyzed. Again, this narrows the vast array of available fabrics from which to choose. Going back to the example of the restaurant and the conference room, the products going into these spaces are different. In the restaurant, the main products to be upholstered are seating options—dining chairs, booths, benches, or lounge chairs, depending on the design parameters. Each type of seating may be upholstered in several ways. For example, a dining chair may have an upholstered seat with a wood back, and the seat of a booth may be upholstered in one fabric and the back in another.

Now consider the contrasting needs of the law firm executive conference room. The products specified for the conference room and other spaces in the law firm will not be the same as those for the restaurant. These might include guest chairs in a lobby, task seating at desks, and executive seating in individual attorneys' offices. Beyond seating, other products in this project will contain upholstered elements, including systems furniture, which is composed of panels (or movable walls 3 to 5 inches thick) and fixed furniture (work surfaces, pedestals, tackboards, overhead bins, or lateral files supported by panels). These are used quite often in commercial projects for individual work areas. Systems furniture creates flexible but private individual spaces within a space. Traditionally, the panels supporting the fixed furniture are upholstered, although panels made of Plexiglas and other plastics allow for acoustical privacy and a more open feel that encourages a collaborative and cooperative work environment. While the panels may not be upholstered as often anymore, most workstations still include a tackboard, which requires that a fabric be specified. Overhead storage bins may also be upholstered. One furnishing trend in commercial design is mobile pedestals on casters. These can roll under the work surface for easy storage and roll out for easier access. The tops of the pedestals can be cushioned and upholstered, creating seating alternatives in tight office spaces to accommodate employee collaboration or an occasional guest.

Analyzing the products specified for a project may not seem at first to narrow the fabric options, as there are so many points to consider. However, keeping in mind the specific products to be upholstered and the application of the fabrics provides direction. Knowing the products, being familiar with them, and being aware of the many options available all help move along the upholstery specification process.

Budget

The budget allotted to a project immediately limits upholstery options. Contract fabrics can range in price from about $15 per yard to over $100 per yard. Determining how many pieces of furniture must be upholstered and the yardage requirements for each piece helps narrow the price range. For example, assume that eight executive chairs are being specified for a conference room. Each chair requires 2 yards of fabric, and the budget is $1,000 for the fabric for these chairs. Fabrics with a net price of around $60 per yard should be considered for selection (8 chairs × 2 yards/chair = 16 yards of fabric needed; $1,000 budget/16 yards total = $62.50 per yard). This assumes tax is included in the cost of fabric but does not account for the costs of upholstering, transportation, and installation.

Figure 8.2 Fine leather upholstery, such as this "Robinson" sofa, is designed in enduring classic form to stand the test of time. *Photography by Jim Koch. Courtesy of Hancock & Moore, www.hancockand-moore.com.*

If a fabric is selected that is a standard with the manufacturer, the price of the fabric is already included in the price of the piece of furniture. If the fabric is not a standard fabric option but rather ordered from another source, it is considered **COM** (customer's own material). This fabric costs more than a standard fabric because additional charges for shipping are applied from the mill or manufacturer of the COM fabric to the manufacturer of the furniture that will be upholstered. It is important to remember that price lists may be printed in either **list** (retail) or **net** (wholesale price), so if the customer is quoted a net price, the design professional obtains neither markup nor profit. Although there may not be a markup for upholstery labor, there should always be a profit on the fabric, unless the professional is charging for design service in another way—per square foot or hourly, for example.

Color Scheme

Another step to specifying upholstery is to consider the color scheme of a project. Often, a space contains materials that must be accommodated, such as paint or wall finishes, flooring, and wood furniture. Upholstery should be chosen to coordinate with the planned color scheme. Some projects may be for a completely new space in which all finishes are yet to be selected. In this case, the design professional may want to refer to the business identity and logo for color inspiration. Additional important factors in selecting a color scheme are the room size, sources of lighting, and the desired ambience of the space. These considerations narrow upholstery options, as some colors will work better and be more appropriate than others.

Upholstery Fabric Composition

The composition of a fabric affects its feel and durability, which are two important factors in specifying upholstery. In contract settings, synthetic fibers such as nylon are often specified as they meet flammability and other testing criteria. Depending on the application of the upholstery, however, the feel or hand of the fabric may be especially important, and many nylon fabrics are less pleasant to the touch. For example, on lounge chairs in a lobby, where clients may be sitting for some time waiting for an appointment, it would be important that the upholstery have a pleasing touch. Polyester micro-fibers are meeting this need.

The fiber content of a fabric has a direct affect on its durability and is crucial for a designer to consider when specifying upholstery for high-use products. Task chairs that clients will sit in every day for hours will receive ex-cessive wear and must be upholstered in durable fabrics. Fabrics tested on a Wyzenbeek or Martindale machine will indicate resistance to abrasion. For example, one fabric may have 15,000 double rubs and another 30,000 double rubs. The second fabric is more durable and will wear better over time. Refer to table 6.7 for abrasion durability tests.

The fiber content and the weave or construction also affect the fabric's susceptibility to pilling, puckering, or snagging, problems that could arise once an upholstered product is being used. **Pilling** is the working loose of threads that form small balls or pills, creating an unattractive visual problem and indicating the fabric appears to be wearing out. **Puckering** is the bunching of fabric that does not lie flat—also unattractive in upholstery. **Snagging** is where yarns are prone to catching on objects and begin to pull loose. This is perhaps the most obvious and most problematic upholstery issue because once the threads break, holes can result, and little can be done to repair them.

Manufacturers' Lead Times

Manufacturers have **lead times,** or estimated lengths of time needed to produce the ordered products. Often, lead times are measured *not* from the time the order is placed by the design professional but rather from the time the order is entered in the manufacturer's computer system, and they extend to the time the product is boxed and ready to be shipped. It is important to factor in shipping time as well as the lead time. Choosing a standard fabric decreases lead time because the fabric is kept in stock at the factory. If a COM fabric is specified, lead time will be longer to accommodate shipping from the textile warehouse and receiving at the furniture manufacturer. Also, if it is the first time a manufacturer will be using the COM fabric, it usually must first be tested on the product and approved for production. A sample of the fabric must be sent to the manufacturer or testing laboratory, the tests performed, the evaluation delivered, and confirmation that the fabric meets the design specification criteria received—all of which takes time. If the schedule is tight, choosing a standard fabric might be wise. Communication about lead time with the manufacturer's customer service department before making the order is essential, as lead times can influence upholstery selection.

Ordering and Installing

After all of the above factors are considered, an appropriate fabric is selected, approved by the client, and then ordered.

Design firms vary in their operating procedures, but the usual basic steps are as follows:

1. The fabric order is assigned a **purchase order number,** which allows the order to be tracked from the time it is placed to the time of delivery.
2. The order is issued a **side mark**—a name, number, or code that cross-references to the project, the specific location, and perhaps the delivery location. For example, a side mark may read "Tanner Co. 5-A," indicating the client name, the floor, and the suite where the furniture is to be installed.
3. Copies of all fabric and upholstery paperwork are filed, along with a record of any conversations via phone or e-mail regarding the order. These records are important in case of problems such as **back orders** (fabric out of stock and awaiting new stock delivery) and delays.

The lead times must be considered in order to estimate a delivery date. Once the order is placed, the manufacturer will send the designer an **acknowledgment number,** another way of tracking the order, which usually includes an estimated ship date. Good communication skills are essential to keeping both installers and clients informed about delivery and the installation schedule once the upholstered product is in production.

Maintenance and Care

The final step in specifying contract upholstery is to educate the client about maintaining and caring for installed products. Some fabrics are easily cleaned; others require specific cleaning products. Clients are more satisfied in the long run when they know what to expect from their products and know how to maintain and care for them. Design professionals also benefit because there will be fewer, if any, maintenance problems to resolve. See www.wiley.com/go/interiortextiles for textile maintenance information.

RESIDENTIAL AND CONTRACT UPHOLSTERED FURNITURE CONSTRUCTION

Frame

Upholstered seating is usually a ten-year investment, so client education concerning the best-quality sofa allowable within the budget is important. The frame is a very important consideration. Although contract seating is often steel-framed to meet durability and flammability requirements, in residential as well as some contract projects, upholstered furniture frames are wood. Less expensive sofas are usually made of hardwood, plywood, particleboard, or some combination of the three. Better frames are at least 1¼ inches thick and made of moisture-resistant, kiln-dried hard woods like ash, birch, maple, or oak. By lifting one end of the sofa one can judge its weight—most often, the heavier, the better. **Joinery** is the method used to join wood frames together. **Splines** are corrugated horizontal nails hammered into **mitered** (45-degree cut) pieces of lumber that fashion the frame. As pieces butt against one another, wood frames may be glued and screwed together in addition to the joint methods that follow. **Dowels** are wood rods cut into small lengths; these are glued into holes in adjoining wood frame members. **Mortise and tenon** joints impart great strength; these are made by interlocking two pieces, one with a square hole (mortise) and the other carved with a projection (tenon). Think of "tab A into slot B." **Corner blocks** are triangular wood pieces glued and screwed into place to reinforce legs.

Springs

The springs are the next consideration. Their quality is a major determinant of the quality of a sofa. Two kinds of springs are generally used in upholstered furniture:

Figure 8.3 The Woodbridge collection captures exquisite tailoring and upholstered details with wood elements reminiscent of the rural wooden bridges of nineteenth-century America. *Photo by Edward Addeo. Produce by Donghia, Inc.*

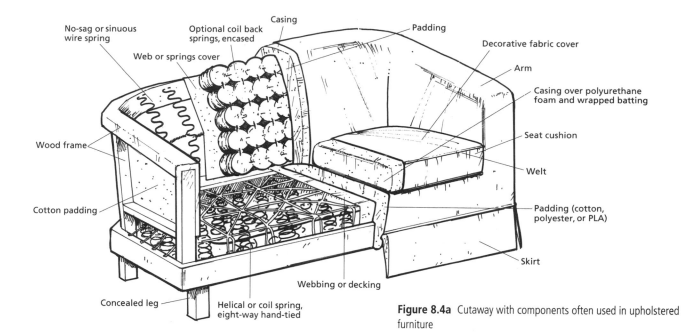

Figure 8.4a Cutaway with components often used in upholstered furniture

Labels (Figure 8.4a): No-sag or sinuous wire spring; Optional coil back springs, encased; Casing; Padding; Decorative fabric cover; Web or springs cover; Arm; Casing over polyurethane foam and wrapped batting; Wood frame; Seat cushion; Welt; Cotton padding; Padding (cotton, polyester, or PLA); Skirt; Concealed leg; Helical or coil spring, eight-way hand-tied; Webbing or decking

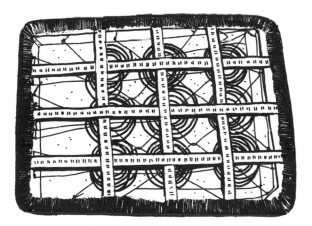

Figure 8.4b Coil springs in high-quality furniture construction are eight-way hand-tied and anchored in place.

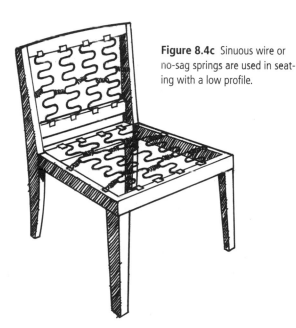

Figure 8.4c Sinuous wire or no-sag springs are used in seating with a low profile.

Sinuous wire or **no-sag springs** are used in chair backs or contract seating with a low profile and where less buoyancy is desired. These are *S*-shaped steel wires bent into a curved or zigzag format and attached to the frame.

Coil springs are helical and cylindrical coils attached to the frame beneath the cushion. Coil springs may be connected to each other in various ways, although the most common is the eight-way hand-tied, wherein the coils are tied to each other at eight points around the top and bottom. High-quality coil springs are made of 8-gauge steel wire. Some manufacturers increase the number or strength of the springs at the edges for a firmer sofa. A simple quality test is to sit on the sofa seat near the arm. The other end of the cushion should sit securely in place without popping up. There should also be substantial support to avoid the sensation of sinking in, no matter how soft the cushions are designed. The springs and cushions should be completely silent—no squeaking sounds.

Seat Cushions

Sofas and chairs are measured in seats, which is a single standard-sized cushion or its equivalent. For longer seat cushions, the number of seats is determined by length—for example, a 5-foot loveseat is two seats, a 6- or 7-foot sofa is three seats, and so on. A seat is often about 20 inches square, although this size and shape vary according to style. Near arms, **end or long cushions** often have a **hurricane clip** installed so the cushion may be attached to the sofa frame to prevent its popping up. The clips may be detached for repositioning, such as turning over and trading positions of the end cushions for even wear.

Inner Cushion Materials

Inner cushion materials are used in tandem to provide the four characteristics of high-quality cushions: support or firmness, compressibility, resilience, and loft. **Support** or **firmness** is necessary at the core of a cushion as a base on which the compressibility and resilience can function. **Compressibility** allows the ability to sink into a cushion, as it gives with weight. **Resilience** is the ability to bounce back or recover from the depression and deformity caused by impact and weight. Cushions are expected to return to their original shape and hold it until further use. This is also referred to as *compressional resilience* or *compressional loft*. **Loft** is the lightness that cushions and pillows must have to be handled, lifted, and managed. One way fiber batting is engineered is by extruding polyester fibers with hollow shafts, which increases loft. A way to increase resilience is to spray resin into the batting.

Coil springs may be at the center of a **Marshall unit seat,** or **spring-down cushion,** surrounded by foam and wrapped in Dacron, then inserted into a muslin bag of channeled blendown (feathers and down). The springs give the unit support, while the blendown gives a luxurious surface feel.

The most common fillings include a solid or slab foam, fibrous batting, loose particles such as down, and casing materials.

Two kinds of foam are used as cushion materials: polyurethane and latex. **Polyurethane foam** is formulated and then baked or heated to give loft and buoyancy. It holds shape well for a long period, resists deterioration from aging, and is resistant to moisture deterioration and microbial growth. **Latex foam** is made from natural or synthetic rubber compounded into a foam slab of specified thickness and then solidified, leaving tiny air pockets or cells. It can be engineered to produce different levels of firmness or softness. When sulfur is added and then heated, stronger chemical cross-links strengthen and stabilize the shape. Latex rubber is a good cushion material for upholstery and for pillows, although it is susceptible to deterioration as it ages.

Solid or **slab foam cushions** are available in various densities and thicknesses, each of which serves a purpose in the creation of balanced cushioning. A dense foam cushion is less resilient and gives firmer support. A less dense cushion with more air and loft is softer and gives comfort. Solid slab cushions have a disadvantage in often being either too firm or too soft. If the cushion is dense, the edges are somewhat sharp or uncomfortable, and if the cushion is less dense, the cushion does not hold its shape. Therefore, a combination of materials is often preferred.

Sandwiched foam cushions are made of layered foam adhered or laminated together into one unit. This is an economical and efficient use of materials. The cushion center is thick, dense foam, and the outer layers are thinner, less dense, and soft, giving the impression of fiber batting. These cushions are not encased in fabric in economy furniture.

Fiber batting–wrapped foam cushions have dense slab foam as a core; this is wrapped with fiber batting. This construction may have a **casing,** a nonremovable or fully sewn lining cushion cover or case, which keeps the fibers from working loose through the seams, the fabric, or the outer zipper. It also holds the cushion materials in place. The decorative fabric covers this unit.

Fibrous batting is used around foam for seat cushions as described above, and it is frequently used alone as back cushions. The most common type is **bonded polyester batting.** For cushion filling used alone, batting is engineered to possess two levels of density—the outer later of finer fibers that are softer, and the lower or inner layer of coarser fiber, which offers better support. Resin is added to enhance resilience. **Cotton felt** is a fiber batting used mostly to lay over arms and backs to soften the frame. Other cellulosic fibers used in this way include kapok and jute. However, all these are flammable, so their use is restricted. **Curled hair batting** is also used in the same way, with disadvantages of odor, mildew, and allergic response. **Spanish moss,** the parasite that grows on live oak trees, has also been used in the southeastern United States. Of all these materials, polyester fiber batting is predominately used in upholstery cushioning.

Loose particle fillings come from natural and manufactured sources. **Down,** or undercoat feathers without quills, long a luxury filling material, and **feathers,** which include quills, are two of the materials that come from waterfowl and nonwaterfowl. As both materials compress but are not resilient, down cushions and pillows require fluffing, replumping, or plumping up by hand after each use. **Blendown** is a combination of down and feathers; it is often wrapped around a foam core and encased in a muslin bag. Other loose particle fillings include **shredded** or **chopped foam,** which has a tendency to clump, and **polyester crimped fiberfill.** Loose fiberfill is encased in bonded olefin/polypropelene fabric, similar to that used as a scrim on the bottom frame of furniture.

Exposed Components

Exposed arms, legs, and frames of upholstered furniture may be made of wood, metal, plastic, or wicker. There is an impressive variety of wood materials and styles; both hard and softwoods are used and frequently add to the character as well as the strength of the piece. Legs and arms are either attached to the frame or extend from it. One quality check for strength is to place one hand on each arm, lean one's weight to a foot placed in front, then push and try to wiggle or skew the chair. The strength and security of the joinery will be evident—give or looseness indicates poor craftsmanship, while a sturdy, unyielding chair will be able to withstand repeated and prolonged use.

Steel is often given a powder coating, a strong and durable coating for contract furniture. Exposed rigid vinyl and thermoset plastic used in contract furniture is also extremely durable and is often used as a finish component over the top of steel inner frame components. These elements are painted or colored prior to extrusion or forming. Wood arms, legs, and trim are stained and finished before upholstering.

Figure 8.5 The "McKinney Arm Dining Chair" features splayed exposed wood legs. The frame is a handsome contemporary style adapted from Neoclassic and Empire period chairs. *Photo courtesy of Jessica Charles Furniture LLC.*

Upholstery Fabric

Considerations for contract upholstery fabric may also apply to residential applications with the following guidelines. Color, texture, and pattern must be appropriate for the style of the furniture. However, many sofa and chair styles are versatile in that many types of fabric look equally acceptable, from velvet to leather to cotton tapestry to chenille, for example. One example is the beloved Rococo fauteuil chair, which has been upholstered in nearly every kind of fabric imaginable. Coordination of upholstery fabric with the interior theme is critical in residential design. And, like contract settings, residential upholstery fabrics should be durable and resist abrasion, pilling, marking, crushing, crocking, and fading.

Durability is the ability of a fabric to endure use and time. Although fabric pricing variables can increase the cost of a sofa dramatically, higher price doesn't necessarily correlate with an increase in durability. In fact, the inverse is often true. Denim, for instance, is a reasonably priced fabric with good durability. Silk, on the other hand, is several times the price of denim and much more fragile. However, silk is a prized upholstery textile for formal settings where furniture receives little use. Upholstery that is exposed to daily wear and tear must be durable.

Abrasion resistance is a key factor in determining durability. Although contract fabrics are tested, residential fabrics generally are not. Hand tests of stretching and bending as well as scrutinizing the denier, or yarn thickness, are some ways to evaluate fabrics. The ability of a fabric to resist abrasion depends on several factors, including the quality of the fiber; the ply, twist, and size of the yarn; and the density and balance of the weave. Sturdy monofilament yarns are the most difficult to break. Backings and finishes can also affect the way a fabric will wear. Even though ability to resist abrasion is the factor most people consider first when determining the durability of a fabric, pilling, fading and soiling are more likely than abrasion to shorten the useful life of the piece. The tighter the fabric is pulled, the more vulnerable it becomes to abrasion. For this reason, upholstered arms and prominent welting or covered cording are areas that wear out first.

Pilling occurs as loose fibers work free, create **fuzzing**, and, with abrasion, eventually roll into tiny balls or pills, which are unsightly and contribute to surface wear. Fuzzing and pilling occur in wool fabrics but tend to diminish as the fabric wears and the loose fibers break. In some synthetics, pilling may be a problem, as the fabric is so strong that it holds the pills and does not allow them to break away. Pills can sometimes be sheared off carefully with a hand razor or a manual sweater defuzzer. Pilling does not occur in fabrics made of filament yarns, which are one length and do not have short fibers.

Marking can occur in fabrics with pile, such as chenille and velvet, where the weight and rubbing of use push pile down or in a different direction than the original, thus leaving a mark in the fabric. Brushing with a brush or vacuum often encourages pile resiliency. Marking can result in pile loss and permanent abrasion damage.

Fading is most often caused by exposure to direct sunlight over time, although indirect sunlight causes eventual fading. Some colors and fibers are more susceptible to fading. Fading damage—color loss and fiber weakening—is irreversible, although it can be prevented by keeping upholstered pieces out of direct sunlight through thoughtful placement, exterior screening devices, and with the application of interior window film and window treatments—sheers and draw drapery, shades, and blinds. Unwitting exposure to sunlight shortens the aesthetic life of upholstery. As it fades, it loses its appeal and ages the piece visually. Artificial lighting may also cause fading.

Crocking occurs when excess dye rubs off the fabric onto another surface. This can happen under both wet and dry surface conditions. **Dry crocking** occurs more often with leather and usually only for a short time, although color loss in leather can be a serious fault resulting in diminished visual value of the piece. **Wet crocking** happens most often in cotton prints, perhaps at a beach house where someone wearing a wet swimsuit might sit on the sofa, for instance.

Dimensional stability is sagging or wrinkling. It is caused by fabrics that stretch but do not recover, occasionally due to humidity changes. It may also be caused by inferior cushion material that breaks down, making the fabric look as though it has stretched or sagged. If the fabric is tufted, buttoned, quilted, or channeled, dimensional stability is increased.

Snagging occurs in upholstery with large or loose yarns or loops that are easily caught and pulled out by rings or buttons, for example.

Soiling shortens the life of fabrics literally by abrasion and aesthetically by stains. Regular vacuuming and prompt attention to spots is the best way to prevent permanent soiling. If stains are left unattended, they may change the composition of the dyestuff so the spot remains even after cleaning. Another way of preventing specific area soiling is to rotate, turn, and trade cushion placement so the wear is not always in the same place. When in doubt about the origin of a stain or the way to remove it, it is best to enlist the services of an upholstery maintenance professional. There is disagreement about the positive and negative effects of soil-repellent finishes, but they do retard absorbency, so soil and stains are less likely to be absorbed into the fabric. These finishes are more effective when they are new; they tend to break with time and age, and the soiling may work under the finish, becoming locked in and perhaps permanent.

Upholstery Color, Pattern, and Texture

Neutral colors tend to suggest a serene, sophisticated look, but they can become listless. Yet strong patterns on large upholstered pieces have the potential to become tiring. Designers often guide clients toward solid fabrics for sofas, as opposed to patterned fabric, allowing more flexibility in other furnishing elements. Color and pattern can be achieved in window treatments and accessories to change interior design themes seasonally or stylistically where the sofa is a neutral color and textured or subtle pattern. A drawback of a neutral sofa is that spots and stains are more noticeable than on a patterned sofa, so owners with children or pets may want to consider the practicality of a pattern. Seams are less noticeable in a patterned fabric; the plainer the fabric, the more noticeable the seam. When motifs are matched in a patterned fabric, seams may seem to disappear, to a large degree. Pattern locks in a particular style, whereas textured fabrics with tonal variations may work well with a sequence of interior design styles, hide soiling, and proving to be long-lived.

Upholstery fabrics are generally more durable than fabrics for other installations, such as draperies or decorative table covers. They are meant to be used for six to twelve years, on average, so they are often stronger fabrics by weave or through treatment or backing. With this in mind, two general types of texture are used: a smooth texture and a texture with a deeper relief or pile. Smoother fabrics, especially those with some sheen, tend to look more formal and restrained and are less prone to snagging. Often, however, smooth fabrics show wear more quickly. Where a smooth fabric is desired but durability is also required, a fiber blend that contains polyester or polyester microfiber, nylon, olefin, or sturdy cotton might be considered. Leather is another durable texture choice; good-quality leather should be expected to last for fifteen years, as opposed to seven for fabric. Leather requires gentle living, as it can be stained and scratched.

Another consideration in selecting upholstery textiles is that the texture or pattern should complement the frame and enhance the line of a piece rather than disguise it. Furniture manufacturers often have guidelines as to which fabrics are suitable for which frames. For example, a heavy, bulky fabric would not be appropriate for a finely detailed piece with welting. Upper-end residential manufacturers de-

Figure 8.6a The "Richmond" sofa is constructed with eight-way hand-tied springs. A nearly endless variety of upholstery fabric selections is available from Duralee® Fine Fabrics and Highland Court Fabrics. *Photo courtesy of Duralee® Fine Furniture, Inc.*

Figure 8.6b Washed Chenille collection upholstery fabrics for residential interiors. From left to right: a pocket taffeta ground weave; a small textured diamond pattern reminiscent of Moorish tiles; and a soft, lush stripe. *Photo courtesy of Highland Court, www.highlandcourtfabrics.com.*

sign their furniture to accept most fabrics. As long as it is strong enough to be applied to the frame without harm to the fabric, the customer's choice will be used.

Scale, the overall size of patterns or yarns, should be considered, as should the scale of the entire piece. The fabric scale must relate in a visually pleasing way to other decorative features and patterns. For instance, a large-scale pattern could overwhelm a small, delicate frame, just as, of course, a heavy weave would not be appropriate for a small frame.

Tautness, the degree of looseness or tension of the fabric application, should be considered when choosing upholstery fabric. The same fabric may appear very different when used in different ways. For instance, a stripe that appears crisp and straight when pulled tightly over the frame may seem much less defined in a loose, shabby chic application that imitates a slipcover. Also, tightly woven fabric, such as taffeta, may show the pulls at the seams if the fabric is pulled tightly. At the other end of the spectrum, if fabric is loosely applied, wrinkles can be produced. Any degree of sheen will accentuate the wrinkles. Some fabrics relax and wrinkle slightly after several months of use; this cannot be prevented or remedied without reupholstering.

Figure 8.7 The Donghia "Berlin Club Chair" features a combination of strong lines and distinctive proportions. This piece was designed to please the body and the eye. *Photo by Edward Addeo. Product by Donghia, Inc.*

Sofa and Chair Selection

Sofas, chairs, chaises longues (long chairs), and ottomans (footstools) are the largest and most visible seating pieces in a room and should be selected wisely, as the average life of a sofa is ten years. Well-built sofas may be reupholstered and used for many years more. The following considerations apply to the selection of sofas and chairs.

Function is judged by how much use an upholstered piece will receive as compared to other types of seating planned in the room. For example, a three-seat sofa usually holds two only people, as the middle seat is often considered undesirable. The sofa should be the correct scale and style for the room; it should look good to be appealing as seating. The cost of the sofa must be within the budget parameters set for the piece.

The adage "form follows function" applies to sofas. First determine function; then the form will follow. How will the sofa be used, and how much seating is needed? Will it be placed in a casual gathering place for family and friends or in a more formal setting? In a casual family room, comfort is paramount, whereas in a more formal room, comfort may be less important, so firmer and shallower seat dimensions may be selected.

Scale should be determined by the size of the room. A common mistake is selecting a sofa that is too large for the room and seems to dwarf other furnishings. This happens because sofas appear smaller in spacious furniture showrooms. One rule of thumb suggests that the sofa shouldn't take up more than 10 percent of the total floor space. The standard sofa is between 72 and 98 inches long. Know the dimensions of the room, draw it to scale, and place the sofa there, perhaps using a furniture-arranging website. Many furniture retailers' websites feature a furniture-arranging tool. Be sure to allow enough room for supporting furnishings such as floor lamps, end tables, a coffee table or sofa table (long and narrow taller table behind the sofa), or other artistic elements such as floor screens or trees. A rolled arm can add up to a foot to the length of the sofa; steer away from this style if the room is small. Another space-saving approach is to select a sofa with a tight back; sofas of this style are usually about 4 inches shallower than those with loose back cushions.

Figure 8.8 Upholstered furniture styles.

Figure 8.8a Lawson (dropped-arm) loveseat with square arms.

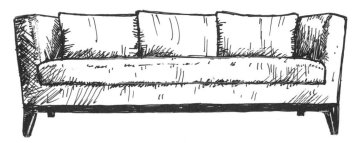

Figure 8.8b Tuxedo sofa (arms same height as back) with loose back cushions, single seat cushion, wood frame, and legs exposed.

Figure 8.8c Lawson sofa with rounded arms, tailored skirt box pleated at corners, single seat cushion, and tight back.

Figure 8.8d Flare-arm tuxedo sofa with sculpted tight back, loose pillows, and two long seat cushions.

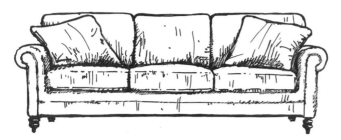

Figure 8.8e Traditional Lawson with rolled arms, exposed legs, three seat cushions, and attached back cushions.

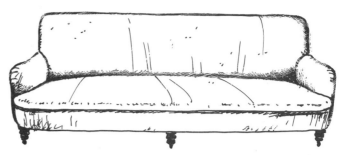

Figure 8.8f English arm sofa (arms roll outward vertically) with tight seat and back.

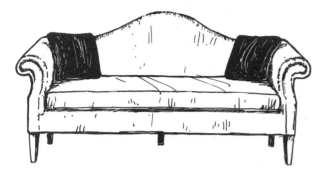

Figure 8.8g Camelback sofa with scroll roll-out arms, single seat cushion, tapered exposed legs.

Figure 8.8h Modified tuxedo with a high angled-arm loose-cushion seat, back, and pillows.

Figure 8.8i Sectional sofa with loose seat and attached back cushions.

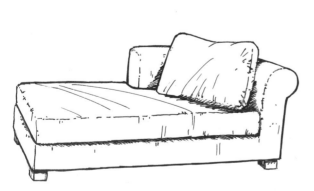

Figure 8.8j Contemporary chaise longue/lounge.

Figure 8.8k Traditional Lawson chair with tight back, roll-out arms, and tailored skirt.

Figure 8.8l Tufted back Victorian wing chair with exposed turned legs.

Residential and Contract Upholstered Furniture Construction **153**

Figure 8.8m Traditional overstuffed club chair.

Figure 8.8n Chair-and-a-half and ottoman, a wide overstuffed Lawson chair.

Figure 8.8o Contemporary tub chair with rounded back and tapered legs.

Figure 8.8p Wood-exposed contemporary neo-classical Bergère (closed arm chair).

Figure 8.8q Wood-exposed French Rococo Bergère wing chair.

Style in sofa design is affected by features that fit the sofa in a certain design category. Exposed legs tend to look sleek, metal legs give the sofa a European or midcentury Modern flavor, and skirted styles are softer and warmer. A curved back gives a more feminine or genteel appearance.

There are several options for back cushions, each adding definition to the style of the sofa. A traditional look is acquired by using three back cushions; two cushions suggest a more current feel. A contemporary look is achieved when the back cushions are squared at the corners. Loose pillows look the most inviting and casual. If the cushions are attached, they can still offer a great degree of comfort, but the sofa is a degree more formal. More formal still is the sofa with a tight back. Chair styling, likewise, is critical to the overall theme. Many handsome formal traditional chairs, such as those illustrated in chapter 15, are used extensively in contemporary interiors to add richness, whereas the sleek styles of the Modern era, as found in chapter 18 are suitable for high-tech interiors.

Figure 8.9 The "Main Street Club Sofa" from Donghia is an example of impeccable design and unsurpassed comfort. This design, inspired by the luxury and clean design of old-fashioned steamships, exudes both Old World elegance and contemporary appeal. *Photo by Edward Addeo. Product by Donghia, Inc.*

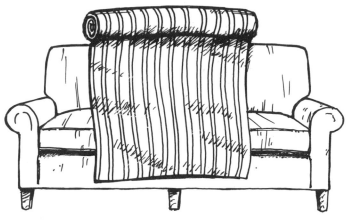

Figure 8.10a Vertical placement, the traditional way to upholster, necessarily creates seams.

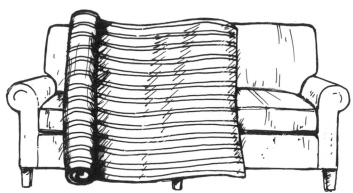

Figure 8.10b A horizontal or railroaded upholstery fabric application offers a different appearance for a patterned fabric and may eliminate seams.

Yardage

Upholstery fabric can be applied in either of two directions. Vertical placement is the more traditional method, as patterns generally seem right-side up when placed this way. Seams are inevitable. Horizontal or **railroaded** fabric application eliminates seams and gives a different appearance to patterned fabrics. It is often used for textured fabrics.

Approximate yardage requirements:

- Dining chair seats—½–1 yard each chair
- Small ottomans or footstools—3–5 yards
- Occasional, wing, club or tub, Lawson or Bergere chairs—5–10 yards
- Lounge/longue chairs—6–10 yards
- Loveseats—6–10 yards
- 6–7-foot sofas—10–14 yards
- 8-foot sofas—14–16 yards
- Sectional sofas—16–25 yards

Pleather is a fabric of polyester or vinyl that imitates natural leather—for example, Ultrasuede®. Many pile fabrics, such as velvet and chenille, can mimic the look of suede (see Figure 8.11). Leather, which is discussed below, is objectionable to clients who perceive its use as cruelty to animals. Many manufactured-fiber textiles appear as leather and may be termed **faux leather**.

Figure 8.11 The Donghia Hudson Collection, designed by Jennifer Hutton and the Donghia design team, reflects form and lines reminiscent of midcentury design philosophy. *Photo by Edward Addeo. Product by Donghia, Inc.*

SPECIFYING LEATHER UPHOLSTERY

Specifying from samples makes it difficult to judge the quality of leather. Cost is not the only indicator of quality —feel is also a good guide—but knowledge about and confidence in the supplier are the most important factors to guide the choice. Leather upholstery must measure 1.0 to 1.2 mm thick or weigh 2 to 2⅔ ounces per square foot. The butt or middling is considered the finest cut; the shoulder also of good quality, although it is uneven and subject to growth marks. Yardage is measured in the following ways:

Leather is purchased by the square foot.

12 square feet of leather = 1 yard of 36-inch fabric

15 square feet of leather = 1 yard of 54-inch fabric

A full-grown European steer averages 52 square feet. **Cattle hides** vary from 42 to 72 inches in width and are about 73 inches long.

Calfskins yield about 32 square feet, vary from 42 to 60 inches in width, and are 62 inches long.

A **bend** is a hide with the shoulder, belly, and butt cut off. Leather from a bend is about 20 square feet cut from the center of the hide; it is generally 46 inches wide and 57 inches long.

Figure 8.12 Jimmy Moore, co-owner of Hancock & Moore, demonstrates the steps in the creation of leather furniture. *Courtesy of Hancock & Moore, www.hancockandmoore.com.*

WORKING WITH MANUFACTURERS

Most manufacturers offer a range of standard fabrics appropriate for their furniture, grouped according to price range. They usually begin with A, the least expensive, and progress to EE, which is several price points higher than A. The manufacturer considers the actual cost of the fabric as well as the waste required for the pattern match to establish its cost. Most upper-end residential manufacturers are willing to accept almost any COM, although they may have restrictions about which types of fabrics will work on certain frames. In making the purchase, COM is specified on the order. Custom upholstery ordered through agent show-

Figure 8.12a Sanding the chair frame.

Figure 8.12b Tracing the pattern for upholstered pieces and seat cushions.

Figure 8.12c Cutting the leather to pattern size and shape.

Figure 8.12d Sewing leather pattern pieces together.

rooms is generally to-the-trade only at wholesale prices intended to be marked up from 20 to 300 percent for resale. Interior design professionals must have a retail certificate or a resale tax identification number for the state where the business is located. A **performa** account is often required; this is the payment of a deposit, generally 50 percent at the time the order is placed, with the balance due on completion. Some textile or custom upholstery sources do accept net 30 terms, which means they bill after the order is placed, or possibly after it is completed, with the balance due within 30 days.

Residential showrooms and upholstery companies with traveling sales representatives feature fabrics that are not rated for contract testing, as listed in chapter 7. Generally,

residential design professionals do not inquire about commercial standards for residential furnishings.

Upholstery companies specialize, some in antiques or customization of frames, in their furniture line. Other companies feature modern styling. Some pieces are on display in the showroom; some pieces are stored in the warehouse on completion before being shipped or before payment is received in full. Some frames of popular pieces are kept in stock in a warehouse.

The **showroom ordering process** begins with a design professional coming to a showroom to pre-shop for a client with whose taste and furnishing needs he is familiar. The designer selects a piece or a few pieces to show to the client. When the designer returns with the client, the designer does

Figure 8.12e Attaching the upholstery leather to the frame.

Figure 8.12f Applying welt trimming.

Figure 8.12g Examining the complete chair for quality and detail.

Figure 8.12h Fine furniture is shrink-wrapped, padded, and placed in a carton for shipping.

Figure 8.13 Showroom

showroom with a sample of the fabric so the staff can ensure the correct product is received from the textile company before it is installed in the furniture frame. Once all the textiles are received by the showroom, they verify that the accurate textiles were received, and in the right amounts. Work proceeds once the 50 percent deposit is received from the design professional. Next, an estimate of time of completion is given the designer and client. Usually the estimate is between 8 and 14 weeks; most showrooms estimate 10 to 12 weeks.

The piece itself is fabricated by local vendors specializing in various construction processes. Some showrooms are associated with over thirty vendors for this purpose. At this point in the custom process, as many as three different orders are placed by the showroom employee. He issues purchase orders for the appropriate vendors: a carver, an upholsterer, and a finisher for staining, painting, or gilding. The showroom associate follows the process closely with each individual vendor as the piece goes through the stages of manufacturing. If the piece is highly customized, very detailed follow-up during construction may be warranted.

When the piece or pieces are complete, the designer receives an invoice and the client must pay for the order. Once payment is arranged, a delivery method is selected. Any damage to the product during delivery is covered by the showroom; the only delay would be the time required to have the piece repaired or replaced. The showroom will not battle with the delivery company while a client is waiting for her goods. After delivery, the design professional places the furniture pieces in their intended locations.

If the piece is damaged by the client after completion, the showroom will arrange for it to be repaired at the client's expense. If the piece was made incorrectly, the showroom will replace or repair it. As this rarely happens, the matter is considered on a case-by-case basis.

To-the-trade showrooms, such as those described here, rarely do reupholster projects, as the cost to reupholster may outweigh the cost of purchasing a replacement item. Only in certain instances is the reupholstering of existing pieces considered: The piece is unique and cannot be rebuilt; the piece is a family heirloom with significant historical value; adjoining pieces make a composite so distinctive that it cannot be replaced. Some showrooms reupholster items that were originally commissioned through them and now need a more modern textile, or if the original textile is worn and needs replacement.

The custom design process varies from company to company. For example, some companies are a franchise and a public showroom not located in a design center. Such companies carry certain lines or styles of furniture and may feature thousands of pieces among all the galleries. Each franchise stocks its showroom floor with pieces selected for the specific region.

the selling of the specific piece and encourages the client to identify style preferences or changes to make to the display piece. Showroom associates answer questions and prepare to take an order once the client has made her final selections and specifications. The showroom representative then works closely with both the designer and the client to be sure the correct product is ordered. This process can take as little as fifteen minutes if the client knows what she wants, or it can take an entire day, or return trips to the showroom.

Some showrooms do not supply the fabric for upholstered pieces but accept COM only, purchased by the client or design professional from another source. The designer must contact the showroom after the order is placed to give specifications on the fabric selected and to determine how much is needed for the project. The showroom sends the designer selections of wood or painted finishes from which he and the client can choose for the finished product.

Once the fabric is selected and ordered by the design professional, he notifies the showroom where the fabric will be coming from. In many cases, the designer also supplies the

Some exclusive companies have furniture manufactured in Europe. In particular, France and Italy have high-quality manufacturing, sometimes called Old World craftsmanship. At the showroom, the client selects the textile to cover the piece from a set of samples distributed by a U.S. textile company. There are often about 400 fabrics to choose from in a showroom. Where furniture construction is in Europe, COM is not encouraged. Fabrics would have to be converted from the imperial system to metric; pattern matching is done slightly differently; the fabric would have to be shipped from the United States to Europe with a 20 percent surcharge to enter the country and taxed again on export, making the price outweigh practicality. Having a COM fabric backed would further increase the cost. This process is suitable for residential projects only. In the manufacturing process, commissioned pieces in a single order may be constructed at different factories, with one factory making a chair and another factory a sofa with the same fabric.

Manufacturing via sales reps is a method used by design professionals who are not near showrooms to obtain custom upholstery. Sales reps travel to cities away from showrooms where interior design professionals are located, bringing to them catalogs and fabric samples, usually twice a year as new furniture lines and fabrics are introduced and older ones are discontinued. For those design professionals who are interested in selling manufactured furniture, it is important to realize that some manufacturers require showrooms, and many require that their dealers invest substantially in these showrooms. Design professionals are hired by the retail store featuring a furniture showroom and paid a commission. Freelance designers may bring in clients and receive a prearranged commission.

Where showrooms are not required, allowing independent design professionals to sell upholstered furniture, it is common to select one or two good-quality manufacturers and use their books, charts, samples, and feature a select number of pieces in a studio or home office as the means of selling goods to clients. In the United States, the majority of furniture manufacturers are located in the East, particularly in North and South Carolina. Prepayment is customary, although net terms are enjoyed by design professionals who have done repeat and reputable business with the manufacturer. Furniture pieces are shipped from the factory **FOB,** or **free on board,** meaning the manufacturer is free of obligation once it has shipped the item. Damage is negotiated between the design professional and the shipping or trucking company. FOB may also mean **freight on board,** meaning the shipment has taken place and final billing is being processed as of that date. If the terms are 30 days net, the bill may arrive with 25 days left for the payment to reach the manufacturer and be posted to the firm's account.

Local manufacturing is yet another method of obtaining custom upholstery. The design professional contracts with a local, independent manufacturer to build the piece using COM. The upholsterer will specify correct yardage for each piece or portion of contrasting fabric. The responsibilities described above to ascertain accuracy fall on the shoulders of the design professional. The time frame is usually 2 to 6 weeks, and costs are generally lower.

REUPHOLSTERING AND RESTORATION

There are several factors to consider when deciding whether to reupholster existing furniture or to purchase a similar item new. These include the style of the piece, its construction and padding condition, financial considerations, sentimental value, and environmental impact.

Construction and padding condition—When a piece needs reupholstering due to long-term wear, the frame is often the only salvageable component. The quality of the frame is never evident until the old upholstery is stripped and the frame stands fully exposed. Depending on the age, type, and amount of use the furniture has received, it is possible that few elements can be reasonably reused for another several years. For example, springs may require repair or replacement. Cushions are rarely in reusable condition and thus require replacement. Even exposed wood may be badly worn and in need of refinishing. All this means that the cost of reupholstering may be substantially greater than the cost of labor per square yard, although minor improvements are usually included in that price. The strength of the frame is the key factor that dictates whether the piece is worth the price of reupholstering it.

Financial considerations—It is important to secure a bid on reupholstering and understand clearly what services or materials are included for the quoted price, including taxes where applicable, and then to compare the price to the cost of a similar new item. If the reupholstering process saves time and money, then, without question, reupholstering is a wise choice. If the cost of reupholstering is equal to or higher than the cost of purchasing a replacement item, then other factors must be considered.

Style—There are two categories of upholstered furniture style. The first includes authentic or adapted historic pieces that are handsome and valued for their excellent proportions. These pieces merit reupholstering, provided the style is an appealing addition to the

Figure 8.14 "Basic Tweed" is a tailored, classic slipcover that gives an existing sofa a new look without reupholstering it. *Photo courtesy of Sure Fit™ Furniture Covers.*

interior where it will be placed. Upgrading fabric and, possibly, upgrading padding or springs and refinishing exposed wood may be all that is required to bring the piece to a contemporary and acceptable appearance.

The second category of style includes pieces that must be remodeled to bring the size or shape up to date. In this case, two options are available: to remodel the piece to update it, or to reupholster it with acceptance of its original style as a unique or period piece. The condition of an existing upholstered piece must be examined to determine the worth of the following:

Sentimental value is relevant where a piece is priceless or irreplaceable. If the piece is an heirloom and highly esteemed by its owner, it is always worth the price and effort to reupholster. Sentimental value has nothing to do with good design.

Environmental impact is perhaps the most compelling reason to keep older upholstered pieces rather than to throw them away. Every piece reupholstered does not end up at the landfill.

SLIPCOVERS

A **slipcover** is a temporary or permanent fabric covering that fits over upholstered or nonupholstered furniture. Slipcovers are specified to enhance an interior design scheme, bring style and character to a room, protect and prolong the life of the upholstery they cover, and give tactile and visual softness to furniture that is not upholstered. It has been said that slipcovers are to furniture what clothing is to the body —coverings for protection and style.

Slipcovers Through History

Slipcovers have been used since the European medieval period and became more important during the formal traditional period (see chapter 15). They originally were very simple and often used as loosely fitted **dustcovers** for fine furniture in rooms that were little used. When a guest room, a spare room, or an entire estate wing of rooms was unoccupied for long periods (months or years), everything of value was covered in white muslin or lightweight canvas (duck, drill) dustcovers. These were plain lengths of fabric, similar to bedsheets, but they often were sewn to approximately fit each furniture piece. When the cotton muslin–type cover was removed, the wooden or fabric furniture piece showed little or no aging that would otherwise have been caused by UV light fading, humidity changes, dust, grime or soiling, insects, or vermin. Such dustcovers protected precious fabrics and thus extended their useful life.

By the eighteenth century, wealthy homeowners in England were using custom-tailored slipcovers fabricated as seasonal furnishing items. Lightweight plain or twill weaves in solid or printed designs, made of cotton, linen, or union cloth (about 50/50 linen/cotton) were preferred. These types of fabric absorbed moisture (sweat) and were breathable, so users felt cooler and comfortable during summer.

Slipcovers have long been used to protect formal dining room chair seats, which were upholstered in precious and costly fabrics. In the formal traditional period, slipcovers were used as decorative and practical elements in many kinds of rooms. They covered sofas and settees, wing chairs, and wood-exposed armchairs and benches, for example. Matching or coordinating fabric was used for window treatments, table covers, linens, and accessories. Attention to detail became a hallmark of English slipcovers during the formal traditional period, when accents were referred to as *dressmaker detailing.* Slipcovers were custom fabricated by tailors and seamstresses, like clothing. Details such as piping, welting, cording, ties and bows, covered and/or contrasting buttons, tiny French pleats, box pleats, banding, and ruffles were examples of artistic craftsmanship found in custom slipcovers.

In France, the châteaux likewise benefited from the fashion for slipcovers. For example, decorators often drenched boudoirs in the beloved monochromatic **toile de Jouy** fabrics by utilizing a single fabric for window, wall, and ceiling treatments, shirred closet or armoire door inserts, bed linens, upholstery, table covers, pillows—and, of course, slipcovers.

Toward the Victorian era, it became fashionably acceptable for slipcovers to be somewhat loosely fitted—what we call today *shabby chic*. This meant the fabric was slightly larger than the furniture and perhaps wrinkled and touching the floor. Slipcovers made of linen or union cloth tended to stretch with summer's heat and humidity and to shrink with the dry interior air of winter. This alternating stretch-and-shrink process resulted in slipcovers' becoming uneven and slightly out of shape. It was only practical that this problem should be solved by altering slipcover fashion from tight and perfect to loose and forgiving.

Immigrants brought the slipcover trade to the United States, and by the nineteenth century, tailors were making custom slipcovers for America's upper class. Much like today, their procedure was to go into fine homes, cut and fit the right amount of fabric, shape the cut pattern to match the furniture item, mark seams with chalk and pins, then take the cut fabric back to a shop to sew into the finished product. This tailoring process resulted in individual coverings known as **loose covers, case covers,** or **dustcovers.** In the nineteenth century, slipcovers were common in all households. In both the United States and Europe, slipcovers of floral printed cotton or linen were popular for use as decorative coverings and to protect upholstery from dirt and sunlight. It was common to use cool, comfortable slipcovers in the warm months, and then remove and store them during the cold months, when the heavier upholstery fabric was warmer and cozier than the slipcovers.

Today, as in eras past, slipcovers are used not only to change the fabric and color of furniture without the time and expense of reupholstering it but also, in many cases, to change the look of the interior design as well. Tailored, contemporary furniture can become ruffled and romantic. Furniture with traditional box-pleated skirts can become sleek and modern; furniture legs can be shown off or hidden. Custom-made slipcovers can be designed to fit any interior; they are designed to be removable and are often washable, except where dry-clean-only fabrics are selected because the right look is more important than ease of maintenance.

Slipcover Considerations

Slipcovers may be an appropriate choice for several reasons, including the following advantages.

Slipcovering is an effective way to create a new style without investing in new furniture. It is often more economical than reupholstering and allows flexibility and the opportunity to have something new seasonally, as well as the option to make variations on furniture through the combination of fabrics, even on a single slipcover. Today, interior design users often have comfort, style, and function as priorities. In addition, change is in the air. Creating new looks "instantly" is a trend made popular through home improvement and decorating television shows. Slipcovers allow designers to develop creative and unique fabric combinations not only through color, pattern, and texture but also through style, form, and shape. Slipcovers provide an affordable and quick way to change the look of nearly any room. Washable slipcovers are good choices for families with pets or small children, as they are removable and can be cleaned easily. Most slipcovers are machine washable and extremely functional. For budget-minded clients, slipcovers can cover secondhand furniture.

Although slipcovers have many advantages and provide numerous options for change in interiors, they have disadvantages that must be considered as well. Slipcovers may shift out of place, depending on the type of use they receive. Adjusting or retucking fabric that works loose can be a regular chore. Slipcovers obscure furniture details and give the piece a simpler appearance, perhaps losing detail and form.

Figure 8.15 "Asian Medallion" slipcovers feature large box pleats and Chinese frog clasp detailing. *Photo courtesy of Sure Fit™ Furniture Covers.*

When to Slipcover

The goals of an interior may fit with the concept of slipcovers. It is important to keep in mind the advantages and disadvantages of slipcovering when deciding whether it is best for an interior. Here are some considerations:

1. **Condition of the furniture** — If a furniture piece is structurally sound or holds sentimental value but the fabric is outdated, slipcovering is a practical consideration. However, if the entire frame and springs need replacement, repair and reupholstery are the better choice.
2. **Style of the furniture** — It is best to slipcover furniture with a separate cushion because less time will be spent pulling and tucking in the fabric after use. Nonetheless, furniture that does not have separate cushions can be made into pillow-back style so a solid streamline can be made.
3. **Details of the furniture** — Details on decorative or wood furniture are concealed by slipcovering. This may be acceptable if the details are outdated or the slipcover is a seasonal or temporary treatment.

What to Slipcover

Slipcovers often make a dramatic fashion statement. Numerous items can be slipcovered to fit any style and any décor, and the options for detailing or mixing fabrics are restricted only by fabric weight and usefulness. Here is a list of items that can be custom slipcovered: sofas, loveseats and overstuffed chairs with attached or loose back pillows, club chairs and ottomans, side chairs and armchairs, dining chairs, Parsons chairs, mismatched chairs, folding chairs, wicker furniture, leather furniture, rocking chairs and recliners, piano benches, backless seating pieces, ottomans, dog and cat beds, and tables.

Style — Custom slipcovers work well with many styles of furnishings. Preferred styles include upscale modern, clean contemporary, American and French country, Asian, retro-Modern bold and graphic, and Victorian romantic, to name a few. For example, slipcovers featuring floral tea-stained fabrics are romantic in Victorian-style homes; neutral, textured, or subtle designs of faded/washed colorations on pale backgrounds, with a gathered skirt, are appropriate for the shabby chic look.

Details — Traditional styles utilize straight skirts. Contemporary style varies from having no skirt to a streamlined skirt. Piping is used on many pieces. If the piping contrasts with the fabric, choose either a solid or a small gingham pinstripe, as large-scale patterns on piping tend to appear as ineffective splotches of color. Contrasting sashes, buttons, or a mix of fabrics can emphasize detailing; this is often a Victorian or country style choice. Solid colors that contrast within the piece are more in line with contemporary elements.

Tiny tucked pleats or French pleats add detail without drawing attention, so the piece becomes more sophisticated and tailored. Fringe and small tassels are also handsome points of detailing.

Fabric Selection

Slipcover fabric choice is as important as the style selection. Considerations include weight, texture, and color. For glossary definitions of fabrics listed below, www.wiley.com/go/interiortextiles.

Fabric Weight and Texture

Lightweight, malleable fabrics are the best choice for slipcovers. Flexibility is required in order for fabric to drape over the curves of the furniture properly, which means stiff fabric is unsatisfactory. Fabric should also be tightly woven, as loosely woven fabric may snag, tear, or stretch out of shape. Select fabrics that will not slip; slippery fabrics will repeatedly demand adjustment. The correct weight and hand in selected fabrics is a crucial element in achieving an appropriate and handsome slipcover. Good choices include lighter-weight fabrics that are lightly textured but not bulky, including cotton, linen, or manufactured fibers blended with natural fibers. Textured or printed polyester is excellent for slipcovers. Lightweight jacquard, printed warp sateen, and oxford cloth work well. These fabrics help the slipcover fall nicely over the furniture and allow a tightly fitted, upholstered look to be specified.

Medium to medium-heavyweight fabrics that fall softly and drape well include denim, drill, duck or sailcloth, and lighter-weight canvas. These are generally solids, though sometimes they are printed. Damask is a medium-heavyweight fabric that, although it is a bit stiff, yields a traditional tailored or perhaps shabby chic look.

Medium to heavyweight pile fabrics should provide a soft, comfortable appearance and feel. Examples of medium to heavyweight pile fabrics include corduroy, chenille, faux suede, and light velvet. Heavyweight fabrics that are possibilities for simple slipcover applications with less detailed tailoring include tweed, novelty or heavy twill, woven plaids, and tapestry. Keep in mind that most heavyweight fabrics are difficult to tailor; the better choice may be to reupholster.

It is wise to select a fabric that can be laundered, unless the client is accepting of a dry-clean-only fabric.

Color

Slipcovers are often preferred because color becomes an effective element that can be changed as desired. Slipcover colors might blend with existing furnishings, or they may establish a new color scheme.

It is important to understand the room the slipcover will be in. Is it an active room? Will children and pets often be in the room? Will the slipcovers need to be cleaned often? If the answer is yes to any of these questions, then durable fabrics that are inherently stain resistant, such as Crypton, or machine-washable fabrics should be specified. White and natural fabrics treated or laundered with detergent and bleach are often suitable for slipcovers. Solid-colored fabrics are not demanding and are often selected so other elements can become focal points. Patterns that are subtle in coloration are also relatively comfortable to the eye. Bold colors seen in stripes, high-contrast plaids, checks, and floral patterns give vibrancy and life to interiors. As slipcovers are viewed as temporary, color schemes can change with the slipcovers.

Custom-Made Slipcovers

A **custom-made slipcover**, otherwise known as a **fitted slipcover**, imitates upholstery; it is often specified to fit furniture contours perfectly. Custom-made back and seat cushion slipcovers are fabricated separately and have zippers for ease of installation and removal. Fitted slipcovers provide many options for decorative skirts and accents such as banding, tabs, buttons, bows, tucks or tiny pleats, skirt pleats or ruffles, or other details. These dressmaker details echo those of the formal traditional slipcovers, still much in demand today.

Fabric—Custom-made slipcovers are typically COM. The interior design professional as well as the client have many options for obtaining fabric—through trade sources as cut yardage, in retail stores with interiors textiles, and online fabric sources. Even high-count bedsheets can be used as slipcover material. Keep in mind that quality and correct fiber, yarn, and construction are critical, as the slipcover may receive much use and frequent laundering.

Yardage—Sofas (6 to 7 feet end to end) require 12 to 15 yards of fabric. If the sofa has loose back cushions, 18 to 20 yards are needed. Loveseats (4 to 5 feet long) require about 10 yards of fabric, or 12 to 14 yards for loose back cushions. Upholstered or wood-framed chairs require approximately 8 yards of fabric, or 9 yards for a pillow-back style. Ottomans usually require 2 to 3 yards, depending on size. These are general guidelines. Slipcover seamstresses or tailors who measure the item will give a firm yardage requirement. This can also be done by sending a photo with measurements to the workroom professional. Digital photographs or scanned photographs sent as e-mail attachments will increase the efficiency of this process.

Cost Factors—Cost depends on the size of the furniture and the fabric selected. Some slipcover professionals have standard prices, whereas others choose to go to the consumer's home and take measurements in order to calculate an estimate. There may be additional charges for estimates, on-site measuring, and pickup and delivery.

Finding the Right Workroom or Tailor

Slipcover workroom seamstresses or tailors are specialized fabricators. They may have a large clientele. They usually do not advertise—nor is it necessary, as word-of-mouth recommendations and repeat business keep them in high demand. Fabric stores and other design professionals may know of slipcover workrooms whose work is excellent. Some may be listed in a local phone book. When making initial phone inquiries, ask for references, contact those customers and inquire about the quality of the slipcover products, on-time delivery, and overall professionalism before committing a project to the workroom.

Slipcovers for Contract Settings

Slipcovers specified for contract or nonresidential installations must be fabricated from textiles that have been tested to meet the codes for the particular interior. These may include flammability standards, microbial specifications, fading, and durability standards. Proof of fabric treatment must be provided to the client by the design professional, who obtains it from the fabric finisher or fabric jobber/supplier. As contract settings often receive high use, slipcovers may be unsuitable, as they are considered less durable and require more hands-on maintenance.

Ready-Made Slipcovers

Ready-made slipcovers are available from mail order catalogs, online, or in department stores in many styles and quality levels. Budget slipcovers may be a disappointing purchase, whereas a high-quality ready-made slipcover may be quite suitable. The advantages are that they are readily obtainable and affordable. Ready-made disadvantages are that they may require a lot of adjusting and pulling in order for the fabric to lie properly. With repeated use, small children, or pets, keeping ready-made slipcovers in place is difficult.

Figure 8.16a This "Lexington" wing chair slipcover offers country or Victorian charm. *Photo courtesy of Sure Fit™ Furniture Covers.*

Figure 8.16b "Perfect Twill Maize Futon" is a clean, handsome futon slipcover. *Photo courtesy of Sure Fit™ Furniture Covers.*

Figure 8.16c "Seersucker Daybed" lends a crisp, fresh appearance to the sofa-cum-bed. *Photo courtesy of Sure Fit ™ Furniture Covers.*

Ready-Made Slipcover Categories

Slipcovers are available in the following product types: sofas, upholstered chairs and wing chairs, dining and folding chairs, oversized chairs, stretch slipcovers, futons, daybed slipcovers, and semicustom slipcovers.

Furniture Throws

Furniture throws are unfitted fabric covers that go on and off with little effort. They are easy to place and remove for instant décor change, are appropriate for shabby chic styling, cover unusually shaped furniture, and, like ready-made slipcovers, may be laundered and are thus suitable for furniture exposed to soiling, pet hair, or food spills.

Sizes

Ready-made slipcovers are available for chairs, oversized chairs, recliners, loveseats, sofas, sectionals, ottomans, futons, and daybeds. Some slipcovers are made as one piece, with elastics placed so they will fit several types and sizes of furniture. To determine which of these sizes is right for a seating piece, decide how many people can be comfortably seated on the furniture. A one-person piece is a chair size, two to three seats requires a loveseat size, and three or more, comfortably seated, is a sofa size. When measuring furniture, simply measure from arm to arm and choose the correct size from the manufacturer.

Furniture Types for Slipcovers

Ready-made slipcovers fit most upholstered furniture with arms. Furniture throws fit armless pieces. Some covers fit furniture with *T*-shaped seat cushions and square cushions, high arms and low arms, and overstuffed styles with loose pillows. Sofa slipcovers are generally not manufactured over 8 feet or 96 inches. One-piece slipcovers are usually about 114 inches from front hem to back hem (over the front and top and down the back side). Ottoman (footstool) slipcovers are also available from ready-made slipcover companies.

The standard measurements for dining chair covers are as follows: from the top of the chair to the bottom, 41½ inches; seat depth area, 17 inches; from seat to top, 22 inches; front seat width, 18 inches; skirt length, 17½ inches; ties on side, 3 by 33 inches, which tie together in the back. Furniture slipcovers generally do *not* cover loveseats and sofas with built-in recliners and chaises longues. Some recliner covers are available, although they do not fit every style. Other guidelines for ready-made slipcovers include the following:

- To fit a slipcover to a piece with wooden arms, wrap polyester batting over the arms for padding and secure it with string or Velcro. This will give softness and the fullness required to fit a slipcover. This also applies to slipcovering dining room chairs with a thin or wood back. Draped batting or a folded blanket, for example, over the back will give an upholstered appearance similar to a Parsons chair. Padding backs and seat cushions before slipcovering can also increase dining chair comfort.
- Dining room chair slipcovers fit most types of chairs, including Parsons, Chippendale, Queen Anne, Colonial, and ladder-back. Measure your chairs to ensure fit. Standard measurements are a maximum height of 41½ inches, seat width of 18 inches, and seat depth 17 inches. Dining room chair covers typically do not fit chairs with arms (host and hostess chairs).
- It is best to cover leather furniture with foam batting to prevent the cover from sliding on the smooth surface.
- Slipcovers can be fitted onto standard double or queen-sized sofa beds, keeping in mind that the slipcover must be removed before opening the bed, un-

less the slipcover has a straight skirt design, which will need only to be lifted in order to unfold the mattress.

- Two-piece sectional sofas with arms can be slipcovered by fitting each piece with an appropriate sized slipcover and then tucking excess arm material in the crack where the two pieces come together.
- Ready-made slipcovers can be used over furniture with loose back pillows. Adjustments to the pillows by overlapping them or removing a pillow or two will assist in achieving an acceptable appearance. Loose pillows can be covered individually by pillow covers made by a local fabricator from matching fabric purchased separately. Generally, fabric is available in 3-yard cuts and is not returnable.
- Slipcovers fit camelback furniture that falls within standard measurements. The measurement from the front of the sofa on the floor, over the seat, up and over the back, and down to the floor again should be 114 inches or less at the highest point.
- Chairs smaller than the standard measurement of 32 inches may still be able to utilize a ready-made slipcover if the cover is securely tucked. Again, foam batting to pad arms helps slipcovers fit better.
- For armless furniture, use throw covers, which are unfitted pieces of fabric without pre-sewn arms. Throws can be folded, tucked, and perhaps held with pins to fit armless pieces.
- Generally, the more a slipcover is tucked, the better it stays in place.

Skirt Design

Two kinds of skirt styles are typical for slipcovers: a straight skirt and an elastic or elasticized skirt. A **straight skirt** design is a more tailored style, appropriate for contemporary interiors. These are usually characterized by ties at each corner that assure a better fit and add detailing. The **elasticized skirt** is slightly gathered, giving a classic ruffled appearance that is appropriate for casual and formal prints and some solids.

Installation

Install ready-made slipcovers by laying the piece over the furniture and then tucking it in place as necessary. Using a wooden spatula or spoon to tuck in excess fabric will do a smooth job and save irritation or injury to fingers. Tuck the fabric deep into the crease where the arm meets the back of the furniture and down where the arm meets the seat cushion. If the piece is wrinkled from the package, fluff it in the clothes dryer. Ready-made slipcovers are machine-washable.

RESOURCES

American Home Furnishings Alliance (AHFA)

www.afma4u.org
317 W. High Avenue, 10th Floor
High Point, NC 27260
Tel 336-884-5000
Fax 336-884-5303

The AHFA website serves the home furnishings industry as a source of information for manufacturers and importers of home furnishings products and their suppliers. AHFA also features a consumer website that serves as a resource on finding furniture for the home by product, style, or room. The site contains review care and safety tips and the latest trends. AHFA also hosts an exclusive website for the media featuring the International Home Furnishings Market in High Point, NC.

Business and Institutional Furniture Manufacturer's Association (BIFMA International)

www.bifma.org
2680 Horizon Drive SE, Suite A-1
Grand Rapids, MI 49546
Tel 616-285-3963
Fax 616-285-3765

BIFMA International is a trade association of over 260 furniture manufacturers and suppliers representing over 80 percent of the value of North American shipments of office furniture. It serves as an information resource and industry advocate and by offering professional and industrywide trade development opportunities.

Upholstered Furniture Action Council (UFAC)

www.ufac.org
PO Box 2436
High Point, NC 27261
Tel 336-885-5065
Fax 336-884-5072

UPAC was founded in 1978 to make upholstered furniture more resistant to ignition from smoldering cigarettes.

Textile Wallcoverings

Figure 9.1a Resolve systems furniture, designed by Ayse Birsel, features textile Multiscrim™ boundary screens and nesting rolling screens. The Reflection Series may utilize digital imaging on textiles. *Photo courtesy of Herman Miller, Inc., www.hermanmiller.com.*

Fig 9.1b Textile wallcoverings upholster these office partitions in this Herman Miller systems furniture. *Photo courtesy of Herman Miller, Inc., www.hermanmiller.com.*

WALLS ARE INCREASINGLY being given textile applications in both contract and residential settings. Although the dictionary spelling of *wallcovering* specifies two words, national associations spell it as one. In this book, therefore, *wallcovering* is used as a single word.

Wallcoverings enrich interiors through color, pattern, texture, and enhanced durability. Wallcoverings may be ad-

hered and left in place for many years, or they may be installed as a changeable application. Textile wallcoverings are applied in several ways. Manufactured wallcoverings include wallpaper and various textiles, predominantly vinyl and natural fibers, such as grass. Fabrics may be applied as a direct paste-up or in a number of suitable ways (see Table 9.1). Wall tapestries are both a historic and contemporary use of fabric on walls. Textile fiber and construction research and development has yielded incredibly strong yet lightweight textile structures where walls and ceilings are made solely of fabric.

Wallcovering applications are used in both contract and residential settings to meet criteria of cost-effectiveness, function, durability, and aesthetics.

SYSTEMS FURNITURE

Systems furniture are contract installations that consist of sometimes movable freestanding walls integrated with other office furniture. Panel systems were first created for use as cubicles and are usually about 5 feet tall. However, they can be customized to any size. Each panel system manufacturer offers standard fabric options. Manufacturers offer tested contract fabrics and are continuously evaluating different fabrics for their panel systems with innovations such as digital images. Lighter-weight fabrics work well on panel systems, while more durable fabrics work well on seating products.

The systems manufacturer forms an alliance with a textile manufacturer; for instance, Herman Miller works with Maharam as a supplier of panel wall textiles. The design professional can select from a specific group of Maharam fabrics that have passed contract testing. A fabric that has not undergone testing may be selected and then tested. This process typically takes a few weeks.

FABRIC WALLCOVERING TREATMENTS

Fabric as a wallcovering treatment offers variety, flexibility, visual comfort, and physical softness to an interior. Fabric-covered walls absorb sound better than nontreated walls. Fabrics may be treated for flammability requirements and coated with vinyl for high-traffic areas. Fabric installations can be temporary, permanent, or semipermanent (see Table 9.1).

As flame resistance is mandatory in commercial codes and sometimes desired in housing interiors, design profes-

---

TABLE 9.1 FABRIC INSTALLATION METHODS

Covered frame method—Fabric is wrapped around a simple lath frame, stapled at the center of each side, and then stapled alternately at each side, working outward. The covered frame can be filled with fiberfill for added temperature or sound insulation. It may be mounted or hung on nails, or the lath may be screwed into the wall and covered with trim.

Direct paste-up—Fabrics are generally finished with a coating or laminated paper in preparation for direct paste-up. The application is similar to that of other wallcoverings but requires more careful handling. A qualified and experienced professional must be selected for excellent results. This method is most frequently used.

Draped wallcoverings—These may be attached at the top and/or bottom in several ways: flat, loose-hung, scallop topped, or pleated in any number of styles. Walls may be treated as windows to soften acoustics and add richness or formality to an interior. Draped installations may be affixed to attached boards or rods, or directly to the walls. Valances, swags, or cornices may be installed over draped walls to enhance the impression of a window treatment.

Hook-and-loop fasteners (Velcro)—Velcro tape is made in two parts. One is sewed or glued to the fabric (usually hemmed), the other part is attached to the wall, and the two are pressed together to mount the wallcovering. An advantage of this method is the ability to remove the fabric for cleaning or replacement.

Lath method—This method involves the attachment of narrow wood lath strips to the wall perimeter. The fabric is then glued, stapled, tacked, or attached with hook-and-loop fasteners to the strips. The wall may be filled with fiberfill. This method eliminates the need to repair damaged walls.

Track/panel method—This method utilizes window covering sliding panel tracks. These may be installed to slide or to be placed side by side.

Shirred application—Shirring is prepared by seaming together the widths for each wall. Next, a rod pocket is sewed top and bottom to form a sleeve or casing, usually ½ inch wider than the rod diameter for small rods. Flat cut-to-measure curtain rods are attached with brackets next to the ceiling and floor. The rod is inserted into the casing and shirred (gathered) to fit, and then affixed to the brackets. Support brackets may be needed every 20 inches or so to hold the weight of the textile. Lighter fabrics are recommended.

Upholstered walls, unpadded method—Textile fabrics can be directly stapled or tacked to the wall surface. Seams can be covered with a variety of decorative methods, such as molding or decorative passementerie.

Upholstered walls, padded method—Fiber batting is stapled to the wall and then covered with fabric, which is also stapled or tacked and finished with trim. See "Upholstered Wall Systems," below.

---

sionals may specify application of flame-retardant compounds or finishes to fabrics composed of cotton, linen, or rayon, or they may select polyester, wool, or vinyl, which generally meets flammability codes. A sample should always be treated first and examined for color and texture change and weakening of fiber.

Upholstered Wall Systems

Upholstered wall systems are constructed on site and can be used for wall or ceiling installations. Framing materials are usually made of wood or plastic. The fabric is held in place by either an extrusion system or concealed fasteners. There are several options for the infill material. Polyester or fiberglass is used for a soft appearance or for acoustic insulation. Plywood is also used for acoustic purposes and tackable areas. Mineral fiberboard is also used for acoustic control. Stable fabrics or upholstery-weight fabrics are required for upholstered wall systems. The selected fabric should not absorb moisture, because changes in humidity can cause rippling and sagging. The fabric should also be snag resistant and self-healing. For areas where tacks or nails may be used, heavier yarn weaves are best. Avoid sateen and satin for these types of projects. To avoid having seams, fabrics up to 120 inches wide can be installed horizontally, or **railroaded.** For light-colored fabrics, a lining may be needed so construction materials behind the fabric are not visible.

CONTRACT WALLCOVERINGS

Contract or commercial wallcoverings differ from residential installations in that they are more durable, more textured, and less patterned, and they must meet testing criteria (see chapter 6): flammability, crocking, colorfastness, physical properties, and abrasion. Notable wallcoverings tests include ASTM E 84-03 Tunnel Test (pass as Class A with flame spread index of 25 or less and smoke developed value of 450 or less); AATCC 8-2001 for wet and dry crocking (grade 3 or lower on a scale of 1 to 5); AATCC 19 Option 1 or 3-2003 Fadometer Test (minimum of grade 4 for 40 hours; a 5 is no fading and 1 is a high degree of fading); ASTM D5034-95 (2001) Grab Test (a 35-pound minimum breaking strength for a pass); and ASTM D3597-02-D434-95 seam slippage (a minimum of 25 pounds is a pass). *Note:* For wrapped panels and upholstered walls, only the breaking strength and seam slippage are tested.

TABLE 9.2 CONTRACT CLASSIFICATIONS

Contract wallcoverings are generally rated in the following manner:

Category I—Decorative wallcoverings

Category II—Decorative and serviceable wallcoverings (washability and some colorfastness)

Category III—Decorative wallcoverings with good serviceability (low to moderate colorfastness, washable, scrubbable, resistant to abrasion, breaking, crocking, staining)

Category IV—Decorative wallcoverings with full serviceability (moderate colorfastness, washable, scrubbable, resistant to abrasion, breaking, crocking, staining, tearing)

Category V—Medium commercial serviceability wallcoverings (very good colorfastness, washable, scrubbable, resistant to abrasion, breaking, crocking, staining, tearing, heat aging, cracking, shrinking)

Category VI—Full commercial serviceability wallcoverings (same as category V with greater resistance to tearing)

TABLE 9.3 VINYL WALLCOVERING FABRIC BACKING MATERIALS

Type	Backing Material	Typical Backing Weight oz/sq yd (g/sq m)	Fiber Content	Wear Resistance
Type I	Scrim backing	1.0/1.5 (33.9/50.9)	Polycotton blend	Light
Type I	Nonwoven	1.0/2.5 (33.97/76.3)	Polyester/cellulose	Light
Type II	Osnaburg	2.0/3.0 (67.9/101.7)	Polycotton blend	Medium
Type II	Nonwoven	2.0/3.5 (67.0/118.6)	Polyester/cellulose	Medium
Type III	Drill	2.5/3.0 (84.7/101.7)	Polycotton blend	Heavy

Note: Contract wallcoverings are wider than residential—generally 52 to 54 inches with about 30 square yards in a roll—and thus more economical and convenient for large installations. Check width and square yards on each product, as these numbers can vary.

Functional Features

For both contract and residential settings, wallcoverings provide functional values such as acoustical control, increased temperature insulation, durability, and longevity.

Acoustic Control

Hard-surface walls often echo and amplify sound. Even in theaters, acoustics must be carefully planned. A space that is **acoustically lively** will enhance and augment noise. In many contract and residential spaces, lively acoustics are undesirable, not only for those who hear well but for those who are hearing impaired. For those who struggle to hear conversation, background noise can make the task nearly impossible. Noise becomes a screen impairment, jumbling words.

The intensity of a sound is expressed as a ratio comparing the sound to the least audible sound. Sound intensity level is measured in **decibels (dB),** named in recognition of Alexander Graham Bell.

Loud sounds can result in hearing loss. The louder the noise, the less time required before hearing loss occurs. According to the National Institute for Occupational Safety and Health (1998; see Resources), normal hearing is affected at 85 dB in 8 hours, and at 110 dB, damage can occur in 1 minute and 29 seconds. A rating of 85 dB is loud, and continued exposure to this or higher levels over time causes hearing loss.

> **Decibel (dB) levels**—Normal conversation, 50–65 dB; laughter, 60–75 dB; shouting in ear, 110 dB.
>
> **At home**—sewing machine, 60 dB; vacuum cleaner, 60–85 dB; hair dryer, 60–95 dB; alarm clock, 65–80 dB; TV audio, 70 dB; blender, 80–90 dB. Prolonged exposure to any noise above 90 dB can cause gradual hear-

ing loss. Examples include garbage disposal, 80–95 dB; noisy squeeze toys, 135 dB; recreational vehicle, 70–90 dB; motorcycle, 88 dB; lawn mower, 85–90 dB; and train or garbage truck, 100 dB. Regular exposure of more than 1 minute at over 100 dB risks permanent hearing loss. Examples are a jet flyover at 100 feet, 103dB; jackhammer, power saw, 100 dB; boom box, 120 dB; loud stereo, 110–125 dB.

Contract—quiet office or library, 40 dB; large office, 50 dB; diesel truck 84 dB; noisy restaurant, 85 dB; shouted conversation, 90 dB; school dance, 100 dB; discotheque or symphony concert, 100 dB (percussion section, 130 dB); rock concert, 110–140 dB; ambulance siren, 120 dB. Some listed above under residential are also experienced in contract settings.

Textile wallcoverings, carefully selected, are effective in sound control and direction. Three-dimensional wall textiles disrupt horizontal sound wave travel, making it easier to contain and limit sound from reflecting into a room (echo) or transmitting into adjacent rooms. Many concert halls and auditoriums have fabric-paneled walls for this purpose. The amount of acoustical control depends on the textural relief and porous qualities of the surface. **Relief** is the difference between the high and low levels of a surface. Textiles, therefore, absorb sound while flat surfaces reflect it. The type and installation also affect sound absorption. Heavily draped rooms, for example, can give significant quietude to interiors.

Acoustic wallcoverings are engineered specifically to absorb sound energy and are intended for contract applications. These specialized coverings are also finding their way into home theaters to balance and enrich sound systems. Cork wallcovering has natural sound-absorbing qualities.

Figure 9.2 Fibrous wallcovering enhances sound control. "Mulberry," from the Innvironments collection of eco-friendly wallcovering, is made from the natural fibers of mulberry bark laminated to metal leaf to create an organic look with unusual luster. *Photo by Fumiaki Odaka; courtesy of Innovations in Wallcoverings, Inc.*

Increased Temperature Insulation

Textile structures are also used for managing room temperature. Adhering textiles to walls helps control heat transfer and minimizes air infiltration. Installing padding behind a fabric increases insulative value. Leather wallcovering provides particularly effective insulation, as it does not allow airflow. Conserving natural resources is a side benefit.

Textile wallcoverings impact temperature in two visual ways as well—through texture and color. Textures can be regarded as warm or friendly. Wallcoverings occupy so large a space that the dominant color has a strong psychological impact on the room's occupant. Colors are generally experienced as warm or cool. **Warm colors** are yellow-green, yellow, yellow-orange, orange, red-orange, red, and red-violet. **Cool colors** are violet or purple, blue-violet, blue, blue-green, and green. Be aware that colors are often mixed, so warm colors may have cool undertones (influences) and cool colors may have warm undertones. Wallcovering aesthetics also discussed later in this chapter.

Functional Finishes

To increase the serviceability of textile wallcoverings and the likelihood the product will meet fire codes, finishes may be added to textiles. These are discussed in chapter 4. Sometimes fabric finishing treatments alter colorfastness, strength, dimensional stability, and hand. However, they can also increase durability, flame resistance, soil resistance, and washability.

Indoor Air Quality and Environmental Concerns

Wallcoverings and floor coverings cover the two largest areas in an interior. As many textile products have finishes that emit fumes suspected of having a negative health impact, they come under particular scrutiny. The Wallcoverings Association has teamed with the Chemical Fabrics and Film Association and the Vinyl Institute (see Resources) to produce a brochure entitled "Vinyl Performance Everyday: Environmental Profile: Vinyl Wallcoverings" to address these concerns.

For example, vinyl wallcovering VOC (volatile organic compounds) emissions are a focus of controversy concerning indoor air quality (IAQ). Many manufacturers now offer low-emissions products, and many of these are Greenguard Indoor Air Quality Certified™ (see Resources) or approved through other certifying programs.

Ventilation following installation to allow time for off-gassing enhances IAQ. Immediately following installation, airing out through ventilation (preferably up to 100 percent natural ventilation—fresh, clean air from outside that moves through the space toward other outside openings such as doors or windows. This may be augmented with fans.) Airing out through interior HVAC (heating, ventilation, and air-conditioning) systems tends to keep the emissions indoors longer. This is generally true of all new textile products. The new smell of vinyl, although strong, does not indicate the presence of VOCs. Vinyl wallcoverings do not impact IAQ adversely when installed according to the manufacturers' recommended procedures.

The growth of mold between vinyl and wall is another health concern, as some molds emit dangerous toxins. Research indicates that although mold growth may be present in wallcoverings in homes and other buildings, the wallcoverings themselves do not cause mold to grow. Strategies for minimizing or eliminating mold growth include abolishing the moisture source, taking into account the climate and design features of the building, and using permeable wallcoverings.

Other environmental concerns have been expressed concerning vinyl, including chlorine (no chlorine is emitted from vinyl wallcoverings), dioxin (less than 3 percent dioxin is emitted during all vinyl manufacturing), flammability behavior (vinyl wallcoverings often contain flame retardants and are rated Class A with excellent fire ratings; see individual product specifications), and combustion toxicity (similar to materials such as wood). Hydrogen chloride gas (HCl) emits odors long before burning and can act as an early warning of fire. As the U.S. death rate has dropped dramatically in recent years, health concerns about vinyl wallcoverings have also decreased. It is interesting to note that vinyl wallcovering installation has increased dramatically, possibly due to this decrease in vinyl wallcovering health concerns. Further, phthalates and other plasticizers have not been found a significant health concern. In vinyl, phthalates are tightly bound and have a low volatility (do not evaporate) and so do not contribute to sick building syndrome.

Regardless of accusations, vinyl use has risen dramatically in both the contract and residential marketplace due to its durability, longevity, and aesthetics.

Vinyl is easy to clean; its durable surface can be scrubbed (with detergent and sponge) to eliminate allergens, including dust and pet dander, which in turn improves IAQ. In healthcare, vinyl wallcoverings are compatible with antimicrobial and disinfectant cleaning agents to eliminate bacteria and disease-causing microorganisms.

Figure 9.3 "Mosaic" is a 54-inch type II viny with an Osnaburg backing that meets or exceeds industry standards. It also meets or exceeds the ASTM E-84 Tunnel Test with a Class A fire rating. *Photo by Fumiaki Odaka, courtesy of Innovations in Wallcoverings, Inc.*

Wallcovering Economy

Installed textile wallcoverings can be somewhat costly as an initial investment, yet they play a role in energy conservation through temperature control. This translates to financial savings in the long run. Where a textile wallcovering is in place for several years, it can potentially pay for itself in lowered utility bills. Durable wallcoverings such as vinyl are often a wise economic choice. Improved and durable vinyl wallcoverings may last up to five times longer than paint under normal conditions. Many vinyl wallcoverings maintain aesthetic appeal and functional durability for up to fifteen years, compared to painted surfaces, which are often repainted about every three years. Over the life of a high-quality vinyl wallcovering, a 30 percent savings over paint is possible in contract design, and in home furnishings the savings may be even greater.

Longevity also depends on wise aesthetic choices. Pattern and dramatically in-fashion colors generally lose their appeal after two to five years. If wallcoverings are selected and then removed in a short time frame, they do become the more costly treatment.

Function can also be preparatory. Wallpaper liner and other special blank wallpaper are used to cover a textured or damaged surface. Wallcoverings can then be installed over the blank paper.

TEXTILE WALLCOVERINGS AESTHETICS

Textile wallcoverings are a source of unlimited aesthetic possibilities. The aesthetic appeal of modern wallcoverings is unmatched by that of painted surfaces. Wallcoverings are available in a single color, as textures from subtle to dramatic. **Faux wallcoverings** are made to imitate nearly every surface material, including wood paneling and all paint faux-finish techniques. Some wallcovering textures are authentic, such as cork or metallic flecks. Wallcoverings are available as murals, photography, digitally generated designs, authentic historic patterns including anaglypta, a pressed, three-dimensional paper that can be painted to give the effect of embossed tin or other metal or to economically replicate intricate molding.

Textile wallcoverings vary in weight, color, styling, tactile characteristics, construction, and textural features. These are useful tools in creating an ambience or thematically designed interior. Wall textiles may coordinate with or match textiles used elsewhere in the room, such as upholstered furniture, accessory items, or bedspreads. As it is may be difficult to obtain exact color matches between paper and fabric because the different dyestuffs applied show different color characteristics, it may be necessary to use fabric instead of wallpaper as a direct paste-up wallcovering.

Some guidelines for choosing textile wallcoverings that add to the aesthetics of an interior are also found at www.wiley.com/go/interiortextiles.

TYPES OF WALLCOVERINGS

The types or categories of wallcoverings are as follows:

Wallpaper—A paper substrate printed with a decorative pattern. True wallpaper is not coated, although some have a fine coating seal in the dye or pigment. As wallpaper qualities vary, check the label for specific attributes and placement guidelines.

Coated fabric—A fabric substrate covered with acrylic or liquid vinyl coating on which is printed the design. This is considered more volatile (breathable) than vinyl-coated wallcovering and so is recommended for low-moisture interiors. Washable.

Vinyl-coated wallpaper—A decorative wallpaper sprayed or coated with an acrylic vinyl or polyvinyl chloride (PVC) to resist moisture and grease better than plain wallpaper. This is appropriate for kitchens and bathrooms because it is scrubbable and strippable.

Paper-backed or solid-sheet vinyl—A decorative solid-sheet vinyl surface laminated to a paper substrate backing. It is scrubbable and peelable. Solid-sheet vinyl resists moisture, grease, and stains, so it may be used in kitchens, baths, and other areas of the home.

Solid vinyl—Wallcovering made of two layers: a heavy-gauge poured (hence, solid) vinyl film laminated to a fabric or paper substrate. Solid vinyl is scrubbable, which is important for areas of high traffic or offices and high-traffic areas within the home. More durable than paper-backed vinyl.

Expanded vinyl—Wallcovering with a raised effect. It is especially useful for covering damaged walls.

Vinyl—Wallcoverings categorized as Types I, II and III (see Table 9.2).

WALLCOVERING TERMS

Appliqué—Cut-out designs applied to plain, textured, or figured backgrounds.

Grass cloth—Wallcovering made of dried grasses or plant materials, either left their natural color or dyed, that are woven into a textile. When woven with fine cotton threads, the product looks very refined, and when woven with other grasses, the product has a more coarse look.

Jute—Wallcovering made of yarn or string, slack twisted and in neutral or natural colors.

Bamboo—Wallcovering of cotton warp with wefts of split bamboo adhered to a paper.

Cork—Wallcovering made of natural flexible bark that is cut into thin layers and adhered to a paper backing. Without the paper backing, it is called *corkboard* and used as bulletin board.

Fiberglass—Wallcovering made of woven glass strands applied to a backing, originally meant for fragile or deteriorating wall surfaces. Fiberglass can be directly applied over cracks and small holes. Fiberglass is flame resistant. It is also permeable and thereby intrinsically mold and mildew resistant, so it is appropriate for use in humid and hot climates or in any location where moisture control and mold are a concern. Fiberglass is not colorful; it provides texture only and requires painting

Figure 9.4 "Grasscloth," woven from the honeysuckle vine, is a popular part of the Innovironments collection. It is made from renewable or recyclable materials using water-based ink and is free of heavy metals and harmful solvents. *Photo by Fumiaki Odaka, courtesy of Innovations in Wallcoverings, Inc.*

after installation. Generally, latex paint is used to ensure breathability. Fiberglass is a durable material.

Linen, wool, and **polyester**—Wallcoverings made of these standard natural materials meet most flammability requirements for installed wallcoverings. Linen has high stiffness and low elasticity, which, while limiting its use for furnishings, creates a highly dimensionally stable wallcovering that resists sagging.

Flocked—Wallpaper created by gluing tiny fibers of pattern to the surface of a paper. Flocking can be highly decorative and made to imitate a cut velvet look.

Foil or Mylar™—These wallcoverings have a reflective quality because of their shiny surface and can enhance any décor. They can come brushed or polished.

Anaglypta—These wallcoverings are paper compounds embossed to produce a raised pattern resembling sculptured plaster, tooled tin, hand-tooled leather, or hammered copper. All of these can be painted.

Leather and **suede**—Wallcoverings made of these natural materials are luxurious textiles that can quiet an interior. Leather can be embossed with special tools to create a pattern, while suede can be printed to resemble animal skins like snake, ostrich, and crocodile.

Natural fiber wallcoverings—include bamboo, rice paper, and raffia, and are installed much like traditional vinyl papers using an adhesive backing.

Customized—Such wallcoverings are available as machine-printed papers or hand-printed papers (also known as silk screen art). Hand-printed papers are expensive but provide a unique and rich appearance. Machine-printed wallcoverings are customizable if the run is sufficiently large—for example, a hotel where wallcoverings are used in guest rooms. Reproductions are also customized.

See www.wiley.com/go/interiortextiles for a glossary of wallcovering terms used throughout the manufactured wallcovering industry. These terms apply to prepackaged bolts of wallcoverings in paper, vinyl, and natural materials.

WALLCOVERING PACKAGING

Wallpaper is manufactured in long production lengths and then cut into shorter lengths for packaging. This package is a **roll** or **bolt** and is produced in varying widths and lengths by each manufacturer. There are two systems on the market, the American and the European (Euro or metric). American bolts or rolls contain about 25 percent more wallpaper than Euro bolts. The trend, however, is toward Euro rolls.

Wallcovering is packaged in single, double, and triple bolts. An **American Single Roll (S/R)** is 18 to 36 inches wide and 4 to 8 yards (12 to 24 feet) long, and it contains 34 to 36 square feet of wallcovering. **Double rolls (D/R)** contain 68 to 72 square feet, and **triple rolls (T/R)** contain 102 to 108 square feet. Double bolts are twice the length and triple bolts three times the length of the single. This assures less waste where larger quantities are required.

Metric, Euro, or **European** single rolls contain 27.5 to 29 square feet. Double rolls are 56 to 58 square feet.

A **pattern number** and **dye lot** or **run number** are included in the packaging of each roll. This number identifies a particular group of rolls that were printed on the same print run. Different dye lot numbers could signal variables such as a possible tonal change of color, a change in the vinyl coating, or a change in the embossing process. It is therefore important to check each individual roll in the job to ensure uniformity in color and pattern and to record pattern numbers and dye lot or run numbers in case additional rolls are needed to complete the project. Once the dye lot run is sold, it may be difficult or impossible to get an exact match for additional needs. It is best to buy a little more than the amount required, even with careful calculations.

UNDERSTANDING PATTERN REPEATS

Patterns on wallcoverings are motifs repeated in sequence. Murals may be an exception. A pattern repeat is measured from the center point (or top or bottom) to the same point in the next pattern. Vertical pattern repeats range from less than 1 inch to about 23 inches. Horizontally, the pattern may be less than 1 inch to the width of the wallpaper or more, as in scenic wallcoverings. The three pattern match types listed below are random, straight or straight-across, and drop match (half-drop and multiple-drop).

Random match is a pattern, such as a stripe, that matches no matter how adjoining strips are positioned, generating less waste. When every other strip is reversed, shading or variations in color are minimized. Note that any random match produces less waste than other match types because there is no repeat distance to take into account.

Straight or **straight-across match** has motifs that match on adjoining strips. Each strip begins the same at the top.

Drop match is where the patterns vary. A **half-drop** match takes three cuts or strips to repeat the pattern; every other cut begins at the ceiling. Odd-numbered strips are identical, and even-numbered strips are identical. A **multiple-drop match** requires four or more strips before the vertical design is matched.

CALCULATING WALLCOVERINGS

Taking accurate measurements is the first priority in wallcovering calculations. A steel tape measure is recommended for best accuracy. Write the measurements on a sketched diagram that includes windows, doors, fireplace, and built-in bookcases. Write each measurement as it is taken. Be sure to read the measurement rather than have it read to you; fewer mistakes are made this way. Rounding up to the nearest half-foot or foot is customary.

Packaged Bolt/Roll Wallcoverings

1. Measure the height from the top of the ceiling to the bottom of the floor, not including baseboards.
2. Measure the width of each wall.
3. Multiply the height by the width to calculate the square footage for each wall.
4. Add the square footage for each wall. If two or four walls are the same size, the first wall may be multiplied by the number of same-size walls.
5. Subtract areas such as windows and doorways that will not be covered by the wallcovering. For example, a 3- × 7-foot door is 21 square feet, and a 3- × 4-foot window is 12 square feet. Generally, small openings are not deducted, although larger doors and windows or closet openings are. Find the square footage of the larger deductible areas and subtract it from the total square footage.
6. Divide the total square footage by the square footage in the single roll of the selected wallcovering. Round up to the next roll.

    Example: Walls are 8 feet high and 12 feet wide. Multiply 8 × 12 = 96 square feet per wall, and then 96 × 4 walls = 384 square feet.

    Subtract the square footage of the door and two windows (assuming they are standard size): 384 − 21 − 12 − 12 = 339 square feet.

7. Check the pattern repeat size and type of match. Keep in mind that pattern matching, odd shapes, or altered strips for beginning or ending a job will increase the waste and therefore the square footage.
8. If the usable yield for this area is 30 square feet (American roll, 7- to 10-inch pattern repeat), divide the total or room square footage by 30. Next, divide 339 by 30 = 11.3; round up to 12 single rolls or 6 double or 4 triple rolls (less waste).
9. Obtaining help for calculations is convenient. Many wallcovering stores and manufacturers are more than willing to go over the figures to ascertain the estimate for the project. Qualified installers also assist and, for a fee, will do the measuring and calculating. Website resources assist in calculating rooms with special considerations (such as a hallway with stairs). Several websites include calculators to assist in roll/bolt calculations. The user enters the measurements, and the website program computes the square footage and amount of material needed. The Paint and Decorating Retailers Association's website (see Resources) also offers instructional books and videos.

TABLE 9.4 APPROXIMATE SQUARE FOOTAGE FOR PATTERNED WALLCOVERINGS

AMERICAN ROLLS

Pattern Repeat	Usable Yield
0–6 inches	32 square feet
7–12 inches	30 square feet
13–18 inches	27 square feet
19–23 inches	25 square feet

EUROPEAN (EURO OR METRIC) ROLLS

Pattern Repeat	Usable Yield
0–6 inches	25 square feet
7–12 inches	22 square feet
13–18 inches	20 square feet
19–23 inches	18 square feet

Note: European rolls are packaged in metric; this chart converts to square feet.

Fabric Yardage Calculations

When calculating fabric yardage for direct paste-up, the procedure is similar to calculating for window treatments.

1. Measure and record the width of each wall; round up to whole feet. These are horizontal or *linear feet*.
2. Add the number of linear feet for a total number.
3. Multiply the total linear feet by 12 inches to yield total inches around the room.
4. Divide total linear inches by the fabric width for the number of widths. Round up to the next whole width.
5. Measure the height from the ceiling to the top of the baseboard. Record in inches.
6. Divide the height by the pattern repeat.
7. Calculate the **adjusted cut length**—that is, the number of complete pattern repeats × pattern repeat inches.

8. Multiply the number of widths by the adjusted cut length.

    Example: Using the above room dimensions of 4 walls, each 12 feet wide = 48 linear feet. Multiply 48 feet by 12 inches = 576 total linear inches. Divide by 54 inches (the width of the fabric) to obtain 10.7 widths; round up to 11 widths.

    Divide the 96-inch height by the 25-inch pattern repeat = 3.84 patterns. Round up to 4 pattern whole repeats, or 100 inches adjusted cut length.

    100 inches adjusted cut length × 11 widths = 1,100 inches. Divide by 36 inches to obtain 30.5 yards; round up to 31 yards.

Note: For shirred or pleated installations, the width of the fabric becomes the shirred or pleated width, or 20 inches in the above formula. Also, adjusted cut length is increased by about 8 inches to accommodate the top and bottom casing for shirred treatments, for example.

WALLCOVERING INSTALLATION

Surface Preparation

Correctly preparing the wall surface prior to installing any type of wallcovering is essential to a successful outcome. Poor surface preparation accounts for a majority of wallcovering problems. The wall must be structurally sound, clean, dry, and free of stains, mildew, and grease. Irregularities in the drywall, such as holes, must be properly plastered, sanded, and primed before applying the covering. Previous wallcoverings must be completely removed and the surface cleaned of residual adhesives or other chemicals. Adhesive removal solutions are available that make wallpaper removal easier and less time consuming. Any damage from this step must also be repaired.

New drywall should be free of dust, dirt, and other contaminants. All drywall, including the joints, should be sanded smooth. Wait at least 60 to 90 days for new plaster to cure, and then apply an acrylic wallcovering primer to minimize moisture on the surface in order to help the wallpaper to bond to the wall.

Sealers

Sealers make a paper more strippable without damage to the wall. A sealer may be painted onto new or existing surfaces. If a surface has ever had water damage, a sealer helps hide the moisture. Sealers are also used to prevent alkali from penetrating the paper.

Sizing

This is a thin liquid painted onto the wall. It is used to reduce the amount of paste absorbed by the wallcovering and to give the wall "tooth," or a slight roughness that increases adhesion. It helps the adhesives stick better and also seals the surface. A primer, which assures proper adhesion, is the most commonly used wall preparation, especially for commercial installations. Some products seal, size, and prime all in one, so only one coat must be applied. Make sure the product has adequate time to dry before installing the wallcovering. When wall damage cannot be adequately fixed, wall liners (plain paper) can be installed to prevent holes, cracks, and gaps from getting bigger.

Tools

In addition to proper lighting and a flat work surface, required tools include the following: paint roller or brushes, scissors, measuring tape or ruler, sandpaper, level, bucket, pencil, seam roller, ladder, drop cloth, masking tape, seam sealer/roller, a 6- to 7-foot straightedge (used to trim selvage), and a breakaway knife. Tools may vary slightly with the type of wallcovering. Wallpaper installation kits are available; tools can also be purchased or gathered individually.

Adhesives

There are two general performance characteristics to look for: the strength of the bond the adhesive creates between the surface and the wallcovering, and how it is applied to the wallcovering. Adhesives are formulated for specific applications. Some are for heavyweight vinyl, while others are intended for lightweight or delicate fabrics. Adhesives are generally applied to the back of the wallcovering with a brush or a pasting machine.

Normally, adhesive is already applied to paper and vinyl wallcoverings. These are water-activated prepasted adhesives. Clay-based adhesives are used by some installers, although cleanup is difficult. Clear adhesives are usually made of corn or wheat; these allow for easy cleanup and are designed for both residential and commercial applications.

Hanging Wallcoverings

Although design professionals hire qualified wallcovering installers, it is useful to understand wallcovering basics. For any installation, it is best to start in a subtle location—in a corner, an area behind a door, or an area next to a door-frame, for example. It is also important to start out with a straight line. Either mark a line with a pencil and level or start against a doorframe or other flat edge.

Plumb Bob/Line

A **plumb bob** is a weighted line used to produce a vertical line to assure that each strip is hung perfectly straight. Measure the height of the wall and add a few inches. Unroll a second strip and match the pattern to the first strip. Sometimes it is a good idea to cut more than a few strips of wallcovering at one time. Align the top of the first strip to the ceiling, letting some of the excess hang over. Smooth it into place, but do not force out any wrinkles. Using a sharp blade, trim the excess wallpaper at the baseboard and the ceiling line. After each strip is added to the wall, wipe it off with a damp cloth to keep the surface clean. Continue to put up all of the strips until the entire surface is covered. Roll a seam roller over the seams to make sure they are tightly sealed to the surface. Textiles that have foam or paper backing can be applied the same way.

CEILING TREATMENTS

Contract ceiling treatments must meet all flammability codes in both fabric and method of installation. Fabric as architecture, discussed below, is worth investigating for contract installations. Wallcoverings and many of the fabric installation methods may be used as ceiling treatments. In addition, fabrics may be hung in a tentlike fashion in flat panels secured to the wall or shirred at the wall and attached in the center of the room (shirred to a hoop, for example). Flat fabrics may be attached at a parallel point across the room and anchored at the middle of the ceiling in a relaxed swag fashion. Used on all four walls, this method results in a right-angle crisscrossing of fabric.

Ceiling treatments can add elements of drama and sophistication while absorbing sound or camouflaging damaged or unacceptable ceilings. Dark or bright colors, complex or bold patterns, and textures make the ceiling appear lower, while light or dull colors and smooth surfaces can visually raise it. However, even light colors will enclose a space and give a sense of coziness, except for light, sheer fabric, which may create a billowy or cloudlike, ethereal effect. Ceiling treatments are generally made from materials that are light in weight.

PROFESSIONAL INSTALLATION

Finding a wallcovering installation professional whose work is excellent is the goal of all textile design professionals. A new search may begin by asking other professionals for recommendations. The Yellow Pages and the online lists of wallcovering associations (see Resources) are good places to start. Ask the installer for references; check these and inspect his or her installations. Check with the Better Business Bureau for complaints registered against the installer.

Bids should be in writing and describe accurately the work to be accomplished, including a comprehensive plan, estimated costs for material and labor, and experience specifications. Obtain two or three bids, but do not accept the lowest bid without clarifying what services are included. A higher fee indicates extra services or better quality. Be clear in understanding precisely what methods the installer uses and what materials are required for a successful project.

Upon accepting a bid, the design professional prepares a contract to be signed by both parties; this includes the client's name, the address of the installation, a time or date for scheduling, or a place where this is to be filled in upon oral confirmation. A contact number for the client is optional. Installation details include each product by brand, name, and number; the areas where the installation will take place; and their measurements. Be specific and detailed. Contracts should include financial terms and limits, including method and timing of payment schedule and the cancellation policy and penalty, if applicable. A contract should outline what is expected of the installer, from protection of furnishings and equipment to cleanup and the disposition of leftover rolls or yardage. Applicable warranties by manufacturer or installer should be in writing. Time frames for all warranties should be clearly specified. The installer should provide craftsmanship warranties and evidence of current certificate of insurance covering workers' compensation, property damage, and personal liability. Changes or amendments to the original contract are to be agreed upon by both parties in writing before work is begun or continued. Be certain the contract is complete and terms and conditions fully understood before signing it.

WALL TAPESTRIES

Tapestries are decorative fabric compositions hung onto or in front of walls. Traditional European tapestries are typically heavy jacquard woven pictorials featuring scrolling floral patterns from a specific period such as the baroque, Rococo, or Arts and Crafts eras. Wall tapestries typically have a pocket or tabs through which a wooden dowel or decorative metal rod is threaded for hanging. Tapestries were hung on walls as insulation in European castles and estates and to indicate wealth or status. They also provided artistic beauty to interiors and were revered as an upper branch of cultural achievement. Tapestries were then and are today a fiber art form. Although some tapestries were woven by hand in centers such as those in Aubusson and Savonnerie, France, and are

Figure 9.5 This "Eighteenth-Century Antique French Tapestry," from the Antique Masterpieces collection, measures 13 feet, 7 inches × 10 feet, 6 inches. *Photo courtesy of David and Jay Nehouray, Caravan Rug Corp., www.caravanrug.com, (310) 358-1222.*

costly treasures, replicas are available today at modest prices through jacquard weaving. Many machine-made reproductions are woven in Belgium and other countries where skilled labor and technology have merged for high output.

Contemporary tapestries may be woven, painted, tied or knotted, layered, appliquéd, or combined with beads, glass, or other hard materials. Tapestries may be yarns, cables, or any structure made of fabric components, hanging from wall or ceiling. Design may be naturalistic, stylized, or abstract. Natural and manufactured fibers may be incorporated as contrasting components. Fiber artists may be commissioned to create tapestries for public spaces in much the same way a sculptor or painter is, given parameters, a budget, and artistic freedom.

FABRIC ARCHITECTURE

Fabric is an element that improves light and environmental qualities, reduces solar heat and energy costs, and provides design solutions. The materials, compared to standard wall and ceiling building materials and labor, are lower in cost, higher in energy savings, and quickly installed. Fabric architecture allows architects to do more with less. Fabric roofs are durable and can last for many decades with little maintenance. They feature new synthetic fibers in combination with high-tech treatments that guard fabrics against mold, mildew, UV degradation, and fading. Flame retardancy treatments enable architectural fabrics to pass stringent California fire code standards.

Fabric architecture is a popular new construction technique. The Industrial Fabrics Association (see Resources) suggests that fabric as architecture reduces project costs, saves time, enhances sustainability, and increases visual appeal. Fabric architecture is durable and, with new technology, is being produced to last much longer. It is engineered to withstand wind and snow. It requires little maintenance and is protected against fading, mildew, mold, and fire.

Fabric architecture is used for heating, ventilating, and air-conditioning (HVAC) systems as well as custom fabric structures designed for almost any event or purpose. Adding fabric to aluminum or fiberglass frames creates endless possibilities. Walls can be created with fabric, as can cubicles, changing rooms for apparel shops, ceilings, and large-scale fabric art within a space. Fabric architecture may even be used as part of light fixtures.

Another innovative trend that is being used more and more is fabric duct air dispersion, which is basically using fabric architecture for HVAC systems instead of metal. It provides many advantages and is also a new fashion statement in the interior design industry. The vents provide an air-flow that isn't drafty for the entire length of the air duct. Metal air ducts allow vents only every few feet, which creates a draft. Fabric duct is faster to install than metal and is quieter, lighter, and requires less maintenance. Materials differ; low-end fabrics usually last anywhere from three to eight years, which is ideal for temporary locations (tents and construction sites). More expensive fabrics can last up to twenty-five years, depending on how much the HVAC system is used. Fabric costs less to clean than metal duct

Figure 9.6a The Denver Airport is a dynamic example of fabric architecture; it features walls and ceilings of flexible textile. *Photo courtesy of the American Manufactured Fiber Association, FiberSource.*

Figure 9.6b A hallway was created in this office/showroom with fabric walls. *Photo courtesy of Eventscape, Inc.*

and doesn't require frequent painting or other maintenance. Fabric HVAC systems are ideal for gymnasiums because the fabric is not damaged as metal systems are by sports objects (balls, bats, etc.). Fabric HVAC systems are much quieter than metal ducts and work best in open-ceiling applications.

Basic fabric colors are offered in blue, red, black, or white, but others can be custom ordered to match any color scheme. Logos can easily be silk-screened onto the fabric. The systems can hang from the ceiling or be installed with one side flat against the wall/ceiling surface. Fabric duct is considered a green product because it conserves natural resources and improves the thermal, acoustic, and air environments.

RESOURCES

Paint and Decorating Retailers Association (PDRA)
www.pdra.org
403 Axminister Drive
Fenton, MO 63026-2941
Tel 636-326-2636
Fax 636-326-1823

The PDRA supports the independent paint and decorating products dealer and builds supportive relationships between dealers and suppliers. It provides information and offers educational programs, sales training, and business operations programs. It was formerly the National Decorating Products Association (NDPA).

Wallcoverings Association
Wallpaper Council
www.wallcoverings.org

The Wallcoverings Association website lists publications and articles covering how-to's, contract and residential categories, and member information. The Wallpaper Council website, accessed through the Wallcoverings Association website, provides current information, trends, and news.

Chemical Fabrics and Film Association
www.chemicalfabricsandfilm.com
1300 Sumner Avenue
Cleveland, OH 44115-2851
Tel 216-241-7333
Fax 216-241-0105

This chemical trade association represents manufacturers of polymer-based fabric and film products.

Vinyl Institute
www.vinylinfo.org
300 Wilson Boulevard, Suite 800
Arlington, VA 22209
Tel 703-741-5670
Fax 703-741-5672

The Vinyl Institute is a U.S. trade association representing the leading manufacturers of vinyl, vinyl chloride monomer, vinyl additives and modifiers, and vinyl packaging materials.

Acoustics FAQ
www.faqs.org

This educational website is geared toward making acoustics accessible to a wider public and encouraging cooperation within the acoustics community. Articles, research, and findings are posted on many acoustics subjects.

National Guild of Professional Paperhangers (NGPP)
www.ngpp.org
136 S. Keowee Street
Dayton, OH 45402
Tel 800-254-NGPP
Fax 937-222-5794

The NGPP provides continuing education, resources, and networking to assist in the management of small to medium-sized businesses and public exposure to the craft of professional wallcovering.

Industrial Fabrics Association International
www.ifai.com

Lightweight Structures Association
www.lightweightstructures-ifai.com

Professional Awning Manufacturers Association (PAMA)
www.awninginfo.com
1801 County Road B W.
Roseville, MN 55113
Tel 800-225-4324
Fax 651-631-9334

The Industrial Fabrics Association sponsors the "Fabric Structures" conference, which explores fabric as a building material—a new architectural ingredient. At this conference, participants can learn about advancements in technology and examine a variety of designs and applications. The Lightweight Structures Association is a division of the Industrial Fabrics Association International; its purpose is to further the use and development of lightweight structures and to represent the interests and concerns of the lightweight structures industry in the Americas. The Professional Awning Manufacturers Association is also a division of the Industrial Fabrics Association International and is the single international trade association dedicated to the awning industry. PAMA offers an opportunity to exchange information, solve common difficulties, and develop valuable associations.

Greenguard Environmental Institute (GEI)
www.greenguard.org
1341 Capital Circle, Suite A
Atlanta, GA 30067
Tel 800-427-9681
Fax 770-980-0072

The GEI is an industry-independent, nonprofit organization that oversees the Greenguard Certification Program for Low-Emitting Products.

National Institute for Occupational Safety and Health (NIOSH)
www.cdc.gov/niosh
Hubert H. Humphrey Building
200 Independence Avenue SW, Room 715H
Washington, DC 20201
Tel 202-401-6997; 800-356-4674
Fax 513-533-8573
24 Executive Park Drive, Room 1103 MS E-20
Atlanta, GA 30329
Tel 404-498-2500

NIOSH is the federal agency responsible for conducting research and making recommendations for the prevention of work-related injury and illness. NIOSH is part of the Centers for Disease Control and Prevention (CDC) in the Department of Health and Human Services.

League for the Hard of Hearing
www.lhh.org
50 Broadway, 6th Floor
New York, NY 10004
Tel 917-305-7700
TTY 917-305-7999
Fax 917-305-7888
2800 W. Oakland Park Boulevard, Suite 306
Oakland Park, FL 33311
Tel 954-731-7200
TTY 954-731-7208
Fax 954-485-6336

A nonprofit hearing rehabilitation and human services agency for infants, children, and adults who are hard of hearing, deaf, and deaf-blind.

Window Treatments

Figure 10.1 The cartridge shape of these draperies is formed by threading a designer rod through grommets in linen fabrics. *Photo courtesy of Masters of Linen: European Linen of Quality.*

ARCHITECTURAL SPECIFICATIONS

In new nonresidential construction, architects write window treatment specifications to meet code, function, or aesthetics. These are addressed by the design professional who selects or sells the product specified. Window treatment specifications may be general or for a specified product. These are the criteria areas:

1. *The type of treatment*—draperies, horizontal or vertical blinds, shades, window film, or solar screens or motorization

2. *The maximum or estimated allowable cost* per item or per project

3. *Fiber or material, finish, and other details* required, such as durability for headrails or mechanical features

4. *Minimum acceptable ratings for health and safety* (see chapter 6).
   - Flammability: fire ignition, flame spread, smoke density tests
   - Microorganisms: resistance to mold, mildew, bacteria

5. *Guidelines for durability*
   - Dimensional stability (resistance to sagging or elongation and hiking)
   - Inherent strength or tenacity
6. *Aesthetic standards* (see chapters 6 and 7)
   - Colorfastness or resistance to fading
   - Drapability or hand (good body, ease of maintenance)
7. *Daylighting*
   - Fabric or treatments that allow natural light so as to diminish electrical consumption
   - Operable treatments that may be opened easily, possibly by remote control or wall switches
8. *Privacy and light control*
   - Daytime privacy with screening fabric or operable shades or blinds
   - In hospitality, layered treatments for both day and nighttime privacy
   - Blackout lining for hospitality hotel suites

PLANNING WINDOW TREATMENTS—RESIDENTIAL AND NONRESIDENTIAL

Planning furnishings for an interior is not complete without planning from the beginning for window treatments. Window treatments are an essential component for many reasons. Today, the inclusion of more and larger windows than ever before in homes and other buildings means increased exposure to the intensity of the sun's heat, ultraviolet rays, and harsh glare that can damage costly furnishings and make the interior uncomfortable and less livable. Window treatments protect the people who occupy the space against UV light danger, heat, and glare. Window treatments that are sheer or translucent soften daylight and can assure daytime privacy. Opaque window treatments can darken rooms for daytime sleeping, home theater, and temperature and brightness control in warm climates or seasons. Window treatments that provide nighttime privacy gives users a sense of well-being and may play a key role in keeping them safe against burglary or personal harm. Layered treatments can accommodate all these needs.

A design professional who fails to plan for and advise about protective window coverings where an occupant later is harmed or the interior burglarized or otherwise damaged may be guilty of negligence, which can justify litigation against the professional. A tort is where harm to person or property is a result of action or lack of action on the part of another person or firm. Personal safety and welfare, along with protection of the furnishings against UV and heat fading or damage and vandalism, give window treatments paramount importance in interior design. In nonresidential settings, employee productivity can be directly affected by window treatments, and sunlight damage to computers or other equipment is a potential hazard.

Another practical function of fabric at the window is to absorb interior and exterior produced sounds. This quieter, lusher-feeling interior produces a sensory phenomenon that is more than audible; rooms with fabric literally feel quieter. This is desirable in many settings. A sound-absorbent window treatment makes an interior more comfortable and livable than where bare walls and naked windows amplify sounds, turning them into irritating noise.

Visually, textile window coverings are effective at softening the hard lines of architecture. The pleasing juxtaposition of hard and soft materials makes a complementary and complete statement, just as does the balance of angular and rounded shapes and the straight, angular, and curved lines window treatments can provide.

Window treatments can establish fashion and thematic authenticity. When planning backgrounds and furnishings, there is usually a theme that lends itself to ideas for creative window treatments—from traditional to contemporary, ethnic to country, window treatments are as much a part of the entire plan as any other element, from carpeting to furniture to accessories. Look to decorative elements in upholstery, shapes of furniture, or patterns in area rugs, wood or metal furniture, and wallcovering designs for sources of inspiration for the window treatment. Clip magazine photos where window treatments are featured, and group them according to style, period, or category, or use a window treatments software program. Photos can be placed in sheet protectors and organized in a binder so clients can see the gamut of choices and possibilities. Present the window treatment along with the other furnishings for budget consideration, and for the sake of not only the design elements but safety and peace of mind, put the window treatment at the top of the furnishings priority list.

SELECTING TEXTILES FOR WINDOW TREATMENTS

Textile Weight and Opacity: Function and Beauty

Textiles at the window have much to offer an interior. According to their weight and opacity levels, groups of fabrics perform in similar ways. From lightest to heaviest:

1. Transparent: window film
2. Transparent sheers* and semisheer and casement fabrics*

Figure 10.2a Harsh UV light, evident in this office setting, can fade interior furniture and produce glare that is harmful to eyes and skin. *Photo courtesy of Vista Window Film.*

Figure 10.2b Window film, as shown here, can eliminate glare, 99 percent of UV light, and reduce solar heat by 38 percent, thus reducing interior fading and increasing comfort. *Photo courtesy of Vista Window Film.*

3. Lightweight* and medium-weight* semi-opaque fabrics
4. Heavyweight* fabrics

*These fabrics are listed in the accompanying website (www .wiley.com/go/interiortextiles) under "Decorative and Supportive Textiles," which includes a glossary cross-referenced to these categories.

Window film is a transparent extruded polymer textile applied directly to the interior of a window. It is sometimes referred to as *window tinting.* Look for products that are natural gray rather than tinted bronze or green, as colored film tends to unduly influence the light source, whereas gray is neutral and will not affect the appearance of furnishing colors. High-quality window film eliminates at least 99 percent of harmful UV light, reducing fading of interior furnishings and harm to human skin. It eliminates glare without darkening the interior. Good window film decreases solar heat by at least 38 percent and is effective at keeping heated air indoors, thus creating a more even temperature throughout the building. Window film should be resistant to scratching and window cleaning products. It will prevent impacted glass from exploding, thus increasing safety. Look for a product with a lifetime residential guarantee and a ten-year nonresidential guarantee. Window film does not replace other window treatments where privacy and light control are requirements.

Sheer and **lightweight translucent** or **casement fabrics** screen bright light, thereby decreasing or eliminating irritating glare. They screen the harshness and temperature intensity of direct sunlight, making the interior more comfortable. Sheer, translucent, and casement fabrics provide

Figure 10.3 Sheer window coverings provide daytime privacy and reduce the intensity of direct sunlight, making interiors more inviting and comfortable. *Photo compliments of Comfortex Window Fashions.*

Selecting Textiles for Window Treatments **183**

daytime privacy, as one can see toward the light source through them. However, at night, a person outside can see directly through these fabrics to the interior. An opaque treatment is required for nighttime privacy. Sheer, translucent, and casement fabrics absorb interior and some exterior sound, making the interior quieter and audibly more comfortable. Visually, this group of fabrics softens architecture but does not obscure it. Sheer fabrics that are artistically draped are sensuous and romantic; textured casement and semisheers offer visual security and textural interest to daytime working conditions. The screening of light helps the occupant focus on furnishings or computer screens without discomfort, thus making the interior more visually pleasing and functional. See the fabric glossary at www.wiley.com/go/interiortextiles for a list of sheer and semisheer translucent fabrics. Sheer and semisheer fabrics are also offered as pleated and cellular shades and shading systems.

Light- to **medium-weight semi-opaque fabrics** are used for nearly every type of soft custom window treatment: draperies and curtains, soft shades, and all top treatments. They may or may not be lined, but lining is almost always recommended to protect the fabric from fading, to provide a uniform appearance from the outside (if there are no alternative treatments beneath), and to give body and substance to the treatments. These groups of fabrics drape well, but individual fabrics may vary dramatically in performance — in other words, some are sturdy, some are fragile, some are stiff, and some are soft. Select a fabric with the hand and drapability that matches the window treatment. Stiff fabrics are good for pleated draperies, roman shades, and some valances; soft fabrics are suitable for balloon shades and swags, for example. If a fabric is selected that is not compatible with the style of treatment, the results can be disappointing. Some medium weight textured polyester fabrics are used as vertical blind vanes.

Heavyweight fabrics for window treatments include leather, tapestries, and velvets, for example, and are used for panels where heaviness equates with richness. Generally, these fabrics are used as flat treatments: drapery panels, flat shades, and pelmet-like valances. They usually work best where the look is somewhat flat or lower on the fullness scale — up to 200 percent fullness (double fullness). These fabrics can be insulative and are often prized for their heavy tactile and visual texture, appropriate for rich historic, traditional, or rustic interiors.

Custom Window Treatment Fibers

Fibers most commonly used for custom fabricated window treatments are cotton, linen, silk, rayon, acetate, modacrylic, and polyester. Alternate or manufactured shade products are primarily polyester. Residential usage of cotton, linen, silk, polyester, acetate, and rayon is higher than other fibers, and nonresidential usage of wool and polyester, acrylic, and modacrylic is higher than other fibers.

Window Treatment Categories

All window treatments are made of textiles, with the exception of wood, aluminum, and vinyl blinds and shutters. (Vinyl is technically a manufactured textile as well.) There are two main categories of textile window treatments: **soft window treatments** and **alternative window treatments.** Soft window treatments include **draperies, curtains and hardware, top treatments,** and **soft shades** or **shadings.** Some are available as ready-made or stock items, and all can be custom fabricated. Alternative window treatments include blinds, shades, and shutters — also in ready-made but ordered in custom sizes and in a variety of options and styles by the design professional. Alternate window treatments are discussed later in this chapter.

Ready-made soft treatments are mass-produced in factories in specific styles, sizes, and a limited number of fabrics to be sold by mass merchandisers. Draperies, curtains, valances, and swags, as well as some alternative window treatments, are available in retail stores and through mail-order catalogs. Although primarily purchased as an economical and easily obtainable window covering by consumers for their homes, they can be utilized by residential interior professionals where the budget is tight and the product is suitable, or when the product is needed immediately.

Custom soft window treatments are those custom-made to specifications. The design professional (and client) select the style, fabric(s), trimmings, and hardware; the order is confirmed; and a work order or specification sheet is filled out and delivered with the textiles to a workroom that fabricates (cuts, constructs, sews, trims, and finishes) the treatment. This is known as *custom fabrication.* These treatments are typically installed by a professional installer. Custom window treatments are made as one-of-a-kind installations, although for hospitality, health care, offices, institutions, and public buildings, one treatment may be mass-fabricated for multiple or repeat window installations.

In each of the following sections — draperies, curtains, top treatments, and soft shades — styles are defined and illustrated, and information is given to calculate yardage and specify work orders.

Draperies and Curtains

Generally, draperies are long, formal, or custom window treatments, and curtains are those that are cottage-looking.

Figure 10.4 An inverted French pleat gives a sleek look to these custom draperies installed over Silhouette® shadings. *Photo courtesy of Hunter Douglas.*

Draperies are usually pleated but may also have tabs or shirred headings.

Pleated Draperies There are many styles of pleated draperies. Some are intended for operation with a traverse rod, and other pleats are ornamental and planned for stationary panels only. The most common and functional pleat is the French or pinch pleat. It is made by interfacing the drapery top or heading with buckram (also known as buchram or crinoline) and then folding and stitching in place a cartridge-shaped loop. Then three or four small folds, called *fingers*, are folded and bar-tacked (with single reinforcing stitches) at the bottom. This causes the drapery to fall into precise folds and the pleating to fan out handsomely at the top. If the fingers are pressed flat into sharp folds, the pleat is a pinch pleat, and if they are left unpressed, a trifle more relaxed, then it is a French pleat. This type of pleat is best for draperies installed on conventional or traverse rods, where hooks are inserted into the back of each pleat and installed on carriers in the rod. The buckram between each pleat is carefully creased vertically so the draperies can open and close with perfection and dignity. Pinch-pleated draperies result from 200 to 250 percent fullness, with 300 percent fullness used for sheer draperies.

Pinch-pleat applications and variations consist of **pinch** or **French pleats; architectural, accordion,** or **single pleats;** and **pinch-pleat variations,** as follows.

Pinch- or **French-pleated** draperies have long been a standard treatment for residential windows. Generally, pinch pleats are precise, folded, and pressed, whereas French pleats are not pressed and are less precise. Sheers with overdraperies that are opened and closed by a traverse rod still have much application and versatility; they can be utilized in nearly any room and in any weight of fabric from very sheer to heavy. They are often lined for consistent exterior appearance, to protect the life of the fabric and prevent drapery fading, and to insulate against heat gain and loss and noise. Pinch pleats are also used as valance headings.

The pinch pleat is also utilized in many nonresidential settings from offices to health care. However, when this approach results in too much fabric, the **architectural** or **accordion pleat,** sometimes called a **single pleat,** may be used (see list below). In hospitality design and especially hotels and resorts, pinch-pleated draperies are used almost exclusively because of their consistent appearance and durability. In hotel rooms and suites, they are often blackout lined, or a separate blackout lining drapery is constructed and installed on its own rod. Often, pinch-pleated sheers or semisheer draperies are also specified. However, a wand is attached, grommet-style, to the leading overlap edge on each side so no traverse mechanism is needed. This eliminates damage to rods by abuse or misuse of the mechanism. The wand is used in place, and the guest can open and close each side separately.

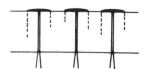

Figure 10.5a Inverted box pleat

Figure 10.5b Exposed or front-faced box pleat

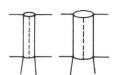

Figure 10.5c Cartridge pleats in small and large sizes

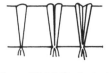

Figure 10.5d Single, double, and butterfly pleats

Figure 10.5e X-pleat and inverted French pleats

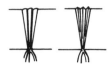

Figure 10.5f French pleat, soft, rounded fingers; pinch pleat with crisp, folded fingers

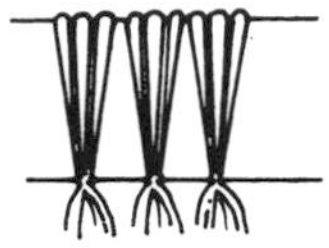

Figure 10.5g Grouped French pleats

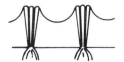

Figure 10.5h French pleats alternated with scallops

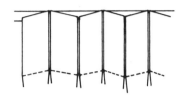

Figure 10.5i Architectural, accordion, or single pleats. This heading requires little fullness; a sleek, spartan office look can easily be accomplished. It often is hung on special architectural rods.

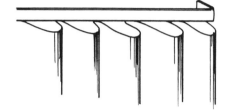

Figure 10.5j Spring-rod pleat. This pleat is made with a flat rod-pocket seam threaded onto a special spring that expands to close and contracts to open. Second in popularity to the French pleat, it gives a tailored, sleek look.

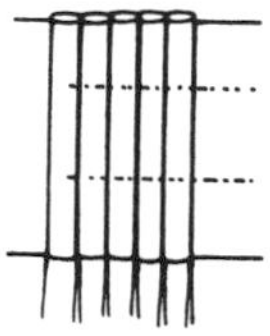

Figure 10.5k The pencil pleat is accomplished with sewn-on or fused-on tape. Strings are pulled to form the pleats.

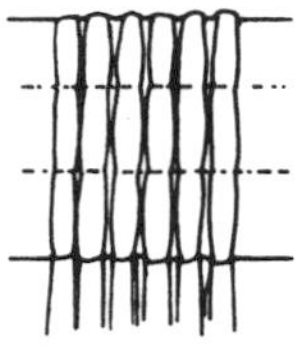

Figure 10.5l A shirred heading, such as this, is usually accomplished with tape.

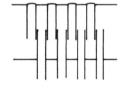

Figure 10.5m A spaced pencil-pleat heading can be sewn or fused on.

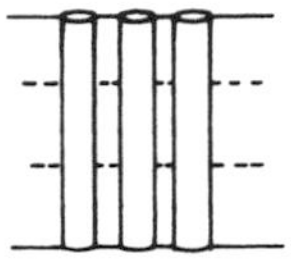

Figure 10.5n Alternate pencil-pleat heading

Figure 10.5o Shirring tape also gives the look of a shirred heading.

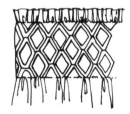

Figure 10.5p Ruffled smocked pleat

Figure 10.5 Standard drapery headings.

Variations of the pinch or French pleat have become a way of designing variety and individuality in draperies. These are some of the common variations:

The **inverted pinch pleat** is created by bar-tacking the pleat fingers at the top. This is stiff where buckram (interfacing) is used, and can be spaced and made into a slouch heading if no buckram is used. Inverted pinch pleats are appropriate for stationary panels and wand-drawn draperies. They should not be specified for traverse rod applications.

The **X-pleat** is accomplished by bar-tacking the pleat fingers in the middle of the 4-inch buckram rather than at the bottom. This makes the pleat flare out both top and bottom, like an X, and is most satisfactory for stationary draperies. The X-pleat is not recommended for conventional traverse rods.

The **butterfly pleat** does not utilize buckram or crinoline. The unlined heading is therefore limp. The bar-tack is either in the center or about one-third the distance from the top. To form the butterfly, the heading between the folds is pulled forward and down, creating a small scallop or dip, and the outer fingers of the pleat naturally fan out. The butterfly pleat is most satisfactory for stationary draperies; it is not recommended for conventional traverse rods.

The **single, architectural,** or **accordion pleat** is a single, narrow finger pressed flat, resulting in a drapery with less fullness—typically about 150 to 200 percent (1½ to 2 times) fullness. This pleat is used in hospital cubicle cur-

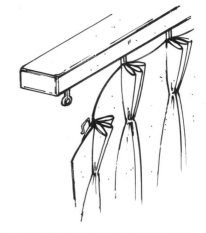

Figure 10.5q Pinch pleat installed on wand-drawn institutional or contract rod

Figure 10.5s Roll pleat installed on wand-drawn institutional or contract rod

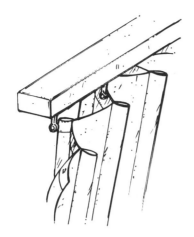

Figure 10.5u Stack pleat installed on wand-drawn institutional or contract rod

Figure 10.5r Pinch pleat with drapery hook and carrier on institutional or contract rod

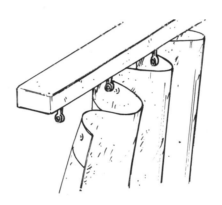

Figure 10.5t Roll pleat and carrier on institutional or contract rod

Figure 10.5v Stack pleat and carrier on institutional or contract rod

tains and some office and institutional draperies. Such draperies are installed on simple architectural rods and drawn with a wand by hand.

The **large** and **small cartridge pleats** are made by forming the loops for a pinch pleat and then stuffing the loop with tissue or plastic to create a perfect cylinder or cartridge. The cartridge size is according to designer specifications. These pleats are best applied to stationary draperies; they are not recommended for conventional traverse rods.

The **goblet pleat** is a cartridge pleat gathered and bartacked at the bottom and stuffed at the top. There may also be a bubble tacked and stuffed trapunta-style just below the large goblet, as often seen in stemware drinking glasses. This is an elegant pleat that may be trimmed with cording or fringe along the bottom. Goblet pleats work best with stationary draperies; they are not recommended for conventional traverse rods.

The **pencil pleat** is a single small pleat repeated across the face of the heading. It is usually formed with shirring or pleater tape sewn onto the back and formed by drawstrings. These draperies are often hung with rings and drawn by hand. The drapery body does not fall in precise folds, but that is part of the charm of this style. It is also appropriate for stationary panels.

Shirring tape pleats usually create a smocked or tightly shirred look. They are also used for draperies intended to look imperfect. The draperies may be stationary or hung by rings on a rod and hand-operated.

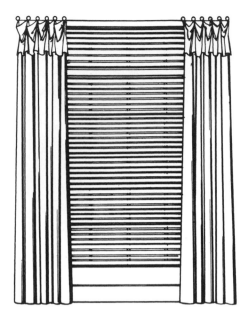

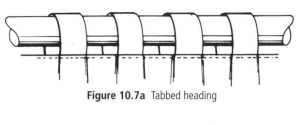

Figure 10.7a Tabbed heading

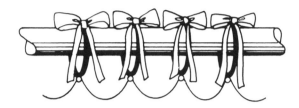

Figure 10.7b Ring headings

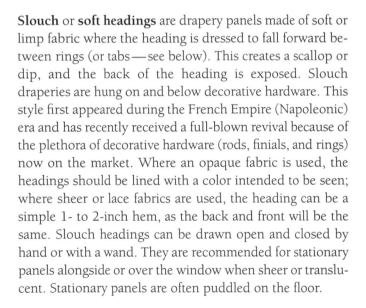

Figure 10.6 When dressed to fall forward between rings, a soft, limp fabric creates a scallop called a slouch or soft heading.

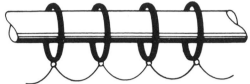

Figure 10.7c Tied/ring headings

Slouch or **soft headings** are drapery panels made of soft or limp fabric where the heading is dressed to fall forward between rings (or tabs — see below). This creates a scallop or dip, and the back of the heading is exposed. Slouch draperies are hung on and below decorative hardware. This style first appeared during the French Empire (Napoleonic) era and has recently received a full-blown revival because of the plethora of decorative hardware (rods, finials, and rings) now on the market. Where an opaque fabric is used, the headings should be lined with a color intended to be seen; where sheer or lace fabrics are used, the heading can be a simple 1- to 2-inch hem, as the back and front will be the same. Slouch headings can be drawn open and closed by hand or with a wand. They are recommended for stationary panels alongside or over the window when sheer or translucent. Stationary panels are often puddled on the floor.

Tabbed Draperies and Curtains Tabbed or tab-top draperies and curtains come in many varieties, with strips of fabric sewn onto the top in various widths and spacings. They can be tied in knots or bows, fanned out into Empire styling, ornamented with buttons or jewelry, or be simple and straight. Tabbed draperies and curtains reveal the decorative hardware that replaces top treatments when desired; they are versatile, appropriate in both formal and informal rooms, depending on the fabric, the style of tab, and the hardware; and they are fitting for relaxed styles of interior design where the fabric is sculptural and even sensuous.

Tabbed curtains originated as medieval window coverings and are still appropriate to country settings. Tabbed draperies or curtains can be as provincial or as sophisticated as the fabric and interior design dictate. The finished look depends on not only the style of tabs but the hand, weight, and drapability of the fabric. A stiff or crisp fabric will look more tailored and can be fashioned into folds that hold their shape, whereas a limp or soft fabric or sheer or lace are good choices for the slouch tabbed look. Be certain to match the fabric weight and texture to the desired finished effect. Here are the types of tab headings:

- **New England tab headings** were originally used as a means of easily sliding the curtains in colonial New England homes. The rod was a wooden dowel or, in some cases, a piece of twine. The tabs were about 2 inches wide, and the loops were 4 to 6 inches long and placed 4 to 8 inches apart. Today, the width and length of the tab and its placement vary according to the intended proportions.
- **Buttoned and tailored tabs** are those where the top stitching appears tailored or that are embellished with a button or other jewelry.
- **Tie-tab variations** include these:
  - **Knotted tab headings** are constructed with two straps sewn into the heading. The straps are then tied over the top of the rod in an informal knot, such as a square knot. The remaining strap length hangs down askew. The tabs may be of contrasting fabrics.

- **Bow-tie headings** are accomplished like knotted tabs, except the straps are tied into bows. Another variation is to construct bows and attach them to the top of looped tabs.
- **Spaghetti-strap tie headings** are made of narrow strips of fabric and are usually longer, so the knot of the bow is tied and the extra length hangs down in irregular fashion. Consider cording or ribbon in place of fabric, or utilize a contrasting fabric.
- **Empire-style tabs** are gathered or tacked at the bottom so they flare outward at the top over the rod. They can be combined with a slouch or scallop heading.

Tabs of other materials such as belting or cording add interest and character to tab headings. Woven leather belting, for example, can form the tabs as well as the ties.

Shirred Draperies and Curtains Shirring means gathering a panel onto a rod by sewing a rod pocket into the top of the drapery, curtain, or valance. Often there is a ruffle, called a **header,** above the rod pocket. For good proportion, the header is usually the same size as or a little smaller than the rod pocket, unless a crown or tiara-shaped ruffle is desired or special circumstances dictate. Rod-pocket draperies without headers are more contemporary in appearance; those with ruffles are more country or traditional. Shirring is often thought to be less formal, but the fabric can determine the level of formality, and shirring can produce a fairly formal ef-

fect. A rod sleeve can also be constructed for the rod itself, if the shirring panels are to be stationary side panels and the design calls for the fabric to be visually connected at the top. Shirred curtains, or cottage curtains, are those we think of as ready-mades—meant for kitchens, for example. Of course, cottage curtains can be custom constructed as well. These include café curtains with valances, priscilla curtains, and tiered curtains. Shirred draperies are longer, usually to the floor or puddled on the floor, and more sophisticated than curtains.

Shirred treatments typically are used with curtain rods, from very small brass café rods to flat or oval white curtain rods; the most common measure ⅞, 2½, or 4 inches in diameter. Wood pole rods, plain or fluted, are also selected for shirred treatments. Multiple rod pockets and rods can add variety to the treatment, such as two or even three rod pockets next to each other or spaced a few inches apart. A word of caution here: Be certain the overall heading size stays in good proportion to the rest of the drapery or curtain, as multiple rods can make a treatment top-heavy and somewhat awkward.

Flat-panel draperies and **curtains** are sometimes called *handkerchief panels* because they are typically lined and then folded back to reveal the lining, much as a handkerchief is folded on the diagonal. A rod pocket can be sewn into the top and slide flat onto a wooden or metal rod. The panel may also be stapled to a mounting board. Different effects can be achieved by different placement of the folded portion (low, high, symmetrical, or asymmetrical). The flat panel is typically tailored in appearance. Because there is no gather-

Figure 10.8 In this pool room, fabric is gathered onto a rod to create shirring. *Photo courtesy of ADO Corporation.*

Figure 10.9a Shirred curtains flank this French window.

Figure 10.9d Shirred treatments, such as these panels and swags, fall softly in sheer lightweight fabrics. *Photo courtesy of Comfortex.*

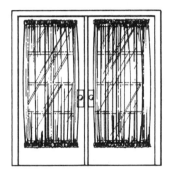

Figure 10.9b Sash curtains are attached to these French doors, assuring daytime privacy and glare control for seated interior occupants.

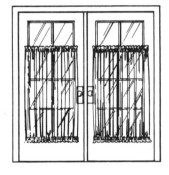

Figure 10.9c Shirred sash curtains are affixed to the French door frame. This allows light and view above; daytime privacy below.

ing or pleating in flat-panel draperies or curtains, the calculations vary from those for gathered drapes. The finished width is not multiplied by the fullness but simply divided by the width of the fabric, less side seam allowance.

Victorian lace panels and **glass curtains** generally hang under long curtains or top treatments and may have these options for installation: shirred onto a rod, pleated on a traverse or decorative rod, attached by Velcro to the window frame, or finished with fringe. Where the standard length is too long for a window, the excess may be folded for a self-valance or cut off and sewn as a valance or accessory item. Victorian glass curtains are short curtains that go inside the casing. They are usually hung on a small rod, with a privacy shade or blind beneath them, next to the glass. Glass curtains are usually polyester sheer or semisheer.

Sash curtains are usually made to cover three-fourths or the whole of the lower sash. They may be used for the glass of French doors, and they may be shirred (gathered onto a small rod) top and bottom. On sash windows, they are often called *café curtains* and may have a variety of headings. They are often unattached at the bottom and therefore operable.

HARDWARE

Hardware is the metal, wood, resin, plastic, or vinyl rods, brackets, and holders that support installed window treatments. See www.wiley.com/go/interiortextiles for links to drapery hardware websites.

- **Conventional traverse rods** are operable via hand or remote-controlled cord-and-pulley mechanisms. They come in standard white and brown and as designer or decorator rods.
- **Designer** or **decorator rods** are made of metal and composite materials to operate as conventional traverse rods but look like wood or several metal finishes.
- **Hand-operated rods** are used in hospitality and healthcare settings, where multiple users raise the odds of inadvertent breakage to the mechanism. These rods may be identical to conventional traverse or designer rods but operated via a sturdy plastic rod attached to the master carriers and guided or drawn open and closed by hand without cords.
- **Cut-to-measure rods** are bendable metal channel rods that hold drapery carriers for hooks. These rods are used for ceiling or unusually shaped windows in stationary or hand-operated installations.
- **Wood rods** utilize wood rings with eye screws through which the drapery hook is fastened, then drawn by hand or with a wand or rod.
- **Metal rods,** in a wide variety of styles, have hooks or rings of metal to which the drapery is attached.
- **Curtain rods** are metal—white and brass two of the most common finishes—used for shirred, tabbed, or other stationary headings.
- **Brackets** are used to project all kinds of rods from the wall about 3 inches per layer of drapery. Along the face of the rod, a bracket is generally installed about every 24 inches.
- **Hooks** and **rings** are the usual means by which fabric is attached to hardware. Hooks are inserted behind the pleats and inserted into the ring or carrier.
- **Swag** and **tie-back holders** are metal or resin decorative drapery hardware that secures fabric draped over or through them. Fabric may also be secured with drapery hooks or cord, attached to the swag or tie-back holder.

MEASURING FOR WINDOW TREATMENTS

Many design professionals avoid window treatments because of the considerable responsibility of measuring correctly. The following is advice on how to do the job without error.

- Use a sturdy 25-foot steel retractable tape measure, and be in the habit of carrying it to each job site.

- Windows are always measured first horizontally and then vertically. The horizontal measurement is the width and the vertical measurement is the length or height.
- Never allow anyone except a drapery installer to take measurements for you. For example, it is typical in the building industry to take the height or length first, then the width. One real-life example of what can go wrong happened to a design professional who allowed the builder to submit measurements for blinds for a 100-unit condominium development. While the dimensions were right, they were backward, as the builder listed the length first, then the width. As a result, all the blinds were the wrong sizes! The designer "ate the job." Many professionals take measurements, calculate and give prices to the client, close the sale, and then send the installer to double-check the measurements. Be sure to charge the client for the measuring fee and trip charge of the installer.
- Always measure window treatments in inches, not feet plus inches.
- Record each measurement as it is taken.
- Do not take two measurements and then write them down at the same time; it's simply too easy to reverse numbers. Remember, you are responsible for accuracy of measurement and product.
- If you get to the paper or laptop and are not sure you recall the measurement you just took, then by all means take it again!
- Be certain each measurement is correct and properly labeled on your measure sheet, so there is no guesswork when you return to your office or studio to order or specify the product.
- If the width is longer than your arm span, ask someone to hold the tape end at 0 inches while you read the measurement.
- While measuring and recording, avoid visiting with anyone. Chatting breaks concentration and adds to the error factor. Tell others you are careful to make accurate measurements and ask them to excuse you for a few moments while you measure.

Window treatment measurements include these:

1. Window width.
2. Wall space on each side, in order to stack draperies off the glass (one-quarter to one-third window width on each side for a two-way draw or pair of operable draperies).

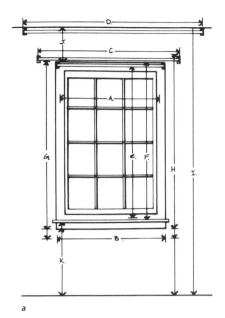

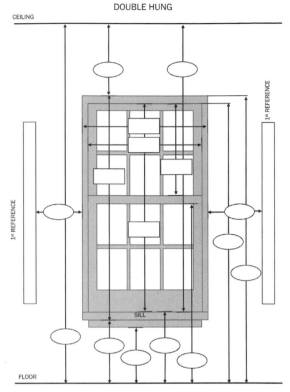

Figure 10.10a Possible measurements for window treatments for a double-hung sash window.

Figure 10.10b Computer software assists interiors professionals in the custom design of window treatments. *Illustration by DreamDraper®. Copyright by Evan Marsh Designs, Inc.*

Figure 10.10c Measuring and design tools for window for custom window treatments. *Illustration by DreamDraper®. Copyright by Evan Marsh Designs, Inc.*

Figure 10.10d An example of a measuring guide for draperies, including rod width dimensions to stack on or off the glass. *Illustration by DreamDraper®. Copyright by Evan Marsh Designs, Inc.*

3. Length of finished drapery (you decide).
4. If the drapery is ceiling to floor, take the exact measurement three times across the width and use the shortest length (floors and ceiling are not always plumb). Subtract 1 inch for clearance—but tell yourself by notation if that deduction has been taken or if the measurement is exact.
5. Note height from ceiling to window or area above window (optional).
6. Note length from window to floor (optional).

Calculating Draperies and Curtains

Calculating comes naturally to some and is a genuine bane to others. Some people have a mind-set that makes calculating feel too hard. Yet cultivating a good attitude about learning can be empowering. Competence in calculating yardage, fabrication, trimmings, hardware, and installation is often a lucrative part of a textile design business. An overview of the steps of calculation appears here; details follow:

1. Calculate the **finished width.**
2. Calculate the **number of widths required.**
3. Determine **finished length** and add **hems and headings** to calculate **cut length** (including pattern repeat for **adjusted cut length,** if applicable).
4. Multiply the number of widths by the cut length, then divide to find **yardage.**
5. Multiply the yardage by price/cost per yard for **total yardage price.** (*Note:* The term *price* usually means retail; *cost* is wholesale.)
6. Calculate **fabrication** (labor to sew) charges.
7. Calculate yardage amount and fabrication for **trimmings,** if applicable.
8. Select and price drapery **hardware.**
9. Calculate or look up **installation** charges.
10. Add all figures, including commission, if applicable, then add appropriate sales tax to arrive at **total.**
11. A deposit of 50 percent with signature approval is customary for retail sales. The balance is due upon installation. For cost plus fee or commission, the entire amount is due with the order.

Calculations in Detail

1. Calculate the **finished width.** Take the window width and add any extra width necessary. These options include:
   a. Stack off or stack back (one-quarter to one-third of the window width on each side).
   b. Returns to the wall. On a conventional traverse rod, this is imperative in order to cover the bracket projection. Try to do this even on designer rods with carrier rings to avoid a light strike. A single return (one drapery layer) is about 4 inches, and a double return (two drapery layers or a valance over one layer) is 6 inches. A valance over two layers has a return of 9 inches. An underdrapery (sheer) will not have any returns.
   c. Where the drapery will draw closed and meet in the middle, add 4 to 5 inches for overlap to avoid a center light strike (that's 2 or 2½ inches on each side).

   The window width and other width additions, such as stack off, returns, and overlap, yield the finished width.

   For example, a window width of 40 inches + one-quarter stack off each side of 10 inches (× 2) = 60-inch rod width + 12 inches for overlaps and returns = 72 inches finished width. (*Note:* You could also use 40 inches + one-third stack on each side of 13 inches (× 2) = 66-inch rod width + 12 inches for overlaps and returns = 78 inches finished width).

2. Calculate the **number of widths** required. A width is one panel of fabric from selvage to selvage. When two widths are required for a pair of draperies or curtains, each panel of the pair is one width. If three are required, then each panel of the pair is one and one-half widths (with the half-width sewn on the outside—and yes, half-widths sometimes look awkward). If four widths are required, then each panel of the pair is two widths, serged together, and so on.

   To calculate the widths, decide first how full the panels will be; 2½ times, or 250 percent, or 2:1 or 2.5:1 fullness is standard for most designer fabrics. This means that for every 1 inch of pleated or gathered/shirred fabric across the drapery rod, 2½ inches is required for fullness. Tab curtains may require only 2 times, 200 percent, or 2:1 fullness, while sheer pleated or shirred draperies/curtains are typically specified at 3 times, or 300 percent, or 3:1 fullness. (Seamless sheers are discussed below.)

   To find the number of widths of fabric required, multiply the finished width by the fullness (use a cal-culator or computer program). Divide that number by the width of the fabric and round up to the next whole number. Designer fabrics are typically 54 inches wide, but other fabrics may be 45, 48, 60, or 72 inches wide. (Widths over 100 inches are usually calculated as for seamless sheers, below.)

   For example, finished width = 72 inches × 2.5 (or 250 percent) = 180 inches. 180 inches ÷ 54 inches = 3.33 widths, which rounds up to 4 widths. If the answer is a 0.1 fraction, round down. For fractions above 0.2 (as in this example), round up. This assures generous fullness and accommodates the side seams.

3. Determine **finished length** and add hems and **headings** to calculate **cut length** (including pattern repeat for **adjusted cut length,** if applicable). For pinch-pleated draperies, add 16 inches. For shirred draperies, add 8 inches for bottom hems and the rod pocket and header twice plus 1 inch to turn under at the back heading (Example: shirred heading 3½ inches + 2-inch header = 5½ inches × 2 + 1 = 12 inches.) For the following working example, we'll use 16 inches, as for a pinch-pleated drapery. (*Note:* Some design professionals prefer to round up to 20 inches.) For finished length, 84 inches + 16 inches = 100 inches cut length. This drapery requires 100 inches for each width or cut of fabric.

   Many decorative fabrics have large patterns. It is crucial that each width of fabric be serged or joined so the pattern is in the same place horizontally from width to width. This means the top pattern must be in the same place on each width regardless of where the pattern ends at the bottom of the cut. To allow for this, complete pattern repeats must be ordered if the fabric is ordered unfabricated (and then taken or sent to the fabricator). Using the example above, a 100-inch cut length in a fabric with a 27-inch pattern repeat (typical for large patterns) would yield 100 ÷ 27 inches = 3.7 pattern repeats, which must be rounded up to 4. The new adjusted cut length will be 4 × 27 inches = 108 inches. When ordering, specify that 4 complete pattern repeats are required for each cut or width. (It may be necessary to cut the fabric into lengths because of flaws.)

4. Multiply the number of widths by the cut length and then divide by 36 inches to find the **yardage.** In the example above, 4 widths of fabric × 100 inches (no pattern repeat) = 400 inches ÷ 36 inches = 11.1. It is wise to round up to 12, even though it is possible to get by with only 11 yards. If the adjusted cut length were 108 inches × 4 = 432 inches = 12 yards exactly, many professionals would choose to round up to the next

yard in case of flaws or problems in cutting the fabric. If 12 yards are ordered, once again, remember to specify the complete pattern repeats required per cut.

5. Multiply the yardage by price/cost per yard for **total yardage price** (*Again: Price* usually means retail; *cost* indicates wholesale.) 12 yards × $30 per yard (for example) is $360. If the drapery is lined, then 12 yards at, say, $6 per yard is an additional $72. The fabrics together total $432.

6. Calculate **fabrication** (labor to sew) charges. Cost to sew is based on linear inches or widths. In this example, widths are used. 4 widths at, say, $25 per width (lined, retail) is $100. If the drapery or curtain is unlined, the price will be lower per width or per inch. Price per width is higher for extra-long draperies. Consult the fabrication workroom for costs. The fabrication profit margin between cost and retail should be between 30 and 50 percent. (*Note:* It is customary to mark up fabrication by double. Create a retail list from the workroom charges that the customer can see, unless you sell at cost and charge a percentage for a design fee.)

7. Calculate yardage and amount and fabrication for **trimmings,** if applicable. For example, if a fringe was selected to trim the leading inside edges and bottom hems of the drapery in this example, the calculations would look like this:

> finished length 84 inches × 2 (each panel of the pair — leading edge) = 168 inches
>
> 4 widths × 54 inches each (for bottom edge) = 216 inches
>
> 168 inches + 216 inches = 384 inches
>
> 384 inches ÷ 36 = 10.7 or 11 yards
>
> 11 yards × $25 (retail price per yard) = $275
>
> labor to sew fringe 11 yards × $6 per yard = $66
>
> fringe total $220 + $66 = $286

Other fringe and trimming items often selected include tassels and rope, used as tie-backs or as ornament. Add in the price per tassel and rope selected. *Note:* Fringe can vary from a few dollars a yard to several hundred dollars a yard. Likewise, rope and tassels range widely in expense.

8. Select and price drapery **hardware.** Designer hardware is sold by the finished width (sometimes called *length*). In this example, the rod width is 60 inches, or 5 feet. A rod price might be $100. (Note: As with trimmings, the price for hardware varies dramatically.) Decorative hardware replaces valances and

then becomes an important fashion statement worthy of investment.

9. Calculate or look up **installation** charges. Installers may charge by the width or by the horizontal foot across the rod. In the example above, 4 widths at a charge of, say, $10 per width installation fee would come to $40. However, the installer may charge a minimum trip charge of $50 to $100. If this drapery is the only one the installer must handle, then the minimum trip fee must be charged. (*Note:* It is customary to double the installation charges to arrive at retail.) If the installer charges by the foot, then the rod width (see Step 8 above) yields 5 feet at a charge of, say, $8 per foot, so the charge would still be $40. It is crucial to obtain a list of installation charges in order to create your own retail list for your customer to see. Not that you would ever offer to show it to the customer, certainly, but always be prepared with retail lists, unless you deal at wholesale and mark up your services by a percentage, as discussed in chapter 1.

10. Add all figures, including commission, if applicable, and add appropriate sales tax to arrive at the total.

In the example given above, this is how the addition would look:

> Decorative fabric 12 yards × $30 per yard = $360
>
> Lining fabric 12 yards × $6 per yard = $72
>
> Labor to sew 4 widths × $25 per width = $100
>
> Fringe 11 yards × $25 per yard = $275
>
> Fringe labor to sew 11 yards × $6 per yard = $66
>
> Installation 4 widths × $10 per width = $40 (or minimum trip fee)
>
> Subtotal = $913

Add applicable sales tax to arrive at total purchase price. A deposit of 50 percent is customary, with the balance due upon installation.

Layered Draperies

Draperies are often layered over alternate treatments (blinds, shades, or shutters) or with an underdrapery of sheer fabric. When calculating an underdrapery, the fullness can vary; heavy lace may be specified at as little as 200 percent, or 2 times fullness, whereas very sheer or even semisheer fabrics are routinely 300 percent, or 3 times fullness (the standard 250 percent used for overdraperies looks skimpy in sheers). When the fabric is 48 to 72 inches wide, calcu-

Figure 10.11a Custom-layered window treatments: upholstered cornice, tied-back draperies, sheers, and Roman shade.

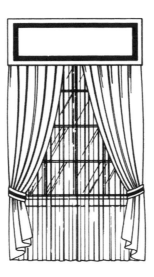

Figure 10.11b Custom-layered fabric window treatments: sheers drawn for daytime privacy and light protection/control.

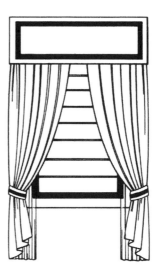

Figure 10.11c Custom-layered fabric window treatments with Roman shade closed for insulation and nighttime privacy.

late sheer vertical widths in the same manner as the example above, except delete the returns, keeping the overlaps (there is no return on the under rod). When the sheer or lace width is over 103 inches (118 inches is typical), then that fabric is termed **seamless** and meant to be **railroaded,** or turned on its side, width for length. This works when the vertical cut length of the sheer or lace drapery does not exceed the width of the seamless fabric. If, in the example above, a seamless sheer were selected as an underdrapery, then the cut length would be 83 + 16 = 99 inches. The finished length of sheer should be 1 inch shorter than the overdrapery to prevent it from showing below the hem or above the heading (overdraperies are more likely to shrink with cleaning than sheers). The 99 inches is less than the width of the seamless fabric, so it may be railroaded. To do this, finished width 60 inches × 3 (300 percent fullness) = 180 inches, then divide by 36 inches = 5 yards. The fabric is cut into two panels to make the pair, but no seams mar either side. *Note:* The workroom will likely charge labor based on every 18 inches, so even though no widths are specified, divide the finished width by 18 inches to arrive at the number of widths of labor charged to this job.

Specifying Draperies and Curtains

Specifying is the process of translating the calculation to a work order sheet. Information must be accurate and understandable, as it will be used by someone who cannot read your mind. Included here is a sample specification sheet or work order. Items required:

name of fabric

color of fabric

source of fabric (optional)

rod width (RW; optional)

finished width (FW)

returns (Ret)

finished length (FL)

cut length (CL)

pair or panel (Pr or Pan; 2 or 1)

number of widths (W)

total yardage (Ydg)

lined (yes or no)

The worksheet below is information from the examples listed above. Some design professionals use their own work order forms; others use a form developed by the workroom. Most workroom fabricators prefer to consistently use a form with which they are familiar.

Single drapery (one layer) Fabric name/color; RW 40"; FW 72"; Ret 4" ea.; FL 84"; CL 100"; W 4; Lined: yes (specify name/color).

Overdrapery Fabric name/color; RW 40"; FW 76"; Ret. 6" ea.; FL 84"; CL 100"; W 4; Lined: yes (name/color).

Sheer underdrapery RW 40"; FW 64"; Ret. 0; FL 83"; CL 99"; W Seamless/4 (labor charges); Lined: no.

Drapery hardware as selected.

DRAPERY ORDER AND WORKROOM SPECIFICATION SHEET

NUMBER:

STORE NAME:

SALESPERSON/   SALESCHECK #:

DESIGNER: DATE:

CUSTOMER'S NAME:

ADDRESS: HOME PHONE: SPECIAL DELIVERY:

CITY: WORK PHONE: APPROXIMATE DELIVERY DATE:

Top table column headers (rotated):

NUMBER | ROOM | FABRIC SOURCE OR COMPANY | FABRIC NAME | FABRIC COLOR | PAIR PANEL SHADE OR VALANCE | ROD, BOARD WIDTH | LEFT RETURN | RIGHT RETURN | FINISHED OR PLEATED WIDTH INCL. RETURNS AND OVERLAPS | CLOSE RIGHT OR LEFT OR CENTER | LINED? YES OR NO | LINING FABRIC | LINING COLOR | CUT LENGTH | FINISHED LENGTH | TYPE OF PLEAT | NUMBER OF WIDTHS | TOTAL YARDS | PRICE PER YARD | TOTAL FABRIC COST | ROD COL. AND NO | ROD PRICE

Rows numbered 1. through 10.

SPECIAL INSTRUCTIONS AND ILLUSTRATIONS:

INSTALLATION

ITEM INSTALLED	HOW MANY WIDTHS/ FEET	PRICE PER WIDTH/ FOOT	TOTAL COST
DRAPERIES & RODS			
DRAPERIES ONLY			
VALANCES & SHADES			
TIES & MISC.			

FABRICATION

ITEM SEWN	HOW MANY WIDTHS/ FEET	PRICE PER WIDTH/ FOOT	TOTAL COST
UNLINED DRAPERIES/ CURTAINS			
LINED DRAPERIES/ CURTAINS			
TIES & TRIMS			
SHADES & VALANCES			

SUBTOTALS

FABRIC COSTS, INCL. TRIM	
FABRICATION	
HARDWARE	
INSTALLATION	
SUBTOTAL	
LESS DEPOSIT	
BALANCE DUE UPON COMPLETION	

APPROVED AND ACCEPTED BY CUSTOMER:

I DO / DO NOT DESIRE INSTALLATION

SIGNATURE

Figure 10.12a Drapery order and workroom specification sheet

SPECIFICATIONS FOR:	ROOM	OVERDRAPERY	SHEER	PRIVACY	VALANCE	SHADE
Name						

Name

Address   City   State

Phone (Residence)   (Work)

Date Windows Measured   Job Sold?   Yes   Call Back

Approximate Date Draperies to be Installed

SPECIFICATIONS FOR:	ROOM	OVERDRAPERY	SHEER	PRIVACY	VALANCE	SHADE
Finished Width (FW)						
Finished Length (FL)						
Left Return (LR)						
Right Return (RR)						
No. of Widths* (W)						
Cut Length (CL)						
Fabric Company						
Fabric Name						
Fabric Color						
Fabric Width						
Trim or Banding						
Fabrication Cost						
Hardware & Cost						
Installation Cost						

	ILLUSTRATIONS AND SPECIAL INSTRUCTIONS:
Subtotal	
Tax	
Total	
Less Deposit	
Balance Due	
Sales Ticket No.	

Figure 10.12b Fabric treatment specification sheet

TOP TREATMENTS

Top treatments comprise the following categories: **valances, pelmets, swags and cascades, jabots, tabs, rosettes,** and **cornices.** Each is described below.

Valances and Pelmets

Valance is a general term for any fabric top treatment, excluding swags and cornices. Valances may be pleated, shirred, or tabbed; have a floppy or any other type of heading; or be fabricated into balloon, Austrian, or Roman shade variations and mounted onto a covered wooden board or attached to a drapery rod. If a drapery rod is selected, be aware that extended brackets are required if the valance is over a drapery. Where one or two draperies are placed beneath a valance, the valance is typically stapled or attached with hook-and-loop fasteners onto fabric-covered boards mounted to the wall or ceiling. Valances can be attached to stationary or operable draperies. They may be attached to a decorative rod or capped with a cornice.

A **pelmet** is a type of valance made of a flat piece of fabric, straight or shaped on the bottom, that is lined or interlined and, typically, mounted onto a board.

The variety of styles and options for valances is nearly endless. Inspiration for styling may come from the fabric pattern, furniture shapes, historical periods, or contempo-

Figure 10.13a French-pleated valance

Figure 10.13b Bell-pleated or scalloped-pleated (spaced) valance

Figure 10.13c Shaped valance with ground pinch pleats

Figure 10.13d Festooned valance with tabs or pleats

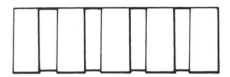

Figure 10.13e Flat shadow-pleated valance

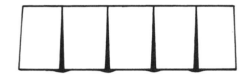

Figure 10.13f Box-pleated valance

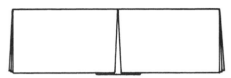

Figure 10.13g Valance with box pleat in center and layered box pleats at corners

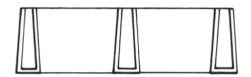

Figure 10.13h Valance or pelmet with tabs

Figure 10.13i Shaped pelmet valance with banding on the face

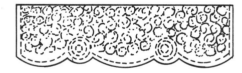

Figure 10.13j Custom-quilted shaped pelmet

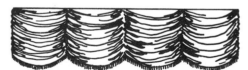

Figure 10.13k Austrian valance with trim

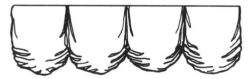

Figure 10.13l Box-pleated balloon valance

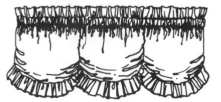

Figure 10.13m Shirred, ruffled balloon valance

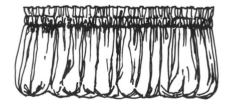

Figure 10.13n Bloused, shirred pouf valance

Figure 10.13 Top treatment valance and pelmet styles

rary creativity. When selecting a style, measuring, calculating, and ordering, here are a few points to keep in mind:

- Look to the overall theme of the interior for inspiration; select a style that is in harmony with the architecture, furniture, colors, and level of formality.
- Carefully select fabric with the level of drapability (stiffness versus softness) appropriate for the style of valance.
- Valance rod or board width is 2 inches wider than the underdraperies on each side to allow access to the drapery rods (4 inches total).
- Valance return (face to wall measurement) is 3 inches deeper than the return of any underdraperies. A valance alone or over an inside-mount alternative treatment has a return of 3 to 4 inches.
- Railroaded (horizontal) fabric may appear a slightly different color than vertical draperies beneath them. Vertical widths need seams, which may be visible.

Calculate valances and pelmets in one of two ways: as vertical cuts or railroaded, per instructions above. Unless the valance fabric is sheer, it is advisable to fully line valances, as an opaque quality is often desired to hide the rods or drapery headings beneath the valance. The rod or board width (fascia) should be wider than the draperies by 2 inches each side, if possible, to allow access to the rods beneath. If the valance is placed over a single layer of drapery, the returns are 6 inches deep; the returns are 9 inches if there is a double drapery and 12 inches if there are three projecting layers under the valance. The length should cover the pleats entirely. Valance lengths should be no less than 8 inches and no longer than about 20 inches unless circumstances dictate otherwise. Most valances are 12 to 18 inches deep. Obtain a pricing list from the selected workroom for valance fabrication styles. To price, calculate yardage, labor to sew, trimmings and labor if applicable, hardware or rods, and installation.

Balloon, Austrian, and Roman valances are calculated in the same manner as their soft shade counterparts, discussed below. Roman valances are usually flat-hobbled. Keep in mind that the workroom can help with yardage calculations, and unusual treatments will probably require a special quote for labor from the workroom. With experience, calculating yardage and labor costs will become easier and more familiar.

Swags, Cascades, Jabots, Tabs, Rosettes

This grouping of top treatment components may be combined in many ways. Such traditional top treatments are used in many interiors today. Whereas a swag can be used alone, it is more often the case that swags are coupled with a pair of cascades, with optional embellishments possible through the addition of jabots, tabs, rosettes, and passementerie. There is a tremendous variety in swags; it is advisable to review with your selected workroom the styles it prefers. Always take a sketch or photograph of the selected swag style to the workroom unless the workroom gives names to specific styles of swags it fabricates.

Traditional swags are mounted on a fabric-covered board with folds on the top or at the corners. They may be trimmed with fringe calculated at 1½ times the top width. Select a fabric with a soft hand; sheer fabrics can be made into swags and are self-lined. A swag is generally between 20 and 40 inches wide and 15 to 24 inches deep, with 34 inches wide by 18 inches deep being perhaps most typical. Traditional swags should be cut on the bias to hang nicely. They can also be cut straight—a useful tip when you want fabric (striped fabric, for example) to run vertically rather than diagonally.

To calculate swags, first determine the number desired for the treatment. In traditional symmetrical or running swags, each swag overlaps the one next to it by half the width. The best way to determine swag is to sketch the treatment with the number of desired swags; multiply the total width by 1.5 then divide by the number of swags, adjusting as necessary.

Smaller sizes require 1½ yards per face and 1½ yards for lining (3 yards for sheers), and larger sizes require 2 yards each for face and lining (4 yards for sheers).

Pole swags are constructed to expose a pole over which they are installed. Typically, that pole is wood, although metal or other types of rods may be used. Pole swags are as carefully constructed as traditional swags, and the cascades are attached via hook-and-loop fasteners (Velcro).

Scarf swags are hemmed or lined lengths of fabric, tapered on the ends, which are looped over or around a pole or swag holder and dressed into folded and swagged shapes by the installer. They may have contrasting lining and can be of any fabric that is soft and flexible. A formula for calculating yardage is as follows: Measure the desired length for each cascade. Add 20 inches for each pouf to be formed or knot tied around the rod. Measure the length of the pole or the distance between the swag holders and add 20 inches to form the swag. Graphically, the calculation looks like this:

Cascade length × 2 + number of knots or poufs × 20 inches + width of each swag + 20 inches each swag = total inches. Divide by 36 and round up to the next whole yard to obtain yardage. Add same yardage for lining.

Cascades are folded, tapered top treatments that connect to the end of swags. They cover the return and give a finished look. They can be folded to expose each fold, with a fascia 12 to 18 inches wide, or they can be stacked in a narrow fashion from 4 to 8 inches. The ends are usually ta-

Figure 10.14a Pole swag installed over a rod or dowel. The draped fabric on the sides may end in cascades, as seen here, or extend to the floor.

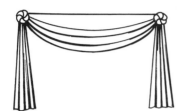

Figure 10.14d Rosette festoon or scarf swag. This may be a finger festoon with attached rosette trim.

Figure 10.14h Single swag over an asymmetrical cascade.

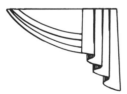

Figure 10.14i Asymmetrical cascade over a single swag.

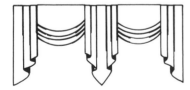

Figure 10.14m Cascades and center jabot over symmetrical swags.

Figure 10.14b A single swag, scaled for a narrow window. Pleats or tucks are on the top.

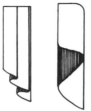

Figure 10.14e Three styles of fabric rosettes, used for trimming top treatments.

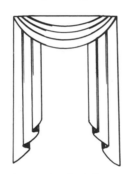

Figure 10.14f Small cascade, large cascade, and jabot with a tab overlay and fringe trim.

Figure 10.14j Single swag with long cascades beneath.

Figure 10.14n Symmetrical swags with cascade and center jabot.

Figure 10.14c Finger festoon without cascades. This may be mounted on festoon hardware or constructed as fabric over a wood cornice.

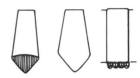

Figure 10.14g Examples of tabs used to trim or overlay top treatments.

Figure 10.14k Lifted swag over cascades. The swag would be effective even without the cascades.

Figure 10.14l Symmetrical swags with cascades and longer center swag behind.

Figure 10.14o Running swags over cascades.

Figure 10.14 Swag, festoon, and cascade top treatments.

pered to a point, although they can be squared at the point where the cascade returns to the wall. Cascade lengths vary. They can be as short as the swag—say, 15 inches—or a bit longer—36 inches, for example. They can be 60 inches long, perhaps to the windowsill, and can even take the place of side panels and reach the floor.

Jabots (zha-bow) are folded in a symmetrical fashion, with a long center point and folds graduating shorter on the sides. They are used between swags, and are typically about the length of the swag or may be longer. The lining is exposed as the folds reverse back and forth on cascades and jabots, so it must be a decorative fabric, either self-lined or

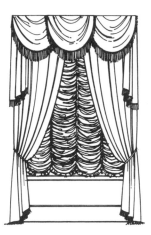

Figure 10.14p An Austrian sheer shade edged with a tiny ruffle repeats the generous depth of these formally balanced swags and cascades. Heavy fringe and deep top treatments were hallmarks of the Empire and Victorian periods.

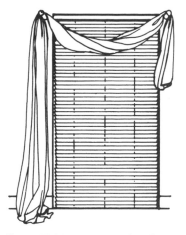

Figure 10.14q Asymmetrical scarf swag over blinds or shades.

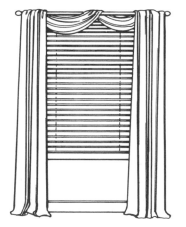

Figure 10.14r Pole swags over 2-inch blinds.

Figure 10.14s Lace fabric installed in a softly swagged top treatment over 2-inch wood blinds.

Figure 10.14t Custom swag top treatments. *Photo courtesy of Lafayette Window Fashions.*

contrast-lined. If the face fabric is patterned, the lining is typically a solid coordinating colored fabric.

To calculate yardage for cascades and jabots, each one requires a single width of fabric. If the cascade or jabot is self-lined, multiply the finished length by 2 and multiply that by the number of cascades. Divide by 36 and round up to the next whole yard. The extra inches as you round up allow for the flap attached to the top of the mounting board.

Example: Cascade finished length 48 inches × 2 = 96 inches × 2 cascades = 192 inches. 192 ÷ 36 inches = 5.33 yards. Round up to 6 yards.

For a contrast-lined pair of cascades, the example looks like this: Cascade finished length 60 inches × 2 (front of 2 cascades) = 120 inches. 120 ÷ 36 inches = 3.33 yards. Round up to 4 yards. Also order 4 yards of lining fabric. To add fringe to the front edge of a cascade, double the finished length. The trim may also be attached to the back edge of the cascade (this technique appears more finished and luxurious). For example, to trim the front only for the example above: 60 inches × 4 (2 cascades) = 240 inches. 240 ÷ 36 inches = 6.67 yards. Round up to 7 yards. 14 yards will trim both sides.

Tabs are short self-lined or contrast-lined flat fabric embellishments used between swags or where desired. They may be pointed or squared off at the bottom. They may be fringed along the bottom and carry ornaments such as rosettes, jewelry, key or small rope tassels attached to the face of the tab. The width can be doubled for the lining. Add 4 inches to the finished length to seam the bottom and add a flap to the top. More than one tab can be cut from a single width of fabric.

Rosettes are made of fabric folded serpentine-style to form a floral embellishment. Allow ½ yard per rosette or as instructed by your workroom. Other rosette styles include a fabric prize ribbon–style folded rosette where the center is a covered flat circle laid atop looped folded fabric pieces. Or a ruffle can form an edging around a covered circle, which can in turn be laid atop the folded ribbon-style fabric.

Calculations for 5 swags, each 36 inches wide, 2 self-lined cascades 40 inches long, trimmed, and a rosette atop each cascade. (*Note:* Labor to sew cascades and swags includes mounting on a fabric-covered board, ready for installation.):

1½ yards per swag × 5 = 7½ yards face fabric

2 cascades, self-lined, each 36 inches long, × 4 (front and back each) = 4 yards

2 rosettes, each ½ yard = 1 yard

fringe for 5 swags: 36 inches × 1½ each = 54 inches × 5 swags = 270 inches, plus

fringe for cascades (front only): 40 inches × 4 (2 cascades) = 160 inches

270 + 160 = 430 inches

430 inches ÷ 36 inches = 11.9 yards, rounded up to 12 yards

total decorative fabric 12½ yards, rounded up to 13 yards, × $30 per yard =$390

lining fabric 7½ yards, rounded to 8 yards, × $6 per yard = $48

labor to sew swags: 5 × $40 = $200

labor to sew cascades: $50 the pair = $50

labor to sew rosettes: $30 × 2 = $60

12 yards fringe × $30 per yard = $360

labor to sew fringe: 12 yards × $3 per yard = $36

labor to install: 91 feet (108 inches) × $5 per foot (estimate) = $45 (or minimum trip charge)

subtotal = $1,189 plus appropriate sales tax

Cornices

Cornices are solid wood top treatments, straight or shaped at the top and/or bottom. They may be stained wood but are usually upholstered—that is, layered with polyester batting and covered with fabric, including a welt or trim at the bottom edge and optional welt at the top. Options include overlaying the cornice with swags, shirring the upholstered fabric, dividing the face fabric into flat and shirred, cutouts in the cornice with fabric draped through, and so on. Consult first with your workroom to identify standard or custom styles and options that may work. Fabric should be railroaded where possible; however, remember that some patterned fabrics cannot be turned horizontally, and some fabrics appear to change color when quarter-turned.

Ordering Top Treatments

Specification sheets or worksheets are filled out for top treatments much the same as for draperies and curtains. The finished dimensions, rod or board width, finished length, long and short points where applicable, trimmings or passementerie, lining information, and any details to assure accuracy in fabrication should be sent to the workroom. Where possible, include a swatch of the fabric, and always the name, color, and source of the fabric on the worksheet. This helps prevent potential mix-ups, which can prove disastrous. It is wise to double-check the status of the order about halfway through in case problems or shortages have arisen.

Top treatments mounted onto a fabric-covered board are usually completed in the workroom, so the installer need only pick it up from the workroom—or from the designer, if the product is shipped to you.

Installation is usually charged by the running foot across the board, but the installer may charge per job, per width, or even per bracket. Take time to become familiar with and to make a retail printout of the installer's charges.

Figure 10.15a Upholstered cornice in a French Rococo style over tied-back draperies.

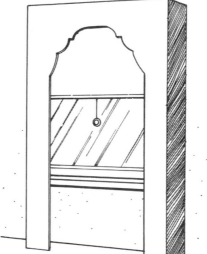

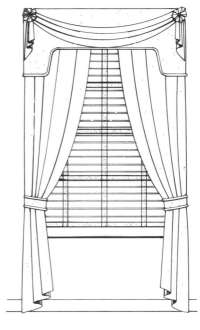

Figure 10.15c Welt-trimmed upholstered cornice with swag, cascades, and rosettes attached to the face

Figure 10.15d Custom-upholstered cornice matches wallcovering fabric. *Photo © Lafayette Venetian Blind, Inc.*

Figure 10.15 Upholstered cornices.

SOFT SHADES

Soft shades include these types, with latitude for customizing: **Austrian, Parisian, balloon** or **pouf,** and **Roman** shades. Of these, balloon or pouf and Roman shades have variations in the way they are shaped when down and as they are pulled up.

Austrian and Parisian Shades

These full, vertically gathered or shirred shades (and top treatments) are primarily used in formal settings. For light-screening requirements, they are usually made of sheer or semi-sheer fabric, and for theatrical settings, from opaque light to mediumweight fabrics.

Austrian shades are constructed by sewing vertical tapes that are then drawn up, pulling the fabric into scallops the entire length of the shade. The fullness is three times the length of the shade, so the shirred scallops are visually very rich.

Parisian shades are less precise, having a looser fold or pouf, but they are similarly gathered up and down vertically.

Both Austrian and Parisian shades can be either operable or not. Both have scalloped bottoms. Typically, the Parisian is untrimmed, but the Austrian often is edged in fringe.

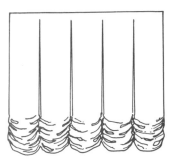

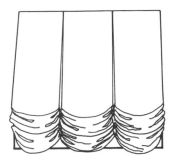

Figure 10.16a The vertical gathers of Austrian shades become fuller as the shade is drawn up. Bottom fringe is optional but commonly used.

Figure 10.16b Box-pleated pouf, balloon, or cloud shade

Figure 10.16c Large poufs with smoothly tailored box-pleated heading

Figure 10.16d Smocked heading on a fringed balloon shade

Figure 10.16e Layered shades are seen here as fringed London-style flat pouf shades or valance over "Vignette" window shadings in Satin Stripe. *Photo courtesy of Hunter Douglas.*

Figure 10.16 Custom fabric shades

Calculating for Austrian or Parisian shades is simple. Double the finished width and divide by the width of the fabric to determine the number of widths needed, and multiply the length by 3. Scalloped hems needing fringe require 1½ the width in yardage.

Example: Finished width 48 inches × 2 = 96 inches. 96 ÷ fabric width 54 inches = 1.8, or 2 widths. Finished length 60 inches × 3 = 180 inches cut length × 2 widths = 360 inches. 360 ÷ 36 inches = 10 yards decorative fabric and 10 yards lining if specified.

Trimming is 1½ times the finished width. In this example, 48 inches × 1.5 = 72 inches. 72 ÷ 36 inches = 2 yards. *Note:* Always round up; in this case, the yardage is exact. Rounding up to 3 yards, if economically feasible, allows room for error, exact placement, and greater fullness. As custom treatments are not always exact, a little extra may be needed, and running short means reordering for a longer length and wasting the original.

Balloon or Pouf Shade

Balloon or **pouf shades** are similar to Austrian shades in that they have scalloped hems that draw up from the bottom in a gathered fashion. This shade offers a less constructed look and optional headings and stringing techniques. Headings may be flat, inverted pleated, gathered with pleater tape, or shirred. Hems can be plain or trimmed with fringe or ruffles. Shades that are strung to have higher scallops in the center and longer ones on the side are sometimes referred to as *London shades.*

Calculating balloon or pouf shades begins by determining the fullness: flat, 2:1 fullness or 2.5:1 fullness (200 to 250 percent). At 200 percent, or 2:1 fullness, a 54-inch width of fabric will cover 27 inches of board, and at 250 percent, or 2.5:1 fullness, a 54-inch width of fabric will cover 21 inches of board. The number of widths of fabric is determined by dividing the finished width by 27 inches or 21 inches, respectively. Round up to the next whole width if the answer ends with 0.3 or more. Next, calculate the cut length. Measure the finished length and add at least 20 inches for the bottom gathers, or pouf. Multiply the number of widths by the finished length, and then divide by 36 inches.

Example: 36-inch board width divided by 21 inches (250 percent fullness) = 1.7, or 2 widths. If finished length is 60 inches, add 20 inches for pouf = 80 inches cut length. 80 × 2 widths = 160 inches. 160 ÷ 36 inches = 4.4 yards. Round up to 5 yards decorative fabric and 5 yards lining if specified.

Bottom hem trimming: 36 inches × 1.5 = 54 inches. 54 ÷ 36 inches = 1.5 yards. Round up to 2 yards.

Fabrication prices are usually per square foot; fabrication to sew trimming is per linear foot or yard. Board-mounted is best; installation is per linear foot to mount the board and attach a cord cleat.

Roman Shades

Roman shades are flat or horizontally folded shades that draw up by cord through rings sewn to the back. **Flat Roman shades** have seams that allow the face of the fabric to lie flat when down and to fold up accordion-style. **Pleated Roman shades** have front and back seams held in

Figure 10.17 Roman shades

Figure 10.17a Flat Roman shades

Figure 10.17b Insulated Roman shade. The look is puffy and cushioned.

Figure 10.17c–d A modestly scaled window seat and bay window arrangement is successfully treated with Castec's " Laguna Roman Shade." *Photo courtesy of Castec.*

Figure 10.17e Vignette® Waterfall Roman Shades roll up into a sleek headrail. *Photo courtesy of Hunter Douglas.*

place by the ring placement on every other pleat. **Waterfall** or **hobbled Roman shades** have looped folds on the face of the shade and fold up by overlapping the loops—except in manufactured alternative waterfall Roman shades, which fold down flat and roll up as a roller shade. **Relaxed Roman shades** have rings toward the outside so the center folds up in a slightly scalloped or loose manner. **Insulated flat Roman shades** have a layer of insulating batting, a film textile moisture barrier fabric, or reflective film and a lining. These can be fitted with magnets to seal the sides of the shade against the window frame when down and are, obviously, appropriate for cold climates.

Calculating Roman shades is done by measuring the width and adding on for hems, generally 1 to 2 inches on each side, and then dividing by the width of the fabric. The shade is flat, so there is no horizontal fullness. Flat and relaxed Romans require only 12 to 24 inches extra length for seams, whereas pleated and waterfall or hobbled Roman shades require double the length plus 12 inches. Relaxed Romans are 1½ times the finished length. Multiply the number of widths by the cut length and divide by 36 inches to obtain yardage. If a pattern is used, calculate for pattern repeat. Specify the same amount of yardage for lining.

Passementerie is typically not used, but occasionally banding is placed around the perimeter with a margin to contrast. Banding is usually cut on the bias, so the width of the banding is calculated and then doubled, and then a length at least as long as the finished length is specified for the yardage.

Example: Flat Roman finished width 30 inches divided by 54 inches = 1 width. Finished length 72 inches + 24 inches for seams = 96 inches × 1 width = 96 inches. 96 ÷ 36 inches = 2.7 yards. Round up to 3 yards decorative fabric and 3 yards lining.

Fabrication is priced per square foot. In this case: finished width 30 inches × finished length 72 inches = 2,160 square inches. 2,160 ÷ 144 square inches (per square yard) = 15 square feet. Installation is priced per horizontal heading board foot (across the top) or the minimum trip fee, whichever is greater.

Measuring for Soft Shades

Soft shades are mounted either on the window frame or on the wall, referred to as an **outside mount,** or inside the window frame, called an **inside mount.**

Specify outside mount for shades that are scalloped on the bottom that do not provide complete required privacy, for shades that take generous stacking space where the window should be fully exposed, and to give greater privacy by protecting against the **light strike,** or sliver of light on the sides of an inside-mount shade.

Specify inside mount for shades that neatly fit the shape of the window, for a privacy installation where bulk inside the room is undesirable, and for a sleek, structural appearance.

TRIMMING DRAPERIES AND CURTAINS

Window treatments throughout history have been enriched, enlivened, and made more beautiful and sometimes more easily operable through passementerie and trimmings. Although midcentury Modern, Colonial, and country styles are not trimmed, the formal styles do benefit from embellishments, which add a touch of luxury, a bonding and blending of colors and textures with other furnishings, and the mark of custom luxury that gives individuality to the room. The trend away from lavish patterns toward texture has also been a call for more trimmings. The cord, tie-back, tassel, or fringe becomes the subtle but essential decorative element that turns an ordinary window treatment into an extraordinary one. The quantity and type of trimmings is a matter of individual taste and level of appropriateness compared to interior furnishings. For draperies, top treatments, and shades with a measure of elegance or tradition, the trimmings often make the aesthetic difference. There are two categories of trimmings: passementerie and fabric trimmings.

Passementerie are hand- or machine-produced trimmings made of threads or woven into narrow strips of decorative textiles. The category includes fringe, tassels, tie-backs, cord, rope, braids, galloons, borders, rosettes, tufts, frogs, and bows. Passementerie is produced in the United States by some fine companies and is also imported from many countries, including England, France, Italy, and South Africa. Passementerie can be made of silk and very costly, but they are also made of rayon and cotton and modestly priced.

To calculate passementerie yardage, add the number of linear inches where the passementerie will be sewn, divide by 36, and round up to the next whole yard. Then multiply the total yardage by the retail cost per yard and add in the labor per yard times the total yardage. For rope or tassel tie-backs, figure the length of the cord as two-thirds the width of the drapery being tied back (or measure around the space where the tied-back drapery will be and add a few inches). Never order short on trimmings. It is far, far better to have a little left over than to run short.

The book's accompanying website (www.wiley.com/go/interiortextiles) contains an extensive glossary of passementerie. Those used specifically for window coverings include various types of fringe, tassels, tie-backs, festoons, cord, rope, braid, galloons, and borders. **Lace and apparel**

Figure 10.18 The Arthur collection, applied to drapery, is seen here as edging fringe, braid trim, and luxurious tie-back tassels on braided rope. *Image courtesy of Houlès U.S.A.*

trimmings for window treatments include pleated, plaited ribbon and edging, and lace of many types—Chantilly, Battenberg, and eyelet, for example. Buttons, belting, appliqués, and other items can be creatively incorporated into trimmings.

Ornament: Jewelry and Floral Accents

Jewelry for window treatments is made of many materials, from resin to rolled steel to seashells to costume jewelry such as beads and brooches. These can be used as or with tie-back holders, hung as pendants at the end of jabots or tabs, or be stitched or glued onto the face of the fabric. Magnets are used to secure jewelry manufactured from drapery ornamentation, which means their placement and effects can be changed as often as desired. Silk greenery and florals, and even dried flowers, can form top treatments, be looped over drapery hardware, and be used as or with tie-backs. Small objects of art from any source can be cleverly used to accent window treatments. *Advice:* Don't allow enthusiastic creativity to usurp good judgment.

Fabric trimmings include custom-fabricated ruffles, banding, and items such as rosettes. These items can be complicated to calculate for yardage and pricing for the labor to sew. As a general rule, add 1 to 2 yards for ruffles and banding and ½ yard for each rosette. Be certain to meet with the fabricator or seamstress on pricing as well as yardage requirements for ruffles, banding, and rosettes. You may need a little practice to calculate these items. Remember that banding is added in linear inches and that pricing usually must be converted to feet or yardage for fabrication. Both ruffles and banding are strips of fabric cut from the yardage. **Banding** is flat and top-stitched or fused; it is often cut on the bias to lie flat better. **Ruffles** are gathered or shirred to 2 to 3 times fullness. The amount of yardage depends on the number of strips needed and the cut width (finished width plus turn-under hem allowances).

Both passementerie and fabric trimmings can add substantially to the price of the draperies. They can also add luxury and beauty to the window treatment, giving it an exclusive, custom look. Don't be afraid to suggest trimmings to a client; trimming is often the difference that sets your designs apart from the competition. However, do use good judgment in trimming placement, color coordination, and amount. Be sure the trimming is appropriate for the level of formality and the theme of the interior—it should be both compatible and complementary. Braid, cord, gimp, and fringe are usually sewn or glued onto the drapery treatment. Banding is either sewn on or fuse-bonded with a heat-sensitive fabrication tape, and it may be layered. Ruffles vary considerably in size and the way they are applied. They can also be layered and are often added to create depth and luxury, or to sound a country or feminine note.

ALTERNATIVE OR MANUFACTURED WINDOW TREATMENTS

Alternative or **manufactured window treatments** are pleated and cellular shades, roller shades and shading products, and vertical blind vanes. Nonfabric alternatives are wood, aluminum, and vinyl blinds and wood and vinyl shutters. When alternative treatments were first introduced, they were commonly known as hard window treatments. However, in recent years, polyester textiles have been engineered into an impressive array of functional soft treatments: pleated and cellular shades and new types of roller shades and vanes for vertical blinds. These products are manufactured by an authorized fabricator according to the manufacturer's exact specifications in custom-ordered sizes. The term *alternative* evolved because they are window cov-

Figure 10.19 "Jubliance®" Roman shades, from the Designer Screen Shades collection of residential screen fabrics, offer a clean, sleek heading cassette system. *Photo courtesy of Hunter Douglas.*

erings that are neither draperies nor curtains nor top treatments.

These products are offered by national window coverings manufacturers in a number of materials, weights, colors, slat/vane widths, and options but assembled by regional fabricators with whom the designer deals directly. Generic products are also produced by some independent fabricators or distributors. Sample or product books are purchased by the design professional and are frequently updated by the manufacturer with new products or options. The alternative window treatments industry is innovative and competitive and widely known by the public because of advertising campaigns that have made some brands household names.

Alternative window treatments have a common set of advantages or qualities in addition to the unique features of each type of product. They are, in general, sleek and handsome and can fit inside or outside the window frame (see "Measuring and Ordering Alternative Treatments" below). They are easy to specify (help from the rep or fabricator is always available) and simple to install. They provide a uniform appearance from the outside, filling needs for privacy (depending on the product and options), glare control, protection against heat loss and gain (also varies), and heat/UV control for protecting not only the user but the furnishings. Once basic requirements are met, the professional can confidently design and specify creative draperies, shades, and top treatments without priority concern for their operability. Stationary or tied-back side panels, those that puddle on the floor, a host of top treatments, and nonoperable shades are all possibilities when combined with alternative window coverings.

Alternative window treatments are just that: options prior or in addition to custom soft treatments. Interestingly, the alternative treatments industry today is valued at over a billion dollars annually. Alternative treatments are mainstream, commonly used in homes and nonresidential settings around the world. They are found as products offered by architects and interior designers, window treatment retailers, paint and flooring stores, decorating and home improvement centers, through mail-order catalogs, and online. Although alternative window treatments are a highly competitive retail product, professionals who form a healthy partnership with a manufacturing fabricator and are serious about providing this product to their clientele or customers can find alternatives financially rewarding. *Note:* The manufacturer often refers to the parent or nationally known company, whereas a fabricator is a regional manufacturing plant with which the professional deals directly or through a sales representative.

Alternative treatments are specified for both home and nonresidential use. Nonresidential alternatives, in order of greatest to least use, are (1) horizontal blinds, especially mini-blinds; (2) vertical blinds; (3) pleated and cellular shades; and (4) other shading products.

The first step is to become familiar with the alternative treatments and their options. Following is brief overview of the products most commonly specified in residential and nonresidential design. Next, contact one or more manufacturers to obtain pricing and literature catalogs and sample books and to set up a dealer's resale account. Finally, find a drapery installer and make installation a part of the product/service package.

Figure 10.20a Cellular or pleated fabric shade

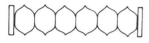

Figure 10.20b Top: pleated shade in cross section; bottom: double-pleated shade with honeycomb construction

Figure 10.20c Printed Oriental design on these pleated cellular shades provides mystique and visual interest. *Photo courtesy of Comfortex Window Fashions.*

Pleated and Cellular Shades

These shades are accordion-folded heat-set polyester fabric shades. A pleated shade is a single layer or a lined single layer and available in a variety of opacity levels and textural fabrics. Cellular shades are sometimes called *honeycomb shades* because they have a cell that increases energy efficiency. This honeycomb cell may be a single layer or smaller double or triple layers. The size of the pleat or fold varies from about ½ to 3 inches wide. As are pleated shades, cellular shades are available in a selection of fabrics that vary in weight and opacity. Options include two shades on one headrail—side by side, clutch/continuous cord loop lift mechanism, specialty shapes, track guides for angled installations, motorization or operation with a wand, as for skylights, and a traveling rail that allows two different shades to be mounted one on top of the other—so, for example, one can be sheer, the other opaque, of different colors. Some cellular shades can be fabricated so the pleats run vertically and the shade operates horizontally, opening and closing like an accordion door. This is a good option for sliding glass patio doors, for example, and other windows can be covered in the same shade fabric in the traditional up-and-down operation. Although most pleated and cellular shades are installed in residential settings, they can also meet criteria for nonresidential interiors.

Figure 10.20d Duette® honeycomb cellular shades trap air for superior energy efficiency and provide softly diffused light that cuts glare and heat. Here, the shades are combined with the Vertiglide™ hardware system, which allows the honeycomb fabric to be oriented vertically. The shade operates sideways up to 120 inches in height with no bottom rail, stacking to only 6 inches. *Photo courtesy of Hunter Douglas.*

A new innovation in cellular shades is disconnected cells that flatten to appear as blinds and give light and view, and then close to form a cellular shade appearance. These can also be stacked or drawn up to the top of the window.

Roller Shades and Window Shadings

Roller shades are made either of a vinyl roller shade material or of a stiffened or laminated designer fabric. The manufacturer's materials vary from screening material that filters light to solid, opaque fabrics that are highly energy-efficient. They can be specified regular roll, where the roll is exposed at the top, or reverse roll, where the roll is on the back of the shade so the front is smooth top to bottom. The skirt can be straight or scalloped, trimmed, and have pull hardware attached. A continuous cord loop or clutch mechanism option is superior to the pull/spring variety, which can break if the shade is pulled too hard. A clutch cord loop can stop the shade at any level.

Window shadings have been developed to combine the roller mechanism with clutch continuous cord mechanism (known by names such as Easyrise and Rollease) with innovative methods of heat-binding polyester fabrics. One sheer/privacy shading combines front and back vertical

Figure 10.21 Fabric roller and panel shades

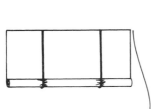

Figure 10.21a Bottom roll-up shade with exposed cords similar to those seen in bamboo shades

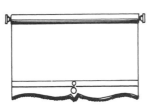

Figure 10.21b Spring-roller fabric shade with optional scalloped and trimmed hem

Figure 10.21c Insulating shade on sealed track

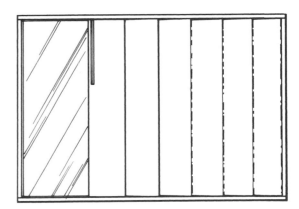

Figure 10.21d Sliding fabric panels are a cross between flat-panel shades and shoji screens. The baton, or wand, is used to draw them, one after another, across the window opening.

Figure 10.21e A roller shade from Castec's Solar Solution product line cuts down on heat and glare while allowing a spectacular ocean view. *Photo courtesy of Castec, Inc. North Hollywood, CA.*

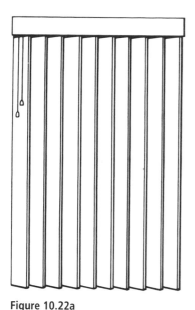

Figure 10.22a

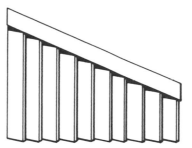

Figure 10.22b Vertical louvers are well suited for angled installation.

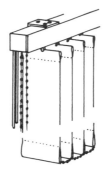

Figure 10.22c Headrail and weighted vanes.

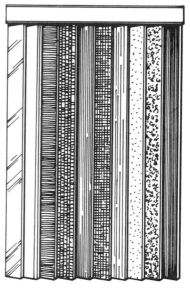

Figure 10.22d A variety of vane textures from which to choose are illustrated here.

Figure 10.22 Vertical-louver blinds open and close like draperies and may rotate 180 degrees with a separate cord or chain control.

sheer panels with slats that open and close as horizontal blinds do. The sheer fabric gives daytime privacy and screens glare while allowing a view to the outside, and, when closed flat, provides nighttime privacy and room shading. Another shading product, manufactured by a few companies, is a hobbled Roman shade created by fusing the back of each loop to a flat vertical polyester fabric. This shading product does not allow a view when the shade is down, but it is both handsome in appearance and light-diffusing; it also provides nighttime privacy.

Vertical shadings of two layers of sheer fabric and fused slats or louvers offer ease of use and maintenance. They can serve as both sheer undercurtains or draperies and privacy draperies, saving space and providing a sleek, handsome appearance.

Vertical Blinds

Vertical blinds are made of slats or vanes that are 2, 3, or, most typically, 4 inches wide. They rotate open and closed for light and glare control, and they can draw on and off the windows like a traverse drapery. They are available in wood, vinyl, or polyester, with the option of combining a vinyl slat with a polyester vane fabric, or wallpaper that slides into side channels. The polyester vanes come in a wide variety of textures, from rough and nubby to smooth and silky, and in a variety of weight and opacity levels from sun-screening to heavy. COM/custom fabrics selected to

slide into the groove should not be bulky but rather have a crisp hand or be stiffness-treated. The advantages of inserting fabric into channeled or grooved vertical blinds include the look of draperies without worry of sunlight damage or having to send them to the dry cleaner; coordinating fabrics with wall coverings or companion fabrics in a durable, alternative treatment; and ease of maintenance, as vertical surfaces collect far less dust than horizontal ones do. Vinyl or PVC blinds are energy-efficient and room-darkening.

Horizontal blinds and **shutters** are not textile treatments. Horizontal blinds are made of wood, metal, or plastic/polymer, and shutters are made of wood, engineered wood (a combination of wood and polymers to prevent warping), or plastic/polymer.

Alternative or manufactured treatments are ordered as inside or outside mounts, with specific order forms and training provided by the fabricator or manufacturer. Regional training seminars and sales representatives are available to assist the design professional in learning the details of their products and how to place orders.

SELLING WINDOW TREATMENTS

Selling window treatments is a natural part of any interior design project. To make the process as smooth and efficient as possible, this format is suggested:

1. **Assess and measure windows** — The first step is to do a walk-through to determine which windows are to be treated; assess the need for light and glare control, temperature, and sound insulation, privacy, view enhancement or camouflage; architectural and mechanical features, color, form, pattern, and textural needs; and possible manipulation of the window size appearance. Ask the client to identify needs and wants.

   Make notes and confirm findings with the client. Then measure the windows and surrounding wall space, including space to the side and above the window. You might suggest the client leave you alone for the measuring, to avoid chatting and writing down incorrect measurements.

2. **Select a style appropriate to the interior** — Select the type of window treatment — alternative treatments and/or custom soft treatments that are appropriate to the theme and level of formality in the room or room plans. Use pictures, layovers, vinyl static clings, portfolio examples, or computer program illustrations to make the style selection. Discuss and confirm the merits or advantages of the selections. Also, at this point, a budget should be established.

3. **Select fabrics, hardware, and embellishments** — Select the decorative and support fabrics, hardware, and trimmings or other embellishments. A good method is to choose, with knowledge of client preference or design parameters, about five fabric selections. With client input, narrow the list to one first choice and one alternate choice in case the first choice is back-ordered or no longer available. Giving the customer or client choices is a great way to accomplish small closes or confirm selections, which makes the final sale or confirmation of order much easier for everyone.

4. **Calculate costs: yardage, hardware, embellishments, fabrication, and installation** — Calculating by hand or even with a calculator, as shown in the examples given in this chapter, is a laborious process. Again, it is best to do this alone to avoid mistakes in figuring the retail prices. Some fabric companies with workrooms have price charts that simplify the process, and computer software programs are also available that do all the calculating for you. With practice, calculations can be completed at the site, a price quoted, and the sale closed at the same time. Some design professionals choose to take information back to calculate at the office or perhaps feel a need to do more materials research and then do a

second presentation. Certainly this latter direction should be the approach if a complete presentation, including renderings, is a part of the larger, complete interior package.

5. **Close the sale** — Asking for the order is, for some design pros, the most difficult part of the entire process of interior design. Giving the customer a choice is a great way to close the sale. Asking "Would you like to use a credit card or personal check to begin these window treatments?" makes saying "yes" much easier. Avoid words like *buy, purchase,* and *signature;* instead, replace them with *select, invest,* and *authorize* to put the customer at ease and feeling in control. You will need an authorizing signature on the sales form, confirmation of order, or sales agreement and a deposit of at least 50 percent before placing the order.

6. **Place the order** — Because, by law, a purchaser has three days to cancel a purchase agreement, it is most judicious not to place the order until the three days have elapsed and until you have cash in hand from the credit card or check. With buyer's remorse, some people have been known to put stop payments on a check without telling the design professional, and others may have insufficient funds in the account. As a general rule, the higher the price tag, the more caution you should use when ordering custom merchandise.

7. **Produce and communicate** — Production begins when the orders for window treatments have been faxed, phoned, or mailed. Fabrics can be drop-shipped to the workroom or shipped to the design/decorating company for checking first, then delivered to or picked up by the workroom. The correctness of the work order form is the responsibility of the design professional. Following through means checking with the fabric company and/or workroom fabricators to ensure timely completion of the job. When a substantial back order (longer than one or two weeks) or slowdown in production is experienced, it is wise to inform the customer to avoid frustration. Schedule the installation when the drapery job is finished and ready for installation.

8. **Install and collect balance due** — When the installer picks up the window treatments, be certain all necessary items are sent together. This means rods, accessories, and all other items needed to complete the job. It is a good idea to use a written checklist rather than to rely on memory. The installer may pick up draperies from the workroom but should still

double-check everything with you before leaving for the installation.

Some design professionals prefer to be present during the installation, although it is not always necessary. Ideally, the customer should not be in the room during installation. It makes some people nervous to see holes being drilled in their walls, and they tend to become picky or anxious as the installation proceeds. It's much nicer for everyone to invite the customer to walk into the room to see beautifully completed window treatments. The drapery installer may be instructed to collect the balance due and then return the monies to the design firm. Installers love to be paid immediately on completion; however, it is wise to make certain the job is complete by checking with the customer first.

9. **Follow up: customer satisfaction**—Placing a phone call the day after the installation is good customer service. If a problem is discovered, it should be remedied immediately. If one blind has a flaw, for example, the replacement should be ordered without delay. Occasionally a customer will refuse final payment until the job is perfect, so immediate attention to detail can be crucial for cash flow. A thank-you note sent to the customer with two or three business cards and perhaps a thank-you gift such as a gift certificate or coupon is also excellent customer service. Ask the customer for referrals at the completion of the job. Sending an additional thank-you gift for a referral who becomes a client is also a nice gesture.

PROFESSIONAL TOOLS

Window treatments are intimidating to some professionals, yet they need not be with the help of fabricators, installers, sales representatives, and seminar leaders. The many tools available for designing, measuring, and calculating make this part of interior textiles a positive and productive experience. Such tools include:

- Magnetic room planners for the residential and commercial design industry. Known in the design industry as the designer's toolbox, The Board™ Space Planning Systems are a series of interior design tools to create scaled, accurate furniture plans using graphically detailed magnetic furniture symbols.
- Measuring and calculating tools
- Style, idea, portfolio, and instruction books for creating unique and artistic window treatments
- Forms, both hard copy and on CD, for window shapes and measuring, and for ordering

- Space planning templates
- Online ordering, which is becoming more available from jobbers/fabricators
- Window treatment software programs. Features to look for in such software include:
  - Online or CD or booklet tutorial CD
  - Ability to create window treatments and fully coordinated room design with fully developed resources of style, fabric, trimmings, and hardware plus window styles and hard or alternative treatments
  - Ability to import or scan room photos and selected fabrics, color window treatments, and add passementerie
  - Ability to print, fax, or e-mail finished presentations, enlarge while maintaining integrity, and save in JPEG, TIFF, or GIF file format
  - Ability to save components separately so brochures, ads, and literature can be produced without other software editing programs
  - Software license that allows for installation on a desktop and laptop for a PC or Mac
  - Free e-mail or phone support, online forum, user-friendly features, and a money-back guarantee

LIFESPAN FACTORS AND MAINTENANCE

The average lifespan of window treatments is six to twelve years, although some people replace them only about every twenty years. Often the treatment becomes outdated and new fashion is sought before the treatment literally wears out. Lifespan factors include sunlight protection, airborne impurities, and cleaning and care.

Sunlight protection—Sunlight can deteriorate fabric window treatments through excessive heat and UV light. Ways to protect against damage include window film, exterior shading devices such as awnings, overhangs, and foliage, and lining fabric treatments.

Airborne impurities—Air that contains oil from frying or smoke can soil fabrics and weaken fibers.

Care and maintenance—Proper care and cleaning can ensure the longest possible lifespan of window treatments. Besides protecting against sunlight damage and airborne impurities, keeping the fabric clean is a protective measure. Avoid handling fabric treatments, as oil and soil on the hands are hard on draperies. See www.wiley.com/go/interiortextiles for specific suggestions for proper window treatment maintenance.

RESOURCES

Window Coverings Association of America (WCAA)

www.wcaa.org
2646 Highway 109, Suite 205
Grover, MO 63040
Tel 636-273-4090; 888-298-9222
Fax 636-273-4439

WCAA is an independent organization for window coverings retail dealers, decorators, designers, and workrooms. The goals of the association are to make available educational and motivational opportunities, to encourage a code of ethics for fair business practices, and to work for the betterment of the interior fashions industry. WCAA sponsors the Certified Window Treatment Consultant Program (CWTC), which works to enhance the knowledge and skills of window treatment specialists and certifies window treatment consultants. WCAA provides a solid foundation of product knowledge. WCAA also sponsors the Certified Workroom Professional Program (CWP), which offers both a solid foundation of knowledge geared to enhance confidence and sewing skills and continuing education.

Draperies and Window Coverings Magazine

www.dwconline.com
840 US Highway 1, Suite 330
North Palm Beach, FL 33048-3878
Tel 561-627-3393
Fax 561-694-6578
Circulation and Production
Tel 561-627-3661
Fax 561-627-3447

To-the-trade magazine for independent design professionals in the window treatments industry. It provides education and connects the professional with the industry.

Draperies & Window Coverings Custom Home Furnishings Conference & Trade Show

A division of: LC Clark Publishing
840 US Hwy One Suite 330
North Palm Beach, FL 33408
Tel 561-627-3393
Fax 561-627-3447

This conference and trade show features education, special events, and activities for fabricators, retailers, and designers.

Custom Home Furnishings Academy (CHF)

www.CHFschool.com
13900 South Lakes Dr., Suite F
Charlotte, NC 28273
Tel 800-222-1415; 704-333-4636
Fax 704-333-4639

The CHF Academy has trained thousands of people all over the world to begin a career fabricating, designing, and selling custom window treatments, fabricating bedding, pillows, slipcovers and upholstery and installing a full range of window treatments. It is also the home of the highly acclaimed Career Professional program.

DreamDraper® Evan Marsh Designs, Inc.

www.evanmarshdesigns.com
PO Box 664
Bethlehem, PA 18106
Tel 610-868-5067; 866-56-DREAM

State-of-the-art window treatment design software system.

Window Fashions Magazine

www.window-fashions.com

Fashion-forward trade magazine that sponsors events including the Window Coverings Expo and the Window Fashions Certification Program.

Window Coverings University

www.WindowCoveringsUniversity.com
Tel 888-333-8981

Training courses for understanding and sales of soft window treatments.

Figure C-1 The wallcovering on this magnificent stairway is a hand painted scenic mural "Flowers and Birds" in the Chinese style. Carpet: "Highgate Aqua."
Interior design by Scott Snyder. Photo courtesy of Stark Carpet and Wallcovering.

Figure C-2 The before image of a window to be given a fabric window treatment custom-designed by Dream-Draper® copyright by Evan Marsh Designs, Inc.

Figure C-3 The finished layered window treatment, "Jester." *Design by Nika Stewart, The Window Dresser. Designed on Dream-Draper® software. Copyright by Even Marsh Designs.*

Figure C-4 Custom shutters in this traditional home are layered with Austrian valance with tabs and cascades, edged with tassel fringe trimming. Double tie-back stationary drapery treatments pool onto the floor near the Persian Oriental rug. Fabric pattern is in the traditional Chinese vine and flower motif enhanced with a Chinese cinnabar red. Chairs are Chinese Chippendale in red-lacquered mahogany. *Photo courtesy ©Layfayette Venetian Blind, Inc.*

Figure C-5 Set against American Early Georgian walnut-stained paneling and crown molding, this single French door with transom window and recessed window with built-in window seat are expertly treated with a rich gold Georgian tied-back stationary drapery with deep folds in a high quality fabric from ADO. Drapery heading is box pleated overlaid with pencil pleats. Sheer underdrapery has a tiny single pleat and is operable. Both treatments are installed on brass designer or decorator rods. The Neoclassic armchair upholstery is an example of Late Georgian deep jade green. *Photo courtesy of ADO Corporation, www.ado-usa.com.*

Figure C-6 The valance and drapery treatment in this lavish bedroom is in "Silk Flora" color Golden and "Acolade" color Golden. Bedding fabric "Leaf Time" color Acorn lined with "Encore" color Maize, all from Carole Fabrics. Hunter Douglas Luminette® Privacy Sheers feature a sheer fabric facing backed by vertical fabric vanes that rotate, allowing the view to be retained with complete privacy with a touch of the control. *Photo courtesy of Hunter Douglas, Inc., www.hunterdouglas.com.*

Figure C-7 A tightly woven, high quality Oriental rug is often the basis for fine interior design. Here, Persian Oriental rug "Tabriz 306" from the Tabriz Collection is courtesy of David and Jay Nehouray, Caravan Oriental Rugs, www.caravanrug.com

Figure C-8 The Caravan Rug Corporation showroom with an extensive selection of Oriental rugs serves interior design professionals and clients, 8725 Wilshire Blvd., Beverly Hills, CA 90211. *Photo courtesy of David and Jay Nehouray, Caravan Oriental Rugs, www.caravanrug.com.*

Figure C-9 This London Style flat pouf shade and matching Early Georgian Queen Anne side chair upholstery is made of a high quality striped brocade ADO fabric, combining Early Georgian-scaled damask with Late Georgian/Baroque colors and wide Empire-scale stripe. *Photo courtesy of the ADO Corporation, www.ado-usa.com.*

Figure C-10 The Hunter Douglas Duolite ™ (two shade fabrics fashioned into one shade), Duette® honeycomb shades featured here are in Majestic™ semi-opaue fabric with UltraGlide® proprietary retractable cord lifting system on the lower shade portion, and on the top, Whisper Sheer fabric in PowerRise battery-powered motorization. These features assure both day and nighttime privacy for peace of mind plus ease of operation for convenience, and for hard-to-reach window treatments. *Photo courtesy of Hunter Douglas, Inc., www.hunterdouglas.com.*

Figure C-11 This hospitality flooring is Soroush Ultra-Weave Axminster carpeting, produced with infill, borders, outfill and door drops in one piece, eliminating up to 80% of seaming, reducing maintenance and increasing carpet durability. *Copyrighted and registered Soroush Custom Rugs & Axminster Carpet, www.soroush.us.*

Figure C-12 A strikingly beautiful hospitality Axminster carpet installed in the Ballroom of a Marriott Conference Center was a 1200 square yard project with less than 9 square yards waste; saving on cost, time to install and materials with stunning results. *Copyrighted and registered Soroush Custom Rugs & Axminster Carpet, www.soroush.us.*

Figure C-13 A custom carpet design taken from the "Soroush Design Book," where designs can be used with Axminster, hand-knotted or hand-tufted carpet, suitable for hospitality and residential settings. Using the design book, the procedure is as follows: upon selection of design and color palette, a full color rendering is sent for preliminary approval followed by a carpet sample for final approval. Finished carpets are ready in approximately 14–16 weeks. Here, the Soroush design was colored to the project specifications, scaled and adapted to the 20' X 20' size. *Copyrighted and registered Soroush Custom Rugs & Axminster Carpet. www.soroush.us.*

Figure C-14 This Soroush hand-tufted carpet edged with a paisley design and featuring an Empire snowflake central medallion on the ground floor of this spectacular circular staircase was given a first place International Rug Design Award. Hand-tufted carpets are extremely durable and are used in any luxury public or private settings where a quality, custom look is desired. Hand-tufted carpet can be used as an area rug, inlaid into a variety of hard surfaces or installed wall to wall. *Copyrighted and registered Soroush Custom Rugs & Axminster Carpet. www.soroush.us*

Figure C-15 Stark carpet, "Apsley Sky Blue" from the Diamond Baratta Collection. Modern Art Deco-inspired upholstery pieces are "Corazon" chairs with "Satin Provencal-Blanc" fabric. Pillow is appliquéd in the same fabric. The "Nenuphar" table features adapted French Rococo metal legs. *Photo courtesy of Stark Carpet and Furniture.*

Linens and Textile Accessories

Figure 11.1 Luxurious custom quilts, pillows, and dust ruffles coordinate beautifully with custom cornice and side draperies. Soft fabric Alouette® LightLouvers, with an elliptical, cellular shape, soften and diffuse light and tilt 180 degrees to control light, glare, and privacy. *Photo courtesy of Hunter Douglas.*

LINENS CONSTITUTE a broad category of fabrics used as bedding, toweling, table linens, and bath linens. Textile accessories are woven items, sometimes custom fabricated, that complement and add beauty and fine design detail to many interiors, primarily residential. Many types of linens are found in both contract and residential interiors.

Contract or commercial differences are found in local code or safety parameters that dictate precise quality and performance specifications for each product. It is important to recognize that the contract market is highly specialized. Specifications for textile products within each specialty are detailed and precise. For example, toweling for hospitality is based on loft and absorption, whereas healthcare toweling for surgery must be tightly woven and lint-free. Both types require high durability for frequent laundering. Manufacturers respond to requirements by fabricating high-quality textiles and testing them to be sure they meet stringent specialty criteria. Contract design professionals usually choose to become expert in one area in order to stay abreast of continually evolving criteria.

The term **institutional linens** refers collectively to textiles used in hospitality (hotels, restaurants), healthcare, correctional facilities, dormitories, and similar places where many people are temporarily or permanently housed. The term is less often used today because specialty terms have largely replaced it.

Residential linens selections have fewer restrictions and, as such, offer much greater latitude for creativity.

In bedrooms and sleeping areas, nearly all components of bedding are textile. These include mattresses, bedding components, and accessory items such as pillows, table covers, and covered screens. In dining areas, tabletop linens are used; in kitchen and bath, toweling linens and floor textiles are relevant.

The extent to which an interior design professional is involved in each of these areas varies. For some categories, such as mattresses, sheets, pillows, toweling, and bathroom rugs, the role may be purely advisory, and knowledge will augment client selections. However, custom work that involves creativity as well as technical knowledge is a part of linens and accessories—and, for some professionals, a profitable part. Custom work includes bed ensembles and accessory items, such as decorative or accent pillows, and table covers or dining tablecloths. Slipcovers are closely related to linens and accessories, as both involve placing a textile over a larger furnishing item.

MATTRESSES AND BED LINENS

Mattresses

Although mattresses, technically, are not bedding, but closer to upholstery, they are included here in the linen category. Keep in mind that when a design professional is involved in selecting mattresses for contract, specific criteria will apply. In residential settings, advice may be given, although the person who sleeps on it ultimately should make the decision which mattress to buy. Mattresses are supportive cushion units generally placed over box springs and sold as a set. For rollaway beds, foldable flat spring units support the mattress, and for futon mattresses, the base unit is the sofa itself. **Foundations,** formerly called **box springs,** are usually made of hundreds of coiled springs attached to wooden slats and a boxed wooden frame. **Ticking** is the cover fabric for mattresses and box springs. In sets, this fabric is the same, often a damask or other beautiful fabric that reflects the fashion-forward, upscale features of contemporary mattress marketing. Historically, ticking, or a **tick,** was a feather mattress and pillow casing made of sturdy cream or gray twill with navy or black stripes; the heavy fabric prevented quills from working through to the surface.

Mattress components consist of a variety of textiles. Mattresses have become a consumer-driven market based on comfort, luxury, and relief from pain and discomfort in order to produce a good night's sleep. *Choice* and *comfort* are key words in contemporary bedding. Traditional inner-spring mattresses are available in a seemingly unlimited range. Foam-core mattresses offer a wide variety of choice, including refinements to solid-core latex, new types of foam that may be constructed in laminated layers, and advanced "memory" visco-elastic foam, as well as gel mattresses, air beds, water beds, and high-tech adjustable sleep sets. Pillowtop mattresses offer an extra layer of soft cushioning, and single-sided no-flip mattresses are common. This broad spectrum encompasses attractive, high-quality alternatives.

There is no "best" mattress, as individual taste is a determining factor. In making selections, eliminate by lying down on mattresses in the retail store or showroom, paying attention to comfort, support, and space. Most people quickly find some mattresses they like and others that are less comfortable. Conduct the SLEEP Test on each mattress:

Select a mattress.

Lie down in your sleep position.

Evaluate the level of comfort and support.

Educate yourself about each selection.

Partners should try each mattress together.

Pay attention to the shoulders, hips, and lower back. If the mattress is too hard, you will experience some uncomfortable pressure.

If one-third of one's time is spent in bed, that means spending 220,000 hours over the course of an average lifetime on a mattress, the most-used piece of furniture in the home or institution. This much use encourages a routine twice-a-year rotate-and-flip check (if applicable) for visible signs of wear and tear and to evaluate if the night's sleep is as good as it was a year ago. If you experience stiffness and poorer sleep, it may be time for a new mattress. A warranty does not indicate how long to keep a mattress and foundation but rather protects the consumer from product defects. Material quality and construction determine how long comfort and support will last. Standard mattress sizes are:

Crib: 28 × 54 inches

Twin: 38 × 75 inches

Full/Double: 53 × 75 inches

Queen: 60 × 75 inches

King (Eastern King): 76 × 80 inches

California King: 72 × 84 inches

Folding mattresses are generally trifold twin-sized (38 × 78 × 4 inches) foldable units made of layered foam, such as a 1½-inch top layer of visco-elastic "memory" foam and a 2½-inch base layer of dense, resilient foam. Look for a cover made of hypoallergenic, machine-washable 100 percent cotton with a zipper and a five-year warranty.

Air mattresses are made of heavy vinyl, often with a soft suede polyester top and bottom layer. They may be inflated with an electric pump; some are attachable to an automatic power source.

Correctional facility mattresses are thin, lightweight foam pads covered with heavy-duty, durable vinyl envelope-style covers that are waterproof, tear resistant, flame retardant, bacteria resistant, and easily cleanable. They are sometimes called **prison mattresses.**

Bed Linens

Sheeting

Bedsheets are in standard sizes: crib, twin, double, queen, king, and California king. However, dimensions can vary, especially in depth. Today, mattresses are different depths; the pillowtop depth requires a deeper fitted sheet. It is best to measure the width, length, and depth of the mattress before shopping for bed sheets, and then compare the actual mattress size to the printed size on the sheet package label. An excellent way to get an accurate measurement of mattress depth is to place a stiff piece of cardboard between the mattress and box spring, place a piece of cardboard on top of the mattress, and measure the distance between the two pieces. Although manufacturer sizes may vary, and the size is before hemming, Table 11.1 of standard sizes can be helpful.

Bedsheet Terms and Types

Thread count is a number often used to indicate the quality or softness of bedsheets. Thread count is determined by the number of warp and weft threads (fine yarns) in 1 square inch of sheeting fabric. In sheets, thread count can range from 80 to 700, although most stores sell sheets with counts between 180 and 320. In general, the higher the thread count, the softer the fabric feels, but that doesn't necessarily mean the sheet will last longer.

Muslin is a sheeting fabric made of carded but not combed threads and with a thread count from 80 to 180.

Percale yarns are carded and combed. The combing process removes up to 70 percent of the bulk of the fiber, resulting in a higher-priced yarn. A thread count of 180 to 220 is most common and holds up well to wear; 230 to 280 is better, and 300 to 400 is best quality. A thread count of 320 is the average for costly high-quality percale sheeting. Higher thread counts indicate finer threads, resulting in a softer hand or feel and, usually, less pilling. Thread counts above 380 are sometimes misleading, as two threads may be twisted in a way that allows manufacturers to double the thread count. Thus, a sheet labeled "400 threads per square inch" may actually have 200 doubled threads. The hand or

feel of the sheet should reveal its true thread count, as a 400-thread fabric is lustrous and very smooth, with a soft hand.

Flannel sheets are cotton or cotton-blend sheets brushed into a light flannelette fabric that is soft, comfortable, and effective at holding in body heat.

T-sheets or **jersey sheets** are made of cotton or cotton-blend single-knit fabric, similar to T-shirt fabric. They are comfortable and soft and, when of good quality, can be long-lasting. However, snags can result in a broken knit loop that becomes a hole or run, as in nylon stockings.

Satin sheets are made with smooth, lustrous yarns in a satin weave. These sheets are smooth and silky. They are, however, prone to snags, which become unsightly. They are also slippery.

Flat sheets have selvage sides and hems at the top (about 3 to 4 inches) and bottom (about 1 inch). In the hospitality industry and military, flat sheets are used as bottom sheets because they can be tucked and folded to precision. In the residential market, flat sheets, also called *top sheets,* are usually companions to fitted bottom sheets and sold as sets or separately. The head hem is deeper and sometimes decoratively trimmed. Flat sheets are creatively used for other applications, including curtains, wall coverings, and accessories, by professionals and residential users alike.

Fitted sheets are elasticized at the edges to fit the mattress snugly. Elastic all the way around is considered the best

TABLE 11.1 BEDSHEETS AND PILLOW SIZES

Bed Size	Flat Sheet	Fitted Sheet	Pillowcases
Crib/Youth	45 × 68 inches	29 × 54 inches	Pillows not recommended for babies
Twin	66 × 104 inches	39 × 75 inches	Standard: 21 × 35 inches (use one)
Full/Double	81 × 104 inches	54 × 75 inches	Standard: 21 × 35 inches (use two)
Queen	90 × 110 inches	60 × 80 inches	Queen: 21 × 39 inches (use two, or use two standard for greater sleeping comfort)
King	108 × 110 inches	78 × 80 inches	King: 21 × 44 inches (use two)

TABLE 11.2 SHEETING FIBERS

Bedsheets or sheeting fabrics historically were cotton until the mid-twentieth century, when manufactured fibers began to be developed and blended with cotton. As there are several grades of cotton that take into account the length and quality of the cotton fibers, not all sheeting fibers and hence not all sheet qualities are identical.

Upland American cotton is the mid- to short-length cotton used in muslin and more economical percale sheeting.

Egyptian cotton, originated in Egypt, feels softer than other cottons, generates less lint, and is more durable. It is a smooth, long, high-quality fiber with a refined and luxurious feel.

Pima cotton was previously called American-Egyptian. This high-quality cotton, developed from Egyptian cotton, is grown only in the southwestern United States. The cotton is exceptionally soft, and the fibers are strong and firm.

Egyptian and pima cottons connote luxury. In the past, sheets made of those cottons were sold in high-end stores only. Now, luxury cottons are sold in most bedding stores and departments and online.

To determine the amount of cotton in sheets, read the packaging carefully. "Cotton rich" may be misleading; the actual amount of Egyptian, pima, or other cottons is probably small, and the rest of the fabric is polyester or other manufactured fibers. 100 percent cotton is often preferred. Today's all-cotton sheets are unlikely to shrink, and they wrinkle much less than in past decades. Cotton sheeting has become more popular than cotton/polyester blends in recent years as the fashion trend toward natural materials from renewable sources has affected consumer purchases.

Polyester: The most common polyester for fiber purposes is polyethylene terephthalate, or PET. This is a strong synthetic fiber that resists shrinking, stretching, mildew, abrasion, and wrinkling, and it washes easily and dries quickly. Polyester is blended with cotton for these qualities. Polyester microfibers are soft to the touch and blend into potentially luxurious sheets through processing and finishing. Cotton and polyester blends outsell cotton sheets largely because they wrinkle less and cost less.

Modal®: Sheets made of Modal do not fibrillate, or pill, and they resist shrinking and fading. They are more smooth and soft than sheets made of mercerized cotton, but they may require ironing after laundering.

Lyocell Tencel®: Lyocell is similar to cotton. It dyes well and is breathable, absorbent, and generally comfortable, smooth, wrinkle resistant, soft, strong, and durable; in fact, it is the strongest cellulosic when dry and stronger than cotton when wet. It can feel like silk or cotton.

Note: Personal choice is paramount in bedsheet selection. Some people prefer very soft sheets, and others like sheets that are somewhat crisp. It is best to be able to feel sheets before buying, keeping in mind that finishes may wash out and the fabric will become softer with use.

---

quality; elastic along the sides is a step down in quality, and elastic at the head and foot or on the corners only is the lowest. The more elastic, the more snug the fit and the more likely the sheet is to stay in place. A fitted sheet should encase the mattress and grip all four corners with just a bit of room left over.

Pillowcases are sewn on three sides with an opening at one of the short ends that is hemmed and perhaps trimmed or contrasting. Sheets come in standard and king sizes. Queen-size pillows and pillowcases are less common today.

Pillow protectors are inner pillowcases, sometimes waterproof. They fully encase the pillow and may be closed with a zipper.

Hospitality Linens

Bedspreads must meet flammability codes for hospitality. Polyester is the fiber most often specified for hospitality guest room decorative bedding.

Figure 11.2 Twill weave blankets of sustainable PLA Ingeo™ fiber. *Photo courtesy of Ingeo Fibers.*

BEDDING TERMINOLOGY

Bedding is a topic with which many people are already familiar as consumers. The following terms apply to decorative bedding components. Bedsheets are discussed separately above.

Bed drapery components are installed at the head or pillow area of the bed permanently or may be drawn to enclose the entire bed. They were used historically to retain heat and now are largely decorative.

- **Canopies** are decorative fabric elements installed near ceiling height above canopy or tester beds. They also may be suspended from the ceiling from drapery hardware. Mosquito netting or tulle is sometimes thus suspended. Canopies may be opaque, semisheer, or sheer.
- **Valances** or **pelmets** are installed around the top of tester or canopy beds, or attached to ceilings.

Bedspreads are one-piece decorative fabrics, often lined, interlined, and quilted. A bedspread covers the top of the bed and falls over the sides to the floor. Bedspreads are most likely to be a single decorative fabric with a straight hem and rounded or split corners. Most bedspreads include an extended length of fabric (14 to 20 inches) at the head called a **pillow tuck** to wrap and neatly tuck the sleeping pillows in place. The pillow tuck is optional and may not be specified when decorative pillow shams are used.

- **Throw style** — A bedspread, coverlet, or comforter style with rounded bell corners at the foot. Square corners may also be specified; these form a pointed bell corner. A throw style is a flat spread, coverlet, or comforter when laid out.
- **Contour style** — Similar to a throw style but with seams in the corners to lessen the fullness of the bell. Cover hugs the bed slightly.
- **Fitted style** — A bedspread or coverlet sewn into a boxlike shape to fit the mattress snugly. Sleek, contemporary look.
- **Split-corner style** — A fitted bedspread or coverlet with a split corner and gusset. This is a flexible style. Gussets are left out for footboards or poster beds.
- **Gusset split-corner style** — A bedspread, coverlet, or comforter style, the bottom or foot of which is cut and hemmed to expose a gusset or accommodate for a footboard or poster. The effect is flat and tailored.
- **Gusset** — A tab or small, flat panel of decorative fabric sewn into a bedspread to conceal the bed; used in split-corner style.
- **Waterfall style** — A smooth construction wherein the bedspread or comforter flows off the foot of the bed without a seam. The sides tuck under the waterfall.

- **Coverlet** — A shorter version of a bedspread ending just below the bottom of the mattress; it is used with or without dust ruffles. As the spare design of contemporary retro or midcentury modern beds have come back into fashion, coverlets are often used without a dust ruffle. A coverlet, like a bedspread, may have extra length at the top for a pillow tuck, although this is optional.

Blanket — A thick fabric that may be constructed in a number of ways, including woven, knitted, knitted fleece, tufted, needlepunched, or flocked. A blanket is used for warmth on the bed beneath a decorative cover such as a bedspread. Some blankets are covered with duvet covers to become the decorative top layer. Blankets may be woven loosely for lightweight warmth and sewn into double layers for reversible décor appearance. Blankets may also be woven with two colors, one on each side. Patterns such as classic plaids are woven, although some blankets are rotary screen–printed. Electric blankets contain insulated wires connected to a disconnectable control and cord that plugs into a wall outlet. They are washable but not dry-cleanable, which can harm the wires. Some have dual-side controls.

Comforter — Similar to a coverlet in size, a comforter is a single decorative fabric top with a solid back or decorative fabric back, when reversible. Comforters are filled with a generous fiberfill (typically polyester) batting and machine-quilted to become thick and resilient. Edges are generally hemmed or corded. The top goes just to the headboard and has no pillow tuck, as comforters are too fluffy to tuck around pillows. Decorative pillows are used with comforters. Bottom corners are generally rounded, bell-shaped, or square, particularly for reversible comforters. Comforters can be custom-made and are an important part of the custom bedding market. Comforters are also mass-manufactured and sold at retail, filled typically with 8- to 9-ounce fiberfill batting and sewn in straight squares about every 10 inches. They are typically part of ensembles sold as separate items and in **bed-in-a-bag** sets, which include a comforter, dust ruffle, fitted and top sheets, pillowcase(s), and pillow sham(s). Optional coordinated items include draperies, table covers, pillows, and rugs.

Comforters available in plain white sheeting may be called a **duvet** (French for "comforter"), although today the term *duvet* generally means a comforter cover. These comforters are filled with polyester batting, feathers or goose down, or both (a combination of 25 percent down and 75 percent feathers is common), or a newer manufactured fiber batting such as polylactic acid (PLA). They are light and very warm and offer the advantage of slipcover-like changeability.

Dust ruffle or **bed skirt** — A three- or four-sided skirt that covers the space between the top of the box spring and the floor. The purpose is to hide the underbed area from view and to keep it free of dust. There are several styles of

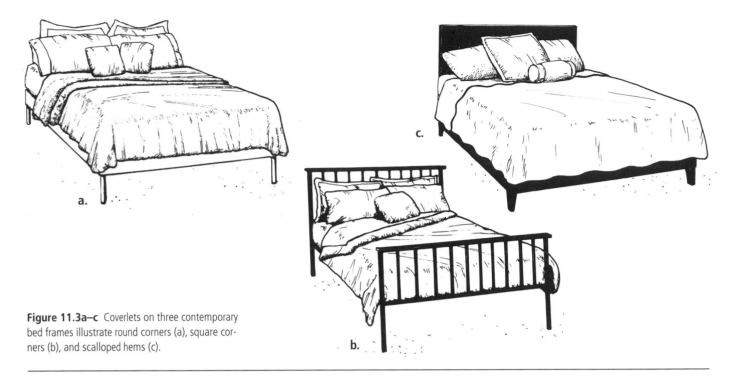

Figure 11.3a–c Coverlets on three contemporary bed frames illustrate round corners (a), square corners (b), and scalloped hems (c).

Figure 11.3d–i Coverlets and ensembles: (d) petite scalloped edge with rounded corners, (e) long square corner throw style, (f) short square corner style, (g) bell corner throw style, (h) fitted style, and (i) tucked captain or trundle bed coverlet.

dust ruffles or bed skirts. Shirred or gathered styles are the most common, followed by flat styles with box pleats of various sizes. See Figure 11-4.

Duvet or **duvet cover**—A decorative cover for a comforter. These covers were originally made for down comforters but are used also for fiberfill comforters with decorative or nondecorative covers. They can also be used over blankets. A duvet cover protects the comforter and is a way to redecorate without having to buy another comforter. Duvet covers can be changed seasonally—for example, using heavier or warmer duvet cover fabric in winter and cooler fabric in summer. They are similar to sheets sewn together and can be folded and stored in a small space. Mass-produced duvet covers are typically 100 percent cot-

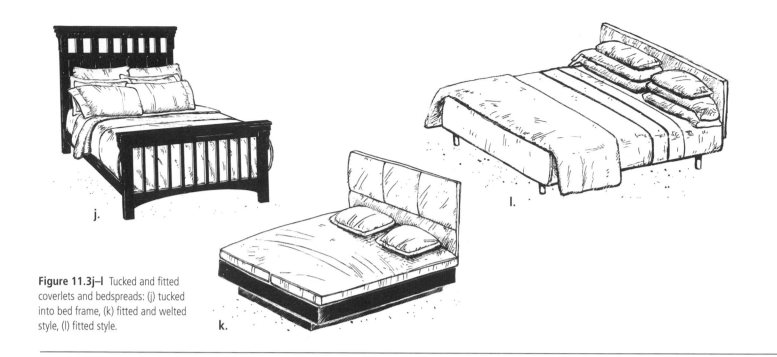

Figure 11.3j–l Tucked and fitted coverlets and bedspreads: (j) tucked into bed frame, (k) fitted and welted style, (l) fitted style.

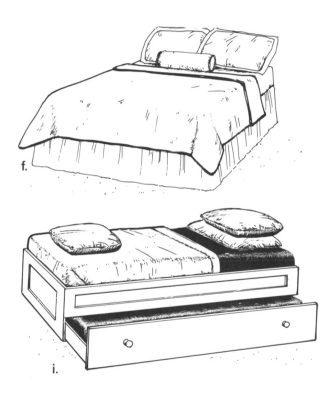

ton and machine-washable; custom-sewn duvet covers can be of any designer fabric and may be dry clean only. If the comforter it covers is down, cotton will allow the down to breathe. Duvet sizes vary by manufacturer. These sizes are general guides: twin, 68 × 88 inches; full and queen, 88 × 88 inches; king, 104 × 88 inches. Oversized duvet covers are available from some manufacturers.

Figure 11.4 This coordinating bed ensemble features square corner comforter, straight bed skirt, and flanged decorative pillows. Custom window treatments include Luminette® privacy sheers. *Photo courtesy of Hunter Douglas.*

Feather bed, feather tick, or **eiderdown** — A comforter encased in a lining fabric without a decorative cover and meant to be used in a removable duvet cover. In very cold European climates, people often sleep between two feather ticks for extra comfort and warmth.

Futon covers — Slipcovers for futon mattresses. See chapter 8.

Hem styles are the various ways the edges of decorative bedding are finished.

- **Contract hem** — The decorative face of a bedspread or comforter is folded and blind-stitched. Alternatively, the face and lining fabric are folded and matched along the folded sides in a pillowcase hem.
- **Corded hem** — A covered cord or welt, small, medium, or large. May be shirred.
- **Scalloped hem** — A semicircular shape along the sides and bottom hemline.

Mattress pads are woven or nonwoven layered and quilted pads that cover the mattress in a way similar to fitted sheets. Woven pads are considered higher in quality. Mattress pads may also enclose the entire mattress. Their purpose is to make the mattress more comfortable and to be absorbent. Some mattress pads have a waterproof bottom layer.

Mattress protectors are waterproof mattress casings that either are fitted or encase the entire mattress so both sides are protected for mattress rotation.

Mattress cushions include a variety of products placed on top of the mattress or on top of the fitted sheet to increase comfort. In Europe, eiderdown, feather beds, or feather ticks are used as mattress tops and as the mattress itself. In the United States, mattress cushions usually are placed on the mattress beneath the mattress pad and the fitted sheet.

Mattress foam cushions are of slab foam, which is a solid piece.

- **Memory foam** pads conform to body contours to relieve pressure points and provide an ergonomic fit.
- **Egg crate** foam cushions are formed in a bumpy manner, like an egg carton, to respond to the different weights of different parts of the body.
- A **wedge foam** piece is available to join two twin beds that are then topped with a king-size mattress cushion, pad, and fitted sheet to form a king-size bed.

Mattress bed pads are made of wool fibers or sheared yarns attached to a knitted or woven fabric. Similar to flokati rugs, these pads are comfortable and warm.

The **pillow tuck** is the extra length of a bedspread or coverlet that folds over and tucks under the sleeping pillow.

Pillow — See "Bed and Accessory Pillows," below.

Quilts are composite bedcovers made of a top layer, an insulating layer of wool, cotton, or fiberfill batting, and a bottom layer. The layers are secured with tiny, even quilting stitches made by hand or machine, or they are hand-tied or stitched with yarn. A quilt is used for warmth but also may serve as a decorative coverlet. Handmade quilts are often pieced or appliquéd.

- **Pieced quilts** or **patchwork quilts** have tops made of small pieces of fabric, such as printed calico, stitched together to form a single piece. In premodern eras, pieced quilts were examples of recycling, often made of scraps of fabric from outgrown or worn clothing. Both traditional and new patterns are created in pieced quilts.
- **Crazy quilts** are pieced or patchwork quilts without a pattern or design; rather, the pieces are joined in a random manner. Especially popular during the American and Victorian Empire and westward movement era, crazy quilts were made of previously used fabric scraps.
- **Appliqué quilts** are similar to pieced quilts except that small pieces of fabric are stitched onto a base cloth. Appliqué is a fiber art medium wherein many patterns and designs are created.
- **Puff quilts** are contemporary pieced or patchwork quilts made in medium-size squares stuffed individually, as in trapunto, and then stitched together. The squares are filled with a generous amount of batting, so they are puffy.
- **Friendship quilts** are pieced quilts where each square is customized by a friend as appliqué, piecework, fabric painting, photography on fabric, or embroidery. The squares are then pieced, joined, and quilted, sometimes with a variety of stitches.

Quilting is the securing together of two or more layers of fabric. Stitches often follow the pattern of the fabric or may form the pattern. See also chapter 4.

- **Hand quilting** is the joining by hand of the layers of a quilt, bedspread, or coverlet. Stitches are tiny, and as the quilter becomes accomplished, the stitches are even and consistent. Sturdy quilting thread and a relatively short needle are used to produce straight or curved lines and plain or **fancywork** of decorative stitches that form a three-dimensional pattern. Words and numbers may be quilted.
- **Hand-guided machine quilting** is used for bedspreads, coverlets, comforters, and decorative pillow shams. The two types of hand-guided machine quilting are outline quilting and freehand quilting. In **outline quilting,** the quilting loosely follows the outline

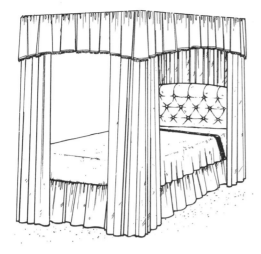

Figure 11.5a Bed draperies with shaped, shirred valance and bed skirt with tufted upholstered headboard.

Figure 11.5b Poster bed with scalloped overhead canopy and shirred bed skirt.

Figure 11.5d Ceiling-suspended sheer canopy (mosquito netting style) and flat bed skirt and feather tick bedding.

Figure 11.5e Flat wall/ceiling mounted canopy and throw style bedspread and upholstered headboard.

Figure 11.5c Headboard draperies with flat, corner-pleated valance and flat bed skirt and comforter.

Figure 11.5f Tied heading stationary bed draperies and tucked coverlet and shirred bed skirt.

Figure 11.5g Tab-heading bed draperies, stationary and puddled or pooled onto the floor.

Figure 11.5h Inverted French pleat bed draperies on sliding rings, scalloped edge on coverlet and flat bed skirt.

or shape of a bedding pattern. In **freehand quilting,** the quilting forms an artistic pattern.

- **Automated machine quilting** is computerized for mass production. A select number of patterns are used; most are simple and based on squares, curves, or ogive (sculpted onion dome) designs.
- **Trapunto** is the custom quilting of a piece that is then stuffed within the outline of the quilted area.

Sheets—See "Bedsheet Terms and Types," above.

Trimmings—Used to finish hems or as embellishment, include banding and fringe. See www.wiley.com/go/interiortextiles.

Sleeping Pillows; Bed Pillows—See below.

Throw—A blanket sized for one person and used for warmth. It is also used as an accent or accessory item on beds and upholstered pieces. It may be a plain or jacquard woven blanket, a fleece, or a crocheted or knitted afghan.

Custom Bedspreads

Custom bed ensembles have several advantages over mass-produced *stock* bedspreads or ensembles.

- Custom ensembles can be made from an almost limitless array of decorative fabrics as COM, which assures the components are one of a kind.
- Custom fabric can be of a higher quality and therefore more durable. Likewise, the thread is often of better quality.
- The style or pattern selected is likely to be the best choice for the installation.
- The client can choose the quilting pattern and type. Hand-guided machine quilting in outline makes the pattern look close to three-dimensional. The pattern may also be freehand.
- Custom measurements assure that the bed ensemble will fit perfectly.
- Fiberfill can be specified—generally a 9-ounce bonded fiberfill. This means a thicker, more luxurious cushioned effect.
- The thread can be matched to the color of the face or top of the bedspread, coverlet, or comforter rather than settling for clear monofilament or white thread.
- Higher-quality lining in white or a coordinated color or reversible designer fabric can be selected.
- Matching coordinating fabric may be used for any style of window covering, tablecloth, upholstery or slipcover, bedding, and accessory items such as pillows.

Quality Checks for Stock or Custom Bedspreads
- Quilting is lock-stitched for durability.

- Fabrics are pattern-matched and then seamed together.
- Bedspreads are framed or outline-quilted in one piece, affording total continuity of both fabric pattern and quilt design.
- Bedspreads are finished with a self-faced tape for a less bulky hemline.
- Bedspreads are fabricated with a lofty 9-ounce per running yard polyester fiberfill and tightly woven, high-count cotton/polyester backing.

Specifying Custom Bed Ensembles

As for all custom textile applications, measurements and specifications must be accurate. Even when a costly custom application is beautifully executed by skilled workroom personnel, it loses all its value if it doesn't fit the installation for which it was intended. This poses a threat to all profitability and credibility for the design professional. When in doubt, remeasure. Be thorough; take more measurements rather than fewer. Take nothing for granted.

The charts that follow are general and not intended to serve the requirements of every custom workroom or manufacturer, as these may vary. Confirm yardage charts according to the workroom's requirements before ordering fabric.

BEDSPREAD, COVERLET, OR COMFORTER MEASUREMENTS

Mattress Width (MW) _____ Mattress Length (ML) _____ Pillow Tuck (PT) _____

Bedspread Finished Length (BFL): Mattress Top to Floor _____

Coverlet or Comforter Finished Length (CFL) _____

Style (circle or explain): Round Throw, Square Throw, Contour, Fitted, Split with or without Gusset, Waterfall.

Reversible: yes/no

Hem Features (circle or explain): Straight Contract Hem, Cord, Shirred Cord, Scalloped, Ruffled, Double Ruffle, Underlay/Petticoat

Four-Poster Bed Bedspread or Coverlet Measurement will be a split corner without gusset. Decorative hems are options.

Mattress Width (MW) _____ Mattress Length (ML) _____

Bedspread Drop (BD) _____ from top of mattress to floor

Coverlet Drop (CD) _____ from top of mattress to bottom of rail

For bedspread or coverlet, also need an inside post width measurement at foot of bed from inside of post on one side to inside of post on the other side (IP) _____

Hem Features (circle or explain): Straight Contract Hem, Cord, Shirred Cord, Scalloped, Ruffled, Double Ruffle, Underlay/Petticoat

DUST RUFFLE MEASUREMENTS

Measure Drop: top of box springs to floor on both sides (may vary) (TBSB) side A _____ side B _____

Width of box springs (WBS) _____ Length of box springs (LBS) _____

For four-poster beds, also need an inside post measurement. Measure at foot from inside of post on one side to inside of post on the other side (IP) _____

Quality Checks: Luxury Dust Ruffles

- Luxury dust ruffles are completely lined.
- The foundation has matching banding on the edge.
- Shirred dust ruffles have 2½ times fullness.
- Each pleat is matched and tailored or box-pleated.

TABLE 11.3 BEDSPREAD YARDAGE

Bedspreads	Solid/Print 48-Inch Fabric*	Solid/Print 54-Inch Fabric*
Twin	8/9½ yards; same for back	8/9½ yards; same for back
Full/Double	12/13½ yards; same for back	9½ yards; same for back
Queen	12/13½ yards; same for back	12/13½ yards; same for back
King	12/13½ yards; same for back	12/13½ yards; same for back

Suggestion: Round up to whole yard. Add 20 percent more for pattern match.

OPTIONS REQUIRING ADDITIONAL YARDAGE		
Scalloped hems	Add 1⅓ yards	
Scalloped round with cord	Add 1½ yards plus 1½ yards (3 total)	
Top cord at mattress edge	Add 1½ yards	
Bottom cord at hem	Add 1½ yards	
Shirred cord at hem	Add 4½ yards	

*This chart lists yardage for solid fabrics and print fabrics in two standard widths: 48 inches and 54 inches. This is for the face (top) decorative fabric only. Yardage for lining or back is the same as for the solid yardage unless the bedspread is reversible in pattern, in which case the back yardage is the same yardage as for a print face (top) fabric.

TABLE 11.4 QUILTED COVERLET OR COMFORTER YARDAGE

Twin	8 yards; 8 yards lining
Full/Double	8 yards; 8 yards lining
Queen	15 yards; 15 yards lining
King	15 yards; 15 yards lining

Add 20 percent more for pattern match; round up to whole yard.

Note: Comforters are generally filled with a standard 9-ounce bonded fiberfill. Additional fill (up to about 14-ounce) can be added for additional charge.

Note: For reversible comforters, these limitations generally apply: Throw-style bell-shaped rounded corners only; contract hem—no cord, ruffle, scallops, or other options, as thread will not match reverse side.

TABLE 11.5 DUVET COVER YARDAGE

Duvet	Top	Back
Twin	2½ yards	2½ yards
Full/Double	6 yards	6½ yards
Queen	6 yards	6½ yards
King	9 yards	9½ yards

Note: Less yardage is required for duvets than coverlets and comforters, which are quilted. For unquilted coverlets, this duvet chart will suffice. For covered cord or other specialty trims of fabric, add 1½ yards extra fabric. For shirred cord, add 2½ yards extra fabric.

TABLE 11.6 DUST RUFFLE OR BED SKIRT YARDAGE, 48-INCH OR 54-INCH FABRIC

SHIRRED (GATHERED) AT 200–250 PERCENT FULLNESS OR BOX-PLEATED		
	Twin	6 yards
	Full/Double	6½ yards
	Queen	7 yards
	King	7 yards
	Flat/Tailored King	5 yards
	Extra-Full King	8½ yards

Note: If drop is more than 14 inches, yardage will increase. For every 20 inches around the bed, add 1½ times additional length. For example: An 18-inch drop will require 6 inches more fabric (4 inches longer than 14 inches × 1½ for every 10 inches around the bed).

BED AND ACCESSORY PILLOWS

Bed pillows come in two basic choices: natural or synthetic fill. Natural consists of feather, down, or a combination of both. Synthetic fill is most commonly polyester. These are described below. A high-quality pillow has a high thread count and should come with a warranty—and the higher the quality, the longer the warranty.

> **Standard pillows**—20 × 26-inch pillows are used singly for a twin-size bed or two for a double bed; three on a king. Many people prefer this size for sleeping.

> **Queen pillows**—20 × 30-inch pillows are used in pairs for a queen-size bed. They also may be used in the same way as standard pillows—one for twin, two for full, and three for king. There is not a queen-size pillowcase, so the standard-size pillowcase is used, with a snugger fit.

King pillows—20 × 36-inch pillows are used in pairs for either standard/eastern king and California king mattresses, although many users prefer standard pillows for sleeping and king-size pillows as decorative, sham-covered *stuffer* pillows. Pillowcases are available in king size.

Euro—26 × 26-inch square pillows are standard throughout Europe and Asia. These make excellent back pillows for reading or watching television in bed. Euro pillowcase sizes are not available in the United States, where such pillows are typically treated as accent pillows or covered with a custom pillow sham.

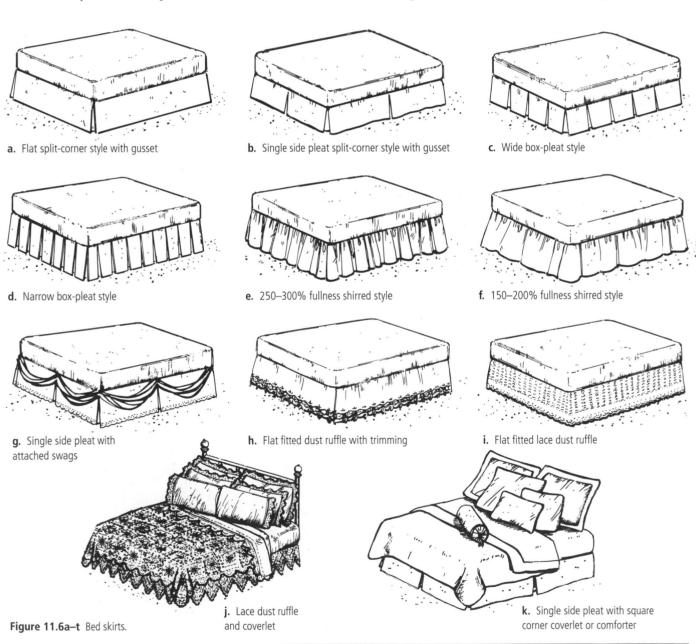

a. Flat split-corner style with gusset

b. Single side pleat split-corner style with gusset

c. Wide box-pleat style

d. Narrow box-pleat style

e. 250–300% fullness shirred style

f. 150–200% fullness shirred style

g. Single side pleat with attached swags

h. Flat fitted dust ruffle with trimming

i. Flat fitted lace dust ruffle

j. Lace dust ruffle and coverlet

k. Single side pleat with square corner coverlet or comforter

Figure 11.6a–t Bed skirts.

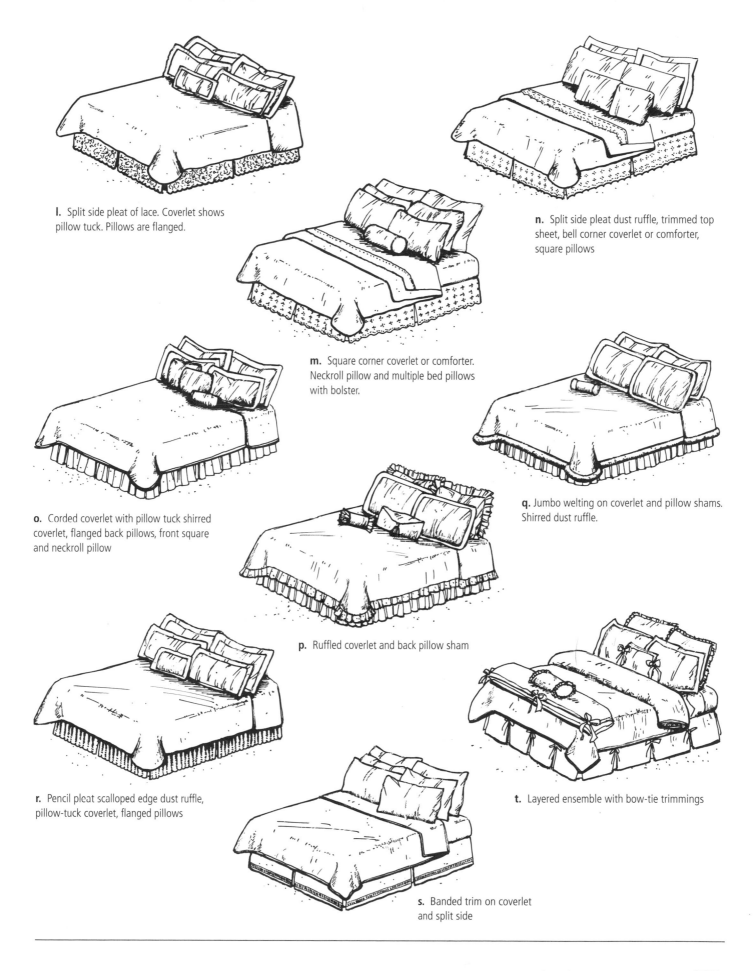

l. Split side pleat of lace. Coverlet shows pillow tuck. Pillows are flanged.

n. Split side pleat dust ruffle, trimmed top sheet, bell corner coverlet or comforter, square pillows

m. Square corner coverlet or comforter. Neckroll pillow and multiple bed pillows with bolster.

o. Corded coverlet with pillow tuck shirred coverlet, flanged back pillows, front square and neckroll pillow

q. Jumbo welting on coverlet and pillow shams. Shirred dust ruffle.

p. Ruffled coverlet and back pillow sham

r. Pencil pleat scalloped edge dust ruffle, pillow-tuck coverlet, flanged pillows

t. Layered ensemble with bow-tie trimmings

s. Banded trim on coverlet and split side

Neck roll pillows, bolsters, and French bolsters are, respectively, short to long cylindrical pillows.

Neck pillows are *U*-shaped pillows that provide neck support for reading or sleeping in a semi-reclined position.

Side sleeper pillows are *I*-shaped pillows used to support the body.

Butterfly back pillows give extra support to the lumbar and lower back when one is seated upright or reclining.

Wedge pillows are triangular pillows used to incline and support the back.

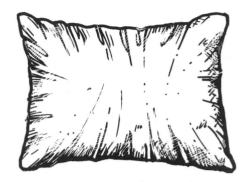

Figure 11.7d Standard, 20 × 26 inches

Figure 11.7e Lumbar or back rest, 9 × 18 inches

Figure 11.7a Small square, 14 × 14 inches

Figure 11.7f Boudoir, 12 × 16 inches

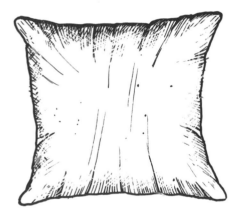

Figure 11.7b European square, 26 × 26 inches

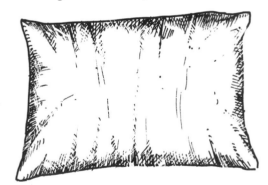

Figure 11.7g Queen, 20 × 30 inches

Figure 11.7c Continental square, 26 × 26 inches (softer form)

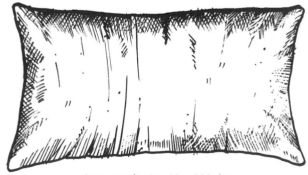

Figure 11.7h King, 20 × 36 inches

Figure 11.7a–h Square and rectangular bed pillow forms.

Figure 11.7i Neck roll, 6 × 14 inches

Figure 11.7j Bolster, 8 × 20 inches

Figure 11.7k French bolster, 8 × 34 inches

Figure 11.7l Wedge, 20 × 19 inches

Figure 11.7m Neck pillow, 19 × 20 inches

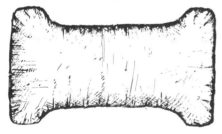

Figure 11.7n Side sleeper, 20 × 26 inches

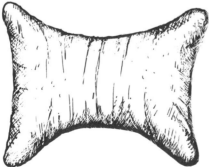

Figure 11.7o Butterfly back, 20 × 26 inches

Figure 11.7i–o Bolster and support pillow forms.

Pillow Filling Materials

Down pillows are considered soft and luxurious; they conform comfortably to head and neck. High-quality down pillows are durable and should be guaranteed (fifteen years is good). They are available in several qualities and covers, including hypoallergenic covers. Covers may be cotton or cotton/polyester with a high thread count to prevent the down from working through the tick. Down pillows are more expensive than others but may last longer and be more comfortable, so life-cycle costing may be lower than for other types of pillows.

Down and feather sleeping pillows are filled with a blend of down and feathers. A premium ratio is 25 percent down and 75 percent feathers. The ticking must be downproof, meaning the filling cannot work loose. Look for a pillow cover with a high thread count.

Hypoallergenic side-sleeper pillows are filled with fine polyester gel fibers that simulate down.

Viscoelastic memory foam pillows are available as bed pillows and neck rolls. The foam molds to the contours of the body, provides cradling support for the neck and head to relieve pressure points, and allows muscular and skeletal relaxation. A 5-pound memory foam is standard high-quality foam. Neck roll sleeping pillows of memory foam are contoured into a peanut shape to support the neck arch. Sizes: petite (about 3½ × 15 inches); standard (about 4½ × 15 inches); extra loft/large (about 5½ × 15 inches).

Polyester fiberfill pillows are made of a silicone fiber filler and a polyester or cotton/polyester tick. Synthetic varies in its level of quality, the most supportive and conforming being a poly-cluster pillow, which is most like down.

Natural latex pillows are made from pure latex rubber with no synthetic additives. They make excellent sleeping pillows.

Specialty Bed Pillows

Body pillows are extra-long pillows meant to support the entire body and to relieve pressure from the back, hips, and knees by propping up the leg and arm in a side position.

Formed specialty support pillows are generally foam pillows in a sculpted, round bolster or half-round shape; they are meant to give special support to the neck and sometimes back.

Neck roll or **bolster pillows** are made in several sizes; some offer neck support only, and others are meant as a finish element across a twin-size bed for a traditional or French neoclassic (formal or informal) styling. Bolsters may be filled with fiberfill, latex, micropellets, or natural hulls.

Lumbar pillows are portable, firm foam pillows shaped to provide lower back support for seating. They may be used at home or taken along for use in a car, at work, or in public seating areas. Lumbar pillows should have a fifteen-year warranty to hold firmness and shape.

Other Pillow Terms

Pillow shams are decorative covers for stuffer pillows. There are several styles of pillow sham; the two most common are the flat flange, which is tailored, and the ruffled style, which is more feminine. There are also two common methods for inserting the pillow: The envelope style opens in the center back by means of overlapping sides, and the zipper style opens in the back via a zipper.

Sleeping pillows are bed pillows that are not decorative but rather used for sleeping. They are placed under the pillow tuck or behind decorative pillows or shams with stuffer pillows.

Stuffer pillows are sleeping or square pillows used solely for decorative purposes so as to not become flattened. They are stuffed inside pillow shams.

Pillow protectors are zippered or envelope closure cases, generally 100 percent cotton and machine-washable. They are placed directly on the pillow to protect it, and the decorative pillowcase is placed over the protective layer.

Microfiber pellet pillows use tiny polyester pellets as filling. Generally the fabric is a soft microfiber velour. They are sometimes used as accent or massage vibrating pillows.

Quality Checks for Luxury Pillow Shams

Zipper closure; single cord between body and ruffle; 2½ times fullness on ruffles; layer of fill in flange for body; optional double cord between body and flange. No loose threads.

Accessory Pillows: Accent or Designer Pillow Forms

Although custom pillows may be stuffed by hand with chopped foam or fiberfill pellets, for example, various foam and fiberfill pillow forms are available for single or quantity purchase at retail or wholesale. For custom applications, one of a kind may be the specification. Figure 11.7 illustrates the styles, shapes, and sizes of standard pillow forms.

Accessory Pillow Styling

Custom pillows are often treated as a signature detail by residential interior design professionals. A fabric that is exquisite and costly is a small indulgence that amounts to the frosting on the cake in many upholstered furniture groupings and bed appointments. Many options from styling to trimming are possible. Custom accent pillows are a rich, detailed expression of the luxury of a space. Passementerie trimmings such as braid, gimp, tassels and jewelry, contrasting fabrics and banding, ruffles, and flanges are some of the many options in detailing custom pillows. Figures 11.8, 9, and 10 illustrate examples.

Throw Pillow Yardage

PILLOW SIZE	REQUIRED YARDAGE
14 × 14 inches	½ yard
16 × 16 inches	½ yard
18 × 18 inches	¾ yard
20 × 20 inches	1 yard
24 × 24 inches	1 yard
26 × 26 inches	1½ yards
36 × 36 inches	2 yards

TABLE 11.7 BED PILLOW AND SHAM MEASUREMENTS AND YARDAGE

	Size	Sham Front	Size	Sham Back
PILLOW SHAM MEASUREMENTS	Standard	30 × 36 inches	Standard	30 × 28 inches
	Queen	30 × 40 inches	Queen	30 × 30 inches
	King	30 × 48 inches	King	30 × 34 inches

PILLOW SHAM YARDAGE	Corded sham; no flange — 2½ yards
	Flanged sham; standard yardage — 2½ yards
	Options: Additional Yardage per Sham

Reverse sham	Add 2 yards (face 2 yards)
Reverse sham with cord	Add 2 yards
Reverse sham with scallops	Add 3 yards
Reverse sham with shirred cord	Add 2 yards plus 1 yard for shirring
Reverse sham with ruffle	Add 2 yards for reverse plus 1 yard for ruffle
Double ruffle	Add 1½ yards
Quilted sham	Add 1 yard

Envelope Back Pillow Yardage

PILLOW SIZE	REQUIRED YARDAGE
12 × 12 inches	12 × 28 inches
14 × 14 inches	14 × 32 inches
16 × 16 inches	16 × 36 inches
18 × 18 inches	18 × 40 inches

BASIC PILLOW COVER YARDAGE FORMULA

(W inches + 2 inches) + (L inches + 5 inches)

THROW PILLOW FRINGE YARDAGE

1. Measure four sides or circumference of pillow.
2. Add ½ inch to all edge measurements or 1 inch to circumference.

Note: To find circumference, multiply the diameter by 3.3.

UPHOLSTERED FOOT OR VALET BENCHES

Queen—4 yards

King—5 yards

UPHOLSTERED HEADBOARDS

Twin—4 yards

Full—4 yards

Queen—5 yards

King—6 yards

Note: Yardage may vary according to style. Consult upholsterer.

Figure 11.8a Square pillow with 1-inch ruffled trim

Figure 11.8b Rectangular pillow with 1½- to 2-inch ruffled trim

Figure 11.8c Rectangular pillow with scalloped fabric-edge trim

Figure 11.8d Cord or jumbo welt rectangular pillow

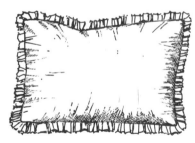

Figure 11.8e Rectangular pillow with 1-inch ruffled trim

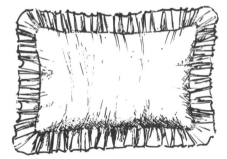

Figure 11.8f Rectangular pillow with 3-inch ruffled trim

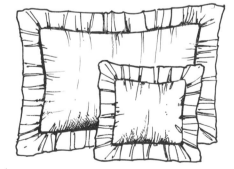

Figure 11.8g Slightly ruffled or gathered flanged pillows

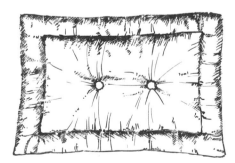

Figure 11.8h Padded flanged pillow with button tufting

Figure 11.8a–h Ruffled and flanged pillows.

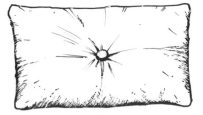

Figure 11.9a Single-button tufted pillow

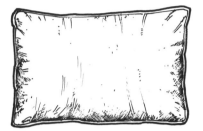

Figure 11.9b Corded knife-edge

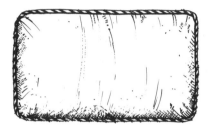

Figure 11.9c Braided cord with rounded corners

Figure 11.9d Front braid trim

Figure 11.9e Custom-embroidered pillow

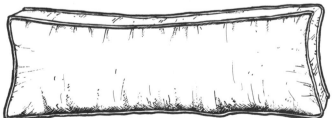

Figure 11.9f Corded box-edge extended back rest pillow

Figure 11.9g Tassel fringe trim

Figure 11.9h Decorative lace or passementerie trim

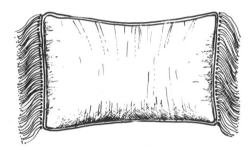

Figure 11.9i Boulle fringe on ends, cord on knife-edge perimeter

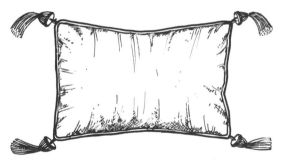

Figure 11.9j Cord and corner tassels

Figure 11.9k Box edge with braided and tassel trim

Figure 11.9a–k Decorative rectangular pillows

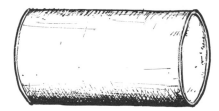

Figure 11.10a Tailored bolster with welt

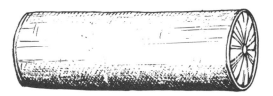

Figure 11.10b Bolster with buttoned sunburst end

Figure 11.10c Round structural pillow

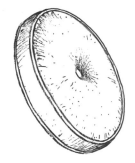

Figure 11.10d Round box-edge pillow with welt

Figure 11.10e Oval decorative fabric pillow with cord

Figure 11.10a–e Decorative bolsters and round pillows

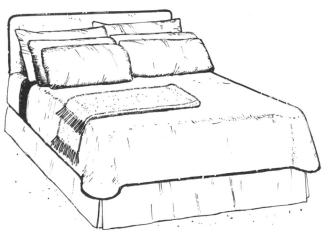

Figure 11.11a Small throw on side of bed

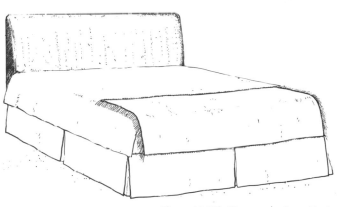

Figure 11.11b Throw across foot of bed

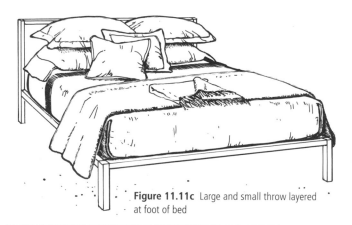

Figure 11.11c Large and small throw layered at foot of bed

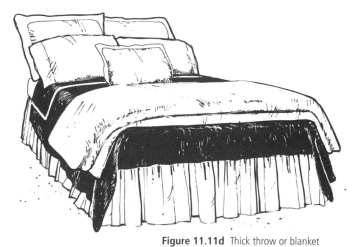

Figure 11.11d Thick throw or blanket

Figure 11.11a–d Throw blankets are used for extra warmth, for single use without other bedding, and for aesthetic accents.

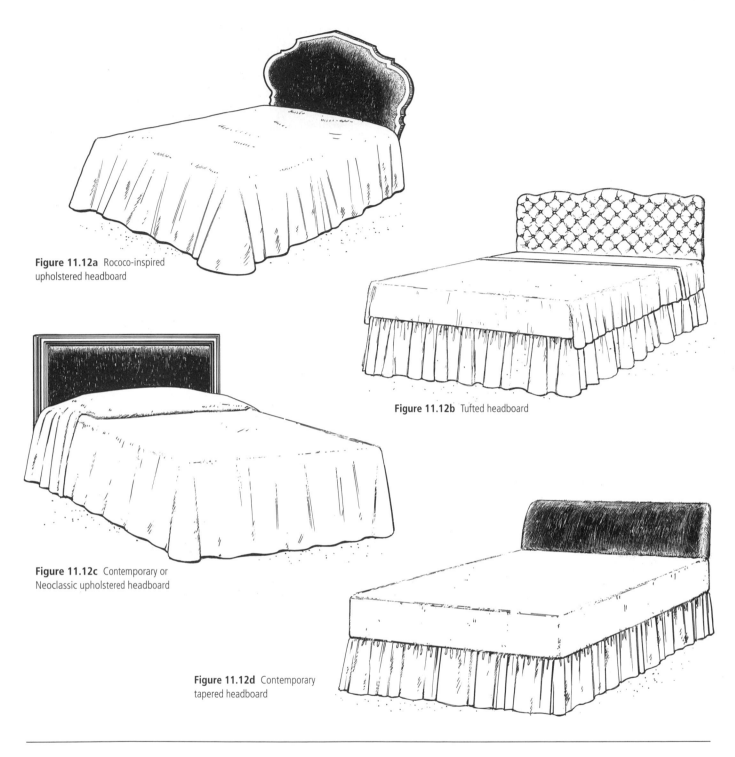

Figure 11.12a Rococo-inspired upholstered headboard

Figure 11.12b Tufted headboard

Figure 11.12c Contemporary or Neoclassic upholstered headboard

Figure 11.12d Contemporary tapered headboard

Figure 11.12a–d Upholstered headboards

Bed Draperies, Canopies, and Top Treatments

In healthcare, **cubicle curtains** are flat draperies that provide privacy for patients. These are attached to a ceiling track rod and are hand-pulled. They are made of polyester or a blend and must meet flammability codes.

In residential settings, bed draperies include straight and tied-back panels, which are specified and calculated similarly to window draperies; canopies, which cover the top of a poster or canopy framed bed or are attached to the ceiling; and valances, which are also calculated as for window top treatments.

TABLE LINENS

Hospitality Specifications

Tablecloths are used for dining and convention meeting or display tables in rounds, rectangles, and squares. In fine restaurants, **dinner napkins** are generally made of the same fabric as tablecloths. Often, restaurants feature white linen tablecloths and napkins. A white square of coated Kraft paper may be placed over tables and removed when the patron has finished dining. This saves cleaning costs and conserves water and detergent. In some restaurants, only tablecloths are used, and they are changed after each meal, if necessary. Hospitality dining and convention table linens may be polyester, polyester/cotton, or cotton. Options:

1. Select 100 percent polyester for flame resistance, stain and liquid resistance, hydrophobic quality, and machine washability and dryability with little or no wrinkling. The potential disadvantage of 100 percent polyester is its smooth, somewhat slick or hard hand, and the fact that stains are sometimes difficult to remove, as explained below.

2. Select polyester and cotton blends, predominantly polyester, for the qualities of the combined fibers. The hydrophobic (water-resisting) and oleophilic (oil-absorbing) nature of polyester may, in some fabrics, cause the fabric to hold stains; particularly if the washing does not remove the stain, the heat of the dryer will lock in or set the stain. Cotton is hydrophilic (water-absorbing), which allows the yarns to fill with water and detergent to interact with the soiling to lift the stain. Polyester as the blend fiber contributes wrinkle-free performance.

3. Select 100 percent cotton, which is preferred by many fine restaurants, for its cleanability and its pleasing hand. Preshrunk long-staple combed cotton is less likely to wrinkle than cotton that is not preshrunk.

Table skirting wraps around standard tables used for three major purposes: buffets, conference classrooms, and trade show displays. Generally made of 100 percent polyester, table skirts are typically attached to tables via Velcro-lined header, sewn to the back of the header or shirring tape heading at the top of the skirt. This fastens to Velcro table clips (clear plastic clips with Velcro outside on the table face edge—use one clip for every 12 inches of skirting to fit tables ¾-inch thick). Standard skirting sizes are 13 feet × 29 inches to fit tables 8 feet × 2½ feet, and 17½ feet × 29 inches to fit tables 12 feet × 2½ feet. Table skirts are available from manufacturers in standard colors, including dark red, cream or off-white, dark green, dark teal blue,

Figure 11.13 This linen "Pond" tablecloth has a cheerful, crisp stripe. *Photo courtesy of Libeco Home.*

and gold. These are generally clipped onto the front, sides, and sometimes back of tables covered with white or matching tablecloths.

Residential Table Linens

Table pads—Both hospitality and residential table linens include table pads. These may be made of washable polyester or blend with an elastic fitted skirt or straps, or may be a felt-backed vinyl pad. Table pads give a soft, quiet, luxurious dining experience, absorb spills, and protect the table surface.

Tablecloths—The majority of residential tablecloths are packaged factory tablecloths that come in the following standard sizes:

Round: 70 inches diameter and 90 inches diameter

Oval: 60 × 84 inches

Oblong (round corners) or rectangular (square corners): 52 × 70 inches; 60 × 84 inches; 50 × 102 inches; 60 × 118–120 inches; 60 × 140–144 inches

Such tablecloths are generally made of 100 percent polyester, 100 percent cotton, or a cotton/polyester blend. The majority of manufactured tablecloths are washable and machine-dryable, although dry cleaning is recommended. Washing tends to shrink and wrinkle some jacquard woven fabrics, causing the fabric to lose body.

Matching or coordinating napkins, placemats, and table runners are also marketed. New linens are introduced at retail each season—spring, summer, fall, and winter. Holiday themes are also a part of each season; hence, table linens can be seasonal accessory items.

Tablecloth protectors—These are sheet vinyl or plastic table covers used over tablecloths to protect against spills and stains. They are intended to show off the tablecloth while keeping it clean. This saves continual laundering and premature wear and tear on the tablecloth. Protectors may be cut to fit exact tablecloth proportions. Objections might be the artificial look and feel of dining on plastic.

Vinyl china protectors—These are zippered, top-loading quilted storage chests meant to protect delicate china from chips, dust, and damage A set of protectors might include one 7-inch saucer plate case; one 8-inch dessert plate case; one 9½-inch salad plate case; one 12-inch dinner plate case (all with cushioned dividers); one platter case, 18 × 12 × 1 inch, with foam dividers; and one cup chest, 4 × 11½ × 13½ inches, with chipboard dividers.

Table leaf storage bags—These are washable bags, about 25 × 54 inches, meant for storing and protecting table leaves from scratches.

Custom Table Linens

Tablecloths, table runners, placemats, and napkins are custom made for residential and, less often, nonresidential use. Designer fabrics (see chapter 6) may be custom fabricated to fit dining tables. Fabrics may be pretreated (chapter 5) to enhance stain release or stain resistance, or they may be laminated. When items will be laundered, they should be prewashed. This is unnecessary when the items will be dry-cleaned.

Table covers may be constructed for decorative purposes in a semipermanent application. Tables can be round, square, or rectangular. Covers can also be made for furniture other than tables—for example, sturdy wooden boxes, short shelves, or even a sturdy metal trash can with a round plywood or pressed wood circle attached to the lid. These kinds of covered items can function as storage and can be changed according to décor or season.

In calculating for rectangular tables, measure the table. Add to the width at least 12 inches for a 6-inch drop on each side (or more, if desired), plus 3 inches for hems (1½-inch double-turned hem on each side). This yields a cut or unhemmed width. If this width is over the width of the fabric (excluding selvages), then a seam at the edge of the table will be appropriate on each side and two cut lengths will be required. Lengthwise, take the measurement plus 12 inches (6 inches or more on each side for drop) plus 3 inches for hem (1½-inch double-turned hem on each side) to obtain the cut or unhemmed length. If the cut or unhemmed width requires only one width, the cut length can be divided by 36 inches to yield yardage. If the width requires two widths, double the cut length and then divide by 36 inches, keeping the pattern repeat match in mind. Always round up to the next whole yard. Prices for fabrication are separate according to workroom charges.

Round tablecloths are measured as a diameter from the floor (or finished point) up, over, and down to the floor or other finished point on the other side. Add 3 to 5 inches for hems to yield the cut or unhemmed diameter. If this measurement is more than 54 inches, a second width will be needed. However, by sketching the round table cover to scale, you may find that a full second width may not be required, depending on the size of the tabletop and the length of the skirt drop. Trimming the bottom of a round skirt is calculated in this way: diameter in inches × 3.3 divided by 36 inches = yards of trim. Often, a square of a complementary or contrasting fabric is laid over round table covers. Add 3 inches per side (for hems) to measurements to obtain the yardage requirement; the minimum is usually 1 yard.

TOWELING

Healthcare toweling—Heavy, absorbent surgical linens are used for towels and drapes. Towels must be low-linting so loose fibers do not adhere to surgical instruments. They are generally made of high-grade mercerized cotton; huck or huckaback piqué are towels designed specifically for surgical use. Sides are lockstitch-hemmed to prevent unraveling. These towels are subject to tough use, and long wear is expected. Healthcare toweling is available in white and soft versions of greens and blues. Healthcare toweling may be certified and assigned a Class I or II rating. Healthcare towels generally measure 18 × 33 inches.

Restaurant toweling—Similar to the huck style described for heathcare toweling. This general rule applies to all institutional toweling.

Terry cloth—Most bath towels and many residential kitchen towels are made of cotton terry cloth, which is a looped cut (velvet texture) or uncut pile weave in various levels of fineness, from a velvety finish to a coarse looped texture. Cotton is a highly absorbent fiber, able to absorb up to 27 times its own weight in water, and it can be sanitized without damage in very hot water using strong bleach and detergent. Terry cloth's looped pile performs like very small sponges, holding water as the loops expand. Looped pile can also withstand the stress of rubbing, pulling, twisting, and tugging. Loosely twisted loops are softer and more absorbent than tightly twisted loops, and long pile is more absorbent than short pile. Terry cloth is most absorbent when it has loops on both sides. A velvet (cut) surface is perceived to be more luxurious, although it is less absorbent. Bath towels may be customized with applied strips of fabric sewn at or on each end in a designer fabric. The fabric must be machine washed and dried before application to prevent shrinking and crocking.

Piqué weave toweling—An important kitchen toweling fabric. It is a three-dimensional weave that includes huckaback or bird's-eye, generally woven of high-grade 100 percent cotton for both institutional and residential use.

Hot pads, oven mitts, and toweling—These items are often sold as coordinated sets featuring a seasonal or thematic designer look. Many style choices are available.

Shower Curtains

Hospitality shower curtains are generally a high-grade vinyl, although in luxury settings they may also be overlaid with designer fabrics. Residential shower curtains are available as machine-washable vinyl products and in machine-washable polyester fabrics. The standard shower curtain size is 70 inches wide by 72 inches in height.

Shower curtain liners are available in several grades. A high-quality hotel fabric shower curtain liner is made of vinyl or mildew-resistant polyester with reinforced metal grommets, a weighted bottom hem, and four suction cups for anchoring the liner.

Custom designer fabric shower curtains are specified for high-end hospitality and custom residential design. They are installed either with the shower curtain liner or on a separate rod and may include decorative trimmings and valances.

OTHER TEXTILE ACCESSORIES

In addition to textile accessories such as accent blanket throws or afghans, pillows, and china protectors, other furnishing items that are made from or enhanced by fabric include the following:

Fabric-covered screens have long been a favored furnishing item. Historically used to provide privacy for changing clothes in a bedroom or multipurpose room, custom fabric screens are now used in private and social residential areas and in some custom upscale contract hospitality settings. Frames can be custom fabricated by a finish carpenter of solid wood or lath. In lath framework, the center may be filled with soundboard, fiberfill, or other material. Fabric may completely wrap the panels, or the panels may be upholstered to reveal a painted, stained, or faux-finished wood trim. Passementerie such as gimp, beadwork, or nailhead trim may be used to cover upholstery staples or provide a distinguished detail.

Licensed textile accessory items are offered to coordinate with or match sheets, toweling, or thematic designer looks. They are stock merchandise. **Custom textile accessory items** are made of COM into products such as shirred or flat trash can covers, toilet paper covers, and tissue box covers. Creativity and manufacturing capability are the only limiting factors in design and specification of custom textile accessory items.

RESOURCES

Home Textiles Today
www.hometextilestoday.com
360 Park Avenue South
New York, NY 10010
Tel 646-746-7290; 800-395-2329 (subscribe)
Fax 646-746-7300

Home Textiles Today is a weekly newspaper that covers all facets of the home textiles industry, from product announcements and personnel changes to financial and fashion news, for manufacturers, retailers, and suppliers.

National Home Furnishings Association (NHFA)
www.nhfa.org
3910 Tinsley Drive, Suite 101
High Point, NC 27265
Tel 336-886-6100; 800-888-9590

National Home Furnishings Association (NHFA) is the nation's largest organization devoted specifically to the needs and interests of home furnishings retailers. NHFA assists home furnishings retailers by providing information, education, products and services they need to remain successful.

"Home Textiles Today: The Online Business and Fashion News Source for the Home Textiles Industry"
www.hometextilestoday.com

A website that features manufacturing, retailing and executive news, quarterly results, monthly retail sales and e-catalogs.

Juvenile Products Manufacturers Association

www.jpma.org is a national trade organization for a wide range of juvenile accessories and decorative items. JPMA developed a Certification Program evidenced by their seal on product packaging to help identify safe juvenile products. JPMA sponsors the International Juvenile Products Show. The website keeps consumers, the industry, and JPMA members up-to-date and well-informed with reliable information.

Hospitality Index

www.hospitality-index.com
120 W. Grayson Street
Galax, VA 24333
Tel 276-236-1076
Fax 276-236-9568

Website featuring lists of and links to hospitality suppliers and manufacturers of products for the hospitality industry including linens.

National Sleep Foundation (NSF)

www.sleepfoundation.org
1552 K Street NW, Suite 500
Washington, DC 20005
Tel 202-347-3471
Fax 202-347-3472

NSF is dedicated to improving public health and safety by achieving understanding of sleep and sleep disorders, and by supporting sleep-related education, research, and advocacy.

Sleep Products Safety Council (SPSC)

www.safesleep.org

The Sleep Products Safety Council is a nonprofit service organization established in 1986 by the International Sleep Products Association. SPSC's mission is to provide consumer safety information, support research, and promote activities aimed at reducing hazards associated with mattresses and other sleep products.

International Sleep Products Association

www.sleepproducts.org
501 Wythe Street
Alexandria, VA 22314-1917
Tel 702-683-8371
Fax 703-683-4503

The nonprofit trade organization representing the mattress industry.

Broadloom and Modular Carpeting

Figure 12.1 This Ingeo™ fiber modular carpeting, "Cabana," utilizes repeated circular and rectilinear design elements. *Photo courtesy of NatureWorks*.

BROADLOOM CARPETING is the general term for soft floor coverings that are woven, knitted or tufted, and generally manufactured in widths of 6, 12 or 13, and sometimes 15 feet. Custom orders can be tufted or woven to specified widths. Modular carpeting or carpet tiles are typically tufted into 12- to 27-inch squares. Modular carpet squares are removable and replaceable to compensate for traffic wear patterns.

In the United States, over 70 percent of the floors in contract and residential design are covered in carpet; over 1.6 billion square yards are installed annually. Broadloom carpeting and modular carpet tiles constitute a substantial segment of the interior textiles industry. As the demand for carpeting has grown over the past half-century, soft floor coverings have gone from a luxury rarely budgeted into con-struction loans in the mid-twentieth century to a dominant current textile in contract and residential interiors. Today, tufted or woven broadloom carpet is planned into the construction budget of the majority of new buildings and homes.

To maximize carpeting performance, the first step is to decide where it will be installed; the second is to determine what type of carpet is most appropriate for the installation. With location in mind, many factors govern carpet selection; sustainability, indoor air quality, maintenance and replacement costs, and worn carpet disposal are the leading concerns in the soft floor covering marketplace. To accommodate these factors, leading carpet manufacturers are heavily invested in developing new generations of easily cleaned fibers, modular carpeting with increased durability and higher aesthetic value, materials that emit lower levels of off-gassing fumes, and options for recycling.

CARPET FUNCTIONAL FEATURES

Carpets can be a high-functioning design element, offering much practicality in contemporary lifestyles and working environments. Functional advantages include the following:

Carpets moderate temperature—Carpeting insulates against cold infiltration, resulting in warmer and more comfortable interiors. In carpeted spaces, occupants feel psychologically warmer than in rooms with hard-surfaced flooring. In hot climates or seasons, carpet offers absorption and softness underfoot, which are cooling effects. These qualities enhance energy conservation and represent thermal savings. The rate at which a material conducts or transfers heat is referred to as *heat conductivity* or *heat resistance*. The *K*-value or *K*-factor measures the rate of heat transmittance. Textiles are poor heat conductors and contribute insulative value, and therefore have low *K*-values. *R*-values or *R*-factors tell how well structures resist heat flow (how effectively they insulate). Carpeting increases *R*-value, which is determined by this formula:

R-value = thickness ÷ *K*-value

Carpeting moderates lighting—Light colors underfoot reflect natural and artificial lighting and can reduce the need for supplemental lighting, thus conserving energy consumption. Darker colors are effective in setting a serious mood, as they absorb light.

The color of carpet also determines how much energy the floor covering consumes. Lighter-colored textiles reflect high quantities of incident light waves.

Carpet refracts lighting, thereby reducing glare. This makes interiors more pleasant and increases productivity.

Carpeting absorbs sound and effectively controls acoustics—Quiet interiors are pleasanter places to work, resulting in higher employee productivity and in peace of mind both at work and in the residential environment. In offices and places of public gathering or passage, where levels of airborne and impact noise can be distressing, carpet is critical.

Cut pile, increased weight or height, separate cushions, and higher permeability (ability to trap air) enhance NRC (noise reduction coefficient). Cut pile coverings are more efficient than loop-pile coverings, at increasing permeability. Pile yarn fiber content has little or no effect on sound absorption. Concrete floors, generally used in commercial structures, are not effective in controlling impact sounds, but wood joist floors are; these are generally used in residential construction.

Carpeting enhances safety—Fewer falls take place and far less injury and damage to people and furnishings occur in carpeted interiors. Carpeting is safer than hard-surface flooring, which becomes slippery when wet, and area rugs, whose sides and corners present the dangers of tripping and falling. As carpet reduces the incidences of slips and falls, it also reduces liability.

Carpet is comfortable—The cushioned effect of carpeting—compression and resilience—reduces fatigue where people must stand or walk for long periods. Carpet resiliency reduces backaches and foot and leg problems, and it may increase productivity.

Carpet camouflages imperfections—In the remodeling market, carpeting is especially useful where flooring is imperfect, although subflooring should be properly prepared as evenly as possible. Carpet cushion or underlay is recommended for such installations.

Carpeting enhances accessibility—Low, dense pile decreases slipping for people who use crutches or canes, where the body weight shifts with swing-through movement. Direct glue-down is preferred for wheelchair accessibility to prevent shearing, where carpet and underlay cushion move in opposite directions, resulting in drag on the wheels and carpet rippling or warping. Slight changes in texture can be useful to people with sight impairments, and limited-vision users may be helped with bright colors where stairs or hallways begin, for example. The Americans with Disabilities Act (ADA), which applies to public, government, commercial, and employment facilities, specifies that carpet or modular carpet tile be level loop, textured loop, level

TABLE 12.1 APPROXIMATE *R*-VALUES FOR MANUFACTURED FIBER CARPETS	
R-Value	Carpet Thickness
0.6	⅛ inch
1.0	¼ inch
1.4	½ inch
1.8	¾ inch
2.2	1 inch

Note: For wool carpets, multiply *R*-value by 1.5.

cut pile, or level cut/uncut pile, and measure ½ inch (13 mm) or less from the bottom of the tuft. Carpet is to be securely attached; have a firm cushion, pad, or backing, or no cushion or pad. Exposed edges should be fastened to floor surfaces with trim along the edge. No trim is required if carpet pile is ¼ inch thick or less. A height change of more than ½ inch requires a ramp. These design features are also helpful for accessible and transgenerational (aging in place) residential facilities.

Carpet hides wear and soiling—Soft floor coverings that feature sturdy contract-level construction, textured pile, variable color, and pattern are effective at hiding wear and soiling, and thus extend the physical and aesthetic life of the carpet. For example, patterned carpets are practical at camouflaging food particles, spills, and traffic patterns in restaurants, whereas plain carpeting readily reveals soiling, which negatively affects business. As worn or soiled carpets diminish the aesthetic and functional quality of interior spaces, careful selection is imperative to avoid frequent replacement.

Carpet is easy to maintain—Maintenance includes regular vacuuming, spot cleaning, and deep cleaning when required. Overall, carpet is easier to maintain than many hard surfaces, thanks to excellent vacuum cleaners and deep cleaning equipment. See "Textile Maintenance" on www.wiley.com/go/interiortextiles for extensive carpet maintenance information.

CARPET AS DESIGN ELEMENT

Soft floor coverings are among the most powerful tools used to create well-designed spaces. The visual impact of carpet color, pattern, and texture is pronounced due to high visibility and the sheer quantity of surface yardage. Carpet is effective in meeting the demand for aesthetically pleasing interiors. It plays several roles in contemporary interiors, yet a coherent focus in the planning stages will help ensure design success for the entire project.

Carpeting may be considered a subtle background that is undemanding and neutral. Subtle and natural earth tones or soothing, cool water colors are often selected for carpeting in corporate offices and spaces, where carpeting is a low-key yet sophisticated element. Carpeting may blend handsomely and be an equal partner with other furnishings. Custom-designed carpet may echo interior elements such as natural or faux stone textures, laminates, wallcoverings and paint, upholstery, and window coverings.

Approached from a different design angle, carpeting may be a vital and vibrant element. Highly contrasting color and dramatic patterns are visually stimulating and often beautiful. In luxury interiors and high-end residences, custom-designed carpeting bespeaks prestige and elegance. In contract settings, patterned carpet, sometimes called visual noise, motivates workers by keeping them awake, alert, and focused on the job. The contrast or change of color, design configuration, or texture can differentiate departments or areas of varying use or purpose. A strip of color can indicate a stairwell, hallway, or designated use area. In healthcare facilities, Alzheimer's patients remember color better than numbers. For example, in a retirement center or assisted-living facility, a carpet color change for each wing assists in wayfinding. Care must be taken, however, to avoid visual confusion or three-dimensional effects that can cause dizziness or reduce orientation.

Much carpeting today is so well designed that it can be a stand-alone design element. Well-chosen carpet makes a statement that impresses and psychologically prepares the user for the purpose of the visit or the direction of the work that takes place in that interior. Custom carpeting designed and shaped into a corporate logo or image via woven or printed tufted carpet establishes identity and employee unity while impressing the visitor.

Carpet design is based on color and pattern psychology. For example, in retail, carpet is often understated so the eye and mind will focus on displayed merchandise. In healthcare, neutral carpet colors promote physical healing and peace of mind. In some hospitality and resort spaces where many people congregate, high-contrast colors and vivid designs are used to create dramatic floor coverings. These luxurious and stimulating carpets help people keep moving through the facility. Advanced technology has produced beautiful offerings, many of which are revived or inspired by historical motifs (see Part III: "Period Styles"). Motifs include plaid and lattice patterns, ribbons and bows, swirling patterns, pin dots, and historical designs such as the French fleur-de-lis. Patterns in both tufted and woven carpeting may be one hue, subtly shaded hues, or tone-on-tone—variations on a single color that pop out as loop and cut yarns and as high and low loop yarns. These carpet patterns are perceived as textural interest on the floor that does not detract from patterns in upholstery, draperies, and wallcoverings.

Carpet pattern and texture have the power to enhance value perception and become a handsome contrast or complement to other furnishing elements. The vast array of subtle patterns, textures, and coloring options has made carpet a center-stage design element. Wilton and Axminster carpeting are woven with dramatic, bold contrast in unlimited pattern variety in custom configurations, shapes, and unlimited design capacity. In addition to expressing authentic and adapted historical design in prestigious interiors, woven carpet can be the canvas for new, creative design.

STOCK AND CUSTOM-DESIGNED CARPETING

Stock carpeting is manufactured and sampled and kept as **stock keeping units**, or **SKUs**. This means that a particular carpet is kept in warehouses in a *colorway* or in specific colors, ready to be cut and shipped to the site, receiving dock, or warehouse. Samples are maintained in architectural or design studios and in retail stores where selection takes place and orders are placed for a product identical to the sample. When the SKUs are depleted, the manufacturer or distributor may opt to not replace the carpet and instead discontinue it. Occasionally the carpet is a current SKU but stock is depleted and awaiting new production, or back-ordered. Dye lots may also vary for stock carpet. Woven, knitted, and tufted constructions may be stocked carpet.

For contract and high-end residential settings, Wilton and Axminster patterned carpet, discussed below, may also be accomplished as new and unique patterns in custom color combinations. In contract settings, 75 yards is usually the minimum yardage order required to custom-specify the manufacture of carpeting. Manufacturers with custom capabilities work directly with design professionals in the specification and manufacture of unique carpets that coordinate with other furnishing elements of individual projects. Design professionals work directly with the manufacturer's design team to specify custom carpets. Territory sales representatives for each of the major carpet manufacturers may be the liaison between the design professional and the manufacturer and can assist in educating, connecting working relationships, and following through on manufactured and installed product. Carpet company websites are linked through the *Interior Design Textiles* website (www.wiley.com/go/interiortextiles) to guide the user to current sales reps, with several ways to contact each. Customer service in the carpeting industry is generally excellent, as competition is highly motivating.

Color is the most flexible carpeting element, limited only by the palette selected for the installation. General rules include the use of cool, soft, neutral, or earthy colors for settings planned for quiet work or concentration. Warm colors—the red, orange, and yellow families—are stimulating and invigorating, especially when contrasted with dark, cool colors within a design or pattern. Mid-range colors are often livable and friendly and can be either warm or cool. Accents in a contrasting color enliven and give interest to a carpet color scheme. Where high traffic results in soiling and matting, particularly near entrances, color and texture together are strong allies. Both light and dark colors show soil and debris readily, while midtone/mid-range colors, particularly in patterns or variegated colors, hide soiling. Colors cannot do it all, however. Entrance mats are highly recommended to absorb tracked-in soil from the outside to about eight paces or steps in from the door. Appearance retention is a performance issue, and avoiding heavy foot traffic prevents carpet discoloration. This simple fact should influence design decisions.

Figure 12.2 This contemporary modular pattern is suitable for both residential and contract installations. The fiber is durable, highly renewable PLA Ingeo™. *Photo courtesy of Ingeo Fibers.*

CONTINUING CARPET EDUCATION

This chapter discusses the types and terminology of carpeting most often specified in interior design. In addition, contract carpets must pass flammability and other functional and aesthetic standards. These were considered in chapter 6. However, carpeting is a vast subject with continual technological development. Design professionals who specify or sell soft flooring should not only acquire basic knowledge of carpeting but also continually be learning about developments in the field. To stay on the cutting edge of product development, professionals should be in close contact with their sales representatives; attend trade shows, CEU (continuing education unit) courses, and flooring seminars; keep up with the literature; and peruse carpet manufacturers' websites. Continuing education assists in selecting the best available product for each installation, which reflects well on the design professional.

A beginning point for study of broadloom carpeting is a comparison of fibers used in its manufacture. Table 12.2 lists the major fibers and their advantages and disadvantages in broadloom carpeting as well as in handmade rugs.

Figure 12.3 This Axminster carpet with contrasting border was custom manufactured for an upscale residential installation. *Photo courtesy of Patterson, Flynn & Martin/Rosecore.*

TABLE 12.2 CARPET FIBER COMPARISON

Acrylic—Man-made fabric that is soft and lightweight, with a wool-like texture. It thus offers the appearance of wool at a lower cost. It is a weaker fiber that crushes more easily than wool. It also tends to hold oil-borne stains. It is sometimes blended with other fibers and occasionally used in bath rugs and mats.

Cotton—Natural fiber manufactured from the seeds of the cotton plant. Cotton is most often used as throw, scatter, or small area rugs, such as bath rugs and fabric rag rugs. As a pile bath rug, cotton is soft and absorbent. It dries slowly, so it requires good ventilation. Cotton is strong and cleans easily. It is used for the warp and weft of Oriental rugs and some folk rugs, such as the original dhurries. Cotton wall-to-wall carpet has two main drawbacks: It costs about $100 per square yard, and the backing is usually fixed with a highly toxic glue, although some sources offer a natural latex. Pesticides may also be a concern.

Nylon—A synthetic fiber produced from petroleum products. It is resistant to wear, abrasion, and soil, and it is easily cleaned. Nylon is resilient and withstands heavy traffic and the weight and movement of furniture. The most durable of the manufactured fibers, nylon accounts for over 90 percent of the carpets sold in America. High-quality bulked continuous-filament nylon, the most durable fiber, can be made into yarns with a pleasant hand, rivaling wool in luxury. Further, it is favorably priced. Each time nylon has undergone an engineering improvement, it is termed a new generation of nylon. Fifth-generation nylon fibers may have the following advantages over earlier generations: enhanced dyeability, which yields appealing, nongarish colors; solution dyes, which resist sunlight fading and harsh cleaning chemicals; the near or complete elimination of static electricity; a pleasant hand; inherent (solution-added) stain repellence; and excellent crush resistance.

Nylon types 6 and 6,6 are most frequently used in carpeting. The difference between the two is within the manufacturing and dyeing processes; both are excellent for contract facilities. Nylon 6 can be recycled or generated into new carpets or other products. One example is a trade name for nylon 6, eco*solution Q, utilized by Shaw Carpet Industries, which can be recycled over and over into new recycled carpeting. Pickup is guaranteed at the end of the carpet life.

Another example of excellence in nylon carpeting is Ultron® nylon fibers, labeled as EverSet Fibers™ by the Mohawk Group, which resist all anionic (acid) stains, neutral stains, color transfer from wear or abrasion, color change or bleeding, color bleed, and color loss when exposed to alkaline (high pH) solutions. EverSet carpets are cleanable with cold water. These, along with other newest-generation nylons, are typically the best fibers for contract settings.

Olefin or **polypropylene**—As an alternative to nylon, olefin/polypropelene carpets are affordable, strong, and colorfast, with a softer, more wool-like feel. Generally, this fiber produces a more pleasing aesthetic than most commercial nylons. For moderate contract traffic and for residential applications, olefin resists wear and stains. It is also used for artificial turf carpeting. It generally does not wear as long or as acceptably as nylon. Olefin/polypropylene is used where static minimizing or sunlight resistance is important. Because it is usually comparatively inexpensive, it is used where a short replacement cycle is anticipated. It is resistant to cleaning chemicals and stains.

(continued)

Polyester — Polyester carpeting is most useful in low-traffic residential areas, as it is prone to crushing and staining. Recycled carpet is made with polyester fiber from recycled plastic (soda pop or water) bottles. Although this is an ecological approach, the design professional should obtain documentation concerning the carpet's durability, lifespan, future recyclability, and ability to disintegrate in a landfill.

Rayon — Synthetic silk-like fiber made of regenerated cellulose. Historically, this fiber is used for scatter or accent rugs or as a shiny substitute for wool in domestic Oriental rugs.

Wool — A natural fiber produced from the fleece of sheep, wool is an excellent insulator noted for its softness and resilience and a compact, smooth weave with little to no nap. Because of its higher cost, it is used as a higher end fiber in custom tufted or woven carpets. For the millennia before the advent of manufactured fibers, wool was the standard of excellence against which all other carpet fibers were compared. The design professional should inquire about the length of wool carpet fibers and the warranties associated with manufactured wool carpeting. Merino fibers are half the diameter of — that is, twice as fine as — traditional carpet wool fibers. It is important to note that when a fiber's diameter is doubled, the area of its cross section is quadrupled. Thus, using a fiber twice as thick provides about four times the abrasion resistance. Many beautiful Oriental carpets (see chapter 13) are woven of yarns spun from highly lustrous, large-diameter, wavy wools. While these wools can have a gentle hand, they are also very strong. These lustrous wool carpets seem to glow and actually show off the dye colors to great advantage. This is due to the larger scales that cover their larger fiber shafts. Carpets of these fibers last longer, and hence more older carpets survive. As the fibers have greater resilience, the pile, the weave, and the design all have greater integrity and definition; there is no matting.

However, some wool carpets have stain repellent applied, and some are constructed with toxic adhesives, and stain repellents may contain formaldehyde, a potent toxin. Wool may be bleached, causing dioxin pollution, before being dyed. Also, people with sensitive skin can feel the microscopic scales on the wool fibers, which can cause irritation and rash, although wool does not create allergies per se. Some wool carpet may feel softer than others to the touch.

Note: Fibers are listed alphabetically, *not* in order of greatest to least usefulness.

Note: Nylon, olefin (polypropylene), and wool are the primary fibers used in commercial carpet. Occasionally, carpet fibers are blended. A blend is two or more fibers, with the predominate fiber listed first on the label. For example, wool may be blended with acrylic or nylon to control cost. Acrylic is softer and less resilient than wool. It also is more vulnerable to stains. Nylon blended with wool does not flex in the same way as wool, so it may cut the wool as the carpet is walked on, giving it a much shorter life.

YARNS

Yarns can be either **bulked continuous filament (BCF)**, which is texturized to increase loft and give texture, or **staple,** which are short fibers spun into yarn. **Ply** refers to one unit of yarn or to the combining and twisting of two, three, or four yarns. Finer denier yarns result in a smooth and often harder surface in loop construction, whereas bulky or lofty yarns are more appropriate for cut pile.

Yarn twist is the winding of yarn by itself or in groups of strands. The more winds or turns per inch, the tighter the twist. A rug with tighter yarn twist is less bulky and more durable. This is especially critical in cut pile to prevent the yarn ends from untwisting and matting together during use and maintenance. Twisted yarns must be **heat-set,** or taken to a high melt-point temperature and then quickly cooled. The twist then becomes relatively permanent. Heat-set yarns offer long wear and resilience.

Density is the closeness of the stitches in woven carpets. The denser the pile, the better the carpet will wear.

Gauge is the number of ends of surface yarn per inch, counting across the width of the carpet. For example, "⅛th gauge" means "eight needles per inch." This is one factor used to determine a rug's density.

Pitch is the distance between rows of tufts or woven stitches.

Pile is the combined cut or looped yarns that form the top surface of a rug. Rounded loops are called **uncut pile.** Cut loops are called **cut pile.**

Pile height refers to the depth of the yarn above the backing, from its base, where it is woven or tufted into the backing, to the tip of the loop or cut. Pile height is usually 0.19 to 1.25 inches.

Pile weight is the mass per square yard of the pile yarn, including the buried portion. In other words, pile weight is the total weight per square yard of the yarn above the backing.

Total thickness or **total height** is the pile height plus the height of the backing.

Texture is the style of surface yarn that yields visual and tactile effect. Texture is determined by three factors: whether the yarns are looped or cut, the tightness of the yarn twist, and the level or height of the yarns compared to one another. Carpet pile and texture terms are listed in Table 12.3.

TABLE 12.3 CARPET PILE AND TEXTURES

Loop construction — Carpet face or pile formed with uncut loops of yarn. Also called **uncut pile**.

Level-loop or **round wire construction** — Low, even, round, uncut loops that produce a relatively flat surface. Generally, loop carpeting is for the contract market. Level-loop texture or pile is one of the most durable surfaces, as the loops are resilient and have an inherent ability to bounce back. Thus, level loop is durable under heavy traffic.

Multilevel loop — Loops at varying levels may form a pattern or appear random. Generally durable contract carpeting.

Cut-and-loop construction — Type of construction in which a rug is formed with a combination of looped and cut yarns. This process creates many patterns. These, in combination with color, create a distinctive sculptured effect.

Level tip shear — Round loops interspersed with cut loops to form a velvet or plush texture. The contrast may form a pattern, or the surface may appear velvet-like, with the loops somewhat hidden and able to give the pile greater resilience. Textured or variegated yarns may give the impression of pattern.

Cut-pile construction — The yarn is cut as part of the production process, and the surface reveals the cut ends of the yarns. It may be smooth, as in a velvet/plush, or heavily textured, as in Saxony.

Multilevel cut-and-loop — Construction showing a high-contrast variation in pile height.

Velour — An extremely short (about 0.25 inch), dense pile, often fuse-bonded into place.

Velvet or **plush** — Short (0.625 to 0.750 inch) cut pile in a woven or tufted carpet. Originally designed to imitate the dense, short pile of Oriental rugs, a velvet or plush texture is a smooth surface similar to a freshly cut lawn. It is often solidly colored. It shows footprints, and vacuuming leaves a distinct pile lay. These are deemed luxury features, although to some they are undesirable. Velvet or plush yarns have a low twist that flares at the top, producing a smooth effect. However, it may be damaged with repeated pivoting action, resulting in shading, pooling, watermarking, or pile reversal.

Saxony — Similar to velvet in pile and density, but with more tightly twisted yarns that don't flare and thus remain thick and stable.

Frieze — Yarns are highly twisted so they do not remain parallel or upright but rather lie in several directions, creating a low shag effect. Frieze yarns obscure footprints.

Shag — A less dense deep pile (up to 1.3 inches) face yarn that lies in any direction, giving the illusion of a more dense face.

Berber — Carpets made of either natural wool or a manufactured fiber, such as nylon, that imitates the coloration of natural undyed wool — a blend of white, beige, brown, or charcoal gray. The result is a flecked yarn, fairly light in coloration, that may be woven or tufted in a looped or cut pile. Yarns are usually medium to large. The term *Berber* is often used to describe a texture, although it is a designation of the yarn itself.

Figure 12.4a A level-loop pile is made of uncut pile yarns of the same height.

Figure 12.4b Multilevel loop pile is made of uncut pile of different heights, yielding a sculpted effect.

Figure 12.4c Random-tip sheared pile features loops of different heights that are randomly cut.

Figure 12.4d Frieze pile is made of lightly twisted heat-set yarns. The grainy appearance hides dirt well.

Figure 12.4e Cut-and-loop pile forms a carved or sculptured effect.

Figure 12.4f Velvet or plush pile yarns blend together for a consistent surface appearance and a smooth cut pile.

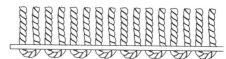

Figure 12.4g Saxony pile is similar to plush pile with cut loops, but its twisted, heat-set yarns give definition to the tufts.

From Maryrose McGowan, Specifying Interiors, *2 ed., John Wiley & Sons, Inc., 2006.*

CONTRACT CARPETING

Carpet is divided into two distinct markets: contract (commercial or nonresidential) and residential. Contract carpet is a major installation in offices, retail stores, public buildings, hospitality and healthcare facilities, and schools. For each of these, codes and criteria exist that must be adhered to by the architectural or interior design firm. Specific tests are required to assure the durability of the product. Often, the carpet manufacturer provides guidance on the best carpet within a given budget and with appropriate construction for the installation.

Contract carpet selection begins by evaluating the location of the carpeting to determine what kind of carpet will be best. Although many carpets are selected from in stock, carpet for large contract installations is often a custom-made product. **Carpet construction specifications** are documents that inform the carpet mill or manufacturer, in exact terms, the style or look of the carpet, the quantity, yarn type and size, face and overall weight, construction type, and coloring method. Dense, low-height loop-pile carpet is best for areas of heavy traffic. In areas with lighter foot traffic, cut pile can be a good choice. Loop pile, cut pile, or cut-and-loop is appropriate for moderate-traffic areas.

Figure 12.5 "Fresh Tapestry" carpet from Mohawk is an understated broadloom carpeting that meets contract specifications. *Courtesy of Mohawk Carpets, www.mohawkcarpet.com.*

Performance specifications are guidelines for carpet selection that assure acceptable appearance retention. The goal is to keep carpet looking as close to new for the longest period possible by matching the projected amount of traffic to the carpet face weight and density, or the amount of pile yarn in a measured part of the carpet. These measurements include yarn size/thickness, pile height, gauge, or stitches per inch across the carpet width, yarn size or thickness, and pile height. A fat (larger) yarn can be tufted at a wider gauge and receive the same density as a fine yarn at a small gauge. For areas where heavy foot traffic is likely, a density of 5,000 to 7,000 or higher may be necessary.

Two areas where performance specifications are high are healthcare and educational facilities. Moisture resistant or impervious backings keep spills on top of the carpet. Carpet may be vinyl-backed for areas of especially high traffic such as entrances and corridors. **Delamination** is the separation of the secondary backing or attached cushion. **Colorfastness** is the loss of color due to crocking or fading. **Static generation** is the tendency of a carpet to generate static as a person or piece of equipment moves through the facility. **Tuft bind** is the force required to pull a tuft from the finished carpeting, which can result in loss of pile in a run or strip, or in a section or area. **Wear resistance** is the ability to maintain pile bulk under repeated use.

Tests and ratings, such as the **Appearance Retention Rating (ARR)** system, identify the degree of appearance change in a carpet surface as a result of foot traffic. Tests and ratings ensure carpet products meet stringent standards. Contract carpeting lists product specification data as a *data list,* enabling design professionals to check fiber, construction type, pile/face weight, density, backing, and other features, as well as the results of tests and ratings such as those listed in chapter 6, against the new construction or refurbishing specification list. These *carpet specs,* or data list, along with the product name and color/number, constitute the manufacturer or distributor label, which is glued to the back of the sample or inside the carpet library sample folders (hardbound binders with one large and several small or all small swatches).

Chapter 6 discussed carpeting tests, including flammability, static generation, colorfastness, wear or abrasion resistance, and many other properties that determine the performance of textile floor coverings.

Contract Carpet Timeline

In contract interiors, timelines are a critical part of the design process. When selecting carpeting, a timeline such as the one suggested here is followed for both new and replacement carpeting:

TABLE 12.4 SUGGESTED PHYSICAL REQUIREMENTS OF FINISHED COMMERCIAL CARPET

Characteristic	Requirement (Based on Finished Carpet)	Test Method
Average pile yarn weight (oz/sq yd)	No less than 6%, as specified	ASTM D418, *Method of Testing Pile Yarn Floor Covering Construction*
Tufts/sq in	As specified	ASTM D418, *Method of Testing Pile Yarn Floor Covering Construction*
Pile height and/or pile height differential	As specified	ASTM D418, *Method of Testing Pile Yarn Floor Covering Construction*
Tuft bind	10.0 lbf (44.5 N) for loop pile only (minimum average value)	ASTM D1335, *Test Method for Tuft Bind of Pile Floor Coverings*
Dry breaking strength	100 lbf (44.5 N) for loop pile only (minimum average value)	ASTM D2646, *Standard Test Methods for Backing Fabric Characteristics of Pile Yarn Floor Coverings*
Delamination of secondary backing	2.5 lbf per inch (11.1 N per 25.4 mm) (minimum average value)	ASTM D3936, *Standard Test Method for Resistance to Delamination of the Secondary Backing of Pile Yarn Floor Covering*
Resistance to insects (wool only)	"Resistant"	AATCC-24, *Resistance of Textiles to Insects*
Colorfast to crocking	4 minimum, wet and dry, using AATCC color transference	AATCC-165, *Colorfastness to Crocking: Carpets—AARCC Crockmeter Method*
Colorfastness to light	4 minimum, after 40 AFU (AATCC facing units) using AATCC gray scale for color change	AATCC-16E, *Colorfastness to Light*
Electrostatic propensity	3.5 kV (maximum value) for general commercial areas, 2.0 kV (maximum value) for critical environment	AATCC 134, *Electrostatic Propensity of Carpets*
Dimensional tolerance—width	Within 1% of specifications—specifications	Physical measurements

Reprinted with permission from the Carpet and Rug Institute, *Specifier's Handbook*.

- Four months before occupancy, specifications are written for carpet and installation, and proposals are requested.
- Three months before occupancy, proposals are received and reviewed, and carpet companies' and installers' references are checked. The company and installers are selected, and the order is placed. A maintenance plan is prepared.
- Two months before occupancy, the carpet mill confirms the order and shipment date. Delivery to a warehouse or other holding site is scheduled. Installation date is confirmed.
- One month before occupancy, the shipment is confirmed and a correctness check conducted: the carpet style, pattern, and color and dye lot, as is a check for

defects, as manufacturers will not replace installed carpet. The facility is properly prepared and construction is complete. The carpet is nearly the last thing completed prior to furnishing placement. Carpet is installed according to guidelines. Ventilation for off-gassing is complete. Inspection takes place; carpet representative reviews punch list (items that need correcting or completing).

Contract Carpet Applications and Use Life

It is imperative to select carpeting that will maintain its initial appearance, providing for lower life-cycle costing. The **use life** is the number of years the carpet is used, which may be before it is physically worn out due to redesign or refurbishment. Costs factored in to determine the use-life cost or life-cycle cost include installation and removal costs, maintenance labor, and cleaning supplies, cleaning equipment, and their maintenance.

RESIDENTIAL CARPETING

Residential carpeting is installed in primary and secondary residences, apartments, and home rentals. Architectural codes generally do not apply to residential carpeting, so testing is not required. Contract carpeting is sometimes selected for durability or to meet requirements deemed important to the homeowner. Most residential carpeting is tufted, and the quality varies dramatically. From the customer's point of view, residential carpet selection is often based on four factors: color, cost, appearance or texture, and touch. The client or customer often is unaware of the many quality levels of carpeting. Thus, retailers are reluctant and often refuse to allow samples to leave the store or studio, as they are aware that these four criteria may be

Figure 12.6 This Berber carpet is installed wall to wall in this cozy family room. Wood blinds and leather furniture complement the natural theme established by this residential carpeting. *Photo courtesy of Lafayette Venetian Blind, Inc.*

applied to lower-quality carpets and the sale lost when a visually comparable piece is found for lower cost. Cushion is likewise not regulated in residential carpeting, and some customers unknowingly receive a lower-quality cushion than they pay for. For both design professionals and consumers, an understanding of quality checks is useful insurance in making decisions. A high-quality carpet may last many more years than an economical one, and life-cycle costing should always be a key factor in decision making.

New home construction is generally given an allotment for carpeting that, by its modesty, usually dictates lower-quality carpeting that may beg replacement long before the budget allows for new carpeting. With a moderate increase in allotment and careful quality and guarantee comparisons, a carpet can be installed that will last for many more years than the economy carpet.

Life-cycle or **life-use costing** is a method of calculating the value of a product over its lifetime (also discussed in the material on contract carpeting above). For residential carpeting where cost is usually the only considered factor, here is a simple example: If 300 square yards (2,700 square feet) of carpet is installed at $12 per yard, including pad and installation, the cost is $3,600. If the carpet wears prematurely due to low quality and requires replacement in five years, the cost per year is $720. Compare these data to 300 square yards of carpet with greater density and resiliency that costs $15 per yard installed, or $4,500. If this upgrade carpet lasts twelve years, it costs $375 per year. Other lifespan or life-use factors include the quantity of traffic and maintenance expected and the selection of a "nice, dirty color" (neither light nor dark, which tends to show everything, but midtone and dull). Also consider varied texture or subtle pattern that will hold good looks for more years.

Quality Checks

The quality of residential carpet cannot be judged by appearance and color alone. A high-quality carpet is one that will withstand wear and tear with resilience and durability. Hand-conducted quality checks for residential carpet include the following:

- Bend the carpet sample so the front of the carpet is folded back to expose the primary backing. If the tufts (tufted carpet) or stitches (woven carpet) are close together, or dense, little backing is exposed. If the carpet "grins" back, showing its primary backing, then the carpet is less dense. The old adage "united we stand, divided we fall" applies to this hand test. Less dense carpeting crushes more easily.

- A test for resilience can be conducted by hand or by foot. Press down on the carpet and rotate it back and forth while pushing with the thumb or palm of the hand or the heel or ball of the foot. Then examine the carpet for crushing; watch to see if the carpet rebounds, or is resilient. If the recovery is slow, the carpet will likely crush.
- A hand tuft-bind test can be useful. Grasp a yarn tuft (cut loop) with the thumb and forefinger and pull hard. Examine what comes loose. Many fibers pulled loose indicate a poor-quality yarn that may unravel and become fuzzy, or even lose its pile.
- Placing a sample on the floor and dropping onto it a bit of debris, such as lint, thread, or tiny pieces of paper, reveals how a carpet shows or camouflages soiling. Keep in mind that soil takes on the color of outside dirt, which can vary from medium light to very dark, depending on the location.

Depend on the Label

Another carpeting quality assurance measure is to specify brand names from manufacturers where the carpet has an impressive guarantee. Look for a long wear and stain-resistance guarantee, easy soil removal, resistance to static electricity, and guarantees against matting, crushing, or even fading. Contract carpeting quality assurances are found through warranties and via testing results.

CARPET COLORATION

Dyeing methods include **solution-dyed yarn,** where color pigment is inserted into the melted polymers during extrusion. The color permeates throughout the yarn, offering excellent cleanability and colorfastness to sunlight fading or spills; this is particularly important in contract carpeting. Other dyeing methods are **stock dyeing,** which is applied after extrusion but prior to spinning; **yarn dyeing** of the finished yarn; **printing,** where color is applied after the carpet is tufted; and **piece** or **continuous dyeing,** where dye is injected into the face of carpet in a continuous process after the secondary backing is affixed.

Color is the key factor in residential carpeting choice. Consumers are aware of innovation, and to meet their expectations of freshness and change, more color plus distinctive textures, patterns, and styling options are available, resulting in thousands of different carpeting looks. Some of these options include layered color combined with texture and soft patterns based on geometry and organic shapes economically accomplished through weaving technology.

These not only enhance fashion appeal but also minimize soiling and vacuum marks. Multicolored loops, cut/loop surfaces, and Saxony, often textured, feature a broad color selection. Neutrals remain strong choices, although some consumers select neutral carpets with patterns such as trellis, floral, or geometric patterns. Natural-looking Berber is still a popular floor-covering choice, but the trend is toward Berber-influenced flecked styles in vivid commercial colors. New color-based Berber or tweed-like neutrals with flecks mask spills and spots and lower maintenance. New families of neutrals include livable greens, dull yellows, and neutral blues. Neutral colors provide a calming effect in interiors, and strong accents and high contrasts provide drama and excitement. Carpet colorations also translate into heavier textures that counterbalance smooth textures on other surfaces.

CARPET CONSTRUCTION

Understanding carpet construction assists in specifying elements that will provide the best performance in a particular location. Commercial carpet is primarily manufactured by tufting, weaving, and fusion bonding. All three processes can produce high-quality floor coverings, but tufted carpet accounts for 95 percent of all carpet construction. The tufting process is the most efficient and has advanced technologically to allow myriad patterns and styles.

Woven Broadloom Carpeting

Woven carpet is created on looms that simultaneously weave face (top or pile) yarns and backing yarns into a complete product. A latex backcoating is usually applied for stability and a separate carpet cushion is usually used, although attached cushions are available for various performance needs. Principal variations of woven carpet include velvet, Wilton, and Axminster. Carpet performance is associated, in part, with **pile yarn density** (closeness of the pile stitches), or the amount of pile yarn in a given volume of carpet face. For a given carpet weight, lower pile height and higher pile yarn density give the highest performance for the money. Density is also influenced by the number of stitches per inch when counting across a width of carpet— for example, a 1/8 gauge carpet has eight stitch rows per inch of width, and a 1/10 gauge carpet has ten rows per inch of width—and the size of the yarn in the tufts. Extra-heavy traffic conditions require a density of 5,000 or more. **Pitch** is the distance between woven rows of weft stitches. **Velvet weave** is a woven carpet without design, in a solid color or of variegated yarns. It is typically a smooth, cut-pile carpet.

Wilton Carpets

Wilton carpet is a type of luxurious cut-pile carpet first woven in Wilton, England, in the mid-eighteenth century. Wilton carpets are known for their velvety quality, made possible when the pile is cut open and then sheared. The weaving process is similar to that of Brussels carpeting, with the face yarns carried in the body of the carpet, meaning some yarns do not appear on the surface of the pile. (The presence of the so-called dead or buried yarns in Wilton construction is what distinguishes it from Axminster weaving.) By this means, all colored yarns used in the pattern are carried under the face of the carpet and pulled to the surface pile as each color is used in the pattern, then submerged again. Wilton carpets are thick and durable and thus a good choice for heavy-traffic areas.

The construction of Wilton carpet differs from that of other carpets. The pile yarns run continuously through the carpet, adding weight, strength, and durability to the backing and significantly extending the life of the carpet. Although the hidden lengths contribute weight, cushioning, and resiliency, they also add to material costs. The textile professional should look for a manufacturer that uses solution-dyed nylon yarns, which can be repolymerized into new nylon at the end of each carpet life cycle, 100 percent wool, or a blend of wool and nylon.

Most Wilton carpets are made of intricate patterns in a variety of colors. A **frame** is a rack at the back of the Wilton loom, a variation of the Jacquard loom, holding spools from which yarns are fed into it. Each frame holds a separate color; thus, a three-frame Wilton has three colors in the design, and a six-frame Wilton has six colors. When the colored yarns on the frames are not being used in the design, they are carried in the backing layer. These are referred to as the dead or buried yarns.

Wilton carpeting features a variety of surface textures, from level cut pile to multilevel loop pile. Computers are used to control the pattern and feeding of yarns to the pile surface. The two types of Wilton production are wire weaving and face-to-face weaving.

Figure 12.7 Three major types of woven carpet construction. *From Maryrose McGowan,* Specifying Interiors, *2 ed., John Wiley & Sons, Inc., 2006.*

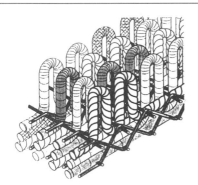

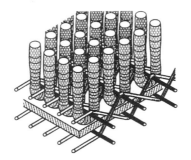

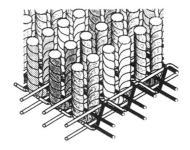

Figure 12.7a Wilton carpet construction   **Figure 12.7b** Velvet carpet construction   **Figure 12.7c** Axminster carpet construction

Figures 12.7d and e This Wilton carpet has been woven to exact specifications for this complex curved staircase. *Photo courtesy of Patterson, Flynn & Martin/Rosecore.*

Figure 12.8a Axminster woven carpet mechanism showing bobbin yarns threaded through feed tubes to protect against breakage. *Copyrighted and registered, Soroush Custom Rugs & Axminster Carpet, www.soroush.us.*

Figure 12.8b Broadloom Axminster carpeting as a finished woven textile *Copyrighted and registered, Soroush Custom Rugs & Axminster Carpet, www.soroush.us.*

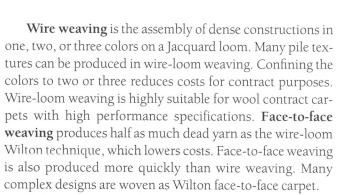

Figure 12.8c Installed Axminster carpeting in this hospitality dining area camouflages soiling while it provides underfoot design luxury. *Copyrighted and registered, Soroush Custom Rugs & Axminster Carpet, www.soroush.us.*

Wire weaving is the assembly of dense constructions in one, two, or three colors on a Jacquard loom. Many pile textures can be produced in wire-loom weaving. Confining the colors to two or three reduces costs for contract purposes. Wire-loom weaving is highly suitable for wool contract carpets with high performance specifications. **Face-to-face weaving** produces half as much dead yarn as the wire-loom Wilton technique, which lowers costs. Face-to-face weaving is also produced more quickly than wire weaving. Many complex designs are woven as Wilton face-to-face carpet.

Wilton carpets may be woven in strips and then fabricated or seamed together for larger floor coverage. A precise repeat pattern assists in side matching. Yardage ordered should take pattern repeats into account.

Quality construction factors to look for include a high-quality wool yarn woven into a cotton primary backing. The secondary backing should consist of high-quality latex applied to polypropylene, which provides lateral and horizontal stability and ensures durability, making these carpets practical for residential and commercial applications. The designer works with the client and the rug manufacturer to create or select a design for Wilton area rugs. Standard patterns are also available for selection. Once a Wilton order is placed, the rug is woven to specifications, with a delivery time of up to six months.

Axminster Carpets

Woven Axminster has become a popular commercial carpet; it is widely specified because of its strong construction and enormous design capabilities. Axminster carpeting is

Figure 12.9 The carpet in the lobby of this Shakespearean theater is custom woven to fit the space. Axminster carpeting performs well as a distinct and unifying design element and as a durable and long-lived soft floor covering. *Copyrighted and registered, Soroush Custom Rugs & Axminster Carpet, www.soroush.us.*

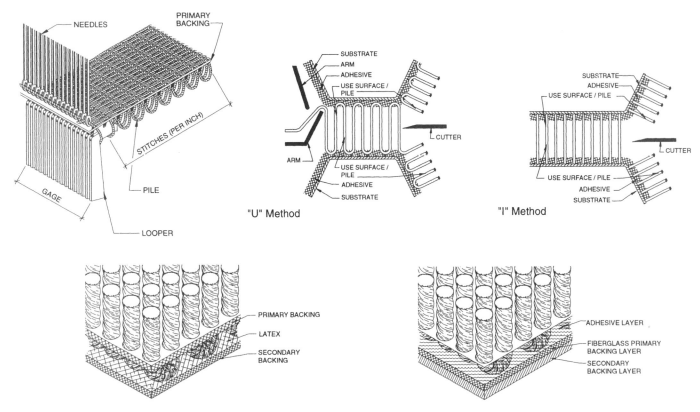

Figure 12.10 Tufted carpet and fuse-bonded carpet construction showing the manufacturing process and cross section. *From Maryrose McGowan, Specifying Interiors, 2 ed., John Wiley & Sons, Inc., 2006.*

widely used in hospitality design in hotels, restaurants, casinos, and cruise ships, and in theaters, prestigious government and corporate settings, retail businesses, passenger aircraft, and high-end residential design.

Axminster carpet was first produced in 1839 by James Templeton of Glasgow, Scotland. Templeton was able to produce a room-size seamless rug with precision and good quality on a Jacquard loom, which became known as an Axminster loom when used for carpet production. Early Axminster patterns tended to imitate Oriental carpets and were woven in large, seamless pieces. Axminster carpets utilize all of the pile yarn effectively for design, with no dead pile yarn, as found in Wilton carpets. During the nineteenth century, two new looms were invented for faster, easier production of Axminsters: the spool and the gripper Axminster looms; both are still used today. Spool looms were invented in the United States in 1876, and the gripper Axminster loom was developed about 1890.

Spool Jacquard looms are most appropriate when long runs of colors and designs are required. Although the setup cost of preparing the spools is high, the production rate of modern spool looms is higher than for gripper Jacquard looms. Gripper Jacquard looms are mostly used for their relatively quick production. Designs can be changed efficiently by changing books of Jacquard cards, which set the design of each rug. Length of time has been reduced even more with the electronic Jacquard. Colorways can be altered simply by adding more colors to the main bobbin frame. Gripper Axminster weaving produces little waste of pile yarn and offers a level surface. Gripper Jacquard looms are the more versatile of the two types manufactured.

Most Axminster carpets are made 7 and 8 pitch per inch, where 8 pitch is the higher and preferred quality. Weave density ranges from 6 to 12 rows per inch. Axminster carpets are often produced in 80 percent wool, 20 percent nylon blends, but can be produced in 100 percent wool or in man-made fibers.

Axminster carpeting techniques are complex and intricate. The backing is made of heavy jute, cotton, or a manufactured fiber. Spools of yarn deliver the colors to the fixed patterns in the weaving area. The carpet has a smooth cut-pile surface.

Axminsters have broad design potential. The art department of a high-quality Axminster manufacturer can create colored art renderings, usually via computer software programs, for custom design from blueprints, fabrics, and color samples.

Acquiring Wilton and Axminster Carpeting

Major manufacturers of Wilton and Axminster carpeting work directly with interior design professionals through design showrooms located in major cities across the United States. Carpeting typically can be ordered in three ways: email, telephone, and ordinary mail sent to the main offices. Traditional designs in mass production from the company, as well as a selection of custom patterns created by manufacturers' designers, are also available. Carpeting manufacturers will accept personally or professionally designed orders after each design is approved by in-house design consultants, who often work with the designer to create the rug motifs and scale and to select colors, yarn type, and height.

Line drawings are prepared within a few days for approval. Once the line drawing is approved, the art department creates a computer color rendering for approval. A color rendering may be prepared in as little as 72 business hours. Upon approval of the color rendering, a pegboard sample (20 × 20 inches) is prepared that presents the final selected coloration, yarn type and weight, face height, and texture. It takes approximately 15–30 business days to prepare a pegboard sample, which is then shipped to the designer, along with a price estimate. This model illustrates the quality, design, and color

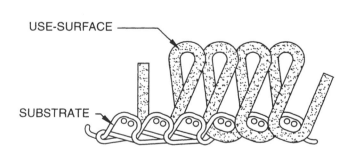

Figure 12.11a Knitted carpet construction showing use surface and substrate. *From Maryrose McGowan,* Specifying Interiors, *2 ed., John Wiley & Sons, Inc., 2006.*

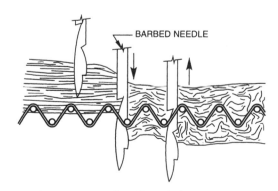

Figure 12.11b Construction of needlepunched carpet. *From Maryrose McGowan,* Specifying Interiors, *2 ed., John Wiley & Sons, Inc., 2006.*

of the carpet to be manufactured and is useful for the design professional or specifier to show the client, who can then confirm the order. At this point, production of the carpet begins.

TUFTED CARPET

The tufting industry is relatively young, yet it has grown into one of the largest in North America. A brief history illustrates the dynamic growth in the past century. At the beginning of the twentieth century, a young woman named Catherine Evans Whitener of Dalton, Georgia, sewed thick cotton yarns with a running stitch onto unbleached muslin and clipped the ends so they would fluff out. Then she washed the fabric in hot water to shrink the muslin and hold the stitches. Thus began the hand-tufting industry. In the 1930s, as the machinery was developed, the automated chenille bedspread industry grew with the addition of multiple sets of needles that made parallel rows cut by attached knives. By the 1950s, cotton chenille rugs were produced in widths of 12 and 15 feet, called broadloom. Following World War II, research and development of manufactured fibers paved the way for new carpet fibers for the tufting industry—nylon in 1947, polyester in 1965, followed by olefin/polypropylene in 1949. With the development of bulked continuous filament nylon yarns, economical tufted carpets could rival the luxury and durability of wool. Today, Dalton is called "the carpet capital of the world," manufacturing over $10 billion in carpeting annually at the mill level. Over 90 percent of carpets manufactured in the United States are tufted carpet.

Tufting is a rapid and economical method of producing 12-, 13-, or 15-foot carpet widths on machines similar to sewing machines. The yarns are threaded into several hundred needles, pushed through a primary backing, and then secured with an adhesive. Tufted carpeting consists of four layers: pile, primary backing, latex, and secondary backing. Pile yarns are tufted as loops into a *primary backing*. The yarn is caught by round wires called loopers and held in place for loop-pile carpet or cut by blades for cut-pile carpet. The yarns are secured with a layer of synthetic latex, which holds the loops in the backing, and then adhered to a *secondary backing*. **Latex** is a rubber-based synthetic polymer frequently used as a coating or backing to hold stable woven fabrics or tufted rugs.

Most primary backing and secondary backing is olefin/polypropylene. Jute is used in some carpeting, although it is seen less frequently today, as it is susceptible to moisture damage, will rot and stretch.

The term **tuft bind** refers to the level of security of the tuft—how well it stays put when a yarn is caught and pulled—by a wheel or a shoe, for example, or when a single tuft works loose and is pulled or yanked. This could result in a row of tufted yarns being pulled out, resulting in a run similar to a run in nylon hosiery. To enhance security, tufts may be placed in a zigzag arrangement, making this problem less likely. The density or tightness of the tufts is another factor in durability.

Other alternatives are attached cushion backings for greater resilience, acoustical insulation, and comfort underfoot. The advantages of attached cushioning are lower cost than separate cushioning and direct glue-down for contract installations where cushioning is required.

Most tufted carpet is produced as 12-foot widths and some as 15-foot widths, hence the term *broadloom carpeting*. This size is versatile, whether seamed in large rooms or cut into shapes. Six-foot widths are increasing in use and available in many designs with a variety of backing systems to accommodate performance needs. Six-foot-wide carpet is often a benefit in high-rise buildings, where transporting a 12-foot roll is difficult or expensive. The narrow width may also provide a cost savings in buildings with many hallways or other narrow spaces. However, careful planning is needed to avoid more seams than necessary. Tufted carpet may also be cut into modular tiles, discussed below.

For much of the short history of tufted carpets, designer effects relied heavily on solid or variegated color. Today, tufted patterned carpeting has become both elaborate and durable. Patterns that were once achieved through weaving or printing only are now achieved through advanced tufting technology. This dramatically expands design options.

Figure 12.12 Modular carpet or carpet tiles are practical, economical, and aesthetically flexible. *Photo courtesy of NatureWorks.*

Figure 12.13 Tufted carpeting provides pleasing aesthetics, comfort underfoot, and absorbs sound, making this bedroom a quiet and peaceful environment for relaxation. Vista window film on the French doors cuts glare, heat, and undesirable UV rays which could fade or damage carpet and textiles. *Photo courtesy of Vista Window Film.*

Needlepunched carpet—The yarn is needlepunched into a polypropylene or jute mesh. Glue is then applied to the back of the mesh and then a secondary backing applied.

Fusion-bonded carpet—Yarns are implanted into a coated backing. The cut pile is produced by slitting two parallel sheets of face-to-face carpet down the middle of the pile. Fusion-bonded carpet is most often die-cut as modules or tiles and is usually backed with a polymeric material to provide stability.

MODULAR CARPET TILES AND 6-FOOT CARPET

Modular carpet, modules, and carpet tiles produced in squares of 18 to 36 inches have become highly popular in contract and even residential interiors in recent years. Offices and schools are full of electronic cabling, and modular carpeting is designed to provide easy access to the narrow space required for low-profile (2½-inch) cable placement or flat electronic wiring. Raised flooring allows the space needed to accommodate extensive wiring and even ductwork for heat and air systems, so modular carpet or 6-foot broadloom is a logical solution. As raised floors sound hollow beneath foot traffic, modular and narrow carpets offer attached softback polyurethane cushion for noise insulation and increased stability and comfort. *Modular hardbacks* are made of polyvinyl chloride (PVC). Hardbacks are used where there is no need for cushion and noise control and budget is lower. Amorphous resins are dimensionally stable, with seam and edge integrity for easy pattern matching. PVC backings are most often used with polymeric compounds, and amorphous resins are used as alternatives to PVC backings.

Carpet tile has many advantages. Modules are tested for and often meet performance requirements to become fully acceptable in the contract markets. Installation, reconfiguration, and removal of modular tile respond to changing configurations of open-plan systems office furnishings, which can be jacked up to install tiles without moving the divider panels. Tiles may be rotated along traffic paths to evenly distribute wear. Individual modules that become soiled can be replaced at a fraction of the cost of removing and reinstalling large broadloom pieces, which also contribute to landfill. Installation labor and old and new carpeting are saved, as are the time and inconvenience of moving furniture and disrupting work to recarpet. Changing out modular tiles may be accomplished in one overnight shift, rather than disrupting an office for days.

Modular tiles can be handsomely designed, duplicating a broadloom pattern, or be custom arranged to contrast colors or patterns. Tiles can be of contrasting colors; they can be quarter-turned to form seemingly new patterns. Installation may be via standard adhesives, releasable adhesives, or mill-applied peel-and-stick adhesives, or produced without adhesives.

Moisture barriers may be engineered into modular carpet tile from the bottom of the pile to the back of the carpet, preventing spill penetration to the subfloor. A moisture barrier is an advantage where spills and therefore cleaning are frequent. In healthcare environments, a moisture-barrier seam-sealing technique lessens the potential for bacterial growth.

Residentially, carpet tiles may be used in indoor/outdoor installations such as porches, decks, and garages. They are also an alternative to single-roll broadloom in home offices, activity rooms, and informal bedrooms. Carpet tiles can be installed by the homeowner. An arrow on the back of the tile facilitates lining up the pile with that of neighboring tiles to create a finished floor that may look like broadloom carpeting.

CARPET BACKING SYSTEMS

Carpet backing systems increase tuft binds and moisture resistance and add stability and resistance to edge raveling. Backings can be ordered to meet functional requirements. **Tufted carpet primary backings** are nonwoven polypropylene or polyester or woven polypropylene slit film. **Adhesive layer** or **backcoating** may be synthetic SBR latex, polyurethane, polyvinyl acetate, ethylene vinyl acetate, PVC, amorphous resins, or thermoplastic polyolefin. **Secondary backings** include leno-weave polypropylene, nonwoven polypropylene or polyester, woven jute, and fiberglass reinforcement.

Woven carpet construction yarns may include cotton, jute, polypropylene, polyester, viscose rayon, and blends or combinations. **Woven carpet adhesive layers** are similar to but thinner than tufted coatings.

Bonded carpet backings include fiberglass matting and are backcoated with PVC.

Needlepunched carpets typically do not have a secondary backing. Backcoating includes SBR latex, acrylics, ethylene vinyl acetate, and SBR latex foam.

PADDING OR UNDERLAY CUSHION

Carpet padding or underlay cushion augments acoustical value, improves insulation, and extends the life of rugs and carpets. Padding quality is judged by chemical composition, thickness, compressibility, resiliency, resistance to moisture and microbes, and cost. These factors should be taken into account when considering environment and traffic. Underlay cushions can be installed separately from the floor covering or permanently attached to the carpet back.

There is an entrenched belief in the floor-covering industry that a lot of cushion in a carpet is a good thing, but this is not always the case. A carpet that sinks under every step will stretch and grind carpet fibers, wearing them down more quickly. The density of the pad is more important than its depth, and guarantees should be sought. A pad protects the fibers from being ground into the floor and breaking. Carpet cushion for contract settings is assigned a class rating. Here are typical installations for each class.

Class I—Moderate traffic: private, executive, and administrative offices in office buildings and healthcare facilities, banks, and schools

Class II—Heavy traffic: public areas, clerical areas, corridors, patient rooms, lounges, classrooms in healthcare facilities, libraries, museums, hotels, motels, and schools

Class III—Extra-heavy traffic: airport or transportation terminals, lobbies, ticketing areas, reception and nursing stations in healthcare facilities, and cafeterias

There are three types of cushions, and each has two or more names. These are **fibrous** or **felted fiber cushions, rubber** or **sponge rubber cushions,** and **foam, polyurethane,** or **urethane foam cushions.** Each type is divided into two or three varieties, the characteristics of which make them useful in particular types of carpet installation. Each variety also has **grades,** which vary by weight (also called density), thickness, and the amount of force required to compress the cushion.

Density is one of the most important qualities of carpet cushion. It is calculated by dividing weight by thickness and measured in pounds per cubic foot. Cushion can be made dense with more material, light with more air, and any grade in between. This means carpet cushion can be soft or firm, resilient or supportive, according to the type of carpet, the location, and expected traffic. For example, Berber carpet requires a thin, firm cushion specified by a manufacturer as suitable for Berber carpet. Another example of specific cushion needs relates to radiant heating, which is being installed more frequently. Carpet cushion for radiant-heated floors should allow subfloor heat to penetrate the carpet system and heat the room. A relatively thin, flat cellular sponge rubber or synthetic fiber cushion works best here.

Fibrous Cushions

Fibrous cushions are made of natural hair or fiber, synthetic fibers, rubberized hair, or jute needlepunched into feltlike structures. Fibrous cushions are often preferred for area and Oriental rugs, where cushion is required to extend the life of the rug but where less resilience or bounce is less damaging because it prevents the backing from stretching and potentially breaking, or where pointed heels may puncture the backing. Most fibrous cushions are bonded between sheets of latex.

Natural fiber cushions include felt, animal hair, and jute (the material used to make some kinds of rope and heavy burlap bags). This is one of the oldest types of carpet cushion, dating to the earliest days of machine-made carpet. As natural fiber cushions age, they crumble and disintegrate. The fibers are susceptible to moisture damage, so latex sheets are often used as protective barriers. Often, a loosely woven jute scrim is added in the batt prior to needlepunching. To delay the growth of mildew, fungi, odor, and overall deterioration, antimicrobial agents are recommended. Fibrous cushions may be purchased in rolls up to 12 feet wide and weights from 32 to 86 ounces per square yard.

Figure 12.14b Nonslip doubled-sided rug underlay for hard and carpeted floors. *Photo courtesy of Leggett and Platt, Incorporated.*

Figure 12.14a Carpet underlay, pad, or cushion, top to bottom: fiber (top five); urethane foam (next two); rebond foam (next two); and rubber carpet underlay (bottom three). *Photo courtesy of Leggett and Platt, Incorporated.*

Figure 12.14c Nonslip rug underlay for all hard floors. *Photo courtesy of Leggett and Platt, Incorporated.*

Synthetic fiber cushions may be recycled fibers made principally of post-industrial scrap synthetic carpet material with no outside additives. Fibers include nylon, polyester, polypropylene, and acrylics needlepunched into relatively dense cushions. Synthetic fiber cushions have a firm feel and may be made in any weight to withstand light, medium, or heavy traffic.

Rubberized hair is a needlepunched felt made from clean, sterilized natural fiber coated with skidproof resin on top and bottom. **Rubberized jute** is a needlepunched felt of fiber (no hair) sealed on both sides with filled latex and embossed.

Rubber Cushions

Rubber cushion is a compound made with chemicals, oils, and fillers added for weight. The mixture is expanded into flat sheets or other forms. Generally, the forms are waffle, ripple, or bubble, while the flat form can be found in thicknesses between 0.125 and 0.3125 inch. Rubber cushion consists of flat rubber, textured flat rubber, rippled waffle (Class I only), and reinforced rubber. Sponge rubber is less likely to retain odors than foam rubber. It also has buoyancy and softness, characteristics that are enhanced by foam cushion. Rubber cushion manufacturing processes can be varied to produce different levels of density and firmness. The usual measurement is weight in ounces per square yard.

Flat rubber cushion is made by converting liquid latex and fillers into flat sheets that range in thickness from 0.125 to 0.6 inch. Flat rubber cushion has a finished appearance on both sides. It provides a firmer, more uniform support than sponge rubber. Unfortunately, it also has a greater tendency to retain odors. The thinner forms are often permanently bound to the back of carpets. Flat rubber is normally used in large-scale commercial applications and with loop-type or Berber carpet. These cushions are available in rolls up to 12 feet wide and in weights from 28 to 65 ounces per square yard.

Waffled rubber cushion is made by molding natural or synthetic rubber. Heat cures the rubber and forms a waffle pattern. This produces a soft, resilient cushion whose luxurious feel is particularly useful for residences.

Rippled rubber is a natural or synthetic rubber cushion manufactured with an appearance of bubbles on the surface. It usually contains nonwoven or paper scrim on the top side.

Textured rubber is a natural or synthetic rubber cushion with a finely textured appearance on the bottom and nonwoven or paper backing on the top. Sponge rubber cushions may be purchased in rolls up to 13 feet wide and in weights from 41 to 120 ounces per square yard.

During installation, a spun-bonded fabric may be attached to rubber cushion to allow the carpet back to slide over it without stretching and distorting the cushion.

Polyurethane or Urethane Foam

There are four types of polyurethane or urethane foam cushion: **prime polyurethane, densified polyurethane, bonded polyurethane,** and **mechanically frothed polyurethane.** All are used for both contract and residential use, and all have the same basic chemical composition. However, they are manufactured in different ways, causing their cellular structures to differ. Polyurethane foam cushions can be found in thicknesses of 0.375 to 0.750 inch and usually have a spun-bonded facing, which eases installation. These cushions generally have a density of 2.4 to 5 pounds per cubic foot. They can be used for skid resistance with area rugs and runners because they minimize the problem known as **rug walking.**

Prime urethane foam cushion is the original or prime urethane foam (not the leftover trim of urethane in bonded foam, discussed below). Prime foam consists of large cells in the shape of ellipses. The foam columns of these cells are vertically oriented. The cushions provide varying compressibility, depending on their density. Their biggest problem is that they may bottom out or flatten under heavy loads. Filling the cells with powdered fillers, which add weight and stability, often prevents this. Prime polyurethane foam is a firmer version of the thick foam cushion used in upholstered furniture, mattresses, and automobile seats. The foam is sliced into sheets for carpet cushion.

Densified prime urethane or **polyurethane foam** cushions have a greater density than prime urethane foam cushions, as the cellular structure is finer and elongated, with a horizontal orientation. Densified prime urethane/polyurethane foam cushion utilizes no fillers, is odorless, resilient, and resistant to mildew, and it doesn't bottom out.

Bonded or **rebond urethane foam** cushions are made by forcing together granulated pieces of prime urethane trim or scrap. It is a recycling of product in that the foam becomes useful cushion product rather than ending up in the landfill. Bonded or rebond polyurethane foam combines chopped and shredded pieces of foam in different sizes and usually different colors, and it often merges different types or levels of firmness into one solid piece of varying thickness. It frequently has a surface net for ease of installation and improved performance. Bonded foam is recyclable.

Froth polyurethane foam cushion is thin, dense foam useful for commercial installation of wide carpet expanses. It may be a separate cushion but, more often, is flowed directly onto the backing of a commercial carpet as an attached foam cushion backing.

Specification Data

Specification data assures that the cushions meet the requirements of the producer, design professional, architect, or specifier. It deals with the composition, construction, and performance features of the cushion structure. The data reported from the evaluated cushion includes values obtained from accelerated laboratory testing of the product. The laboratory performs tests specified by the professional, who lists the characteristics and properties their clients prefer or those that are mandated for textile products. These tests must achieve specific levels of performance to ensure the structure's accordance with the standards established by the authority that has jurisdiction. These levels depend on the type of cushion selected, the anticipated traffic conditions, the carpet selected, and the mandated features.

Accelerated aging is taken into account with rubber cushion compounds because they can be affected by heat, which causes them to crack, crumble, and stick. The tests performed in the laboratory are designed to assure the cushion will not behave this way.

Compressibility is the degree of resistance a cushion offers when crushed under a static load. With the percentage of deflection used, the average number of pounds per square inch required to compress the cushion material is reported to the nearest pound. Specific levels of compression load deflection (CLD) are mandated by several federal agencies and vary with the type of cushion and the facility it will be used in.

Compression loss is the extent a structure fails to recover its original thickness after compression. The compression set is calculated by the following:

Compression set = (original thickness – thickness after compression) $\times$ 100 $\div$ original thickness

The higher recovery of the cushion thickness, the better. A minimum recovery level of 85 percent is recommended and often mandated. This level of recovery also helps the carpet recover.

Tensile strength is the force per unit of cross-sectional area necessary to cause rupture. Generally, the minimum tensile strength values are between 8 and 20 pounds per square inch.

Elongation is how far a cushion structure extends before rupturing. This is part of evaluating tensile strength. It is calculated by the following formula:

% elongation at break = length stretched $\times$ 100 $\div$ original length

Contemporary carpet cushions are generally environmentally friendly, with low levels of volatile organic compounds (VOCs). Testing identifies low-emitting products

TABLE 12.5 CARPET CUSHION R-VALUES

Carpet cushion R-values are added to the R-value of carpet for a total R-value of soft floorcoverings. Manufacturers supply actual R-values for tested cushion on request. The following are approximate R-values.

FIBER CUSHION	6–8 lb/cu ft	¼ inch thick	R = 1.00
	6–8 lb/cu ft	⅜ inch thick	R = 1.40
	6–8 lb/cu ft	½ inch thick	R = 1.90
FOAM RUBBER	25 lb/cu ft	¼ inch thick	R = 0.60
	25 lb/cu ft	⅜ inch thick	R = 1.00
	25 lb/cu ft	½ inch thick	R = 1.30
WAFFLE RUBBER	33 lb/cu ft	¼ inch thick	R = 0.30
	33 lb/cu ft	⅜ inch thick	R = 0.50
	33 lb/cu ft	½ inch thick	R = 1.30
PRIME URETHANE	2.2 lb/cu ft	¼ inch thick	R = 1.10
	2.2 lb/cu ft	⅜ inch thick	R = 1.60
	2.2 lb/cu ft	½ inch thick	R = 2.10
BONDED URETHANE	4–8 lb/cu ft	¼ inch thick	R = 1.00
	4–8 lb/cu ft	⅜ inch thick	R = 1.60
	4–8 lb/cu ft	½ inch thick	R = 2.10

Note: From this table, it is evident that prime and bonded urethane have higher R-values and are the more insulative cushion. For radiant floor design, however, carpets with lower R-values should be selected so the heat will transfer from the subfloor up through the cushion and carpet to heat the room.

by requiring representative product samples to meet emissions standards. Products displaying the CRI IAQ Testing Program label have met the Carpet and Rug Institute testing and labeling program criteria for carpeting, cushion, and adhesives. See Resources, chapter 6.

Some tests evaluating the cushion, such as for noise reduction and insulation, are performed with the carpet for greater accuracy. Often, the carpet and cushion both contribute to functional value.

DETERMINING CARPET YARDAGE

It is important to determine the correct amount of yardage required for an installation. Carpet and separate pad/cushion for tackless strip installation usually require equal yardage, although where extra carpet yardage is required for pattern matching, for example, cushion yardage will be less than carpet yardage. Inevitably, scraps of carpet result from any broadloom installation, as the carpet must be cut to fit. Excessive wasted yardage from careless calculation is not in line with professional ethics and should be avoided by means of responsible measuring and computation. Miscalculations that result in the need for additional yardage pose financial, scheduling, and reordering problems and are likewise irresponsible. If a firm bid is given and accepted, additional carpet yardage will not be paid for by the customer but rather by the retailer or design professional who sold the product. The exception is where a specifier is in-house as an employee and responsible for ordering. If carpeting yardage is short, the installation may be put off until the total yardage arrives or, in the case of beginning an installation and then discovering the yardage is short, installation is interrupted, potentially putting other furnishing installations behind or disrupting the occupants while the remaining yardage is ordered and delivered and installers are once again available. Also, where yardage is reordered to complete an installation, the risk of dye lot variation can become a matching nightmare.

For design professionals just learning the skills necessary to measure carpet, many installers are willing to measure and calculate for a fee. Installers should never become carpet sales competitors.

CARPET YARDAGE MEASURING GUIDELINES

- When measuring a space, obtain a floor plan or draw a diagram showing walls, doorways (indicating a door or an opening), halls, closets, and stairs with the actual number of steps, and fill in dimensions as you go in a method that is consistent and makes sense.
- Use a retractable steel tape measure at least 25 feet long. Have someone hold the beginning, and you read the measured dimension where needed.
- Be consistent in using inches or feet plus inches (or the metric system).
- When in doubt, take the measurement and record it. Be thorough enough that return trips for missing measurements are unnecessary.
- Between opposite walls, the distance from baseboard to baseboard must be measured if the space is uninterrupted.
- If the space is interrupted by an opening, the measurement must be from the baseboard to the midpoint of an archway or to the point halfway under a closed door.
- When measuring stairs, add 2 to 4 inches to each lengthwise and crosswise measurement. The extra inches may be required for fitting and trimming.

Carpet yardage can be calculated for large spaces within contract or residential interiors only by plotting the direction in which the carpet will be installed and then plotting where the cuts and seams will be. This is often done with a floor plan or blueprint where the placement can be drawn or plotted; this plan may become a part of the installation instructions or documents.

Additional Considerations

Other considerations that affect the plotting or placement of carpet, seams, and yardage calculation include carpeting nap and pattern repeats.

Nap—A mechanical finish that results in a raised fiber surface. Nap usually has a direction, where yarns lean slightly to one side. This is called **pile lay.**

Pile lay—The direction of the nap, which almost invariably is discernable, is critical in installation. The pile lay viewed from one side will be more lustrous or light-reflecting, which may cause the carpet to appear a different color. It is important to have the lay of the pile or the direction of the nap the same with all adjoining pieces of carpet. The lay should parallel the longest dimension in the largest room being carpeted rather than crossing it. Also, the pile lay should be toward all entrances and, at the same time, away from the strongest source of light in an interior to minimize luster. This creates uniformity in the quantity of light reflected by each section of carpet and causes all of the carpet to have the same apparent color. Sometimes, however, professionals may vary the pile direction in adjoining pieces of carpet for aesthetic reasons or to create marked differences in their brightness, depending on what a particular room requires for atmosphere. Sometimes the direction of the pile lay should correspond with a pattern on the carpet. This applies more to modules than to roll goods.

Consider these rules when planning the pile lay on stairs. The pile lay should always be in the same direction toward the stairs. This means that with angled stairways, the carpet must be turned proportionally to the turn in the stairway. This avoids exposure to the backings, which is more important to avoid than shade variations. The width of the carpet paralleling the width of the stairs is important to minimize the carpet grin; the grin is the exposure of the backing on the nose edges.

Seam placement—Seams blend in better when they run lengthwise, parallel with the pile lay. Seams that run crosswise interrupt the pile sweep and stand out more with incidental light. It is not recommended to have a seam perpendicular to a doorway. Also, seams that saddle, or parallel seams on each side of a doorway, are discouraged. They can be avoided by shifting the carpet, and hence the seams, to a different location. Most important, it is best to avoid placing seams in high-traffic pivot areas and on stair treads.

Matching patterns for pattern repeat—The measurement between a point in a design and the next point where the design begins again. Patterns on floor coverings have either a set-match or a drop-match pattern repeat. The yardage required to fill a space is determined by the type of match and the lengthwise and crosswise dimensions of the repeat. Set-match patterns repeat across the width of the carpet. Such carpets should be laid so the pattern has the complement of the incomplete part of the design on the opposite side of the room if the pattern ends incompletely. The patterns can be laid to be either fully or partially completed. Cut patterned carpet at the beginning or the end of the pattern only; never cut before it has reached the end of its repeat. This way of cutting the carpet supplies the yardage required for side matching.

Drop-match patterns diagonally repeat across the width of the carpet. Half-drop-match patterns are those where a portion complementing another part of the design is located at a point up or down one-half the length of the repeat. Cutting these types of carpet can be tricky. One method, used to cut the carpet on multiples of the repeat, minimizes waste. The second method is to cut on multiples of the repeat plus half a repeat. This method uses the extra half to advantage. The quarter-drop pattern is another type of drop-match pattern. It was most common during the colonial era, consisting of four blocks to a repeat, with figures that match one-quarter of the repeat at the opposite edge.

Keep in mind that once the carpet is received, it must be inspected for flaws, color variations, and quantity. Once the carpet is cut, most manufacturers won't be held responsible for these defects. The pile lay, placement of the seams, and the size of the pattern repeats must be considered in this process.

CARPET INSTALLATION

The evaluation of the site from the floor plans or in person is the first step in making decisions about the direction in which to install carpet. It is the responsibility of the design professional or specifier to supply in writing all instructions concerning installation procedures, including the specifics of how the carpet will be installed, the cushion type and weight, and delivery and installation schedules. The interior design professional should request and include in the specification the manufacturer's installation instructions for patterns, unusual shapes, and borders. Carpet should be installed according to industry standards, available in the standards published by the Carpet and Rug Institute (see

---

TABLE 12.6 QUICK CARPET YARDAGE ESTIMATING

Most carpet is sold in widths of 12 or 15 feet and priced per square yard.

Here is a simple formula for calculating yardage in uncomplicated spaces:

1. Multiply the interior's length in feet by the width in feet, rounded up.
2. Multiply the total by 1.1 to avoid undercalculating.
3. Divide the total by 9 to calculate square yards.

For example, for a space 9 feet 8 inches by 11 feet 2 inches:

1. $10' \times 12' = 120$ sq ft
2. 120 sq ft $\times$ 1.1 = 132 sq ft
3. 132 ÷ 9 = 14.6; round up to 14.7 sq yd

Carpet price per square yard + cushion price per square yard + installation price per square yard = installed price of goods per square yard

14.7 square yards $\times$ installed price per square yard = total installed cost + applicable sales tax = total price of installed carpet

Actual carpet piece size will be 12 feet wide (4 yards) $\times$ 11.025 feet (3.675 yards)

Resources below). This guide for installers, "Standard for Installation Specification of Commercial Carpet, CRI 104," outlines proper procedures and terminology used in specification writing, planning, layout, and installation. This document also includes guidelines for floor preparation and installation in special areas, plus diagrams and charts.

The Carpet and Rug Institute also makes available its "Residential Carpet Standard for Installation of Residential Carpet, CRI 105" (see Resources below), which outlines workmanship standards for residential carpet installation and includes guidelines for floor preparation and installation in special areas, plus diagrams and charts. Responsibilities of the manufacturer, installer, dealer, builder or general contractor, and consumer are listed.

Carpet installers or contractors should be bonded or insured and offer credentials. Always check these credentials. Carpet installation contractors should be certified by organizations such as the Certified Floorcovering Installers (see Resources).

Carpet installers can make or break an installation. Excellent installation reflects positively on the design professional. Professional installers should know what installation method will be best to use with the features of the carpet, including pile lay and pattern repeats. Installers should also be able to plan the carpet layout, determine the yardage required, and estimate the cost. A qualified installer can also solve problems, communicate well, look, speak, and perform in a clean way, and work efficiently. For residential installations, the installer may collect the balance due at the completion of the installation. Typically, installers prefer to be paid at the completion of the job. High-quality installation includes sealed carpet edges that will not fray and are power-stretched rather than kicked in with a knee-kicker or a spike tool (positioning tools); patterns that are matched; no staples or bubbles in either stretch-in or adhesive installations; and seams that are hidden and perfectly sealed.

Site Preparation

The site must be prepared before the professional installs the carpet. The first step may be removal of the previous floorcovering assembly. The floor must be dry before installation; this is crucial for glue-down installations. This step includes making sure that if the carpet is to be installed on concrete, the concrete has had adequate time to dry; this may take up to four months. If concrete is not completely dry, ground moisture will move upward through the slab, which will prevent adhesion of the carpet and create other serious problems. Also, if installing on a concrete floor, alkaline substances must first be neutralized. These substances, found in concrete, can react with the adhesive that secures the carpet in position, creating degradation and loosening the carpet. The area must be clean (free from dust, lint, and grit), smooth (sanded down where rough), and free of cracks, crevices, and holes. The goal is a uniform support for the floor assembly.

Wall-to-Wall Installation Methods

Three methods are generally used in a wall-to-wall installation: **stretch-in**, **glue-down**, and **free-lay**. Broadloom carpets typically come in rolls 12 feet wide; when a room is wider than this, the carpet must be seamed. Seams should be minimally visible and placed inconspicuously, as determined by the installer. Sometimes, seams can be used to delineate space by splicing different carpets together. When a seam is necessary, the pattern of the fabric must be matched, and the two sections of carpet must face the same direction. The edges must be aligned and trimmed to fit together; using the factory edges is not recommended, as they are likely to be irregular. After the carpet is cut, a thin bead or

an adhesive strip should be applied to prevent the edge from raveling and fraying in the future. The seams are created by hand sewing or with tape, such as hot melt, which is often used for lengthwise seams. The professional installer should be able to provide carpet maintenance instructions. The following are methods of installation:

Direct glue-down—This involves simply securing the carpet or tile with an adhesive. The adhesive, chosen by the professional based on the floor type and the carpet weight, pile height, and material, is spread on the floor with a trowel; then the carpet is set in place and pressed down. Direct glue-down decreases the chance of ripples, which are likely to occur in high-traffic contract areas. This kind of installation method is best used where softness and padding are not required or where the subfloor is cement. It is cost-efficient.

Stretch-in or **pad and tackless strip**—This installation method uses a tackless strip, a thin strip of plywood with sharp protruding tacks that face the wall. The plywood strips are approximately 1½ inches wide and have rows of rust-resistant metal pins or tacks that stick upward at an angle of 60 degrees. If the carpet is to be placed in a high-traffic area, three rows of pins should be used; in residences, two rows of pins are adequate. The thickness of the boards should coordinate with the thickness of the cushion to be used. The boards are placed around the perimeter securely by nailing or gluing them to the floor, with a space slightly narrower than the thickness of the carpet between the wall and the strip. The pad is set in place next and stapled, nailed, or glued down, filling the entire floor to the tackless strip. The carpet is then placed over the pad, using a power stretcher to create a uniform stretch. After the carpet is seamed, it will be stretched from 1 to 1.5 percent in length and width in the process of anchoring it to the pins. A knee-kicker is used to anchor the edges over the pins.

Free-lay—The most often used method of installing carpet modules. To prepare for this installation, a grid is planned of the perimeter modules. Specific crosswise and lengthwise rows are secured to the floor to minimize shifting. In this type of installation, the tiles are held by gravity. When high traffic is expected, modules are not recommended because the edges of the modules can easily be raised and worn. Modules require tiles to alternate layers of gauge vinyl and glass fiber scrims with the free-lay tiles, which helps the stability of the floor assembly. Free-lay offers the same conveniences as the direct glue-down method when releasable adhesives are used.

Figure 12.15 *Photo courtesy of Certified Floor Covering Installers Association, Kansas City, MO, 816-231-4646.*

Alternative installation systems—The advantage is the flexibility of a nonpermanent fixture that can be selectively replaced. Tile and broadloom can be installed with a **releasable adhesive** or a **hook-and-loop** fastening technology. With both methods, carpet can be easily removed, allowing the carpet structure to be lifted and rebonded multiple times; being able to do this allows access to wire or piping systems located in the floor. This approach also allows the rotation or removal of the modules as needed. Adhesive modules are not used with pad or cushion unless the carpet tile has an attached cushion.

Determining Installation Method

As mentioned above, factors such the composition of the subfloor must be considered when specifying an installation method. Other considerations include traffic conditions, including both foot and wheeled traffic. Where traffic will be heavy, no pad, or a thin cushion, may be best as a backing, and the best installation methods are glue-down and stretched-in. Where traffic will be lower, most types of cushions will be used with stretched-in carpet.

Planned space—Cubicles or wall partitions adjust to changes in workstations. Sometimes wall partitions can be moved to reveal a bare strip in the floor, which requires patching in a roll good. The wall partitions can also leave lines, which are not professional-looking and require a large amount of replacement carpet. If releasable modules are used, these problems are less severe. Modules adapt to environmental changes and are much more convenient to replace.

Cost—Comparing installation costs should include long-term upkeep and considerations such as acoustical benefits and long-term energy saving. Installation is priced per square foot or per square yard, as is carpet cushion or underlay.

Carpet Maintenance

Extensive carpet maintenance information is found on www.wiley.com/go/interiortextiles.

RESOURCES

The Carpet and Rug Institute (CRI)
www.carpet-rug.org
Street Address: 730 College Drive, Dalton, GA 30720
Mailing Address: PO Box 2048, Dalton, GA 30722-2048
Tel 706-278-3176
Fax 706-278-8835

The CRI is the national trade association representing the carpet and rug industry. Its membership consists of manufacturers representing over 90 percent of all carpet produced in the United States and suppliers of raw materials and services to the industry. There is continued coordination with other segments of the industry, such as distributors, retailers, and installers. CRI is a source of extensive carpet information.

International Flooring Sciences Resource Center (IFSRC)
www.flooringsciences.org

Sponsored by the Carpet and Rug Institute, the IFSRC is a source of technical information on a variety of carpeting subjects, including product formulation and chemistry, ergonomics and human response, environmental attributes, cleaning science, and product and materials recovery, recycling, and reuse. The IFSRC produces the *International E-Journal of Flooring Sciences.*

World Floor Covering Association (WFCA)

www.wfca.org
2211 E. Howell Avenue
Anaheim, CA 92806
Tel 800-624-6880; 714-978-6440
Fax 714-978-6066

The WFCA serves to advance the hard and soft floor-covering industry and reinvests in the industry. It sponsors the Surfaces Annual Trade Show and offers certification programs.

National Association of Floor Coverings Distributors

www.nafcd.org
401 N. Michigan Avenue, Suite 2400
Chicago, IL 60611-4267
Tel 312-321-6836
Fax 312-673-6962

Fosters trade and commerce in the floor-coverings industry and offers training and information to members.

Carpet Cushion Council

www.carpetcushion.org
PO Box 546
Riverside, CT 06878
Tel 203-637-1312
Fax 203-698-1022

The Carpet Cushion Council educates carpet retailers, carpet manufacturers, distributors, and cushion manufacturers about the benefits of carpet cushion and provides tools for carpet retailers to improve communication skills with customers and increase sales.

Polyurethane Foam Association (PFA)

www.pfa.org
9724 Kingston Pike, Suite 503
Knoxville, TN 37922
Tel 865-690-4648
Fax 865-690-4649

PFA educates about flexible polyurethane foam and promotes its use.

Radiant Panel Association

www.radiantpanelassociation.org
PO Box 717
Loveland, CO 80539
Tel 970-613-0100

Facilitates communication and cooperation among those interested in the advancement of the radiant panel heating and cooling industry, primarily in North America.

Floor Covering Installation Contractors Association (FCICA)

www.fcica.com
7439 Millwood Drive
West Bloomfield, MI 48322
Tel 248-661-5015
Fax 248-661-5018

FCICA consists of professional firms working together to bring leadership and support to floor-covering installation contractors.

Certified Floorcovering Installers Association

www.cfi-installers.org
2400 E. Truman Road
Kansas City, MO 64127
Tel 816-231-4646
Fax 816-231-4343

Trains and certifies floor covering installers.

InformeDesign

www.informedesign.umn.edu

An online research and communications tool for designers, sponsored by ASID and created by the University of Minnesota. Research results and published papers on specific topics serve to augment standard information from other sources.

Hand- and Machine-Made Area Rugs

Figure 13.1 This fine hand-knotted Persian Oriental rug is a dynamic focal point, enhancing the beauty and value of this interior. *Photo courtesy of David and Jay Nehouray, Caravan Rug Corp., www.caravanrug.com.*

HAND AND MACHINE-MADE AREA RUGS comprise a very large category of study that could fill multiple volumes. This chapter presents rug types and associated considerations. For those with a particular passion for rugs, this knowledge can be a springboard to a lifetime of learning. Design professionals who love area rugs always counsel, "Begin with the rug!" A high-quality decorative rug is often the foundation of a stunningly beautiful room setting. This chapter discusses the following types of rugs: Oriental, folk, European handmade, Colonial American, designer, natural fiber, and machine-made area rugs. It concludes with a section on ob-taining area rugs. Resources for and information on rug maintenance is found on www.wiley.com/go/interiortextiles.

Area rugs offer the following commonalities in interior design:

- Oriental and decorative area rugs function as prestigious focal points for interiors because of the character and richness they add to a room. Rugs are an aesthetically valuable soft-surfaced floor covering.
- Area rugs cover a portion of an interior, leaving a peripheral border of hard or soft flooring. They can be

replaced easily as style, room function, or primary user changes.

- Rugs anchor furniture arrangements, uniting pieces both thematically and aesthetically.
- Rugs draw users together through common appreciation of visual richness and interest.
- Area rugs provide effective acoustical absorption and temperature insulation underfoot; they make the room quieter and more comfortable.
- Rugs can often be repositioned or rotated to distribute wear, moved to other areas, or rolled and stored for later use.
- Rugs can be lifted or removed for professional cleaning and restoration.
- Authentic Oriental and folk rugs may be resold or traded at some rug dealerships. Antique and high-quality new rugs may increase in value and are, in fact, among the few furnishing items that have the potential to hold and appreciate in value.
- Rugs may be specified to cover an entire room; custom-woven Oriental and area rugs can be fitted to accommodate jogs, angles, and features such as fireplaces.

ORIENTAL RUGS

By definition, handmade Oriental rugs, also known as Oriental carpets, are hand-knotted or hand-woven by native craftspeople in many countries. These include countries of the Balkans and Caucasus in southeast Europe; the Near and Middle East, with emphasis on Turkey and Iran; North Africa; and the Far East, including the "-stan" countries, India, Tibet, and China. Thus, Oriental rugs represent many cultures. Considered by many to be works of art, these rugs are more than textile art on the floor; they are a tangible journey through time and space to an ancient realm of beauty that bridges centuries, spans cultures, and captivates admirers around the world. The history of Oriental rugs is complex and fascinating. An overview of this history is found on www.wiley.com/go/interiortextiles.

Oriental Rug Design

It has been said that the history of the world is woven in tapestries and Oriental rugs. Early patterns consisted of stripes, which slowly evolved into more complex geometric shapes and patterns. Nomadic weavers most often worked from memory of designs passed down through the generations; these may be traced to specific geographical locations. Originally, Oriental rugs served as family utilitarian items such as tent floor coverings, blankets, sleeping mats, and saddle blankets and bags. Rugs were also bartered or traded for goods needed to sustain life. Designs were like trademarks that could be traced to their region, village, or even family of origin. All family members were involved in the business of rug weaving; they tended sheep or goats, sheared them, dyed, carded, and spun the wool, wove the rugs, and bartered. Young girls and boys became adept at tying knots with their slender, nimble fingers—a skill highly revered in nomadic cultures. Tribes migrated, intermarried, and copied one another's traditional patterns, and rugs evolved into regionally definable patterns and weaving styles.

Throughout the Orient, workshops evolved where semi-nomadic and settled family craftsmen worked under the direction of a master weaver. Younger craftspersons sometimes left families to apprentice and work as weavers in city manufacturing facilities, where the mass production of rugs began to be lucrative for business owners. In this setting, well-developed motifs became somewhat homogenized, although rug styles maintained their identity and names.

In some countries, entire communities are involved with cottage-industry rugmaking, with each family carrying out specific rugmaking duties, similar to the nomadic tribes. In cottage-industry rugs, the Western rug purveyor often specifies both design and coloration. In this circumstance, specific rug designs are produced in varying sizes so they can be easily marketed from brochures and websites by Western rug dealerships. Given the high-profile human rights issues of recent years, designers and clients may seek rugs not made with child labor. As in Tibet, some domestic rug dealers may commit a percentage of their sales to the country of origin for the education of the rug weavers' children.

In general, today's **Persian rugs** are often considered the finest, with curved, flowing lines accomplished with high knot counts. **Caucasian rugs** are often have angular, simpler, or more primitive patterns that result from a lower knot count.

Through the centuries, rug weavers have incorporated their interpretation of nature in their products. Motifs and design compositions represent local aesthetic traditions, lifestyle, natural flora (trees, vines, flowers, shrubbery) and fauna (animals, birds, insects), architecture (mosque domes and arches, summer pavilions or gazebos), formal garden forms, and water elements. One beautiful design is the tree-of-life motif, which may be expressed in the ogive-shaped Cyprus tree or another type of tree where leaves and flowers do not repeat in design or color; each is a unique and beautiful element that represents the life-giving flora of the oasis where nomadic families traded rugs for food and supplies. Sometimes a large, central tree-of-life design is surrounded by animals, which also represent the support of life in an often harsh desert climate.

Other designs are inspired by clouds, trees, and mountains. Objects such as vases, lamps, and porcelain items may be used as design motifs. Scenes from folklore and conquests may inspire compositions. Family crests and fretwork are seen on many Chinese rugs. Many of the thousands of symbols or motifs used in Oriental rugs are tiny and isolated—a small stylized flower, for example, or a miniature crest. These individual elements become part of a whole composition. Some motifs are simple and primitive and others fairly sophisticated, yet the skillful incorporation of individual motifs into a pleasing whole is the essence of an Oriental rug masterpiece. The design of Oriental rugs is nearly always symmetrical and often mirrored at all four corners.

Many traditional Oriental rug designs include two elements: a field and a border. The border may consist of a wide band and a few lines, or multiple lines that form a wider border. A **closed border** is a straight line that defines the edges, whereas an **open** or **broken border** is foliage-like, revealing background areas between its leaves or abstract open designs, as seen in many traditional Chinese rugs. The background is termed a **ground** or **field**; it may be fairly open, moderately filled, or completely covered with motifs.

Contemporary hand-woven Oriental rug compositions begin with a graphed representation called a **cartoon.** Each tiny square represents a knot, colored as a standard for dyed yarn. The same cartoon design can be colored differently for other rugs—same pattern, different color scheme. This is an efficient use of the labor to produce cartoons. New rugs are inspired by the thousands of Oriental rugs made during the past four centuries, so the potential for varying designs and color combinations is limitless. In large manufacturing facilities, a caller reads the cartoon and instructs multiple weavers in the quantity of specific colors and their sequence. In this way, several identical rugs can be produced simultaneously.

Custom designs planned on computer programs are utilized by design professionals who contract with rug weavers or own Oriental rug manufacturing facilities in Tibet or India, for example. Computers assist the design professional in creating a customized design that can be executed as a handmade Oriental rug specified in a shape and dimension to fit a particular interior precisely and that, with proper maintenance, will last much longer than many other types of rugs. This approach combines the best of high-tech design and high-quality Oriental rug weaving.

Oriental Rug Materials and Construction

Authentic Oriental rugs consist of a set of cotton (or linen, jute, or wool) warp yarns around which are tied pile wool knots. Occasionally the pile knots are of silk, camel hair, goat hair, or horsehair. The source and quality of the wool pile is a major determinant of the rug's quality and value. Some countries, such as India, that require the use of indigenous wool produce lower-valued rugs because the wool is of lower quality, whereas wool from New Zealand and Tibet is considered superior because the sheep are raised in higher altitudes, thus developing higher lanolin content and stronger wool—and increasing the value of the rug.

Rugs are produced on a vertical loom, at which the rug weaver sits and ties the yarns from a small skein, cutting the yarn at the completion of each knot. After every two rows of knots, a weft yarn is inserted in a plain weave and tamped down tightly. This dual construction method is why Oriental rugs are identified as both hand-knotted and hand-woven.

The knotting techniques primarily used are the **Turkish** or **Ghiordes knot** and **Persian or Senneh knot.** The Turkish knot is characterized by its symmetrical nature. The two ends of the yarn are brought forward together between two adjacent warps. In contrast, the Persian knot is asymmetrical. The knot differs from side to side so it can be tied in two different ways. Lightly running a hand over the surface of a rug will reveal the use of the Persian knot, as the pile will lie in one direction. Most often, the Persian knot is tied open on the left with the loop on the right. The yarn encircles two warp threads, passing under one and around the other. There is no difference in appearance between Persian and Turkish knots because in both, two strands are always left showing.

Figure 13.2 Oriental rug designs are first drawn on paper as a cartoon, where each square is a single knot.

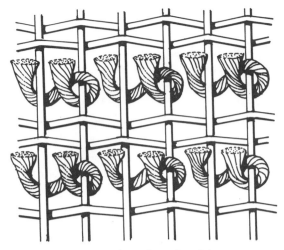

Figure 13.3a The Persian or Senneh knot

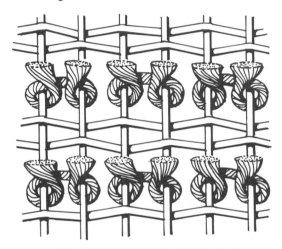

Figure 13.3b The Turkish or Ghiordes knot

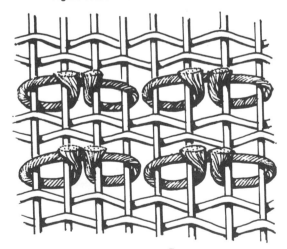

Figure 13.3c The Jufti knot

The edge knot is found in the terminal (last) rows of knots and is tied to the left or right depending on the size of the rug, always so the rug pile inclines inward. When the knotting is completed, several weft yarns are woven and then tied, and warp yarns are cut past that to form a fringe. To gauge the fineness or density of the knotting in a partic-

ular rug, examine the quantity and diameter of the warp threads that form the fringe. The finer the fringe yarn, the more knots will be tied into the rug. Note that fringe may be attached separately in imitation or machine-made rugs, so take care to determine that the fringe really is the warp. Also, consider that a vintage rug whose fringe has become worn can have a new fringe attached as a restoration service (see www.wiley.com/go/interiortextiles).

The **Jufti knot** is like the Turkish or Ghiordes knot in that it is symmetrically tied. However, the knots are placed around two warp yarns on each side. Thus, yarns may be more coarse with half the knots. The lower knot count produces a simpler, more abstract pattern suitable for Caucasian-style rugs. Lower knot counts also mean a rug that is less costly and less durable.

The rug is finished by shearing the pile to a perfect, even finish. In rugs with deep piles, such as Chinese or Indo-Aubusson rugs, the finish also includes cutting a mitered or beveled angle around the designs.

Dyes and Colors

Natural dyes are obtained from leaves, bark, and other vegetable matter, and only small kettle batches or dye lots are produced at one time, as the process is long and difficult. Colors between dye lots will not match. This dye lot striation is called **abrash,** subtle irregularities that add charm and character to the rug. Abrash is copied in modern dyeing techniques such as dip-dye, where the yarn skein is dyed more at one end than the other.

As weavers migrated to rug-weaving centers, colors began to change from tribal or nomadic or natural dyes to chrome-based dyes developed to meet the fashions dictated by the Western market. Today, both natural and chrome synthetic dyes are used to dye Oriental rug wool. Previously, aniline dyes were used beginning in the 1860s. Within a decade, aniline dyes were used nearly worldwide, but unsatisfactorily. Color loss from bleaching and running resulted from poorly developed dyes. Aniline dyes also weakened the wool fibers. Over time, the tone of colors can shift to change the composition of the rug. Chrome dyes, on the other hand, have nearly been perfected. They are fast, or fadeproof, when exposed to water, alkalis, and sunlight, and they seem to cause minimal impairment to the wearing qualities of the wool and to provide a greater variety of shades.

There appears to be only one flaw attributed to the chrome dyes: Their fastness limits the rug's ability to age and mellow gracefully, if at all. These new dyes have led to a controversy over which dye is the best and most valuable. Many rug experts favor natural dyes and snub the chemi-

Figure 13.4 This fine Oriental rug from the Ushak Collection illustrates "abrash," the streaked effect of fine Oriental rugs woven over time with slight dye-lot differences. *Photo courtesy of David and Jay Nehouray, Caravan Rug Corp., www.caravanrug.com.*

cally developed dyes. Regardless of dye type, however, rug weavers are able to create miraculous colored designs.

Color is a critically important element because it unifies the design composition. The same rug composition can be executed in different colors; the results appear to be completely different. Some rugs are washed to remove excess dye or given a chemical wash to soften the colors and perhaps give the rug an antique finish or appearance.

Color is also dependent on the type of wool. Sheared wool takes dye differently than wool taken from dead sheep. Wool from lower altitudes has lower lanolin content, resulting in colors that are a bit brighter or more brash. Wool of high-altitude sheep, such as that from Tibet and New Zealand, is higher in lanolin content, and whether dyed with natural vegetable or chrome dyes, it yields a deeper luster and mellower coloration, which be-

comes a patina as it ages. In traditional Tibetan yarn production, this lanolin is not completely scoured out. This results in a sensual, soft wool that also accepts the dyes in a soft manner, yielding an appearance that holds much appeal in today's market.

Valuing Oriental Rugs

The value of Oriental rugs is dependent on several factors: the age and/or rarity of the rug, its condition, the pile depth, the yarn composition and fineness, the color richness, and the fastness of the dye. Other value determinants include the quality of artistic composition, the subtle symmetry of the pattern, the harmony of the composition, and texture—especially the appeal of soft yet strong wool.

Figure 13.5 This "1900 Antique Mahal" from the Antique Masterpieces Collection indicates the enduring appeal of traditional Persian Oriental rug designs. *Photo courtesy of David and Jay Nehouray, Caravan Rug Corp., www.caravanrug.com.*

Oriental rugs are often divided into age categories as follows. (Bear in mind that experts do not always agree among themselves.)

- **Antique Oriental rugs** are over 75 years old (some contend that antique begins at over 100 years).
- **Semiantique Oriental rugs** are 25 to 74 years old (or 99 years old).
- **New** or **contemporary Oriental rugs** are under 25 years old.

Generally, an older rug is more valuable, but only if the rug is well preserved. New or contemporary rugs that are finely woven will hold their value and should not be overlooked as a wise investment. High-quality contemporary rugs are more widely available than antique or semiantique rugs. The quantity of knots per square inch is a key factor in determining the value of Oriental rugs. The more intricate the design, the more knots per square inch. Good rugs have up to 200 knots per square inch, whereas fine rugs have 400 or more knots per square inch and take months to weave in a rug-weaving center—or years, if the weaver works alone.

Rugs often increase in value over time, even with the effects of some wear. It can be difficult to date Oriental rugs. Occasionally, dates are woven into rugs. The figures are arranged from left to right and usually correspond with the Islamic system of timekeeping. These dates should be accepted with caution, as dates can be easily copied in new rugs.

The value of an antique or semiantique rug is variable. If the carpet is exceptionally well preserved relative to its age, the value dramatically increases. For example, a skillfully restored 150-year-old carpet typically has significantly greater investment potential than a 70-year-old piece in unblemished condition. The rarity of the rug is also a factor. When trying to assess the value of a rug, it is wise to use the help of experts, as the evaluation process can be tedious and difficult. Interior design professionals often work with one or more reputable rug dealerships.

For discriminating clients, fine rugs are much more than floor coverings: They are precious works of art to be valued and respected, maintained, and perhaps resold, traded, or bequeathed to heirs. **Art-level rugs** are those where quality counts. For finely woven Oriental rugs, for example, selection as an art-level rug is often based on these criteria:

- Rugs are woven traditionally, without the constraints of the international commercial market. These rugs have higher artistic merit because of the rich cultural heritage from which they stem.
- Rugs woven with pure natural dyes, as opposed to chemical dyes, become softer and mellow or mature over time; this increases variety and depth and

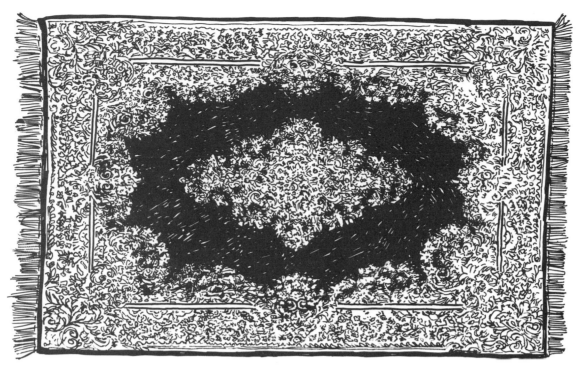

Figure 13.6a Perslan Oriental rug

Figure 13.6b Turkish Oriental rug

Figure 13.6c Chinese Oriental rug

Figure 13.6a–c Oriental rugs

therefore the carpets' beauty. (Note that some people, even experts, prefer chrome dyes for their greater consistency.)

- High-quality materials raise a rug's value. A wool face is soft yet resilient and durable. The wool possesses a luster that enhances the quality of its colors and ensures great resiliency and durability.
- Uniqueness in the rug raises its value. In contrast, standardized commercial Oriental carpets are copied as rote themes and color combinations. Art-level rugs reveal an artistic vision whereby the weaver either masterfully reinvents traditional regional motifs and colors or achieves an innovative, captivating departure.
- The design and color are fluid and artistically beautiful, with substantial visual depth and texture. Such a rug invites the viewer's gaze to move over a continually varying composition.
- The rug is well designed, with a sense of unity, balance, and harmony. All elements—pattern, color, texture—are fully developed and work together as a harmonious whole.

The Naming of Rugs

Oriental rugs are named for the **rug-weaving district** where the individual style was developed and became famous, even when the district no longer exists on a map. An explanation of rug names is found on www.wiley.com/go/interiortextiles.

Figure 13.7a–g Steps in the production of hand-knotted Tibetan rugs. *Photos copyrighted and registered, Soroush Custom Rugs & Axminster Carpet, www.soroush.us.*

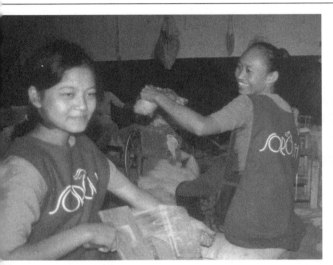

Figure 13.7a Tibetan women carding wool fibers

Figure 13.7b Hand-spinning Tibetan wool

Figure 13.7c Drying the hand-dyed carpet fibers

Figure 13.7d Tibetan rugs are hand-knotted on a vertical rug loom.

Oriental Rug Restoration

Oriental rugs that become worn, faded, or damaged are often repairable, thus preserving their monetary and artistic value. See www.wiley.com/go/interiortextiles for information.

Categories of Oriental Rugs

Handmade Oriental rugs are divided into the following categories: Persian, Caucasian or Turkish, Chinese, and Tibetan.

Persian Rugs

Persian rugs originated in the region that used to be known as Persia, now primarily Iran, and are replicated in nearly every Oriental rug-weaving country. Persian rug designs are characterized by intricate curving and floral patterns, made possible with very fine yarns and high knot counts. Despite their reputation for outstanding quality, Persian rugs do vary in quality. It is somewhat difficult for a layperson to correctly identify Persian rugs because of regional variations in design, weave technique, dyes, sizes, and yarn quality. Persian rugs are produced using both the Persian and the Turkish knotting techniques and in a variety of sizes. Well-known Persian styles include the Hamadan, Hereki, Herez, Isfahan, Kashan, Kerman/Kirman, Nain, Qum, Sarouk/Saruk, Senneh, Sereband, Shirvan, Soumak, and Tabriz.

Persian prayer rugs are distinctive because their design includes a Moorish arch imitative of those found in mosques, often with a hanging lamp. Above the arch is a

Figure 13.7e Washing handmade Tibetan rugs prior to inspection

Figure 13.7g Close-up view of contemporary midcentury modern designs woven into handmade Tibetan rugs. *Photo courtesy of Patterson, Flynn & Martin/Rosecore.*

Figure 13.7f Hand-knotted Tibetan rug in the Viking Hotel, Historic Hotels of America, Providence, Rhode Island. *Copyrighted and registered, Soroush Custom Rugs & Axminster Carpet, www.soroush.us.*

rectangle. There are borders and usually a complex design in the field. Many of these rugs were gifted to the mosques and, representing the mosque itself, used for worship in areas where no mosque was located. Prayer rugs are small enough (2 × 3 feet to 3 × 5 feet) to be rolled and carried on the back. At designated prayer times, they are unrolled and laid down with the arch pointed toward the holy city of Mecca; the devout then can prostrate himself and pray. The rectangular band is designated for the bowed head. Larger prayer rugs can anchor furniture groupings. Some luxurious, high-knot-count prayer rugs are woven with a 100 percent silk face pile (400 to 600 knots per square inch). Because of their high quality and design complexity, prayer rugs are valued as wall hangings and as accent rugs.

Persian garden rugs are replicas of the walled gardens of ancient Persia, the domain of the sultan and his family. They consist of a series of squares or rectangles, each containing a design with outdoor scenes of trees, flowers, birds on branches, and fish in pools. Within the geometric panels are walks, streams, and fountains, all representing the palatial Persian walled garden.

Persian hunting rugs feature animals and hunters or men engaged in combat.

Persian tree-of-life rugs display a large tree with lush fruits, flowers, and foliage.

Persian pictorial rugs show figures from history and folklore or familiar landscapes.

Caucasian or Turkish Rugs

Caucasian or Turkish rugs originated in the Caucasus region and Turkey, areas considered the northern Middle East and southern Central Asia. These rugs originated with nomadic tribes. Their patterns are less formal than those of Persian rugs. Caucasian or Turkish rugs may be coarser as well, with a lower knot count than Persian rugs (fewer than 200 knots per square inch), and feature geometric patterns and abstract designs with little or no shading. Caucasian rugs often use vivid and appealingly bright colors; however, rugs in muted colors are also available. Types of Caucasian rugs include the Afghan, Belouch, Bokhara, Cabistan, Daghestan, Derbend, Karabagh, Kasak/Kazah, Kurd, Malagaran, Qashqa'i/Kashkai, Shirvan, Tekke/Turkoman, and Yomut/Yamout.

Chinese Rugs

Chinese rugs have a deeper pile than other Oriental rugs, coarser yarn, and fewer knots per square inch. The number of knots per square inch in contemporary Chinese rugs is mandated by law. There are three categories of Chinese rug design: traditional, Persian- or French-influenced, and contemporary. The traditional design is characterized by an open background, central medallion, large-scale broken or open border with uncomplicated motifs such as fretwork, dragons, phoenix birds, lotus blossoms, flowers, and foliage on large branches or trees, waves or clouds, vases, chariots and horses, and perhaps Buddhist, Taoist, or Confucian religious symbols. Traditional Chinese rug colors include cream (used for the open, plain field), Ming blue (dark royal), sky blue, gold, and cinnabar red. Rugs that copy other Oriental patterns are usually simplified, and contemporary designs might reflect natural objects, architectural history, or abstract patterns.

Tibetan Rugs

Tibet has become a major producer of rugs that are in high demand in the West for several reasons. Tibet's high-altitude wool offers superior strength and resilience. The scouring process is simplified to leave some lanolin residue, resulting in lustrous, sensuously soft wool. Tibet has been responsive to the Western market and produces many custom-designed rugs. The Tibetan rug-weaving technique, dating to the eleventh century or earlier, differs from other methods. It involves looping the pile yarn around the warps on the loom and then around the gauge rod held parallel to the wefts; when a row is finished, the loop is cut. Many rugs are woven with coarse yarn in abstract patterns with streaked **abrash** effects.

Other Oriental Rug Types

Indo-Aubusson rugs are woven in simplified European Neoclassic or French motifs and typically in pastel colors on a fairly plain cream background. Thus, the designs often imitate the Aubusson rugs of the Neoclassic period. They are hand-knotted Oriental rugs with plush, deep pile similar to a Chinese rug, with beveled outlines around the simplified patterns. They are often mass-produced or cottage- industry rugs made in India or other Eastern countries.

Mass-produced and cottage-industry rugs are made in several countries, with India and Egypt as major suppliers. These standardized rugs may imitate fine Persian, Turkish, or Chinese rugs, or feature a combination of styles. They are less valuable due to their lack of uniqueness and lower-quality wool. Their typically flat colors are another shortcoming. However, cottage-industry and mass-produced rugs are popular in the West, mainly because of their competitive price. Clearly, there is a wide range in the quality of rugs.

Domestic Oriental rugs are machine-made reproductions of hand-knotted Orientals and are often incorrectly called Oriental rugs. Domestic rugs are woven as Axminster or Wilton carpets. High-quality domestic rugs, such as those produced by Karastan and Couristan, have a wool pile and are likely to last more than a lifetime. They are difficult to distinguish from authentic Oriental rugs.

FOLK RUGS

A folk rug is any rug woven by an ethnic or indigenous group or that reflects the native heritage of a country. Folk rugs are most often flat weave and may be reversible. Some have a pile weave. Folk rugs are produced in nearly every country in the world and known by names that relate to their origins. Here, the best known are discussed.

Oriental flat tapestry rugs include the **kilim** and **Bessarabian** rugs of Asia and southeastern Europe, and the **dhurrie**, largely from India. **Navajo** rugs from the southwestern United States are distinctive. In Scandinavia, the **Rollikan** rug is a flat weave and the **rya** is a pile weave. Many countries replicate authentic folk rugs by hand or machine. These are sometimes referred to as *area rugs*, and in the trade they may be called *knockoffs*. See "Machine-Made Area Rugs," below. Flat tapestry rugs from France are discussed under "European Handmade Rugs."

Folk rugs are believed to have originated in the need of nomadic tribes for shelter from rigorous weather. The Seljuks, Ottomans, Mongols, Safavids, Mamelukes, and Berbers influenced the development of flat tapestry rug weaving during their respective reigns. Weavers and dyers from across the Middle East and Asia were gathered to work in workshops to create beautiful flat rugs as well as pile Oriental rugs, as described above. Flat rugs were practical items used as bedding, blankets, and insulating coverings for floors and walls. In work life, flat rugs were used as saddleblankets and bags or satchels. They also represented wealth and formed an important part of wedding dowries, particularly when the rugs were finely woven and beautiful.

Folk Rug Composition and Technique

Authentic folk rugs are composed mostly of sheep wool, goat, camel, and horsehair, and cotton. The warp is typically cotton, and the weft, which constitutes the pattern, is generally wool or hair. Flat-weave folk rugs are tapestry (plain) weaves executed on a horizontal or vertical loom. The artisan changes colors in a design by one of two methods:

In **shared and Soumak warp weaves**, the artisan reweaves the cut or continuous yarns into the preceding warp yarn, with some overlapping. Variations are known as balanced plain weave, weft-faced plain weave,

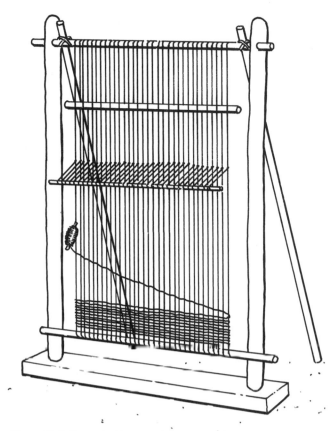

Figure 13.8 The vertical loom used in weaving folk and Oriental rugs

warp-faced plain weave, twill, dovetail, and double-interlock weave.

Slit tapestry or **slit-weave** yarns do not overlap, leaving small slits in the rug. Coarse yarns reveal these slits, whereas in fine tapestry-weave rugs, the slits are barely discernible.

Folk Rug Designs and Colors

Euro-Oriental folk rugs share many similar designs. These include simplified, stylized flowers and foliage, branches of trees and bushes (sometimes a tree of life), garden designs, simplified domestic and wild animal designs, people in native dress, and abstract designs in geometric patterns. Folk rug colors and designs tend to be typical of a given area, making it relatively easy to identify the origin of a rug. Other identifying characteristics include asymmetrical designs and irregular color combinations. Color is a key factor, and regional colors are traditional, enhancing the design and hence the character of the rug. Weavers of authentic rugs express their imagination and creativity with distinctive color combinations and unique patterns.

Many folk rugs today are mass-produced as a cottage industry. Thus, a large number are produced, but they lack

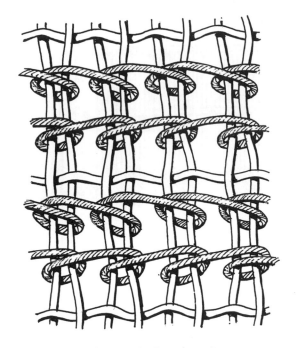

Figure 13.9a Soumak weaving

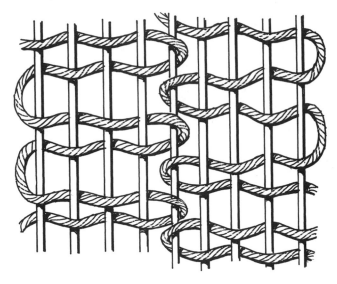

Figure 13.9c Shared warps

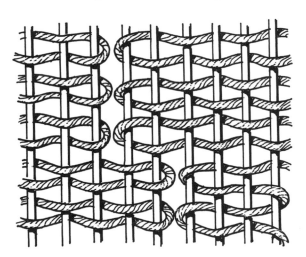

Figure 13.9b Slit tapestry

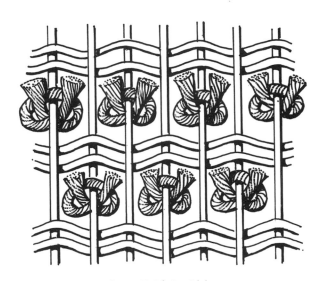

Figure 13.9d Spanish knot

Figure 13.9a–d Folk rug construction methods

in originality and distinction. Today, folk rug designs may respond to the Western interior fashion market, where designs and colors are dictated by color trends.

Valuing Folk Rugs

Folk rugs can range in value from a few hundred to a few thousand dollars; generally, however, they are far less valuable than Oriental rugs. Because they take less time to weave, have no pile, and are less durable than knotted rugs, they are less expensive to purchase.

The value of a folk rug can be assessed in a variety of ways. One is to lift the rug; the lighter the rug, the finer the yarn and hence the more valuable the rug. The high yarn count in the weft indicates higher quality, as does the fineness and high count of the warp yarn. Dye and color-fastness are an important factor in judging value; high-quality colors will not fade easily when washed, and when a damp white cloth is applied, no color should crock (come off). Visible warp threads indicate inferior quality. Age is another criterion; older rugs are of greater value, although determining the age of folk rugs is sometimes difficult.

Types of Folk Rugs

Folk rugs are constructed in every developing nation and in many developed nations. For example, folk rugs from Africa are prized as indigenous tribal art. Folk rugs are an important artistic achievement in many cultures worldwide.

Kilims (kelims), bold, colorful rugs, are credited to Romania and other countries in areas surrounding the Black and Caspian seas. Bessarabian rugs, which are similar, originated from a region of the Ottoman empire known as Bessarabia. Today, kilims are made in many countries and regions, including Turkey, Kurdistan, the Caucasus, Iran, and western Turkestan. Kilim rugs are characterized by long, narrow slits in the fabric, arranged in a stair-step pattern to avoid weakening the rug. Kilim rugs usually are reversible. They are made in bold colors and a variety of designs typical of the regions where they were woven. Kilims may be constructed of wool, camel hair, goat hair, and/or horsehair.

Dhurrie rugs are also flat and reversible. They were originally made in India of cotton warp and weft, so antiques are nearly nonexistent. Dhurrie rugs are characterized by distinctive reversible patterns—but not, however, by color, as they are woven into virtually every style and pattern and coloration imaginable, from imitations of Oriental rugs to contemporary abstract or geometric patterns. Generally, the dhurrie comprises paler, more subdued colors than pile Oriental rugs. It is most often a shared warp weave.

It is interesting to note that dhurrie and kilim rugs are often difficult to distinguish from each other, given the wide spectrum of designs and colors used in both types. Some designs are geometric, while some are based on floral patterns, and yet others employ shades of color to invoke texture in their design. With the **ingrain** method, the yarn is dyed before weaving and then woven so the pattern shows clearly on both sides.

Navajo Rugs

Navajo rugs are produced in the southwestern part of the United States, primarily in Arizona and New Mexico. A true Navajo (Navaho) rug is made of wool in a shared warp tapestry weave. Some twill weaves and basket weaves are also used. Navajo weavers learned the art from the Pueblo and became adept weavers of blankets, apparel fabric, and rugs. A Navajo loom consists of a crosspiece, upright warp beam, warp threads, shed rod, heddle rod, and web beam. It is a simple device strung so the completed rug slides to the back side of the upright loom and the weaver sits in front, working comfortably and composing the design as she works.

Navajo rugs reflect Native American motifs and natural colors. However, the rugs are named for the trading posts to which entrepreneur traders came in the mid- to late 1800s, established rapport, and encouraged and influenced the design of a particular style that would create a market and assure them some measure of fame. The traders knew that if the Navajo prospered through the sale of their goods, so would they. Some of the early traders published mail-order catalogs, and all improved wool quality and spinning techniques, encouraged higher-quality weaving, and hired weavers and sold rugs from the area surrounding their trading posts. Until the traders came, demand for Navajo blankets was sufficient to make swift production necessary, thus dramatically decreasing the quality of the products. Thus, the traders deserve credit for their development of both style and insistence on quality.

Today, Navajo weavers are considered artisans and are highly revered. Within their regional styles, they still con-

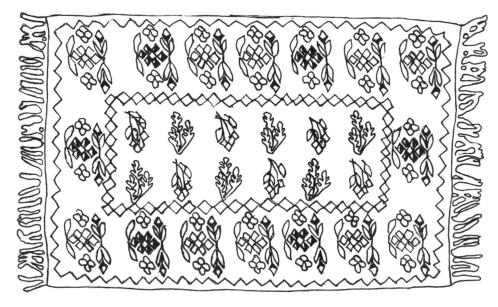

Figure 13.10 Dhurrie or kilim folk rug

Figure 13.11a Two Gray Hills Navajo rug

Figure 13.11e Teec Nos Pos Navajo rug

Figure 13.11b Ganado Red Navajo rug

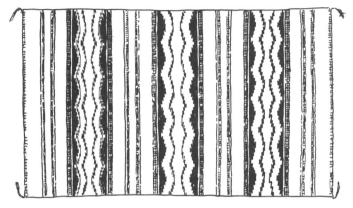

Figure 13.11f Wide Ruins Navajo rug

Figure 13.11c Storm Pattern Navajo rug

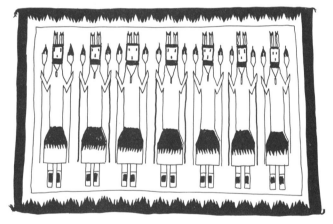

Figure 13.11g Lukachuki Yei Navajo rug

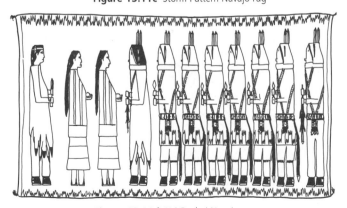

Figure 13.11d Yei-Bechai Navajo rug

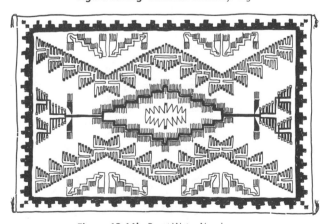

Figure 13.11h Burnt Water Navajo rug

Figure 13.10a–i Navajo rugs

struct their designs as they work. The design of Navajo rugs is characterized as simple, geometric, and angular.

Navajo rug yarn is from the mixed breed of sheep introduced at various points during the colonization of the Southwest. The wool is sheared, carded, cleaned, spun, and dyed by hand with natural dyestuffs from the surrounding landscape or with aniline dyes. Historic Navajo rug yarn, dyed naturally, may be sensitive to water, making cleaning difficult. Bleeding and shrinkage are common problems, although they have has lessened as contemporary wool-dyeing techniques produce more colorfast yarn. Some weavers use commercially produced yarn.

Navajo rugs are largely associated with the weaving district in which they were produced:

Two Gray Hills rugs have the finest weave and are considered the most valuable; they are sometimes referred to as *precious gems*. The yarns are carded and spun carefully to produce a fine quality and a weft count of 100 or more wefts to the inch. This is highly refined compared to the 35 to 50 wefts to the inch of most Navajo rugs. The rugs feature a solid border, generally black, with center designs that have a stair-step architectural feeling. The corners are filled with triangular ziggurat shapes. Colors are natural (undyed) black, brown, and gray. Some grays are achieved by spinning black and white together.

Chinle rugs are borderless striped rugs that contain horizontally paneled bands featuring the squash blossom design, T-shapes, crosses, ziggurat designs, and connecting diamonds. Colors include natural white, gray, gold, brown, orange, green, and rose.

Crystal rugs are borderless striped rugs with bands of solid, wavy lines (alternating two or three wefts of contrasting color in a band) and bands of angular designs, stylized arrows, feathers, cornstalks, and stacked diamonds. Colors are earth-toned brown, gold, orange, green, gray, and maroon.

Ganado-Klagetoh (Ganado Red) are the best recognized of the Navajo rugs. They feature a well-woven brilliant red background surrounded by strong, angular crosses, diamonds, stepped terraces, and serrated forms in gray, white, black, and red outlined with black borders. Sizes range from small and intricate to large, simple, and bold.

Storm Pattern rugs are highly symmetrical, with a square or rectangular center from which radiating lines lead to the four corners in a stair-step manner. Patterns include zigzags, diamonds, swastikas, stepped lightning-like terraces, and arrows. Colors are black, gray, and white, with some red or yellow-gold.

Teec Nos Pos and **Red Mesa** rugs feature a contrasting colored outline around a busy field of zigzags, serrated diamonds, triangles, and boxes. These rugs are bright with multiple colors and sometimes flamboyant accents. Colors are bright green, blue, orange, and red on backgrounds of tan, brown, gold, black, and dull green.

Wide Ruins rugs are simple, finely woven striped rugs with repeated designs in wide bands, often in three sections. Colors include neutral backgrounds of natural white, tan, and gray and beautiful design colors including orange, gold and yellow, deep and pale coral, dark gray, olive green, and tan. There are no borders on these rugs. The patterns include wavy lines, stylized chevrons, and small multiple squash blossoms.

Shiprock Yei and **Lukachukai Yei** rugs are small to moderate-size rugs with slender front-facing figures sometimes framed by a rainbow goddess that forms a border on the sides and bottom of the rug. The rug depicts Yei religious figures but has no intrinsic religious significance. It is frequently used as a wall hanging.

Yei-Bechai rugs feature copies of Navajo sand paintings complete with human figures and wildlife. Yei-Bechai rugs illustrate Navajo dancers in profile. The figures are geometric, angular, and simple in gray, cream, white, black, gold or yellow, brown, green, turquoise, and rust red.

Pine Springs/Burnt Water rugs are visually busy or complex rugs. They usually feature serrated or stepped borders and are filled with diamonds, crosses, serrated steps, and triangles. Colors include gold and yellow, tan, dark gray, turquoise, and bright coral.

Pictorials are rugs that feature a variety of designs including stylized animals, birds, insects, corn and foliage, patriotic symbols, Navajo dancers, hides, architecture, and monograms.

Navajo rugs must be carefully evaluated because knock-offs are created in Mexico by skilled labor. These imitations do not share the value or quality of Navajo rugs. Machine-woven area rugs also may have similarities in design and color to authentic Navajo rugs.

Scandinavian Rugs

Scandinavian Rollikan rugs are flat-weave tapestry rugs that reflect modern tastes influenced by the folk arts and flowers of Scandinavia. Rollikan rugs, which are reversible, are similar to kilims in construction. Most of the designs are modernized by the weaver according to contemporary style preferences.

Scandinvaian rya rugs have their origins in Viking bedding used in farm homes and fishing boats. In the early 1400s, the rya was mostly used by royalty to keep warm. The technique developed to incorporate more color and for use in wedding ceremonies, primarily in Finland. Because it takes great skill and strength to create a rya, weavers would be commissioned to weave in celebration of a wedding. The rya involves Ghiordes knots tied in an alternating pattern within several rows of plain weave. The rya is a hand-knotted deep-pile rug characterized by abstract designs or wedding motifs in contemporary colors. The knots are farther apart, larger, and longer than those of Oriental rugs. Finished rugs feature selvages, tassels, fringe, and other ornamentation.

EUROPEAN HANDMADE RUGS

Handmade rugs have been produced historically in every country in Europe. However, the most notable are the French **Savonnerie** and **Aubusson** rugs and the Portuguese **needlepoint** rug. France has a rich history of rugmaking. The Louvre Museum shows a stone carving of a threshold rug with a pattern that is still being made today. The Apus statue, also in the Louvre, depicts God in full decoration with a carpet on his back. The history of rugs in France began with Louis IX (1226–1270), who defeated the Moors who had migrated to France from Spain. The bounty included fine rugs and carpets. By the end of the fifteenth century, Louis XII (1498–1515) had brought in many Italian craftsmen to train French artisans. Francis I (1515–1547) continued patronizing the arts; he invited Leonardo da Vinci and Andrea de Sarto to his court to produce works for the royal family. From 1547 to 1589, textile arts waned, but in 1589, weaving production began a dramatic increase. Henry IV (1589–1610), founded a rug factory in his palace to create rugs for the French market. However, he liked the rugs so well that he never shared them with the population. Louis XIII (1610–1643), his successor, established a workshop outside the palace for the people called Savonneries. **Savonnerie** rugs were initially influenced by Persian Oriental patterns. However, by the time of Louis XIV (1643–1715), the flamboyant, large-scale, and dramatically rich and vivid colors of the Italian and French Baroque period created a demand for French designs. The larger-than-life designs were then and are still today woven in the same manner as Oriental rugs. They are expensive, mainly because of high European labor costs, which are much higher than those of Asia.

Aubusson rugs take their name from the city of that name, located in the Creuse Valley of France, where the waters have the renowned property of rendering dye colors that are unusually pure in tone. Aubusson became the headquarters for tapestry-weave rugs made for the French aristocracy. The rugs are finely woven flat tapestry made using the slit-weave technique. They were especially favored during the French Neoclassic era, when tapestry was in high demand. Aubusson rugs are also woven in contemporary designs. High quality coupled with high labor costs make these rugs expensive. As a result, Aubusson-style rugs are

Figure 13.12 French Savonnerie rug

Figure 13.13 "Le Jardin" collection of petit-point carpets, constructed in delicately fresh botanical motifs. This 15-mesh petit-point weave is a finer version of needlepoint carpet construction.*Photo courtesy of Costikyan™ Carpets, Inc., www.costikyan.com.*

also produced in countries such as China and India where skill is high but labor and wool costs are lower. Today's rug purveyor collections may consist of tapestry-weave adaptations of time-honored French Aubusson and Savonerrie rug designs as well as modern versions of traditional English designs. Finely crafted Aubusson rugs utilize forty or more colors of fine woolen yarn, blended to add subtlety to the palette and create an overall softness in the design.

Portuguese needlepoint rugs are not created by weaving but rather by decorative needlework. The process involves sewing a design into a piece of fabric such as canvas or scrim. Needlepoint is considered to have originated from the desire for embroidered upholstery. The canvas is stretched across an embroidery frame to keep it taut. Sewing the design into the fabric allows for different types of stitches to be used, resulting in a variety of textures and appearances. The majority of needlepoint rugs feature floral designs and are European in flavor. They are sturdy, graceful rugs specially suited to traditionally styled interiors. Detailed floral patterns and other intricate designs are found, as are custom-designed modern patterns. Usually, individual panels are created, and then many panels are sewn together to make a large or specially shaped rug. Finely worked needlepoint rugs are called **petit-point** rugs and consist of a 10-mesh cross-stitch background and 15-mesh petit-point design elements. Smaller design stitches make possible exquisitely colorful and detailed botanical motifs. Petit point may contain from forty to sixty colors.

Spanish rugs are referred to as **mantas** and are characterized by bright colors and bold patterns in a pile weave. Yarns are relatively coarse and patterns simple and large in scale. Yarns are tied by hand, but not on every warp yarn. For example, see Figure 13.9d. Thus, the pile is relatively sparse, like a contemporary shag carpet. Thus, Spanish mantas have far less value than authentic Oriental rugs or Portuguese needlepoint rugs.

MACHINE-MADE AREA RUGS

Many types of machine-made rugs are available to both the trade and the public. They are obtained online, through catalogs, and in retail stores. Names are created for identification purposes by the merchant. Imitations of Oriental and folk rugs can also be machine-woven. Imitation folk rugs can be so well made it is difficult to differentiate them from authentic folk rugs. Mass-produced machine-made area rugs provide instant color, pattern, and texture to support the interior theme or style. They give softness and comfort, enhance temperature and sound insulation, and can serve as a room's focal point. These rugs, however, are not investments. They depreciate in value, so when they become dated, they should be sold, donated to charity, or, if very damaged or worn, discarded. Hundreds of thousands of modestly priced rugs belong in this category.

Figure 13.14a A large-scale custom-designed rug being hand-tufted. *Copyrighted and registered, Soroush Custom Rugs & Axminster Carpet, www.soroush.us.*

Figure 13.14b Trimming and finishing a rug custom-designed for a high-quality contract interior. *Copyrighted and registered, Soroush Custom Rugs & Axminster Carpet, www.soroush.us.*

Woven Area Rugs

Whereas the majority of Wilton and Axminster carpeting is specified as wall-to-wall installations, occasionally broadloom carpets are bound and used as area rugs. Borders may be woven separately and seamed to the main body of the rug or field, or they may be attached with heat tape (glue is melted as tape is applied; then cools to secure tape to the back of the rug). Separate borders are ordered by the linear foot. Square-footage pricing is based on the total square footage of the order. Borders can also be woven into the field of the rug.

Custom Designer Rugs

Custom designer rugs are made by hand or machine. The yarn is typically wool and custom dyed to match a designer fabric, wallcovering, or other element in a planned interior. A rug may also be created as the focal point around which all other decorative or structural elements revolve. A custom designer rug is the result of collaboration between the interior designer, the client, and the artisan or the design team of a rug manufacturer. Hand-tufted rugs are designed domestically but often executed in Asia; they are tufted by hand with automated tufting guns. Custom designer rugs can also be executed as hand-knotted Tibetan Oriental rugs. These two methods produce a high-quality product that typically withstands many years of traffic in both residential and nonresidential settings.

In each kind of manufacture, the design begins by hand or computer. A pattern is created and colored, then presented and accepted by the client. Often, the interior designer works carefully with the manufacturing company to create the design. The rug company then creates a computer-generated to-scale pattern, possibly in several colorways for the designer and client to consider and from which to select. Texture and relief are also selected. Tufts of yarn are dyed to match the selected colors. Next, a carpet sample or **strike-off** is created, compared to the computer-generated design, and presented for a final signature approval by designer and client.

Some professionals also place custom-designed broadloom carpeting in this category, although it is typically installed wall to wall and therefore is not, technically, an area rug. Custom-designed Wilton and Axminster rugs are discussed in chapter 12.

Custom designer rugs can also be created from cut pieces of broadloom carpeting. This method is somewhat like creating a stained-glass composition, where colored elements are joined. Interest is created by selecting pieces of varying color, pile depth, and yarn texture. The pieces are cut into shapes and heat-taped together. Then the entire composition is glued onto a heavy canvas and backed with a jute or polypropelene secondary backing. These edges are bound with cotton tape.

AMERICAN HANDMADE RUGS

Rag rugs are sturdy, colorful rugs hand- or machine-woven from cotton scraps or wool. An overview of handmade rag rugs is on www.wiley.com/go/interiortextiles. There are several types of rag rug: **Wool warps** are made in a weave in which the yarn runs lengthwise in the carpet. **Pile rag** rugs included **shirred** rugs and **pleated** rugs, historical (or contemporary) rag rugs made by gathering or shirring the materials and then stitching the result to a backing according to a pattern. **Braided** rugs are made of strips of fabric braided and sewn in a circle or oval. Like woven rag rugs, braided rugs were historically a homemade, handmade

product. Braided rugs are constructed of wool, cotton, or linen fabric or heavy wool rug yarn. Individual lengths of braid or a continuous braid may be stitched or laced together into the desired shape. Braided rugs are associated with colonial New England interiors and are appropriate for Colonial or country styles (see chapter 16).

Braided shag rugs are strips of fabric knitted into a string base with a shaggy top.

Crocheted rugs are a variation on braided rugs that involves hand knitting or crochet. Long strips of fabric are still used, but more freedom in color and design is possible. These rugs are often colorful and made in hit-or-miss round, heart, oval, or rectangular shapes. They are completely reversible and wear moderately well. Underlay padding or double-faced tape is recommended to prevent sliding.

Needlepunch rugs are made of yarns in a looped pile punched with a handheld instrument into a background of burlap or heavy cloth. A pattern is printed or composed on

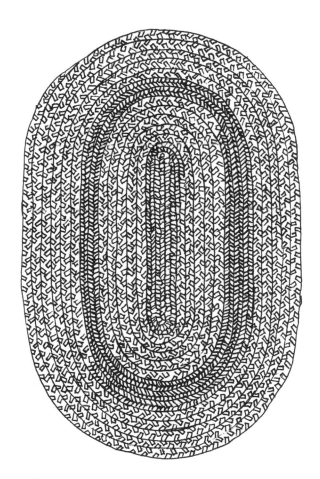

Figure 13.15a A braided rag rug, made historically of strips of used clothing. This rug is hand braided then hand-stitched into an oval.

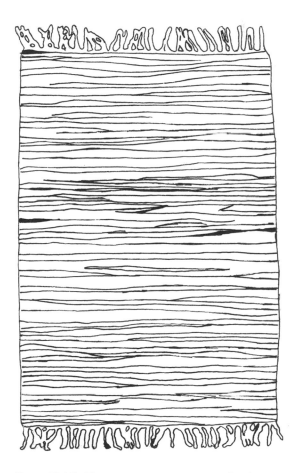

Figure 13.15b The woven rag rug is woven on a hand-operated loom with strips of fabric as weft and cotton yarn as warp. Today these rugs are made from a variety of fabrics custom chosen for a specific interior. Lower quality woven rag rugs are also available as ready-made in-stock items.

the cloth, guiding the artisan in the creation of the design. Historic pieces may be fairly valuable and large. Kits are available for needlepunch rugs today.

Hooked rugs are simple hand-tool-tufted rugs with a burlap or canvas base. They are often found as needlecraft kits online and in stores. A few hooked rugs are historic.

Floorcloths are floor coverings used both historically and today. During the American colonial period, canvas or oilcloth fabric was used; this was sometimes painted and sealed so it could be swept and lightly mopped. Today, floorcloths are often executed as a craft item in much the same way. A heavy fabric is painted or stenciled, then sealed with a product such as polyurethane. It is an economical and artistically creative floor covering.

NATURAL FIBER RUGS

Woven or tufted natural fiber area rugs include protein and cellulosic woven broadloom and tufted rugs. The categories include flokati/floccati rugs, wool area rugs, cotton rugs, sisal rugs, coir mats, jute rugs, and Japanese tatami mats. Also in this category are sheep or lamb fleeces and big-game animal skins.

Flokati/floccati woven rugs are originally from Greece and named for the flokati or floccati goat. They have a fluffy wool pile with very long fibers. The average-quality flokati rug has a pile height of about 3 inches, and the higher quality flokati rug has an average pile height of 5 inches and is 3 times the knot density. **Turkish Angora rugs** are similar, but the hair is from the Angora goat. These rugs are historically favored in modern Scandinavian interiors and are broadly available. They are primarily used in homes. See www. wiley.com/go/interiortextiles for specific cleaning instructions.

Sheep and lamb fleeces are the tanned hides of domesticated sheep slaughtered for their meat. Fleeces are small, very soft, and comfortable year-round—seemingly cool in summer and warm in winter. They are used as accent rugs and car seat covers.

Big-game animal skins are considered trophy rugs and are the result of big-game hunting. New animal trophy skins are scarcer than in the past, as laws have been enacted to protect species, and hunting is by permit only. The animal skins most popular for interior design have been zebra and bear. Imitation zebra rugs are made of manufactured printed fibers, and horsehides are sometimes printed to imitate zebra skins.

Wool area rugs are often choices for neutral and natural area rugs in plush, Saxony, or shag textures. Examples are Berber rugs, made of blended undyed yarns (white, gray, brown, black) in plain or hand-beveled textures. Wool broadloom carpeting is cut to size and shape, and, when finished with a binding and sometimes an attached fringe, becomes a neutral, natural area rug.

Cotton rugs are generally small and used as bath rugs. They are highly absorbent and slow-drying, and are handsome in natural hues, or unbleached. The advantage of cotton underfoot is its comfort; cotton fibers do not irritate the skin as can wool or wiry cellulosic fibers.

Sisal is a natural fiber derived from the *Agave sisalana* cactus plant, which grows in semi-arid regions in Brazil and Mexico. Sisal is not the same fiber as coir or jute; it is stronger and more durable than other natural fibers and is, therefore, preferred. Other natural fibers used in making rugs that may be labeled as "sisal" include coir, jute, hemp, and sea grass and mountain grass from China. Sisal rugs are for indoor use only and are sometimes used in enclosed and screened-in porches. They should never be exposed to rainfall or allowed to become saturated with water.

Coir mats are made of coconut fiber and may be natural brown in color or printed with a design. They are generally used at doorways rather than as interior flooring.

Jute rugs are in tones of natural beige, as jute is not a colorfast natural fiber. Jute area rugs are typically executed in plain, flat, reversible weaves.

Tatami mats are traditional Japanese woven mats made of sea grasses and edged with black silk fabric. They are woven 1 to 3 inches thick and in 3- by 6-foot modules that can be arranged in a number of geometric configurations.

Machine-Made Area Rugs

Area rugs encompass a broad range of moderately priced, machine-made, mass-produced rugs. They are referred to as *designer rugs* when the design is original; sometimes they are custom designed by a well-known living designer, artist, or architect, or derived from the work of a designer no longer living. Area rugs that are copies of Oriental rugs are referred to as *domestic Orientals*. Woven and oval rag rugs are available from area rug purveyors at retail locations, online, and through mail-order catalogs. These rugs are woven primarily in the United States, Belgium, India, China, France, and Egypt. There are many quality levels and hence many price levels of designer area rugs. While some are authentic in coloration, some are contemporary adaptations and colored to meet a modern market.

Machine-made designer rugs are made of wool, wool/rayon, wool/acrylic, acrylic, olefin and nylon, and sometimes cotton. They are generally not washable and thus

Figure 13.16a Natural fiber woven rugs or mats are practical and handsome where natural texture underfoot is desirable. Luminette® Privacy sheers filters and diffuses light. *Photo courtesy of Hunter Douglas.*

Figure 13.16b Plain and novelty twill weaves emphasize the natural quality of these sisal carpet samples. *Landry & Arcari Oriental Rugs and Carpeting. From Maryrose McGowan,* Specifying Interiors, *2 ed., John Wiley & Sons, Inc., 2006.*

require spot cleaning and do best when protected from heavy traffic. Shapes include square, rectangular, circular, and unique, in sizes varying from approximately 2 by 3 feet to 10 by 13 feet. Rug catalogs may categorize their offerings along the lines of this list: traditional, tropical, exotic, porch/patio, braids/rag, lodge, country, children's, contemporary, mats, shags, transitional, and natural.

Scatter or Accent Rugs

Scatter or accent rugs comprise a variety of small rugs tufted with a latex backing, or woven and intended for use in front of kitchen and bath sinks, by tubs, showers and toilets, by entrances (usually back doors), in laundry rooms or other workrooms, or scattered wherever useful. They are more serviceable if they are washable; check labels before buying. If scatter or accent rugs have a rubber or latex nonskid backing, they should not be exposed to heat during cleaning. Even so, latex ages, becomes brittle, and breaks loose, eventually leaving a slippery rug that requires replacement. As such, these rugs are temporary rugs and meant to serve a need while the color and style are in fashion. Scatter or accent rugs are often solid colors or slightly mottled patterns and of various yarns and textures, from very fine cut pile to cable yarn looped. The most common fibers for scatter rugs are polyester and cotton. Polyester is nonabsorbent and quick-drying; cotton is highly absorbent and slow-drying. Other fibers are also used and are indicated on the label.

PADDING/UNDERLAY FOR AREA RUGS

Over time, shifting and slipping of rugs laid directly on hard floors and carpeting can cause stress to the rug construction, break the stitching on the backing, and cause excessive wear and stretching. Rug pads increase the life of rugs and make them safer. Urethane and rebond foam pads are generally not recommended for area rugs, as their resilience or bounce allows heels, particularly women's dress shoe heels, to stretch and even break the rug warp or backing. However, the right padding or underlay is important for area rugs to extend the life of the carpet, to protect it against abuse, to keep it from sliding, and to help prevent dangerous falls. There are four types of area rug underlay: flat open-mesh grid, open-mesh pad, carpet-to-carpet, and thin, dense fiber pad.

- **Flat open-mesh grid** holds a rug in place and does not add height to the rug, thus avoiding a shoulder on which heels can catch, resulting in trips and falls. This mesh is used on hard surfaces.
- **Open-mesh pad** also anchors the rug, but it adds cushion and insulation, plus increased height or shoulder. This pad is also used on hard surfaces.
- **Carpet-to-carpet pad** holds a rug securely in place on carpeting. It also protects the carpeting beneath, so the rug backing will not abrade the carpet pile.
- **Dense fiber pad** is generally flat or a medium-fiber cushion. This pad may be combined with the flat open-mesh grid to hold the pad in place.

For all types of grid mesh or padding, seek warranties for nonallergenic and mildew-resistant materials. High-quality grid underlay features safe adhesives that stick to the back of the rug and to the floor. Good underlay does not stain the floor or leave a residue on rugs, and it prevents colors from transferring from the rug to the carpet or floor beneath. Open-grid construction allows the rug to breathe and prolongs its life while protecting its construction integrity. It makes vacuuming more efficient. Airflow construction also deters damage from mold, mildew, and vermin. Standard sizes of no-slip grid padding are 3 × 5 feet, 4 × 6 feet, 5 × 8 feet, 6 × 9 feet, 8 × 10 feet, and 9 × 12 feet and can be cut to fit. Guarantees for good-quality underlay are ten to twenty years.

Rug Installations

A loose-laid or room-sized rug used in combination with a cushion calls for a thin cushion that is 1 or 2 inches smaller than the rug size. The edges of the rug must be cut and bound to the runners by sewing tape over the raw edges or by serging them together. These tactics are especially important to use if the rug is to be laid on stairs because they help prevent the rug from moving off the cushion and because it is not as raised from the ground.

OBTAINING AREA RUGS

Many resources exist for the purchase of handmade and machine-made area rugs. Oriental rugs are purchased from dealers who have buyers in the countries of origin and who select and supervise the shipment to merchant showrooms and warehouses. These rug dealers also take custom orders to locate an Oriental rug to a client or interior designer's specifications (colors, pattern, size, type). Designers who bring clients to Oriental rug merchants or dealers are paid a commission for sales or are given a discount if they purchase and resell rugs.

Custom-designed rugs are obtained through manufacturers whose work is done domestically or abroad. These rugs are sold to the design professional, who resells them to the client, or they are sold directly to the client and the designer charges a fee for liaison services.

Other kinds of rugs available in showrooms, online, or through catalogs may serve the trade only where designers purchase product for resale. In some cases, the source may sell both to the trade at a discount and to the public at retail. Additionally, many rug retailers sell directly at retail only to the customer. Designers often use these sources, and then charge for their time or for their design work. A glossary of Oriental, handmade, and area rug terms is available on www.wiley.com/go/interiortextiles.

RESOURCES

See Bibliography and www.wiley.com/go/interiortextiles for rug purveyors.

PART III

PERIOD STYLES

14

Oriental and Asian Styles

Figure 14.1
Chinese interior

CHINA

Period Overview

The Chinese Ming and T'a Ch'ing dynasties date from 1368 to 1912, when the Chinese revolution ended them. The homes of the royalty and very wealthy as well as religious buildings were made of wooden post-and-beam construction. Dark brown Persian cedarwood was carved or pierced in symbolic, complex fretwork or lattice patterns, or painted with colorful designs. These components formed exposed architectural members and sliding screens used as wall partitions. Seating pieces were human scale and dignified, and Chinese rugs gave much elegance and softness. Rich Chinese textiles are a hallmark of this period. Some designs still in use today are over 4,000 years old, and were fully developed during this historic era. China was an artistically and architecturally well developed nation long before the European Renaissance.

Textiles: Colors, Motifs, and Textures

Color

Classic Ming and T'a Ch'ing colors include ivory; Ming blue (a medium-value royal blue); cinnabar red (a slightly dulled red); mandarin or Manchu red (a warm, deep red), which symbolizes good fortune and long life; coral; Chinese or (a somewhat faded, medium-tone, rich, slightly greenish gold); jade green (light to dark shades of this natural stone); and peacock blue, which is rich and clear. Flowers imported from China added peony pink and chrysanthemum gold to the Chinese palette as it became popular in Europe during the Rococo and Late Georgian eras. Bright pink is said to bring romance into one's life, and red is still the color considered most propitious or favorable. Historically, brides dressed in red, as the color symbolized good luck and fertility. White is the color of death, as ashes of the cremated family members are kept in vases; therefore, it is avoided as an interior color in favor of pale gold or cream. Blue—dark, bright, and pale—symbolizes heavenly blessings. Gold suggests money or wealth, which is highly regarded in Chinese culture.

Chinese wallpaper, described below, and many fabric colors came from a lighter palette of apple green, yellow, rose red, and ultramarine blue, as well as the coral, pale green, lavender that had become popular in China in the late eighteenth century, and a pale version of turquoise blue. Chinese wallpaper colors are light and airy, an interesting contrast to the heavy woods and deep Ming blue and cinnabar red.

Motifs and Symbolism

Folklore and superstition, ceremonies, and ancestor worship combine as the basis for the symbolism of many Chinese motifs. Reverence for nature and the seasons, the intimidation of evil spirits, and the quest for special personal benefits all have had a profound effect on this symbolism. The mythological **chimera**, a fierce dog with a dragonlike head, represents power and dignity. The five-clawed dragon is the symbol of the emperor, often seen clutching the pearl of wisdom in one claw. The four-clawed dragon is a protector against evil and a disseminator of wisdom for the commoner. The patterns of chrysanthemum and other enduring, sturdy plants symbolize both longevity and patience. Water, waves, and cloud patterns symbolize heavenly blessings. The phoenix bird represents life and success; pine trees, old men, and the tortoise shell suggest longevity; birds and old coins bring fortune or money; and circular and hexagonal shapes bring good luck and the warding off of evil spirits. Textile design and scrolls also included full landscape scenes such as the vertical mountains

of the Gang-Zhou province and the Yellow River winding around bends where houses were placed to receive the prosperity of living waters. Pagodas or open, columned pavilions with turned-up eaves, arched bridges, and willow trees are frequently seen in these pictorials. Chinese fretwork is also seen in textiles—as angular, complex components that often represented family crests.

Feng Shui Feng shui is an ancient Chinese philosophy that is integral to many of today's Asian interiors. In order to ensure health, happiness, and prosperity, feng shui dictates the arrangement of buildings, graves, furniture, and even entire cities in favorable positions. The name of this ancient art of placement literally means "wind" and "water." Integral to the feng shui philosophy is the Chinese term **ch'i** (pronounced "chee"), which represents a life force or energy that moves the universe, makes water run, creates mountains, breathes life into plants, trees, and humans, and pushes humans along a life course. Feng shui addresses the flow of this life force on a micro level, bringing energy and balance into the interior environment. Successful feng shui brings to the occupants vibrant ch'i, encompassing health, energy, balance of mind and body, vitality, and regeneration of the spirit, resulting in harmony, growth, and success. Many principles of feng shui are based not only on Chinese tradition but also on common sense, and they are parallel to the wise use of principles and elements of design.

Tao In the vast literature of Chinese painting, there is continual reference to a **tao**, or "way," also interpreted as "road," "path," "method," "standard," "doctrine"—in sum, the Way. It is not a personal way; it is the fundamental concepts and the manner in which they have long been represented by the Chinese brush and ink on silk or paper. The great unifying aim is to express the Way—the basic Chinese belief—as the order and harmony seen in nature. The Chinese word for *landscape* is written as "mountain" plus "stream," which symbolizes all aspects of nature. This Taoist philosophy is seen in mystical painting on silk scrolls, and in artwork and even in textiles—the guiding principle of achieving beauty and harmony.

Motifs: Hand-Painted Wallpapers

One of China's most influential exports was the wallpapers that appeared in Europe as early as the seventeenth century. They were highly prized both there and in America in the eighteenth and nineteenth centuries.

Chinese wallpapers were made of joined sheets of mulberry paper forming panels, mostly a standard 47 inches

Figure 14.2 a–t Chinese textile motifs
a fretwork borders on floral fabric;
b–g tree branches, exotic birds, peony,
chrysanthemum, and other blossoms;
water elements; **h** clouds in stylized form

a.

b.

c.

d.

e.

f.

g.

h.

Figure 14.2 i, j lattice work; **k, l** tortoise shell lattice and fretwork; **m** tortoise shell, ocean waves or clouds; **n** chimera; **o** phoenix birds; **p** deer; **q** male protector dragon with imperial scepter/ball symbolizing emperor on lattice fretwork field

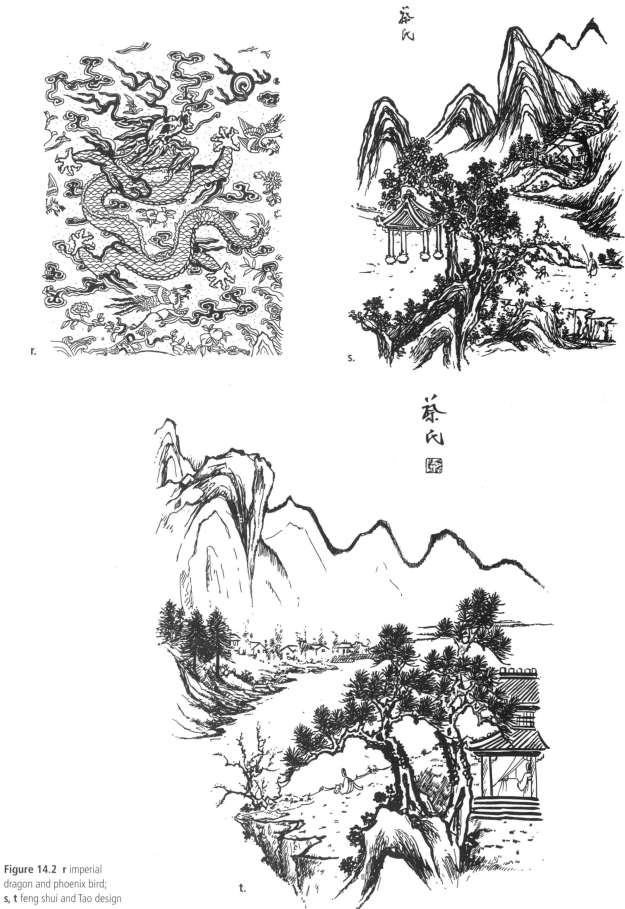

Figure 14.2 r imperial dragon and phoenix bird; **s, t** feng shui and Tao design

wide and 10 to 12 feet high and usually sold in sets of 20 to 25. Mounted on silk, heavy cartridge paper, or linen, they were shipped in rolls to the West. Outlined by hand in simple carbon ink and then filled in with colored washes, the images never used repeat patterns, making every set essentially unique and prized. The most common type of paper featured highly stylized, antiperspective scenes of blossoming trees or bamboo, often growing from fantastic rock formations, with animals, birds, and insects depicted in great detail, and all in bright, naturalistic colors. Extra sheets of birds or butterflies were often sold with each set; these could be cut and pasted over torn or stained sections.

In general, the Chinese designs were painted on ungrounded papers so less surface paint would flake off when rolled and transported. The resulting soft white or cream-colored grounds that characterize the oldest papers were a large factor in the airiness these papers would lend a room. Sometimes, however, the paper was tinted in the pulp stage, creating soft blues and pinks equally effective at setting off the strong black calligraphic lines and subtly changing the mood from warm to cool. This tinting method was replaced by a vogue for laid-in grounds in the early eighteenth century.

Everyone who was anyone wanted at least one room decorated with the "India papers," as they were often known, as Britain's East India Company was the largest importer. People even went as far as to build rooms to fit the standard panels exactly. George Washington, who was fashion-conscious, ordered a set for Mount Vernon in 1787. Many American interiors were graced with these fine decorative papers. Designs could be custom ordered as well.

Textures: Silk

Exquisite and luxurious hand-embroidered, printed, or painted Chinese textiles have given silk the title "queen of fibers." Silk velvet was used for temple hangings in China.

The Chinese were the first to weave silk from cocoons and to embroider in silk. Chinese silk fabrics were printed, painted, or embroidered in complex patterns as far back as 2,000 B.C. Ancient Chinese silk textiles were divided into two grades; the thicker variety was called *lo* and the thinner variety *ling*. Today there are many grades, such as *ch'ou,* a general name for silk cloth; *chiian,* or damask; *lo* and *sha* for thick or thin gauze; *tuan,* or satin; *jung,* or velvet; and *chin,* or brocade. Each of these is divided into subcategories according to design and form of weaving. Examples of supreme artistic interest are brocade, tapestry (*k'ossu*), and satin embroidery. Many silks are enriched with hand-painted decorations and colored and metal threads.

Textures: Embroidery

The Chinese have always excelled at embroidery, embroidering objects such as robes, purses, shoes, spectacle cases, banners, and altar cloths and using an infinite variety of threads, patterns, and stitches. It is said that on a spectacle case, 6 × 2 inches, there are sometimes no fewer than 20,000 stitches. Theatrical costumes, mandarin robes, and ladies' dresses could take ten or twelve women four or five years' constant work to finish. Embroidery was also used in ancient China for the decoration of silk flags and banners distinguishing marks of rank. It gradually developed into a pastime for wealthy ladies. A princess of the T'ang dynasty excelled at this art and worked with her needle 3,000 pairs of mandarin ducks on a single coverlet.

Textures: Velvets

It is probable that the technique of velvet-making was introduced to both China and Japan from the West. In China, velvet was used for cloaks and riding coats as well as for cushions and Buddhist temple hangings. The most common design is a lotus flower surrounded by scrollwork. The flowered velvets are among the most dramatic of Chinese textiles; even when the colors are the same throughout, the raised pattern contrasts in its fuller depth of tone with the smooth glow of the rich silk ground.

Textures: K'ossu *Tapestry*

Apart from brocades, the Sung period was particularly famous for its silk tapestries, known as *k'ossu*. The term has been written in various ways, to denote "crossing-threads," "weft-woven threads," or "weft-woven colors." The characters now used in writing *k'ossu* mean "cut threads," referring to the separation of the weft thread of various colors, these terminating at the margin of the colored areas instead of running through the width of the cloth.

K'ossu is an ancient method of tapestry weaving, now applied to very fine silk threads.

Textures: Cotton Prints

Finely woven imported cotton printed fabrics with Chinese designs became a European vogue during the Early and Late Georgian eras and during the French Rococo period. Many Chinese-like or chinoiserie designs were roller-printed in France in imitation of the lovely patterns imported from China. These cotton prints often depicted old, gnarled trees with lavish blossoms hanging down as does a fully blossomed peony; often, each flower differed from the next. Exotic birds perched in the branches. Other printed designs include those discussed under "Motifs and Symbolism," above.

Figure 14.3 a–c Chinese chair, sofa, and bed

Upholstered Furniture

Chinese upholstered furniture was largely dignified chairs with upholstered seats. Persian cedar was used as the complexly carved legs, arms, and backs. The **banti** leg is a slightly turned-in foot. The seat and back are flat; some **Tsu** chairs have simple, straight slat backs with curved arms and back frames. The size of Chinese furniture is similar to the size of Western furniture; the chairs and chests are tall, for example, and dignified in appearance. Woods such as rosewood and teak, polished to perfection, are in themselves works of art.

Window Treatments and Beds

Although some silks and cottons were used as draping fabrics, most were hung around or at beds and rarely used at the window. Instead, the Chinese rice- or mulberry-paper sliding screen was used extensively, with intricate fretwork designs. Another treatment that originated in China was the bamboo shade, used to filter light and provide some privacy. Both of these classic treatments offer an element of intrigue because they are translucent. Latticework screens were similar to the Japanese shoji screen discussed below, but with more complex and intricate symbolic designs.

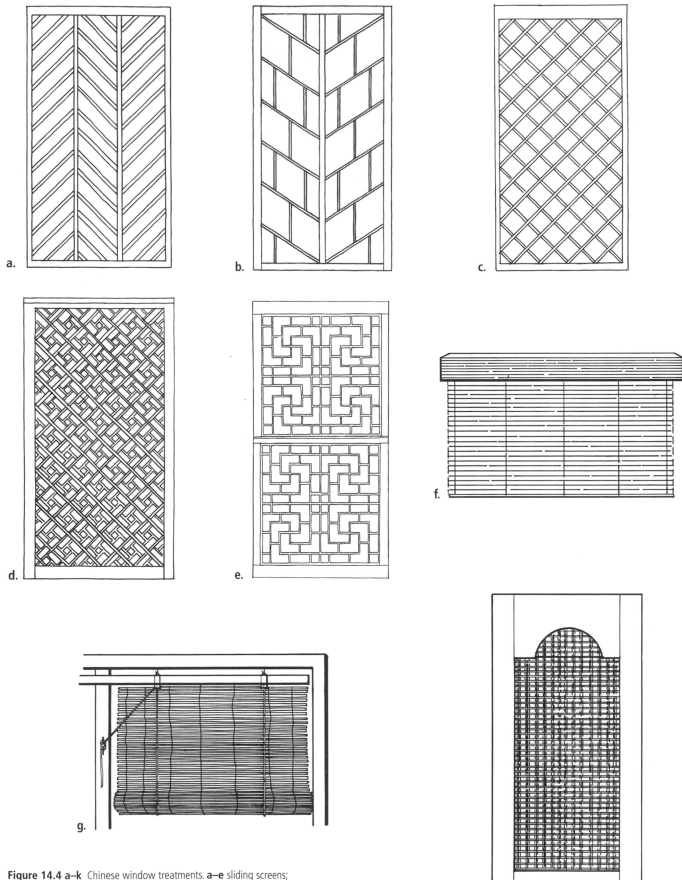

Figure 14.4 a–k Chinese window treatments. **a–e** sliding screens;
f, g, j, and k bamboo shades; **h, i** lattice work insets

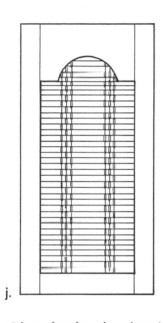

i.

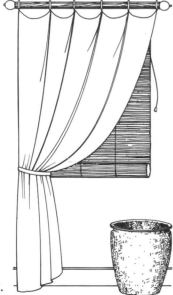

j.

k.

Rugs

Rugs play a large part in the floor coverings in China. Each magnificent Chinese rug is an authentic work of art. Many thousands of hours are spent on hand-knotting, hand-washing, hand-carving, and self-fringing by weavers skilled in the ancient art of Chinese rugmaking. The exquisite beauty of these rugs is indeed long-lived.

Chinese rugs are filled with bold and simple patterns. Chinese rug pile is deep, dense, and cut at a beveled angle to yield striking patterns.

Chinese carpets are made of wool or silk. Wool is prevalent in Chinese rugs, which adds comfort by warmth to interiors. Warp and weft yarns of cotton hold the hand-knotted wool pile in place.

The earliest Chinese wool rugs to have been preserved are felt; some of these felt rugs are silk, others wool.

Figure 14.5 Traditional Chinese rug or carpet

Felted woolen rugs were made to furnish the fire-heated brick bed or *k'ang* (a bench with room for two people) used by the peasants of northern China. These rugs were either divided to be placed on either side of a table on the *k'ang* or designed to cover the whole *k'ang* in a single piece measuring about 9 × 12 feet. Camel hair was used in the manufacture of felt rugs, which had dyed black and red borders and, sometimes, colored woolen insertions. See also chapter 13, "Hand- and Machine-Made Area Rugs," for more information about Chinese rugs. Also, www.wiley.com/go/interior-textiles has Oriental rug terms and history sections.

Chinese Influence Today

Chinese design has a great influence on today's contemporary settings. Many designers look to the style for inspiration. It is important for us to understand this particular style and to appreciate its beauty before we can go on to create new ideas. Classic designs last forever, and fine designs are even more beautiful. It is the exquisite design and fine workmanship of Chinese pieces that make the style so distinctive and admirable.

In recent years, feng shui has become a major philosophy used in creating interiors with balanced energy, light, color, and overall good design. Some contemporary methods of increasing good ch'i in the home are to add water or fountains, candles, aromatherapy, and so on. Many people have embraced the tenets of feng shui, claiming it does affect the physical and psychological health of people. Feng shui consultants assist those who are seeking better ch'i, peace, and harmony in their environments. Countless fabrics on the market today are inspired by or adapted from Chinese textile textures, designs, and color schemes.

JAPAN

Period Overview

Japanese architecture and the interiors described here date to the enduring style that originated in the Muromachi and Momoyama periods, A.D. 1392 to 1603. Japanese architecture from these periods is mainly wood, frankly exposed and used in structural designs with predominant horizontal lines. In palaces, the wood was ornately carved; in the homes of the wealthy, the decoration resulted from simple posts and beams and carefully arranged latticework. Open floor plans made rooms look larger. Rooms were divided by shoji or fusuma partitions (see "Window Treatments and Beds," below). Some areas were partitioned with painted rice-paper **byobu screens** or lacquered wooden **coromandel screens**

(hinged, freestanding lacquered panels with decorative designs applied in colored lacquer with mother-of-pearl inlay). Wall composition was somewhat cubist, with long planks of hinoki cypress used to frame wooden walls. Interior walls were few in number; they often consisted of sliding **fusuma** partitions made from plain or painted mulberry paper or wood that was block-painted or hand-painted.

Decoration and furniture were sparse, although every home had its **tokonoma**, a niche the size of a modest clothes closet without the door. This area was a focal point of two or three items asymmetrically arranged to show honor to the homeowners or guests. The tokonoma contained rice-paper or silk scrolls painted with scenes and calligraphy, and often a stylized floral arrangement, known as **ikebana**, which was rotated or refreshed regularly.

Japanese design focuses on the form and the way it is expressed in the composition. It simplifies and beautifies by excluding insignificant details and focusing on the message of the composition. Beauty is viewed in terms of design and pattern and interpreted with the utmost vigor and earthiness. This beauty is what makes Japanese design timeless and interesting throughout the world.

Textiles: Colors, Motifs, and Textures

Traditionally, Japan has always been a country of fine-quality goods. This includes its textiles. Many Japanese textiles are so beautiful they can be considered works of art. In fact, textile and interior component craftsmanship in Japan is very highly regarded. The techniques used to create textiles are intricate and difficult to master. The textiles produced by weaving and dyeing are called kasuri and are the most common in Japan. Color is incorporated to create different esteemed aesthetics, as listed below.

Color: The Shibui Aesthetic
(Note: *Shibui* is the adjective form of the noun *shibusa*.)
Shibusa may be defined as understated beauty that is never obvious, is deceptively simple, while being based on thoughtful, complex design. The shibui object never proclaims itself—not in color nor line nor material. It must wait for its depths to be discovered. In traditional Japanese interiors, shibusa is the most sought-after aesthetic value, representing both the aesthetics of nature and the prized human quality of modesty.

Shibui interiors utilize ratios of color and texture as seen in nature as backgrounds and furnishings. It is based on the principle of optical interrelationships, where every object affects the pleasing power of the whole. No object, color, form, or texture is seen in a vacuum—rather, the intrinsic beauty of each furnishing selection affects the entire

Figure 14.6 Japanese interior showing floor tatami mats and zabuton pillows. Shoji screens at the window and sliding fusuma screens are made of rice or mulberry paper.

interior. This means each item must be selected carefully to evoke qualities of tranquility, simplicity, gracefulness, yet complexity. No item or material demands attention. Philosophically, the colors, patterns, and textures evoke the following qualities:

- Simplicity—often based on thoughtful, complex design
- Humility—something is left to the imagination of the viewer
- Silence—quiet serenity or tranquility
- Naturalness—use of nature's colors and materials; things that are born, not made

Shibui interiors inherently possess high quality viewed with an innate understanding of fine design and a quality of the old, meaning the furnished space will stand the test of time through innate graciousness and naturalness.

Six aesthetic laws of nature govern the application of shibui color, texture, and pattern in interior design:

1. In nature, color is not distributed evenly.
2. No color is matched in nature; thousands of greens are seen in a landscape, and thousands of other colors are seen in soil, bark, stone, and foliage.
3. Color intensity is distributed in ratio; muted colors are more abundant and form backgrounds, while brighter colors are accents and provide interest, and in very small ratio to the overall scene.
4. Pattern and texture are integral and seen in profuse application, yet they are subtle and understated. The viewer must examine and is thereby rewarded with an experience of lovely patterns that waited for their depths to be discovered.
5. Although nature possesses an abundance of pattern, those patterns never monotonously repeat. Rather, variety is seen blending together seamlessly to provide a quiet, interesting whole.
6. Interest is created with ratios of shininess versus dullness. Backgrounds are muted, dull, matte finishes.

Added to this dull background are tiny flecks of sparkle, similar to sunlight backlighting leaves or the sparkle of sunlight on water. The sparkle can be accomplished with light, reflecting textiles such as silk or metallic *lamé* threads. These tiny scintillations provide a dash of excitement in an otherwise calming interior.

These qualities are incorporated into fabrics, furniture, artwork, lighting, and accessories.

The law of value distribution is expressed in flooring elements being darker and more solid in appearance, medium values appearing around the walls, and lighter colors showing above, as in nature.

Color: The Hade Aesthetic

The **hade** aesthetic utilizes the brightest colors of nature to create exciting designs. There are no neutrals or soft colors. It is usually associated with theater and celebration.

Color and Philosophy: Yin-Yang Aesthetic

The **yin-yang** aesthetic is a contrast of two elements. The yin is the female or negative element, force, or principle, seen in interiors as shade, dark, cold, moistness, water, blackness, and nighttime. The yang is the male or positive element, force, or principle, represented by clarity, light, heat, dryness, fire, and daytime. These two principles interplay and give character by contrast. They are dynamic, meaning they are never static—one is increasing, or waxing, while the other is decreasing, or waning—thus giving life flow and energy to interiors. The dualism is found in all art forms in Japan and in China, where it originated.

Color and Philosophy: Zen

Zen is a form of Buddhist mediation introduced into Japan at the end of the twelfth century. It is a training intended to emancipate the mind from the worries and troubles of life and to help the soul thus purified and pacified attain a truly transcendental view of the world. The teaching emphasizes the identification of the soul with the vast universe and treats human emotions and passions as things to be suppressed. The innate simplicity of Japanese interiors is a fitting expression of Zen philosophy. The three methods of achieving Zen are **Mondo** (questions and answers), **Koan** (a device; sitting motionless and in silence and trying to solve riddles proposed by the Zen master), and **Satori** (spiritual awakening and thereby the attainment of enlightenment).

Color and Philosophy: Shinto

Shinto is defined as "the way of gods," and **Kami**, which should be worshipped, is the entity that is invisible to the human eye in the normal state of consciousness and that is capable of exerting an influence on the visible universe.

Kami, men, and all nature are born of the same parents. This belief is a primary factor in Japanese life, meaning that all mankind and nature are one in harmony and purpose. This philosophy finds expression in the modesty and subtlety of the shibui aesthetic, and is a primary influence on Japanese social patterns, individual behavior, ethics, and attitude—and especially art and architecture.

Color and Philosophy: Japanese Moods

In addition to the influence of shibui, Zen, and Shinto, other Japanese moods include **Mono no Aware,** or "sympathetic sadness," which implies that the world will go on and that mutability, change, and the evanescence of all things yield their elegiac satisfactions; that as with environment, one lives with, not against it. **Sabi** mood is the moment of solitude or quiet, a type of thrilling loneliness. **Wabi** is where the artist or designer feels depressed or sad, and in this peculiar emptiness of feeling catches a glimpse of something rather ordinary and unpretentious, an incredible "suchness." **Aware** is when the moment evokes a more intense, nostalgic sadness, connected with autumn and the vanishing ways of the world. **Yugen** is the vision or moment, the sudden perception of something mysterious and strange, hinting at an unknown never to be discovered. Each of these moods can be captured in interior design as a philosophy and through artistic materials.

Color: Indigo and Cotton

The most common dye is indigo, which is applied to cotton; the two complement each other. Cotton is easily dyed by indigo, and indigo strengthens cotton fibers in the dyeing process. Indigo can dye in a variety of shades. The shade is determined in two ways: the strength of the dye and the number of times the yarn is placed in the dye solution. This combination of dyeing and cotton historically allowed citizens of the lower classes to enjoy high-quality material without breaking the law, as they were forbidden from wearing silk.

Motifs

Two types of motifs are employed by the Japanese: abstract and figurative. Both are important to the clean, simple style and symbolism of Japan. The abstract is more formal and masculine, while the figurative tends to be more feminine.

The abstract motifs usually consist of straight lines. The vertical, horizontal, and diagonal lines can form trellises, basket designs, or fencing. More complex line patterns include the tortoise shell (joined hexagons), lightning, and swastikas. The most popular abstract design during the Muromachi and Momoyama periods was

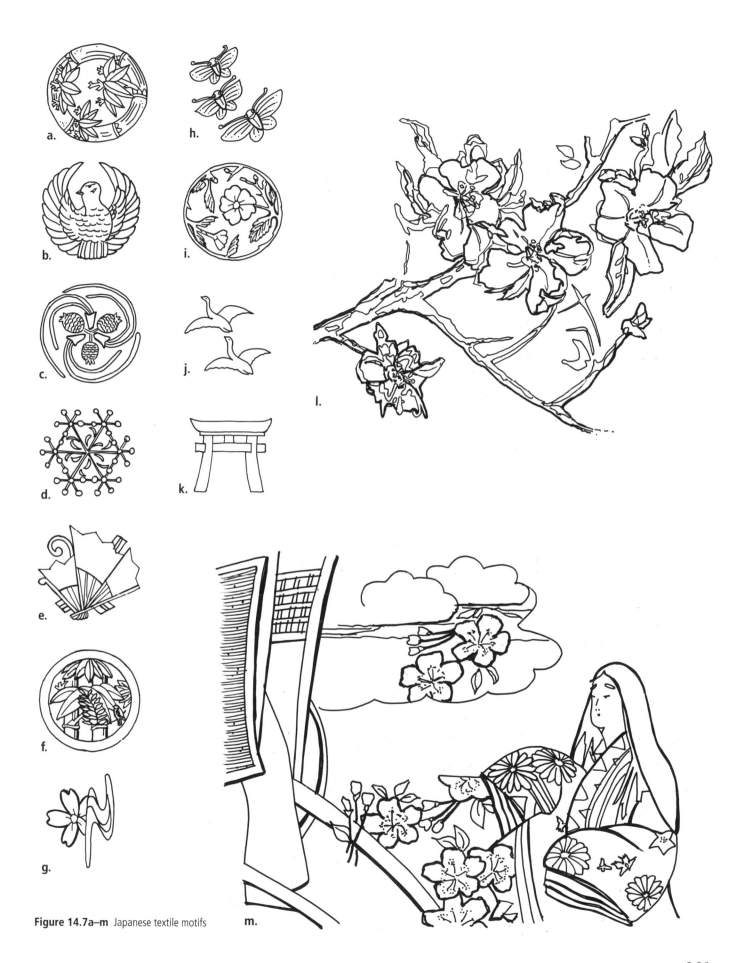

Figure 14.7a–m Japanese textile motifs

the lozenge, a diamond-shaped pattern. The lozenge was usually created from pine, and thus is referred to as the *pine-bark lozenge.*

The curved, expressive lines of figurative motifs provide contrast to Japanese abstract design and incorporate an appreciation for nature. The Japanese used the floral motif as accents to abstract designs, but flowers were a popular motif for any material. Blossoms, such as plum, cherry, wisteria, and bush clover, were also used, along with flowers, trees, leaves, animals, and natural scenery in textile design. The trees were usually in the form of pine, bamboo, willow, and vines. Animals included cranes and mandarin ducks. During the Muromachi period, herons, cormorants, sparrows, swallows, and quail were added to the animal motifs. All of these could be added to a natural scenery motif to create a beautiful print. Common natural scenery motifs were boats, bridges, clouds, mist, and especially snow and water. Water was important because it expressed power and fluid motion. This feeling was usually conveyed in a waterfall or ocean scene. Snow became more popular in the Momoyama period.

Last, the Japanese are well known for their art in characters. The Japanese use the characters of their written language as beautiful design motifs. Many times, old poems were written on textiles. The lines of Japanese characters are free-flowing and express the same feeling of nature and beauty that the figurative designs achieve.

Painting and Calligraphy

Ancient Japanese (and Chinese and Korean) people considered painting and calligraphy the only true art forms, and both are still popular today. The most common painted theme is the "bird and flower." This consists of plum trees, cherry blossoms, or peonies, with mandarin ducks, cranes, or sparrows incorporated the same scene. Each of these involves symbolism. Two examples are the mandarin duck, which symbolizes fidelity and commitment because these birds mate for life, and the plum tree, which symbolizes the arrival of spring because it is among the first to flower.

Other frequently painted scenes depict mountains whose tops are left unfinished or hidden by mist. Unseen paths are also used in these landscape scenes to allow the viewer's imagination to finish the painting.

Tie-Dyeing

Tie-dyeing, or **shibori,** is common in Japan. Shibori is a type of resist-dyeing. Fabric is pinched or twisted, tied to keep it in place, and then placed in the dye solution. **Yuzen** is another resist method of dyeing; it is created with a paste applied with a fine brush along the line of the pattern. After the paste is applied, dyes of several colors are painted onto the material, or the material is dipped in a vat of dye. The paste is rinsed out, and the dyed pattern, outlined in white where the paste resisted the dye, is revealed. This material is known for its beautiful color and attention to detail. **Yukata** is a similar technique known for its stark contrast and mainly geometric patterns. These three forms of dyeing are most common. Other forms exist that are are similar to yukata and yuzen.

Textures: Weaving

Types of weaves most often utilized in Japan are the plain weave, the twill weave, and the satin float weave. The plain weave is most common and has been used longest. A pattern is created by using different warp and weft threads. Some of the threads are dyed by placing them in large vats. Others are resist-dyed using the methods mentioned above. The dyed warp threads and plain weft threads create geometric patterns called *tategasuri,* dyed warp and weft threads create *yokogasuri,* and resist-dyed warp and weft threads create *tateyokogasuri.* Later, a variation was introduced by weaving a gold or silver warp into the kasuri. The kasuri produced in this method can be seen in clothing and accessories for formal occasions. Even today, this shiny fabric is popular.

The twill weave is accomplished by running a weft thread over or under at least two warp threads. These materials are often referred to as *brocades* and are woven on a Jacquard loom. This weave yields two effects: *nishiki* and *kara ori.* Nishiki is woven on a loom and is characteristic because its weft threads run from selvage to selvage unbroken. It uses silk and odd numbers of different colored threads to create a brocade-like material. It can employ more colors and variety than the plain weave. The most common motif found in this fabric is the flower. Kara ori looks a lot like embroidery because it has colored threads that float on top of the material. It is a very formal and rich material.

The third weave, the satin float weave, is the most elaborate and formal. This one was popular during the Momoyama period, when Japan was under the influence of China's Ming dynasty. In China, the colors are brighter and bolder. The Japanese used this weave to design clothes for the noble class. The satin float weave consists of a weft thread that floats over the warp threads, creating the appearance of embroidery. This weave includes *donsu,* a damask-like fabric. The common motifs of this weave are checkerboard squares, clouds, spirals, and plum blossoms. This material was used most often in costumes but can be applied today to an interior for a traditional formal look.

Textures: Surface Ornamentation

Embroidery, quilting, and appliqué were, and still are, used in the Japanese production of fine textiles. During the Muromachi period, embroidery was used instead of expensive brocades, notably on the *Noh* costumes. By the end of the Momoyama period, embroidery had reached a peak, and costumes entirely covered with embroidery were used in the theater and as kimonos. Many times a thread was wrapped with gold or silver paper and stitched to the material with another filament, a method of embroidery called *couching*. Because of the expense of embroidery, it was soon replaced with appliqué.

Quilting, used to stitch two layers of fabric together, has several variations, of which *sashiko* is the most common. Sashiko is quilting on cotton. The process is as follows: Cotton that has been dyed with indigo is quilted with white thread in varying patterns. Usually, the stitches are in long rows and take on motifs like hemp leaf or tortoise shell. This fabric was both useful and durable; firemen, for greater protection, wore this thicker material. Today the motifs are more curvilinear, and textiles other than cotton can be used.

The Ainu people used appliqué. These people live on a northern island in the Japanese chain. The women created beautiful garments as gifts to their husbands. The husbands, who were wood carvers, gave gifts of their trade to their wives. The women stitched the basic design and added details with several types of embroidery. The motifs were always symmetrical to protect every part of the wearer equally. Also, every opening had a special design to protect the wearer from evil spirits that might try to enter. The motifs on the openings were usually spirals, thorns, or something similar.

Upholstered Furniture Styles

A Japanese home is sparsely furnished. Most of the cupboards or chests are built-in. The Japanese sit on a cushion or mat called a *zabuton*. Zabutons come with or without backs. The only other upholstered piece is the *futon*, a foldable mattress that functions as a sofa during the day and a pull-down bed at night. Historically, futons were rolled or folded and kept in cupboards and out of sight during the day.

Screens and Scrolls

Byobu and *fusuma* are beautiful Japanese painted silk or paper screens, still used today. Screens are panels with an antiqued paper, fabric, or cork application. After one of those materials is applied, a metal-leaf edging of pewter, silver, or gold is added. Once the hinges are joined, the screen is painted by an artist. A highly artistic textile, both symbolic and interpretative, is the painted silk scroll traditionally hung in Japanese interiors in the small nook called a *tokonoma*, usually a sacred focal point of the home that also include flowers or other accessories placed simply and neatly.

Window Treatments and Beds

Japanese architecture is made up of connected oblong cubes. The panels that divide the interior from the exterior are called *shoji*, and a similar treatment, called *fusuma*, is used as a partition. Fusuma may have a transom for light and ventilation. They can also be decorative. Shoji screens consist of a wood frame with geometric paneling. This paneling can be left open but is usually covered by pressed rice paper or mulberry paper. The wood frame is usually made of softwood, such as clear pine or fir, redwood, cedar, Alaskan cedar, and port or ford cedar. Hardwood does not work as well as the joints used in building the frame. The shoji screen is usually mounted on a track to slide horizontally. This track can be made of hardwood, such as ash, maple, birch, or oak. Another option is a track made of aluminum. These tracks are less expensive but less durable. The track can be set into the floor so the screen is flush with the tatami mats or wood.

Simplicity of lifestyle is exemplified in the Japanese sleeping mats. These mats are larger versions of the zabuton, the mat used for sitting on. Sleeping mats are called **futons.** They are kept folded or rolled in a closet or cupboard during the day and brought out at night for sleeping. The futon is covered with muslin and filled with cotton or feathers. They are frequently used today in Western interiors, usually on a sofa that folds down into a bed. Futon covers may be of many decorative fabrics.

Rugs

The floor of a Japanese house is part of the wood frame. The house sits above the ground and is mostly surrounded by a deck. In humid areas, pebbles are set under the house to help with water drainage. On top of the wood floor are mats made of rice straw or sea grass called **tatami mats.** Before the Muromachi period, these mats were used only for sitting. Beginning in the Muromachi period, they covered the entire floor. These mats are usually 6 × 3 feet in area and 2 inches in depth. Each mat has a dark banding around the edge. Japanese are careful not to walk on the banding so the mat lasts longer. Tatami mats are a modular division; the size of the room is measured by how many mats cover its floor. Tatami mats must be kept dry and ventilated. They can also be used for sleeping mats, but they are firmer than futons.

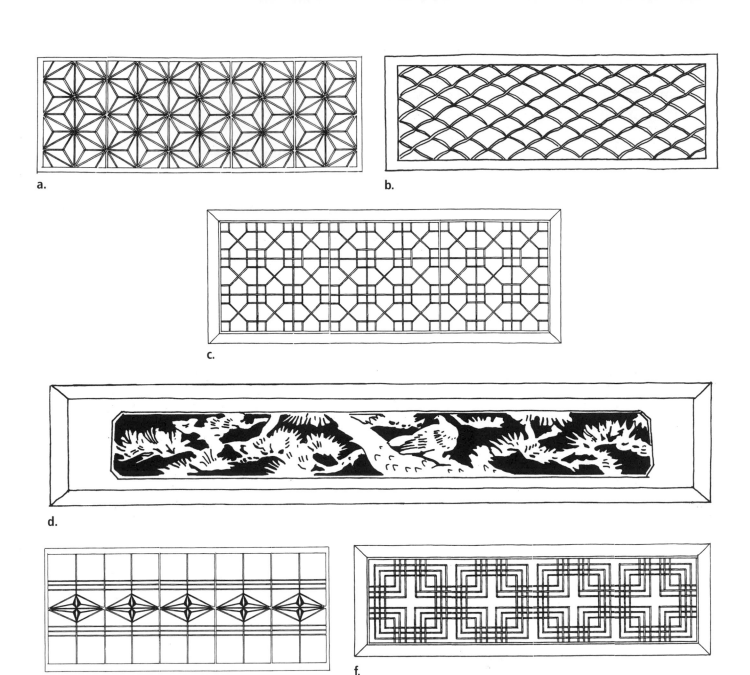

Figure 14.8 a–f Japanese window treatment transoms, fitted or carved wood, often with rice or mulberry paper as glazing material

Floor coverings that are also seating pieces also include **zabuton pillows,** which sit on the floor and add accents of bright color. This is another way the shibui aesthetic is applied to the traditional Japanese interior: through small accents of brilliant color.

Japanese Influence Today

Since 1870, Japan has had a design influence on other countries. It began with *japanning,* the use of lacquer on furniture. Since the close of World War II, the Western world became interested in the applicable aspects of Japanese culture, and there is now much borrowing of general ideas, if not of actual details. Many people in both East and West enjoy relaxing in a room with tatami mats on the floor. Shoji screens are functional and beautiful. They may be used inside as folding sliding screens and, in warm areas, as exterior doors. The shoji screen was the inspiration for the sliding glass door that is so prevalent in Western architecture. The naturalness and simplicity of Japanese design are evidenced in the Early Modern bungalow style, created by architects Charles and Henry Greene, with its exposed beams, and many of the American

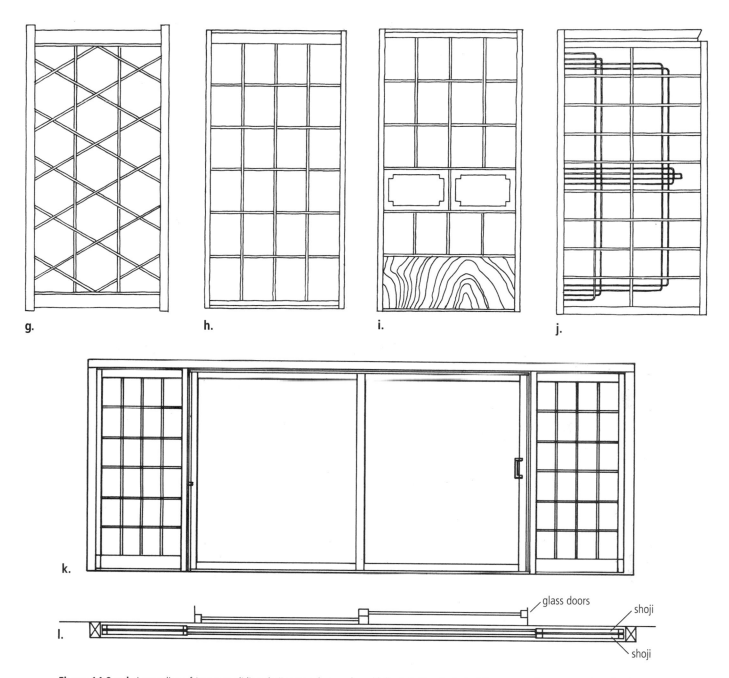

g.   h.   i.   j.

k.

glass doors

shoji

l.

shoji

Figure 14.8 g–l A sampling of Japanese sliding shoji screen designs. **k** and **l** illustrate the stacked sliding screen placement and mechanism.

architect Frank Lloyd Wright's homes. This style is of tremendous import today. The Early Modern style is examined in chapter 18. Roofs of tile or thatch are also evidence of the influence of Japan today.

Japan's shibui and Shinto philosophies of nature-and-mankind-as-one continue to influence Western design ideals. Zen interiors bring peace to an overly stressed Western world, which reveres the exquisite simplicity of Japanese design.

Contemporary as well as historic Japanese philosophy ensures that all aspects of an interior design work together. Whether in a textile pattern or an entire home, an admirable balance of simplicity and beauty is achieved. The harmony, peace, and beauty created by these spaces are appreciated around the world. In contemporary Japanese interiors, the robes and fabrics described above are displayed as artwork, a visual treat, and an exciting focal point amid the serenity of the background elements. Likewise, coromandel and byobu screens, shoji and fusuma screens, are decorative elements utilized today. Silk and cotton textiles continue to be welcome additions in contemporary Japanese homes, appreciated for their exquisite beauty as cushions, upholstery, and accent fabrics.

THE KOREAN INFLUENCE

Korean design is often based on both function and long-lasting beauty, as many activities may take place within small spaces. Korean design is often aware of the latest trends but does not necessarily follow them if they are not functional. Like Chinese and Japanese design, simplicity is a key element, and nature is one of the biggest influences. From this stems feng shui, which plays a big part in Korean design. Korean feng shui espouses that specific areas of the house pertain or correspond to different areas of the residents' lives. It is based on the idea of balance, harmony, and unity in life.

Korean space planning is often based on the status and size of the family; for example, *sarang-chae* is the male quarters; *ahn-chae,* the women's quarters; and, for those of higher class, *hangrang-chae,* or the servants' quarters. Many Korean families have three or more generations living under one roof. Houses for these families are bigger and have more rooms.

ASIAN STYLE TODAY

Contemporary Asian design is a mix of elements from Japan, China, Korea, Southeast Asia, and the interior Asian countries, including Tibet, Mongolia, and Kazakhstan. This mixing of styles is referred to as *Pac-Asian* or *PacAsian.* Elements from the Pacific Rim, including Japan, Hong Kong, Taiwan, Southeast Asia, and the Philippines, is referred to as *Pac-Rim* or *PacRim.* Although the United States and Japan today enjoy great material abundance, which has resulted in excessive consumerism, the effect of PacRim and PacAsian design has been the opposite in the design community.

The age-old tradition of seeking peace, enhanced spiritual enlightenment, and the flow of ch'i is highly prevalent. Further, the concept of Zen, the doctrine of silent illumination and its offshoot, Tao, from which the tea ceremony is derived, encompass elements of inner peace. Today, a calm mind-set is sought by many who are repulsed by the consumption of materialistic societies. Today, Zen is both a place to go in one's mind and a literal place where the interior is simple and free of clutter and demands. The white lotus symbolizes minds pure and free of the stains of the world, enlightened by a quest for that which is somehow unfathomable. Interior design elements today that are influenced by Zen and Tao doctrine yield new forms that employ old and new elements, giving meaning and balance to those who live and work in twenty-first-century environments. These are venues of escape for people who need places to retreat from everyday existence. Simple, elegant, and beautiful PacAsian objects bring ch'i—good energy plus the benefit of momentary release and bliss—which fosters a sense of balance between the ordinary and the exquisite.

15

Formal Traditional Styles

Figure 15.1 Italian Renaissance interior

The Renaissance, Baroque, Georgian, Neoclassical, Empire, and Victorian periods are considered "formal traditional." These styles appeal to conservative taste and are elegant, beautiful, and finely trimmed and detailed. Formal traditional interiors are often lavish or elaborate when created with authenticity, although many contemporary formal traditional interiors are less complex even when inspired by these rich period styles.

ITALIAN AND FRENCH RENAISSANCE

The Italian and French Renaissance was the rebirth of art and architecture dating from A.D. 1420 to 1650. This period reintroduced many elements of classical design—copied and adapted architectural and interior design elements of ancient Greece and Rome. Renaissance interiors

Figure 15.2 French Renaissance interior

and furniture were heavily scaled. The style and materials of rooms, textiles, and furniture reflected the new era of enlightenment.

Period Overview

The Renaissance began in Florence, Italy, the center of culture and wellspring of new materials, designs, and manufacturing. Italy became a focus of trade and merchandise in Europe, exporting exquisite fabrics and materials, including rich damasks and sumptuous velvets. The many immigrants to Italy who left Constantinople when it fell in 1453 included numerous Greek scholars and craftsmen who possessed a knowledge of Classical architecture. The writings of Dante, Petrarch, and Boccaccio also contributed to the resurgence of Classical ideals. With this information, and by patronizing the skills of the new craftsmen in Italy, Europe's prominent families began to incorporate classical motifs into their furniture and architecture. The de' Medici family were among the patrons of the arts, meaning they funded artists in return for ownership of the artisans' work.

A middle class emerged during the Renaissance, and some prominent families slowly gained more power and influence in society. With the rise of the middle class, many peasants gained enough financial security to improve their home lives. These people felt a need to change their interiors to more aptly fit their new lifestyle.

With the changes in design that occurred during the Renaissance, art also took great steps forward. Artists learned how to use perspective. Art became more realistic, creative, and less symbolic. Some of the great artists of the time were Brunelleschi, Leonardo da Vinci, Botticelli, Michelangelo, and Raphael. Their artwork instigated the spread of the Renaissance to France. Evidence of the new style appeared in France during the reign of Francis I in 1515.

Interior Architecture

Andrea Palladio was one of the greatest architects of the Renaissance. His famous villas in northern Italy incorporated many of the Classical forms, such as Doric, Ionic, Corinthian, Tuscan, and composite columns as well as pilasters, entablatures, moldings, and pediments. These served decorative, ornamental, and structural purposes. Used for specific functions, the rooms seemed large and dark, and were more formal and symmetrical than previous designs. If moldings were used, they exhibited motifs such as the acanthus leaf, tongue-and-dart, egg-and-dart, egg-and-leaf, and tongue-and-leaf designs. Walls were sometimes paneled; panels mostly extended from floor to ceiling and were sometimes divided by pilasters. French panels were larger and more heavily molded, carved, or painted. Marble slabs were sometimes found on walls, though this was not common. Wall decorations included frescoes, embroideries, velvets, and tapestries.

Ceilings were high and heavy during the Renaissance. Many were treated with wood, plaster, or both. Most had walnut, oak, cedar, or cypress beams, and some were painted. Wood-paneled or coffered ceilings were common. Some curved arches came from brackets that resembled pilaster capitals. The doors often had broken pediments, carving above them, or pilasters beside them. The doors themselves were plain slabs, or had panels. Strapwork (interlacing straps) was used during the reign of Henri II, arabesque was used under Francis I, and the cartouche was used under Henri IV.

Renaissance floors were made of tile, stone, or brick in an ashlar pattern. These were best for the warmer climates. There were a few tile and leather floors. Thick Oriental rugs sometimes covered the cold brick and tile floors, but they were expensive and found mostly in the homes of the wealthy.

Textiles: Color, Pattern, and Texture

Colors

The colors of the Renaissance became noticeably more bold and dramatic. Many of the new, vivid colors represented power and wealth. These colors were first applied in Italy and then spread northward to France, Germany, the Lowlands, England, and America. Most colors were jewel-toned. Some also resembled shades found in marble, which became more popular during the Renaissance. This period favored gold and red. These two dominant colors were often complemented with royal blue, emerald green, bright copper, Pompeii red, garnet red, dull brown, ivory white, rich brown, golden ocher, metallic gold, ceramic blue, soft gold, and creamy yellow. The colors used for wall hangings were of softer hues rather than bold reds, blues, and greens. Creams and golden yellows were often used for wall hangings, particularly in France.

Pattern and Texture

In Italy, textiles were often controlled by prominent families such as the de' Medicis. Fabrics such as silk, linen, and cotton damask featured large, scrolling, floral printed and woven designs. Velvets were among the most important and frequently used fabrics, and included plain and antiqued, voided, cisclé, jardinière, and ferronière velvets. Some velvet fabrics were woven with metallic threads, and some were multicolored. Velvets woven in complex designs and embroidered with gold were considered prestigious and exclusive. Centers of velvet weaving included Venice, Lucca, and Genoa, Italy. Other Renaissance textiles included satin brocade and brocatelle. All fabrics were woven with cotton, linen, wool, or silk. Silk was one of the most favored fibers.

a.

b.

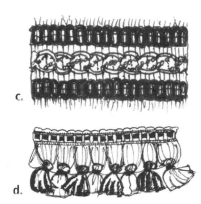

c.

e.

f.

g.

Figure 15.3a–g Italian/French Renaissance textile motifs

France was renowned for fine silks during the Renaissance. Sericulture began in both Italy and France after Olivier de Serre wrote a book about silk production. Patterns and motifs on silk included the acanthus leaf in framed large floral sprays, vases with naturalistic flowers, and pomegranate seeds. An elongated scroll, or S-shape, became common. This motif later became the ogee arch. The pomegranate was a classical motif that slowly changed into the artichoke motif, which the people of the Renaissance favored. Thistles and pineapple spikes were also applied as patterns. Flower designs primarily featured carnations and roses, other than the naturalistic arrangements that were depicted in vases or tied together in bunches. The chrysanthemum was often used alone as a motif.

Upholstered Furniture

Most Renaissance furniture followed a general furniture style set by influential cabinetmakers, such as Jacques Androut du Cerceau. Cerceau created a pattern book during the time of Henri VI detailing the general design that furnituremakers followed. The book depicted engravings and styles through both drawing and description. Jacques du Cereau's furniture styles became popular during the height of the Renaissance in France, between 1550 and 1610.

The chairs of the early Renaissance still resembled thrones with small chests underneath. This was when châteaux were sparsely furnished with few but massive pieces of furniture. Very few upholstered pieces were created during the Renaissance, with only a small number of benches and chairs gaining upholstery toward the end of the period. Only then did chairs and tables become a little less massive and eventually padded for comfort. The chairs that were upholstered had square backs and seats, were typically made of velvet, and

may have displayed some sort of fringe. If they possessed arms, they were mainly scrolled in design. Also, a few chairs were upholstered with leather made from sheepskin.

Wood Furniture

During the early Renaissance, furniture displayed only simple detailing. Furniture moldings, applied sparingly, featured Classical acanthus leaves and animal forms. Toward the end of the period, designs became more ornate. The ornamentation was usually found on the backs of chairs and the doors of furniture pieces. As this trend increased, gesso was introduced. Gesso is a mixture of glue and plaster of paris, cast to create ornamental forms in low relief for application to wood panels prior to gilding and painting. It was not applied until the late Renaissance, and then was carried over into the Baroque period.

Tables sat on bases that resembled columns, balusters, caryatids, and scrolls. Many of the furniture pieces maintained pilasters, paneling, broken pediments, or flat carving that framed the doors. Panels often exhibited geometric designs with stars and diamonds in bold relief. Others displayed large cartouches and flat strapwork.

Beds

Beds became significant pieces of furniture during the Renaissance. Built to make a statement about style and status, beds were massive and heavy. Most had some type of canopy. Those that did not still boasted four tall, heavy, carved, wood posts. At the top of each post rested a carved urn, vase, or similar object. With or without a canopy, the headboard was always a dominant feature. The headboard could be left plain but often exhibited Renaissance paneling

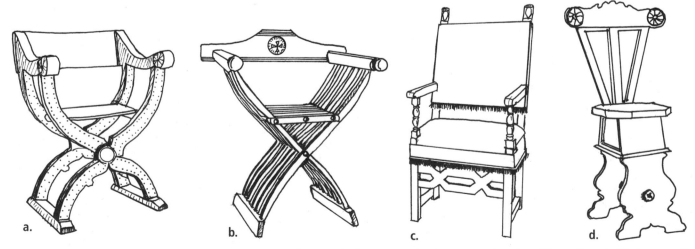

Figure 15.4a–d Italian/French Renaissance furniture. **a** Dante chair; **b** Savanarola chair; **c** French Renaissance court chair; **d** small throne-like chair with chest beneath

Figure D-1 This contemporary Asian interior features Japanese zabuton pillows and natural fiber floor mat, a Chinese chair and cabinet, calligraphy screen, vases, and potted bamboo. Windows that echo traditional Japanese sliding screens and transom frame the spectacular view of the California coastline. Crowning the view is an Asian-inspired fabric valance. Windows are treated with "Rollstar" sunscreen shades from Castec's Solar Solutions product line. *Photo courtesy of Castec, Inc., North Hollywood, CA.*

Figure D-2 Black lacquered French doors create a feeling of Japanese shoji screens, treated with Castec's "Natural Woods" Roman shades in the manner of Asian/Oriental bamboo shades. On the floor, zabuton pillows lay astride a low Japanese table. *Photo courtesy of Castec, Inc., North Hollywood, CA.*

Figure D-3 Renowned interior designer Mario Buatta created this French Neoclassic-inspired interior with a sumptuous Victorian flair. Bed canopy is "Austin Stripe" beige/rose/blue, canopy lining is taffeta "Carreaux" color blue, slipper chair "Les Perdrix" color multi on crème. The rug is "Aubusson 43498B" from the Veronica Collection. *Photo courtesy of Stark Carpets.*

Figure D-4 This "Nineteenth Century Antique French Tapestry" measures seven feet by six feet, an ideal size for an impressive wall covering tapestry. French Rococo colors include apple green, French turquoise, rose Pompadour, and powder pink on a lightened Chinese gold background. *Photo courtesy of David and Jay Nehouray, Caravan Oriental Rugs, www.caravanrug.com.*

Figure D-5 This "Chateau Collection" Aubusson-style rug features delicate Neoclassic era arabesque, oval and floral bouquets in carnation pink, pale pink, pale yellow, and browned light gold. *Photo courtesy of David and Jay Nehouray, Caravan Oriental Rugs, www.caravanrug.com.*

Figure D-6 "Antiqua Bow Tieback" features extraordinary attention to fine detail. A looped guimpe trim with tiny tied tassels edges this rich coral silk drapery fabric. Large-scale boulle fringe contrasts with the fine moss-edge dainty tassels, creating a sumptuous juxtaposition of refined passementerie elements. *Photo courtesy of Houlès-U.S.A.*

Figure D-7 This handsome Rococo fauteuil holds layered pillows finely trimmed with Houlès "Antiqua" fringes and braid. Rococo apple green and coral duBarry red are both light-hearted and passionate hues. *Photo courtesy of Houlès-U.S.A.*

Figure D-8 Expert quilters Lynn Lonsdale and Lee Bromley created this vibrant 39" x 39" "Pinwheel Pattern" pieced quilt, replete with vivid greens, corals, browns, with touches of lavender. Tiny curved stitches atop the angular blocks enhance the visual delight of this practical fabric art work. *Photo by Gordon Lonsdale*.

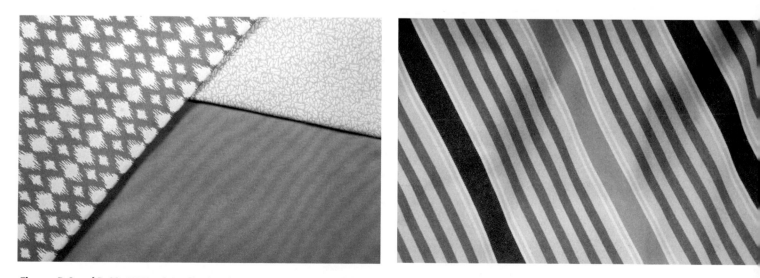

Figures D-9 and D-10 100% solution-dyed acrylic "Currents" from Currents boasts a 3-year guarantee against cracking, splitting, peeling, and fading. The collection, including these bright colorways, is sunfast, water and mildew resistant. For residential and commercial applications. *Photo courtesy of Giati Designs Inc.*

Design #Br-001

Figure D-11 The "Soroush Design Book," features designs such as this one that may be executed in Axminster, hand-knotted or hand-tufted carpet for hospitality and residential settings. This design features motifs from the Neoclassic and Empire periods, such as griffins and modillions in the outer border, round center medallion including eagles, and modillion-filled interlocking ovals. This page show the stages of design—from black and white drawing to the filling of layered colors as the rug coloration becomes finished. *Copyrighted and registered Soroush Custom Rugs & Axminster Carpet. www.soroush.us.*

Figure D-12 This historic interior has been furnished in an American Empire style, with gold and red color scheme taken from the satin upholstery fabric of isolated snowflake motifs on a smooth red ground. Broad gold and cream Empire stripes on pillows are edged with long boulle fringe. Generously full gold draperies of ADO fabric are contrast-lined with bold red to match the wall paint and upholstery fabrics. The writing desk is inlaid with leather and rests atop a fine Persian Oriental rug. *Photo courtesy of ADO Corporation www.ado-usa.com.*

Figure D-13 American Empire is the inspiration for this luxury high-rise suite interior. Silhouette® shadings by Hunter Douglas assure day and nighttime privacy and protection against sunlight damage. Tied-back overdraperies feature inverted pleat headings and bold Empire style motif braid. The arm chairs are Percier and Fontaine Josephine swan-backed chairs, black laquered, gold-leafed, upholstered in smooth satin with tiny isolated laurel leaf and trimmed with upholstery guimpe/gimp. A rich brocatelle fabric has been edged with braid banding to become an elegant tablecloth, overlaid with a fine linen runner. The Wilton or Axminster Empire-style carpet has been custom executed for this interior. *Photo courtesy of Hunter Douglas, Inc.*

Figure D-14 This Early Georgian raised-paneled interior features an exquisite room-sized Persian Oriental rug. The Elizabethan/Jacaobean arm chair features garnet red figured velvet with lathe-turned legs similar to the writing desk. Formal traditional swags and shirred cascades are top treatments over Late Georgian tied back draperies in a parchment colored ADO damask fabric. Renaissance sapphire or cobalt blue and ecru gold pillows rest in the window seat. *Photo courtesy of the ADO Corporation. www.ado-usa.com.*

Figure D-15 This Soroush hand-tufted designer rug is a stunning Empire-styled focal point visible through the glass-topped table. Fully upholstered side dining chairs feature a moiré fabric on seats and scrolled backs. The tailored box-pleated skirts of echo the anthemion designs in the wide border of the commanding, perfectly executed rug. Semi-sheer underdraperies overlaid with stationary panels are also in the Empire style. The unique asymmetrical festooned top treatments use generous amounts of this lustrous fabric. *Copyrighted and registered Soroush Custom Rugs & Axminster Carpet. www.soroush.us.*

Figure D-16 This Modern-styled interior is an artistic interpretation of the International and Organic Modern and Art Deco styles. In this living area, a Soroush Hand-Tufted carpet displays the flexibility available in texture, shape, design, and color, conveying the look and feel of old world rug craftsmanship even in the most contemporary designs. *Copyrighted and registered Soroush Custom Rugs & Axminster Carpet. www.soroush.us.*

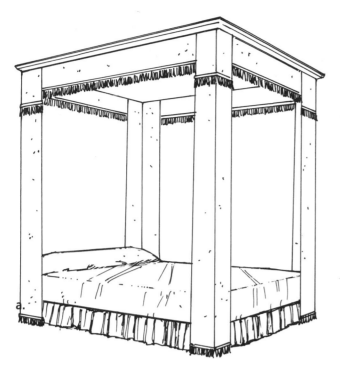

Figure 15.5a, b Italian/French Renaissance beds

or carving. Many canopy beds included a cornice above the posts. The cornices were usually flat and heavy-appearing. There was some carving, but less than during the later Baroque period. The posts under the cornices were either simply carved wood or columns highlighting elements of Classical design. During the late Renaissance, posts and cornices became more intricately carved.

Beds also had pelmets or valances along the top, many of which were made with Venetian velvet. They were usually flat, with ornate passementerie. Typically made of silk, trimmings took the form of gimp, banding, braids, decorative ropes, fringes, or tassels. Sometimes beds also displayed drapery at the four corners or along the sides of the headboard. These usually featured decorative tie-backs and trimmings. Beds with enhanced headboard draperies, fully enclosed draperies, and decorative valances signified wealth and power during the Renaissance era.

Window Treatments

Renaissance windows were shaped as vertical rectangles, some with pilasters to divide them. Some others featured lintel stonework or Roman arches. Many were casement windows with small panes, sometimes in decorative patterns and sometimes with green-tinted lights or panes. In the homes of the wealthy, rich tapestries hung over or beside the windows. Many were furnished with flat pelmets made of velvet with carved wooden cornices, on which rested urns or vases at the outer corners. These increased in intricacy later in the period. Draperies were usually tied back or hung vertically, but they were not full compared to modern standards. The ties and trims for draperies consisted of banding, braids, decorative ropes, fringes, and tassels made of silk. Some windows were left untreated or simply covered with wood panel shutters.

Figure 15.6a–u Italian/French Renaissance window treatments

The Renaissance Influence Today

The Renaissance colors, textiles, furniture, materials, and room styles have had a long-lasting effect. Interiors of the Baroque and Early and Late Georgian eras were based on Renaissance designs. The Renaissance influence can be seen in modern interiors, achieving a dignified and formal look. Deep jewel tones and the large Renaissance floral patterns are often utilized in upscale interiors. Renaissance fabrics such as silk, velvet, and damask are still considered formal and beautiful, and they are widely available today.

THE BAROQUE PERIOD

Period Overview

The Baroque period, marked by flamboyance, drama, and boisterous ornamentation, dates from 1580 to 1750 and is an energetic continuation of the Renaissance style. Italy, France, Spain, and England are particularly credited for the Baroque style. The term *Baroque* originates from the Portuguese word *barocco,* meaning "a misshapen, irregular pearl." The Baroque style began as a form of revolt, a breaking away from the frigidity of earlier design periods. Carrying on the tradition of Renaissance style, Baroque became even more ornate and ostentatious.

Italy and Spain

Baroque began its ascent in Italy. The first applications of Baroque can be found in St. Peter's Cathedral in Rome, dating from 1506. The style did not reach its zenith until 1650. Baroque moved out of Italy after 1650, spreading into Spain and Portugal. The popularity of Baroque was short-lived in these regions, where the theatrics never equaled those of Italy. Spanish Baroque, however, is well known and was imitated and even revived in the Beaux-Arts era.

England

The dates of the English Baroque period range from 1660 to 1714. The architect Inigo Jones, who studied the Renaissance, introduced the Baroque style to England. Sir Christopher Wren was famous during this period for his design of Baroque churches and interiors in London. Wren, the surveyor of the king's works, was the royal architect in 1666, when London was destroyed by fire. He was commissioned to rebuild St. Paul's Cathedral, along with over fifty other buildings. Because of this significant influence, Baroque took hold strongly in England. English and French Baroque have many similarities.

French Baroque

The French Baroque style developed under the reign of Louis XIV, the so-called Sun King. It was a vision of glory and grandeur well suited to his ego. He wanted impressive riches to surround himself and his court. Louis XIV thought of himself as a god over the nation he ruled, and thus his settings were designed to flaunt his power to the rest of the world. Baroque was precisely the style to achieve this end. The period in France dates from 1643 to 1730, though true manifestations of the French version of this style did not emerge until 1660. The most renowned example of French Baroque is the Palace of Versailles. One of the most impressive rooms to display this style is its famed Hall of Mirrors.

Figure 15.7 French Baroque interior

Figure 15.8 English Baroque interior

The decline of Baroque popularity in Italy directly corresponds with the transfer of cultural, political, and financial control of Europe to Louis XIV and later to Queen Anne of the House of Stuart in England, when Baroque slowly began its transition to the more feminine Rococo period.

Interior Architecture

Some modest-size interiors were built during the Baroque period in France, but most were built to grand scale. An example of large scale, the Palace of Versailles is one of the most duplicated buildings in the world. It is an inspiration to interior ornamentation in the French Baroque style. The Renaissance used curving forms and intricate detail, but Baroque took ornamentation a step further. Much of the detailing found in Baroque interiors had no special function or structural value, except to increase the appearance of the king's importance.

Walls featured wood paneling ornately carved with Classical designs. Surfaces were painted and gilded or applied with inlays and marquetry. Richly ornamented moldings and cornices surrounded both doors and windows. Ceilings were decorated with frescoes, angels, cherubs, and genies in various forms of relief, often colored to appear lifelike. Gilt was used to ornament the sculptured plaster in unrestrained abundance.

Floors were primarily made of highly polished oak parquet or black and white squared marble. Parquetry is the arrangement of short planks of wood in decorative geometric patterns. Oriental and French rugs were also used as floor treatments during the Baroque period. Savonnerie and Moquette rugs were common.

Textiles: Color, Pattern, and Texture

French Baroque textiles were as lavish as the interior surfaces. Emphasis was placed on scale; the larger the motif or pattern, the more Baroque it was considered.

In 1662, Louis XIV purchased the Gobelins tapestry looms for the purpose of producing high-quality textiles to

Figure 15.9a–f French Baroque textile motifs with large-scale floral and acanthus patterns seen in **a–d**; **e** and **f** show architectural and furniture patterns woven as textile designs.

decorate his interiors. He also purchased the Beauvais looms and appointed a man named Charles LeBrun his chief designer and the director of these facilities.

Colors of the Baroque period can best be described as florid. Louis XIV possessed a special preference for rich reds and rosy pinks. These red hues were used in abundance in interior color schemes. Medici blue (a turquoise shade), palace cream (a pinkish yellow), and Medici green (a deep mint green) were all readily applied in interiors. Coral, peach, and shades of brown, with black as an accent color, were also common. Gold and silver were woven into textiles and used in both furniture gilding and wall ornamentation. All of these colors were rich, vibrant, and intense, and used in large scale.

Motifs of the Baroque period influenced later periods and even modern textiles. They include large scrolls, heavy garlands of flowers and fruit, and scrolling acanthus leaves encompassing fruits such as pineapples and pomegranates. Repeating trellises, fountains, and baskets were also common. The patterns on textiles were bold, with dramatic interplays of dark and light. Two common motifs typifying Louis XIV included back-to-back *L*s on a coat of arms and a radiant sun or sunburst, representing him as the Sun King. The European Baroque period saw the development of new "bizarre" motifs in textiles; these shapes had no exact equivalent in nature, although they sometimes resembled shrimp bodies and metal pieces. Lace was produced in motifs that replicated damask and brocade designs.

Textures included rich, complex, and luxurious velvets that continued the tradition of the Renaissance velvets. Moquette velvet, cut velvet, and multicolored velvets were especially beautiful. Damask, brocade, and brocatelle fabrics sometimes became heavier and utilized larger-scale motifs. Silk was used extensively in luxurious interiors, having become the "queen of fibers." Also of note were finely woven cotton, linen, and wool textiles. Some of the common fabrics utilized in this period were tapestries, brocades, damasks, needlepoints, heavy silk fabrics, and both plain and complex velvets. Court textiles were often woven with designs in gold and silver, producing exquisite velvet, damask, brocade, broché, and brocatelle fabrics. This contributed extra richness and sumptuousness to the court textiles.

Upholstered Furniture

Furniture and other movable objects were considered secondary in importance to interior architecture. Although furniture was not the primary locus of flamboyance, it did receive its share of ornamentation. Due to the large scale of Baroque rooms, furniture had to maintain the effect of heavy proportion. Rectangular forms in furnishings dominated the

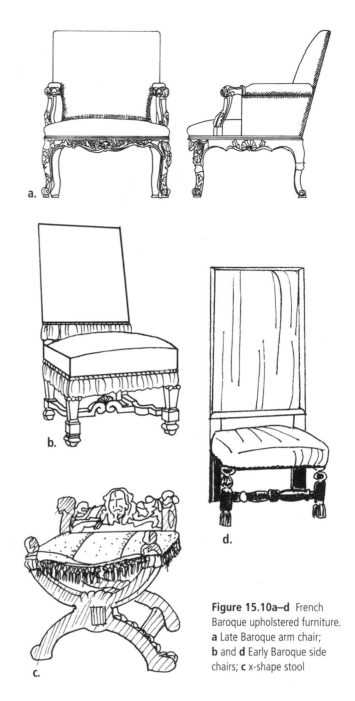

Figure 15.10a–d French Baroque upholstered furniture. **a** Late Baroque arm chair; **b** and **d** Early Baroque side chairs; **c** x-shape stool

period, although curves were used where necessary. Symmetry of furniture was strongly emphasized by Louis XIV. Wood carving was heavily gilded in court pieces. Materials often used in the construction of furniture were oak, walnut, ebony, sycamore, cherry, and chestnut. Tabletops were commonly made of marble. The beautiful textiles manufactured at the Gobelins works were used on upholstered pieces.

Common ornamentation that appeared on furniture included leafy boughs, guilloches, lozenges, shells, and flowers embossed in high relief. Festoons, scrolls, garlands, and myriad other decorations produced the appearance of luxury and elegance.

Figure 15.11 French Baroque bed

Beds

Bed appointments of the Baroque period were lavish and rich. They were similar to the window treatments, with low tie-back draperies falling from the canopy, upholstered pelmets or cornices richly adorned with passementerie, and gilt used as the top treatment. Luscious textiles embroidered with gold were often seen in bed appointments. King Louis XIV's bed was so adorned he often used it as his throne while receiving foreign dignitaries at his side.

Window Treatments

Window treatments were as elaborate as any other aspect of Baroque interiors. Sumptuous draperies were typically tied back low and accompanied by a top treatment such as a valance, pelmet, or cornice. Pelmets were elaborately ornamented with embroidery and passementerie—fringe, braids, ropes, and tassels. Pelmets often exhibited cutout shapes and were scalloped or sculptured along the lower edge. They were sometimes decorated with Louis XIV motifs at the top or the center of the cornice. These motifs included back-to-back *L*s, sunbursts, and seashells. Gilt was also ap-

a.

b.

c.

d.

e.

f.

Figure 15.12a–w French Baroque window treatments

plied on upholstered chair wood trim and window and bed treatment cornices as a means of enriching the carved designs and the textiles attached to wood components.

Rugs

Exquisite rugs and carpets used over parquet and marble flooring were standard in court Baroque interiors. In 1673, the expenses of the Gobelins factory works and the Savonnerie manufactory—which eventually merged—were assumed by Louis XIV. Thus began the era of Baroque rugs. The two rugs that gained the most prestige were the Savonnerie and Moquette rugs.

One of the most common rugs to come out the Baroque period is the **Savonnerie**. This is a pile rug woven with a symmetrical knot and exhibiting great detail. One interesting characteristic of the Savonnerie is that it has two warp threads superimposed on top of each other and three weft threads—the symmetrical, hand-tied knot, and the taunt— that keep the warps on two levels. Except in rare instances where silk was and is used, wool is the primary fiber for the Savonnerie rug. During the reign of Louis XIII, however, hemp was used to make the rugs. Sometimes the weft thread was hemp and the warp was wool. Common motifs used in Savonnerie rugs were those that glorified the king, including the lyre, a symbol of Apollo, the ancient Greek

Figure 15.13 French Baroque rug or carpet

sun god, and the sunflower. Some of the carpets featured figures of Classical mythology, virtues, heroes, allegories, allusions to the arts and sciences, and the four elements—earth, fire, air, and water. Scrolling acanthus leaves were used frequently to unify the entire rug.

Moquette rugs were first produced in France in 1667. The moquette is a thin rug with a low pile, with either cut or uncut loops. It was made primarily of wool and sometimes of cotton or silk. The loom width was approximately 27 inches. The strips of rug were then sewn together to form larger pieces. The joining produced the pronounced striped effect characteristic of this rug.

The Baroque Influence Today

The Baroque period, though never revived to the extent of its peak in France, has strongly influenced other periods. The Rococo period, which followed Baroque (1730–1760) was greatly affected by its immediate predecessor. Rococo is considered the female or feminine version of the Baroque. The Baroque style also influenced the Regency period in its grace and curvilinear elements. Though America never experienced a Baroque period, Baroque influence is manifested today in the grand scale of homes and rich interiors now being constructed. The motifs and textiles of that period are still being woven into modern society. The influence of Baroque furniture is seen in armoires, the Louis XIV armchair, and the ever-popular fauteuil. The Baroque period, elaborate and ornate, earned its place in history and will continue to inspire interiors for years to come.

AMERICAN EARLY GEORGIAN

Traditional interior design furnishings that originate with the formal historic European periods were heavily influential in the American colonies. The Early Georgian (c. 1699–1750) and Late Georgian (c. 1751–1774) styles were two of America's most formal periods of the eighteenth century. During these periods, beautiful furnishings were combined with elegant wallcoverings, Turkish and Persian Oriental rugs, and window and bed fabric treatments to create gracious, upscale rooms where genteel lifestyles reigned. The Early Georgian period is divided into two subperiods: the William and Mary era (1695–1702) and the Queen Anne era (1704–1750).

Period Overview

Prince William of Orange, who was from the Netherlands, and his English wife, Mary, crossed the English Channel in 1688 to assume the British throne. They brought with them colonial tastes in architecture, which had a major effect on both English and American style. William introduced the styles and the workmanship of the Low Countries, which were on a more genteel, human scale than the Baroque. Mary was skilled at needlework, and several of her works were used as chair coverings. Together, the two created a style that was a version of Baroque design stemming from the influence of the Italian Renaissance. The furniture of the new period was made almost exclusively of walnut; thus it is sometimes known as the Age of Walnut.

Queen Anne's reign lasted from 1704 to 1714. Although she was on the throne for a brief period only, her influence on furniture design extended into the 1750s. A new architectural style evolved from Sir Christopher Wren, the English architect responsible for rebuilding much of London after the Great Fire of 1666. Wren was influenced by the ideas of an early English architect, Inigo Jones, who reintroduced the styles and influences of the Renaissance and the Palladian era. Wren transformed Jones's architectural renderings into middle-class manor house designs that adapted to both the common house and the elegant manor. Wren architecture and Queen Anne furniture style flourished in tandem during the reigns of George II and George III; therefore, it is also known as the Georgian style.

Textiles: Color, Pattern, and Texture

Throughout the Early Georgian period in America, textile mills were just beginning operation. Professional weavers and linen stampers produced simpler versions of European fabrics. Some households did produce cotton, woolen, and linen goods for their own use (mainly in clothing), but they

Figure 15.14 American Early Georgian interior

imported the more elegant home furnishings fabrics from Europe. Fabrics from England dominated because high tariffs were placed by England on goods imported into the colonies from other countries. The quality of the imported fabrics varied, but generally they were superior to those made domestically. Due to the cost of importing textiles, only the wealthy were able to afford finer textiles. Silk was the most valuable fabric of the period, followed by wool and then cotton. Calico and chintz gained popularity, and in fashionable homes leather upholstery was common. Those who paid close attention to the finer points of textiles focused on color coordination, and often a single fabric was used as window treatment, upholstery, and bedding.

Colors

Colors were subdued and conservative and, therefore, bright, bold colors were rarely used. Grayed colors of medium value were popular, such as faded rose, dull olive green or dull blue (Williamsburg colors), and teal blue. Indian red, green, gold, and mustard also proliferated. The blue and white Delftware from Holland was popular, as was the Ming blue and white china from China. These colors added flavor to the Early Georgian period in America. A prime sign of the fashion during this time was the color coordination of textiles within bedrooms and social rooms.

Motifs

Popular imported fabrics included the Renaissance cotton damasks and the English block-print florals, which were based on the English garden designs created during the reign of Queen Anne. Typical fabric designs of this era included handsome large-scale flowers and birds as well as endless stems in open white grounds symbolizing the Tree of Life. Delicate Rococo scrolls and shells and some Chinoiseries were also popular. Some carryover from Medieval needlework was also seen in small floral patterns and motifs from that era, many of which were hand-embroidered.

a.

b.

Figure 15.15a–d American Early Georgian textile motifs

c.

d.

Textures

Textures included silk brocatelle, brocade and damask, printed linen, wool, crewel embroidery, and cotton prints and damask. Some fine Renaissance and Baroque velvet fabrics were imported to the colonies as well, and they were highly valued. Embroidered textiles such as hand embroidery, crewel, needlepoint, and hand-loomed tapestries were also popular. Calico and chintz gained popularity. Leather was used on masculine pieces as a smooth-textured, elegant fabric carried over from the medieval era. Cottons, particularly damasks and tapestries, were common upholstery textiles appreciated for their beauty and durability.

Upholstered Furniture

Furniture styles of the Early Georgian era include William and Mary and, particularly, Queen Anne. Furniture began to be designed in more sophisticated forms in response to the demand for greater comfort and beauty in home furnishings. For the first time, furniture was made and sold in sets of matching pieces intended for use in the same room.

In the English court, the furniture prototypes had more Baroque ornamentation, even gilt, whereas in America, the style was a simple elegance, better suited to the craftsmanship skills of cabinetmakers (furniture builders) and in line with

Figure 15.16a–i Queen Anne American Early Georgian upholstered furniture. **a** settee; **b** wing chair; **c** corner or roundabout chair; **d** arm or host chair; **e, f** splat-back dining side chairs; **g** gentleman's reading or straddle chair; **h** camelback sofa; **i** footstool

the egalitarian creed of Colonial Americans. To be ostentatious and showy was in poor taste and politically incorrect. Queen Anne furniture was sleek and genteel and offered a great opportunity to display quality upholstery fabrics because relatively little was required. The style expressed a unity of curved lines, a restraint of ornamentation, and a good technical understanding of design. The principal characteristic of the time was the use of the curved line, especially the *S*-curve, as a dominant motif. The Queen Anne wing chair, which evolved from the seventeenth-century sleeping chair, was introduced and became extremely popular. Considered a lavish use of precious fabric, the wing chair was thus a symbol of wealth and status. Comfort became noticeable in this chair, whose wings were designed to cut off drafts while providing support for the nodding head. The wings also aided in holding the warmth of a fire close to the body.

The settee, or sofa, also became quite fashionable. The settee was fully upholstered, so it also showed prestige. It had rolled arms like a wing chair and was most often found in a walnut frame. Two other chairs were also introduced, the corner or "roundabout" chair and the reading or "straddle" chair. The reading chair, with an elegant mahogany frame and leather upholstery, was a gentleman's favorite. The corner chair had an upholstered seat and cabriole legs, both common characteristics of furniture at the time. It had a rounded armrest supported by two pierced splats.

The delicate Queen Anne chairs were very popular at this time. The Queen Anne side chair and armchair both had upholstered seats. The backs of these chairs had a curved top and were made slightly concave at shoulder height. They were given a splat in the center of the back that ran from the seat to the crest. This back design was often called the fiddleback in America. Piercing the splat with simple curved cutouts occurred late in the Queen Anne period. The frame of the seat was curved on the sides and front. The legs were designed in the cabriole fashion with a slipper pad, or club foot. The Queen Anne side chair was armless, and the armchair had open arms in most forms. The most common arm for the armchair was the gooseneck or shepherd's crook arm, with a shaped curve. These chairs were gracious, genteel, comfortable, and flexible seating pieces in the American Early Georgian period.

Beds

The daybed and the tall or short four-poster bed were popular. Also common were half-headed bedsteads or half-canopied beds and trundle beds. Ready-made bed hangings could be imported from London. Bed draperies were simple and functional, similar to those in the Medieval period. The basics consisted of tester cloth, head cloth, valances, and

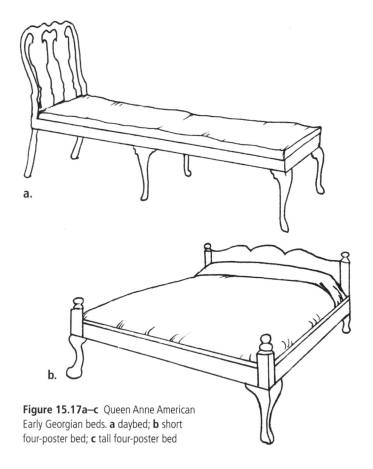

Figure 15.17a–c Queen Anne American Early Georgian beds. **a** daybed; **b** short four-poster bed; **c** tall four-poster bed

bases—these were nailed to the bed frame—plus movable head and foot curtains. The scrolls of the valances were often outlined with decorative border tapes or fabric used as trim. Swag and cascade treatments were popular; sometimes the selvages were not hemmed. Shaped pelmets and a version of a poufed top treatment surrounded by wooden Georgian moldings were also used.

Window Treatments

When they existed, bedchamber window treatments were often of the same fabric and style as the bed hangings. Window treatments included raised panel shutters and two-inch blinds with wide tapes. During the Queen Anne era, a curtain was defined as a piece of cloth that could be expanded or contracted when desired to admit or cut off light. Window treatments were either functional or decorative. Draperies ended at the windowsill or were extended to the floor. A simple top treatment was a way to conserve the rare and expensive fabrics. Many top treatments were used over paneled shutters that could be opened and recessed into the surrounding wall. Shaped pelmets, Parisian shade valances, and swags with or without cascades were handsome and effective to treatments often enriched with passementerie.

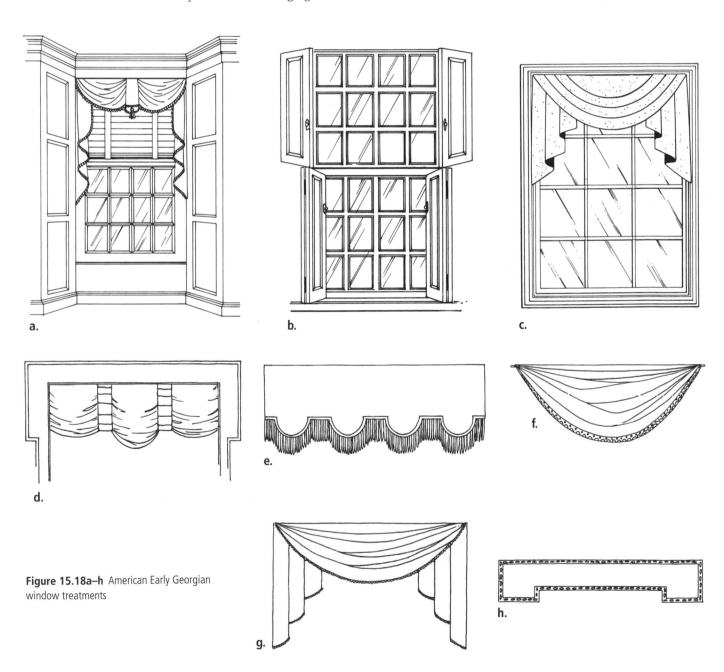

Figure 15.18a–h American Early Georgian window treatments

Figure 15.19 American Early Georgian rug/carpet — "Turkey rug" or Turkish Caucasian rug.

Rugs

Because fine textiles had to be imported from England, France, and Italy, few were used as carpeting. The "Turkey rug" or Turkish Oriental rug was highly popular and was used atop a wooden plank floor. Floor cloths, rag, braided, and hooked rugs were used in less formal settings.

The Early Georgian Style Today

The American Early Georgian style is a popular and important style today because of its beauty and sophistication. Simple yet formal window treatments are again in favor, together with the swags and cascades that have gained popularity. The combination of hard treatments paired with draperies is a look of great contemporary appeal. Traditional interiors, including Early Georgian furnishings, contribute elegance and refinement to residential and nonresidential interior architecture.

FRENCH ROCOCO

Period Overview

French Rococo, also known by the name of King Louis XV, dates from 1730 to 1760. Louis XV had very little interest in architecture, although Madame de Pompadour and, later, Madame du Barry were largely responsible for influencing the color, design, and tastes of the Rococo period. Madame de Pompadour helped create the rising enthusiasm for the exotic Oriental style. Known as *Chinoiserie*, meaning Chinese-like, this style became an extremely important phase of the Louis XV era.

Madame du Barry introduced fine, delicate silks, the light and dainty patterns, and the delightful stripes. These styles led to a great desire for small and dainty things. Freed from the antiquity of the Baroque and the Italian Renaissance, room sizes were reduced and specialty rooms created. The idea of exquisite ornamentation and elegance allowed for feminine ideas of romance to be implemented in the frequent use of curved lines where shells, originally

Figure 15.20 French Rococo interior

called **rocaille,** gave rise to the term *Rococo.* This was the age of romance, pleasure, comfort, and convenience. The beloved Rococo style, despite its brief thirty years, lives on as a perennial favorite, revived continually by those who love gentility. In its pure form, Rococo is very formal, with excessive ornamentation. Its influence is most often seen in the countrified version, known as Country French or French Provence, presented in chapter 16.

Leading Rococo designers Pineau and Meissonier created *genre pittoresque,* the frivolous phase characterized by intricate curves and C-scrolls in asymmetrical decoration. Under the direction of Boucher, *Manufacture des Gobelins* produced magnificent Rococo tapestries.

Interior Architecture

Parquet wood floors were made in patterns such as the framed basket weave or herringbone design. Walls were plain plaster overlaid with **boiserie,** or carved, curved anaglypta molding. Where walls met ceiling, the sharp angle disappeared in favor of a coved connection, with moldings at the bottom, top, or both, or sometimes unadorned.

Textiles: Color, Pattern, and Texture

Colors

Colors softened considerably from the Renaissance and Baroque eras to medium and lighter-valued colors, producing a refreshing subtlety of muted tones and pastels. The soft hues lent an intimate, soft-spoken, and cultured sophistication to the playful curved lines and excessive gilt ornamentation. They included Pompadour blue (slightly gray-violet medium blue), French turquoise, Sèvres blue (medium-value turquoise, named for the porcelain factory), French lilac (slightly blue medium-value), apple green (a crisp yet creamy yellow-green), powder green (grayed lightened yellow-green), cloud white (very pale green), oriental gold (Chinese gold with a greenish cast), rose Pompadour (a strong, deep pink), du Barry red (more vivid and coral than rose Pompadour), and powder pink (soft, very light grayed pink).

Motifs

Fine detailing highlighted this era of luxury, romance, and extravagance. The dismissal of straight lines and the extensive use of *C-* and *S*-curves in patterns gave way to a feeling of intimacy and femininity. A proliferation of floral patterns, often woven or printed in vertical scrolling patterns, was focused on bouquets. Swagged vines with delicate leaves and carefully placed single or grouped flowers gave a garden theme to many fabrics. Floral bouquets were romantic—and appropriate, as the ideals of romance were at fever levels.

Some fabrics were printed in scenes from mythical settings or gardens in historic ruins, with men and maids at work and play in coy poses, sometimes surrounded with quaint farm life. These flowers were either strictly European, such as roses, or inspired by the rich floral traditions of Chinese textiles, with mature, woody climbing vines, full, heavy-headed peonies, and chrysanthemum, with exotic birds perching on branches. Other common designs were pastoral scenes with the shepherdess's hat, crook, and basket. Musical instruments such as the horn, violin, and bagpipes, and the well-known Cupid, with his quiver and bow, were also typical of the period. The importation of Chinese textiles established a rage of fashion the French labeled Chinoiserie. Textiles featured Asian gazebos or pavilions, monkeys, Chinese men or maids in long, fluid robes, fishing boats (junks), Chinese landscape scenery, and latticework designs.

Textures

Textures were lustrous and sometimes slightly irregular, as evidenced by the extensive use of silk fabrics: damask, brocade, brocatelle, and hand-embroidered broché (brocade) fabrics. Sheer and semisheer fabrics such as voile, batiste, and chiffon softened window views. Very fine petit point was a favored upholstery fabric. Fabrics occasionally were interwoven with gold and silver threads. Tapestries from the Gobelin and Aubusson works, which were patronized by royalty, gave a heavier, more substantial hand to upholstery textures, and carpeting and area rugs were also finely cut in pile or finely woven. The whole process of needlepoint and needlework was considered a fine art, and finished pieces received attention and respect. (*Note:* The extraordinary skill of the French Huguenots, who sought religious freedom in France, was a key factor in the production of exquisite textiles for the *bourgeoises,* or upper-class French.)

Upholstered Furniture

General characteristics of furniture were portability and comfort. The continued use of the dominant *S*-curve was seen in legs and the general shape of each piece, imitating the feminine body, although straight lines also were employed in the structure of the furniture pieces. There were two types of chairs: the ornamental, which was placed against walls, and the usable, found in the middle of the room. The ornamental chairs were hard, straight-backed, and lacked arms, whereas the usable had cushioned and/or curved backs for greater comfort, and often had arms as well. Seating was said to be impossible to improve upon, as seen in the two chair classics, the *bergère,* which was an upholstered armchair outlined in wood, with arms filled in with upholstery, and the *fauteuil,* an open armchair. Occasionally the fauteuil was given a woven cane back and rush seat upon which were

a.

b.

c.

d.

Figure 15.21a–d French Rococo textile motifs **a** C- and S-shaped forms in foliage; clustered flowers; **b** nosegays on fluttering ribbons; **c** chinoiserie or Chinese-like design; **d** free-form trellis of foliage and flowers in asymmetrical composition.

placed down cushions in luxurious fabrics. French wing chairs are also a part of the upholstered family, as are settees and foot cushions. In the madam's boudoir, or bedchamber anteroom, was nearly always found a *chaise longue,* or long chair, usually resembling an attached bergère and footstool.

All upholstered Rococo furniture is outlined in wood and carved with Rococo motifs, such as shells carved into the knee and perhaps the center skirt of the frame.

Beds

Rococo beds were designed with fully upholstered curved headboards and footboards. They were often used as daybeds—for sitting, lounging, napping, and nighttime use in pairs on either side of a fireplace. The *lit clos,* or bed in a closet, with curved, carved paneling known as *boiserie* surrounding the opening and perhaps as a cornice across the

Figure 15.22a–k French Rococo upholstered furniture. **a–d** settees or canapes;
e–g chaise longue (chaise lounge) as one or two pieces (bergère and extended footstool);
h fauteuil; **i–j** bergère; **k** bergère wing chair

front, was a common feature in Rococo court interiors. A valance and side draperies around the *lit clos* and perhaps upholstery on the walls gave greater richness to this important piece of furniture. As this was a period that focused on romance, these beds in the wall made convenient hiding places and were sometimes made complete with hidden compartments!

Window Treatments

At the window, scalloped Parisian or Austrian shades in sheer or semisheer (batiste) fabric were often placed beneath full or generous tie-back draperies held with scalloped ties; the purpose was privacy, as for wood shutters. Pelmets or upholstered cornices were curved, shaped, or scalloped on the top as well as on the bottom. Fabric

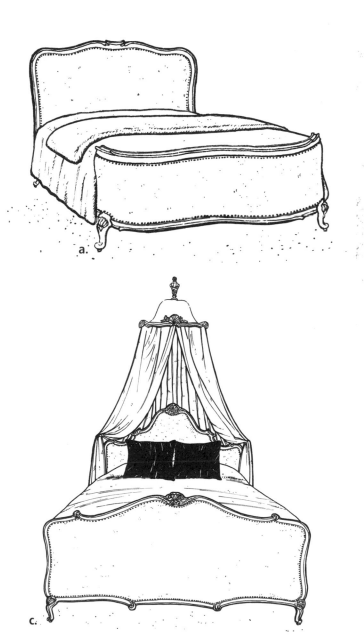

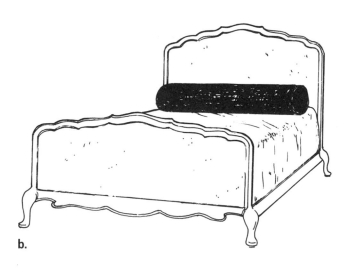

Figure 15.23a–c French Rococo beds with upholstered head and footboards.

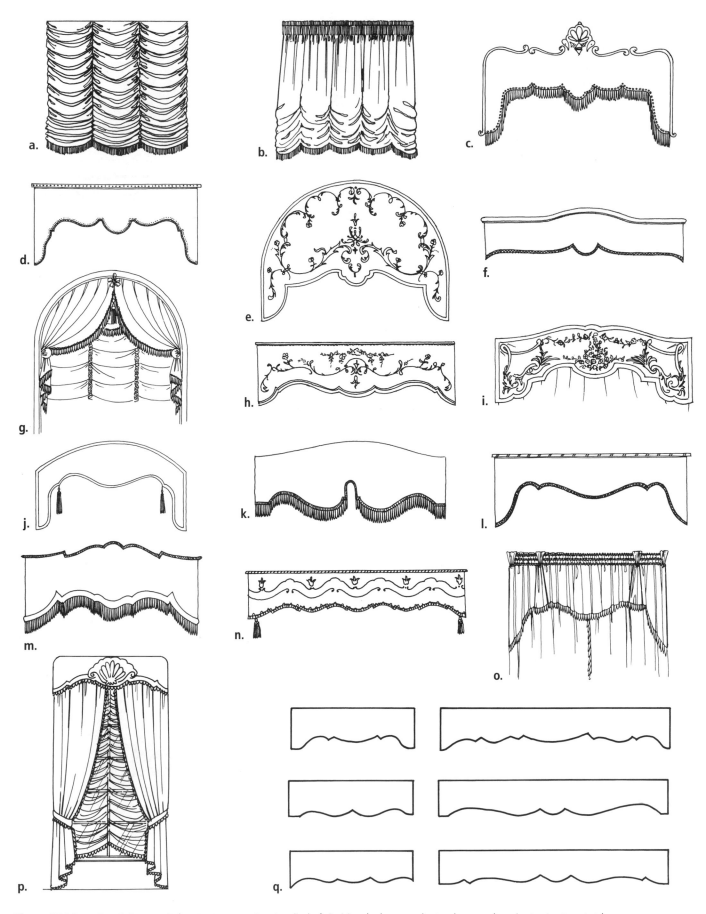

Figure 15.24a–q French Rococo window treatments. **a** Austrian shade; **b** Parisian shade; **c–q** pelmet, valance, and cornice top treatment styles

valances made their debut in shirred styles with scalloped or curved lower edges; they were later combined with embroidered pelmets. Exquisite embroidery and dressmaker detailing, a French tradition by now, were completed with a large selection of trimmings and tassels. The embroidered designs were mostly based on Chinese motifs and Asian compositions.

Rugs

Two main types of rugs were produced during this time: French Savonnerie and Aubusson. Savonnerie rugs were woven in the same manner as Oriental rugs, with a plush pile that produced greater warmth. These rugs were especially popular during the Baroque or Louis XIV era, and their use continued into the Rococo period (see Figure 13.11).

Aubusson rugs, woven in a flat tapestry weave, were considered the height of simple elegance and charm. The motifs were floral, with wreathlike swags and open backgrounds. Colors were soft and pastel. Aubusson tapestry rugs were produced on the Jacquard loom. Aubussons also were produced as wall hangings or tapestries; paintings by artists were used as inspiration for these carefully crafted designs.

The French Rococo Influence Today

The feminine curves of Rococo textiles, motifs, colors, window treatments, bed styling, upholstery, and carpeting are used extensively in upscale hotels, residences, and restaurants primarily to show comfort and elegance with a historic atmosphere. In spaces ranging from exquisite bedrooms and ornate lobbies to grand entrances and sophisticated dining rooms and living rooms, even upscale retail interiors, French Rococo gentility is expressed through the use of curves, romantic textiles, Chinese-influenced motifs, and soft colors. The Rococo influence is part of elegant society today.

AMERICAN LATE GEORGIAN

Period Overview

The American Late Georgian period dates from 1751 to 1790. Named after King George III and King George IV, the style in America ended with the Revolutionary War, which occurred during the reign of George III. The Late Georgian era was hallmarked by increased wealth, decoration, and

Figure 15.25 English Georgian interior in the "Chinese Chippendale" manner

Figure 15.26 American Late Georgian interior

blue, and green—in rich imported textiles such as silks, fine cottons, linens, and in the increasingly popular Oriental rugs. As trade was established between the Western world and Asia, Chinese color influence expanded. The Chinese palette included the warm cinnabar red, peacock blue, Ming (royal) blue, cloisonné teal, deep jade green, bright chrysanthemum yellow, gold, coral, and peony pink (fuchsia). The "Chinese Chippendale" Asian-inspired furniture was enhanced with these exotic colors. However, neither the Renaissance nor the Chinese palette were used in large quantity nor in proximity to each other in American mansions, with the exception of large wall murals. These often depicted scenes from a real or imagined time and place, a result of the shipping industry's trade and adventure, and painted where a chair or sofa was placed near draperies.

The second avenue reflected the trend in the later period to lighten color, undoubtedly influenced by the colors discovered at Pompeii in 1754. Although vivid Imperial Roman colors were discovered at Pompeii in the *a'fresco* walls and floor mosaics, the resulting fashion rage turned to Neoclassic pale colors—peach, light olive green, grayed teal blue, gold, beige, gray-violet, Wedgwood blue, opal, pink, and green—with clean and creamy white backgrounds. This interesting scenario resulted in fabulous English garden florals on light backgrounds in subtle versions of Chinese or Pompeiian colors—all beautiful and appropriately proportioned.

Motifs

Rich textiles, reflecting Italian Renaissance damask (large floral spray) designs, were imported to America during the Late Georgian period. These patterns gradually gave way to Rococo and Chinese designs. The Chippendale Rococo style added to the damasks and embellished shell motif, adding scrolls and elaborate designs. Chinoiserie fabrics—woven or printed on fine cotton or silk—reflected the Western fascination for all things Chinese. *Chinois* (shin-wah) motifs included fantastic geographic shapes (soaring isolated mountain forms), pagodas set in exotic gardens of stylized trees, flowers, and birds, and paths trod by Chinese men and women in native costume. Overscaled, climbing branches with a variety of leaves and lavishly full flowers—peonies and chrysanthemums (flowers first imported from China during this era), whose heavy heads hung downward in full bloom, and with large, exotic birds perched artistically on them—was a Chinese textile design that became enormously popular. Climbing vines in a diamond pattern, known as *garden lattice,* was a Chinese- and Indian-inspired design adopted by the Rococo period and then the Late Georgian. Chinese fretwork and fine dotted work were used to accentuate individual motifs, to fill in an entire back-

the influence of the Baroque and Rococo styles, and through them the influence of China. English architect James Gibbs designed homes that were more elaborate than the Early Georgian style. Through published pattern books, the Late Georgian architecture of Gibbs and the furniture designs of cabinetmaker Thomas Chippendale reached America, where they became standards of design excellence. The American Late Georgian is historically concurrent with the English Palladian and English Middle Georgian styles.

Textiles: Color, Pattern, and Texture

Colors

The colors of the American Late Georgian period were divided into two avenues: brilliant and subdued. Intense colors from the Renaissance palette were used—vivid gold, red,

Figure 15.27a–d American Late Georgian textile motifs. **a** Oriental influence; **b** Renaissance spray design; **c** Queen Anne floral; **d** Colonial or European toile pattern

ground, or on their own. The fashion for Chinese decoration was evident in the ornamental detail on chairs, tables, and mirrors as well as fabrics and wallpaper.

Textures

Although fine damask, velvet, brocatelle of silk, wool, and cotton were still imported from Europe, the textile manufacturing system in America came into its own. By the 1760s, cotton and linen factories were copying the crewel and chintz designs of the English Palladian period. As time and style progressed, the textures became smoother and more refined. Polished cotton, broadcloth, chintz, and cretonne and satin weaves were ideal textures for the plethora of Chinese and Rococo motifs. Wallpapers were first imported in 1737, and from that time onward, scenic and allover patterns were used to complement and enrich the elegant textiles.

Upholstered Furniture

Thomas Chippendale, an English cabinetmaker, revolutionized furniture fashion during the American Late Georgian period. His book *The Gentleman and Cabinetmaker's Director*, published in 1754, contained 160 engraved plates of designs for furniture. This book played a key role in developing the furniture of the American Late Georgian era.

Chippendale's furniture pieces are known for their grace and elegance. His chairs usually had upholstered seats, cabriole legs with a claw and ball foot, and/or a straight square leg known as the Marlborough leg. Settees—wood-framed upholstered sofas—were popular because of the variety of back, arm, and leg styles. Chippendale's humped camelback sofa was fully upholstered with cabriole or Marlborough legs. The Chippendale wing chair had the same features, plus tall arms and deep wings, all in larger scale than the Queen Anne wing chair. In fact, many of the shapes and features of the Queen Anne style were retained, but considerably more carved Rococo ornamentation and Chinese details were added, reflecting the optimism and increased wealth of the period.

Beds

When Chippendale began to influence furniture design, the mahogany tester bed with tall, slender, delicately carved posts and headboard became important. Although most of these wood-framed beds were restrained, some tester cornices were ornately shaped in Rococo/Chinese designs or carved with acanthus foliage. The Late Georgian bed was frequently handsomely draped, and in lieu of a wooden cornice frame, many beds were capped with pelmets. Sometimes the drapery panels were used merely to frame the foot and/or head testers or posts. In other cases, the draperies could be drawn closed around the bed, a long-standing technique for keeping in body warmth in the winter. False ceilings of fabric were created where a lavish use of textiles was justified, often shirred laterally above the bed or brought to

Figure 15.28a–f American Late Georgian upholstered furniture. **a** Triple pierced slat-back settee; **b** Chippendale camelback sofa with Marlborough legs; **c** Pierced slat-back scholar cap chair with cabriole leg; claw and ball foot; **d** Chinese Chippendale side chair; **e** Chippendale wing chair; **f** Lattice work chair

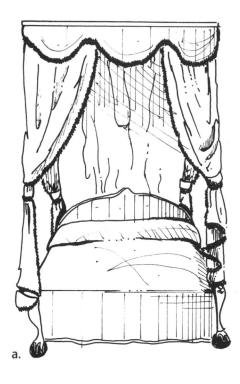

Figure 15.29a–d American Late Georgian tester or poster beds.
d shows Chinese Chippendale influence.

a center point. Beds of the well-to-do were appointed with the most luxurious of textiles and trimmed with the finest fringe. Lace and handmade trimmings were used as accents. Dust ruffles and bed skirts (taller beds required a step stool, accommodating trundle beds for small children) were common. Coverlets were textiles that often showed off the needlework skills of the mistress of the household. These included crewel embroidery, appliqué quilting, and finely hand-stitched patterned or outlined quilting.

Window Treatments

Pairs of long draperies, sometimes pooling onto the floors, topped with elaborate pelmets or upholstered cornices, graced windows in more formal settings. Tied-back fabrics finished with silk tassels and fringes were an indication of wealth and prestige. Top treatments largely reflected Chinese Chippendale designs—pagoda-like flaring corners and elaborate trimmings. English Middle Georgian window

Figure 15.30a–j American Late Georgian window treatments

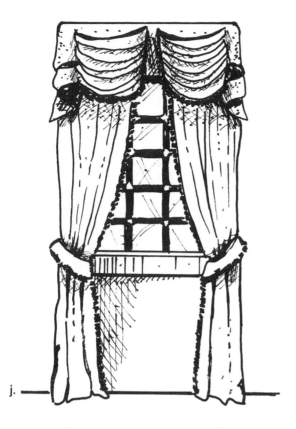

j.

treatments were used in America, although the complexity of the design was sometimes simplified. Vertically drawn Austrian shades as undertreatments indicated a rococo influence. Two-inch wood slat blinds, known as *Venetian blinds,* were commonly used, overlaid with floor-length draperies and/or beautiful top treatments. Raised-panel shutters were the other means of establishing privacy, alone or in addition to other treatments. These shutters were stacked off and set flush into the deep-set window frame to appear as traditional raised paneling.

Rugs

Carpets were plentiful during the Late Georgian era; many kinds were utilized, and they represented both status and practicality. In formal and sophisticated rooms, Oriental rugs were an imposing presence. Elaborate and complex Persian rugs began to replace the Caucasian "Turkey" rugs of the Early Georgian era. In the spacious entry halls and up the stairs, Oriental rug runners added desirable color and pattern as well as comfort. Motifs seen in area rugs or carpets included European floral designs. Two types of woven carpet were imported from England; broadlooms (4 feet wide) in the towns of Axminster and Wilton produced high-quality wool carpets. Handmade rugs were also

present during this period; examples are rag, braided, and needlepunched rugs. These rugs were also used in less formal settings and where economy dictated, along with painted canvas floorcloths and haircloth rugs.

The American Late Georgian Style Today

The American Late Georgian style offers appealing options for today's stately interiors. It provides a template for upscale traditional interiors in the lavish use of textiles as a counterpart to richly appointed architectural design (stained wood complemented with white trim and balusters). Most varieties of Chippendale's furniture design are available and sought after as reproductions, antiques, or adaptations. Window treatments of the period appeal to us today because of the combination of fabric shades with fabric draperies and top treatments or wooden blinds or shutters with similar overtreatments. Puddled draperies, straight or tied back, are reminiscent of Late Georgian treatments. The influence of both Chinese and Rococo styling adds charm and character to these window treatments. Beds lavishly draped and embellished with precise and ornate detailing are hallmarks today of textile application excellence. They still provide privacy, quiet, and emotional support in addition to beauty. Oriental rugs over wood floors are also classic; they will likely never go out of style.

FRENCH NEOCLASSIC AND AMERICAN FEDERAL

Period Overview

Neoclassicism dominated European and American interior design in the latter half of the eighteenth century. The roots of Neoclassicism were in the excavation of the ancient Roman cities of Pompeii and Herculaneum, located across from each other on the Bay of Naples in Italy. Pompeii was destroyed in A.D. 79 by the violent eruption of Mt. Vesuvius which rained poisonous gases and filled the city with debris and ash, which remarkably preserved architecture and even carvings, tilework, and a'fresco colors applied to walls. Herculaneum was destroyed by earthquake and mud slides at the same time and also well preserved. In 1754, the discovery and subsequent excavations began, which continue today. The new discoveries made there brought the time-darkened classic forms of the Greeks into the light of the new century. Such was the pull of Neoclassicism that Louis XVI adopted and incorporated the style into his surround-

Figure 15.31 French Neoclassical interior

Figure 15.32 English Neoclassical interior

Figure 15.33
American Federal
interior

ings. This style became the fashion late in Louis XV's reign and was well established when Louis XVI came to the throne. Today we associate the Neoclassical period with Louis XVI.

When Neoclassicism took hold in England, Robert Adam, embraced the style and dedicated all of his energies to its expansion. By the late 1780s, the Neoclassical style bridged the continents and began to influence the fledgling United States. It arrived just as America began to experience life with the new federal government, a government based on "classic" principles and ideals. In part because of this timing, the Americans were more than willing to adopt the Neoclassic style; in the United States, it became known as the Federal style.

Adam, a Scottish architect, designer, and cabinetmaker, was the most influential architect of the period. His work was greatly inspired by the art and architecture in France and Italy, and after his visit to Pompeii and Herculaneum, he used Roman and Renaissance design. He enjoyed creating original new ideas from old ones. Working as an interior designer as well as an architect, Adams is most remembered for his design of Wedgwood Jasperware, upholstery, fabrics, anaglypta architectural trim, delicate and exquisite window treatments, broadloom carpets, and refined, detailed furniture. Adam contributed by bringing lightness and grace to interiors. Many of his works can still be seen today, preserved in their original state of beauty.

Textiles: Color, Pattern, and Texture

Color

The Neoclassic period saw colors lightened to creamier values. Aubusson pastel tapestry colors included a yellow that was pale and light, a deeper yellow color that was light gold-orange, a carnation pink that was dulled to a grayish pink, and a cream used to highlight molding. Some Gobelin colors were adapted as well, including light blues with a green tint, pinks with a bold orange tint, and grays with a great deal of brown. The colors excavated at Pompeii were bold and bright, but they did not become fashionable until the Empire period. Other colors of the period were Wedgwood's jasperware red, which was softened to a deep coral color; a deep, dull brown; a vibrant, strong cane yellow; a lilac that was soft and dulled to a gray-violet; pale to deep Wedgwood blues that went from a light royal blue to a deep aqua; and especially Adam's pale to deep greens, which varied from a light softened green to a deep avocado green. Adam created bold materials using richly colored backgrounds for his walls and ceilings, and he

decorated them with delicate white plasterwork details. American Federal hues included Federal blue (light, slightly grayed), Federal yellow (clear, clean, light), light coral, and grayed medium green.

Pattern

Many of Robert Adam's carefully copied and designed classical motifs became the basis for the Neoclassical textile patterns. Adam used these motifs on furniture, ceilings, and walls in the form of painted decoration and plasterwork. His focus on decorative detail enhanced interior architecture dominance more than previous historic styles. Adam even invented a style of anaglypta that could be mass produced for moldings to be used as wall trimming. The ceilings of many Neoclassic and Federal homes are ornately decorated with anaglypta. The cast plaster decorations on interiors and textiles included Grecian human figures, garlands of flowers and fruit, urns and statuary, ancient musical instruments, and paterae (oval or elliptical shapes). Greek designs were seen in every aspect of an interior, including moldings on walls and ceilings, intricate color schemes, carpet designs, upholstery, and especially textiles. This mass coordination was the style of the interiors of Neoclassical and Federal homes.

Textures

Most fabrics of the Neoclassic and Federal period displayed themes of ribbons, wreaths, garlands, acanthus, medallions, lozenges, festoons, and vases, all delicately trimmed with silk tassels and braids. Many of the fine textiles of the period were plain, smooth satin cotton or polished cotton, finely blended stripes or small-scale striped fabrics, or beautifully designed silk brocades and damasks.

A relatively new development was copperplate roller printing. This technique allowed for larger repeats and better definition. With this invention, the first toile (a linen fabric with scenic designs printed in one color) was printed. Toile featured rich Neoclassic motifs and was used as wall panels in order to express the intricate details of a scene. Trimmings were also an important element in decoration with textiles. Most trimmings of the Neoclassic period were made of silk. Tassels began leaning toward a smaller arrow shape with rectangular heads in the middle of the eighteenth century. Many tie-backs were made of satin with a braid trim.

One aspect of the Neoclassic and Federal period was the refined detail used in both decoration and textiles. Textiles were used to depict graceful living, elegance, and beautiful classical design. The prints and trimmings of the period made it a step apart from all others.

Figure 15.34a–q Neoclassical and Federal textile motifs. **a** vase and floral spray; **b** swag and bouquet; **c** lozenge and laurel wreath; **d** agricultural symbols including patterae and honeysuckle flower; **e–g** lozenge borders; **h** Arabesque—scrolling, interlacing foliage and tendrils; patterae and honeysuckle also seen here; **i** laurel wreath, scepters, fluttering ribbons, swags and cascades; **j** torch and floral design; **k** guilloche scroll pattern; **l** Federal pineapple—symbol of hospitality

m.

n.

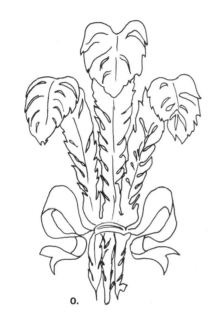

o.

p.

q.

Figure 15.34 m griffins, rinceau, and center honeysuckle flower; **n** half-patterae in "spider web" design; **o** Prince of Wales plumes; **p** stylized acanthus leaf; **q** Adam patterae and urn

Upholstered Furniture

Much of the upscale furniture of the period was made from satinwood, mahogany, and occasionally curly maple used in imitation of satinwood. Cherry and other fruitwoods were used for less costly furniture. The furniture style was delicate and refined, yet it expressed a quality of simplicity. Brass ornamentation was in the form of ring handles and, occasionally, feet. The two most influential furniture designers of the period were the English cabinetmakers George Hepplewhite and Thomas Sheraton.

These designers had similar styles, and both published books on upholstery and furniture patterns. This helped spread the influence and popularity of Neoclassical furniture design in the United States.

Sheraton is known for his square-back chair and Hepplewhite for his shield-back chair. Both are delicate chairs with upholstered seats. Other great upholstered furniture pieces were the bow-back sofa, the Martha Washington armchair, and the Phyfe chair. It is noteworthy that this period saw a trend toward comfort in furniture design. Those elements of comfort are evident in the works of other influential Neoclassical and Federal furniture designers, such as Duncan Phyfe and the architect Samuel McIntire.

Beds

In France, beds were an established status symbol, with flowing draperies installed, most often, from a short canopy above the pillow area. Pelmets or shirred fabric were used as top treatments around these rectangular or circular draped applications. Fabrics were either soft and fluid—the gamut of sheers—or they were brocade, damask, or other heavily formal fabrics cut and shaped into pelmets and trimmed with exquisite passementerie. In less formal settings, printed fabrics were used, often lined or double-paneled in printed companion fabrics. Coverlets or bedspreads were smooth and fitted, and long bed-width bolsters were indispensable.

The bed appointments of the period, one of its most important manifestations, gave new light to the use of textiles. With the coordination of window treatments, upholstery, and bed appointments, a new look came to interiors. A perfect sense of classical balance was often achieved with elaborate embroidery and excessive fabrics. The bed pelmets or valances expressed a delicate Neoclassical styling. Elegant fabrics adorned the bed and could be pulled off by cords to display the simple shapes and refined carvings on the bedposts, giving a type of double-festoon look. Often silk, printed cottons, and velvets were used for bed treatments.

Figure 15.35a–h Neoclassic and Federal upholstered furniture **a** French sheaf-back settee; **b, c** French Neoclassic fauteuil; **d** French Neoclassic bergère; **e, f** Hepplewhite shield-back chairs **g** French Neoclassic footstool; **h** Neoclassic bow-back sofa

In both England and America, the Sheraton and Hepplewhite designed pencil-post beds fast became perhaps the most beloved of the Neoclassical beds—straight and tapered, simple and enduring in design. The rice poster bed had round fluted posts carved with a rice pattern, symbolizing fertility and hope of posterity.

A variety of bedding styles was seen because of the various levels of formality. In formal settings, silk woven into satin was hand-quilted into exquisitely artistic coverlets. Abbreviated or short swags sometimes were attached to the coverlet along the sides and foot of the mattress. Appliquéd quilts were sometimes used as bedding, and printed smooth cotton fabrics became coverlet tops with attached skirts in a shirred or gathered fashion. Dust ruffles became fashionable. Canopies for beds also came into style, either flat or, more often, a graceful elliptical arch covered with a semisheer fabric with shirred panels. These were often trimmed in silk or more affordable cotton fringe and tied back at the posts. Sleeping pillows were tucked in, and a round bolster in the French style was appropriate.

Figure 15.36a–e Neoclassical and Federal beds
a French partial canopy bed with draperies, swags, and cascades; **b** upholstered head and footboard with French bolster pillow; **c** Rice-poster bed and formal bed ensemble with full canopy; valance and bedskirt both feature trimmed swags and rosettes; **d** partial canopy and tied-back draperies; simple coverlet with trundle bed; **e** Pencil post bed with shirred bedskirt and quilt. Exposed pillows are a contemporary application.

Window Treatments

The style of Neoclassical curtains, draperies, and bed appointments was restrained and formal. The motifs of window treatments and bed appointments followed the others of this period with classical decoration. The wide range of fabrics available during this period allowed a broad selection of styles and designs. Trimmings and tassels were used extensively and to great detail. Many bed appointments were appliquéd and embroidered to a degree hard to achieve today. Of all historic periods, Neoclassical and Federal treatments and appointments are perhaps the most refined and delicate with the greatest attention to detailed trimmings.

Symmetry and asymmetry were important characteristics of the whole Neoclassical period, and evident in the window treatments. The windows of this period were English sash windows. Slender tie-back draperies were used with a sheer and/or translucent semisheer fabric, and overdraperies with a muslin lining to protect fabrics from fading or sun rotting. The overlap used where the curtains met gave a finished look. Top treatments included Austrian shades, pelmets, fabric valances, and upholstered

Figure 15.37a–q French and English Neoclassical and Federal window treatments

cornices ornamented with modest-scaled fringes, tassels, and ribbons.

A major invention of this period was the full cord-and-pulley system for opening curtains and drawing them closed. This innovation minimized inconvenience and saved fabric from the wear and tear of handling.

In the 1790s, Thomas Sheraton designed a light, refined curtain that was tied back with rope, ornamented with large rosettes, and topped with straight cornices softened with swags and cascades. The refined and subtle folds and delicate fabrics used in such Neoclassical drapery designs represented the gowns of Greek goddesses. Neoclassic swags and festoons were used in top treatments. A common style of draperies was called *Bishop's sleeves,* involving fabric of slender proportion and symmetrical design tied back between slight poufs that puddled onto the floor. In America, window curtains were rare before the Revolution due to the expense of the fabrics. However, in time, many of the French and English window treatments were repeated with the United States Federal style.

Neoclassical and Federal style window treatments featured a slender or elliptical curve in pelmets and swags or festoons layered on or against a straight-lined frame.

Beds

One of the most important features of the English and American Neoclassic period was the bed appointments. The style of this period gave the bed pellets or balances a delicate Neoclassic styling. Elegant fabrics adorned the bed and could be pulled back by cords to display the simple shapes and refined carvings on the bedposts, giving a type of double-festoon look. Often silk, printed cottons, and velvets were used for bed draperies and top treatments. Draperies were often operable for keeping in body heat during the nighttime.

Rugs

Generally, in the Neoclassic and Federal periods, the absence of a carpet was not uncommon. Wood flooring was used, while carpet was a luxury. Common floor coverings included stenciled/painted floors, floorcloths, mats, needlepoint and Aubusson rugs, and broadloom carpeting.

Painting floors became popular in New England, where the typical pine floor was often finished with paint—mainly the yellows, dark reds, grays, and brown. Patterns consisted of narrow borders and centered swirls, pinwheels, and oak leaves. Often, geometric shapes took form in squares, diamonds, and cubes.

Floorcloths were also stenciled or painted. Floorcloths were made by layering four to seven coats of an oil-based paint onto a canvas and topping that with a decoratively designed pattern. These cloths were often placed in entries, parlors, and dining rooms. Floorcloths were painted to imitate carpeting, and the design was often tailored to their location.

Matting was a popular covering during the Federal period. George Washington originally used it in his beautifully designed Federal home, Mount Vernon. Matting was made of materials such as grass and straw that were woven in strips and stitched together to form larger carpeting.

Textile carpeting was a luxurious commodity few had the chance to enjoy during the Neoclassical and Federal period. Carpeting was a sign of status as well as comfort in the home. Aubusson rugs were common in France, along with Wilton and Axminster weaves, in traditional Neoclassical motifs. Robert Adam actively designed broadloom rugs for his interiors, giving them grace and charm to complement his style.

By the 1750s, English weavers had begun producing Wilton and Axminster carpets (the names originated with operating weaving centers). These were some of the first machine-woven pile carpets, known collectively as *broadloom*. Carpeting of the period also came from the hand-knotted Orientals and European handmade needlepoint rugs.

The Neoclassic and Federal Period Influence Today

The Neoclassic and Federal period produced an elegant and refined style of window treatments and bed appointments that is still widely seen today in many interiors. The tall, slender bishop's sleeve and tie-back curtains with swags and festoons are common in cultivated homes today, giving a graceful and artistic feel to an interior with a splendid historic touch. As the centuries have passed, the Federal treatments gained a simple and refined look that is still exquisite. The furniture design of the period has lasted into the twenty-first century and can be found in many upscale homes. The refined style gives these pieces a feeling of delicacy and sophistication. Carpeting is also seen in most homes and nonresidential interiors.

The Neoclassical is a distinctly *formal* style. Postmodern Neoclassical-styled furniture is clean and fresh, retaining elements of the stately and elegant look yet also being comfortable and casual.

Figure 15.38 Neoclassical and American Federal rug/carpet or floor cloth design

FRENCH AND AMERICAN EMPIRE

Period Overview

The French Empire period was a natural development of the Neoclassical, although the style was dictated heavily by the personal tastes of Napoleon Bonaparte. The period dates in France from 1804 to 1820. In the United States, the Empire style began in 1820 and extended until the onset of the Civil War in 1861.

Napoleon Bonaparte wanted to add grandeur and splendor to his reign, a purpose he found best served through the arts. "Men are only as great as the monuments they leave behind," Napoleon said. He enlisted some of the best artists and architects in Europe to help accomplish his goal.

As emperor, Napoleon restored most of the royal palaces of the ancient regime, and he bought castles and hotels that he renovated and gave to family members. Napoleon's chief architects were Charles Percier and Pierre-François Leonard Fontaine. Because much of the work was renovation rather than building, Percier and Fontaine worked much more as interior designers than architects. Some of the buildings they renovated were Malmaison, the Tuileries, the Louvre, Fontainbleau, Compiegne, and Rambouillet.

Percier and Fontaine worked as a team, working first for Josephine Bonaparte and then for Napoleon himself. Their interiors featured majestic architectural elements in the ceiling and cornices. Walls were covered with wallpaper, often with a marbled effect. Some walls were draped, although this became less common as the period progressed. Colossal orders were used, including classical columns and pilasters. Textiles and Savonnerie rugs were bold in both color and form. The style had an overall masculine feeling, with stark geometric forms.

In the United States, the Greek Revival or American Empire influence was embraced throughout the country, but particularly in the South. The wealth of the planters, the size and elegance of the plantation mansions, the ample space for expansion, and the luxurious style of living all created an atmosphere that welcomed the new style.

The American Empire interior, like the French Empire, was characterized by heavy architecture of primarily Roman design. One of the most prominent furniture designers of the era was Duncan Phyfe (1768–1854), a Scottish cabinetmaker. His Regency-style furniture was first made popular in the Directoire period, which immediately preceded the Greek Revival. The look and feel of Phyfe's work, as well as many of his actual pieces, played a strong role in setting the American Empire interior. His designs frequently displayed the harp or lyre as a motif.

Figure 15.39 French Empire interior

Figure 15.40 American Empire interior

American Empire interiors showed the strong influence of the classical orders, including columns and pilasters, often painted white or gray. Scenic wallpaper became popular, as did patterned broadloom carpets. The draperies were heavy in scale, especially in the top trimmings.

Textiles: Color, Pattern, and Texture

Throughout the Empire period, textiles softened the stark lines of the otherwise imposing, rigid architecture and furniture. They also added color to the wood, which was often dark or gilt.

Napoleon paid special attention to the textile industry. For a time, he allowed only French fabrics to be used in order to promote the growth of the industry in France. He made sure the necessary help was given to the industry, which had almost come to a halt during the Revolution. He contributed massive commissions that revived the silk industry in Lyons and the cotton industry in Normandy, Ile de France, and around Paris.

Napoleon encouraged technical advances in the textile industry. Research was done on dyes to improve colorfastness. At this time the Jacquard loom was invented by Joseph-Marie Jacquard, which dramatically improved silk weaving. Christopher-Philip Oberkampf had introduced to France the roller cylinders for printing cotton cloth.

Although production increased during this time, quality was not always the best, even for the imperial interiors. The lack of quality was due in part to young and inexperienced workers, continual wars, and the Continental Blockade. In addition, the industry was composed of artisans rather than of factory workers. In the Lyons silk industry, the chief manufacturers of fabrics were the *chamberlains*, who worked at home (in their chambers). This made quality control difficult. Cotton manufacturing had similar problems. The industry was scattered throughout the countryside among peasant families who rented looms from industrialists. As industrialization increased, these factors disappeared, and the quality of textiles in turn increased.

During the French Empire period, walls were sometimes draped with silks and tapestries, often to imitate the interior of a luxury military tent. The hangings were loose in an effort to look antique. Many materials were embroidered with gold, and Greek and Roman fretwork borders were used in the imperial palaces. Printed cottons were popular and usually printed in one of three ways: woodblocks, copperplates, or cylinders. Designs of the Empire period began as light and airy but became progressively dense throughout the era.

French and American textiles included smooth satins, fine woolen fabrics, and woven jacquards. Cottons were smooth, plain, or satin weave, and were often printed.

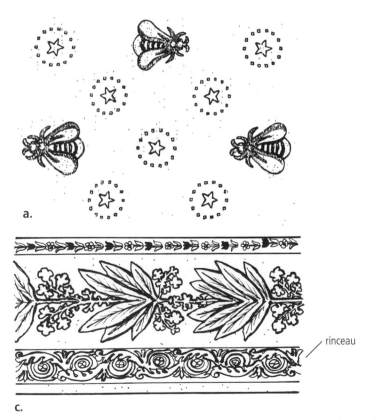

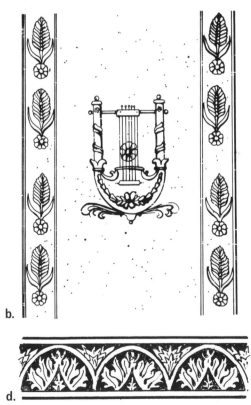

Figure 15.41a–t French and American Empire textile motifs. **a** honeybee and star; **b** lyre framed with laurel leaves and rosettes; **c** laurel leaf bordered with honeysuckle and rosettes (above) and rinceau of acanthus leaves (below); **d** arcaded border of acanthus leaves and carnations

e Greek fretwork f grotesque arabesque with animal/human forms, here swan's head; g laurel wreaths and anthemion; h wreath and bee; i, j wide/narrow stripes k–n rinceau borders o swag/anthemion border; p architectural grotesque; q anthemion; r acanthus leaf; s griffin; t laurel leaf and pearl

Colors

The Empire color palette was varied. The Directoire period was strongly influenced by the Empress Josephine's taste for lighter materials and colors. Her interest in nature and love of flowers had a strong impact. Among the most popular colors were bois de citron (lemonwood), aurora (dawn), terre d'Espagne (earth of Spain), poppy red, and hazelnut.

Between the Directoire and the end of the Empire period, the colors grew darker as life became more formal. Many of Napoleon's rooms featured bold red, green, and gold. The American Empire closely followed the colors of the French Empire. The colors found in upholstery, draperies, and carpeting were predominantly bright royal red, emerald and olive green, imperial purple, gold, and rich coffee brown. Where intense color was unsuitable, paler neutralized versions were used, particularly in the United States. Among these were pale mauve, cream, white, black, azure blue, salmon, and gray-blue.

Pattern

Common patterns of the Empire period included stylized antique patterns such as anthemion, cornucopias, and florals, foliage such as ivy, Greek acanthus leaves, and vines, woven or printed as garlands, scrolls, or laurel wreaths; and wide stripes in solids or multicolors.

Among the more common motifs of the era were imperial emblems. Stemming from the strong influence of Napoleon Bonaparte, these included the eagle, the *N*, the bee, the snowflake and Greek laurel leaf and pearl, the lozenge and guioche. Also seen were swags or festoons, the five-pointed star, honeysuckle, and the griffin (lion's body, eagle's head and wings, or the Josephine griffin, a swan body and a creature head, usually similar to a Chinese dragon). Motifs were often isolated (printed or woven) on a smooth background or incorporated into complex compositions. Frequently seen were tiny floating motifs on refined silks and cottons used for upholstery and drapery, which contrasted dramatically with large, bold, carpet patterns.

Texture

Popular fabric textures of the Empire period included:

Satin—Smooth satins were in high demand, along with moiré (textured, with a watermark design) and polished satin.

Jacquard—This loom attachment produces large and intricate woven patterns, making possible the production of brocade, brocatelle, figured velvet, and tapestry.

Brocade—This Jacquard-woven fabric gives the appearance of being embroidered. It is traditionally a formal fabric.

Brocatelle—This Jacquard-woven fabric is similar to brocade. It can be found as a tightly woven, formal, traditional fabric, or with a slightly puffed surface.

Lampas—Another Jacquard-woven fabric, lampas has a ribbed background and raised figures or motifs woven with the warp threads and contrasted with small streaks of colored thread.

Sheer wool—Sheer wool is woven of very fine threads, such as fine nun's veiling.

Printed fabrics—Printed fabrics created visual texture that varied from very small to quite large patterns.

Upholstered Furniture

The personal taste of Napoleon, together with Percier and Fontaine, determined to a large degree the style of Empire furniture. The industry was dictated by Napoleon because of the financial support he offered. The furniture commissions given by the emperor determined the style of not only France but also a great part of Europe overall.

The strict etiquette encouraged by Napoleon led to very stiff furniture. At official gatherings, only the emperor, empress, and the emperor's mother were seated in armchairs. A few important dignitaries were given chairs, and the remaining guests were seated on stools—if at all. The only exceptions were made for pregnant women in the emperor's family. At the onset of the Empire period, this was the rule for all official palaces, but as the period progressed, more chairs were brought into court life.

Many women began running salons, which were gatherings of typically feminine activity where women and some intellectual or artistic men met and did a great deal of philosophizing, political debating, and social entertaining. These led to more functional interiors with increased seating for entertaining.

Larger sofas and armchairs known as *meubles meublants* were introduced. These large pieces were accompanied by *chaises volantes,* which were smaller chairs that could be pulled up to a table or brought near the fireplace, where much of the entertaining was centered. For more formal rooms, the wood was usually gilded, and in more comfortable settings, mahogany was common.

Scrolled backs and saber legs were common at the onset of the period. Later, however, the furniture became heavier, the scrolled backs turned straight, and the legs became thicker. Chairs were upholstered in vivid colors. Some Beauvais tapestries were found in the more luxurious interiors. Seats were often covered in silk or silk velvets. Arm pads were common, and backs and seats also were padded.

Figure 15.42a–g French and American Empire upholstered furniture
a, b Napoleonic chairs with griffins;
c vernacular American Empire chair;
d x-back chair; **e** stool with cornucopia legs; **f** empire sofa with bolster pillows;
g fainting sofa or recamiér

Some dining chairs were grand, while others were quite simple. Seats varied from generously padded to cane. Stools, similar to those of previous periods, were generally in the shape of an *X*. The legs were sometimes arched on claw-feet or made in the shape of crossed swords. They were usually upholstered with velvets accented with fringe and tassels. Seating pieces were tightly upholstered, giving empasis to often intricately carved exposed wood.

Sofas were elaborate and dramatic. The plush seating was upholstered in tapestries and silks. Frequently, two sofas were set on either side of the fireplace. Some smaller sofas were generally more square and sometimes found with rolled ends. Sofas were heavily carved and sometimes gilded. The American fainting sofa is an example of Empire asymmetrical design.

Figure 15.43a–d French and American Empire beds with lavish fabric appointments

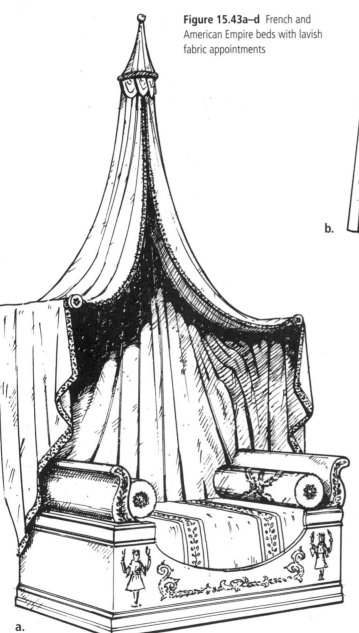

Beds

Prestigious beds of the Empire period were heavily decorated. Generous yardage of draped silk or muslin crowned the bed with a canopy—sometimes round, sometimes rectangular—flowing down to encompass the bed as a side drapery. Bed-width bolsters enhanced formality. Along with the excessive fabric were found high-quality bronze mounts.

On the wooden bedframes were applied military symbols such as the spear and the letter *N,* as well as mythological motifs—winged figures, chariots, wreaths, and torches —or symbols of sleep and night, decorated the lavish beds. On either side of the bed were found *sommos,* night tables in the shape of classical pedestals, decorated with bronze mounts to match the canopy.

Window Treatments

Empire window treatments were often layered and asymmetrical. They were commonly made of silk, fine wool, or cotton, and either tied back symmetrically or overlapped at the center, perhaps with one straight panel to balance. This was a common Roman *toga* effect. The heavier side also may have had another deep, swagged fabric layered on top. The top treatments consisted of heavy fabric draped over a metal rod. Some were precisely pleated into goblet pleats or floppy headings. Treatments were heavily trimmed with fringe and tassels. The rods often displayed decorative ornaments in a spear or rope shape. American top treatments were also deep, sometimes swagged, and of heavy proportions often trimmed with beaded passementerie. In America, opaque fabric as elaborate pelmets or festooned swags was often placed over semisheer draperies. Tied-back draperies, whether heavy or sheer, were nonoperable. Shutters or Austrian shades provided privacy.

c.

d.

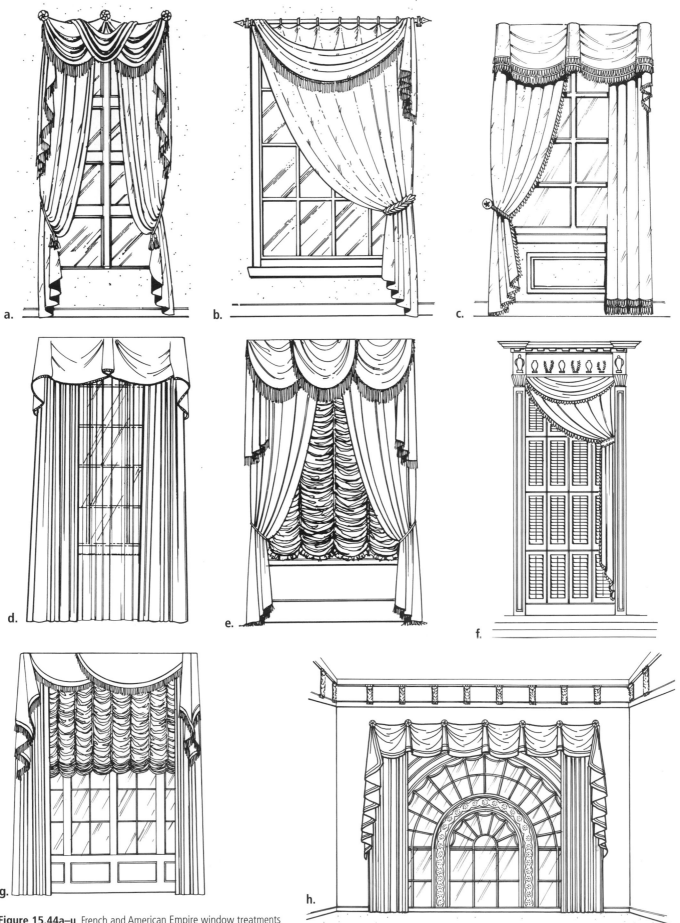

Figure 15.44a–u French and American Empire window treatments

i.

j.

k.

l.

m.

n.

o.

p.

q.

r.

s.

t.

u.

Rugs

For many years, during the reign of the kings, a strong tradition of tapestry weaving had flourished in France. This went into a decline at the start of the Revolution. Although some chairs were still upholstered with Beauvais tapestry, and doors were sometimes hung with an Aubusson, as the period progressed, it was no longer the style to cover entire walls with great tapestries. Making tapestry rugs was a slow and costly process. Unlike in the textile and furniture in-

dustries, state commissions were insufficient to keep the weaving industry going full force. The makers of the tapestry rugs therefore looked for more lucrative work. Following the Revolution, their production turned to carpets. It was the first time that wall-to-wall carpeting was seen. Most Empire rugs were Savonnerie or Wilton or Axminster broadloom. Later in the period, nearly all carpeting was broadloom Wilton or Axminster, and installed wall-to-wall.

Carpets of the Empire period generally had the following characteristics: bold, large-scale patterns, bright colors,

a.

b.

c.

d.

Figure 15.45a–d French and American Empire rugs/carpets

flowers, foliage, swans or griffins, military and imperial emblems, the Napoleon *N*, stars, and fabric motifs.

The brilliant carpets added to the Empire interiors strong, bold pattern that complemented the strong colors of the other textiles. The Manufacture de Savonnerie, which originated in the seventeenth century and was famous for a knotting technique that gave Oriental carpets a velvety texture, acted as the primary source for both carpets and rugs. Many of the grand carpets could be found only in Napoleonic residences, buildings owned by the state, or in homes of the higher upper class. The designs were often custom-made.

The Empire Influence Today

The pure American Empire influence can be seen today in the White House—in the Red Room, the Green Room, and the Oval Office, for example. Many preserved interiors still function and are formal, dignified, and commanding in appearance. In these traditional settings, an authentic French and American Empire influence can still be strongly felt today. The heavy furniture styles are finding wide acceptance as antiques, and many are being reproduced in mass quantities, particularly as adapted furnishings for large-scale and upscale contemporary interiors. Similar window treatments are still found in today's formal settings. As a classic style, the Empire influence promises to continue influencing interiors into the future.

AMERICAN VICTORIAN

Period Overview

Named after the reign of Queen Victoria of England, the Victorian era dates from 1837 to 1901. The Industrial Revolution allowed interior products to be made without the influence of trained designers or architects. Motifs were borrowed from previous historic periods and known as revivals: Gothic Revival, Neoclassic Revival, Rococo Revival, Islamic, East Indian influences, and Italianate.

This familiarity and ease with furniture and products encouraged the emergence of curving forms, ornamentation, and complex design. Two prominent designers who opposed the usual Victorian tastes were Charles Eastlake and William Morris. Eastlake's 1868 book, *Hints of Household Taste in Furniture, Upholstery, and Other Details,* promoted simplicity in interiors, although his tastes were lavish in comparison to current standards. Similarly, Morris was opposed to machine-made products and advocated a return to handmade simplicity and artistry. His style was

Figure 15.46 Victorian Rococo Revival interior

important to what came to be known as the Arts and Crafts Movement.

Another significant influence on Victorian society was the growing middle class, a result of the economic activity generated by the Industrial Revolution. A new market suddenly emerged for goods that had previously been available to the wealthy only. These products were now conveniently attainable through new avenues such as department stores and mail-order catalogs, leading to the spending spree. The middle class was suddenly able to add culture and beauty to their homes; however, the results were not always cohesive due to the untrained eye.

England's Great Exhibitions and world's fairs also lent a hand in unveiling Victorian design. The 1876 Exhibition in Philadelphia and the 1893 World Columbian Exposition in Chicago dazzled visitors with bewildering technological inventions, including the telephone, carpet sweeper, typewriter, and elevator. The people of the Victorian era were confident in their abilities, and the furniture of the time reflected this assured attitude. The Victorian love for novelty was indicative of this thinking; the credo was "If a little is good, a lot must be better."

Textiles: Color, Pattern, and Texture

Colors

Until about 1865, muted fabric colors were made from vegetable dyes derived from plant roots, bark, leaves, flowers, seeds, and other natural materials. Then William Perking invented chemically produced dyes, which were a distillation of coal tar. These dyes generated striking colors such as Prussian blue, malachite green, and chrome yellow. Normally, though, the brightness of the color selected was dependent on the tastes of the owner.

Other popular colors included olive and sage green, chocolate brown, pale (federal) and navy blues, light yellow, and creamy and dark gold. Red, magenta, and mauve were so widely used that the Victorian era has been referred to as the "mauve decades."

Motifs

Some critics feel the greatest contribution of the Victorian era was the variety and beauty of its fabric designs. Pattern copies or revivals of the time included Gothic, Baroque, Rococo, Oriental, Georgian, Renaissance, Celtic, Islamic, English Regency, and French styles. The hallmark of Victorian

Figure 15.47a–f Victorian textile motifs influenced by **a** Rococo; **b** India and the Orient; **c** Queen Anne and English gardens; **d** Islamic/Oriental

design was a brightly colored Queen Anne floral chintz. Patterns were often overscaled, elaborate, and repetitious. By this time, almost all fabrics were machine-made on the Jacquard loom, and some were block- or roller-printed.

Textures

Textures were most often floral chintz, with stems creating silhouette portraits of Queen Victoria and her consort. Damask, printed sateen, silk, rayon, sheers, and horsehair materials were also common selections. Muslin or silks were used in the earlier part of the era, with heavier fabrics such as velvets applied later on. Embroidery, applique, and patchwork were hand-made textiles.

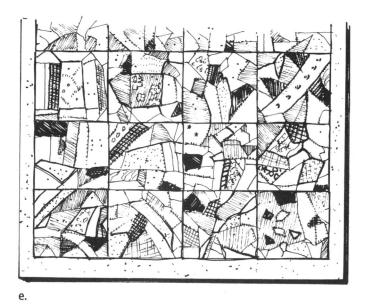

e.

f.

Figure 15.47 e crazy quilt pieced quilt pattern; **f** applique and quilted pattern

Upholstered Furniture

Rosewood furniture was popular toward the beginning of this era, and mahogany began to rise in popularity as time moved on, and rooms began to acquire the familiar cluttered look.

Charles Eastlake's Gothic Revival style and Japanese influence increased interest in Medieval motifs. A popular style of the mid-Victorian years was Rococo Revival with naturalistic ornamentation. German immigrant John Henry Belter was one of the leading furnituremakers of the time. He made chairs, sofas, and case pieces in fanciful designs that appeared to be hand-carved but were typically machine- or mass-produced. His furniture included the important development of coiled-spring supports for the seats, making physical comfort a reality. These were topped with horsehair padding and tufted silk upholstery trimmed with elaborate fringe and tassels. Popular fabrics were bright red, green plush, and black horsehair, with patterns everywhere. The Turkish divan also became an important decorative feature.

Toward the end of the period, with the influence of the Civil War and Darwin's 1859 theory of evolution, people no longer looked to the past or to nature for sources of artistic inspiration; they looked instead to science and technology. Furniture began to have a combination of functions, such as the bed-wardrobe, desk-bookcase, and table-chest. With wide claims for therapeutic value, platform and spring rockers were popular, as were as jolting and reclining chairs.

Beds

The Victorian bed had no springs, making a soft feather mattress a necessity. Later, the French spring mattress was introduced, the precursor of today's box spring mattress. Four-poster frames were still being used, and the half-tester—a wood- or iron-lined canopy upholstered with tufted fabric on the underside, with optional draperies hung on either side—grew in popularity. Bed draperies were often fringed but rarely draped the entire bed, because that was considered unhealthy. Sheets were made of muslin or colored silk and layered with patchwork quilts or puffy comforters, pillow shams, and bolsters. Damask bedspreads were also used. Dressing tables were sometimes covered with white muslin over a colored foundation fabric.

Bed coverlets were mass-produced on powered Jacquard looms in the nineteenth century; these were ideal for homes without central heating. They were made of cotton, wool, and, less frequently, linen. In the middle of the nineteenth century, patterned Jacquard or handmade coverlets became the primary source of decorative color in many American households, reflecting domestic life, business, and politics

Figure 15.48a–g Victorian upholstered furniture
a Rococo Revival side chair; **b** Turkish ottoman; **c** Rococo-style fauteuil; **d** Rococo-influenced tufted sofa;
e Gothic-style gentleman's chair; **f** Chesterfield sofa; **g** contemporary Victorian styled ottoman

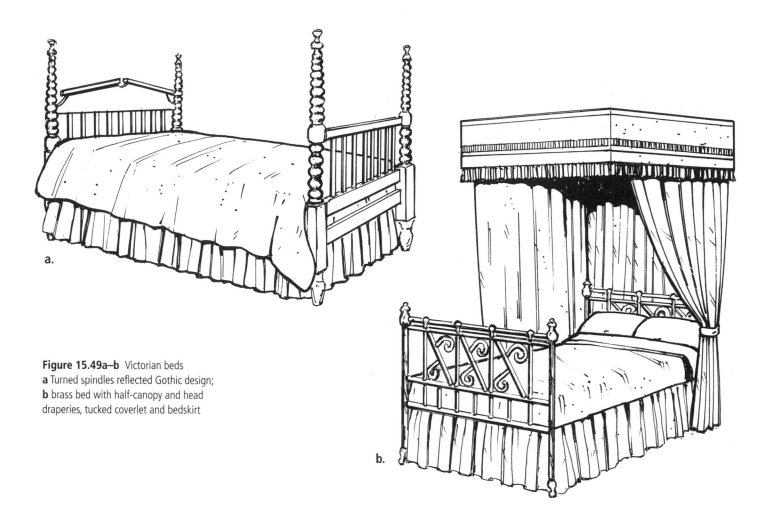

Figure 15.49a–b Victorian beds
a Turned spindles reflected Gothic design;
b brass bed with half-canopy and head
draperies, tucked coverlet and bedskirt

in small towns and rural communities. Patterns included gorgeous floral medallions of roses, lilies, violets, and ferns. They also celebrated the building of railroads, ships, and grand houses. Other patterns expressed patriotic themes such as hymns and slogans, Miss Liberty, Old Glory, George Washington on horseback, and the eagle from the Great Seal of the United States.

Window Treatments

Near the beginning of the Victorian period, window curtains were often made of lightweight materials that hung from gilded wooden or plaster cornices. Later on, draperies evolved into several layers of heavy damask or velvet with Nottingham lace curtains underneath. Deep valances or swags were commonly trimmed with heavy fringes and tassels and hung from large drapery rods of wood or metal with a gold-leaf finish.

Home manuals of the time advised hanging curtains in bedroom doorways in order to increase privacy when the door was opened. Known as *portières,* these draperies also closed off rooms and minimized drafts.

Rugs and Carpets

A design manual of 1865 advised that it was customary to carpet every room of the house. The process included covering the seam of a wood floor with brown paper, then spreading out old newspapers (instead of straw, which was previously used), with the carpeting on top.

Carpets were often Axminster and Wilton broadlooms and Oriental rugs. Broadloom carpet designs tended to be naturalistic patterns, such as trellises composed of stripes alternating with simple clusters of flowers. Contrasting backgrounds, trompe l'oeil effects, borders, and corner patterns were common. Victorian producers also borrowed patterns from the designs of Oriental rugs. Small hearthrugs with designs complementing the larger carpet pattern were sometimes applied.

Recommended colors included light blue grounds with figures of crimson or purple, and salmon or buff colors with shades of green or red.

As carpetmaking was becoming mechanized, Eastlake and his followers began to condemn wall-to-wall carpeting, instead favoring authentic Oriental rugs because they illustrated the weaver's skill rather than the machine's regularity.

Figure 15.50a–f Victorian window treatments featured swags, elaborate fabric valances, sheer or lace undercurtains and generous, often tied-back overdraperies.

Figure 15.51a–c Victorian rugs/carpets
a oilcloth in simplified Turkish Oriental rug design; **b** simple oilcloth or hooked rug design; **c** bearskin rug with roaring mouth, often placed over broadloom patterned carpet or Oriental rugs

Commonly used rugs included Orientals, hooked rugs, Berlin works rugs, and rag rugs made from reused apparel textiles in the kitchen. Animal skins were also utilized, sometimes on top of an Oriental rug or other carpet. The head of a lion, tiger, or bearskin often displayed an open, "roaring" mouth.

Generally called oilcloths, floorcloths were made of treated heavy canvas. These were dyed in a solid color or printed with a design, then sealed with a type of varnish. These rugs were rarely found in formal rooms such as parlors, but they were considered practical for the kitchen because they were easy to wipe clean and maintained warmth in the kitchen without collecting noticeable dust or grease. Eastlake suggested that these oilcloths be all one color and placed in halls or passages, using only floorcloth-like designs, which were simple and naturalistic.

The Victorian Style Today

The popularity of the Victorian style today can be seen in the enthusiasm for restoring nineteenth-century homes and in the growing number of bed-and-breakfast inns decorated with the opulent Victorian look. Generally, the lighter side of the style is popular today in lace accents and cheerful patterned fabrics. Nostalgia accounts for some of the passion and romance, as well as a longing for a time free from the pressures of today's hectic lifestyle. In the 1980s and early 1990s, there were more floral fabrics than could be counted. Today we see somewhat fewer prints, but there still exists—among enthusiasts—a keen interest in things Victorian, from elaborate draperies to lace and lovely floral prints.

RESOURCES

National Preservation Institute (NPI)

www.npi.org
P.O. Box 1702
Alexandria, VA 22313-1702
Tel 703-765-0100

NPI is a nonprofit organization that provides professional training for the management, development, and preservation of historic, cultural, and environmental resources. Seminars include historic property management and design issues. NPI offers limited scholarship opportunities for tuition only to participants in its seminars. Applications are available online.

National Trust for Historic Preservation (NTHP)

www.nationaltrust.org
1785 Massachusetts Avenue NW
Washington, DC 20036-2117
Tel 202-588-6000

The NTHP is a nonprofit organization with more than a quarter million members. It is the leader of the vigorous preservation movement that is saving the best of our past for the future. It provides leadership, education, and advocacy to save America's diverse historic places and to revitalize communities. It publishes *Preservation* magazine, operates a nationwide collection of National Trust Historic Sites, and promotes travel to historic destinations through its National Trust Study Tours and National Trust Historic Hotels of America. The NTHP provides technical and financial assistance to state and local organizations, works on legislative issues and initiatives, sees that preservation laws are upheld, and sponsors the annual National Preservation Conference.

United States General Services Administration: Historic Preservation

www.gsa.gov
D.C. Service Center
Seventh and D Streets SW
Washington, DC 20407
Tel 202-401-2521
Fax 202-708-0229

16

Medieval, Colonial, Country Styles

Figure 16.1 English Medieval interior

ENGLISH MEDIEVAL OR ELIZABETHAN

Period Overview

English Medieval dates from 1500 to 1625, during which time Queen Elizabeth I successfully navigated the transition of her realm from the Dark Ages to the Renaissance. English Medieval, sometimes called *Early Renaissance,* includes the reigns of the Tudors, Henry VII, Henry VIII, Edward VI,

Mary, and Elizabeth I, from 1485 to 1603. *Jacobean,* the latter portion of the period, is given the Latin name for King James I, who ruled from 1603 to 1625. During the Jacobean period, the Italian Renaissance was introduced to England. Through both the Jacobean and Elizabethan eras, people emerged from poverty, created domestic comfort, and added decoration to their lives.

Queen Elizabeth I was the most important sovereign of the English Medieval era. During her reign, the population became enlightened. Peace and domestic stability increased. Exploration of new concepts and foreign lands was encouraged. Prosperity resulted from increased trade with other nations. Shipping commerce, conducted by such entities as the East India Trading Company, brought beautiful furnishing items from the exotic ports of Turkey, India, and China.

Domestic brick or stone and half-timbered manor houses were built by the new gentry class of the Elizabethan era. Interiors developed distinctive characteristics. In the great halls, hammer beam ceilings were trussed upward into Gothic arches, often elaborately carved in patterns of oak-tree stems, leaves, and acorns. Thick stone walls were painted with frescoes and adorned with hanging tapestries, or arras. Paneling was applied to some walls, carved in linenfold, strapwork, or diamond-shaped geometric patterns. In smaller cottages, walls were exposed or half-timbered (half outside, half inside) in post-and-lintel construction with rough stucco wattle-and-daub infill. The small windowpanes, made of crystal-bright crown glass cut into diamond shapes, were set in casement frames or Gothic or Tudor openings. Later in the period, the Renaissance windows were widely used—vertically rectangular panes set in casement windows and, eventually, in vertically sliding sash window frames. Art glass heraldry—symbols such as the Great Lion of Scotland and coats of arms —replaced much of the religious-themed stained glass when Henry VIII broke with the Roman Catholic Church, formed the Church of England, and became the head of both church and state. Upper floors sometimes featured projecting oriel bay windows. Slate floors and, later, marble were used in manor houses for their durability; smaller cottages featured wood floors as well as stone.

Textiles: Color, Motif, and Texture

Color

Overall, color was limited during the English Medieval era. The island's relative isolation from Europe, a colder climate, and a struggling economy early in the period were reflected in somber colors and neutral hues. Yarns were hand-dyed from natural sources such as flowers, leaves, bark, and earthen compounds. Consequently, the color palette was limited, though the colors used were warm and natural. Mellow gold, yellow, orange, madder red, and warm green were most popular in the flame-stitch design and were also common for tapestries and crewel embroideries. Seating cushions were often made with solid colors on an off-white background.

Late in the period, Renaissance damask, brocade, brocatelle, and velvet textiles began to be imported from France and Italy, influencing Elizabethan and Jacobean textiles toward richer, deeper, and higher contrast fabric color schemes,

including garnet and persimmon red, warm yellow-based greens, royal blues, and lavish gold.

Motifs

English versions of the Asian Tree of Life were often seen on crewel embroideries. Bedspreads frequently incorporated this motif, a symbol of fertility and renewal; the leaves die in the fall and then regenerate in the spring.

Biblical stories were depicted in fabric. The white unicorn was a common tapestry motif, viewed by some as a symbol of the resurrected Christ during this period of Christian religious conversion. Portraits of great leaders were also frequently found woven into tapestry designs, as were coats of arms and family crest symbols, cultural scenes, and mythical tales and fables carried over from the British Isles' Celtic clan heritage. Floral motifs included the Tudor rose, carnations, peonies, climbing (often rose) vines, morning glories, and the fleur-de-lis (lily flower). Other popular motifs were pomegranates, birds, branches, leaves, and scrolls. An important motif was the flame-stitch design, inspired by the ever-present leaping flames of the fires kept burning to allay the damp, cool climate. An irregular chevron pattern, it was typically executed as a fully embroidered design on heavy fabric or as tapestry cloth done in earthy yellows, oranges, reds, and greens.

Tapestries and embroideries of the Jacobean period were like those of the Elizabethan, except the expertise of the workers increased.

Textures

Fabrics were primarily woolen during the reign of Elizabeth I, and as the East India Trading Company imported Indian crewel embroidery, these goods spawned an intense interest in wool and silk hand-needlework. The Elizabethan era became known as the Age of Embroidery. Crewel (woolen chain stitch) embroidery on plain linen or woolen cloth imitated imported Indian crewel. Fancy stitches were accomplished in both domestic wool and imported silk, which was embroidered into fine, luxury fabrics. All textiles of the Elizabethan period were made of wool and silk. Printed fabrics, cotton, and linen were not seen in England until the eighteenth century.

Until 1561, when William Sheldon brought experienced workers from Flanders, no manufacturers of tapestries existed in England. Tapestry was a new fabric construction, initially affordable only by the nobility and the very wealthy. The high cost of tapestry was due to the labor intensity of its production, relating particularly to the extensive color selection and copious detail. Rich patrons used tapestries as wall hangings and bed curtains. When a tapestry covered a cupboard or table, it was called a carpet.

Figure 16.2a–r English Medieval and English Early Renaissance textile motifs. **a, d, e–h** Indian/Oriental tree-of-life designs, sometimes with English rose (**a**) or carnations; **b** Renaissance pomegranate with seeds; acanthus leaf; **c** flame-stitch

Figure 16.2i, k Oriental influence in crewel patterns; **j, m** oak leaves; **l** carnation or fully opened climbing rose; **n** Renaissance column with tree-of-life crewel motifs; **o** English bouquet; **p** monogram, acorns, and foliage; **q** strapwork; **r** linenfold

Leather was used as the structural seating material, and for settee cushions, trunk coverings, and floor and wallcovering tiles.

In interiors, embroidery was used for Bible covers, pillow covers, valances, draperies for beds, curtains, table carpets, and cushions. A woman's embroideries were often used as her dowry. The wealthy frequently hired an artist to draft unique and original patterns, while commoners gained ideas from pattern books. The prestigious Medieval embroidery guilds were founded for both apparel and domestic applications. In one example of the quality control function of the guilds, the Borders Company guild required that member women present their embroidered work for the guild members' approval. If the quality was unacceptable as a consensus, the piece was cut up, burned, or destroyed. If approved, it was stamped and sold. Learned at an early age, embroidery provided the sole source of income for many women. They thus spent much of their lives learning and perfecting the skill. For the wealthy class, embroidery became a symbol of achievement and esteem.

Upholstered Furniture

During the early Tudor era, it was rare that anyone, even the upper class, owned many pieces of furniture. What items people were able to collect were small, collapsible, portable, and typically made of oak, which was a high-quality yet affordable material. The lower classes made their furniture out of ash, elm, and beech woods, which were not as strong; thus, few pieces in the Tudor style have survived.

Furniture became more of a household item for many people during the Elizabethan period. The average member of the middle class possessed two cupboards, a counter, a chair, two benches, a long settle, and a press or clothes cupboard. Chests and trunks were often used as tables or beds.

Decorations became an important new concept through the advent of the lathe. Beds, chairs, and tables became ornate and heavily designed. The linenfold, named for its resemblance to a folded piece of linen, was carved into cupboard panels. Strapwork, a repetitive curled carving re-

Figure 16.3a–g English Medieval upholstered furniture. **a** corner spindle chair; **b** upholstered settee; **c, e** English Danté chairs, **e** with footrest or tuffet; **d** lathe-turned open armchair with stretchers; **f, g** side chairs

sembling back-to-back scrolled valentines, was found on walls, moldings, and furniture. When used on furniture, strapwork was called fretwork. Large melon-shaped turnings made possible by the newly invented wood lathe were used on tables, beds, and chairs; these bulbous designs were often referred to as *cup and cover* because they resembled a cup with a lid.

Comfort also increased. The daybed or couch, a new furniture item, was a padded and upholstered trunk or chest. Cushions became more prevalent in households and seemed necessary for hardwood chairs. Although upholstered chairs were seen during the Elizabethan era, they were rare. It was not until the seventeenth century that upholstery became a common sight.

The Italian Renaissance influenced the Jacobean period. Comfort became increasingly important. Cushions were seen attached to chairs, and upholstered furniture fully emerged at the onset of the seventeenth century. Although chairs became lighter in scale, decoration and carving became increasingly ornate. Many fabrics, including leather, solid fabrics, detailed embroidery, and damask, were used as upholstery. The new upholstered chairs came to be called *farthingales*.

Beds

During the early Tudor period, beds were built into one or two walls and had a canopy that hung from the ceiling and drapes that pulled across the bed frame. The drapes were used for two reasons: privacy and warmth. Regardless of

b.

c.

Figure 16.4a–c English Medieval beds
a crewel embroidery bed hangings or drapery, coverlet; **b** walled bed with canopy; **c** details of bulbous turnings, podium lower posts, elaborate carving on headboard, cornice, and posts or testers

a.

economic situation, warmth was a definite concern. Cottages lacked sufficient insulation, and the castles where members of the upper class often lived had large and drafty rooms. Beds were enclosed to keep in the warmth at night, which created a room-within-a-room effect.

Beds became more common in the sixteenth and seventeenth centuries. Although they were still expensive, a larger proportion of people could afford them because prosperity had increased. Beds became increasingly more decorative. Toward the end of the Elizabethan period, the bed frame became a part of the end posts, and the headboard became intricately decorated with carvings and strapwork. As the Medieval period progressed toward the Renaissance, the bed became the most important piece of furniture a person could own. People spent many years saving for such a piece of furniture.

The Jacobean period had three types of beds. The first, the four-poster bed, was attached to a frame and occasionally had a paneled headboard. The second, with paneled head- and footboards similar to the Elizabethan style, had the head and foot panels open on two sides instead of one. The third piece was designed with the paneled head and foot, but with the addition of heavily draped fabrics. Holes were incorporated in the frame so ropes could be pulled across to hold the mattress of straw or goose down in place. Closer to the Renaissance era, drawers were also attached to accommodate clothing.

Draperies that covered the sides of the bed were full and long, reaching to the floor. Valances often were used to cover the rod from which hung the draperies. Wealth at this time was essentially determined by the ownership and display of silverware and gold, banners and wallcoverings, and the number of blankets on a bed and bed hangings or draperies. Draperies and valances on the beds were often tapestry or embroidered fabrics, used as insulation to increase interior warmth.

Window Treatments

The window treatments of the period included heavy textiles such as crewel embroidery, leather, or homespun woolen fabrics, hung on rods with small tabs or grommets. They were pulled across the face of the window by means of tasseled braids. Long draperies helped insulate against the damp, cold British weather. Later in the period, shaped, flat-topped treatments or pelmets, edged with gimp or braid, were developed. Crewelwork and flame-stitch designs abounded in the Jacobean age of embroidery of woolen yarns on linen cloth.

a.

b.

Figure 16.5a–b English Medieval window treatments
a Oriel or bay window with diamond-paned glass, linenfold below. Draperies with tab-top headings are drawn closed with braided cord and tassels.
b Late Medieval/Early English Renaissance low tie-back draperies on rod; pelmet with tassels top treatment behind draperies. Elaborate cornice above window.

Rugs

Floor carpets were mostly unavailable in England until Elizabeth's reign, when opportunities materialized to import Oriental rugs from Turkey and the East through the East India Trading Company, which the queen established. During this early part of the Medieval era, precious Oriental rugs were more often used on walls. Carpets were rarely used on floors, although in castles fabrics were laid around beds on raised wooden platforms to insulate bare feet. In less formal settings, floorcloths and rag rugs were used in the latter part of the era. Late in the period, a few Oriental carpets were used on floors, though this was rare. Floors largely remained hard surfaced, as the damp climate made the tracking-in of mud and dirt entirely too common to justify the wear and tear on beautiful carpets.

Medieval Style Today

Although styles have changed, the influence of the Elizabethan period persists today. While the style is rarely completely and accurately applied, upscale homes and some contract and hospitality settings incorporate replicas of Medieval beds, chairs, and tables to add distinction and prestige. Actual pieces of furniture from the sixteenth century can be viewed in museums, in museum homes in Europe and, less commonly, in America, and in restored or historically preserved English castles and palaces.

Country English–styled interiors with a provincial rather than a formal theme often display Elizabethan window treatments. From the simple tab-top draperies in cottage or casual settings to the plastic wands utilized in hotel room draperies, this influence is felt.

Textiles that are substantial in weight, such as flame stitch, crewel embroidery, and those with rough and nubby textures that look hand-woven, are appropriate choices. Historic interiors from the early Colonial period often have a strong Elizabethan influence, as this was the style when the first English immigrants journeyed to America. Today's extensive use of hand-forged wrought iron where aesthetically wonderful fabrics hang in a somewhat informal manner recalls the English Medieval tradition.

AMERICAN COLONIAL

Period Overview

The term *Colonial* refers to the political time frame of the New England and Eastern Seaboard American colonies, about 1620 to 1776. *Colonial* is an umbrella term that also

Figure 16.6 American Colonial interior

encompasses the formal Early and Late American Georgian styles. Here, the term refers to the country style as it developed in the United States. The major influence on American Colonial interiors is from the English Medieval style, although it became uniquely its own and has continued without interruption to be a popular vernacular style. American Colonial homes belonged to the working class, mostly farmers. Families provided for their own necessities and comforts. What they owned was mostly made at home, including furnishings and textile applications.

Common wall treatments were half-timber wattle-and-daub (exposed posts and stucco) or plain plaster walls with an optional chair rail. Many homes featured a palisade wall made of board and batten (wide planks with narrow wooden strips to cover the joints) surrounding a large brick fireplace; all the cooking took place over this open fire or in beehive ovens. Doors were often made of vertical planks with hand-wrought iron hardware as a decorative and functional feature. Floors evolved from earth to stone to the classic broad, random planks of pine or oak. The wooden plank ceilings were also the upstairs flooring, held in place by exposed beams, the largest, load-bearing *summer* beam carrying the smaller crossbeams. Originally, small windows were set in threes, of which the center casement sash was the only operable unit. Later in the period, vertically sliding sash windows with individual, true divider lights or panes were commonly three or four panes or lights wide and four or five panes long. Staircases were narrow and straight.

Shaker furnishings later added to the style. The Shakers were a religious group that flourished during the nineteenth century, which postdates the Colonial era. They have since died out, yet their influence continues. Their simple lines, high-quality craftsmanship, and exquisite structural design are very much in keeping with the authentic Colonial style. Chairs, embroidered textiles, quilts, and rugs are Shaker products that have become a part of this style. Likewise, the Amish, another group that continues as a subculture today, have produced pieced quilts that are treasured textiles for Colonial interiors.

Textiles: Color, Pattern, and Texture

Colors

The colors of the American Colonial period were derived from indigenous plants: madder and cranberry red (dark, dull red), indigo blue (deep violet-blue), goldenrod or mustard yellow (mellow orange-yellow), olive green (dull yellow-green), flax (light grayish off-white), and small amounts of black. Apparel colors reappeared on rugs as the material was recycled (see below). These colors were accents to neutrals or natural, undyed cotton, wool, or linen textiles. Besides fabric colors, much wood was used, giving the interiors a warmly colored appearance.

Patterns

As most fabrics were homespun and hand-loomed, simple checks, plaids, and stripes were the common patterns. Simple patterns such as the Scandinavian wig rose, the snowflake pattern, or dobby-like patterns could be executed on hand-operated looms.

Plain or piqué diaper-weave toweling fabrics were embroidered with cross-stitch lettering and simple, angular folk patterns in the Pennsylvania Deutsch (German) style. The finest examples were often laid over the utility linens and called *show towels*. Samplers, often hung on walls, included stitched quotes or sayings of folk wit and wisdom, the name of the artisan, and the date, and they showcased a sampling of embroidery stitches. These were typically accomplished by girls who were expected to possess needlework skills as they prepared their domestic dowry items.

The crewel embroidery patterns imitated designs from India and China—with less sophistication—climbing branches or vines on old tree trunks in an Asian curved shape (sinuous or twisting); multiple types of flowers in one composition; exotic birds, butterflies, ocean waves, clouds, and fretwork motifs. As many families did not have access to woolen yarns, a suitable substitute was found in the wicking used to make hand-dipped candles, a commodity everyone possessed. This cotton yarn was thinner and less bulky than wool, and therefore, the embroidery was more lightly scaled. Sometimes the candlewick was dyed, but often it was left uncolored, so a natural pattern on an off-white background was a lovely substitute for the more colorful crewel embroidery. Candlewicking also influenced the creation of crewel white-on-white pieces. Needlework as heavy tapestry was sometimes accomplished for seat cushions.

Pieced quilts were a standard as well as a prestigious patterned item during the Colonial era. Three kinds of quilt patterns were used at the time and later. Solid block patterns were one single piece of fabric; this, however, was rare, as most fabric was recycled from worn clothing. Appliqué quilts were made of fabric pieces stitched together to form a pattern and then applied to the top of a solid block or piece. Pieced quilt tops were made of fabric pieces cut and sewn together to form the top. Patterns were formed from small scraps of plain or printed calico fabrics. The pieced quilt top was then layered with an inner batting of wool and a backing fabric. The entire "sandwich" was then held taut on a quilting frame or a handheld, lap-sized circular frame that held a section of the quilt. Thread was used to hand-quilt tiny stitches, often in decorative patterns. The smaller the stitch, the finer the quality of the quilt—and the more durable.

During the 1600s, trapunto was used. This is a quilting technique where batting is stuffed inside the pattern to create a raised effect; it is seen both as block work and as whole-cloth work.

As the period drew to a close, quilting was clearly established as an artistic and individually creative pattern medium. It was also practical as a means of reusing fabric scraps in an important and needed textile. The following patterns, though past the period dates, are acceptable today as Colonial-style bedcoverings or quilts for occasional use. The timeline indicates when each style came into favor. From 1775 to 1789, **appliqué** and **broderie perse** (Persian embroidery) were used in symbols of the Revolution. By 1782, the **eagle** was adopted as the national symbol and become popular in appliqué. The solid **one-patch** was used from 1785 to 1800. In 1790, the **flo-**

Figure 16.7a–I American Colonial textile motifs.
a stencil patterns; **b** cross-stitch embroidery with rooster perched on potted tree; **c–I** embroidery patterns with Asian, English, and vernacular motifs

j.

k.

l.

Figure 16.7j Pennsylvania Dutch tulips and flowers; **k** tree-of-life; **l** peonies, chrysanthemum, or carnation motifs

ral wreath and **basket appliqué** became popular, followed by the **pieced pinwheel** and the **Yankee puzzle** or **hourglass** in 1795. In 1800, the **nine-patch, grandmother's basket,** and **variable star** were added to the American quilting repertoire, and in 1806, the **Irish chain** pattern. From 1810 to 1830, pieced quilt patterns included the **log cabin** and squares made of rectangular strips, while the **barn raising** and **courthouse steps** were variations of the **chimney sweep** (stepped ziggurat) pattern. The **lover's knot** utilized appliqué fabric cut into a tied bow shape with two or three loops and tie ends, and the **wedding ring** consisted of appliqué pieces made into two intersecting circles. A **friendship quilt** was made of square or rectangular panes, each customized by or in honor of a friend with embroidery or piecework. In 1815, the more complex **eight-pointed star** and the **Ohio star** and **hourglass** patterns became popular. By 1820, additional patterns included the **double Irish chain, clamshell,** and **thousand pyramids.** The **crazy quilt,** made popular in the antebellum and Victorian eras, was made of scraps in varying shapes and without regard to color or pattern. The seams were overquilted with large turkey-track quilting or embroidery. Many quilts were unique and did not follow a standard pattern. Rather, they became artistic one-of-a-kind pieces. Antique quilts today fetch high prices as collectors' items.

Textures

A gamut of natural textiles, including woolens, linen, and cotton, were hand-spun and hand-loomed into homespun, huckaback toweling, and muslin. Crewel embroideries and candlewick fabrics were heavily textured. Tweed as a plain or twill weave was created for heavier clothing and later became a recycled interior textile for rugs. Broadcloth, seen as printed calico, was a quilting fabric. Leather was used for several utilitarian purposes, including seating pieces.

Upholstered Furniture

Colonial furniture included ladder-back chairs and trestle tables, some of which converted to benches. Settees or benches often were storage units for extra bedding or items for occasional use. Table runners were a form of furniture textiles, though few tablecloths were used. Settees or benches sometimes had cushions covered with hand-loomed textiles. Seating may have been rush—woven grasses, or strips of sturdy fabric made on backstrap looms and then woven onto the chair. This is seen in Shaker furniture.

Figure 16.8a–c American Colonial Shaker chairs with sturdy fabric strap or braid interlacing upholstery

Beds

Colonial beds were handcrafted and of uncomplicated construction. Most were simple posts with woven straps connected to side and end rails. Boxed beds had deep sides that held the mattress in place, a forerunner of the sleigh bed style. Trundle beds for children were customarily slid beneath parents' beds, which were elevated slightly to accommodate them.

During New England winters, interiors are very cold, so bed draperies were hung from poster or canopy beds to keep in body heat. Draperies were often of muslin and thus a perfect showcase for embroidery skills, including decorative stitches, crewel, and candlewicking. These draperies were usually tabbed and slid along a rope, cord, or wooden dowel between posts. Canopies covered the top of the draperies and helped contain body heat. Canopy frames were generally flat, although during the Late Georgian era, an arched shape can be attributed to Rococo and Chinese influences. The top rails between the posts were sometimes covered with a separate valance, which necessitated a separate pole or cord for the bed draperies. Valances were sometimes made of hand-tatted or crocheted lace, both forms of needlework originating as European folk crafts.

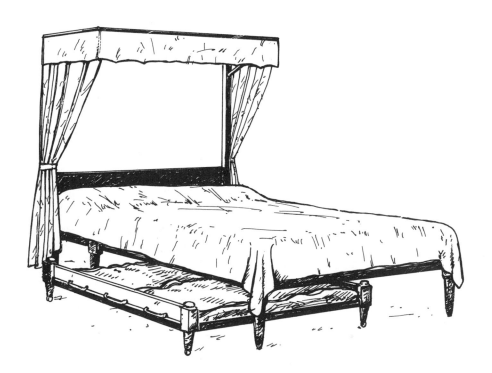

Figure 16.9 American Colonial bed with trundle; partial canopy and draperies beneath pelmet

The quilts discussed above under "Patterns" were used both as decorative coverlets and as layered bedding beneath a more decorative coverlet. Fancy coverlets were often needleworked to match, as were the draperies. This style persisted past the Colonial era; coverlets during the Victorian era also included patterned jacquard coverlets and chenille tufted and fringed coverlets. These covered only the mattress sides plus a few inches or were tucked under the mattress; they did not reach the floor, as a bedspread does, to facilitate access to the trundle or storage space.

Window Treatments

Many rural Colonial homes had no window treatments until the farm family's needs were met. Then short curtains and/or valances were added, generally in plain, lightweight muslin.

Now termed **cottage curtains**, these treatments cover the window and, sometimes, the frame. The two most common kinds of curtain headings were tabbed and shirred. A variety of cottage curtain styles, trimmed or untrimmed, evolved that are appropriate for Colonial-style interiors. This includes full window-length curtains, straight or tied back; tiered treatments; and valances used alone or as a top treatment over café curtains. Valances and tiered curtains softened the window and were yet another opportunity to use decorative stitches or handmade lace.

Ruffles were added to the vernacular Colonial style during the Victorian era, when cottage curtains became more decorative. Cottage curtains with ruffles along the tied-back edge and as an attached valance are called **priscilla curtains.** Trimmings such as cottonball fringe and small tassels also developed in the Victorian cottage era.

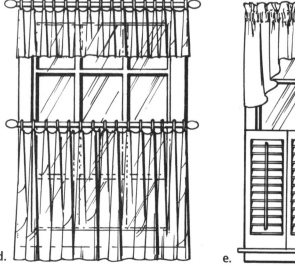

Figure 16.10a–e American Colonial window treatments **a** shirred valance and stencil work; **b–d** cottage curtains; **b** ruffled header and ties; **c** tabbed heading; semisheer fabric; **d** scalloped valance and café curtain; **e** shaped shirred valance and single-hung louvered shutters

German or Pennsylvania Dutch (Deutsche) and Dutch Colonial homes often had roller shades made of Holland cloth, a sturdy, heavy oilcloth that was a forerunner of today's vinyl shades. These shades later were given scalloped or decorative hems, but this touch is not authentic.

Also Germanic and Scandinavian (Norwegian rosemaling) in origin, stenciling around windows was a treatment that required few resources and connected a Colonial home to European folk crafts. Designs included stylized versions of the tulip, carnation, wreaths, meandering or scalloped vines, hearts, leaves, and pinecones.

Rugs

Rugs in Colonial American interiors were made of woolen (or occasionally cotton or linen) fabric scraps cut from worn-out clothing. Women and children wore homespun cloth, muslin, and some calico; men's shirts were muslin, and trousers were generally brown tweed. Worn-out Sunday suits were black, while long-john underwear, which was particularly prized, was always red. Worn items no longer usable as clothing were cut or torn into strips and then stitched together to form a long strip of fabric. These strips were then braided and sewn into small or large oval or round rugs, woven into rectangular rugs on the family loom, or used as yarn needlepunched or hooked rugs to form floral patterns.

Floorcloths were another type of rug that could be kept clean. They were generally a heavy canvas and could be painted and then covered with a coat of shellac or stain to seal the design.

The American Colonial Style Today

American Colonial is a style embraced in all regions of the United States today. Its continuing success may be credited to the genuineness of its materials and its handcrafted country simplicity. Contemporary Colonial is often a lifestyle as well as an interior design style; owners may enjoy handcrafts associated with this era. Quilting, for example, has been resurrected as a fashionable pastime at all income levels, and the availability of Shaker-style furnishings as kits and finished or unfinished furniture has furthered interest in handcrafted products of excellent structural design. Likewise, cottage curtains are widely used today, as are stock and custom-made rag rugs and other folk art items. This style is alive and well and will continue to be a country style of first choice for the foreseeable future.

COUNTRY FRENCH, FRENCH PROVINCIAL

Period Overview

The Country French style dates from 1740 to 1760 and was a provincial outgrowth of the Court Rococo style. Like the American Colonial style, it has really never ended. The original style followed the basic trends of the court or French Rococo style, but simplified and without the pomp, luxury, and embellishment the wealth of royalty could afford. Later,

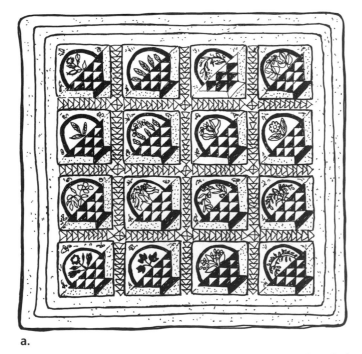

a.

b.

Figure 16.11 American Colonial quilt patterns. **a** grandmother's basket or basket appliqué quilt; **b** floral wreath variations

the French Provincial style also embraced simplified Neoclassical and Empire elements to become a look with many faces. Here, the original Rococo Country French style is discussed.

The term *Country French* is often used interchangeably with *French Provincial*, but the two are actually separate decorating trends that evolved outside court boundaries. *Provincial* refers to the designs that copied the styles of Paris in a simplified version. Country French is less formal and sophisticated, more rustic, with adapted regional characteristics. The farther away from Paris, the more local and regional the style and craftsmanship, due in part to lower awareness of style trends. Country French was designed by and for people of modest means to be functional as well as aesthetically pleasing. It may be said that French people of this period had an innate sense of style.

Although the actual style of the Louis XV court was little imitated beyond the royal palaces because of its extreme grandeur and cost, it served as the motivating agent in engaging the attention of the public in matters of home furnishing, decoration, and furniture style. The Rococo influence of curved lines captured the public imagination and was simplified by local craftsmen who adapted the style according to their own skills, the demands of the climate, and the needs of the people.

With the invention of roller printing, textiles began to be much more influential and prominent in Country French interiors. Fabrics, designs, and motifs that previously required hand-weaving to achieve the design could now be mass-produced in less time via printing. Often, Country French interiors copied costly handmade or hand-silkscreened styles, leading to a wider variety of patterns and designs at less cost.

Textiles: Color, Pattern, and Texture

Colors

With the influence of the French court, colors were closer to modern tastes, with a fresh subtlety of muted tones and pastels. The provinces applied these same hues, for the most part. However, practicality dictated that pale, pastel colors would not stand up to the less refined country lifestyle. The colors used still related in identity to those of the court, yet they were deeper, more somber, and earthier. They were also often set on cream, dark, or colorful backgrounds. Colors included cranberry and brick red, clay and earth-toned orange, goldenrod yellow and dark gold, sage and olive green, blues ranging from dulled royal to navy, and natural off-white (natural linen or parchment color). Neutrals were also extremely important. They blended well with the wooded country ambience and helped cover dirt and wear. The neutrals included gray, brown, beige, and black.

Figure 16.12 Country French interior

Motifs and Textures

Motifs and texture are combined here, as Country French fabrics are integrated. Historically, the selection of textiles depended largely on the wealth of the owner. In some châteaux, court Rococo fabrics were used, but rarely, for owners often desired Provincial styling that differed from their formal city dwellings.

With the invention of roller printing, printed fabrics were more readily available and became central to Provincial and Country French interiors. Roller printing also expanded the variety of motifs and patterns available.

Floral Fabrics Floral fabrics became extremely popular in the provinces because they depicted the flowers and foliage so abundant in the countryside, and because they resembled feminine forms, which were consistent with the theme of curved lines typical of the period. Floral fabrics are divided into three categories: medium- to large-scale bouquets, quaint small-scale floral fabrics, and trellis fabrics. Bouquets were stylized semiformal sprays of isolated flowers, sometimes incorporating woven baskets and fluttering ribbons. Small-scale floral fabrics, also stylized, were calico-like allover designs. Trellis fabrics featured climbing vines in a Chinese-influenced diamond pattern, with abundant small leaves and delicate flowers.

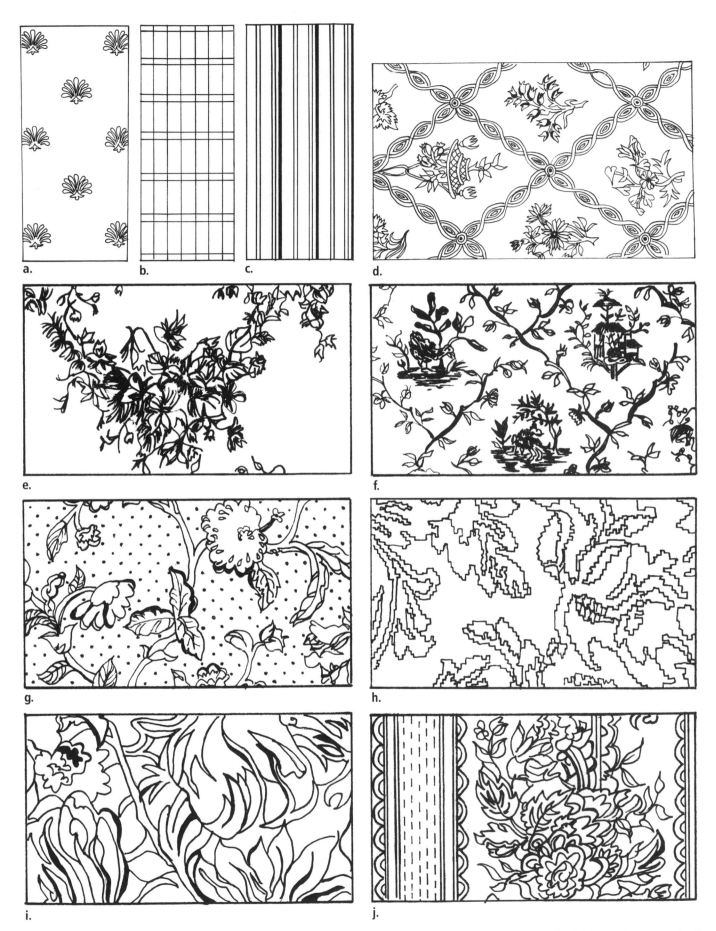

Figure 16.13a–m Country French textile motifs. **a** Rococo shells; **b** plaid, check; **c** stripes, ticking; **d** lattice and floral; **e–i** printed floral designs; **j** Chinoiserie and trellis

Toile de Jouy Toile de Jouy, a printed (occasionally woven) fabric showing pictorial scenes and stylized floral patterns, originated in the town of Jouy, near Versailles. Christophe-Phillippe Oberkampf produced scenes in a single color—black, madder red or burgundy, cobalt or navy blue, goldenrod, or sage green—on a cream-colored muslin cloth. Designs included men and maids at play, châteaux, gardens, isolated architectural ruins, carriages, agricultural landscapes, people at work, and farming.

Chinoiserie Similar to toile de Jouy in idea, the original Chinoiserie fabrics were imported from the Far East and depicted Chinese or *Chinois* scenes such as pagodas, rickshaws, fishing junks (boats), saki trees, floating pavilions, winding paths, and flora—especially chrysanthemum and peony flowers, climbing vines, and old gnarled trees filled with exotic flowers and fanciful birds—Chinese men and women in traditional costume, and landscapes of deep river gorges and soaring mountains. Chinoiserie fabrics were also seen as brocades and used in some châteaux settings.

Other Fabrics Plaid fabrics were woven with fine or coarse colored yarns as plaids or checks in both large and small scale. **Houndstooth** is a novelty twill that looks like a plaid where solid dark squares have a dog's tooth projecting from each of the flat sides. This was a heavy, woven, wool or linen twill upholstery fabric. **Tweed fabrics** in plain or twill weaves regular (even interlacing), or novelty (uneven interlacing), were popular in this time as well. The Country French variety had a slightly uneven coloration or heathered effect. **Herringbone** is a novelty twill in a regular chevron pattern; it is fitting for Country French interiors.

Other textures of the period were **cretonne,** a coarse, plain weave often printed as a floral or toile, and **ticking,** a woven (or printed) stripe in a twill or plain weave, originally used as mattress covers; this later became useful for multiple applications and compatible with the monochromatic toile fabrics, as ticking is also woven in one color with a cream background.

Tapestries also made their way into the décor. They were seen mostly in costlier interiors, as they were handmade of cotton or perhaps silk and were considered the most luxurious textile of the style. Country French tapestry motifs included floral bouquets and scroll-shaped asymmetrical shell motifs, similar to Norwegian rosemaling. Other motifs included shells, ribbons, scrolls, and love knots. These could be printed alone or combined with other motifs, such as floral, toile, or Chinois designs.

Upholstered Furniture

Country French homes were furnished with benches, settees, and ladder-back chairs. These chairs were originally Rococo, but as the Neoclassic period followed quickly, simplified versions included straight legs in addition to the Rococo cabriole legs. Rush seats were often topped with plump cushions, with covers usually made of cotton ticking, toile, or floral fabric. Wood was the dominant element in the furniture pieces, and the added upholstery was considered a luxury when affordable; it was placed on the seats and back only, and the legs and arms were left exposed.

The amount of upholstered furniture in a home reflected financial ability. Some Country French interiors included the **fauteuil,** an open armchair; the **bergère,** a closed armchair that was fully upholstered; the **canapé,** a sofa of exposed

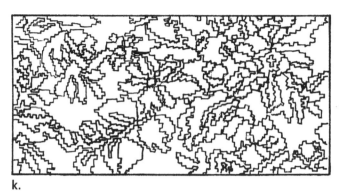

k.

l.

m.

Figure 16.13k, l Country French floral patterns; **m** Toile de Jouy

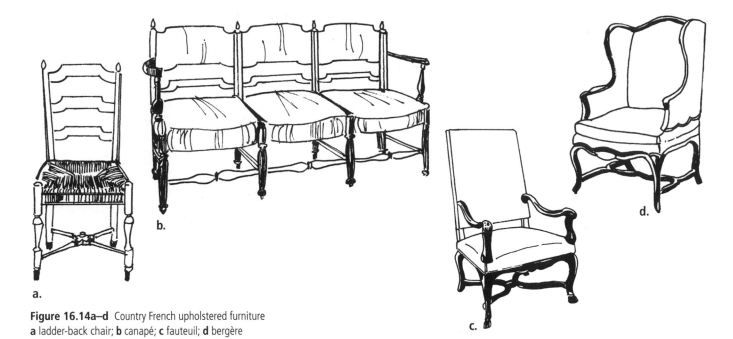

Figure 16.14a–d Country French upholstered furniture
a ladder-back chair; **b** canapé; **c** fauteuil; **d** bergère

wooden frame with a loose or connected cushion running the length of the seat; the **petit canapé,** which is the same as the canapé, only smaller; and the **tabouret,** a footstool unupholstered or topped with a connecting cushion. The ladder-back chair with rush seat was often topped with a cushion held to the frame with ties.

Beds

The **lit clos,** or a bed in a closet, also seen in court French interiors, became a distinctive Country or Provincial French de-

sign. Often, curtains were hung to close off the bedchamber from the rest of the house when doors had not been built in. Country French beds were often four-poster with hanging draperies or simple fabric pieces on all sides that could be pulled shut to completely enclose the bed. When fabric was used, the head- and footboard were sometimes upholstered. Canopies were popular, as were partial canopies, where the fabric was attached to a high frame or the ceiling in a rectangular or circular shape, often with a pelmet valance at the top.

The bed was an object of prestige during this time; it reflected wealth or achievement, indicated by the lavish use of

Figure 16.15a–d Country French beds
a lit clos; **b** four-poster bed, often fully draped and with canopy

fabric. Draped beds often had coordinated fabrics, one on the outside and one on the inside. Canopies and upholstered headboards used one or more coordinated textiles, with bedspread, pillows, and dust ruffles as part of these luxurious bedding appointments.

Window Treatments

Two types of window treatments were popular: shutters and curtains. Operable shutters—painted, stained, or left natural—were often mounted on both the inside and outside of the home to allow light in while providing privacy. White, creamy off-white, and natural were popular choices for the interior shutters, while the exterior shutters were usually either painted in darker colors of the period or stained.

Wooden rods with pleated draperies on rings, often pushed to one side, were among the most common interior treatments. Simple dowel rods used to support valances were often attached to shirred and pleated treatments. The impact of these simple treatments was extended through the use of fabric in a variety of prints and textures. On occasion, the valances were sewn onto the draper fabric, attached together at the top or heading. These dual treatments were drawn open and closed together.

Curtains were long when drawn in front of French doors and short for all other windows except formal chambers. A variety of cottage curtains are appropriate for simple Country French interiors, particularly valances and café curtains, or tiered curtains (a lower and upper café curtain).

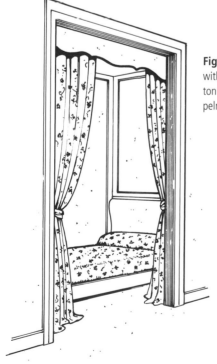

Figure 16.15c Lit clos with matching printed cotton coverlet and drapery; pelmet above.

Figure 16.16a–o Country French window treatments. **a–c** tied-back long curtains or drapery: **a** tab-top; **b** smocked top; **c** Neoclassic/Empire tieback and shirred heading

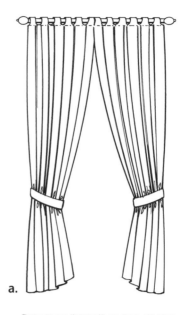

a.

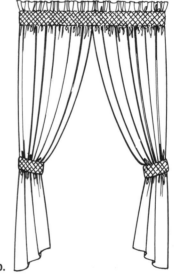

b.

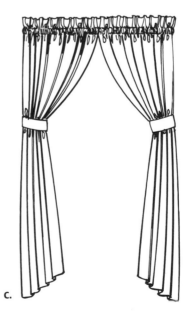

c.

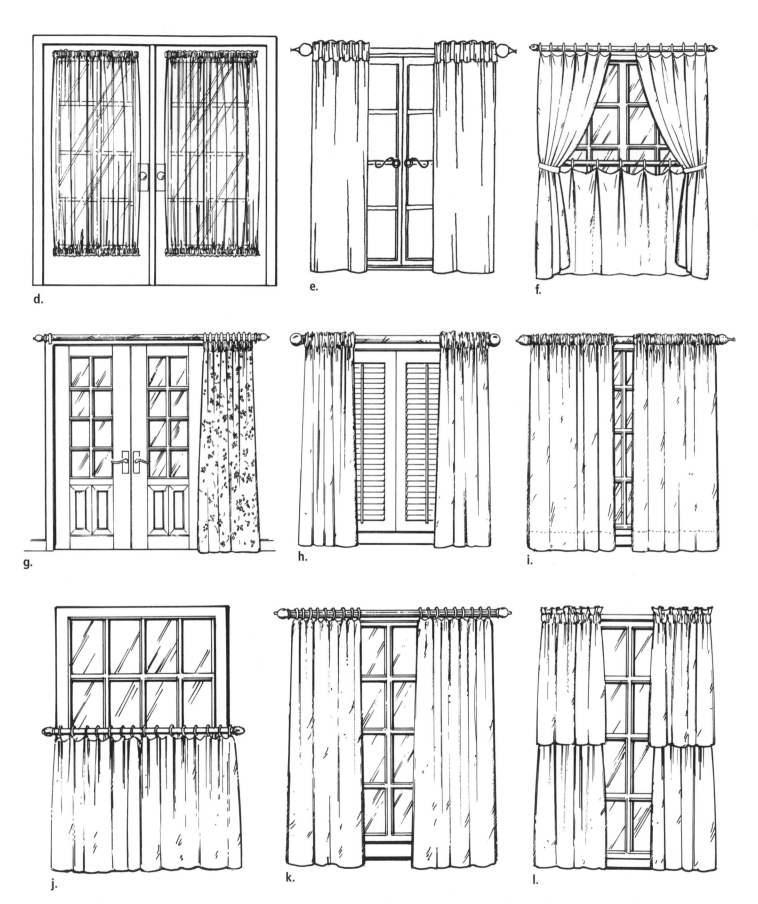

Figure 16.16d semisheer sash curtains for French doors; **e** shirred curtain on casement window; **f** café and scalloped tied-back curtains; **g** one-way printed French door draperies; **h** shirred curtains over movable louvered shutters; **i** no-header tightly shirred curtains; **j** café curtains; **k** single pleat on rings; **l** tiered curtains

m.

n.

o.

Figure 16.16m raised-panel operable shutters; **n** printed curtain, cartridge pleat on rings; **o** single-hung shutters

Rugs

Floor coverings varied in formality, depending on proximity to court influence and funding allocations. The more formal floor coverings included refined wood planking, often set in parquet, basket weave, or herringbone pattern. In less formal areas, terra-cotta quarry tiles were set in hexagonal and honeycomb motifs, or paving brick was laid in basket weave and herringbone patterns.

Close to Paris, the interior might feature a French pile Savonnerie, a flat tapestry Aubusson, or an imported Oriental rug. Farther from Paris, rug motifs were less complex and the rugs themselves often less densely woven, to lower the cost. Flat tapestry folk rugs were considered more practical and easier to maintain than deeper pile rugs. Many of the popular rug patterns and motifs were copied by local people and painted onto floorcloth or stitched into the fabric. These approaches made for inexpensive and simple yet stylish and functional floor coverings.

The Country French Style Today

The Country French style continues to evolve, yet remains constant in appeal. Its graceful curved and straight lines, simplicity of design, and combination of feminine romance with rustic elements yield a distinctive style with genuine gentility. The influence of the French Empire has produced County French window treatment styles in grommet or tabtop floppy headings hung on slender black or verdigris wrought-iron hardware. Printed floral fabrics, which have rarely gone out of style since then, are coupled with stripes and plaids and solids. Colors seen in decoration are more masculine, as in the Country French, but also more muted and natural.

FOLK SCANDINAVIAN DESIGN

Period Overview

The Folk Scandinavian period extended from the mid-eighteenth century into the late nineteenth century. In Denmark, Norway, Finland, Sweden, and northern Russia, the Victorian era was ignored in favor of handmade quality and creative, distinctive style. The Scandinavians historically espouse a simple and charming lifestyle with good design based on simplified Rococo and Neoclassical elements. The detail is colorful, adding personality and visual delight to interiors that were bathed in light day and night in the summer and devoid of sunlight throughout the long winters.

The most influential couple of this time was Carl Larsson, a noted artist, and his creative and artistic wife, Karin Larsson, who wove rugs and fabrics and embroidered folk motifs onto curtains, bed draperies, and coverlets. So accomplished was Karin and so inventive was Carl, his most beloved paintings are those of his family members setting about daily tasks in their artistic home. Their home, Little Hyttnäs, is located in the Sundborn village in central Sweden and is open for tours.

The Larssons approached every part of life with a determination to make ordinary things beautiful. They surrounded themselves with artwork and crafts that have become the model for Folk Scandinavian design. Larsson inherited the house from his father-in-law in 1889, and he and Karin spent their lives improving and building onto it so as to provide a comfortable and warm home for their family of eleven. They built small additions to the home with the help of savings and the tradesmen of the village. The house is relatively small, inviting, and cozy. Little Hyttnäs is truly a masterpiece—a charming Swedish home, not a just a house.

Textiles: Color, Pattern, and Texture

Color

Color gave the Folk Scandinavian room a lively personality; colors were often chosen to create warmth and coziness. There were two main color palettes in the Scandinavian home. One was a set of pale Swedish Neoclassical colors, including peach, cream, pale goldenrod, coral, salmon, mint

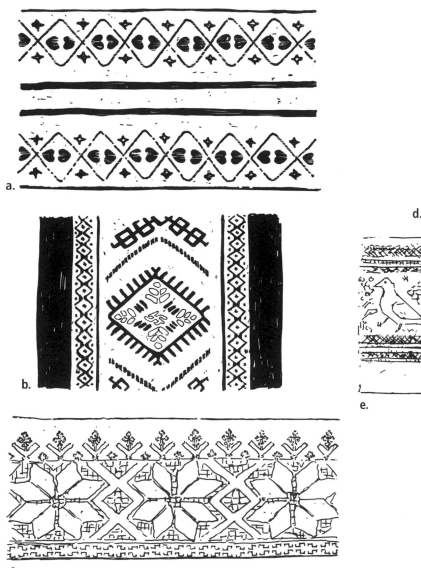

Figure 16.17a–f Scandinavian Country textile motifs
a hearts and diamonds in stripe; **b** lozenge, diamonds, and stripes; **c** summer flowers or snowflakes; **d** heart, leaves, and birds; **e** birds, flowers; **f** stripes

green, dove gray, light steel, cobalt blue, and powder blue. These colors were used primarily as a monochromatic scheme in a white or whitewashed background, kept light to make bearable the long Nordic winters.

The other color palette was a vibrant one of intense bright or deep accent colors. These colors were generally primary, with strong reds such as sienna and brick, blues such as navy, indigo blue, and steel, yellows such as goldenrod, and forest or kelly green. Colors were printed or embroidered into apparel and domestic fabrics for curtains, bed draperies, coverlets, and toweling.

Motifs

Wood was a common material used in homes of this era, and color was applied as painted folk designs, often whimsical and humorous—and always a delight to the eye.

Although the Scandinavian people are known for clean, simple design and lack of ornate detail, they used many motifs in this era. The most common were the crown, parrots, swans, fruits, flowers, monograms, the lion and dragon in battle, the rococo shell motif, most often modified into Norwegian rosemaling, and Scandinavian folk painting on wood and applied around windows and on shutters, cupboards, and other furniture.

Motifs also included deer, birds, conventionalized floral designs—tulips, forget-me-nots, Dutch iris, primroses, summer field flowers—butterflies, and Neoclassical motifs such as delicate vases and climbing or serpentine (curved) tendrils. The heart motif and simple leaf and snowflake designs were often seen as embroidered patterns, sometimes as cross-stitch.

Neoclassicism was embraced, as its lightweight forms and furnishings were already in keeping with Scandinavian values. Thin woven stripes, especially the soft, vertical blue-and-white or more cheerful red-and-white combinations, were used as bed draperies and vanity skirts. Stripes in rag floor rugs were horizontal and multicolored. Simplified geometric designs such as snowflakes and diamonds were sometimes combined with stripes.

Textures

The textiles in this period were heavily embroidered formal applications on muslin curtains and coverlets; gauze or semisheer or lightweight opaque window treatments; and diaper cloth (piqué toweling). Embroidery offered a simple and effective way to add detail. Most fabrics had a natural look and feel and were used for window treatments, table runners, bed draperies, and furniture coverings.

Unique, handmade pieces of art added life to simple interiors. The Scandinvian cultures are industrious and creative, and the people used materials on hand or made by hand to create wonderful details.

Upholstered Furniture

Straight lines influenced by Neoclassic and Empire, tapered legs and distinctive curves yielded furniture that was clean and simple, and hard-wearing. Lightly scaled furniture was well proportioned and increased space visually. Chairs were commonly lined along the exterior of a room to allow seating yet plenty of space for other activities. Furniture was designed not only for style but also for function. Rarely was anything wasted, either space or material.

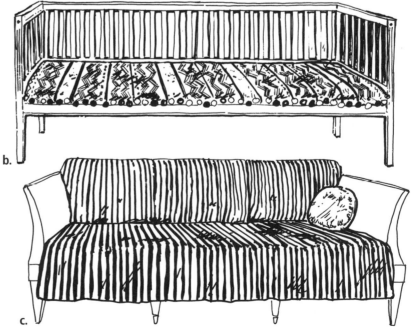

Figure 16.18a–c Scandinavian Country upholstered furniture
a Swedish Neoclassic side chair; **b** bench or settee;
c Swedish Neoclassic slipcovered settee

Beds

Folk Scandinavian beds are often boxed, with a mattress placed inside the raised side rail frame. Hand-woven textiles in simple stripes or angular folk motifs or embroidered muslin were used as coverlets. Posts and unique head- and footboards were often added, some modeled after the Rococo lit clos and becoming charming closet beds. Curtains around beds were straight hand-loomed and embroidered panels with simple headings. The effect is sweet, charming, and clean.

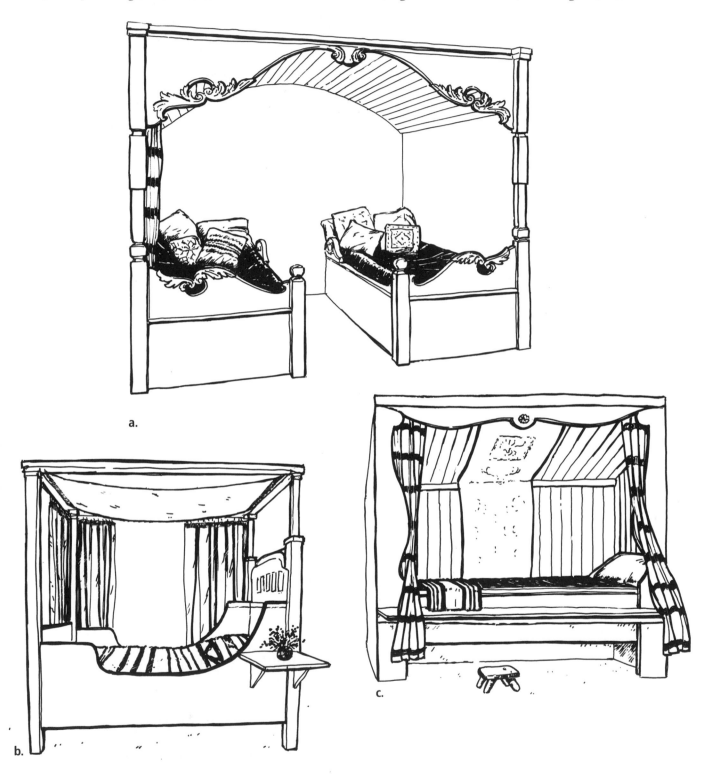

Figure 16.19a–c Scandinavian Country beds
a twin beds in Rococo-influenced lit clos; **b** boxed bed; **c** boxed bed or lit clos

Figure 16.20a–c
Scandinavian Country window treatments **a** valance with Swedish ivy; **b** shutters; **c** asymmetrical curtain

Window Treatments

Common window treatments were loose casement or semisheer fabric, sheer curtains, embroidered muslin, or other lightweight material such as woven stripes or simple checks and plaids. Sheer and semisheer curtains and valances softened architecture without obstructing light. Curtains with tabbed or shirred headings were often pulled to one side of the wooden dowel rod in a relaxed asymmetry. Windows are an important feature in the Scandinavian home; the ability to allow light inside the home is vital. Lightweight fabrics filtered light and diffused glare. In the summers, sheer, semisheer, and lightweight fabrics allowed welcome breezes to circulate through the house to keep it cool.

Some windows had no fabric treatments. Some were left bare, and others were treated with solid, raised-panel, or plank shutters that were closed at night to retain heat and give visual warmth during long, dark periods. Cheerful folk painting was used on raised-panel shutters and around window frames; painted swags and vines and rosemaling were common motifs. Live plants were also an important element in keeping the house lively and cheerful. Swedish ivy was sometimes used to fill the tops of windows to create a valance-type effect. Plants allowed life in the house during winter and created a spring atmosphere.

Rugs

Hardwood flooring, durable and pleasing to the eye, covered a majority of the home. Rugs were commonly laid over the wood flooring. The rugs were generally hand-loomed rag rugs. Some of them were long and narrow; these were folded into right angles to follow the rectilinear outline of a room. Rugs were typically striped with thin rows of pale colors in the Swedish Neoclassical manner or in brighter folk colors.

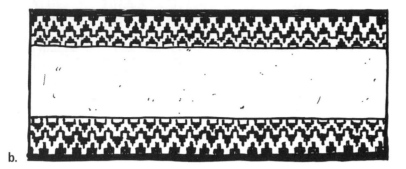

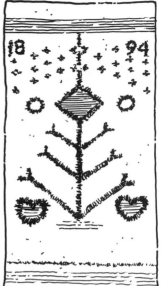

Figure 16.21a–c Scandinavian Country rugs/carpets
a rag rug, often turned 90 degrees on corners; **b, c** simple angular designs

The Folk Scandinavian Style Today

Elements of Folk Scandinavian are seen in many country-styled homes today, where handcraftsmanship is valued and simple motifs in cheerful bright or calming pastel colors are desirable. In contemporary cottage homes, this style has particular application in white painted furniture, blue ticking stripes, and sparse furnishings, all in high-quality design. The style combines well with Country French and Gustavian Swedish Neoclassic elements such as tole lamps with metal lampshades and patterned toile fabrics; the result is a fresh and charming yet sophisticated interior.

17 Regional and Thematic Styles

Figure 17.1 Spanish Colonial interior

SPANISH COLONIAL AND SOUTHWEST INFLUENCE

Period Overview

The term *Spanish Colonial* refers to the influence of Spain in the New World between 1500 and 1840. The conquistadores and priests who brought Spanish settlers to the Americas and explored the great Southwest paved the way for Hispanic architectural style.

From the eighth to the 15th centuries, both Moors and Christians occupied the Iberian Peninsula. The Moors, specifically, the Sunni sect of the Islamic faith influenced much architectural style of Spain during eight centuries of their coexistence there. Their influence, referred to as *Moorish*, was based on abstract designs and geometric form. The patterns were derived from the religious belief that art was to be completely nonrepresentational. Naturalistic or lifelike imagery was considered blasphemous because it imitated the great works of Allah. Although the Muslims, or Moors, were finally driven out in 1492 by the

Christians, their artistry remained and was thoroughly assimilated into a distinctive style. This resulting style was a combination of the Moorish influence and Christian standards called *Mudejar.*

Most Spanish architecture is derived from the **Mudejar** period (A.D. 1250–1500). This architectural style utilized hard materials such as ceramic tiles (azulejos), wooden ceilings with heavy transverse beams (artesonado), and ornately carved plaster friezes (yeseria). Hard window treatments such as raised panels and movable (louvered) shutters were used on the inside, while ironwork grilles (rajas) adorned the outside. Furniture pieces were embellished with intricate carvings and ornamentations based on geometric forms. Common features were canopies, cushions, embroideries, galloons, fringes, cords, tassels, wrought and gilded nailheads on furniture and doors, and leather that was plain, tooled, stamped, embossed, gilded, or painted to soften interiors and counterbalance the hard materials.

The Spanish **Plateresque** period dates from 1500 to 1556. The term is derived from the Italian word for "silversmith," denoting the increase in metalwork during the period. This led to an increased use of stamped or tooled leather studded with nails for covering chests or cabinetry.

The **Desornamentado** period dates from 1556 to 1600 and was greatly influenced by the architect Herrera, who opposed the richness of the Renaissance by eliminating adornment and detail in his work. Consequently, this period can be recognized by its lack of color and ornamentation.

The **Churriguera** period, named after an influential architect of the time, directly followed. Unlike Herrera, Churriguera embraced intricate and elaborate ornamentation and design.

Spanish conquests on the North American continent fused these styles with those of the indigenous peoples of Mexico to form what we now refer to as the Southwest Adobe style.

Textiles: Color, Pattern, and Texture

Colors

The most commonly found colors in Spanish interiors were variations of bright red, gold, yellow, deep forest green, orange, light brown, dark blue, and black. Vibrant colors contrasted dramatically with the earthiness of the architectural style. Walnut, oak, and cedar were common furniture materials. Walls were usually off-white plaster, and tile was often terra cotta–colored.

Influenced by Native Americans, the southwestern palette included earth tones with accents of salmon, ocher, yellow ocher, mica, cocoa brown, terra-cotta, and turquoise (an indigenous stone valued for jewelry and trading). More recent colors from the Mexican heritage that have blended into this style include brilliant hues commonly known as fiesta pink, jungle green, bright blue, and del sol yellow.

Motifs

Originating in Spain under the Moorish influence, the majority of early Spanish textiles incorporated abstract and geometric motifs. After the Moors were expelled, some floral and other natural elements were added, but with a flavor of complex geometric design influenced by Islamic patterns; these included the arabesque, a complex geometric panel motif; the sun, or el sol, usually conventionalized with curving rays; and birds perched in stylized trees with bodies facing each other but heads turned away.

a.

b.

c.

Figure 17.2a–p Authentic Spanish and Colonial textile motifs
a foliage; **b** crown and shield; **c** Islamic arabesque; **d, g** conventionalized floral; **f** intertwining Islamic motifs; **h–p** Southwest

d.

e.

f.

g.

h.

i.

j.

k.

l.

m.

n.

o.

p.

In the American Southwest, the Spanish style merged with the skills of the Native Americans. As trading posts were established in the late 1800s in New Mexico, Arizona, and the connecting corners of Utah and Colorado, the owners or traders helped local Navajo weavers develop a style and encouraged high-quality weaving. (Navajo rug or blanket types are discussed in chapter 13.) These Navajo patterns included stripes, zigzags, diamonds, swastikas, and highly stylized birds, flowers, corn, dancers, and pictorial representations of architecture, people, and celebrations.

Textures

Leather is an important texture in Spanish interiors, as it withstands the rigors of the harsh, arid climate. Early textiles included heavy matelassé, tweed, and twill textiles of cotton, wool, and linen. The Spanish style also incorporated wonderful textiles originating in the Spanish Renaissance and Baroque periods—a variety of rich cotton, silk, and linen velvets, brocade and brocatelle, and damask textiles. In up-

scale applications, semisheer and translucent fabrics of cotton, linen, or wool screened the sun's intensity.

Prior to Spanish conquests in the Western hemisphere, Native American weavers depended on cultivated cotton for their textiles. The Spanish weavers introduced large, horizontal wooden shuttle looms for making cloth for clothing, domestic use, and heavier-patterned Rio Grande blankets and rugs. With the opening of trade to Mexico, many kinds of textiles were brought into the Southwest Territories. Widely accepted textiles originating in Spain included printed calico, corduroy, jean, leather, and more expensive lengths of linen and silk.

Upholstered Furniture

The Spanish designed their furniture to be durable as well as visually appealing. The **frilero,** an original Spanish armchair, was covered with dark, geometrically tooled leather and fastened with hand-tooled or brass nails. Velvet or leather was used for the seat cushion. In later models, the

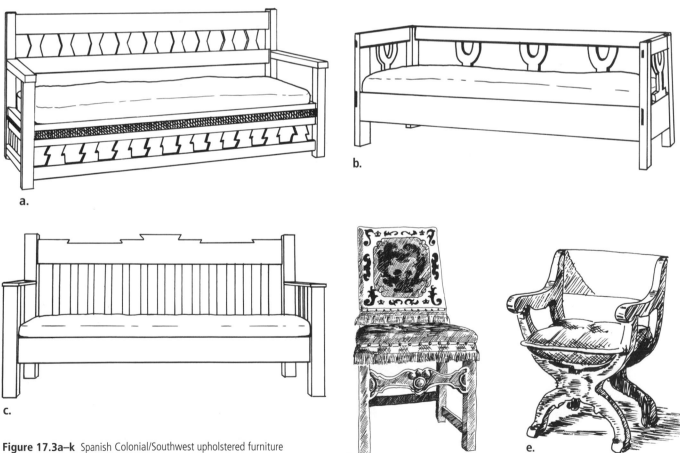

Figure 17.3a–k Spanish Colonial/Southwest upholstered furniture
a–c benches or settees; **d** Spanish side chair; **e** sillon de caderas chair;
f, g lathe or hand-carved frilero chairs; **h** upholstered bench or settee;
i Southwest side chair; **j** leather or velvet side chair with brass nails and fringe;
k leather-covered Spanish chest

leather was covered with silk or velvet and adorned with rich galloon and fringe.

Another style of chair was the **sillon de caderas** (the hip joint), known as "the Moor's seat of dignity." Variations of this scissor-frame style are the Italian Dante and Savonarola chairs, which replaced the sillon de caderas in popularity during the Renaissance.

Because of their ease of construction, benches were found nearly everywhere. Upholstered benches were viewed as luxury furniture and found in the homes of the upper class. Upholstery fabrics included leather, velvet, and matelasse, or "double cloth." Some fabrics were quilted with lozenge or crescent shapes with stitching in heavy raw linen thread.

The Spanish traditionally had several chests in the same residence. These were used as tables or chairs and stored clothing, linens, silver, tools, and grain. One style of chest was covered with leather and studded with nails in intricate patterns following linear or geometric designs consistent with the Moorish influence. The lid was usually arched, and the inside was lined with silk and trimmed with braid. For those covered with silk or damask, the choice of color was usually crimson, although green and blue velvet were also used.

Beds

Spanish-style beds were often substantial in scale and heavily carved or ornamental, and made of wood or wrought iron. Colors were often dark, although sometimes gold leaf or lighter colors indicated a Baroque influence. Wood components included headboards and, occasionally, footboards, and sometimes tester or canopy styles.

Several styles of bedding were uniquely Spanish. These include the Majorca, which featured a linen canopy and a shallow valance and spread made of the same material. The Majorcan style used a blue and white linen woven into a horizontal zigzag pattern known as the Moorish tongue pattern (lengua). A second style, the Catalan, was a low post bed with a coverlet made of knotted linen (colcha) or a block-printed chintz. Headboards were often carved.

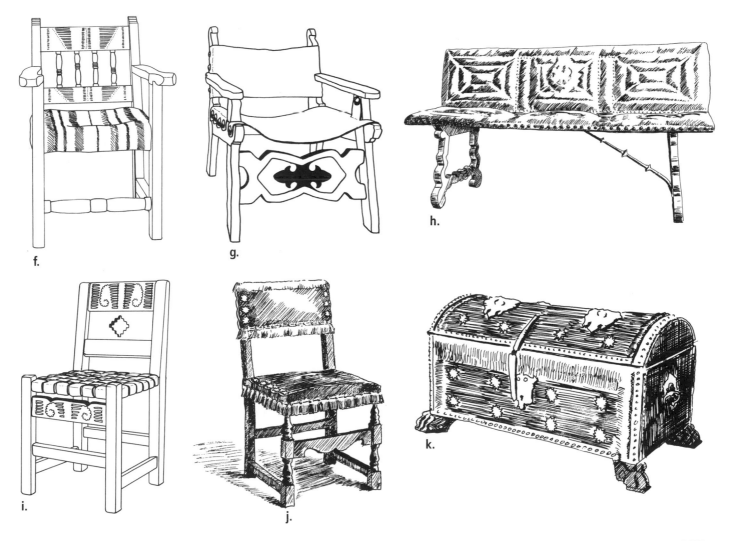

f.

g.

h.

i.

j.

k.

Figure 17.4a–h Spanish Colonial/Southwest beds
a lathe-turned poster bed with deep, fringed valance, coverlet, and bedskirt; **b** elaborate wooden bed frame, beadspread to floor; **c** Southwest head- and footboard, tucked pillows and coverlet; **d–f** bench-style beds; **g, h** carved head- and footboards with coverlets

Window Treatments

Traditional Spanish window treatments such as shutters, blinds, and lattice screens evolved in response to Spain's arid climate. These treatments were long-lived and relatively impervious to both ultraviolet rays and heat damage. The Spanish style also incorporated wrought-iron drapery rods and heavily textured, richly patterned or colored complex textiles. More formal Baroque and Renaissance drapery fabrics such as damask, brocatelle, matelassé, and moiré were heavily trimmed with fringe, passementerie rope, tassels, or patterned braid. These were combined into long draperies topped with ornate pelmets and valances, with semisheer shades or curtains to soften and diffuse the intense glare and bright light. In less formal interiors, plain and oxford-weave fabrics such as muslin, linen crash, osnaburg, and similarly natural and coarse fabrics were pleated simply and attached via wrought-iron

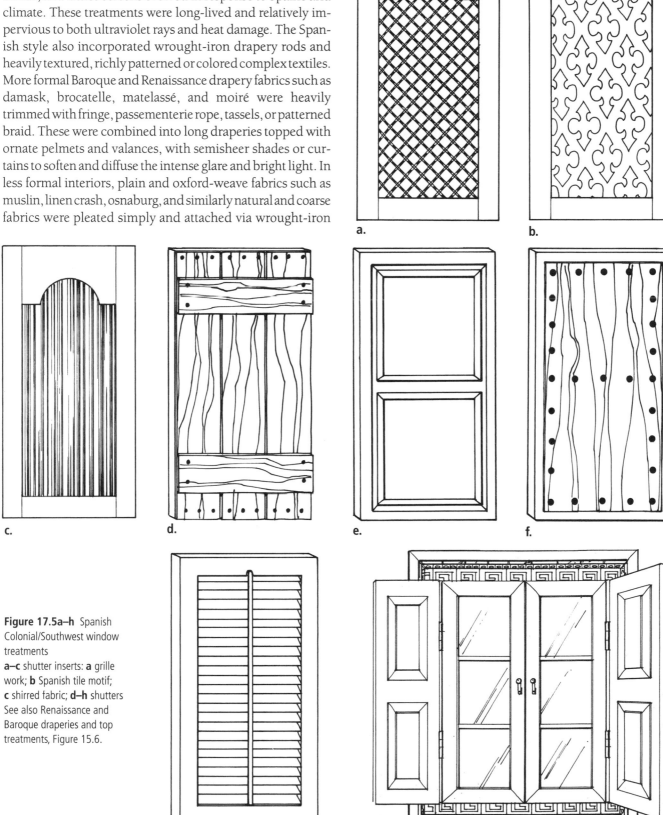

Figure 17.5a–h Spanish Colonial/Southwest window treatments
a–c shutter inserts: **a** grille work; **b** Spanish tile motif; **c** shirred fabric; **d–h** shutters See also Renaissance and Baroque draperies and top treatments, Figure 15.6.

rings to the wrought-iron drapery rods. More than one treatment was preferred—for example, a hard treatment under draw draperies, or a pouf shade under draperies. Occasionally, leather was used as a window covering.

Rugs

The **alpujarra** rug comes from the southern regions of Spain. Wool fibers were knotted thickly as a third pile thread into a two-dimensionally woven linen warp and weft. The rugs most widely associated with the Spanish Colonial style, **mantas,** were deep-pile rugs of coarse wool yarn hand-tied or knotted into abstract or geometric patterns. In contrast, the pile of manta was not nearly as dense as the alpujarra. The bright colors of the rugs added character to the rigid architecture of Spanish homes.

Navajo rugs, with their woven motifs, were used throughout the American Southwest. The patterns and motifs most often applied in blankets and rugs were stripes, zigzags, diamonds, swastikas, borders, abstract patterns, stylized people, foliage, trees, animals, and birds; these are itemized and defined in chapter 13. With the changing styles and designs of the Southwest, different kinds of rugs began to be used. Hooked, braided, and crocheted rugs made of strips of old, worn-out cloth were introduced into New Mexico. These rugs could be handmade, purchased, or obtained through trading. Occasionally a steer hide or skin was placed on hard flooring.

The Spanish Colonial and Southwest Influence Today

Hard materials at the window, particularly shutters (wide-blade) and wood blinds, are enormously popular today because of their excellent light control and durability in direct sunshine. The Spanish Colonial interior has proved a classic in contemporary architecture, particularly with the influence of Southwest Adobe and the handicrafts of native North Americans. In a rustic setting, fabrics and materials are natural and nubby: cotton, linen, and even wool. Cow or steer hide, leather, textured tweed, denim, and other tough twill weaves are just a few of the textiles used in connection with Southwest design. Where a more formal or upscale interior is planned, rich and sumptuous fabrics are used with shaped pelmets that evoke the Moorish influence. Tassels, trimmings, and tied-back draperies with fabric shades or sheers beneath complement this style.

Today, the Southwest Adobe style includes many styles reflecting the westward frontier movement. Navajo patterns and their accompanying color schemes are still widely used. Other motifs include cowboys and their gear—boots, horses, cattle, hats, ropes, guns—and desert and mountain landscape scenes featuring cactus, sand, and rocks. Desert animals, including coyotes, snakes, rabbits, lizards, wolves, birds, and buffalo, are used in today's interiors.

AFRICAN STYLE

Overview

Many styles of ethnic diversity encompass an African look, and there are differences between African Ethnic and African style. Africa is a diverse continent with many cultural influences. Northern Africa, or what is now Arabic Africa, is religious in its art and design. Ancient Christian or Coptic designs still influence many tribal designs. Egyptian, Islamic, Byzantine, and classical Roman and Greek style elements all have influenced the lives and culture of the northern Africans. Here the emphasis is a style that blends the African ethnic tradition with that of European settlers.

African ethnic culture is eclectic, with a thread of each cultural influence woven into the overall fabric of ethnic identity. It would be easy to mistake African Colonial design for the true ethnic without an understanding of the role each element plays—and the philosophy of art. Perceptions of Africa vary. The Europeans who colonized Africa in the eighteenth and nineteenth centuries appreciated the aesthetics of tribal arts and motifs, but not their symbolism.

True African ethnic culture sees Africa as home, as the only world one knows. The land is rich but fragile. There is abundance, but it is given only through reverence to the creating deities and ancestral spirits. To the African tribesman, communal harmony is a major goal. Peace can occur only when all have enough to eat and when prosperity allows the suppression of contentions between tribes. The humility among the people opened their eyes to learning others' ways. This eclectic characteristic has caused difficulties in defining what is indigenous to each cultural region. As well, the Coptic, Egyptian, Islamic, classical, and European influences have been so interwoven into tribal life that they have become integral parts of the culture. In this ironic twist, of each culture's goal of remaining separate, the two philosophies appear in their styles to have grown quite similar. The philosophies behind these closely related styles are what separates them. Why an element is included in an interior is more important than what is included.

The traditional African way of life is far different from how most people live in the Western world. The furnishings are minimal, and comfort gives way to sustaining life through rigorous work. There are, however, ways to incorporate elements of ethnic Africa—a focus on textiles, colors, and the philosophic use of art as a basis for patterned textiles and as tangible elements.

a.

b.

c.

d.

Figure 17.6a–d African textile motifs

Textiles: Color, Pattern, and Texture

Color

Color is important to traditional African design applications. Colors possess mystical properties, yet each tribe uses different colors to express similar spiritual attributes. A Zulu love letter consists of colored beads that express a maiden's emotions for her suitor, for example. Color is exciting and symbolic. Due to the differences among tribal interpretations of a color's symbolic nature, no concrete rules of color can be identified as specific to interior design. Generally, however, these color rules pertain:

Natural colors and earth tones should predominate.

Monochromatic themes work better to draw less attention to the structure and assist in displaying art and functional furnishings.

Bright hues are more traditional, and natural dyes express the beauty of nature. In a drab, often dusty world, great value was placed on the few beautiful, bright natural features such as flowers and sunsets.

Bright hues should only accent interior spaces. Rich textile dyes are predominantly reserved for clothing and ceremonial garments.

Colors often have spiritual meaning. The word *blue* translates literally into Sotho as "the color of the heavens"; it is a holy color.

Green is associated with life and nature.

Red, in some areas, is a symbol of blood and human life.

Black is not necessarily a negative color, and it does not symbolize death and sorrow.

The colors of walls and most floors traditionally depended on the soils native to the builder. Red clay is ever-present and commonly used in the stuccoing of homes. The clay is often mixed with straw and horse manure to cure into a cement-hard treatment that covers sun-dried brickwork. The monotony of walls and floor matching the surrounding terrain has led the artistic spirit of the Africans to decorate homes with different hues of mud in intricate patterns.

Bright modern paints are used today among the Ndebele tribes to decorate their homes in depictions of everything from abstractions of animals to airplanes (which symbolize freedom from oppression).

To the designer, it would be most appropriate to have minor differences in earth tones for walls, or possibly to have a patterned print as trim.

Earth tones should predominate both in textiles and in wall and floor treatments. Bright hues, though appropriate, should be used as accents and only sparingly applied to hard treatments.

Textiles should display their natural beauty, and bright, natural dyes should be used sparingly.

Colors should not stand out against the environment but rather the home with the earth.

Bright colors are used in geometric shapes that display them in combination.

Patterns

The patterns used in African Ethnic interiors should conform to the philosophy of simplicity of life and decoration of common objects. The abstraction found in most of Africa has many influences. For example, the Copts, mainly in Ethiopia, introduced Christian imagery and symbolism to other ethnic African cultures. A great similarity to Byzantine mosaic design can be found in Coptic tapestries. This was countered by Islamic law prohibiting the depiction of living objects. What results is a geometric and patterned repetition of symbolic forms.

Art is primary in the African ethnic culture, and it serves myriad purposes. It is used to decorate functional items of furniture. It is used to teach traditions and legends and to invite spirits to do good as well as to fend off evil spirits. Traditions include the southern African Bantu tribal belief that the image of a carved crocodile under the bed protects the sleeper from being carried off to their realm at night by mischievous demons called Tokalosis. Art serves as the primary communicative device, second only to the oral storytelling or wisdom-disseminating tradition, because few African tribes originally had a written language. The design professional who plans to capture this integral element of African culture should learn about the functions of each icon or carving included in a designed space.

Here are basic guidelines:

Nature is more beautiful than man's creations, so the inclusion of many natural textiles and materials in an interior is indicative of the style.

Images of animals usually represent the power the animal possesses. Here are examples:

Winged birds possess the mystery of flight and carry messages from the ancestors in spiritual domains.

Horns are symbolic of power as displayed on the many horned antelopes of Africa.

Open and toothed mouths in faces or masks show aggression in the associated spirit, not evil or good. Motherly protection, for example, is often expressed in this manner.

Most imagery is abstract, incorporating the essence of a spiritual quality. To the Dogon of western Africa, the forces of nature are expressed in geometric shapes that

piece together to form a checkerboard pattern that shows their influence on one's life.

Geometric shapes are the abstraction of imagery to serve a communicative purpose. As art was a language, the repetition of drawing the images led to the abstraction of the forms to save time and to distinguish one form from another. Individual research on specific pieces of art is recommended, but do not feel a commanding knowledge is necessary, because many interpretations exist.

Textures

It is important to utilize the beauty that natural fibers and materials possess. For example, the Berber tribe of northern Africa blends whites, browns, and blacks into yarn so the colors are equal and no prejudice emerges. Berber carpeting is the result. African cotton batik is also a printed design and a visual texture.

Traditionally, stucco made of mud, manure, and straw was put on buildings with a wooden plank or by hand. In regions where there are mud floors, there is often a spiral pattern of ridges made by fingertips running through the stucco compound. Today, the application of a textured gypsum base or plaster prior to painting mimics this effect. Practicality prohibits mud or plaster floors, but a textured, earth-toned carpet or, better yet, tile or hardwood floor is highly appropriate. These textures are often created or imitated in textiles today.

The techniques for creating textile designs are all based on hand labor. Hand painting is still used, and the imperfection of the pattern repeats is part of the charm. The geometric, simple patterns of few hues can blend to form new colors as they are blended by the human eye.

The wax batik method, introduced to most of Africa by the Dutch, became popular and is mimicked by the Java prints of today. Java prints are simple silk screen prints on cotton made to look like either wax batik prints or hand-dyeing. Java prints are often used for clothing or for accents. Their bright nature makes them ideal for accents, but the thin cotton fabric and bold motifs make them less suitable for large window treatments and large upholstered items.

Hand-woven rugs made from naturally dyed wool and mohair are common, and the abstract representation of natural forms is reminiscent of the conflicting Christian, Islamic, and tribal influences. The result is a beautifully ornate yet simplistic design that is truly African. Kente cloth, from Ghana, is a popular example of a traditional bright geometric pattern. It is noted for a golden yellow base with red, blue, green, and orange stripes woven into alternating bands that form shapes and blocks of blended color.

Africa is home to some of the most beautiful woods in the world. Ebony, sandalwood, and teak, the bright yellow grain of the Savannah umbrella tree, and thorn all contribute to the palette suitable for floors, ceilings, furniture, and trim, although ultrasmooth texture is not a common element for walls. The natural grain of woods is important for use as wall, ceiling, and floor treatments.

Upholstered Furniture

African furnishings rely heavily on outside influences. A tradition of communal society put more emphasis on cultural art than on building or developing new styles for everyday objects. Most beds were reed mats on the floors of huts.

As colonialists arrived, the tribes quickly adopted a new appreciation for the raised bed. This shows the eclectic nature of African culture. If people see a way to improve their life, they incorporate it without pridefully holding on to their previous beliefs. For this reason, no furniture style is distinctly African. Further, styles that were used reflect a culture not easily compatible with that of most of the Western world.

African culture requires that furniture be functional, and the artistic decoration of tools glorifies the work they do. Chairs are more than things to sit on: They are where people in authority sit to teach others, or where the father of the home dispenses law. The concept of chair is more important than the material object the chair is. As well, a structure supporting a beam of a roof, like a tent pole, is symbolic of a protecting spirit upholding the safety of the inhabitants. For this reason, many everyday items are intricately decorated to show their symbolic nature. Something as simple as a water pot, to the Zulu tribe who live in the dry savannas of southern Africa, is an important part of life, so it is decorated with symbolic reference to life-giving spirits.

Furniture should be functional, and the function of the piece should be glorified. In the context of today's interior design, the glory should be subtly achieved in order to conform with Western principles. Small accents, rustication, and the hand-hewn look are appropriate. Furniture is the one element in which modern style can easily be incorporated with otherwise rustic design, as the furniture's modern purpose is completely different than its traditional role. This mismatch works only if the abstraction of the new piece fits the philosophy of the traditional style. Oversized chairs, leather, and natural textiles all are suitable modern additions to the African Ethnic style. Cabinets and armoires should reflect an artistic role. Traditional lines include rudimentary imagery and extensive decoration. The textile motifs neither overpower the lines of the furniture nor detract from its usefulness.

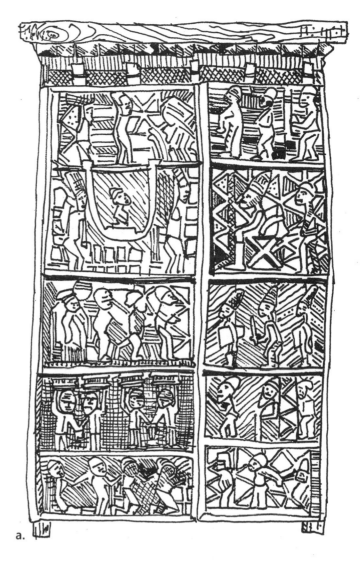

a.

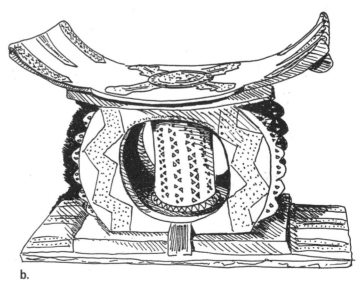

b.

Figure 17.7a–b African furniture

Window Treatments

The window treatments of African Ethnic fail to be incorporated with much of today's interior space. There are ways, however, to bring the materials and styles to current standards.

Africa is known for its harsh sun and dry heat, and to the traditional tribes, the hut was often the only place to escape the weather. Thatched roofs and open windows allowed whatever breeze there was convey the heat out of the house. Window treatments most commonly consisted of woven grass fibers that covered the open holes of the huts. These fabrics and textiles were never elaborate in design, and were often tied up or simply removed when not used to shade the interior. As it is impossible to imitate the function and design of African window treatments, emphasis must be placed on the spirit of the traditional. Here are ways to accomplish the essence of African Ethnic window treatments:

Wooden blinds, specifically with large blind widths, emphasize the function of the treatment.

Thick, coarse, natural textiles such as burlap, oxford cotton, and coarse linen give a clean, bold, rustic look.

Textured sheers, though not traditional, give a sense of the netting used as protection from insects, and thus are appropriate.

Textured cellular shades or shadings control light and provide soft colors and a variety of textures, merging new window treatments with traditional philosophy.

Bold colors should be avoided in window draperies, as the large area of bright hue detracts from the neutral color theme that should predominate.

The function of window treatments should be emphasized. Manual workings are preferred to traverse rod and hidden tension pulleys.

Rugs

Rugs are produced in many African nations, each with unique tribal or traditional designs. Overall, tribal rugs are flat woven with abstract, geometric designs in colors derived from native plants. They have charm and character and are often filled with symbolism. They fall in the category of flat tapestry folk rugs and are generally woven on an upright loom where the artisan creates the design as the work progresses.

In North Africa, two countries deserve special mention. Morocco produces richly colored, deep-pile rugs similar to the Spanish mantas. They combine features of the hand-tufted rya or shag rug and coarse Turkish rugs. Egypt also has many factories that produce rugs, often with child labor, so prices are not high. Egyptian rugs are hand-knotted in the Turkish and Persian styles. In addition, a variety of flat tapestry and other Oriental-influenced rugs are produced in Egypt for the Western market.

African Style Today

To design a space in African Ethnic style, consider the following guidelines. First, nature is beautiful. Incorporate as many natural textiles as possible, avoiding bright hues except as accents and keeping in mind the symbolic spiritual quality of each color. Second, avoid the European approach of African safari motifs. The only appropriate use of this style is for furniture or window treatments, as the Western world's use of these elements is foreign to African culture. Third, the function of furniture and decorative treatments should be emphasized and even glorified. Finally, art is key. The artistic qualities of functional elements, and any exclusively decorative art the client wishes to incorporate, should

Figure 17.8 a–b African rugs/carpets

be displayed individually without overshadowing the major neutral color scheme. In this way, the true African Ethnic style can be incorporated into the demands of today's interior designs.

For adapted African style, focus on materials that imitate handmade textiles or animal-skin prints or man-made designs from existing tribes. Accurate or adapted representations of materials such as woven mat or grass textures, hardened or cracked clay designs, or carved wooden designs, for example, will assist in the creation of an African interior theme.

LOG CABIN STYLE

Overview

The log cabin is credited to Swedish immigrants to the United States during the mid- to late 1800s. However, the Swedes were not the only Europeans who utilized small wooden structures; most northern European city dwellers had small cottages in the countryside where they stayed in the summer while raising vegetables for the family; these cottages were also used as weekend or holiday escapes. For generations, millions of people throughout Europe and Central Asia, including Siberia, have lived or are living, often without electricity or indoor plumbing, in small wooden homes as their only residence.

In the United States, the log cabin became the initial home of choice in New England settlements as early as the mid-1600s, and it was extensively used later as the push into the western frontier required the clearing of wooded lands. As trees were felled, full-flitch or half-flitch logs were found to be plentiful and a strong building material and interior wall in one. The walls, when adequately sealed and chinked, are an excellent insulator for both temperature and sound.

Interior Architecture

As the upper crust of the Beaux Arts (1881–1945) wealthy class became bored with their Eastern Seaboard luxury palaces, magnate families had large custom log residences built in the Adirondack Mountains of upstate New York. Railroads were built to serve these rustic palaces, where peeled log walls and beams with elaborate structural framing, wooden plank floors, and a full staff of servants made roughing it easy for the *nouveaux riches*. These large-scale mountain estate residences influenced the building of lodges such as the famous Old Faithful Inn in Yellowstone National Park. Built in the winter of 1903–1904, the Old Faithful Inn

was designed by Robert C. Reamer, who wanted the asymmetry of the building to reflect the chaos of nature. The lobby of the hotel features a 65-foot ceiling, a massive rhyolite fireplace, and railings made of contorted lodgepole pine. Wings were added to the hotel in 1915 and 1927, and today 327 rooms are available to guests in this National Historic Landmark.

Early pioneers settling on both sides of the Mississippi River built log cabins, many of which survive as historic landmarks today, such as the Abraham Lincoln Log Cabin State Historic Site, 8 miles south of Charleston, Illinois. This was the last home of Abraham Lincoln's father and stepmother, Thomas and Sarah Bush Lincoln. The 86-acre site includes the reconstructed Lincoln cabin and a surrounding living history farm, managed by the Illinois Historic Preservation Agency. The Lincoln family lived in a saddlebag cabin —a cabin of two rooms with a central chimney. As many as eighteen people lived in this cabin in 1845. The home was typical for many subsistence farm families: simple homes, often with packed-dirt floors, small paned windows (if any) set into rough pine logs, and plank doors. Fireplaces were large to accommodate the cooking and baking needs of large pioneer families. Often, the chimney caught fire, so families kept filled buckets of water ready to douse flashover flames. Chimneys were built of brick later, when it became available. Often, a sleeping loft was accessed by a dropdown ladder. Sometimes the cabin was divided into two rooms, a cooking/living space and a bedroom. In the South, log cabins had covered porches created by extending the roof at a less steep angle. Sometimes two-room cabins were made into separate log cabins connected by a roof; these were known as dog-trot cabins. One example is on the grounds of Andrew Jackson's Hermitage estate in Nashville, Tennessee.

Textiles: Color, Pattern, and Texture

Textiles were luxury items in log cabin homes. Many were handcrafted, most were utilitarian, and some were recycled. The colors, patterns, and textures discussed here represent the log cabin historically; they are also appropriate selections for contemporary log cabins.

Colors

Appropriate colors comprise natural colors or neutrals— colors of stone in gray, red, brown in flecks, or composite colors of rock; sand; and dirt in dark brown to light beige, black, or charcoal gray. Natural dyes include indigo blue, madder or cranberry red, goldenrod, light neutralized green, and deep forest greens. Accents are best in wildflower colors: red, yellow, orange, lavender.

Patterns

Many log cabins were built in areas where the former occupants were Native Americans. Hence, the angular and sometimes complex designs of Navajo rugs and other tribal basketry, pottery, and jewelry are all appropriate, as are portraits of great chiefs or scenes honoring the nomadic Native American heritage. Contemporary motifs found in textiles include mountain landscape scenes with pine or aspen trees, foliage and wildflowers, waterfalls, rivers, and lakes. Animal motifs include bears, wolves, small animals, and birds, particularly hawks and eagles.

Textures

As most historic log homes were rural, textiles were hand-spun and hand-loomed. Homespun, muslin, and simple checks and stripes could be woven at home; store-bought textiles included calico and tweed. Toweling such as diaper cloth or waffle weave and plain cotton towels were sometimes purchased. Clothing was often recycled into rag rugs—braided or plain weave, hooked, or needlepunched (see chapter 13). Oilcloth was used at the windows as a roller shade and, because of its weight and durability, as tablecloth. Heavyweight canvas was sometimes painted and sealed as a floorcloth. Embroidered handwork brought life to practical as well as show towels. Immigrants from Europe often brought precious pieces of lace and practiced traditional lace-making skills to make window curtains, table decorations, and accent pieces. Pieced and embroidered quilts were a special pride of frontier women.

Upholstered Furniture

Historic log cabins had no upholstered furniture. However, eventually cushions may have been placed on rocking chairs and, even later, on chairs surrounding the fireplace or table. Because textiles were at a premium, they were used first for clothing.

In contemporary log homes, inns, and lodges, upholstered furniture is a given. Sometimes it is overscaled to match the enormous size and scale of log interiors, and sometimes it is small-scale. In the past, dark colors were used to hide dirt, but today's fabrics can be easily maintained, so medium to lighter fabrics with nubby, suede-like, or luxurious upholstery textures are now acceptable.

Beds

Log furniture beds were found in large or small scale. Later, turned spindle beds and, still later, Victorian brass beds had headboards and footboards. Tester or poster beds or canopy beds were often hand-built. Draped beds were a luxury but gave a measure of warmth and privacy to parents. A trundle bed for children pulled out from under the master bed. Bed skirts of muslin were sometimes used to conceal trundle beds.

Coverlets were made of candlewick fabric, embroidered muslin, and tufted bedspreads, when they became available during the Victorian era. Pieced Colonial style quilts in many patterns showed great skill. Victorian crazy quilts were made of small scraps of worn-out clothing put together in a seemingly haphazard manner with large decorative stitches called turkey tracks.

Window Treatments

Authentic log cabins had very small windows, and when treatments were used, they were simple lace, muslin, or calico curtains shirred or tabbed onto a primitive rod, stick, wire, or string. Today, however, log cabins often have very large windows. Where privacy is no issue and the scenery is spectacular, the only treatment may be window film. Other treatments include traverse or hand-operated draperies, horizontal wood or metal blinds, cellular shades, Roman shades, fabric vane shadings, and vertical blinds. Sometimes top treatments are used as decorative elements featuring small log rods, fishing poles, or boat paddles used as rods.

Rugs

Historic log cabins began with packed-dirt floors which were later replaced with wooden planks. The hearths were often stone or brick. Accent or area rugs gave softness and provided areas of cleanliness. Woven and braided rag rugs, crocheted rugs, hooked and needlepunched rugs, and floorcloths are all examples of handmade rugs used in log cabins. Navajo rugs were also used and enjoyed as focal practical soft floor coverings and artistic elements.

The Intermountain West Log Cabin Style Today

Log cabins today come as "kits" that range from small custom homes to multimillion-dollar estates. The variety of sizes dictates that some interiors are rustic and others elegant and filled with luxurious furnishings, including European furniture and fine Oriental rugs. However decadent or modest, cabins often have an otherworldly flavor, a quietude and naturalness that make them a part of nature. Many resorts are built in log cabin style, from ski lodges to guest cabins, and filled with handsome natural American West art, accessories, and textiles.

ISLAND STYLE

Overview

One style that has become increasingly popular over the years is that of islands and coastal areas. Because beaches generally relay a message of relaxation, beauty, and peace while at the same time being fun, exotic, and mysterious, it is easy to see why people have wanted to bring this theme indoors—to incorporate these feelings into everyday life. The island motif encompasses several styles, however; these can be classified as Caribbean, Hawaiian and Polynesian, and Southeast Asian.

Interior Architecture

Caribbean (British West Indies)

The stereotype of the Caribbean style is a multicolored, stucco-covered bungalow with a perfect lawn surrounded by a white picket fence and sitting next to white sands. The Caribbean style is often simple, lively, and quirky. Architectural elements such as steep gabled roofs, gingerbread fretwork, wide verandas, and shuttered windows are most often seen. Much of the architecture is stuccoed or whitewashed, though some buildings are painted as brightly as the gleaming Caribbean sun. Popular flooring choices include tile, stone, and rough pine. Mahogany is also a popular material. The Caribbean style is a mesh of many cultures and incorporates Dutch, Spanish, and other European influences.

Hawaiian and Polynesian

Historic native Hawaiian and Polynesian architecture included modest homes built of bamboo posts; the roofs were thatched with palm fronds and the walls covered with native grasses or bark. Floors were sand or dirt, packed solid. Open windows allowed sea breezes to enter. Where flooding was frequent, homes were raised and entered through steps or ladders.

The Hawaiian and South Seas theme today is often a part of modest modern homes as well as high-end exclusive settings. As the Hawaiian theme was made popular in America through John Wayne World War II movies, the style became Americanized and celebrated because it represented the sacrifice of lives at Pearl Harbor. Many of the thousands of servicemen and servicewomen who were stationed there learned to love the environment and brought it back to the continental United States with them. Post–World War II homes were modest Beaux Arts or Modern-style cottages that often included the new sliding glass doors or French doors that connected the exterior to the interior.

The Polynesian Cultural Center has succeeded in preserving the culture, architecture, and traditions of the South Seas nations, the basis of our acquaintance with the island style. The Cultural Center is located in Laie on the north shore of Oahu, Hawaii. You can learn more at www.polynesia.com.

Southeast Asian

The style of places such as Indonesia often offers a regal feel, as it is largely based on wealth, royalty, and social class. It is quite functional, though not lacking in ornamentation. There is a strong emphasis on horizontal lines rather than vertical. The picture that most often comes to mind when thinking of Southeast Asian design includes little huts with thatched roofs that are sloped, tiered, or paneled. For the wealthy, the style is highly embellished with intricate wood carvings and other detailing.

Textiles: Color, Pattern, and Texture

Color: Caribbean

Caribbean colors include seashell shades such as coral, peach, yellow, and creamy white. All of these colors, though not necessarily bright in shade, still have a bright, sunny tone. Other natural colors are also popular, including the green of palm fronds, the light tan shade of sand, the earthy brown of bark, and the bright blue-green of the clear ocean waters. Finally, one of the most basic shades, and a true necessity in the warm Caribbean climate, is whitewashed white—never dull. These colors together produce a calm, no-stress feeling that sets one's mind at peace.

Color: Hawaiian and Polynesian

Contemporary colors combine boldness with casual living, resulting in splashes of bright color. These include hot magentas and bright yellows of hibiscus flowers, the bright green of lush foliage, the rich orange of sunset, and the yellow of the tropical sun. The colors often reflect the weather—warm all year round.

Color: Southeast Asian

This style features jungle green, coral, rich, iridescent gold, some soft purples, and, most commonly, solid red with a hint of burgundy. These colors contrast nicely with the use of dark wood. Silks are often produced in red and gold. This style carries a more serene and serious atmosphere than the other island styles, and although bold, the colors still imply royalty and wealth.

Pattern: Caribbean

In the Caribbean, patterns include exotic flora and birds, sea creatures such as turtles and stingrays, dolphins, starfish, fish, crustaceans, and mollusks, especially conch shells. Others are fishing nets, boats, and scenes from the ocean such as approaching storms; and seashore scenes, such as a white sand beach framed in palm trees meeting the tantalizing blue-green of the sea. Parrots and lizards also are island motifs. All these patterns are very much nature-influenced or nature-created. Patterns also appear in woven and thatched straw materials as well as in the shells used for decoration.

Pattern: Hawaiian and Polynesian

The Hawaiian theme involves hundreds of floral patterns —leaves, flowers, and ferns, for example. Most blossom with large representations of hibiscus flowers in every imaginable color. Hawaiian patterns and colors are meant to be highly visible in furniture as well as clothing; they are derived from the *aloha* (welcome) shirts, originally souvenir items for tourists. Hawaiian prints were used on furniture in World War II movies and found instant favor in homes both in Hawaii and on the mainland. In strong colors less likely to fade in the bright island sunlight, exotic prints were made of durable cotton, a breathable and serviceable fabric.

Other contemporary island motifs that suggest a vacation in Hawaii or the South Pacific include starfish, bamboo, tiki or totem pole designs, seagulls, fish and other marine life, ocean scenes with sailboats on the horizon, sunsets through colorful clouds, beach scenes, and beach accessories or clothing.

Pattern: Southeast Asian

Southeast Asian themes are often much more refined than Hawaiian. Wallpapers and fabrics often boast small, detailed designs that show little floral influence but rather many geometric shapes. Bamboo also plays a large part in the patterns of Asia. In the South Sea Islands, where there were few tourists and almost no military presence to take home the style, the influence came from movies such as Rogers and Hammerstein's *South Pacific,* in which motifs included native crafts—perhaps even a shrunken head or two—tiki totems, and the craggy tropical geography of Bali and the mountains of Indonsia. Plantations and farms lent pineapple or rice motifs, native fishing or high seas boats, and the Hawaiian scenes listed above.

Texture: Caribbean, Hawaiian and Polynesian, and Southeast Asian

Texture is seen as printed or natural cotton textiles, breathable and comfortable. Other fibers with a natural hand and appearance are used as upholstery and window coverings.

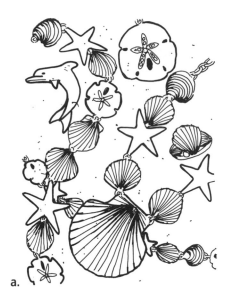

Figure 17.9 a–g Island-style motifs

Soft-to-the-touch fabrics on bedding, including mosquito netting, suggest a cool, clean approach, relaxing fabrics without pattern. Natural fibers underfoot include Japanese tatami mats. Other durable natural fibers for rugs include sisal, piña, or coir mats that can be shaken to remove sand and that are not damaged by water.

Tapa cloth from Polynesia is made by pounding the bark of trees until it is supple and flattened; it is then painted in traditional motifs. Hand-woven mats made of land or sea grass and reeds, are used for wall materials. One example is grass cloth wallcovering.

Upholstered Furniture

Rattan and wicker seating pieces with loose cushions covered with bright floral prints or solid durable fabrics hallmark the island theme. The large, open bamboo- and rattan-framed sofas and chairs reminiscent of post–World War II Hawaiian movie sets have once again become appealing in nostalgic Midcentury Island settings. Wicker furniture may be as traditional as Victorian or as contemporary as tightly woven framed pieces that bespeak the sleek Modern style. Deck chairs from cruise ships are also a favorite.

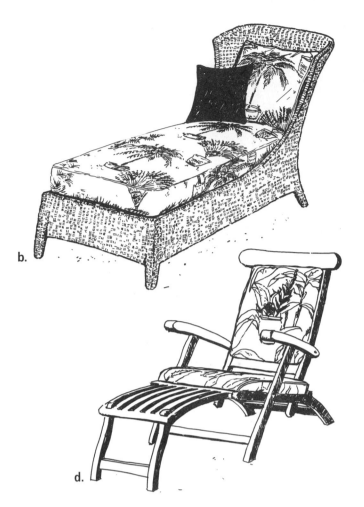

Figure 17.10 a–e Island style upholstered furniture
a wicker sofa; **b** wicker chaise lounge; **c, e** rattan chair and sofa; **d** deck chair

Frames for chairs and sofas may also be hand carved of tropical mahogany to reflect period styles or native motifs. These pieces, particularly popular during the British colonial days, were fitted with loose seat cushions. Today replicas are sought after for their exotic and unique appearance.

Beds

Floor mats and hammocks serve as beds in many native settings, although European and American settlers used mattresses on platforms. Like upholstered furniture, bed frames today may be of rattan or wicker or simply wood. Where headboards or footboards are used, motifs include grasses, bamboo, or geometrically carved wood, but these are not common. Bedding is simple, plain, and lightweight. Mosquito netting hung from a circular frame above the bed forms bed draperies.

Rugs

Japanese tatami mats of woven grass or other forms of matting such as sisal, coir, piña, or other natural fiber, possibly stenciled in simple, abstract patterns inspired by the art of indigenous peoples, are an appropriate flooring. As high humidity precludes the use of floor fabrics that tend to support mold growth, breathable natural materials are often preferred.

OTHER REGIONAL OR THEMATIC STYLES

The **coastal style** may be regionally expressed. Thematic styles may also be determined by the climate and by popular styles of an area. For example, the **Pacific Northwest** region, along the northern California and the Oregon and Washington coasts, often features homes based on natural elements—a high-quality woodsy, modern effect and motifs taken from the ocean or forest. Colors are often neutral, dark, or midtoned. In contrast, a **New England coastal** style might include lighthouses, ropes, fishing boats, and the blues and greens of the ocean. Variations: sailing, voyaging, or ocean exploration themes that embrace all the el-

Figure 17.11 Island-style rug/carpet

ements of boating on the high seas—sails, the ships themselves, compasses, ship wells, and life preservers.

Silver screen style embraces numerous themes. Hollywood star style is regional. More specifically, the stars may come from the rock-and-roll era or from a favorite vintage movie such as the original *Star Wars, The Wizard of Oz,* or any other classic Disney or MGM live-action or animated movies, for example.

Sports themes for specific rooms may focus on a single sport. For example, a room might feature the colors and logos of a favorite collegiate or professional football, baseball, or basketball team. Alternatively, the theme may revolve around the equipment of a particular sport.

Winter sports themes include skiing, snowboarding, ice-skating, and other Olympic events. Snow-covered mountains and winter sports equipment may form the colors, patterns, and textures. Winter sports can be integrated with the log cabin theme, above.

Freshwater or ocean fishing is a sport, as is hunting. Fishing and hunting motifs and colors may come from the animal hunted or the equipment used—fish and fishing gear, for example. Antlers or hunting trophies are often featured in a log cabin theme. African photo or hunting safari expedition themes also fit into this category.

Juvenile themes comprise an area of nearly limitless imagination. Frequently used examples include little-girl themes such as dolls, ballerinas, floral patterns, and storybook fairy tales and little-boy themes such as cars, dinosaurs, sports, and superheroes. Nursery themes may be based on alphabet and nursery rhymes or a contemporary marketed theme.

Juvenile themes also encompass **fantasy** as a theme. Using a fabric or wallcovering as the basis for a foray into the imagination, these rooms are pure entertainment. Juvenile fantasy themes might be generic or include a licensed cartoon character. Little boys seem to gravitate toward themes such as race cars, trains, sports equipment, and rocket ships. For little girls, ballerina shoes, storybook bunnies, and tea party motifs help satisfy their desire for beauty and gentility. Even color without the pattern can be a basis for a child's fantasyland; yards of happy colors can provide fertile ground for a lively imagination.

Far and away is a theme that transports the user to another place and time—the more exotic, the better. Examples include an English Victorian estate, an island in the South Seas, and a trip to Africa, Australia, the great north woods, or the sunbaked isles of the Mediterranean. Fabric is the entry ticket to a world apart where one can feel the ambience of a place far removed. These interiors often combine styles of furnishings that may need to be unified neatly and professionally with yards of thematic and carefully coordinated fabrics.

Casual contemporary is a broad theme where mostly plain or textured fabrics are assigned to calm the mind and refresh the body with subtle, undemanding simplicity. The applications of fabric may be conservative and limited, as this theme is often based on the "less is more" philosophy. Less pattern, less confusion means more mental freedom from stress, more physical room in which to unwind and gently converse, more emptiness that can be filled with people, their projects, their entertainment, their interactions. These are often rooms for busy people with little time or inclination toward decoration as well as little desire for upkeep. They want interiors that serve them and do not demand much attention in return. They may be looking for unusual textile applications that meet these criteria.

Seasonal style is furnishing according to a season; the décor may be permanent, or it may be approached like a theater stage set. For example, interiors with neutral backgrounds as floors, walls, window treatments, and ceilings can be considered a backdrop for a space changed as if by magic through the rotation of seasonal slipcovers, bed, bath, and table linens, area rugs, and window treatments. Off-season items that are carefully stored should require little care beyond an occasional cleaning or pressing. Art and accessories are finishing touches that support a seasonal style.

Helps for furnishing for the four seasons—spring, summer, fall, and winter—are as follows:

Seasonal spring elements: Use clear tinted hues, full and pure or lightened high value, and plenty of white. Patterns include naturalistic or conventional florals, vines, lighthearted graphics, crisp stripes, checks, and plaids. Textures include natural cotton fabrics such as sailcloth, chintz or warp sateen, gingham, muslin, and lightweight manufactured-fiber easy-care fabrics. The effect should be informal or casual, animated, lively, cheerful, or cute, with an unaffected simplicity. Many delightful focal points, with a somewhat cluttered, playful effect, are perfect for spring. This approach enlivens the senses and keeps the eye and brain interested and moving. The theme might be Midcentury Retro, Country French, Island, or simply vernacular country, for example.

Seasonal summer elements: Colors are grayed tones and pastels; midtones dominate. Value is low, as softer colors blend. Accents are fine wood and metal, mirrors and luxury elements. Patterns are formal traditional or noncommittal, stylized, or even mystical. Shibui elements (see "Japan," page 298) may prevail to create a timeless, peaceful beauty. Textures are often matte or smooth, polished, antiqued, and in fabrics may include refined brocade and damask, smooth or antiqued satin or velvet, and chiffon or ninon sheer or batiste semisheer. Elegant and refined or softly relaxing, the overall feeling is gracious, romantic, proper or mannerly and genteel, cultured, and picturesque, without a strong focal point. The theme could incorporate many of the formal traditional styles as well as Asian styles.

Seasonal fall elements: Autumn colors are twofold. For backgrounds, use shades or hues plus black or brown. Browned colors are often earthy and of medium or deep value; they are complex, made of a mixture of hues. Hence, they often elude specific names and may require two or more words to describe them, such as "earthy golden-brown" or "burnished copper." Think of the complexity of leaves that fall to the ground, creating a kaleidoscope of color. Try describing it. It's difficult without more words, more description.

For accents, use brilliant colors such as those of turning deciduous leaves and the backlighting of sunlight through them, always with a touch of vivid gold or orange. Color that scintillates is also autumnal. As the sunlight reflects through fall foliage, it has an iridescence and a visual richness that can be translated into interior accents in metal—gold and copper in lamp bases, chandeliers, artwork, and centerpieces, for example.

As nature is complex, so are the patterns that suggest autumn. They may be overlaid or visually busy, much like leaves that fall and haphazardly overlap. Tightly curved patterns such as paisley are excellent choices to reflect this complexity. Patterns that are masculine or rustic, such as African or primitive tribal designs that connect the viewer to the earth, are effective. Patterns may be angular, suggesting opposition. Geometric patterns on fabrics may be echoed or complemented with three-dimensional geometric shapes—for example, window treatment rods or tie-backs can provide substantially impressive design elements.

Autumn textures are tactile, inviting touch and lingering feel. Fabric textures that are decidedly autumn include chenille, velour, tweed, twill, plaid, matelassé, tapestry, and woven, deeply textured fabrics. Wood is a major autumn element, as seen in flooring, furniture, and window treatments. Wood colors that are natural to darkly stained rather than light create a sense of cavelike or reclusive coziness. Wood elements often produce a psychological effect of safety and security.

Overall, the feeling is solid, often masculine, and powerful. It is practical and physical. It can be primitive. Autumn interiors may create a sense of somberness or seriousness. The effect is earthen—connected to soil, trees, rivers, stones, and wildlife. It may be dynamic, with a heavy, commanding, pedantic effect. It appears anchored, sturdy, and sometimes massive. It is quiet, important, yet filled with patterns and textures that impress.

Seasonal winter elements: Winter in northern climates is a stark time in which white snow contrasts with silhouettes of blackened trees devoid of foliage. The winter palette is a black and white or achromatic interior with splashes of brilliant color that scintillate—like a red cardinal or a bluejay on the bare branch of a tree. White is used generously, black sparingly as dramatic contrast, with brilliance from jewel tones, including ruby or garnet red, sapphire blue, emerald green, topaz gold. Other contemporary strident colors might include persimmon orange, acid or citrus green, and deep fuschia.

Patterns are sleek, disciplined designs, with sculptural vertical or horizontal curves. Designs are abstract, definitive, precise, hard-edged, and sharp. Overall, the period styles that fit winter are classical (Greco-Roman), Empire, International, and Midcentury Modern. Winter spaces may be described as striking, stately, formal, restrained, dignified, intellectual, stunning, dramatic, majestic, monumental, regal, aloof, solitary, suave, mature, exclusive, stark, simple, and refined.

18 Modern Styles

INTRODUCTION

All styles discussed here for the Modern period are influential in contemporary interiors and will continue to be for the foreseeable future. Not every historic style can be popular concurrently, so some Modern styles will be stronger than others at any given point. Contemporary style reliably consists of revisitation, modification, adaptation, and, occasionally, authentic historic style. The Modern era consists of six distinct styles: Art Nouveau (1890–1910), Arts and Crafts (1905–1929), Organic Modern/Frank Lloyd Wright style (1908–present), Art Deco

(1918–1945), Midcentury/International Modern (1932–present), and Retro Modern (revisiting styles from the 1940s to the 1970s).

ART NOUVEAU

Period Overview

Art Nouveau is a decorative and architectural style that flourished primarily in Europe and the United States between 1890 and 1910. *Art nouveau* means "new art" in

French; the name of the style was given by Samuel Bing in Paris at La Maison de l'Art Nouveau, a gallery where much of the work was displayed. The new design style was called *La Floreale* or *Style Liberty* in Italy, *Jugendstijl* in Austria and Germany, and *Art Joven* in Spain.

At the beginning of the twentieth century, Art Nouveau was viewed as a Victorian movement that helped discard old conventions of the nineteenth century and clear the way for post-1918 developments. Art Nouveau was the leader in breaking from historical art and architecture.

The style developed as part of the rebellion against the Industrial Age and its mass production of design products. There was a conscious effort to break from the mold, to borrow nothing from the past. The style militated against traditional architectural values of reason and clarity of structure. Artists and designers sought a unified style in which tableware matched furniture and even fashion and jewelry. This new style design was mainly used for interior decoration, in the design of glassware and jewelry, and in graphic design.

Art Nouveau first developed in France and later was greatly influenced by the popular Arts and Crafts movement in England. In Germany, Jugendstijl was particularly popular. Art Nouveau reached its peak at the Turin Exhibition in Paris in 1902, which brought together works of the finest exponents of the style. Both architects and designers emphasized simplicity and precision, but the function of the design came to seem more important. After 1910, Art Nouveau appeared old-fashioned and limited; it was used only as a distinct decorative style. Not until fifty years later was it rediscovered.

Many artists and designers worked within the Art Nouveau style. The best known were the Scottish architect and designer Charles Rennie Mackintosh, who worked with sinuous and delicate structures; Hector Guimard of France and Louis Sullivan of the United States, who worked with traditional design but used plant-like ironwork to decorate buildings; and architect and sculptor Antonio Gaudi of Spain, one of the most original artists of the time. Other famous artists of the period include Louis Comfort Tiffany of the United States, a glassmaker; Louis Majorelle of France, who dealt with furniture and ironwork; Emile Galle of France, a glass and furniture designer; Rene Lalique of France, who designed glass and jewelry; and Henri de Toulouse-Lautrec of France and Alphonse Mucha of Czechoslovakia, graphic designers.

Art Nouveau artists and designers were influenced by nature's foliage, colors, forms, and lines. Many of them shared the goal of returning to simplicity and implementing nature to design. All furniture, tapestries, wallpapers, fabrics, and pottery was handmade. The idea of unity in design played an important role as the twentieth century proceeded. The ideas from Art Nouveau also contributed to art styles after 1910, including the Arts and Crafts and Organic Modern movements. American artists and craftsmen made a significant contribution to Art Nouveau movements in fields such as glassware, lamps, and ceramics.

Textiles: Color, Pattern, and Texture

Colors

Art Nouveau was expressed in warm afternoon hues and deep, rich colors. A popular combination was Mackintosh rose with black and white, purple, blue, and peacock green. Other colors were the greens, yellows, browns, and oranges that reflected the colors in nature, particularly of the sunset or summer fields.

Motifs

Art Nouveau was characterized by long, flowing lines and wavelike contours. Intricate designs were common. Fabrics featured complex repeated patterns. Nature was a rich source of inspiration. Motifs such as vines, ocean waves, and peacocks were used. Others included plants, stems and tendrils, flowers (Mackintosh rose, honesty plant, iris, poppy, sunflower), seed pods, waving grass or plants bending in a stiff breeze, seaweed, snakes, insects, smoke, reptiles, and swans.

The female form — slender and languorously posed with long, flowing hair—dominated Art Nouveau decorative design. Women were pictured as nymphs, naiads, or undines, and appeared melancholy and somnambulistic. Through women, often pictured on posters, artists personified ideas such as faith, truth, and progress. Sarah Bernhardt and Loie Fuller were two popular women depicted graphically. Although this style sought to break from the past, many women's forms were clad in Celtic dress. Sometimes dreamy castles, clouds, and other ethereal images complemented these female motifs, again seeming to celebrate the pre-Medieval era of magic, dragons, and heroes.

The line was elegant, graceful, and infused a powerful rhythmic and whiplash force. The line created symbolist, abstract, or rhythmic impulses. Charles Rennie Mackintosh introduced geometric and rectilinear lines as well.

Of note also is the patterning of wood furniture pieces. Patterns appeared in wood cutouts, wood burning, marquetry, and stenciling. Marquetry was an intricate part of furniture design; the furniture itself was commonly built of mahogany, walnut, and rosewood. Lighter woods — pear, teak, ash, maple, and jarrah—were used as well, sometimes inlaid with metal, mother-of-pearl, tortoiseshell, horns, and ivory.

Similarly, decoration was seen in glass etching, fabric embroidery, printing, fabric painting, and batik.

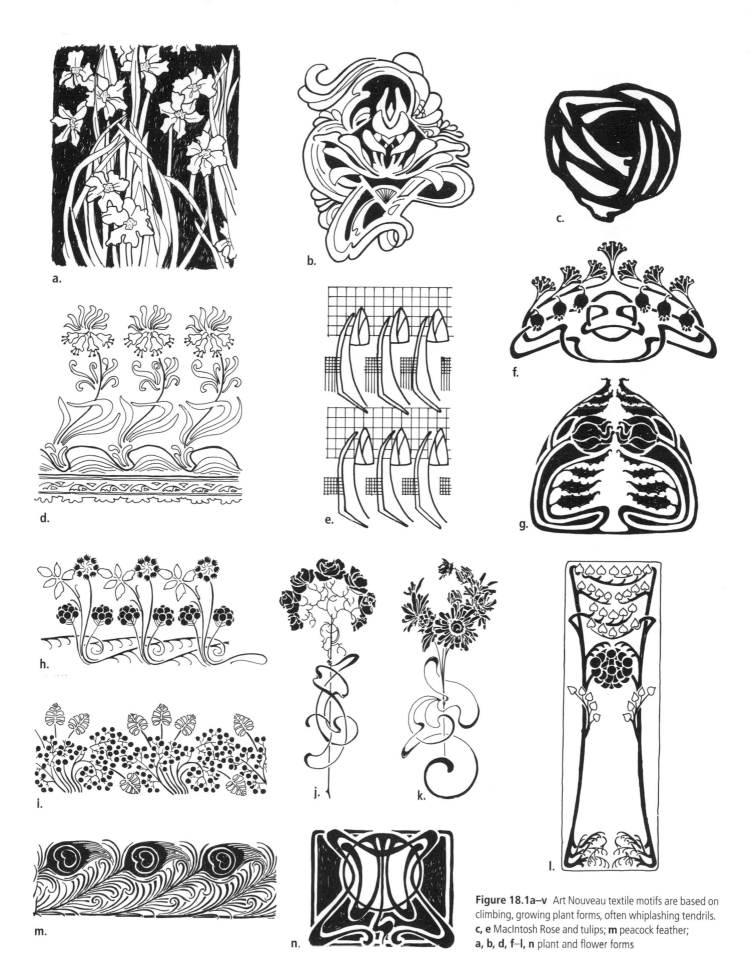

Figure 18.1a–v Art Nouveau textile motifs are based on climbing, growing plant forms, often whiplashing tendrils. **c, e** MacIntosh Rose and tulips; **m** peacock feather; **a, b, d, f–l, n** plant and flower forms

Figure 18.1 o lizards; **p** fish; **q** poppies; **r** female; **s** sinuous forms; **t** seahorses; **u** nymphs; **v** art glass plant motifs

Textures

Art Nouveau fabrics included tapestries woven with the fluid designs described above. Soft fabrics for draped applications were especially important. Sateen, or polished cotton, for example, was an ideal fabric because it draped sensuously and was printable. Sheer fabrics were introduced during this era as a part of the mainstream and were often printed. Art Nouveau designs were also woven into heavier fabrics for upholstery, including tapestry, damask, and sometimes formal brocade or lampas.

Upholstered Furniture

Art Nouveau furniture was well constructed and functional, but decoration was also important. The dynamic quality of line was expressed in the furniture. The curvilinear swing was seen in chair legs and chair backs. The flowing line, called the *Belgian curve,* was used for furniture supports and furniture forms.

Mackintosh's furniture emphasized perpendicularity. Henry van de Velde's furniture expressed his philosophy of

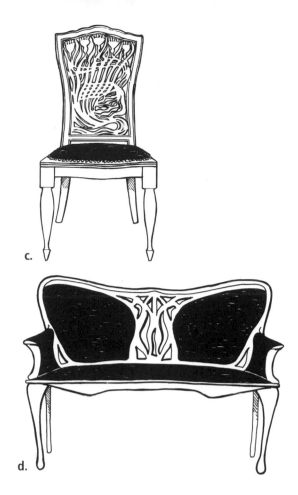

Figure 18.2 a–d Art Nouveau upholstered furniture
a, b MacIntosh Hill and Argyle chairs; **c** side chair; **d** settee

representing nature and organic forms in abstract. Lines in the furniture became more important than ornament. Hector Guimard became one of the first designers of free-form furniture—beautiful, carefully constructed, and functional.

Beds

The headboards and footboards of Art Nouveau beds were sculptured or had marquetry panels, usually depicting nature scenes or animals. Beds were dressed with smooth coverlets, rolled or tucked-in pillows, and, sometimes, bed drapery. Both smooth, plain fabrics and patterned fabrics with Art Nouveau motifs were applicable.

Figure 18.3 a, b Art Nouveau beds

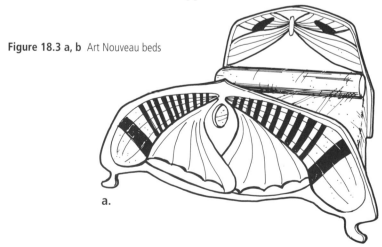

Figure 18.4 Art Nouveau window treatment

a.

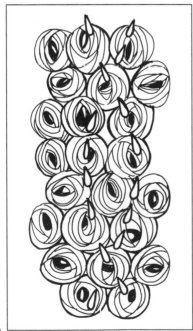

b.

Figure 18.5 a, b Art Nouveau rugs/carpets

Window Treatments

Textile window treatments were used during the Art Nouveau period. Draperies were long and fluid. There were some draw draperies and some panels that were drawn with cords. Draped top treatments such as swags were appropriate in formal settings. Even more common was the use of stained glass as art glass, as the work of Louis Comfort Tiffany became well known and loved. The curving, sinuous designs of hand-forged wrought iron or cast iron were used as a companion to the glass.

Rugs and Carpeting

Most carpet was in the style of William Morris, and almost always wool pile and sculpted. The most common rug patterns were floral, leaf, scroll, and plant designs.

Art Nouveau Today

Art Nouveau continues to influence design today in art glass, textile, and wallcovering design, carpet design, and, occasionally, in furniture design. It is fluid and natural, which will always find a niche, however small.

CRAFTSMAN AND ARTS AND CRAFTS

Period Overview

The Arts and Crafts movement (1905–1929) was a manifestation of the abhorrence of the assembly-line goods resulting from the more-is-better Victorian philosophy. The Craftsman-style house, called a bungalow, was designed by brothers and architects Charles Greene (1868–1957) and Henry Greene (1870–1954), whose work was particularly influenced by the traditional Japanese home in form, material, and construction. Prefabricated versions of the Greene and Greene bungalow could be ordered as a kit for $1,000 from the Sears, Roebuck catalog company, an indication of its wide acceptance during the period. Gustav Stickley was another proponent of the movement, and his Mission-style furniture was a hand-in-glove fit with the structurally exposed, wood-framed Craftsman interiors. Bungalow homes were given emphasis in the details such as the configuration of the glass muntins and mullions (divider bars) above a single large glass lower panel and on stained glass featuring natural forms such as leaves set in an overall rectilinear pattern. The effect was both artistic and earthy.

Arts and Crafts has its roots in the late nineteenth century in Britain. Leading theorists were trained as architects and worked toward unity in the arts, believing all creative endeavors were of equal value. They wanted not only to reform design but also to give quality once more to the work process itself. With its division of labor, the industrial revolution had devalued the work of the craftsman and turned him into a mere cog on the wheel of machinery. The aim of the Arts and Crafts reformers was to reestablish harmony among architect, designer, and craftsman, and to bring handcraftsmanship to the production of well-designed, affordable everyday objects. Through the influence of the designer-philosophers William Morris (1834–1896) and John Ruskin (1818–1900), four principles that forged the Arts and Crafts movement were (1) design unity, (2) joy in labor, (3) individualism, and (4) regionalism.

These principles were adopted in the United States and, to a lesser extent, in continental Europe. Although practitioners had widely differing agendas, they were unified in the belief that design could draw inspiration from the past without slavishly imitating historical models. Buildings were crafted of local materials and designed to fit into the landscape and reflect vernacular tradition. To provide design unity within these structures, furniture was often simple and "honest," left unpainted to display its method of construction, and polished to reveal the beauty of its wood. Nonarchitectural, movable crafts, from printed and woven fabric and embroidery to metalwork, were, on the other hand, frequently far from plain and intended, in an era of economic and social confidence, to equal the technical virtuosity and brilliance of earlier civilizations. High ideals, unfortunately, could not always be reconciled with practice. The movement flourished only where professionals could depend on rich clients who were perhaps gentry but more often industrialists or members of the expanding professional classes.

The Arts and Crafts interior was influenced by the exterior environment. Hence, it encompassed a unity of design from environment to exterior to interior. Ceiling, floors, walls, finished furniture, textiles, and metalwork all played a part in total design. The desired harmony of architect, designer, and craftsman was expanded to include manufacturers and retailers who printed woven textiles, machine-made and hand-knotted carpets, and tapestries according to Arts and Crafts principles.

Textiles: Color, Motif, and Texture

Colors

Colors of the Arts and Crafts era were those of the earth, particularly autumn-inspired colors and geologic tones. Most colors had a warm, golden undertone; yellows, greens, and golds were especially prominent. Rust, families of beige and brown, and warm reds with accents of blues and purples, as seen in shadows or sunsets, created this palette. Morris often used bright colors—turquoise and royal or bright blue, clear red, and bright yellow. Greens, sometimes quite clear and foliage-inspired, also were popular choices for textiles. The complexity of designs allowed much room for color exploration. Often colors were the source of bright accents in interiors filled with ponderous dark woods and straight-lined furniture. Thus, brilliant accents of color within complex textile designs provided visual relief and optimism.

Colors in rugs reflected the patterns of wallcoverings and textiles—for example, blue and red with white or very light outlines on a dark ground. Often the rug patterns were seen in a browned or blackened palette, with dark, practical color choices. A favored rug palette included an earthy sage green, orange, and gold, all dull or somber in value and intensity.

Motifs

William Morris said, "Have nothing in your house that you do not know to be useful, or believe to be beautiful." The most influential surface designer of the period, Morris created beautiful textile patterns that have withstood the test of time. Other influential pattern designers included Kate Faulkner, J. Henry Dearle, and Edward Burne-Jones.

Arts and Crafts patterns were small- to medium-scale complete designs based on leaves and growing plant forms. One of the main characteristics of the textile design was the floral decorative motif and the sense of movement—which, however, remained purely two-dimensional. The sense of movement was created with the addition of meandering stems. These design elements, plus interlacing patterns of rich color and texture, made the finished product highly ornamented. Wallpaper design, influenced by Morris, featured birds, stems, and leaves. Other motifs, such as animals, were also used in stained-glass and tapestry designs. For wallpaper, the use of single-color patterns such as diaper, Venetian, mallow, bird, and anemone was a simple compromise. The yellow and pale green were said to be most suitable. The acanthus leaf, a motif used as early as the Renaissance, folds or curls downward in a layered, complex manner. Hence, utilizing design and color in complex leaves began a new period of rich effects. The vigorous curves and scrolls of foliage and flowers, the deep and somber colors, and detailed hatching and veining gave the design a three-dimensional look.

An overlaying effect in Arts and Crafts textiles was seen as a light or subtle background pattern with a bolder and more brilliantly colored design on top. Both designs were typically based on foliage with complex forms and rigorous curves. This layered complexity was a marked and complementary contrast to the straight lines of Stickley furniture and the bold and heavy forms of the architecture.

Figure 18.6a–h Arts and Crafts textile motifs in the manner of Morris, Faulkner, Pearle, and Burke-Jones, based on complex foliage and animals

Textile art succeeded in developing art needlework as a profitmaking venture for women who worked in crafts. With the benefit of modest labor costs, the carpet factory was established and the craft of hand-knotting reintroduced. Morris's interior furnishing plan for St. Martin's Church showed a powerful design of floral sprigs worked on silk and then cut out and applied to a velvet ground. Another design where the motifs were used repeatedly was the Red House, with its brightly colored daisy clumps. These hangings were embroidered in outline with crocheted wool on a dark blue woolen ground. Morris became engrossed in the dyeing of embroidery threads and background fabrics.

Textures

Fabrics are key elements in expressing the softer side of Arts and Crafts. Hand-loomed fabrics were appreciated and revered, as textiles of the Medieval era, which strongly influenced William Morris, were in vogue. Hand-embroidered fabrics in Morris patterns were useful in settings from bedding to draperies to upholstery to pillows and accessories. Hand-loomed and hand-embroidered textiles were both textural and earthy. Woolen basket weave ground cloth for crewel designs is one example.

Tapestries were typically power-loomed or printed fabrics after the designs of William Morris. Long-wearing woolen velvets proved an alternative furnishing to the balanced twill weave blue and green woolen serge fabrics.

Many textiles were printed in designs similar to wallcovering patterns. Most designs for upper-income customers were block-printed onto fine woolen ground or onto substantial cotton ground cloth. As its popularity spread, broadcloth and warp sateen fabrics were printed via roller printing and made available to the broader public.

Upholstered Furniture

The geometric and linear design of Arts and Crafts furniture reflected the basic concept of unity. The use of built-in furniture, which expressed the principles of simplification and integration, also gave the designers more control over design unity: The more furnishings that could be integrated, the less opportunity the client had to install unsympathetic elements that would interfere with the overall composition.

The Mission designs by Gustav Stickley (1848–1942) were well known, partly because they were associated with eighteenth-century Spanish Colonial churches or missions but also because of Stickley's repeated statement that a chair, table, bookcase, or bed must fulfill its mission of usefulness as well as it possibly can. Most of his furniture was made of quartersawn oak, with the grain emphasized by a finish of fumed ammonia. Seats and upholstery were first made of leather or rush and later upholstered with William Morris–styled textiles. Prominent pieces included Stickley sofas, chairs, lounge chair and ottoman sets, along with unupholstered wooden pieces such as cabinets and tables.

Figure 18.7a–f Stickley-style Arts and Crafts upholstered furniture

Figure 18.8 Arts and Crafts bed

Beds

Arts and Crafts bed styles were primarily those designed by Gustav Stickley. Lines were straight and simple, frank and honest. The bedding was often fabric coverlets or full bedspreads with pillows tucked in, sometimes with a companion or contrasting accent pillow or two. The arrangement was modest and unassuming. Bedding fabrics were in the manner of the William Morris prints or woven textiles.

Window Treatments

Window treatments exhibited refined stained-glass designs based on simple, geometric, and native motifs. Stained-glass panels in window frames acted as screens, allowing

light to enter the house while maintaining a sense of privacy. Where stained glass was not used, large overhanging eaves achieved the same effect of keeping the sun out of the interior. Window treatments were simple — straight pleated or shirred draperies, curtains, and valances on rods.

Pinch- or French-pleated drapery was used most often, drawn by hand with a cord or with a hidden cord mechanism. A favorite approach was an iron rod, usually in a bronze color, with a simple curtain hanging supported by rings. Other choices were simple wooden rods with rings on pleated draperies, flat panels, or tabbed curtains. Curtains and draperies were in earthy colors and usually textured.

Rugs

The earliest Arts and Crafts rug designs were woven by machine, although later many were woven by hand following the Persian hand-knotted technique. The earliest designs had traces of naturalism, but this soon gave way to abstraction; however, as the movement, many continued to produce formal designs. The object of creating rugs and carpets was to make the pieces of color look gemlike and beautiful in themselves. Larger-scale, simplified Arts and Crafts patterns, with or without borders, were often the focal point of the room. As public appeal broadened, the Axminster was employed to mass-produce rugs.

Rugs were made in many sizes. Small rugs were used as accents and placed near doors, by the bedside, and in bathing or grooming areas. Larger area rugs and room-sized rugs anchored conversation areas.

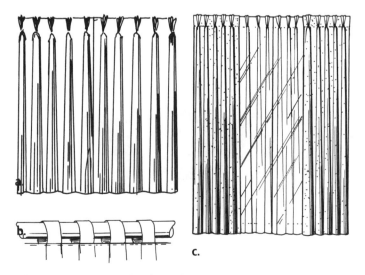

Figure 18.9 a–c Arts and Crafts window treatments

Figure 18.10 Arts and Crafts rug/carpet

Arts and Crafts Style Today

Arts and Crafts enjoyed a resurgence of popularity in the 1990s. This appears to be a long-term trend, as Stickley furniture is being mass-produced and there is great interest in bungalow homes. Today's keen interest is due, in part, to a seeking of simple, low-stress, and earthy or authentic interiors that are casual yet cozy and have the richness of history. Window treatments are pleasant and unassuming, and include simple draperies and top treatments with a variety of headings—shirring, various pleats, and tab tops. The undertreatments, often alternative, consist of blinds, shades, and shutters, with glass exposed wherever possible. Furniture may be Stickley Mission style, although many contemporary homes have interpreted versions and softer furniture with more fully upholstered pieces. Some Craftsman homes simply express a flavor of the style, while others are more strictly authentic.

ORGANIC MODERN AND FRANK LLOYD WRIGHT STYLE

Period Overview

The Organic Modern style dates from 1908 to the present. Its founder and greatest exponent, Frank Lloyd Wright (1867–1959), was a prolific architect, industrial designer, and interior designer; his was the longest career in American architectural history. His style is known as organic architecture due to his use of natural forms and materials. In 1887 he joined Adler and Sullivan, where he apprenticed and developed into a capable architect, then set out on his own, creating his own unique style. His successful part in the design of the Transportation Building of the Chicago World's Columbian Exposition in 1893 secured him prestige and fame, and clients came to him in a steady flow.

Wright was influenced heavily by the art and architecture of Japan, which became a large portion of his philosophical foundation. He turned to nature to develop his unique style of organic architecture. He was also captivated by the Aztec Indian culture of Mexico, intrigued with their stacked cliff homes and large temples. Wright's style also appears influenced by Arts and Crafts and, to a lesser extent, Art Deco. He identified with the Arts and Crafts movement, as he likewise emphasized nature as a primary inspiration. He rebelled against excessive ornamentation, incorporated muted earth tones with a few bright accents, and was determined to utilize fine craftsmanship in all his works. He felt that a home should seem to grow out of the landscape and that the landscape should become an integral part of the interior as well. With this reasoning, he created with and of the earth, not just over it, integrating the site into his floor plans.

A dominant feature was his strong use of horizontal line, as evidenced by his early and successful Prairie architecture, which hugged the landscape in extended horizontality. Wright's ideal was for things to be authentic, meaning that all materials should be used naturally and properly, with a purpose in mind.

Wright did take advantage of new technology in reinforced concrete, glass modern building techniques; however, he avoided unnecessary enhancement, such as paint, by using materials such as stone and wood on floors and walls. He felt the only appropriate treatment was to preserve materials in their natural state.

Wright created a pattern of homes for modest-income families that he dubbed Usonian, or unified. His plan was for entire Usonian communities. Usonian homes typically were one-story, modest dwellings without a garage or much storage. They were often L-shaped to fit around a garden area and constructed with environmentally conscious native materials. Usonian homes had flat roofs and large cantilevered overhangs for passive solar heating and natural cooling. Natural lighting from clerestory windows gave warmth, as did radiant floor heating. The trademark connection between the interior and exterior living spaces was integral to this style. Wright coined the word *carport* to describe an overhang for a vehicle to park under.

Textiles: Color, Pattern, and Texture

Colors

Wright's partiality toward nature influenced his use of colors, such as continued soft, foliage-like reds and greens and watery blues set against large neutral or creamy white grounds. The exterior colors of his buildings and houses are based mainly on the surrounding land, with complementary colors used for the interiors. Other colors often found in Wright interiors are shades of gold, brown autumnal colors, the natural grays found in stone and cement, olive and dull greens, and accents of bright pumpkin orange, bright gold and green, and cerulean blue. Cherokee red was one of Wright's favorite accents; it is now often called Frank Lloyd Wright red. The shade is slightly browned yet powerful and dramatic or theatrical. He also favored a bold yellow-gold or a

Figure 18.11a–s Organic Modern textile motifs in the styling of Frank Lloyd Wright, inspired by machines, pre-Columbian and Japanese architecture

strong pumpkin orange for occasional or accent upholstered pieces.

Motifs

Several patterns are seen in Wright's work. The well-known square is simple and yet captivating, and has been copied in nearly every possible design form. Wright had a liking for geometry, particularly the most basic forms such as diamonds, squares, and circles, which are recurrent themes in architecture, window forms, and furnishing alike. He also used stepped ziggurat patterns and designs based on earth-influenced geometry. Many of his patterned designs are set on a background of straight vertical or horizontal lines. Diagonal arrows, overlapping geometric details, and movement are elements in his designs, suggesting the influence of pre-Columbian architecture. While some Frank Lloyd Wright patterns are simple, many are complex, and all are distinctly architectural.

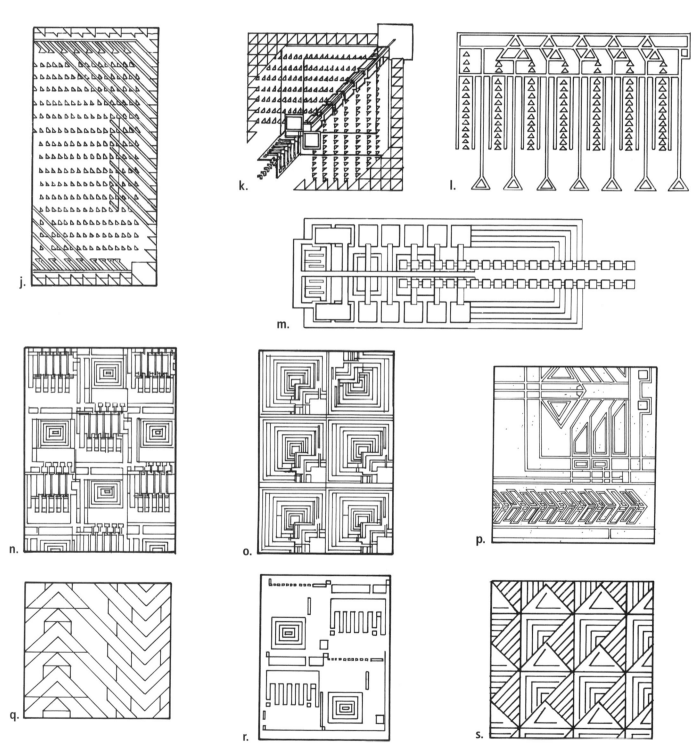

Textures

Although Wright favored natural materials, he did use tactile fabric texture in his work. More refined fabrics included short-napped velvet, satin weave wool, tightly woven linen, and mohair satin in his characteristic soft, earthy colors. As his designs evolved, Wright leaned more toward natural hand-woven fabrics and nubby textures to contrast with the smoothness of his Usonian homes.

He often used leather as a chair covering and animal skins to increase texture and to soften and humanize or balance the hard materials that formed the buildings' construction and interior finish materials.

Upholstered Furniture

Wright incorporated his custom-designed furnishings, which were generally simple and fluid, with the structure itself. He insisted that furniture be consistent in design, construction, and style as an extension of the buildings or homes being furnished. For this reason, he designed all of the furniture and upholstery in his buildings, although many of his pieces were left unupholstered. Each piece was designed for a specific building or residence. All of Wright's furniture embodies the same idea of natural design as do his houses. On an even smaller scale, his textiles and accessory designs are perfect examples of this idea as well. By designing his homes and their components like this, he created among them a unified whole.

Beds

Beds were simple and angular, made of natural wood. Bedspreads were generally of fabrics similar to those described above. Wright also designed pillows, bedspreads, and table and dresser scarves, often in solid fabrics skillfully embroidered in geometric motifs.

Window Treatments

Frank Lloyd Wright at first abhorred the use of window treatments because of his strong desire to make nature a part of the interior. Large horizontal windows helped achieve this purpose. Examples are seen at the Ward Willits House, the Robie House, the Tomek House, the Midway Gardens, the Imperial Hotel, Trinity Church, the Fallingwater house, and the Guggenheim Museum, among others.

As his style developed, however, Wright came to love stained and leaded glass. It fit his belief that ornament should either take architecture to a higher plane of expression or be left out. He felt his stained glass did this; it literally took his artistic architectural designs to a higher plane, to the vibrant world of art glass, becoming living architectural artistry with the changing light of day passing through the light and shadow, color and nuance of beveled and stained glass.

Although Wright did not favor window treatments in general, he did recognize the need of some clients for privacy. Many of his residences were so unusual that passersby frequently peeked in. To protect privacy, he first designed stained glass that was often slightly obscure. When movable window coverings were used for day or nighttime privacy, they were usually simple, straight pleated draperies made of theatrical velvet or nubby or textural casement fabric. Cellophane-like sheers and burnout sheers were acceptable, as they reflected the leaded and stained glass. Pleated draperies could easily be stacked to the side of the window, allowing for light, view, and the artistic enjoyment of art

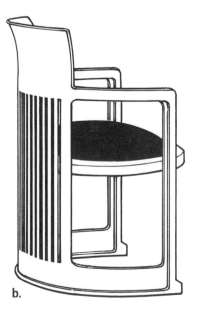

Figure 18.12 a, b Organic Modern upholstered furniture in the manner of Frank Lloyd Wright designs

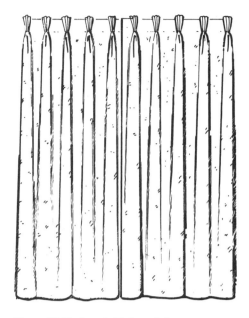

Figure 18.13 Organic Modern window treatment

glass or architectural framing elements. Other window treatments on occasion included wooden shutters, metal blinds, and roller shades.

Rugs

Wright had a special interest in rugs and carpeting, and felt they were extremely important. Like the other furnishings in his buildings and houses, the carpets were custom-made. He incorporated bright accent colors—Frank Lloyd Wright red, blue, gold, or green—to set off the overall warm color scheme of each structure. Each carpet had an earthy solid background, small amounts of geometric pattern, and a linear border or medallions.

Wright used rugs as a substitute for walls in the definition of space, creating a room within a room. He also placed large rectangular rugs under expansive tabletops for emphasis. Carpets were a great way to give texture to the smooth concrete floors and to make the interiors softer, quieter, warmer, and more livable.

Organic Modern Today

Organic Modern has resurged in popularity and is a major style as part of the wider environmental movement. There is a keen interest in all things Frank Lloyd Wright. From his furniture designs to his motifs to his use of natural materials, particularly stone in an ashlar pattern, the Frank Lloyd Wright influence continues to be felt. Earthy background elements, interesting angular art glass, and heavily textured or unusual fabrics all have a place in today's interiors.

Upholstery and drapery textiles, accent fabrics, and custom and stock area rugs and wallcoverings are all materials used for classic Frank Lloyd Wright patterns and colors.

Neutral hues with accents of intense orange, green, or gold are appealing and popular color directions. Cherokee red is a color of passion and often used as an accent in Organic Modern interiors. Many loyal followers, from architectural graduates of Taliesin West, Wright's Phoenix, AZ, school of architecture, to countless aficionados, continue to keep the principles of Organic Modern alive. Its design virtues are timeless.

a.

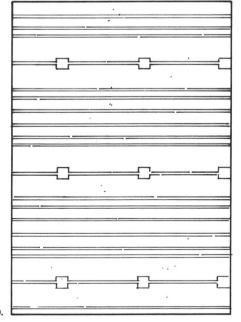

b.

Figure 18.14 a, b Organic Modern rugs/carpets

Period Overview

Art Deco dates from 1918 to 1945; its name derives from the Paris exposition of 1925, "l'Exposition Internationale des Arts Décoratifs et Industriels Modernes." Art Deco represents the rich development of decorative motifs inspired by nature, history, and the machine.

Two major influences in forming Art Deco were the lavish Beaux Arts historical styles and the sleek, pared-back International Modern. The Beaux Arts Paris designers covered every available surface with stylized flowers and fruit, whereas International Modern designers chose purity of line uncluttered by decoration. Designers found inspiration for design and aesthetics from the machine as well, inspired by architect Le Corbusier's dictum, "A house is a machine for living in." The battle of detail versus function was often energetic, yet many times the result was a marvelous combination of the two styles. The idea of total design was increasing in popularity, and every detail was worthy of the designer's attention.

The world wars and unstable economic times seemed to constrain the designs of Art Deco, although toward the beginning of the period, members of the new moneyed class, the nouveau riche, were willing to spend vast sums on their homes. Furniture was at the height of luxury; rare woods were used, as were other costly materials such as ebony, morocco leather, and sharkskin. The upper middle classes seemed preoccupied with taste and elegance. This was the time when those of the new profession called *interior design* were given opportunities to explore new ideas and establish a name for themselves. Through the economic depression of the 1930s, less emphasis was placed on the luxurious style and more on cheaper mass-produced items as the functional aesthetic that emanated from the Bauhaus became more influential. The Bauhaus designers proclaimed that all interior products should be simple, functional, well designed, and affordable within the reach of everyone.

Textiles: Color, Motif, and Texture

Colors

The colors used during the 1920s were earthy, grayed, muted, and soft in appearance. Toned-down interior design colors were livable. The most popular colors were red-violet mauve, peach, gray-green, brown, rust, black, white, gray, and beige. Highlights of silver and gold gave sheen and sophistication to color application.

a.

b.

c.

Figure 18.15a–z Art Deco textile motifs. **a** Egyptian lotus; **b** flowers and lightning bolts; **c** sunburst and cranes in Chinese influence

Figure 18.15d–g sleek haute couture (women's fashions; h sunburst; i circular clouds; j machine/architecture; k angular abstract; j exotic animals; m floral motif

n.

o.

p.

q.

r.

s.

t.

u.

v.

Figure 18.15n–p fashion and floral motifs; **q–r** sunbursts, gazelle; **s** speeding automobiles; **t** abstract floral or geometric; **v** linear movement; **w** gazelles and foliage; **x** ziggurat forms; **y–z** machine shapes

w.

x.

y.

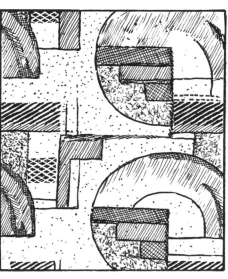

z.

Bright colors were seen in smaller quantities, reflecting the underlying "anything goes" philosophy of the Prohibition era. Accents included clear turquoise, sunshine yellow, tangerine orange, purple, and ruby red. The brilliant accent colors of the 1930s were inspired by Diaghilev's Ballets Russes of 1909, when his Russian dance company brought an explosion of color and boldness of design to the stage — colors that were brilliant if not garish. Inspiration also was found in colors of the jungle, as exotic ports of call became "must-see" places for the new traveling class of nouveaux riches.

Motifs

Fabrics during the Art Deco period were sleek and stylish. Designers were influenced by the simple geometric designs of pyramids; Aztec architecture and Egyptian images spawned patterns that were pyramidal, with stepped ziggurat sides. Travel and speed (automobiles could move at 30 mph) created new excitement to which designers responded eagerly, depicting it with stylized motifs of streamlined ocean liners and racing cars trailing clouds of smoke or dust. Patterns incorporated animals such as gazelles and lizards that symbolized quick movements. Other popular fabric motifs included sunbursts, lightning flashes, circular clouds, flowers, stylized fruit, and the wood-block prints that found fame during the 1920s.

Other influences were the Jazz Age, the glamorous cinema, the fashion world, the new industrial age, and other aspects of modern society. The aesthetics of machinery and pure geometry were the decorative fads of the 1930s, bringing in Fauvism, Cubism, and futurism as well.

Textures

Textures included woven textiles such as brocade, smooth velvet, and sheer fabrics. Plain satin was used to emphasize the prevalent futuristic theme. Hand-worked embroidered textiles and wallcoverings also found a place as stylish and tasteful touches.

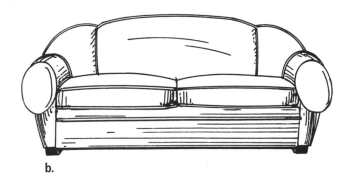

a.

b.

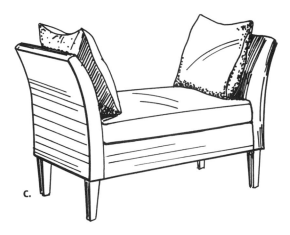

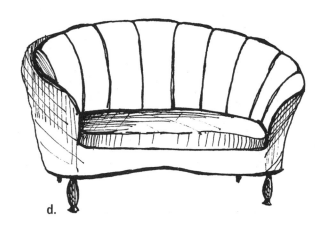

c.

d.

Figure 18.16a–k Art Deco upholstered furniture
a, c benches; **b, d** rounded sofas; **e, f** daybeds; **g** scroll-back side chair; **h** ziggurat-back arm chair; **i–k** round-back arm chairs

Interior designers frequently used pattern-on-pattern repetition in their residential and commercial design, and then found that harmonizing color and texture added a greater appeal. Art Deco fabric and furniture textures were sleek, smooth, polished, and shiny. The goal of the interior designer was to match the fabrics, furniture, and textiles, creating a harmonious interior atmosphere.

Upholstered Furniture

During the Art Deco period, furniture proportions changed. Armchairs became longer, deeper, and stood on lower legs. Sofa backs were heightened, and seats were lowered. Dining room chairs had small, rounded backs, which made for more convenience in serving the diners. Shapes of furniture varied from interior to interior, but as a general rule they were supple, gentle, and curved—made not only for the pleasure of the eye but also for comfort.

All surfaces exhibited special effects, either smooth or decorated. Designers experimented with finishes, colors, and fabrics. Furniture was often painted in popular colors

such as gray, silver, and gold. Fabric patterns were paired with furniture styles of similar lines, such as Modern furniture upholstered in geometric patterned fabrics.

As the period progressed, the furniture continued to evolve, becoming heavier and more geometric. Legs became more solid, and ornamentation tended to be less flowery or disappeared altogether. The functional Art Deco furniture of the 1930s began to mesh with the streamlined style dictated by the rising generation of American industrial designers.

Beds

The early Art Deco style is also known as the boudoir style due to its emphasis on rich detail and intimacy. The taste for anything Asian led to a style of cushions for low divans and daybeds, with long silk tassels and textiles of mixed patterns and vivid colors. Like other furniture fashioned during the Art Deco period, the beds were built low to the ground, and the fabrics used were soft, luxurious, and often had a shiny satin finish. Bolsters and smooth pillows, few in number, were fashionable late in the period.

Figure 18.17 a, b Art Deco beds

Window Treatments

The Art Deco window treatments of the early 1920s were similar to those of the Victorian era. Curtains were made of lace panels that hung straight, tiered, or crisscrossed, and they faced the room when used alone. Lace was used as an undertreatment as the fabric faced outward. Over-draperies were fuller and occasionally lavish, with Austrian curtains, tied-back drapes, and fancy valances. On the other hand, drapery and curtain rods became more functional; decorative rods often reflected the lines of Art Deco. Motifs were sleek, sophisticated, and elongated. High tie-back draperies resembled women's flowing evening gowns.

The Bauhaus philosophy was seen almost everywhere. Architects used glass extensively and left the windows exposed and untreated. Stained glass and art glass became more popular. Plain fabrics on Venetian blinds were used where the Bauhaus or International style influenced the interior and where the need for privacy and light control superseded the desire for untreated glass

Rugs

Decorators during the Art Deco period regarded carpet as an essential part of the décor and often designed the rugs themselves and then matched the upholstery to it for a uniform look. Room-size and wall-to-wall carpets for domestic and public interiors were in high demand. Chinese Art Deco rugs were imported, and Navajo rugs were newly appreciated. Designers often re-created these distinctive patterns for specific settings and clientele.

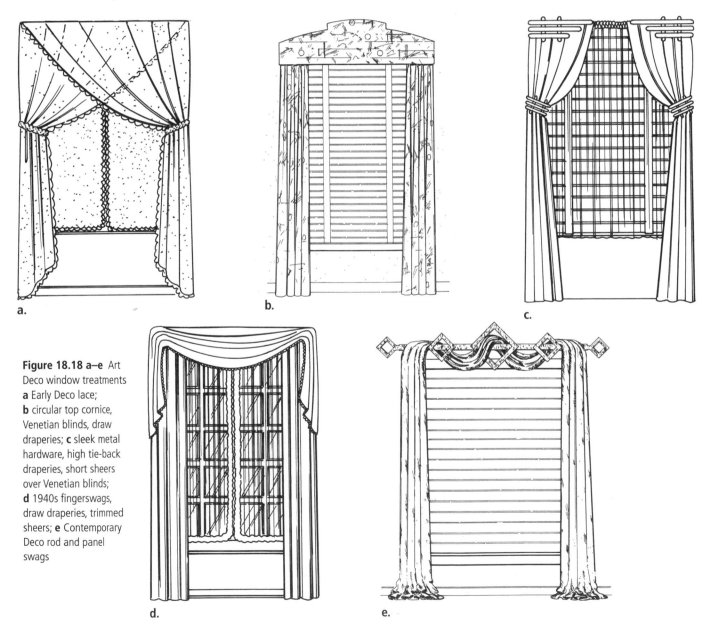

Figure 18.18 a–e Art Deco window treatments **a** Early Deco lace; **b** circular top cornice, Venetian blinds, draw draperies; **c** sleek metal hardware, high tie-back draperies, short sheers over Venetian blinds; **d** 1940s fingerswags, draw draperies, trimmed sheers; **e** Contemporary Deco rod and panel swags

Figure 18.19a–d Art Deco rugs/carpets

Motifs found in the rugs and carpeting were rolls, spirals, and stems in rhythmic abstract patterns, often based on African textiles. Many designers were influenced by the artwork of Cézanne and Picasso, so they created and used sophisticated carpets incorporating geometric, zigzag, skyscraper, animal, and other motifs in a way that created harmony in the setting.

Floral carpets were also used in various ways. Art Deco knotted carpets were covered in flowers, following a strong French tradition. The floral patterns of the students at the Martine Workshop contributed a new look, renewing the total range of colors as well as free and youthful patterns. Styles based on Russian and Asian folklore were successfully interpreted and adapted to the French temperament.

Manufacturers gave new life to their production by turning to classical-contemporary artists for their designs. Area

rugs were one-of-a-kind designer rugs mass-produced in the more broadly appealing motifs, generally in a deep wool pile.

Art Deco Today

Designers today are inspired by the elegance of Art Deco style. The phrase *luxurious minimalist* evokes the feeling of the Modern rooms of the 1920s and 1930s. Rooms are made sensuous with fabrics and other materials but retain a formal, sleek appearance. Designers today repeat the use of design details and Art Deco motifs along with materials such as satinwood paneling, mother-of-pearl accents, iridescent fabrics and wallcoverings, satin, and other smooth fabrics. All designs are flawlessly assembled and meticulously detailed to imitate original Art Deco styling.

MIDCENTURY/INTERNATIONAL MODERN

Period Overview

The Midcentury/International Modern style dates from 1932 to the present. Major influences included the De Stijl movement, the Bauhaus and American architects and designers, Le Corbusier, and Scandinavian Modern style.

In the Netherlands, artist Piet Mondrian's studies of Cubism influenced the development of the De Stijl movement. Bright primary and secondary colors on separate walls were outlined in black in cubistic structural architecture. The same concept was utilized by Gerrit Rietveld in his Red/Blue chair.

The Bauhaus, a design school that existed from 1919 to 1933 in Weimar and then Dessau, Germany, was the main forerunner of the Modern design of the post–World War II era. The Bauhaus brought together architects, furniture designers, artists, and craftspersons as faculty to learn, teach, and invent ways to design for the machine and to use man-made and natural materials in harmony. Excellent, affordable design was the goal—a direct reaction to the poor mass production of the Victorian era. The Bauhaus philosophy incorporated Japanese traditionalism as uncluttered minimalism.

Le Corbusier and Bauhaus faculty were among the first to incorporate the steel of World War I in furniture design; they believed metal was styleless, expected not to express any particular style beyond its purpose and construction. Marcel Breuer, a Bauhaus student and, later, head of its furniture department, said, "The appearance of objects depends upon the different functions they have. Since they satisfy our demands individually and do not clash with each other, they produce collectively our style. They are unified as a whole through the fulfillment of their individual tasks." In the eyes of the Bauhaus, ornamentation could not exist on modern furniture because to the designer/builder, ornamentation is squandered work and material; therefore, it is also squandered capital. Bauhaus architects and furniture designers who came to the United States during World War II included Marcel Breuer, Walter Gropius, and Ludwig Mies van der Rohe. These men influenced the design of the glass-and-steel, curtainwall-construction architectural skylines of American cities and were proponents of the less-is-more philosophy. Artists Josef Albers, Johannes Itten, Paul Klee, Wassily Kandinsky, and fabric artisan Annie Albers also came to the United States, taught at universities, and influenced color and interior design of the Midcentury/International Modern era.

Figure 18.20 Midcentury Modern interior

Figure 18.21 Scandinavian Modern interior

American architects and designers Charles and Ray Eames, Philip Johnson, Richard Meyer, and Harry Bertoia all believed that the practicality of design should be considered before the form. Swiss-born French architect Le Corbusier's dictum (noted above), "a house is a machine for living in," influenced the thinking of post–World War II Americans. Frank Lloyd Wright also accomplished buildings in the International Modern style—the Guggenheim Museum in New York and Fallingwater in Bear Run, Pennsylvania.

The Scandinavian Modern style flourished during this period and had a strong influence on the International Modern style. Scandinavians have a tradition of fine craftsmanship in practicality as well as beauty of design. The Scandinavian countries (Denmark, Norway, Sweden, and Finland) combined their folk craft's hands-on traditions with the capabilities of the machine to create a clean, sculptural, and fully exposed construction design statement. Some noteworthy Scandinavian architects or designers include Eero Saarinen, Alvar Aalto, Gunnar Asplund, Finn Juhl, Arne Jacobson, and Hans Wegner.

Midcentury Modern architecture consisted of hard surfaces, straight, sleek lines, and interesting angles and shapes. It brought together the craftsmanship of the Scandinavian Modern style, the simplicity of Japanese design, the technology of the Bauhaus, and modern building materials such as reinforced concrete, steel framing, expansive, flawless float glass, and natural stone and wood. It was simple, practical, and functional, using natural and manufactured materials together in harmony.

Textiles: Color, Motif, and Texture

Colors

Two color directions typified Midcentury. One was an achromatic background of natural slate, concrete, plain white stucco walls, and glass with black leather. In this direction, the colors were only small accents, or they were brought indoors through visually connecting windows. The second direction involved natural materials in a warmer vein, including much wood in architecture and furniture and expressive, fresh, almost childlike graphic designs in brilliant or happy colors. See the end of this chapter for a more complete discussion of twentieth-century colors.

Motifs

Motifs were kept to a minimum in Midcentury/International Modern. The style used abstract geometric designs affected by Piet Mondrian's studies of Cubism. In less formal spaces such as bedrooms, Scandinavian motifs included large, lively colored geometric shapes or field flowers, ocean waves, boats, animals, and other shapes and designs from nature.

Designs of the period were also affected by the works of artists in the Bauhaus school—for example, Josef Albers's "Homage to the Square" series of juxtaposed studies in simultaneous contrast and Paul Klee's pastel watercolor paintings. Notable Midcentury American designer Alexander Girard created abstract versions of folk art and geometric configurations.

Textures

Textiles of the International Modern style consisted of materials from nature and man-made materials used in harmony. Natural materials included textiles such as leather, cotton, and wool. New durable and versatile man-made materials were acrylic, nylon, vinyl, and polyester. Modern textiles offered many variations in weave, dye, pattern, and weight. The unique texture of leather, the loose feel of casement fabrics, hand-woven fabrics, smooth-felted broadcloth, and the design and texture of needle-constructed "architectural lace" or burnout sheers are examples.

Upholstered Furniture

Scandinavian furniture is known for its excellent craftsmanship and structure as well as its simple beauty and comfort, and has always had a traditional handcrafted touch. Designers such as Wegner, Juhl, and Saarinen, demonstrating this craftsmanship, used bent and shaped plywood and other types of wood to produce beautifully crafted furniture.

While much furniture of the International Modern period demonstrates the Scandinavian handcrafted look, designers such as Breuer and Mies Van der Rohe used steel in their furniture, in the tradition of the Bauhaus. Furniture was functional; materials were durable, expressing function as well as handsome design. New furniture forms were made possible by stronger materials—steel, plywood, and bentwood—which resulted in cantilevered construction and plastic vacuformed shapes. Thus, furniture became art, created to be scrutinized and admired not so much for its comfort as for its genius form and design and triumphal combination of natural and man-made materials.

Leather, vinyl, cotton, wool, caning, and man-made fibers such as nylon, olefin, and polyester were most commonly used for upholstered furniture. Plastic was a new material used in formed furniture construction. Foam was also introduced as upholstery cushioning during this period, which resulted in new forms never before possible. Furniture of the period is practical, functional, often comfortable, and simple.

The Barcelona chair (1929) was designed by Mies van der Rohe. It had chrome-plated steel bars and leather upholstery, and had a huge impact on Modern design. Marcel Breuer's chair (1928) showed the simplicity of the Interna-

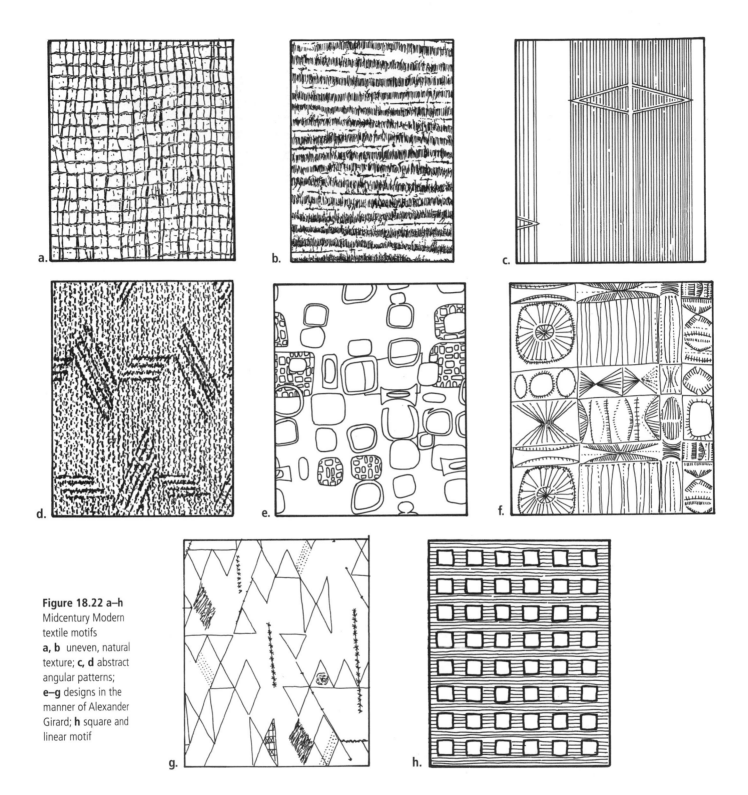

Figure 18.22 a–h
Midcentury Modern textile motifs
a, b uneven, natural texture; **c, d** abstract angular patterns; **e–g** designs in the manner of Alexander Girard; **h** square and linear motif

tional Modern style. It was made of chrome-plated steel tube, wood, and cane. The chair designed by Alvar Aalto (1934) was made of molded and bent birch plywood. The dining chair Charles Eames contrived (1946) was the first great post–World War II chair. It used molded plywood for the seat and metal rods for the frame. It was followed by Hans Wegner's armchair (1949), constructed of oak, teak, and cane. The plastic-coated Tulip chair of Eero Saarinen (1957) is still

seen today. The Grand Confort, also by Le Corbusier (1928), is another famous piece with large cushions and chromium-nickel-plated tubular steel. The armless Barcelona group was contrived by Mies van der Rohe (1931).

The T chair was produced by Katavolos (1953). The side chair was by Harry Bertoia (1951). Bruno Mathsson's lounge chair (1940) was made of laminated bent birch plywood and used fiber webbing form-fitted to human anthropometrics.

Figure 18.23 a–i Midcentury Modern upholstered furniture
a the Eames lounge chair and ottoman; **b** Le Corbusier's grand
comfort sofa; **c** Harry Bertoia's side chair; **d** Mies van der Rohe's
Barcelona chair; **e, i** Midcentury sofas; **h** chaise inspired by works
of Le Corbusier and Mathsson; **f, g** sculptural chair forms

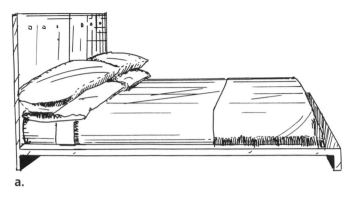

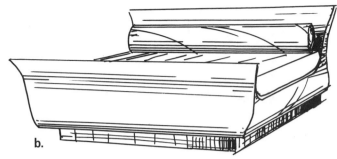

Figure 18.24 a, b Midcentury Modern beds

Beds

Beds were simple and unadorned furniture items made from natural wood, metal, or, reflecting the Japanese influence, painted black. Headboards and footboards were structural in design, although some had great style and unique, sleek shapes. Platform beds came into style late in this period.

Bedding was simple—coverlets without dust ruffles or bed skirts exposed the legs of handsome beds or made the beds appear to float when the legs were very thin. Fitted coverlets, sometimes quilted, gave a neat and trim look to bedding. Round bolsters and square pillows emphasized geometric forms. The bolster was tucked in and the sleeping pillows kept out of sight in closets during the day. Bedspreads, when used, took a tailored approach, such as a fitted bedspread with a split corner and a flap or tab gusset beneath.

Little pattern was seen on bedding, although when the bed became a focal point, contemporary fabrics in printed or woven abstract designs were appealing. Quilting was also used sparingly. In patternless fabrics, the quilting designs were often large squares.

Window Treatments

Many Midcentury/International architects at first insisted that International-style buildings not have any window treatment, as they felt fabric would detract from the pristine quality of the architecture. They did not, however, consider the problems that arose from large expanses of glass, which admitted too much heat, sunshine, brightness, and accompanying glare. At night, occupants felt insecure and vulnerable; the windows became black voids, and the people within lived or worked in fishbowls. Because fabric was required to make these rooms livable, glass walls became known as curtainwall construction. Large plate-glass windows draped

with semisheer fabric, batiste, architectural lace draperies, or lightweight casement fabric softened the interior but still allowed ample light to enter. These fabrics protected against ultraviolet and heat damage, diffused sunlight, and provided daytime privacy. Early window treatments were pleated and installed on conventional traverse rods.

The need for nighttime privacy was met as the decades progressed with the development of alternative window treatments, including horizontal 1- or 2-inch blinds, vertical blinds or louvers, and pleated and cellular shades. The micro-mini-blind, wood slat blind, vertical louver, woven-wood shade, pleated shade, and plantation shutter were developed during the 1970s and 1980s and are all appropriate for an International Modern interior. Alternative treatments are practical, efficient, and durable. They provide light and glare control, some temperature control, and privacy both day and night while assuring a clean, precise appearance of straight lines and light colors.

Rugs

Carpeting and rugs used during this period were originally plain broadloom area rugs with little or no pattern and color in neutral hues. As the style developed and pristine interiors were found to be too stark and unfriendly, a greater variety of rugs was used. Lively folk rugs in bright hues and abstract design became geometric focal points. These included dhurries, kilims, Navajo rugs, and rugs from Africa and South America. Pile rugs, such as mantas from Spain, and Caucasian Oriental rugs as well as the Scandinavian rya rug were deemed fashionable and used in a somewhat formal context. Some Midcentury/International Modern interiors featured the complex and fluid designs of Persian Oriental rugs and a wide variety of designer rugs. All of these rugs contrasted with the starkness of the interior and became works of art.

Figure 18.25 a–h Midcentury Modern window treatments
a, b vertical louvers; **c** one-inch mini-blinds; **d** pleated or cellular shade; **e** shirred side draperies with blind or shade; **f** casement draperies; **g** one-way pinch pleat draperies; **h** flat sliding panels in translucent fabric

Figure 18.26 a–b Midcentury Modern rugs/carpets
a Navajo folk rug; **b** designer rug

Midcentury Modern Style Today

Midcentury/International Modern waned in popularity during the 1980s, but in the early 1990s a resurrection of the style began with the mainstreaming of computer technology into the workspace and homes of the American public. Clean lines and lighter-weight Midcentury/International-style furnishings fit perfectly with the technology era and continue to do so today. Although the style is less stark and more livable in terms of fabric and accessories, many of the furnishing components are fairly true to their sources. Innovation continues to be a hallmark, where the form-follows-function ideal combines with environmental responsibility and continuous advancements in technology.

RETRO MODERN

Period Overview

Retro design, a revisitation of influences from the 1930s to the 1970s, is a compilation of Modern styles, particularly the Midcentury/International Modern and Art Deco styles, but with a twist: Elements are sophisticated and fun at the same time. Retro Modern has gained a substantial following. At the beginning of the twenty-first century, many took a keen interest in turning to history for a sense of nostalgia, and for the younger generation, the 1950s was a long time ago.

Retro prides itself on uncomplicated, simple, light furniture with a long and low emphasis. It is a compilation of many styles, mainly Scandinavian, International Modern,

Bauhaus applied to the postwar era, and Japanese. The specific period for Retro Modern includes two decades, the 1950s and 1960s, although many contemporary designs adapt these styles and are thoroughly Retro. Scandinavian designers started fresh, without the heavy Victorian influences that affected the rest of Europe and America; hence, the Scandinavian version of functionalism came in a more comfortable manner, being minimal, unadorned, and bright. World War II helped Scandinavian design because it created a shortage of building materials, forcing innovation.

World War II also helped open design possibilities for America's Modern form. After the war, the economy rose, and more people bought houses and became interested in the new domestic modern conveniences. The war also spurred the development of new materials and manufactured fibers and color technology. In 1964, at the New York World's Fair, the United States caught its first glimpse. Although still functional and simple, furniture was also made of fine woods, materials, and finishes using curves instead of the straight lines of International-style box shapes. During this exposition, the wood in furniture was finished blonde, usually hand-rubbed to a high finish, with hardware in materials or finishes such as wrought iron, copper, and chrome.

Today's Retro is not as dogma-ridden as the earlier styles, as it originally was not as concerned with reviving the notion of form following function as it is with reviving the free spirit of the mid-twentieth century, the era that gave us hula hoops, suburbs, television, rock and roll, Disneyland, and the baby boomers. The furniture styles of the 1950s, adapted for the 1990s, are mostly dominating Retro, and the color schemes of the 1960s prevail in Retro textiles.

Textiles: Color, Pattern, and Texture

Retro designers chose mainly natural fibers to show raw texture. Chenille and velour were popular once again, as have wild silk, linen, coarse wool, leather, suede, and leopard and zebra prints.

Colors

During the 1950s, color was still suffering from the Bauhausian notion that only primary colors, black, and white could be used to make an environment aesthetically pleasing. However, technology was providing advancements for color through the development of synthetic dyes and fibers such as Dacron polyester, which left a perfect opening for the 1960s to utilize. As the population watched movies in the magic of Technicolor, the younger generation sought a new enlightenment through hallucinatory drugs, producing a more uncommon palette of wild colors in wild patterns that were influenced by the brilliant silks of India and Southeast Asia.

Most of these colors were not used in large quantity but rather as accents or pools of color on a neutral background.

Color schemes were often related or contrasting. An office in New York decorated in 1960 boasted a walnut ceiling panel, moss green carpet, white walls, flame leather-covered armchairs, and a sofa in gold yellow, orange, and brown striped fabric. During the 1960s, many colors were often combined into a single upholstery fabric or into one space. This was before color psychology became a topic of study, so authentic 1960s colors are often judged harshly in light of contemporary color understanding.

Motifs

Retro motifs become more architectural, geometric, and stylized. Lines were silhouetted against mass or solid color. In the 1950s, patterns were abundant. Although they were unsophisticated by contemporary standards, those 1950s patterns often captured a free spirit of new design. In the 1960s, pattern was sometimes considered distracting and

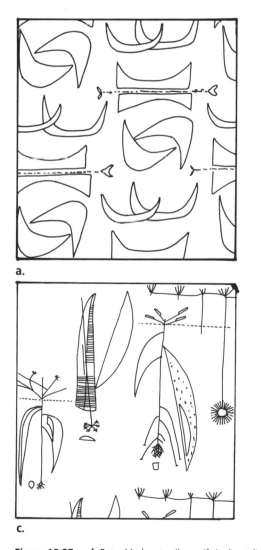

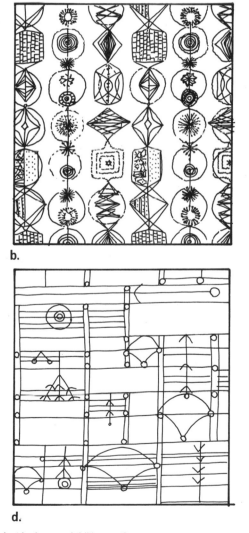

Figure 18.27 a–d Retro Modern textile motifs in the styling of Alexander Girard with abstract childlike motifs

Figure 18.28a–j Retro Modern upholstered furniture inspired by Midcentury and Art Deco designs

often gave way to solid colors. This carried over well to Retro design because the solid colors give a cleaner look to the furniture or room. Visual interest is derived from the texture in the fabric. Patterns are more abundant in accents such as pillows and area rugs, or perhaps an occasional chair. For example, a sofa may be of a solid upholstery fabric and accent pillows of many colored solids, thus creating the pattern. Alternatively, the pillows may be covered in lively colors and designs, either mixed with solid contrasting pillows or blatantly disharmonious and thereby disarmingly delightful, vigorous patterns in bright colors.

Upholstered Furniture

Retro furniture is lightweight and light in scale, with tapering lines. Gone are the days of excessive ornamentation, fabric, and cushions. Retro goes back to the basics with versatile, uncomplicated, yet fluid furniture. Retro furniture prefers the long and low emphasis especially seen in Japanese homes.

Sofas and armchairs seem to float above the floor. Beneath the seat are thin peg legs made of wood or tubular steel or other metal. Furniture once again begins to take on the look of artwork or fine sculpture. If the sofa or chair is covered in a solid-color fabric, the welting may or may not be of a slightly contrasting color for visual interest. Dining room chairs have as little upholstery as possible, concentrating instead on fine craftsmanship. The lightly scaled Danish Modern blonde wood is decidedly Retro; beauty is created through the juxtaposition of the grains, which are hand-rubbed for a naturally rich finish. Retro furniture is sculptural, with sleek and sensuous curves, whether in a sofa, kidney coffee table, or dresser. Casters added to tables and dressers for movability are a Scandinavian influence.

Beds

Retro beds are simple, often placed on a low platform made of wood, theoretically eliminating the need for a box spring. Therefore, the bed can be made to appear even lower, having only the mattress. The headboard is usually made of the same wood as the platform, with little carving, if any. Minimalistic sleigh beds, updated to fit Modern requirements, can have a head and footboard, usually in a light wood. Retro beds also can have a head and footboard, sometimes upholstered. Corners may be rounded, square, or flared outward, reflecting the influence of Japanese architecture. Bedding is solid textiles in clean lines. Accent pillows are simple squares or curves and may soften the angular beds. Bolsters or neck pillows may be the only accent or used in addition to other pillows. Coverlets or short bedspreads are preferred, often with no bed skirt.

Window Treatments

Early Retro interiors of the 1990s left structural window architectural detail exposed. However, homeowners and non-residential users required privacy and safety. Shoji screens, an alternative window treatment, indicate the Japanese influence. Other alternative treatments that work well for Retro design are mini-blinds, vertical blinds (2-inch wood or metal slats), woven-wood or bamboo roll-ups, or Roman shades. In soft treatments, pinch-pleated draperies dominated the homes of the 1950s and 1960s. Tab curtains also can be used because of their simple lines and tailored appearance.

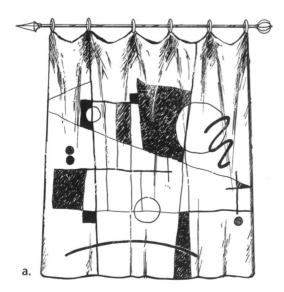

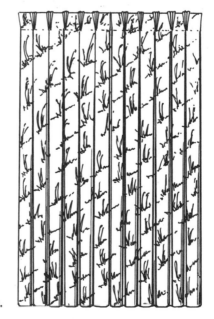

Figure 18.29a–b Retro Modern window treatments

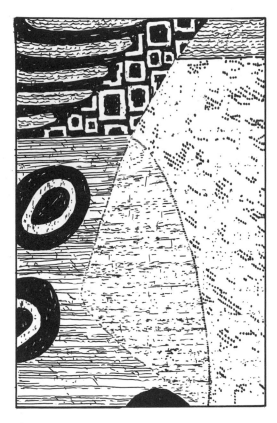

Figure 18.30 Retro rug/carpet

Rugs

Area rugs work best on hard flooring such as wood, stone, or tile. Rug types include Scandinavian rya (deep-pile shag), rollikan (flat tapestry), flossa (thin shag), and flocatti (goat hair), and folk rugs, including dhurrie, kilim, and Navajo rugs. Berber carpet and other dense but low-pile carpeting are good choices, as are tatami mats, sisal rugs, and other natural fiber rugs. The floor covering is used as an accent for the Retro room, and sometimes is highly colorful and abstract. Real or faux zebra rugs as well as custom carpets are good selections. Modular carpet tiles are the perfect Retro floor selection, as the colors and shapes can be arranged to make graphic statements, neutral or bold.

Retro Style Today

Retro is likely to stay in fashion for some time to come, as it suits the techno-generation, whose work is largely computer-based; the simple lines and uncomplicated forms coupled with whimsical patterns and colors are compatible with the new designs that appear daily. Retro still utilizes stimulating colors, although in smaller quantities and with more careful and tasteful coordination than in the 1950s and 1960s.

MODERN COLORS AND TRENDS BY DECADE

As the twentieth century saw more change in style and industrial and technological development than any other time in human history, a further look into influences that particularly affected color is appropriate here. During this wide expanse of Modern style, American colors can be effectively examined by decade, as follows.

The 1940s

The United States was cut off from European influence during World War II. Hence, many interiors were drab and even featured army green. Whites, grays, and dark, dull blues and reds were also seen in interiors. Art Deco colors also influenced 1940s interiors. To keep domestic morale high, designers turned to Latin American colors, which were warm and bright—hot pink, fuschia, bright parrot green, sunshine yellow, warm red, clear blue.

The 1950s

The 1950s witnessed several simultaneous color directions. The purist International Modern colors were often achromatic, meaning without color. As upholstery, black, white, gray, and natural brown leathers were often preferred. Naturally occurring neutrals were used, such as gray stone, steel gray, slate, brick, wood brown, and clay tile. Accents of intense colors, such as a brilliant red, clear yellow, or turquoise blue, were used in some interiors. Many colors that became part of the interior were from the exterior. Expanses of plate glass framed landscapes that became, as it were, visual art and color.

Midcentury Scandinavian colors, influenced by the Danish Modern furniture craze, included nature as seen in the blues and greens of sky, ocean, meadows, and forests. Scandinavian designers introduced blues and greens together, which first surprised and then delighted Americans in the 1950s and 1960s. Other colors in this style are the more vivid flower colors, used as accents; these include clear yellow, pink, red, green, and turquoise.

Post–World War II optimism was reflected in a wealth of "new" colors, which varied from dull to intense. Rose colors included a grayed, medium-value pink, rose beige, sandstone (pinkish beige), flesh, rose (a dirty, dull pink), peach, warm yellow (pinkish yellow), and medium coral (dull pink). Light blue-green, medium blue-green, medium blue-teal, medium green, light green, light jade green, light aquamarine, medium-warm gray, light gray, and nutria (pinkish brown) composed a palette that offered little contrast in value. This palette, although bland by contemporary standards, was intended to create calming, Modern interiors.

Some vivid colors were introduced and used with little real sophistication; they bore names such as flame red (coral), chartreuse (bright yellow-green), sulfur yellow, avocado (bright, browned green), fern green (medium-value avocado), Bristol blue (bright turquoise), hyacinth (medium violet), vermilion (dark coral), flamingo (medium coral), melon (light coral), and sunset orange (bright pinkish orange). These colors laid the foundation for the next two decades of experimentation with bright colors as applied to the new manufactured fibers, such as polyester.

The 1960s

The 1960s witnessed a dramatic increase in color brightness and purity for larger areas such as sofas and beds, carpeting, draperies, and wallcoverings. Vibrant colors such as electric blue, fire-engine orange, shocking pink, vibrant yellow, and Spanish red edged and contrasted with black. All these colors bordered on psychedelic intensity and were seen in broadloom carpeting, loose-weave casement draperies, and upholstery. Influences came from India, Spain, and the broader Mediterranean and were frequently expressed with little restraint.

The 1970s

The 1970s brought new color and design directions to interiors. One was the back-to-nature trend, which brought to the world's attention the necessity of protecting, preserving, and cleaning up the environment. One offshoot of this larger trend was the hippie movement, wherein materialistic decadence was overthrown for a life of "voluntary simplicity." Colors became bland—beiges by the boatload, browns, and natural materials, including beads and macramé. At the same time, psychedelic colors inspired by India were used as accents—brilliant purple, electric blue, shocking pink, sunshine yellow, and lime green.

Another 1970s direction was the result of the U.S. bicentennial celebration in 1976, when America rediscovered formal traditional and Colonial colors and furnishings. On the heels of the psychedelic colors, the red, white, and blue patriotic schemes were far too vivid for livability. As the decade progressed, these colors became more authentic, lovely, and livable, and produced many interiors that were a flattering copy or adaptation of the estates and museum homes of the eighteenth and nineteenth centuries.

Also during the 1970s, the profound influence of Spanish or Mediterranean design developed into a generous use of harvest gold and avocado green, applied to carpets, appliances, wallcoverings, draperies, and bedding as well as countertops and plumbing fixtures. Toreador red became wall-to-wall carpeting and bedspreads, and harsh black and dark wood accents gave drama to this style of color application. Normalization of relations with mainland China brought down long-standing trade barriers and introduced the American public to the rich family of Chinese textile colors, including peacock blue (vivid greenish blue), orchid violet, chrysanthemum gold, peony pink, Ming dynasty blue and white, and jade green (light to dark creamy greens). These were used as fashion accents and established a more authentic sophistication.

The 1980s, 1990s, and Early Twenty-first Century

This twenty-five-year span has many elements in common. It was and still is an era of heavy building of office space. The demand for nonresidential textile products has steadily increased.

Beginning in the 1980s, the gray and dull pink or mauve palette, combined with toned-down and grayed colors, permeated the nonresidential market and affected home décor as well. Some said the United States was "mauved to death" during this time, and later in the 1980s it was "tealed to death" as Chinese peacock blue gave way to a plethora of teals in fabrics and interior applications.

Early in this span, the California influence of neutrals established the calming, natural, colorless interior. This trend has continued with variations of nature-inspired neutral interiors. Application of neutrals was also seen in the reinterpretation of Southwest colors during the 1980s and 1990s. The desert-inspired Santa Fe style produced a palette nearly devoid of real color, but applications of neutralized pastels were seen in all textile applications.

In 1981, the world was swept away with the fairy-tale wedding of England's Prince Charles to Lady Diana Spencer. This event charged an emotional foray into the world of Neotraditional design based on English drawing rooms and the English and American Georgian periods. The United States looked to European manors and fell in love with movies based on Victorian English novels. It became an era of interiors designed for luxury and softness and, often, romantic propriety. Traditional elegance was augmented in the Reagan White House years, when a lavish Beaux Arts California or Hollywood influence resulted in interiors that were full of rich color and lavish fabric applications. This began a flowering of many interior design textile applications.

Rooms were richly appointed with layered window treatments, lavish bedding, patterned wallcoverings, custom carpeting, and beautiful upholstery. Interior designers created signature fabrics, rugs, and licensed accessory items, and made their interiors a brand they could market to a high-end clientele. This trend, well established during the 1980s and 1990s, continues today.

American Country interiors during the 1980s and early 1990s varied from the authentically spare Colonial New England look toward an eventual Upscale Country style that blended comfort elements such as upholstery and carpeting, throws, and draperies with Shaker influence and darker, muted color palettes. Country blue and country red were two favorites, both warm and dull. Earthy darker greens and blackened colors carried over into the twenty-first century.

Victorian floral fabrics of the 1980s to mid-1990s presented a seemingly love-starved America with reason to dream. A host of pink, red, and violet fabrics on backgrounds of green foliage with tiny accents of yellow and orange or rust resulted in a profusion of florals applied to fabric and used in every conceivable application. During the late 1990s, this style faded and was replaced during the early years of the twenty-first century with Cottage style, a Victorian remake that allowed room for pre– and post–World War II cottages complete with Fiestaware colors: dull, lightened blue, red, green, and yellow, with accents of navy and cream.

Organic Modern was revived with the thirtieth celebration of Earth Day in 1992. This made Americans nostalgic for styles of the earlier decades, including a revival of all things Frank Lloyd Wright and the entire Arts and Crafts style. Colors revisited have been green-based and with yellow undertones—warm versions of earlier color palettes.

Retro Modern has taken on a life of its own as the New Modern style for the techie generation. Neutral and quiet or bright and bold, colors are custom-fitted to the occupants' lifestyle or workstyle preferences.

The steady increase in textile products has produced seemingly limitless color, pattern, and texture offerings. Many of these are the consequence of consumer demand and legislative incentives for both sustainability and ease of upkeep. As a result of new technology in the textiles industry, many interior designer professionals are placing contract or nonresidential products in the residential marketplace. This crossover or blurring of the lines between contemporary home and workplace brings color into the house that may have originated in a commercial context. Quiet, sophisticated color and rich midtones are often seen in homes, creating a professional interior appearance. Today much business is conducted from home, so homes may reflect a business persona. Colors for healing have found their way into both healthcare and home environments. Based in the calming green family, the emphasis is on promoting emotional and physical health and repair through muted colors.

COLOR FORECASTING AND MARKETING

The coordinating of in-style colors for the interior products industry is a critical service that benefits manufacturers, retailers, interior design professionals, and the public. Color Marketing Group (CMG), www.colormarketing.org, is perhaps the leader of color forecasting. Founded in 1962, CMG is a not-for-profit, international association of over 1,300 color designers whose profession involves the selection or specification of color in producing and marketing goods and services. CMG members exchange noncompetitive information on all phases of color marketing: color trends and combinations, design influences, merchandising and sales, and education and industry contacts. Textures and patterns are also affected by the research of CMG professionals.

Color designers who participate in Color Directions forecasting are knowledgeable about past and present trends and events. They have color psychology insight and understand the marketplace and the likely reaction of the consumer or user. These skills qualify CMG members to interpret, create, forecast, and select colors that will enhance the salability of manufactured products. This is a reason why a palette of colors can be seen in cross-merchandising, making possible textile coordination for all interior design applications.

Textile Maintenance

Textiles should be kept in a good state of repair, acceptable to all users, as close to the state of newness as possible, even after years of use and wear. Once a textile product is purchased and installed, the responsibility to maintain textiles falls on the new owner(s). Many textile companies issue disclaimers stating strict allowance policies for replacement of textiles, and these are usually only in the case of new flawed textiles. Unless tested and certified with a guarantee, it is customary for textile jobbers or distributors to **not** guarantee against loss of fabric durability due to wear and use, fading, deterioration from heat/UV light, or changes due to atmospheric (gas) fading. Often, it is the type of use and maintenance or lack of maintenance that largely determine durability. It behooves any design professional to encourage good textile maintenance by educating the owner about upkeep. Whether nonresidential or residential, the reasons for good maintenance are similar:

1. A well-maintained environment gives users pride in their surroundings, which helps to produce good attitudes and improves employee or occupant productivity.
2. Good maintenance increases the lifespan of fabrics; they last longer and replacement costs are thereby reduced.
3. Keeping textiles in good repair may be a safety measure. Clean and relatively smooth surfaces are less likely to cause accidents and to catch on fire.
4. Well-maintained interiors make a statement to others, including visitors and clientele about the values and reliability of the owners or the business.

The first rule of upkeep is to keep the textile clean. Soiling from any source, if allowed to stay on the surface, will eventually penetrate and may become embedded, particularly if the textile has been given a soil repellent finish.

These types of finishes hold the spot on the surface for a time, making clean-up easier. However, with wear and use, this thin coating can crack and break, allowing the soil to penetrate. The finish then acts as a barrier, locking the soil into the fabric. Spots are then extremely difficult, sometimes impossible to remove completely. Upholstery fabrics treated by the Crypton, which then become Crypton Super Fabrics prevent moisture, bacteria and stains from entering fibers, so that foreign substances can be easily removed from the fiber's pores and most stains can be wiped away. Moisture does not penetrate through to cushion material preventing microbal bacteria growth inside upholstered furniture.

Horizontal applications—carpets and upholstery are most vulnerable to soiling, augmented with by walking and sitting that tends to push soiling further into the textile. Carpets, for example, should be regularly vacuumed to prevent dirt, grit, sand or minute gravel from working its way to the base of the carpet. Abrasion from walking vibrations can saw-off the yarns at their base. Upholstery, linens and fabric accessories kept fresh, clean and in good order will be more appealing, sanitary, and long-lived. Draperies and wall treatments are subject to dust and air-borne impurities that can become embedded if not kept vacuumed regularly and cleaned when necessary.

CLEANLINESS IN THE INTERIOR ENVIRONMENT

Although many fabrics are surprisingly resistant to soiling and wear, all fabrics do require some upkeep. It requires no more effort than cleaning only when it becomes apparent that the textile is dirty. Keeping textiles clean may also decrease the frequency of major or professional cleaning efforts.

In general, textiles can be kept in a state of good repair in two ways: by being a part of clean, efficient working and gracious living environments, and by proper cleaning. Clean environments include a lack of air-borne impurities such as smoke, grease, dust or other pollutants. It also means that users are instructed in clean behaviors such as eating at a table or removing dirty shoes. Spills should be immediately blotted, wiped up, or scraped off and spot-cleaned where necessary. Crumbs or dry dirt should be quickly brushed off and swept up or vacuumed. These simple procedures will eliminate the need for more extensive deep cleaning later on. Empowering individuals to live or work in a clean way and to be responsible for their own messes is a key to fostering good human relationships as well. It may be said that the way people behave impacts the interior environment and the state of an interior environment impacts behavior.

Professional Cleaning Services

At what point should the services of a professional be contracted? The answer is two-fold:

1. In residential settings, only when necessary. By removing dirt and spots immediately, a major cleaning should be needed infrequently. Repeated major cleaning can weaken fibers and loosen yarn twists and fabric constructions when the cleaning is vigorous and solvents or detergents are strong. It will also remove and soil repellent and anti-static finishes (although some can be reapplied).

2. In nonresidential settings an option may be to contract with a cleaning service company to maintain textiles. These companies provide daily, biweekly or weekly light cleaning services, and major cleaning as necessary.

Professional or contracted cleaning services are available for both residential and contract settings. Look for companies that are licensed where required, and bonded (insured against theft or damage). Some companies specialize in deep cleaning—such as upholstery, carpet, or drapery cleaning. Deep cleaning may be performed twice a year, or where high traffic and usage dictate, as often as monthly or even bi-weekly. Although deep soiling shortens textile life spans, so does over-cleaning. A rule of thumb is to deep clean only as necessary. Another rule is that keeping a textile clean by vacuuming, brushing or dusting and spotting is easier on textiles than rigorous cleaning.

Fibers respond differently to cleaning. Following is a cleaning chart for natural and manmade fibers. The chart suggestions are based on fabrics which can be handled and manipulated as decorative fabrics.

Cotton: Linens may be machine wash and dry with chance of shrinkage unless item is preshrunk. White cottons may be bleached and washed at high temperatures. Cotton releases soil readily. Wrinkling may occur when finishes are washed out. If cotton scorches while ironing, plunge into cold water immediately and let stand 24 hours. The scorched areas will disappear. Dry-cleaning is a good alternative when colors may bleed or fade, and when shrinking and wrinkling are unacceptable. Bright colors will fade. Printed cottons hung at the window should be lined to protect from sun fading. When storing cotton or linen, leave them unstarched as the starch rots them.

Linen: May be machine washed with a mild detergent and dried, which causes the fabric to soften over time and also causes wrinkling, limpness and shrinkage. Placing delicate linen items in a lingerie bag will lessen the damage. Clean stains with hydrogen peroxide. Chlorine bleach may be used, although it causes yellowing; non-chlorine bleach is a good alternative for washable items. Avoid wringing linen when wet as it tends to break the fibers. Gentle cycle in the dryer or line dry. Heat press linen while still slightly damp; pressing from the wrong side on medium-high heat with steam to remove wrinkles and give the surface a sheen. For embroidered linens, use a soft press cloth over the fabric when pressing. Linen may also be dried in place, such as on a table with a pad to protect wood, which gives an antique, formed appearance to tablecloths, for example.

Dry-cleaning is recommended for decorative and heavier fabrics to avoid loss of body and crispness. 100 linen percent tablecloths should be rolled and not folded; the inherent stiffness of the fiber causes permanent creases where the fabric is folded. For napkins or smaller items, fold in a different way each time to avoid breakage in repeated fold lines. As linen needs to breathe, it should not be stored in plastic bags. Rather, store covered cotton muslin or with acid-free tissue paper. Stored items should be kept dry and well-ventilated.

Linen draperies should be lined to protect the dyes from sun fading. Humid climates cause linen to stretch and result in uneven hemlines.

Jute: Hand washable, but must be dried thoroughly and kept dry to avoiding rotting. Dry-cleaning recommended.

Silk: Hand washable or machine washable which may produce variable wrinkling. Must not be bleached. Dry-cleaning recommended. Protect from exposure to sunshine. Silk will disintegrate under prolonged sunlight. Silk is also sensitive to artificial light, particularly fluorescent. Silk is sensitive to chemicals and will become tender if exposed to many pollutants.

Wool: Dry-cleaning is best. Wools may be safely hand washed in cold water but should be laid flat to dry to prevent elongation. Agitation and heat from machine washing and drying will cause severe shrinkage.

Leather: Gently hand wash with a mild solution of soap and water. May be dry cleaned with care. (Find a cleaning company which specializes in cleaning leather and suede.) Ink may be removed with hair spray or specially prepared solvents. Avoid saddle soap or other leather shoe preparations. Some leather spots can be removed with art gum eraser or an emery board.

Rayon: May be washed and line-dried, but washing may cause shrinking, wrinkling and loss of body and draping qualities. Dry-cleaning is the best alternative for decorative rayon fabrics. Iron setting should be moderate to hot.

Acetate: Some acetates are washable, others are not. Dry-cleaning is safest. Iron at moderate temperature. Sunlight sensitive.

Lyocell: Follow labels on bath towels, bed sheet sets and window treatment products.

Modacrylic: Utility fabrics may be washed using mild alkaline soaps, bleached and machine dried. Dry-cleaning is recommended to retain body and finishes for interior fabrics.

Nylon: May be hand or machine washed. Needs little ironing at low heat. May be spot-cleaned. Dry-cleans well. Susceptible to sunlight deterioration.

Olefin: Hand or machine wash in moderate, not hot water. Line or machine dry on low heat settings. Iron at very low heat to avoid melting. May be dry-cleaned. Outdoor carpeting may be scrubbed with soap and water and/or hosed-off to clean.

Polyester: May be machine or hand washed. Sheer drapery fabric of polyester with buckram or crinoline headings are best hand washed (swished around) in a bathtub of mild suds. Use the shower to rinse the sheers and let them drip-dry. May also be dry-cleaned.

Polylactic Acid (PLA): Sponge spots. Professional care recommended.

Saran: Washable at cool temperatures only. Heat will cause fibers to shrink and deteriorate.

Vinyon (Vinyl): Wipe clean with warm sudsy water. Hair spray type solvents will dissolve ink stains. Some vinyl is machine washable at moderate temperatures. Line dry.

Note: Crypton fabrics can be any of the above fibers or combination of fibers. It is a finished, decorative fabric that has been treated to become a Crypton fabric. Therefore no fiber will be listed on a Crypton tag.

Bibliography and Resources

GENERAL BIBLIOGRAPHY

ATMI Educator Package. Washington, DC: American Textile Manufacturers Institute, n.d.

Cook, J.G. *Handbook of Textile Fibres*. Vol. 1, *Natural Fibers*. Durham, England: Merros, 1984.

Hatch, Kathryn L. *Textile Science*. Minneapolis–St. Paul: West, 1993.

Herring, Robert. *The Schumacher Guide to Decorative Textiles*. New York: F. Schumacher, 1991.

Kandolph, Sara J., et al. *Textiles*, 7th ed. New York: Macmillan, 1993.

Ladbury, Ann. *Fabrics*. London: Sidgwick and Jackson, 1979.

Larsen, Jack Lenor, and Jeanne Weeks. *Fabrics for Interiors: A Guide for Architects, Designers, and Consumers*. New York: John Wiley and Sons, 1975.

McGowan, Maryrose. *Specifying Interiors: A Guide to Construction and FF&E for Commerical Interiors Projects*, 2nd ed. Hoboken, NJ: John Wiley and Sons, 2006.

Nielson, Karla J. *Understanding Fabrics: A Definitive Guidebook to Fabrics for Interior Design and Decoration*. North Palm Beach, FL: Clark, 1989.

Nielson, Karla J., and David A. Taylor. *Interiors: An Introduction*, 4th ed. New York: McGraw-Hill, 2006.

Trocme, Suzanne. *Fabric*. London: Mitchell Beazley/Octopus, 2002.

Yates, Mary Paul. *Fabrics: A Guide for Interior Designers and Architects*. New York: W.W. Norton, 2002.

Yeager, Jan I., and Laura K. Teter-Justice. *Textiles for Residential and Commercial Interiors*, 2nd ed. New York: Fairchild, 2000.

Chapter 1: Professional Practices: The Textile Industry, Profession, and Careers

Knackstedt, Mary V. *The Interior Design Business Handbook*. Hoboken, NJ: John Wiley and Sons, 2005.

Piotrowski, Christine. *Becoming an Interior Designer*. Hoboken, NJ: John Wiley and Sons, 2005.

Chapter 2: Sustainable Design and Textile Careers

A Comparison of Indoor and Outdoor Concentrations of Hazardous Air Pollutants. *Inside IAQ* (Spring/Summer 1998). EPA/600/N-98/002.

Bonda, Penny, FASID. "Why Green Design Matters." *Icon* (May 2003): 11–13.

"EconTrade Data." www.atmi.org. Spring 2003.

Environmental Protection Agency. *Introduction to Indoor Air Quality: A Self-Paced Learning Module* (July 1991). EPA/400/3-91/002.

Fishbein, Bette K. "Carpet Take-Back: EPR American Style." *INFORM: Strategies for a Better Environment*, www.informinc.org/carpettakeback.php.

Jennings, Lucinda. "Green Tips: A Basic Guide for Residential and Commercial Designers." *Icon* (May 2003): 20–21.

Jones, Sandy. "Smarter Solutions." *green@work* (May/June 2003): 25–28.

McDonough, William, and Michael Braungart. *Cradle to Cradle: Remaking the Way We Make Things*. New York: North Point, 2002.

———. *The Hanover Principles*. McDonough Braungart Design Community. www.mbcd.com. 1992, 2002.

———. "From Principles to Practices: Creating a Sustaining Architecture for the 21st Century, Using the Enduring Laws of Nature." *green@work* (May/June 2003): 36–37.

Nielson, Karla J., and David A. Taylor. *Interiors: An Introduction*, 4th ed. New York: McGraw-Hill, 2006.

O'Brien, Mary. *Making Better Environmental Decisions: An Alternative to Risk Management*. Cambridge, MA: MIT Press, 2000.

Stenland, Jan D. "Take a Breath: Understanding Indoor Air Quality and Toxicity." *Icon* (May 2003): 14–17.

True Green: The Road to Susainability. Antron Carpet Fiber CD. Jacksonville, AL: DuPont Textiles and Interiors, 2002.

Turning Green: A Guide to Becoming a Green Design Firm. Washington, DC: Associates III and American Society of Interior Designers, 2003.

Chapter 3: Natural and Manufactured Fibers

"Art of Upholstery: Leather, Odyssey from Pasture to Sofa." *Fine Furniture International* (February/March 1999).

Belgian Linen. New York: Belgian Linen Association, n.d.

Bulbach, Stanley. "The Importance of Wool." *Oriental Rug Review* 8, no. 3 (February/March 1988).

"Cotton." www.encarta.msn.com.

Cotton: From Field to Fabric. Memphis: National Cotton Council, 1981.

Edelman: A Leather Handbook. Danbury, CT: Edelman, n.d.

Jacobson, Timorth, Timothy C., and George D.Smith. *Cotton's Renaissance: A Study in Market Innovation*. New York: Cambridge University Press, 2001.

Leather: The Revealing Facts. Lackawana Leather Company, n.d.

"Meet the Azlons from A to Z: Regenerated and Rejuvenated." www.fabrics.net/joan103/asp.

Story of Cotton. National Cotton Council of America, n.d.

Chapter 7: Aesthetic Coordination

Harmon, Sharon Koomen, and Katherine E. Kennon. *The Codes Guidebook for Interiors*, 3rd ed. Hoboken, NJ: John Wiley and Sons, 2005.

Pile, John. *Color in Interior Design* New York: McGraw-Hill, c1997.

Rodemann, Patricia A. *Patterns in Interior Environments: Perception, Psychology, and Practice*. New York: John Wiley and Sons, 1999.

Chapter 8: Upholstered Furniture and Slipcovers

Clifton-Mogg, Caroline, and Melanie Paine. *The Art and Technique of Decorating with Fabric*. New York: Prentice Hall, 1988.

Lang, Donna, and Lucretia Robertson. *Decorating with Fabric*. New York: Clarkson Potter, 1986.

"Measure Guide." Surefit Slipcovers. www.surefit.com.

Sunset Slipcovers and Bedspreads. Menlo Park, CA: Lane, 1987.

"Textiles." www.wikipedia.org.

Walking, Gillian. *Upholstery Styles*. London: Quarto, 1989.

Chapter 9: Textile Wallcoverings

"Abrasion." Association for Contract Textiles. www.contract textiles .org.

Banov, Abel, and Jeanne Lytle. *Wallcoverings and Decoration*. Farmington, MI: Structures, 1976.

Booth, Betty. "Five Hot Trends for Wallpaper." National Guild of Professional Paperhangers. www.ngpp.org.

"Colorfastness to Light." Association for Contract Textiles. www.contracttextiles.org.

"Custom Fabric Environments Catalogue." Toronto: Eventscape, 2004.

"Decibel." www.thetechdictionary.com.

Drabowicz, Barbara L., ed. "Defining Wallcoverings." *Seabrook Journal* 4, no. 2 (1994): 9.

"Duvet Covers." Bed, Bath, and Beyond. www.bedbathand beyond.com.

Fabric: This Century's Building Material. Roseville: MN. Industrial Fabrics Association, 2004.

"Fabrics and Weaves." Salwar. www.salwar.com

"Flammability." Association for Contract Textiles. www.contract textiles.org

"Formulas and Estimating." Wallcoverings Association. www .wallcoveings.org

"Frequently Asked Questions About Wallcoverings." Paint and Decorating Retailers Association. www.pdra.org.

Hanging Wallpaper: Enhancing and Beautifying Your Walls. Cleveland: Sherwin-Williams, 1999.

"How to Hang." Wallcoverings Association. www.wallcoverings .org.

"How to Hang Wallcoverings: Step by Step Guide." Wallpaper Warehouse. n.d.

"How to Hire a Contractor." Wallcoverings Association. www .wallcoverings.org.

McGowan, Maryrose. *Specifying Interiors: A Guide to Construction and FF&E for Commercial Interiors Projects*, 2nd ed. Hoboken, NJ: John Wiley and Sons, 2006.

"Mold Cause, Effect, and Response: A Study of Wallcovering Products." Wallcoverings Association and Chemical Fabrics and Film Association. www.wallcoverings.org.

"Noise Levels in Our Environment Fact Sheet." League for the Hard of Hearing. www.lhh.org.

"Physical Properties." Association for Contract Textiles. www .contracttextiles.org.

Pinkalla, Cary. "Fabric Duct Air Dispersion." *Construction Specifier* (June 2003).

Sofio, John. "Avoiding the Cookie-Cutter Approach to Office Furnishings." *Construction Specifier* 2004: 50–56.

"Sound: Decibel Levels." Physics Tutorials. www.internet4 classrooms.com.

"Wallcovering Installation: Special Considerations for Commercial Wallcovering Applications." Wallcoverings Association. www.wallcoverings.org.

"Wallcovering Installation: Surface Preparation." Wallcoverings Association. www.wallcoverings.org.

"Wallcovering Installation: Wallcovering Adhesives." Do It Yourself.com. www.doityourself.com.

"Wet and Dry Crocking." Association for Contract Textiles. www.contracttextiles.org.

"Why Wallpaper?" National Guild of Professional Paperhangers. www.ngpp.org.

"Vinyl Performance Everyday: Environmental Profile Vinyl Wallcovering." Vinyl Institute, Wallcoverings Association, Chemical Fabrics and Film Association. www.wallcoverings.org.

Chapter 10: Window Treatments

DuBoff, Randy and Deborah. *Hard Window Coverings Made Easy*. San Diego: Randy DuBoff.

Clifton-Mogg, Caroline, and Melanie Paine. *The Art and Technique of Decorating with Fabric*. New York: Prentice Hall, 1988.

Creative Window Treatments. Minnetonka, MN Creative Publishers International, 2000.

"Curtains, Draperies, and Shades: A Sunset Book." Menlo Park, CA: Lane, 1992.

"Drapery Workroom Directory." Window Coverings Association of America. www.wcaa.org.

"DreamDraper® System." Evan Marsh Designs. www.evan marshdesigns.com.

Drew, Melinda, Ed. *A Guide to Window Treatments*. St. Louis: Window Coverings Association of America, 1985.

"Expressions of Style: Window Fashions by Graber." Des Moines: Meredith, 1990. Fishburn, Angela. *Curtains and Window Treatments*. New York: John Wiley and Sons (Van Nostrand Reinhold), 1982.

Forbes, Isabella. *The Ultimate Curtain Book* Pleasantville, NY: Reader's Digest, 1994.

Griggs, Lamar. *Designing Windows*. Arlington, TX: Designing Windows, 1989.

Helsel, Marjorie Borradaile, ed. *The Interior Designer's Drapery, Bedspread, and Canopy Sketchfile*. New York: Whitney Library of Design, 1990.

Merrick, Catherine, et al. *The Curtain Design Director*, 3rd ed. Gainsborough, Lincolnshire, England Merrick and Day, 1999.

Moreland, F.A. "Laces, Glass, and Sash Curtains." *Practical Decorative Upholstery, Containing Full Instructions for Cutting, Making, and Hanging All Kinds of Interior Upholstery Decorations*, 3rd ed. New York: Clifford and Lawton, 1889 and 1899. J.R. Burrows. www.burrows.com.

Nielson, Karla J. *Soft Window Coverings Product Knowledge Manual. Part A: The Basics of Window Treatments*. Grover, MO: Window Coverings Association of America, n.d.

———. *Window Treatments*. New York: John Wiley and Sons, 1990.

———. *Windows of Opportunity: The Role of Window Fashions in Interior Design*. Hunter Douglas, Inc. Upper Saddle River, NJ, 1995.

Randall, Charles T. *The Encyclopedia of Window Fashions*, 6th ed. SanClemente, CA: Randall International, 2006.

———. *Dream Windows: An Inspirational Guide to Draperies and Soft Furnishings*. San Clemente: CA: Randall International, 2003.

———. Charles Randall's Designer Sketchfile: San Clemente, CA; Randall International, 2006

Stoehr, Kathleen. *Dream Windows: Historical Perspectives, Classic Designs, Contemporary Creations*, 2nd ed. San Clemente, CA: Randall International, 2005.

Strickland, Cheryl. *A Practical Giude to Soft Window Coverings*. North Palm Beach, FL: Clark, 1992.

Sunset Ideas for Great Window Treatments. Menlo Park, CA: Lane, 1992.

"Training Guide." Denver: Wesco Fabrics, n.d.

Chapter 11: Linens and Accessories

"Better Sleep Guide." Better Sleep Council. www.bettersleep.org.

"Blankets." Bed Bath and Beyond. www.bedbathandbeyond.com.

"Comforters." Bedlinens.net. www.bedlinens.net.

"Duvets." Bed Bath and Beyond. www.bedbathandbeyond.com.

"Duvets." Bedlinens.net. www.bedlinens.net.

"Mattress Pads." Bed Bath and Beyond. www.bedbathandbeyond.com.

"Safety Issues: Bedroom Air Quality." www.safesleep.org.

"Safety Issues: Chemical Emissions." www.safesleep.org.

"Satin." Bedlinens.net. www.bedlinens.net.

"Sheets." Bed Bath and Beyond. www.bedbathandbeyond.com.

"Sheets." Bedlinens.net. www.bedlinens.net.

"Uniforms, Linens, and Bedding." Hospitality Index. www.hospitality-index.com.

Chapter 12: Broadloom Carpeting

"Axminster." *Encyclopedia Britannica*. Chicago, IL Encyclopedia Britannica 2003.

"Installation: Industry Standards for Installation." Carpet and Rug Institute. www.carpet-rug.org.

Rosenstiel, Helen von. *American Rugs and Carpets*. New York. Walter Parrish International, 1978.

Rosenstiel, Helen von, and Gail Caskey Winkler. *Floor Coverings for Historic Buildings*. Washington, DC: Preservation Press, 1988.

"Rugmaker's Homestead." www.netw.com/-rafter4/history.htm. 2005.

"Selecting Carpet and Rugs: Commercial; Specifying Commercial Carpet; ADA Compliance." Carpet and Rug Institute. www.carpet-rug.org.

"Selecting Carpet and Rugs: Commercial; Specifying Commercial Carpet; Appearance Retention Rating Guidelines." Carpet and Rug Institute. www.carpet-rug.org.

"Selecting Carpet and Rugs: Commercial; Specifying Commercial Carpet; Backing Systems." Carpet and Rug Institute. www.carpet-rug.org.

"Selecting Carpet and Rugs: Commercial; Specifying Commercial Carpet; Carpet in Schools." Carpet and Rug Institute. www.carpet-rug.org.

"Selecting Carpet and Rugs: Commercial; Specifying Commercial Carpet; Construction." Carpet and Rug Institute. www.carpet-rug.org.

"Selecting Carpet and Rugs: Commercial; Specifying Commercial Carpet; Cushion in Commercial Installations." Carpet and Rug Institute. www.carpet-rug.org.

"Selecting Carpet and Rugs: Commercial; Specifying Commercial Carpet; Fiber." Carpet and Rug Institute. www.carpet-rug.org.

"Selecting Carpet and Rugs: Commercial; Specifying Commercial Carpet; Modular Carpet Tiles and Six-Foot Carpet." Carpet and Rug Institute. www.carpet-rug.org.

"Selecting Carpet and Rugs: Commercial; Specifying Commercial Carpet; The Right Carpet for Your Facility." Carpet and Rug Institute. www.carpet-rug.org.

"Selecting Carpet and Rugs: Commercial; Specifying Commercial Carpet; Specification Installation Timeline." Carpet and Rug Institute. www.carpet-rug.org.

"Selecting Carpet and Rugs: Commercial; Specifying Commercial Carpet; Testing Requirements." Carpet and Rug Institute. www.carpet-rug.org.

"Soroush Custom Rugs and Axminster Carpets: Hospitality, Corporate, Residential." Kensington, MD: Saroush Custom Rugs and Axminster Carpets.n.d.

"Wilton." *Encyclopedia Britannica*. New York, Chicago, IL Encyclopedia Britannica

2003. Wool Research Organization of New Zealand. www.canesis.com/Documents/Manufacture.

Yeager, Jan I., and Laura K. Teter-Justice. *Textiles for Residential and Commercial Interiors*, 2nd ed. New York: Fairchild, 2000.

Chapter 13: Handmade and Area Rugs

Allane, Lee. *Chinese Rugs: A Buyer's Guide*. London: Thames and Hudson. 1993.

———. *Kilims: A Buyer's Guide*. London: Thames and Hudson. 1995.

Amesden, Charles Avery. *Navaho Weaving: Its Technic and Its History*. Los Angeles: RioGrande Classic/Southwest Museum. 1991.

Amini, Majid. *Oriental Rugs: Care and Repair*. London: Orbis, 1981.

Arizona Highways 50, no. 7 (July 1974). Phoenix: Arizona Highway Department

Aschenbrenner, Eric. *Oriental Rugs: Persian*, Vol. 2. Woodbridge. Suffolk, England: Antique Collector's Club, 1981.

Bennett, Ian. *Oriental Rugs*. Vol 1, *Caucasian*. London: Oriental Textile, 1980.

Bernardout, David. *Care and Repair of Rugs and Carpets*. Edison, NJ: Chartwell, 1995.

Bosley, Caroline. *Rugs to Riches: An Insider's Guide*. New York: Pantheon, 1980.

Boucher, Jeff. *Baluchi Woven Treasures*. Alexandria, VA:: Jeff W. Boucher, 1989.

cannot locateDenny, Walter. *Sotheby's Guide to Oriental Carpets*. New York: Fireside, 1994.

Eagleton, William. *An Introduction to Kurdish Rugs and Other Weavings*. New York: Interlink Books 1998.

Eiland, Murray. *Oriental Rugs: A New Comprehensive Guide*. Boston: Little, Brown, 1993.

———. *tarting to Collect Oriental Rugs*. Woodbridge, Suffolk, England: Antique Collector's Club, 2003.

Ford, P.R.J. *Oriental Carpet Design*. London: Thames and Hudson, 1989.

cannot locateGarstein, A.S. *The How-To Handbook of Carpets*. New York: Van Nostrand Reinhold, 1979.

Getzwiller, Steve. *Ray Manley's The Fine Art of Navajo Weaving*. Tucson, AZ: Ray Manley, 1984.

Housego, Jenny. *Tribal Rugs*. New York: Inerlink, 1996.

Hull, Alastair, and J. Luczyc-Wyhowska. *Kilim: The Complete Guide*. San Francisco: Chronicle, 1993.

Jacobsen, Charles W. *Checkpoints on How to Buy Oriental Rugs*. Rutland, VT: Charles E.Tuttle, 1969.

———. *Oriental Rugs; A Complete Guide*. Rutland, VT: Charles E. Tuttle. 1976.

James, H.L. *Posts and Rugs: The Story of Navajo Rugs and Their Homes*. Globe, AZ: Southwest Parks and Monuments Association, 1976.

Jerrehian, Aram, Jr. *Oriental Rug Primer: Buying and Understanding New Oriental Rugs*. New York: Facts on File, 1980.

Kent, Kate Peck. *Navajo Weaving: Three Centuries of Change*. Sante Fe: School of American Research, 1985.

Keshishian, James Mark. *Inscribed Armenian Rugs of Yesteryear*. Washington, DC : Near Eastern Art Research Center, 1994.

Kline, Linda. *Beginner's Guide to Oriental Rugs*. Berkeley, CA: Ross, 1980.

Liebetrau, Preben. *Oriental Rugs in Colour*. New York: Macmillan, 1963.

MacDonald, Brian W. *Tribal Rug Treasures of the Black Tent*. Woodbridge, Suffolk, England: Antique Collectors Club, 1997.

Maxwell, Gilbert. *Navajo Rugs*. Sante Fe: Southwest Images, 1992.

McManis, Kent, and Robert Jeffries. *A Guide to Navajo Weavings*. Tucson, AZ: Treasure Chest, 1997.

Middleton, Andrew. *Rugs and Carpets*. London: Michelin House, 1996.

Milanesi, Enza. *The Bulfinch Guide to Carpets*. Boston: Little, Brown, 1992.

Navajo Weaving Handbook. Santa Fe: Museum of New Mexico Press, 1981.

O'Bannon, George. *Oriental Rugs: A Collector's Guide*. Philadelphia: Courage, 1995.

Opie, James. *Tribal Rugs* Boston, MA: Bulfinch Press, 1998.

Parsons, R.D. *Oriental Rugs*. Vol. 3, *The Carpets of Afghanistan*. Woodbridge, Suffolk, England: Antique Collectors Club, 1994.

Pickering, Brooke. *Moroccan Carpets*. Chevy Chase, MD: Near Eastern Art Research Center & Hali Pub., 1994.

"Prodigal Rugs: Makers of Rag Rugs and Wall Hangings." http://www.prodigalrugs.com/history.html.

Rosenstiel, Helene von. *American Rugs and Carpets from the Seventeenth Century to Modern Times*. New York: William Morrow, 1978.

Rosenstiel, Helene von, and Gail Caskey Winkler. *Floor Coverings for Historic Buildings*. Washington, DC: Preservation Press, 1988.

Sala, Maria-Merecedes. (1999). "Trade in Tokens of Heritage: Traditional Carpets and Kilims." *International Trade Forum* 4 (1999): 5–7.

Sakhai, Essie. *Oriental Carpets, A Buyer's Guide*. RI: Moyer Bell, Wakefield, RI: Moyer Bell; Emeryville, CA: Distributed in North America by Publishers Group West, 1995.

Seymour, Liz. "Tibetan Rugs." *Traditional Home* (November 1993): 53–54.

"Southwest Indian Weaving." *Arizona Highways* 50, 1–48.

Stone, Peter. *Oriental Rug Repair*. Chicago: Greenleaf, 1981.

———. *Oriental Rug Lexicon*. Seattle: University of Washington Press, 1997.

Summers, Janice. *Oriental Rugs: The Illustrated World Buyer's Guide*. New York: Crown, 1994.

Tanavoli, Parviz. *Shasavan: Iranian Rugs and Textiles*. New York: Rizzoli, 1985.

Thompson, Jon. *Oriental Carpets*. New York: Penguin, 1993.

Ware, Joyce. *Oriental Rugs: Official Price Guide*. New York: House of Collectibles, 1992.

Weeks, Jeanne. *Rugs and Carpets of Europe*. New York: Chilton, 1969.

Chapter 14: Oriental Style

Chapter 15: Renaissance and Formal Styles;

Chapter 16: Medieval, Colonial, Country, and Provence Styles;

Chapter 17: Regional and Ethnic Styles;

Chapter 18: Modern Styles

Adams, Monni. *Design for Living African Art*. Cambridge, MA: Carpenter Center for the Visual Arts, 1982.

Allen, Phyllis Sloan, Lynn M. Jones, and Miriam Stimpson, *The Beginnings of Interior Environment*, 9th ed. Upper Saddle River, NJ: Pearson Prentice Hall, 2004.

Aronson, Joseph. *The Encyclopedia of Furniture*, 3rd ed. New York: Crown, 1965.

Art Institute of Chicago. *Miniature Rooms*. New York: Abbeville, 1983.

Baca, Elmo, and Suzanne Deats. *Santa Fe Design*. Lincolnwood, IL: Publications International, 1990.

———. and M.J. Van Deventer *Native American Style* Salt Lake City: Gibbs-Smith, c1999.

———. Romance of the Mission : *Decorating in the Mission Style*: Salt Lake City: Gibbs Smith Publisher, c1996.

Benirschke, Max. *Color Source Book of Authentic Art Nouveau Design*. New York: Dover, 1984.

Bossaglia, Rossana. *Art Nouveau Revolution in Interior Design*. New York: Orbis / Crescent, 1973.

Bourgoin, J. *Arabic Geometrical Pattern and Design*. New York: Dover, 1973.

Brain, Robert. *Art and Society in Africa*. New York. Longman, 1990.

Bunt, Cyril G.E. *Hispano-Moresque Fabrics*. Leigh-on-Sea, England: F. Lewis, 1966.

———. *Spanish Silks*, Leigh-on-Sea, England: F. Lewis, 1965.

Byne, Arthur, and Mildred Stapley. *Spanish Interiors and Furniture*. New York: Dover, 1969.

"Carl Larsson: One of the Most Beloved Swedish Artists: Carl and Karin Larsson Family Association. www.clg.se. 2005.

Cavalli-Björkman, Görel, and Bo Lindwall. *The World of Carl Larsson*. San Diego: Green Tiger, 1989.

Chapman, Suzanne E. *Early American Design Motifs*. New York: Dover, 1974.

Cheek, Richard. *Vanderbilt Mansion*. Hyde Park, NY: Fort Church /Hyde Park Historical Association, 1988.

Davies, Colin. "Modernism Shows Its Human Side." *Architect's Journal* (1994): 53.

Deschamps, Madeline. *Empire*. New York: Abbeville, 1994.

Duncan, Alastair. *Art Nouveau Furniture*. London: Thames and Hudson, 1982.

Editors of American Heritage. *Reader's Digest Pocket Guide to American*. Eskeröd, Albert. *Swedish Folk Art*. Stockholm: Nordiska Museet, 1964.

Fehrman, Cherie and Kenneth. *Postwar Interior Design: 1945–1960*. New York: Van Nostrand Reinhold, 1987.

Fiell, Charlotte and Peter Fiell, *Modern Furniture Classics Since 1945*, Washington, DC: American Institute of Architects Press, c1991.

———. *Modern furniture Classics : Postwar to Post-Modernism*: London ; New York, NY : Thames & Hudson, 2001.

Fleming, John, and Hugh Honour. *Dictionary of the Decorative Arts*. New York: Harper and Row, 1977.

Fowler, Penny. "Please Be Seated." *Frank Lloyd Wright: The Seat of Genius, Chairs: 1895-1955*. Ed. Timothy Eaton. West Palm Beach, FL: Eaton Fine Arts, 1997, 29–35.

Friedmann, Rosemary Sadez. *Mystery of Color*. Naples, FL: LandM Publications, 2003.

Garret, Elisabeth Donaghy, compiler, *The Antiques book of Victorian Interiors:* New York: Crown Publishers, [1981]

Geibel, Victoria. "Architect-Designed Furniture." *V and A Album* (Spring 1989): 71–76.

Genaur, Emily. *Modern Interiors Today and Tomorrow*. Cleveland: World, 1942.

Gerspach, M. *Coptic Textile Designs*. New York: Dover, 1975.

Gibbs, Jenny. *Curtains and Draperies: History, Design, Inspiration*. New York: Overlook, 1994.

Gillon, Werner. *A Short History of African Art*. New York. Viking Penguin, 1984.

Gordon, Elizabeth. "Wright's Way with Little Things." *House Beautiful* (October 1959). 232.

Greck, Francis J. *French Interiors and Furniture: The Period of Francis I*. Boulder, CO: Stureck Educational Services, 1982.

———. *French Interiors and Furniture: The Period of Henry II*. Boulder, CO: Stureck Educational Services, 1985.

———. *French Interiors and Furniture: The Period of Henry IV*. Boulder, CO: Stureck Educational Services, 1986.

Griesbach, C.B. *Historic Ornament: A Pictorial Archive*. New York: Dover, 1975.

Hart, Spencer. *Wright Rooms*. New York: Grange, 1998.

Hatje, Gerd, and Ursula Hatje. *Design for Modern Living: A Practical Guide to Home Furnishing and Interior Decoration*. New York: Harry N. Abrams, 1962.

Heck, Sarah. "Frank Lloyd Wright: 1867–1959." *Crystal City Tour: Frank Lloyd Wright*. 1997.

Helsel, Marjorie B. *The Interior Designer's Drapery, Bedspread, and Canopy Sketch File*. New York: Watson-Guptill, 1990.

Henere, Enrique. *Spanish Textiles*. Leigh-on-Sea, England: F. Lewis, 1955.

Historical Colours. London: Thomas Parsons and Sons, 1937.

"History and Philosophy of the Nordic Folk School Movement." Scandinavian Seminar. 2004.

"House Beautiful: Frank Lloyd Wright for Everyone." *Eluehjem Museum of Art Bulletin/Annual Report*. Madison: University of Wisconsin, 1987–1988.

Kardon, Janet. *The Ideal Home: History of Twentieth-Century American Craft, 1900–1920*. New York: H.N. Abrams in association with the American Craft, 1993.108.

King, Julia. *The Flowering of Art Nouveau Graphics*. London: Trefoil, 1990.

Kiracofe, Roderick, and Mary Elizabeth Johnson. *The American Quilt: A History of Cloth and Comfort, 1750–1950*. New York: Clarkson Potter, 1993.

Klein, Dan. *All Color Book of Art Deco*. London: Octopus, 1974.

Koloss, Hans-Joachim. *Art of Central Africa*. New York. Metropolitan Museum of Art, 1990.

Lind, Carla. *Frank Lloyd Wright's Furnishing*. New York: Archetype, 1995.

Loukin, Andrea, ed. *Interior Design* (May 1996). Market Issue.

Mackintosh, Alastair. *Symbolism and Art Nouveau*. London: Thames and Hudson, 1975.

Marberry, Sara O. *Color in the Office, Design Trends from 1950 to 1990 and Beyond*. New York: Van Nostrand Reinhold, 1994.

McCorquodale, Charles. *History of the Interior*. New York: Vendome Press: Distributed by Viking Press, 1983.

Mera, H.P. *Pueblo Design*. New York: Dover, 1970.

Mucha, Alphonse, Maurice Verneuil, and Georges Aruiol. *Art Nouveau Designs in Color*. New York: Dover, 1974.

Muller, Debra. "Design Legacy: Charles Rennie Mackintosh." *Traditional Home* (May 1996): 42–48.

Nielson, Karla J. *Window Treatments*. New York: John Wiley and Sons, 1990.

———. "Cultural Crossroads." *Draperies and Window Coverings* (November 1996).

Nielson, Karla J., and David A. Taylor, *Interiors: An Introduction*, 4th ed. New York: McGraw-Hill, 2006.

Nylander, Jane C. *Fabrics for Historic Buildings*. Washington, DC Preservation Press, 1990. Parsons, Jack. *Santa Fe and Northern New Mexico*. New York: Rizzoli International, 1991.

Pegler, Martin M. *The Dictionary of Interior Design*. New York: Fairchild, 1983.

Pevsner, Nikolaus. *Pioneers of Modern Design*. New Haven: Yale University Press, 2005.

David A. Hanks, et al *High Styles: Twentieth-Century American Design*. New York: Whitney Museum of American Art in association with Summit Books, c1985.

Pile, John. *A History of Interior Design*, 2nd ed. Hoboken, NJ: John Wiley and Sons, 2005.

———. *Furniture, Modern + Postmoder : Design + Technology*: 2nd ed. Hoboken, NJ: John Wiley & Sons, 1990.

————. *Modern Furniture*: Hoboken NJ: John Wiley & Sons, 1979.

Rosenstiel, Helen von. *American Rugs and Carpets from the Seventeenth Century to Modern Times*. New York: William Morrow, 1978.

Rosenstiel, Helene von, and Gail Caskey Winkler. *Floor Coverings for Historic Buildings*. Washington, DC: Preservation Press, 1988.

Savage, George. *A Concise History of Interior Decoration*. London: Thames and Hudson, 1966.

Schottmuller, Frida. *Furniture and Interior Decoration of the Italian Renaissance*. New York: Brentano, 1921, 1925.

.Schroy, Ellen. T., ed. *Warman's American Furniture*. Iola, WI : Krause Publications, c2000

Segerstad, Ulf Hård af, and Karl-Erik Granath. *Carl Larsson's Home*. Reading, MA: Addison-Wesley, 1978.

Sheehan, Sama, et. al. *Mary Emmerling's American Country West*. New York: Clarkson Potter, 1985.

Snodin, Michael, and Elisabet Stavenow-Hidemark, eds. *Carl and Karin Larsson: Creators of the Swedish Style*. Boston: Bulfinch, 1997.

Stewart, Janice S. *The Folk Arts of Norway*. Baltimore: Waverly, 1953.

Stimpson, Miriam. *Modern Furniture Classics*. New York: Whitney Library of Design, 1987.

Swedberg., Harriett and Robert W. *Collector's Encyclopedia of American Furniture*. Paducah, KY: Collector Books, 1994.

Taylor, Lonn, and Dessa Bokides. *New Mexican Furniture, 1600–1940*. Santa Fe: Museum of New Mexico Press.1987.

Walch, Margaret, and Augustine Hope. *Living Colors: The Definitive Guide to Color Palettes Through the Ages*. San Francisco: Chronicle, 1995.

Warren, Geoffrey. *All Color Book of Art Nouveau*. London: Octopus, 1972.

Whiton, Sherrill. *Interior Design and Decoration*, 4th ed. Philadelphia: J.B. Lippincott, 1974.

Wichman, Kerstin. Design for Everyone. *IKEA PS* (1996).

Zahle, Erik, ed. *A Treasury of Scandinavian Design*. New York: Golden, 1961.

NOTE: See www.wiley.com/go/interiortextiles for additional resources.

Index